Investment Analysis and Management

Anthony J. Curley / Robert M. Bear
THE PENNSYLVANIA STATE UNIVERSITY

Investment Analysis and Management

Harper & Row, Publishers
NEW YORK, HAGERSTOWN, PHILADELPHIA, SAN FRANCISCO, LONDON

Sponsoring Editor: John Greenman
Project Editor: David Nickol
Designer: Emily Harste
Production Manager: Stefania J. Taflinska
Compositor: Syntax International
Printer and Binder: The Maple Press Company
Art Studio: J&R Technical Services Inc.

Investment Analysis
and Management

Library of Congress Cataloging in Publication Data

Curley, Anthony J
Investment analysis and management.

Includes index.
1. Investment analysis. I. Bear, Robert Martin, 1943- joint author. II. Title.
HG4521.C96 332.6'7 78-31115
ISBN 0-06-041452-9

To Janice and Anita

Contents

Chapter 3
Return on Investment 51

Chapter 4
Investment Elements 91

Chapter 5
Bonds, Mortgages, and Preferred Stock 125

Chapter 6
Common Stock Analysis 164

Chapter 7
Accounting Data 204

Chapter 17
Investment Maintenance and Revision 512

Chapter 18
Investment Management 535

Appendix
Compound Interest Relationships 557

Preface

Security analysis and portfolio management have changed significantly in recent years, and that process of change continues to accelerate. Refined analytical tools and expanded data bases provide new opportunities and new challenges to investment managers. Security analysis is being redirected from a narrow focus on stocks and bonds to a broader perspective that evaluates the full array of investment opportunities. Portfolio theory is becoming operational, and the integration of security analysis and portfolio selection assumes an increasingly critical role in translating theory into practice. Finally, the structure and operation of capital markets are in rapid transition as traditional markets give way reluctantly to a centralized national market system.

The impact of transition and change is very evident in the academic community, where course work in investment management is continually evolving and adapting in response to new ideas and discoveries. The development of portfolio theory and the emergence of the efficient market hypothesis have resulted in principles and procedures that are sometimes in apparent conflict with those found in more traditional offerings in security analysis. In addition, the increasing rigor of the investments literature creates serious difficulties for students with only an average background in mathematics and statistics. For these and other reasons, course content often differs markedly from one school to another and, in many cases, from term to term at particular institutions.

Consequently, the design and execution of investments course work is a difficult problem, and it was this challenge that motivated us to write *Investment Analysis and Management.*

THE BOOK'S APPROACH AND ORGANIZATION

The book is analytical and is not intended for a purely descriptive course that surveys the investment environment. We have not avoided mathematics, but the book is not mathematical. We use algebraic expressions because there is no better way to describe complex relationships, but virtually all algebraic statements are demonstrated arithmetically. Use of statistics is generally limited to topics studied in a first statistics course; each statistical topic is reviewed in the text as it is needed, because we have found that our students profit from this type of reinforcement. Specific topics in investments are referenced in footnotes and in the end-of-chapter bibliographies for students who wish to pursue them in greater depth.

The text can be used for a one-term or one-semester course that surveys analytical and managerial procedures, or it can be used for sequenced course work exploring security analysis and portfolio selection in greater depth. The organization of the text reflects our preference regarding topical development, but the sequence in which materials are presented may be altered to conform to other views. Each chapter was developed after a careful search of the existing literature, and we believe the coverage of empirical research is reasonably complete. Literature references are included in the text narrative and in footnotes within chapters to accommodate modifications in chapter sequencing. Also, each chapter in our accompanying *Instructor's Manual* was developed concurrently with the content of its corresponding text chapter in order to assure pedagogical consistency and accuracy.

Our most difficult problem in organizing this text involved integrating several investment dimensions that are usually treated separately and, in our opinion, inadequately. Major difficulties exist (1) in extending debt and equity valuation principles to convertible securities, options, futures contracts, and other financial claims, and (2) in reconciling and integrating security analysis techniques with portfolio selection principles. We have attempted to solve the first problem by standardizing valuation procedures in terms of a basic yield model introduced and discussed in detail in Chapter 3. Our approach to the second problem also makes use of that basic model, because we describe the outputs from security analysis—expected rate of return and its variance—as two of the three critical inputs to the portfolio model. We recognize that problems still remain in integrating these elements satisfactorily, but we also believe that the structure we have adopted provides a logical basis for introducing students to the many issues and controversies involved in investment analysis and management.

ACKNOWLEDGMENTS

We are very grateful to everyone who helped us in preparing and completing this effort. Useful comments on several drafts of the manuscript were provided by John A. Boquist, Indiana University; Harvey T. Dill, Iowa State University; John T. Emery, University of Calgary; Michael D. Joehnk, University of Wyoming, later Texas Tech University; Charles O. Kroncke, University of Wisconsin, Madison; Richard W. McEnally, University of North Carolina, later University of Texas, Austin; and Douglas M. Patterson, University of Michigan. Robert Hollerorth, Do-Soung Choi, and Roger Hahn provided research assistance and Anna Peters, Beth Wheland, and Robin Carson provided aid and comfort with respect to hundreds of frustrating details involved in meeting publication deadlines. Throughout the process, Professor Joseph F. Bradley gave us encouragement and helpful advice. We are particularly grateful to our students during the last several terms for their patience, endurance, and penetrating comments as they helped us in class-testing the materials contained in this text.

Anthony J. Curley
Robert M. Bear

University Park, Pennsylvania

Investment Analysis and Management

Chapter 1
Introduction

Investment is a topic which interests millions of investors, from individuals who manage personal assets through professionals responsible for portfolios valued in the hundreds of millions of dollars. It involves relationships ranging from the very naive through the highly sophisticated; investment strategies, for example, include some bordering on myth and superstition and others that require electronic computers to solve complex mathematical models. Investment relies in part on formal principles developed in academic disciplines and in part on intuition and judgment forged through time "on the (Wall) Street." It is often a bewildering area for those who must cope with "random walk," "short sales," "NASDAQ," "weak-form efficiency," and other terms which constitute the specialized vocabulary of the investment community. It is also, perhaps most crucially, a dynamic and developing art; investment principles are based on analytical, managerial, and institutional elements which are currently in a state of rapid and significant change. The complexity and dynamism of the investment environment, coupled with the rational motive to increase personal wealth, account in large part for the fascination which so many persons have for investment topics.

This text studies the process of analyzing and managing investment opportunities. It attempts to reduce complexity by ordering and structuring principles on a common foundation which can be applied to any financial asset: common stocks, preferred stocks, bonds and mortgages, convertible securities, options, commodity futures, or portfolios consisting of two or more of these. Major topics are developed historically to place contemporary procedures in perspective and to provide a basis for evaluating future change. Technical terms are defined and discussed as relevant topics are introduced.

The text recognizes that the investment process is both inexact and incomplete in the sense that a number of important theoretical and methodological problems remain to be solved. Operationality is stressed but not to the extreme of ignoring shortcomings which impair practical application. When deficiencies are recognized they are discussed in light of recent research in investments to establish a basis for incorporating new developments as they occur. More generally, text materials are based on the existing literature in an effort to provide a reasonably complete description of important issues and controversies.

This chapter discusses the purpose, organization, and assumptions on which the development of text materials is based; it also provides a brief historical survey of investment performance. The first section examines the investment process; the organization of text materials is reviewed in relation to elements of that process. The second section considers the relevance of security analysis because some people argue that market efficiency obviates the need for traditional analytical methods. The integration of security analysis and portfolio management, a major objective of the text, is also introduced. The third section describes the educational philosophy underlying specific decisions as to content and level of difficulty. The relationships existing among investment principles and principles of accounting, economics, finance, mathematics, psychology, and statistics are also discussed. Finally, return on investment during the last half century is reviewed to provide an introduction to the challenges and rewards facing investment managers.

Text Organization

Figure 1.1 is a schematic description of the investment process. The relationship described there is continuous but it is convenient to begin with the *screening* problem. Although analysts with access to large computers may attempt to evaluate all possible assets, it is more likely that the population of securities will be screened in order to develop a subset which will then be subjected to detailed analysis. The screened subset is analyzed and risk-return measures are estimated; this process is called *security analysis. Portfolio analysis* follows; risk and return are evaluated for combinations of individual assets. The fourth stage involves *timing and portfolio revision.* As economic conditions vary, and with the arrival of new information concerning individual securities or the capital market in general, resources must be

Figure 1.1
The Investment Process

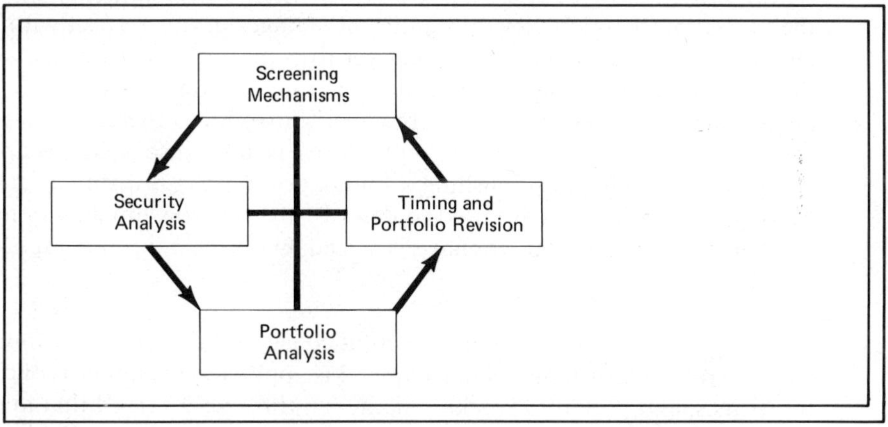

reallocated among cash and other assets. This involves portfolio revision and the first stage in that process is, again, the screening problem.

The text is organized to conform to the investment process, although the order in which materials are presented necessarily differs from the order described above. As summarized in Table 1.1, the text contains five major sections.

Table 1.1
Text Organization

Section	*Chapter*	*Topics Discussed*
Foundations	2	Capital markets
	3	Rate of return concepts
	4	Investment elements
Security analysis	5	Fixed-income securities
	6	Common stock
	7	Accounting data
	8	Price-earnings ratio
	9	Forecasting
Analytical extensions	10	Special situations
	11	Convertibles and warrants
	12	Commodities and options
Portfolio analysis	13	Screening and efficient markets
	14	Diversification
	15	Portfolio models
Investment management	16	Portfolio performance measures
	17	Timing and portfolio revision
	18	Investment strategies
	Appendix	Compound interest relationships

1. FOUNDATIONS. Three chapters are devoted to environmental and analytical foundations. Chapter 2 considers the role, function, and structure of the capital markets; in view of significant changes in this respect within the last few years, and potential changes yet to come, contemporary issues are discussed in detail. Chapter 3 analyzes the rate of return concept; the basic analytical model used throughout the text is introduced there. The development and measurement of market indexes is also discussed. Chapter 4 completes the task of establishing a foundation for the investment process. Management principles are used to describe the relationship among investment elements; particular emphasis is placed on the meaning and importance of risk.

2. SECURITY ANALYSIS. The next section consists of five chapters. In Chapter 5 the rate of return model of Chapter 3 is applied to the analysis of bonds, mortgages, and preferred stocks. Chapters 6 through 9 extend that application to the analysis of common stocks. The equity valuation model is developed in Chapter 6. Chapter 7 provides a detailed discussion of the accounting process, and Chapter 8 considers the difficult problem of the price-earnings capitalization ratio. Forecasting is discussed in Chapter 9; a case study is provided there to illustrate the equity valuation process.

3. ANALYTICAL EXTENSIONS. Chapter 10 examines special situations in security analysis where one or more variables differ from those developed in the basic equity model; in the case of a firm that goes public for the first time, for example, accounting data are likely to be far more limited than the data available for a seasoned firm. Merger and bankruptcy are also considered in Chapter 10.

The next two chapters analyze the forward pricing of goods and claims. Warrants and convertible securities are discussed in Chapter 11, and security options and commodity futures are discussed in Chapter 12.

4. PORTFOLIO ANALYSIS. Chapters 5 through 12 focus upon individual securities; the next three chapters expand upon that discussion by analyzing the combination of securities in an investment portfolio. Chapter 13 introduces the concept of the efficient pricing of assets and discusses the relevance of different types of analysis in that context. The problem of security screening, which is often overlooked, is also discussed. The meaning and significance of diversification are explored in Chapter 14 where a foundation is established for the discussion of portfolio analysis contained in Chapter 15.

5. INVESTMENT MANAGEMENT. The three remaining chapters focus upon problems and details involved in managing a portfolio. Chapter 16 contains an illustration of portfolio selection and then introduces and illustrates a number of portfolio performance measures. Chapter 17 explores the very difficult problem of timing and portfolio revision. Chapter 18 considers

elements which affect the management of individual portfolios; the topics discussed there include income taxes and mutual fund performance.

Compound interest is described in an appendix to the text. This material is included in an appendix because it may have been encountered in other courses and because location at the end of other text materials does not disturb the logical flow of the basic discussion. The appendix also contains compound interest tables and a table of common logarithms.

Security Analysis in an Efficient Market

The relevance of security analysis has been controversial for several decades. Originally the debate centered on the relative merits of "fundamental" security analysis as opposed to a set of charting techniques referred to as "technical analysis." More recently, evidence of efficiency in the capital market pricing mechanism has been interpreted by some to imply the uselessness of *both* fundamental security analysis and technical analysis. Since a major part of this text is a description of security analysis, it is important to consider the question at this point.

SECURITY ANALYSIS

Fundamental security analysis involves the processing of available information concerning a firm in order to arrive at a subjective estimate of the expected return and risk to an investor who purchases the firm's stocks or bonds. Fundamental analysis can also be defined more narrowly as the process of calculating a firm's *intrinsic value*; this is an equilibrium price which can be compared to the current market price in order to identify undervalued and overvalued securities. The term "fundamentalist" is more closely associated with the narrower definition.

Relevant information is both quantitative and qualitative. The former includes the firm's stock price history, financial data generated by accountants, reaction of the firm to changes in macroeconomic variables, and other data which may be used to forecast return on investment. Qualitative information includes such items as the assessment of competence of a firm's management. Information can also be classified as (1) publicly available or (2) inside; the former is generally available at little or no cost while the latter is known only to a limited number of persons. Notwithstanding its usual definition as data available to corporate employees, inside information may be generated externally from publicly available information, through private techniques developed by an analyst.[1]

[1] See Manown Kisor, Jr., and Van A. Messner, "The Filter Approach and Earnings Forecasts," *Financial Analysts Journal*, January–February 1969, pp. 109–115.

Security analysis is not a unique and codified set of techniques. There is basic agreement as to the general analytical formulation, but forecasting techniques and qualitative adjustments will vary from one analyst to another. Research has provided increasingly better forecasting methods but the search for superior techniques continues. A large part of security analysis consists of routine forecasts using a model which is considered to be most reliable by the analyst in question; risk and return elements are estimated on the basis of anticipations formed from existing information. As new information is received, it is compared with anticipated values and the forecasting process is repeated. On occasions new information may concern an unexpected and major event. In this case windfall gain or loss accrues to shareholders as market price adjusts to reflect that information; equilibrium risk-return dimensions may also be altered significantly. The quality of the analytical process depends on the ability to anticipate events; in this respect the value of inside information becomes obvious.[2]

TECHNICAL ANALYSIS

Technical analysis is an alternative methodology in which relevant information is limited to historical market prices and trading volumes. Technicians recognize the importance of basic valuation elements but they assume that information concerning those elements has been completely discounted by investors and it is therefore reflected in the current market price. Accordingly, there would be no rationale for ongoing fundamental security analysis. Technicians also assume dependence in the time series of market prices; that is, they assume that price behavior repeats itself through time. On these assumptions, technical analysis consists of procedures designed to uncover systematic historical patterns which can be used to predict future price behavior. These procedures range from the observation of price trends to computer-assisted trading rules based on past prices and trading volumes.

The relevance of technical analysis has been very controversial. It has a mystique which leads some investors to use it in the pursuit of systematic gain based on simplistic decision rules. Proponents staunchly defend it while critics have subjected it to ridicule.[3] Although interest in technical analysis appears to be waning, there are investors who continue to believe that one of a large number of charting techniques or mechanical trading rules will lead systematically to above average gains.

Unfortunately, technical analysis has no theoretical foundation on which it can be defended. In addition, there is impressive statistical evidence

[2] It is for this reason that federal regulations prohibit corporate insiders from profiting from inside information. Regulation will be considered in Chapter 2.

[3] See Daniel Seligman, "Playing the Market with Charts" and "The Mystique of Point-and-Figure," articles reprinted from *Fortune* Magazine, February and March 1962, in *Elements of Investments*, ed. Hsiu-Kwang Wu and Alan J. Zakon (New York: Holt, Rinehart and Winston, 1965).

which suggests that mechanical rules are not profitable.[4] Finally, the methodology of technical analysis is elusive; stock price charts, for example, differ widely in both design and interpretation. For these reasons technical analysis is briefly summarized in an appendix to Chapter 13; it is included there for completeness because analysts should recognize its basic features.

EFFICIENT MARKETS

The most recent challenge to security analysis arose because of the statement and testing of the *efficient market hypothesis.*[5] An efficient market is defined as one in which security prices fully reflect all available information. As new information arrives it is discounted and price immediately adjusts to a new and correct level. Under the circumstances detailed analysis of existing information would appear to be fruitless. In fact it is not. As Lorie and Hamilton have pointed out, it is the interaction of investors in analyzing new information and in adjusting portfolios which causes price to respond in an efficient market; paradoxically, if investors accepted the efficiency hypothesis, and abandoned security analysis, market efficiency would decrease.[6]

There are three reasons why security analysis remains relevant in a generally efficient market:

1. In an efficient but less than perfect market, there is a time lag between the arrival of information and its subsequent reflection in price. During that interval security analysis provides an opportunity to adjust portfolios profitably. Market efficiency in this respect has not been fully established but evidence which is available suggests that price response is fairly rapid; this may imply that rewards arising from security analysis are captured by institutional investors and others with the capacity to process large amounts of data quickly and efficiently.
2. Superior analytical techniques may allow the analyst to transform publicly available information into inside information. This possibility is difficult to evaluate because there is little motivation for making superior techniques public. But some evidence is available which supports the proposition.[7]
3. Security analysis is critical to the investment process even in the case of instantaneous price response because securities must be evaluated in a portfolio context. Correct pricing of individual assets in an efficient but less than perfect market does not imply investor indifference to the choice of assets which are held in a portfolio. As the price of an individual security

[4] This will be discussed in detail at a later time when the random walk controversy is reviewed. An excellent summary of studies of price behavior is found in Eugene F. Fama, "Efficient Capital Markets: A Review of Theory and Empirical Work," *Journal of Finance*, May 1970, pp. 383–417.

[5] The efficient market hypothesis will be examined in detail in Chapter 13.

[6] J. H. Lorie and M. T. Hamilton, *The Stock Market: Theories and Evidence* (Homewood, Ill.: Irwin, 1973), p. 98.

[7] See Kisor and Messner, "Filter Approach and Earnings Forecasts," and Henry A. Latané, O. Maurice Joy, and Charles P. Jones, "Quarterly Data, Sort-Rank Routines, and Security Evaluation," *Journal of Business*, October 1970, pp. 427–438.

responds to new information, reflecting change in risk and expected return, the security in question may no longer be desirable as part of the portfolio *for some particular investors.* Other investors, in contrast, may wish to acquire the asset *because* of the change in risk and return. Portfolio management is clearly a continuing process with portfolio revision dependent upon evaluation and reevaluation of asset risk-return elements. Security analysis and portfolio selection are therefore complementary; they are both compatible with, and necessary to, an efficient capital market.

PORTFOLIO ANALYSIS

Investment consists of (1) analysis of risk-return elements for individual assets and (2) allocation of available wealth among individual assets. The first step in the process is security analysis and the second is portfolio analysis. Portfolio theory was somewhat vague and elusive until the early 1950s when the pioneering work of Harry Markowitz provided a sound foundation for the construction and application of operational models.[8] Since that time portfolio analysis has changed from a frontier topic in research into an applied area with day-by-day importance. Portfolio theory involves complex and currently unresolved problems and research in the area continues; at the same time, portfolio measures have become familiar in practice and portfolio analysis has become increasingly operational.

With the translation from theory to practice, a process which is still under way, portfolio analysis has been emphasized in the finance curriculum. At first security analysis and portfolio analysis were viewed as competitive, with significance of the latter implying insignificance of the former. More recently, however, as discussed in the preceding section, capital efficiency has been reconciled with security analysis and elements of the analytical process have been integrated. To demonstrate this, the relationship between security analysis and portfolio analysis must be considered in greater detail.

The description of the portfolio model which follows is intended only for purposes of establishing the linkage among analytical components of the investment process. Portfolio will be treated in detail in later chapters of the text. For present purposes, and briefly, there are three inputs to the basic portfolio model; for each security considered for inclusion in a portfolio, required data include:

1. A statistical estimate of the expected return to be realized from investing in that security.
2. A statistical estimate of the variability in return, or risk, for that security.
3. A statistical measure of the covariability among returns for that security and all other securities considered for the portfolio.

Given these inputs, output from the model is a set of portfolios which minimize risk for any level of expected return; this is known as the *efficient*

[8] Harry Markowitz, "Portfolio Selection," *Journal of Finance*, March 1952, pp. 77–91; *Portfolio Selection: Efficient Diversification of Investments* (New York: Wiley, 1959).

set from which investors select the portfolio they desire according to their attitude toward risk and return.

Security analysis provides estimates of expected return and risk and, depending on the adequacy of statistical techniques employed, estimates of covariability as well. In practice the association among returns may have to be inferred from historical data since alternative methodologies are difficult to accomplish even by computer. In any event, the relationship between security and portfolio analysis becomes clear. Security analysis provides statistical estimates of expected return and risk for individual assets; in the second stage of the process, given these estimates, efficient portfolios are defined and wealth is allocated among assets in accordance with an investor's attitude concerning the trade-off between risk and return.

In summary, security analysis and portfolio analysis interact to provide a basis for the selection of assets which will be held for investment purposes. As analytical techniques are perfected and applied, capital market efficiency increases. But increased analytical sophistication also results in increased demands on the talents and training of investment analysts; the next section of this chapter considers the role of formal education in developing professional investment skills.

Formal Training and the Professional Investor

Successful analysts and managers blend formal training and sound common sense with insight gained through on-the-job experience. Only the first of these can be addressed academically although professional competence requires continuing education throughout one's career. In designing formal course work some framework is needed for selecting materials to be included and for determining the level of rigor with which those materials will be presented. The framework adopted here is summarized below.

EDUCATIONAL PHILOSOPHY

Underlying the organization and development of this text is a basic educational philosophy. Simply stated, it adopts the objective of structuring professional training in terms of both the current state of the art and the prospect of future developments which may alter that state. Knowledge of the first is necessary for entry to a successful career and appreciation of the second is required for career advancement and satisfaction.

The development of entry-level skills is the primary objective of this text but frontier issues are also considered throughout. Security analysis and portfolio management is a specialized area in a professional school. For this reason entry-level skills must be emphasized. But entry skills are an inadequate preparation for excellent achievement. At minimum, success requires a willingness to adapt to change and, more commonly, success implies an ability to innovate change to which others adapt. For that reason, and to provide a foundation for continuing professional education, frontier topics will be discussed. Nonetheless, the basic thrust of the text is directed to the entry level.

RELATIONSHIP TO OTHER ACADEMIC AREAS

Principles of investment analysis and portfolio management are very dependent on elements and principles developed in a number of other academic subjects. Difficulties arise in designing coursework and reading materials in investments because backgrounds in related subjects can vary widely among students within a given college curriculum. This text assumes a background in accounting, economics, and statistics at the elementary level. Advanced training in these areas is necessary for professional investors but it is not prerequisite to an understanding of the elements of investments. Forecasting, for example, requires mastery of a number of statistical methods but the role of forecasting in security analysis can be grasped by anyone with an introductory exposure to statistics.

Investment principles are based on elements developed in a number of academic disciplines; these may be classified as basic (economics, psychology, and mathematics) and applied (statistics and accounting) as depicted in Figure 1.2. Computer science is assigned a special classification since it is unnecessary to some parts of the investment process but critical to some others.

1. ECONOMICS. Economics is defined as the art of allocating scarce resources among competing end uses; since this is also an excellent definition of the portfolio problem, it is obvious that investments and economics are closely related. In fact, many of the topics which are called "finance" in a college curriculum can more properly be described as applied economics.

Figure 1.2
Foundations for Investments

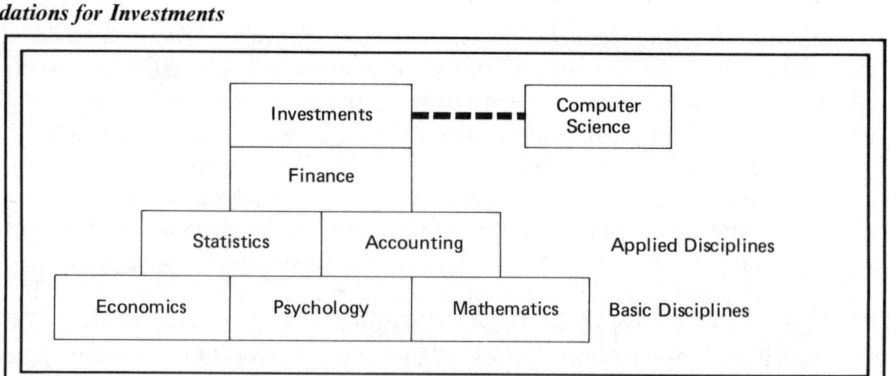

Economics is important to the study of investments for two reasons. First, economics provides guidelines for rational decision making according to rules of logic and arithmetic. This is critical to professional analysts and managers. Second, and more directly, economic variables are an integral part of almost all models used in security and portfolio analyses. For example, sales for a given firm may be modeled as dependent on gross national product, or some other macroeconomic variable, for purposes of forecasting future sales. Alternatively, income estimation, given the level of sales, depends upon cost relationships developed in microeconomics. An in-depth understanding of economics, and economic variables, increases the level of competence of the professional investor.

2. PSYCHOLOGY. Investment is related to another basic discipline, psychology, but this relationship is poorly understood and it has been very difficult to isolate.[9] On one level, it is not uncommon to read of the role of "market psychology" in contributing to sharp fluctuations in the price of individual securities or market averages. But available evidence suggests that investors cannot profit systematically through trading strategies based upon group behavior under unusual circumstances.[10] On a different level, psychology can make a significant contribution to the investment process. Value depends upon investors' expectations as to the future and some believe that psychology is the key to unraveling the manner in which expectations are formed. The point is illustrated by the "beauty contest" analogy set forth by John Maynard Keynes who compared the investment decision with the decision one has in predicting a contest winner: "It is not a case of choosing those which, to the best of one's judgment, are really the prettiest, nor even those which average opinion genuinely thinks the prettiest. We have reached the third degree where we devote our intelligences to anticipating what average opinion expects the average opinion to be. And there are some, I believe, who practice the fourth, fifth, and higher degrees."[11]

The investment decision involves the reactions of other participants, a problem which psychology addresses. Research in this area has been very limited but it is to be hoped that behavioral science will contribute a great deal in the future in explaining the formation of investors' expectations.

3. MATHEMATICS. Mathematics describes complicated structures in a simplified and precise manner. Some assume, incorrectly, that mathematics should be reserved for persons with above average intelligence. But the

[9] A well-known exploration of market psychology, written by a Wall Street professional using a pseudonym, is 'Adam Smith,' *The Money Game* (New York: Random House, 1967).

[10] See Victor Niederhoffer, "The Analysis of World Events and Stock Prices," *Journal of Business*, April 1971, pp. 193–219; Frank K. Reilly and Eugene F. Drzycimski, "Tests of Market Efficiency Following Major Events," *Journal of Business Research*, Summer 1973, pp. 57–72.

[11] John Maynard Keynes, *The General Theory of Employment Interest and Money* (New York: Harcourt Brace Jovanovich, 1935), p. 156.

opposite seems more likely. Brilliance implies an ability to grasp complex relationships without the benefit of tools used by less gifted persons. Mathematics provides a more normal basis for expressing those associations.

To illustrate, consider the mathematical model summarized in Equation 1.1:[12]

$$P = \frac{D}{k - g} \quad (P\uparrow \text{ as } D\uparrow,\ k\downarrow,\ \text{or } g\uparrow) \tag{1.1}$$

where

P = current price per share of common stock
D = current dividend per share
k = rate of return required by investors to purchase the stock
g = rate of growth in dividends per share

From Equation 1.1, price will increase as the numerator of the fraction increases or the denominator decreases. Thus Equation 1.1 specifies a direct relationship between share price P and either dividend D or growth rate g; it also specifies an inverse relationship between price and required rate of return k. Equation 1.1 describes these relationships more easily and precisely than they could be described verbally. This text employs mathematics in the manner described above. Equations are used to simplify the expression of relationships among analytical variables.[13]

4. STATISTICS. Statistics is another essential analytical tool. It is a branch of mathematics which deals with methods for analyzing numerical data. Statistics provides the operational models which, together with data inputs from economics and accounting, are the foundation of security analysis. Although this text requires only an introductory exposure to statistics, analytical competence implies formal training at a far more advanced level. Elements of statistics are introduced and/or reviewed here as the development of text materials requires. The regression model, which is especially important to both security analysis and portfolio theory, is discussed in detail in an appendix to Chapter 8.

5. ACCOUNTING. Among applied academic disciplines none is more important to investments than the study of principles of accounting. The only internally generated record of a firm's activity is provided by accountants and security analysts must be thoroughly familiar with principles and practices employed in generating financial statement data. This is not a simple task. Accounting principles allow a wide variety of methods for

[12] Equation 1.1 is a familiar model in finance. It will be introduced formally in another chapter of the text where its advantages and disadvantages will be discussed. For the moment, it is included only to illustrate the value of mathematics in explaining investment elements.

[13] Mathematics provides an opportunity to do more than this; insights provided by Equation 1.1, for example, can be greatly expanded by application of techniques of calculus. But that is unnecessary here and text materials are developed without mathematical rigor.

recording and tracing selected transactions and these methods are subject to change, often rapid change, through time. Because of the central significance of accounting in the analytical process, and in view of dynamic institutional forces which affect accountancy, Chapter 7 is directed to an in-depth review of accounting from an analyst's perspective.

6. FINANCE. Investment is related to and dependent upon other areas in the finance curriculum. "Corporation finance" is a case in point; variables affecting the value of a firm are identified and normative decision rules are developed to assist the financial manager in maximizing value. In the investments course those same variables are studied historically, and then extrapolated, in the process of security analysis. Familiarity with principles of financial management, and other elements of the finance curriculum, is clearly helpful in studying investments.

This text is self-contained with respect to other areas in finance in that all necessary foundations are independently introduced and developed. Although this policy may result in the inclusion of materials which seem repetitious to some, it is necessary to avoid the more serious error of omitting necessary but unfamiliar foundations. Risk and compound interest relationships are examples of important topics which are completely defined and developed here.

7. COMPUTER SCIENCE. The use of computers has become widespread in all areas of business decision making. In the investment community, major institutions have computerized security and portfolio analysis and complex models employing machine-readable data are now used routinely. For this reason security analysts should be familiar with computer operations.

Although computer science is important in investments, this text is developed with minimal reliance on the computer. There are two reasons for this. First, hardware may be unavailable to students in a particular course. Second, and more importantly, reliance on the computer may lessen comprehension rather than increase it. It is possible to operate "canned" programs using data stored on magnetic tapes with little or no knowledge of the underlying mechanism. For educational purposes it is preferable to study relationships directly. Once mastered, analytical procedures can easily be adapted and converted to a computerized basis.

Investment Performance

This chapter has introduced the text and, in the process, it has also introduced investment analysis and investment management. To be complete, and to provide a perspective for the materials to follow, the long-run performance of the capital markets will be reviewed at this point.

Historical returns have been measured by researchers at a number of universities and financial institutions.[14] Two recent and comprehensive studies were provided by Soldofsky and Max and by Ibbotson and Sinquefield; their studies measured returns on common stocks and bonds over the periods 1910–1969 and 1926–1974, respectively.[15] According to the Ibbotson and Sinquefield study, the value of common stocks increased during the 1926–1974 period at a compound annual rate of 8.5 percent per year. Adjusted for inflation, measured by the consumer price index, common stock value grew at a real rate of 6.1 percent. At that deflated rate $1.00 invested in 1926 was worth $18.53 at the end of 1974, a year in which the third worst market decline since 1926 was experienced. Long-term corporate and government bonds provided compound annual rates of return of 3.6 and 3.2 percent, respectively; adjusted for inflation, they were 1.4 and 1.0 percent. Year to year values for stocks, bonds, and the consumer price index are portrayed in Figure 1.3.

Some specific highlights of capital market behavior over the past half century are the following:

Of the 8.5 percent compound annual return to common stock, 5.0 percent resulted from dividends and the balance was represented by capital gains. Annual stock yields were volatile, ranging from +54.0 to −43.3 percent with a standard deviation of 22.5 percent. Stock returns were positive in two-thirds of the years and the longest period with an overall negative return was the fourteen years from 1929 through 1942. The decrease in stock value in 1974 was −26.4 percent, the worst one-year decline since 1937. The market recovery of 1975–1976 ended the most recent period of overall negative return after an eight-year (1967–1974) duration.

The behavior of corporate and government bond yields was very similar during the 49-year period studied by Ibbotson and Sinquefield. Returns were positive for corporate bonds in 39 of those years and they were positive for government bonds in 37 years; bond yields ranged from 18.4 to −8.1 percent for corporates and 16.8 to −9.2 percent for governments. Bond returns were substantially less than stock returns over the entire period but bonds outperformed stocks on average throughout the 17-year period spanning the Great Depression. Moreover, bond yields were far less variable than stock yields throughout the period.

The investment yields traced in Figure 1.3 provide a realistic interpretation of the investment process which was described schematically in

[14] L. Fisher and J. Lorie, "Rates of Return on Investments in Common Stock: The Year-by-Year Record, 1926–65," *Journal of Business*, July 1968, pp. 291–316; L. Fisher and R. Weil, "Coping with the Risk of Interest-Rate Fluctuations: Returns to Bondholders from Naive and Optimal Strategies," *Journal of Business*, October 1971, pp. 408–431; and *An Analytical Record of Yields and Yield Spreads* (New York: Salomon Bros., May 1975).

[15] Roger G. Ibbotson and Rex A. Sinquefield, "Stocks, Bonds, Bills, and Inflation: Year by Year Historical Returns (1926–1974)," *Journal of Business*, January 1976, pp. 11–47 and Robert M. Soldofsky and Dale F. Max, "Securities as a Hedge Against Inflation: 1910–1969" *Journal of Business Research*, April 1975, pp. 165–172.

Figure 1.3
Value Relatives of $1 Invested (1926–1974)

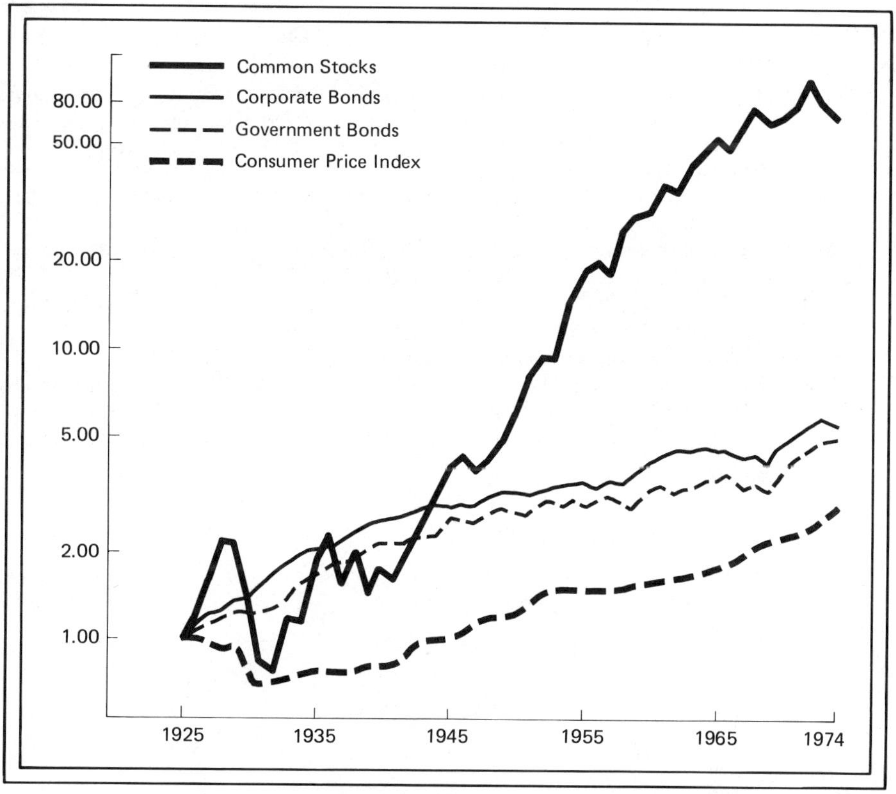

Source: R. G. Ibbotson and R. Sinquefield, "Stocks, Bonds, Bills, and Inflation: Year by Year Historical Returns (1926–1974)," *Journal of Business*, January 1976, p. 36.

Figure 1.1. Underlying stock and bond averages are thousands of individual securities which must be screened to identify candidates for inclusion in a portfolio. Risk and return elements, which are evident in the 1926–1974 record, are analyzed in security analysis; individual securities are then selected with a view toward aggregate levels of risk and return for a portfolio of assets. Finally, as Figure 1.3 clearly demonstrates, relative performance of different types of securities varies widely over time and portfolio revision, or timing, becomes a crucial element in establishing investors' strategies.

Selected References

Bernstein, Leopold A., "In Defense of Fundamental Investment Analysis," *Financial Analysts Journal*, January–February 1975, pp. 57–61.

Blume, Marshall E., and Irwin Friend, "Risk, Investment Strategy and the Long-Run Rates of Return," *The Review of Economics and Statistics* LVI, August 1974, pp. 259–269.

Fama, Eugene F., "Efficient Capital Markets: A Review of Theory and Empirical Evidence," *Journal of Finance*, May 1970, pp. 383–417.

Graham, B., D. L. Dodd, and S. Cottle, *Security Analysis*, 4th ed. (New York: McGraw-Hill, 1962).

Ibbotson, R., and R. Sinquefield, "Stocks, Bonds, Bills, and Inflation: Year by Year Historical Returns (1926–1974)," *Journal of Business*, January 1976, pp. 11–47.

Lease, Ronald C., Wilbur G. Lewellen, and Gary G. Schlarbaum, "The Individual Investor: Attributes and Attitudes," *Journal of Finance*, May 1974, pp. 413–433.

Lev, Baruch, *Financial Statement Analysis: A New Approach* (Englewood Cliffs, N.J.: Prentice-Hall, 1974).

Lorie, J. H., and M. T. Hamilton, *The Stock Market: Theories and Evidence* (Homewood, Ill.: Irwin, 1973).

Malkiel, Burton, "Reports of the Death of Common Stocks are Greatly Exaggerated," *Fortune*, November 1977, pp. 156–160, 164, 169.

Roberts, H. V., "Stock Market 'Patterns' and Financial Analysis: Methodological Suggestions," *Journal of Finance*, March 1959, pp. 1–10.

'Smith, Adam,' *The Money Game* (New York: Random House, 1967).

Soldofsky, Robert M., and Dale F. Max, "Securities as a Hedge Against Inflation: 1910–1969," *Journal of Business Research*, April 1975, pp. 165–172.

Treynor, Jack L., "Long Term Investing," *Financial Analysts Journal*, May–June 1976, pp. 56–59.

Chapter 2
Capital Markets

Capital markets is a term which is used to describe a variety of activities which (1) channel new savings into investment or (2) facilitate the exchange of existing securities. Capital markets include stock and bond markets, commodity markets, option markets, and other markets dealing with claims issued against real goods and services. The importance of capital markets is demonstrated in Table 2.1 where the comparative growth of national wealth and financial claims in the United States is traced from 1900 through 1968.[1] Capital markets have evolved hand-in-hand with other economic sectors and have grown more rapidly than most in response to the relatively greater growth of financial claims and corresponding demands for efficient and highly liquid means of transferring these investments. Individual security transactions, taken in the aggregate, give rise to security values measured in the trillions of dollars. For this reason the market environment in which transactions take place is a logical starting point for a study of the investment process.

[1] The apparent premium of financial claim values over tangible asset values in recent periods results in substantial part from the combined effort of (a) understating tangible assets due to accelerated depreciation techniques and (b) investor optimism regarding future economic growth.

Table 2.1
National Wealth and Financial Assets in the United States, 1900–1968 (1968 values, $ billion)

	1968	*1960*	*1952*	*1929*	*1900*
Tangible National Wealth					
I. Land	716	413	200	113.5	31.0
II. Buildings	1536	925	577	189.9	34.9
III. Equipment	611	368	228	80.6	12.6
IV. Inventory & others	277	190	148	55.2	9.2
Total national wealth	3141	1895	1153	439.2	87.7
Financial Claims					
I. Nonstock claims	2791.2	1555.5	971.8	317.3	44.8
II. Corporate stock	1126.2	445.9	189.7	186.7	13.9
Total financial claims	3917.4	2000.4	1161.5	504.0	58.7
Financial claims/Tangible wealth	1.247	1.056	1.007	1.148	.669

Source: Institutional Investor Study, Report of the Securities and Exchange Commission, Supplementary Volume I, May 10, 1971, pp. 95, 98.

This chapter describes the organization and operations of major capital markets. The first section is a brief introduction to the role of a market system in exchanging financial claims. The next two sections examine *primary markets* where new securities are distributed to investors and *secondary markets* where existing securities are purchased and sold. Security brokerage functions are described in the fourth section and government regulation of market operations is reviewed in the fifth section. The chapter concludes with a discussion of current problems and contemporary trends in capital market activities.

Functions of the Capital Market System

The basic function of capital markets is to provide an efficient mechanism for the exchange of securities but the term "efficiency" has a number of different interpretations in this respect. Efficiency may refer to (1) operating procedures, (2) allocation of available funds among competing uses, or (3) realization of an individual investor's goals and objectives.

EFFICIENT OPERATION. Financial institutions are operationally efficient when the cost of doing business is minimized for services provided and these economies are passed on to customers in the form of reduced service charges.

To minimize operating costs, institutions must be large enough to realize economies of scale and cost-reducing technology must be adopted as it becomes available. The structure of an efficient capital market will remain competitive and adaptive to changing needs.

EFFICIENT ALLOCATION. Allocational efficiency requires that savings are channeled into investment in a manner in which the level of return is justified in terms of the risks involved. Efficient allocation assures promising business ventures of an adequate supply of reasonably priced capital, while at the same time unpromising or obsolete operations are denied or drained of funds. The requirements for efficient allocation of capital include a pricing mechanism that operates freely in response to supply and demand conditions; accurate, low-cost, and broadly disseminated sources of information; and a rational population of investors who seek the highest possible return for the risks that they are willing to assume.

Security prices in an allocationally efficient capital market will adjust rapidly and, on average, properly to all relevant new information. News of an oil strike in an area where mineral rights are held by a major oil company should produce an immediate increase in the price of the common stock. The immediate rise, in this particular instance, may prove to be too little or too much as additional information becomes known, but if the pricing of the stock is efficient the change in price will be fair for the information known at the time. Since new events occur regularly, security prices change constantly in response to a continuing stream of new information.[2]

EFFICIENT INVESTMENT. An efficient investment for an individual is one where perceived after-tax return equals or exceeds all other investments of equivalent risk. An efficient investment dominates other investment opportunities. Since investors differ in their expectations of future values and events and face different tax rates, transaction costs, and investment constraints, an investment may be efficient to one investor and inefficient to another. This will result even if capital markets are allocationally efficient in the sense that investments are properly priced by informed investors. Furthermore, there is no assurance that all investments are properly priced at any given time.

OTHER CRITERIA. In addition to efficiency, capital markets are also responsible for maintaining liquidity, continuity, and order.[3] Liquidity refers to the probability of completing a transaction quickly. An important aspect of

[2] The implications of efficient pricing of investments are considered throughout the book and they are discussed in greater detail in Chapter 13.

[3] These capital market objectives were identified by the U.S. Securities and Exchange Commission, *Report of the Special Study of the Securities Markets of the Securities and Exchange Commission* (Washington: U.S. Government Printing Office, 1962), esp. part 2, pp. 13–15.

Table 2.2
Market Value of Major Financial Claims in 1972 and New Issues, 1973–1975 ($ billion)

	Value 1972	*New 1973*	*New 1974*	*New 1975*	*New 1976*
Corporate stock	1228	9.6	4.6	10.4	12.3
Corporate debt	252.1	12.5	23.3	30.1	28.6
U.S. government (marketable) debt	273.7	29.4	33.5	98.0	87.2
State & local debt	173	13.7	17.4	17.3	17.2
Mortgage debt	565	71.9	54.5	59.0	85.4

Source: Federal Reserve Bulletin, September 1973, February 1976, and July 1977.

liquidity is market depth since the level of demand for a security affects the prospects for effectively executing large-sized orders. Continuity requires that a transaction can be executed at the approximate price of immediately preceding and subsequent transactions for the same security. Order refers to the resiliency of the market in absorbing shocks and crises with a minimum of disruptive consequences. In a sense these objectives are in conflict; full attainment of one precludes full attainment of others. For example, emphasis on continuity and market order impacts adversely on efficient pricing, especially at times when major events induce change in the value of securities. Of necessity, a viable capital market system requires compromise among competing objectives; ideally, this would be accomplished in full recognition of the social costs and benefits involved.

Capital markets are a complex of interrelated and specialized financial activities. Broadly speaking, three major functional areas can be identified: primary distributions, secondary markets, and service intermediaries. Primary distribution of new securities by firms and government agencies is accomplished with the assistance of a network of investment bankers who facilitate, and in many cases guarantee, successful distribution to the investment public. Efficient, competitive distribution of new issues is essential to insure uniform and equitable financing costs to all economic units and sectors. Brokers and dealers serve the needs of investors in purchasing and selling existing securities in the secondary markets. The exchange of securities is conducted in organized, quasi-auction market places or through one of a number of direct systems of exchange among brokers referred to as over-the-counter markets. Finally, a number of specialized institutions exist to act as agent for other investors. Among others these service organizations include bank trust departments, insurance companies, mutual funds, and pension funds.[4]

[4] A complete discussion of these service intermediaries is provided in Chapter 18.

Financial services can also be classified by the type of financial claim in question. For example, primary distribution may refer to new stock or new debt. If new debt is issued, a distinction may be made between corporate and government debt as well as between short-term (money market) and long-term (capital market) investments. Table 2.2 provides a survey of financial claims by type in recent years. The magnitude of these outstanding and new issues highlights the importance of both primary and secondary institutions and markets.

Primary Markets: New Security Issues

Each year billions of dollars of new securities—both equity and debt—are issued by corporations and public agencies. Corporations have favored debt financing in recent years primarily because of depressed stock market conditions through 1974 and the favorable tax treatment resulting from the deductibility of interest payments. The financial intermediary who manages the distribution of new securities is the investment banker. Using extensive communication networks and syndication, which is a cooperative arrangement among a number of individual investment banking firms, large blocks of securities can be rapidly and efficiently distributed. The investment banking firm is generally compensated for its services by the "spread" between the price it pays to issuers and the price received from investors. In some cases the investment banking firm accepts partial payment in the form of additional securities or options to purchase securities at a later date. Nonmonetary compensation may include first refusal rights for subsequent issues and membership on the firm's board of directors.

INVESTMENT BANKING INDUSTRY STRUCTURE

Investment banking is characterized by a large number of small firms which are dominated by a few large ones. There are over four thousand firms who are in some manner affiliated with the investment banking industry. Some (e.g., First Boston Corporation) specialize in investment banking services; others (e.g., Merrill Lynch) offer a wide range of other financial services. Approximately seven hundred investment bankers serve as both originator and underwriter; these firms negotiate with the issuer and they guarantee a minimum value for the entire offering. Remaining institutions limit participation to distributing securities to investors. Some investment bankers specialize in certain types of offerings. Others are restricted in their activities. Commercial banks, for example, can underwrite municipal bonds and they can distribute municipal and federal debt; they are prohibited by law from participating in new offerings of corporate stock or bonds to avoid possible conflict of interest with their other financial services.

INVESTMENT BANKING FUNCTIONS

Investment banking encompasses a number of specific services for both issuer and investor. The most important of these are the following:

FINANCIAL ADVISOR. When a prospective issuer first contacts an investment banker, the investment banker initiates a thorough preliminary investigation of the operations and needs of the client firm. This study examines all operating and financial characteristics of the firm, including the capabilities of its management and the structure, competition, and outlook for the industry. Should the investment banker decide that additional financing is warranted, a positive recommendation is made to the firm which details the characteristics and cost of raising new funds. The type of security, equity or debt, and the type of placement, public or private, will depend upon the needs of the firm and current circumstances in the capital markets. In many cases a negative recommendation is given because of the condition of the firm, conditions in the capital markets, or a combination of the two. While the relationship between a firm and its investment banker is very intense when new financing is contemplated, it is generally an ongoing one for most medium- to large-sized corporations and government agencies. In some cases members of investment banking firms serve on the board of directors of client firms. This direct contact does not preclude competition in the industry, however, because client firms may seek competitive bidding by consulting the services of more than one investment banker, placing the offering where terms are most advantageous. Figure 2.1 portrays the investment banking function when financial advice recommends that an issue should be marketed.

ORIGINATOR. An investment banker who reaches a preliminary agreement with a firm to bring forth a new issue is known as the originator. The originator prepares and manages the preparation and distribution of new securities and assumes responsibility for underwriting or insuring the issue. All of the voluminous paperwork, including Securities and Exchange Commission filings, registration statements, and prospectus, becomes the responsibility of the originator.

UNDERWRITING AND DISTRIBUTION. In the case where a new issue is offered publicly, an investment banker may and generally does underwrite the offering. This amounts to a guarantee that the client firm will receive a stated value for its securities; the investment banker assumes the risk that the offering will be unsuccessful. In some cases an originator may underwrite the entire issue. Usually, however, the originator forms a *purchase syndicate* which shares in underwriting liability and the distribution of securities. A purchase syndicate is a group of investment bankers who cooperate on the joint venture of bringing a particular issue to market. Unsold securities will be purchased and held in inventory by the syndicate until they can be

Figure 2.1
The Investment Banking Pyramid: Public Offering

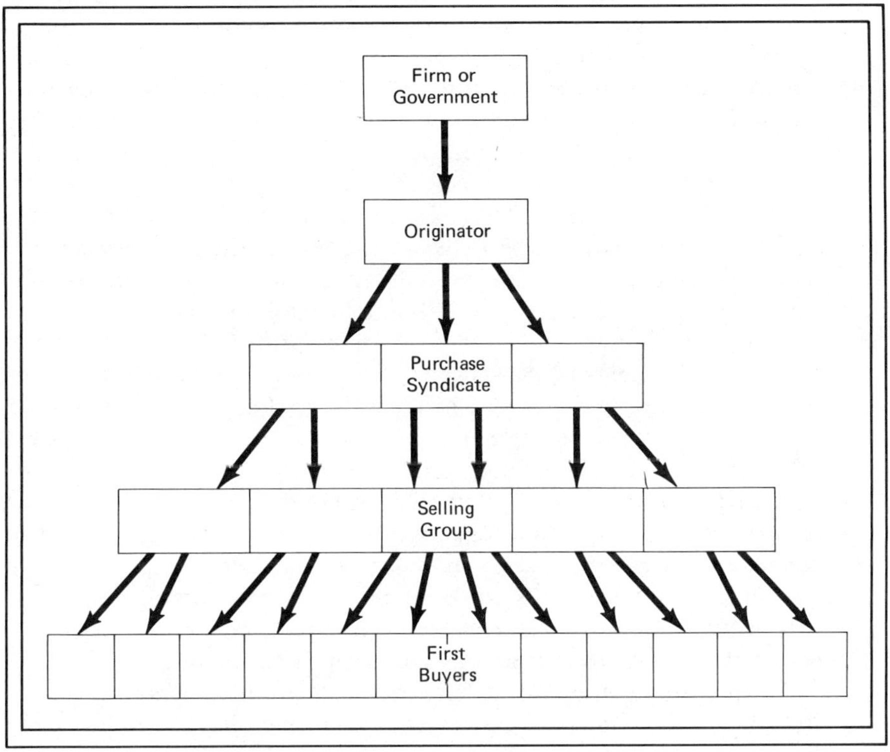

marketed, often at a loss. Each member agrees on the extent of commitment in underwriting and distributing the issue. Depending upon circumstances, a syndicate may be as small as two or as large as several hundred bankers; typically it includes 15 to 30 members. Considerable flexibility exists in the management of a syndicate.

Members of the purchase syndicate usually sell only a portion of the issue directly to their clients. The remainder will be sold and distributed through other bankers recruited by members of the purchase syndicate. This group of bankers is known as the *selling group*. The three-layer process of distributing a new issue which is illustrated in Figure 2.1 (originator–purchase syndicate–selling group) insures wide and rapid dispersion among the investment public and it substantially reduces the extent of possible loss to any one banker should the issue fail to sell as expected.

BROKER–DEALER. Members of the selling group act as agents for the individual investor in the same way as they do for the purchase and sale of existing securities. In many cases, particularly when the issue is not listed on an established exchange, the banker maintains an inventory of the security to facilitate trading. "Making a market" in recently issued new securities is usually considered to be an obligation of the investment banker. For a short time after issue, possibly 30 days but more often only a few days, underwriters provide market support for a new security. This is accomplished by placing orders to buy any shares of the issue that are offered below a determined price. This stabilization activity is legal providing that the banker acknowledges the price support operation. Knowledge that the price will be supported reduces risk to first buyers and increases the probability of acceptance of the issue. In the process, the investment banker's underwriting risk is reduced. An issue that is initially overpriced, however, cannot be supported very long without substantial loss to the underwriter.

Not all issues are underwritten. An investment banker may market an issue on a "best efforts" basis where the issuing firm's proceeds are limited to the portion of the offering which can be sold on the date of issue. As an alternative to public issue, new securities may be privately placed without underwriting with one or more buyers, usually other financial institutions including pension funds and insurance companies. Private placement is sometimes arranged by the issuing firm or government agency but investment bankers generally serve as intermediaries. Private placement avoids Securities and Exchange Commission registration requirements and provides flexible financing arrangements. For these reasons, about one-third of all corporate debt in recent periods has been privately placed.[5]

Most major investment banking firms are members of the Securities Industry Association (SIA), a trade group formed in 1971 by the merger of the Investment Bankers Association with the Association of Stock Exchange Firms. SIA's primary purpose is to provide representation of the common interests of its more than 850 member firms to government, other trade groups and exchanges, and the general public. The association distributes a number of publications relating to the securities industry through its member firms' offices.

Secondary Markets

The primary market for new securities is an important segment of the capital market system but the average investor will more commonly be involved with the purchase and sale of existing securities. The mechanism for the exchange of existing securities is referred to as a secondary market where brokered transactions are executed on an organized exchange or through a network of dealers who are referred to as the over-the-counter

[5] "Direct Placement of Corporate Debt," *Economic Review*, Federal Reserve Bank of Cleveland, August 1970.

Table 2.3
Value of Shares Traded on Registered Exchanges, 1962–1974 ($ billion)

	1962	*1968*	*1974*
NYSE	47.3	145.0	99.2
(Percentage of total)	(86.5)	(73.8)	(83.9)
AMEX	3.6	34.8	5.0
(Percentage of total)	(6.7)	(17.7)	(4.3)
All Other	3.7	16.6	14.0
(Percentage of total)	(6.8)	(8.5)	(11.9)

Source: 1975 Fact Book, New York Stock Exchange, p. 73.

market. The assurance that an investment can be purchased or sold on short notice for a competitively determined price enhances its value; demand for securities would certainly be reduced in the absence of an opportunity for immediate resale and exchange. Lower demand implies higher capital costs and a reduced incentive for new investment. Secondary markets are an important determinant of the nation's economic growth and prosperity because they reallocate available savings to deserving firms in the economy.

Organized security exchanges provide physical trading facilities and formalized mechanisms for exchange. They are "quasi-auction" markets where prices are determined through competitive bidding by numerous buyers and sellers. The term "quasi" is used because security transactions are processed by "specialists" who are responsible for maintaining an orderly and continuous market. Specialist activities will be described in detail shortly. The largest security exchange is the New York Stock Exchange (NYSE) located on Wall Street at Broad Street in lower Manhattan. In 1974 over 80 percent of the value of all stocks traded on exchanges were "Big Board" (NYSE) securities (see Table 2.3). The American Stock Exchange (AMEX), the second largest security exchange in the United States, is located on Trinity Place within a few blocks of the NYSE. The remaining eleven exchanges are regional and they list securities of smaller, less familiar companies.

Between 100 and 900 companies are listed on each regional exchange. The largest regional exchanges have been the Pacific Coast Stock Exchange (PCSE) located in both San Francisco and Los Angeles and the Midwest Stock Exchange (MSE) located in Chicago. The MSE had been the largest regional exchange, rivaling the AMEX in trading activity; however, by 1978 MSE had declined greatly. No company can be listed on both the NYSE and AMEX at the same time but firms listed on either national exchange may also be listed on regional exchanges. In that case prices on regional exchanges are generally based on quotations from the national exchange.[6] A large percentage of transactions on regional exchanges are odd-lot transactions which involve fewer than a hundred shares. An exception is provided by the Spokane Stock Exchange which specializes in very low-priced and typically low-quality oil and mining stocks.

THE NEW YORK STOCK EXCHANGE

The organization and operation of the New York Stock Exchange is followed in most respects by other exchanges. Founded in 1792, the NYSE is an incorporated association of 1366 members who have trading privileges on the floor of the exchange. The total number of members has remained unchanged since 1953. In addition to meeting stringent financial requirements and member recommendations, individuals seeking membership must purchase their "seat" (membership) from a retiring member. Bidding is competitive, and in this century seats on the exchange have sold for as high as $625,000 (1929) and as low as $17,000 (1942). In January of 1978 a seat on the NYSE was valued at $48,000. The value of memberships depends on the expected value to be derived from their ownership. In addition to this initial cost, members are assessed annual dues. The structure of the NYSE is similar to the structure of other corporations. The membership elects a chief executive officer and seven executive officials who manage the operations and affairs of the exchange. Policy issues are determined by a 21-member board of directors which includes 10 public representatives.

MEMBERSHIP. A firm is a member firm of the New York Stock Exchange when one or more partners or stock-holding employees is an exchange member. At the end of 1975 there were 508 member firms, 160 fewer than 12 years earlier. These firms are almost evenly divided between partnerships and corporations but there is a clear trend toward the corporate form of organization. Approximately half of all member firms are known as *commission houses* because they execute buy and sell orders for the public. Many of these are large brokerage firms with regional, national, and, in some cases, international networks of offices. Some commission houses specialize in bond brokerage. Although the majority of bonds are traded over-the-counter, the NYSE has always maintained a substantial market in corporate bonds.

One of every four member firms provides the *specialist* service of matching buy and sell orders. A specialist is charged with maintaining a fair and orderly market in a limited number of exclusively assigned securities, typically five or more. Specialists execute orders for other brokers and they

[6] An exception to this results from time zone differentials which may permit a stock which is listed on a national exchange to be traded through a regional exchange after the market in New York closes. Current trading hours on the NYSE and AMEX are 10:00 A.M. to 4:00 P.M. Eastern Time. The MSE is also open from 10:00 A.M. to 4:00 P.M. Eastern Time, while the PCSE is open from 10:00 A.M. to 5:30 P.M. Eastern Time.

buy and sell stock for their own account. They must maintain an inventory of at least 1200 shares in each of their stocks and they are permitted by the exchange to carry inventory on 25 percent *margin* with 75 percent financed through borrowing. Specialists are expected to subordinate their personal interests for the benefit of the public. When the number of buy orders exceeds sell orders at current price levels, they are expected to sell shares from personal inventory. When there is an excess of sell orders, they will buy shares to equalize supply and demand with minimum impact on price from transaction to transaction. These activities are assigned, regulated, and monitored by the exchange to insure that they stabilize prices. Unfortunately, the public and private roles of the specialist are in economic conflict. As shown in a recent major study, transactions which contribute to market order and continuity also result in a lower and more variable return on invested capital.[7] For this reason the role of the specialist is currently under review and it will probably be modified in the manner discussed in the concluding section of this chapter.

Other member firms and individuals act as floor traders, floor brokers, and odd-lot dealers. Floor traders buy and sell only for their own personal account. Most trading positions are short-term; in many cases a stock is purchased and sold within the same day in what is referred to as *daylight trading*. The floor trader has free access to the trading floor and, as a member, pays no commission, although transactions are subject to exchange clearing fees and stock transfer taxes. The floor trader has been subjected to increasingly strict regulation in recent years in the belief that privilege is enjoyed without matching responsibility. This view overlooks the economic service floor traders provide, within the current exchange structure, in facilitating the rapid and proper adjustment of price to new information.

Floor brokers are seldom affiliated with any one member firm and they do not execute orders for customers. Instead, they serve as a broker's broker, executing orders for other brokers as requested, commonly during periods of peak activity. For this service the floor broker receives part of the commission received by the originating firm.

Shares are exchanged in *round lots*, usually 100 shares; *odd lots* are orders for less than a round lot. Until recently odd-lot orders on the NYSE were executed by one member firm, Carlisle DeCoppet & Co. Other member firms would route their odd-lot orders to Carlisle DeCoppet & Co. for execution at the next round-lot price plus an odd-lot differential of $12\frac{1}{2}$ cents per share. Early in 1976 Merrill Lynch formed their own odd-lot market which operated independently from the exchange.[8] Under the Merrill Lynch plan, odd-lot orders are executed at the current "bid" price to buyers and

[7] *Institutional Investor Study Report of the Securities and Exchange Commission*, Summary Volume, March 10, 1971, pp. 95–98.

[8] Several other major brokerage firms, including Dean Witter & Co., Shearson Hayden Stone, and Paine Webber Jackson & Curtis, have also expressed interest in developing their own odd-lot trading system.

"ask" price to sellers instead of the next round-lot price. A customer who purchased one share of stock with a bid price of $30.00 would pay that amount (plus commission); under the Carlisle system, if the next round-lot transaction cleared at $30.00 the customer would pay $30.125 (plus commission). However, the next round-lot transaction might be lower than the current bid, eliminating or reversing the differential. As a result of Merrill Lynch's odd-lot system the NYSE purchased the Carlisle system with the announced intention of operating it through assigned round-lot specialist firms.[9]

SECURITY LISTING. A firm desiring to be listed on the NYSE must demonstrate to the satisfaction of the exchange that it meets, and has a good chance of maintaining, specified standards. These standards involve size, distribution of ownership, and earnings record. Minimum requirements are:

1. Net tangible assets valued at $16 million or more. The exchange also considers the current market value of all publicly held shares which should also be at least $16 million.
2. A minimum of 2000 shareholders who own at least 100 shares each and a minimum of one million publicly held shares outstanding.
3. Current pretax earnings of $2.5 million and earnings of at least $2.0 million in the two preceding years. Additionally, the exchange considers the outlook and future prospects of the industry and the competitive position of the firm within the industry.

Each firm is considered individually and the requirements listed above are guidelines. Exchange officials must be convinced of the firm's willingness to make full public disclosure of its corporate operations in a fair, orderly, and responsible manner. Timely disclosure of all information which may affect security values is contractually specified in the listing agreement between the company and the exchange. At the end of 1974 there were 1543 common stocks, 537 preferred stocks, 2380 bonds, and 12 warrants listed on the NYSE.

The exchange reserves the right to delist a security when it believes that continued listing is not in the best interests of the investing public. Normally this occurs when the number of shareholders or the market value of the firm falls substantially below initial minimum requirements. The turnover of firms listed on the NYSE is less than on other exchanges where listing requirements are less stringent but the number of firms added or dropped has been substantial. In the 1960–1974 period there were 1077 new common listings while 626 stocks were removed. Many delistings resulted from merger activity which was especially intense in the late sixties. In contrast, 1350 stocks were added to the American Stock Exchange and 942 were removed during 1962–1972. The total number listed at the end of

[9] "Big Board Agrees to Buy Odd-Lot System from Carlisle DeCoppet for $3.5 Million," *The Wall Street Journal*, January 9, 1976.

1972 was 1419. Of the 942 stocks removed, 272 transferred to the NYSE and most of the others were delisted due to merger, liquidation, or failure to maintain exchange standards.

The NYSE reserves the right to suspend trading or to restrict margin transactions for any listed stock. The specialist may suspend trading temporarily when unusual circumstances warrant that action. Margin is the percentage of the cost of a security which must be settled with cash. The exchange established procedures in 1965 for placing individual securities on 100 percent margin, thereby prohibiting the use of credit. This action is taken when the exchange decides that trading activity and price increases are not fully warranted by fundamental conditions; it was originally designed to discourage day trading by floor traders. Through 1970 the exchange imposed 100 percent margins 364 times on a total of 207 different stocks for periods ranging from three weeks to more than a year. One hundred percent margins have been used sparingly since 1970.

THE AMERICAN STOCK EXCHANGE

The American Stock Exchange is also known as the "Little Big Board"; until 1953 it was called the New York Curb Exchange. It has a colorful and somewhat turbulent history dating back to 1850. Reorganized in 1962 following special studies by both the exchange and the Securities and Exchange Commission, the AMEX today is very similar in operation and governance to the NYSE. Most of its listed firms are smaller and younger companies than those carried on the Big Board. The number of common and preferred stocks listed at the end of 1974, 1222 and 83 respectively, was 63 percent of the number listed on the NYSE but their aggregate market value was only 5 percent of the NYSE total. This results because AMEX listing requirements are less stringent than those of the NYSE. As indicated previously, substantial numbers of firms transfer to the NYSE as they grow and prosper; General Motors, DuPont, and McDonalds are a few of these companies.[10]

Unlike the NYSE, the AMEX lists a substantial number of foreign securities as well as numerous stock warrants and options to purchase stock. Only 5 percent of all AMEX stocks are foreign securities, mostly Canadian, but they represent 25 to 30 percent of the total measured by market value. A number of non-Canadian issues are traded through American Depository Receipts, or ADRs, which are certificates representing shares of foreign corporations held by U.S. banks abroad. Originated by the AMEX, ADRs make it possible for U.S. investors to trade in major foreign securities that otherwise, because of U.S. or foreign restrictions, would not be available to them. In addition, the AMEX permits its specialists to make a market in a

[10] The relationship between listing and value is discussed in Chapter 10.

limited number of unlisted stocks. With recent developments in over-the-counter trading, activity in unlisted securities on the AMEX has declined steadily.

OVER-THE-COUNTER TRADING

When securities are traded "over-the-counter" (OTC) no centralized market place is involved; securities are traded directly through brokers and dealers who are linked by telephone and an automated quotation system. Over-the-counter trading involves four distinct groupings or "markets": (1) U.S. government securities, (2) state and municipal obligations, (3) corporate bonds, preferred stocks, and high-grade equity issues, including bank and insurance company stocks, and (4) other unlisted corporate securities. Over-the-counter trading thus covers the range from the least to the most risky of securities. The first three categories represent generally low-risk investment although certain corporate and municipal debt issues are notable exceptions. The majority of corporate bonds, the common stock of insurance companies, banks, and other financial institutions, and all government and quasi-government obligations are traded over-the-counter.

Unlisted common stock is generally more risky than shares listed on exchanges. Most of these securities represent ownership in small local firms where trading occurs on a limited and infrequent basis in the particular geographical region where the firm is located. Some securities, on the other hand, are nationally prominent; unlisted major corporations include Anheuser-Busch, Pinkertons, and Roadway Express. Some eight thousand securities are sufficiently active that at least one security brokerage firm will provide price quotations on a regular basis. Three thousand over-the-counter stocks are traded with sufficient regularity to be included in the automated quotation system which will be described below. In the aggregate, one-quarter to one-third of all shares of common stock traded in the United States, measured by value, are exchanged over-the-counter. Commission rates are generally the same as those charged for an equivalent purchase or sale on the NYSE.

THE NATIONAL ASSOCIATION OF SECURITY DEALERS. The National Association of Security Dealers (NASD) is a trade organization consisting of more than four thousand brokerage firms and 150,000 individual representatives. The organization was formed as a result of the Maloney Act of 1938 which authorized the formation of over-the-counter trade associations for the purpose of self-regulation. The act required the registration of all associations with the Securities and Exchange Commission but NASD was the only one to apply. Although membership is voluntary, the prohibition of trade discounts between member and nonmember firms effectively makes it mandatory. NASD is governed by a board of governors and operational responsibilities are divided into 13 geographic districts. The association's main responsibilities are the management of its information system and the enforcement of its code of fair practices. The code details the responsibilities of members in such matters as advising, advertising, and providing services at a fair and reasonable cost. It also prohibits price manipulation, fraud, and other deceptive practices. Admission standards were tightened recently in an effort to minimize legal violations and the liquidation of member firms. Since no brokerage firm can operate profitably without NASD membership, the enforcement of its code by censure, fine, or expulsion has proven to be an effective deterrent to carelessness or deliberate misconduct.

AUTOMATED QUOTATIONS. NASD introduced a computerized communications system early in 1971 to facilitate trading of over-the-counter securities. Appropriately known as NASDAQ for NASD Automated Quotations (pronounced Naz'dak), the system will be able to provide up-to-the-minute bid and ask quotations for approximately twenty thousand securities when it becomes fully operational. With a central computer located in Trumbull, Connecticut, NASDAQ consists of a network of terminals located in brokerage offices and trading rooms of broker–dealer member firms throughout the nation. Prior to its introduction a customer's broker would have to request price quotations from broker–dealers who were known to "make a market" in that particular security. The procedure was cumbersome and there was no assurance that customers received the best available price. With NASDAQ, a broker can identify the best price immediately, contacting the offering broker directly by telephone or teletype to complete the transaction. Broker–dealers offering securities have direct access to the NASDAQ system to change bid and ask quotations for stocks in which they make a market. Market makers are required to buy or sell reasonable quantities of stock at bid and ask prices they have quoted.

Price quotations on almost all over-the-counter securities are published daily by the National Quotation Bureau. These listings, known as "Pink Sheets" because they are printed on pink paper, contain bid and ask quotations and the name of the broker–dealer(s) making a market for any security. Separate listings, on different colors of paper, are provided by the bureau for securities with limited local or regional interest. Most of the securities which are too small or too infrequently traded to be carried on NASDAQ can be located in Pink Sheets which are available to investors in the offices of most major brokerage firms. Quotations are *nominal prices* because, unlike the case of organized exchanges, they do not represent an actual transaction. In some cases there is very little relationship between a nominal price and actual value.

THIRD AND FOURTH MARKETS. NASDAQ performs the same function for over-the-counter securities that a specialist provides for listed securities.

Indeed, the system is sometimes directly competitive with the specialist since listed stocks may be traded over-the-counter. Over-the-counter trading of listed securities is referred to as the *third market*. Third-market volume has grown steadily; the market value of transactions has equaled or exceeded 7 percent of the value of NYSE transactions each year since 1970. It usually involves a large number of shares, commonly referred to as "blocks," which are purchased or sold by financial institutions. Active third-market trading is concentrated in approximately fifty major common stocks by a dozen or so well-capitalized broker–dealers, with Weeden & Co. generally considered to be the leader. These broker–dealers are not NYSE members; they act as market makers in direct competition with the exchange specialist, buying and selling for their own account in any amount required.

The NYSE prohibits member firms from participating in third-market transactions in a listed common stock. This is required by Rule 390 of the exchange which was adopted in 1957. Interestingly, however, Rule 390 applies only to common stocks; exchange members frequently trade listed corporate bonds and preferred stocks on a third-market basis without restriction. The Securities and Exchange Commission and Congress intend to suspend the rule on grounds that it is anticompetitive. The exchange has argued unsuccessfully that the third market, by fragmenting supply and demand, is not in the public interest and should be eliminated.

The third market developed in response to fixed minimum commission schedules which resulted in transaction costs directly proportional to the number of shares traded. Thus a 1000-share transaction would cost 10 times more than a 100-share transaction in the same stock. Third-market dealers were able to charge net prices which were lower than the exchange price plus fixed commission. Since April, 1971, exchange commissions on large transactions have been subject to negotiation; in May, 1975, all commissions became competitive. Despite these changes the third market has continued to prosper. It has profited from the NASDAQ system and the efficiency of over-the-counter dealers who in many cases enjoy lower overhead expenses than exchange member firms. Investors, particularly institutional investors, will try to acquire needed services at the lowest possible cost. Third-market broker–dealers generally charge no commission on transactions, profiting instead from the spread between bid and ask quotations. For very large blocks, the broker–dealer may act as an agent in locating buyers or sellers for a customer. In this case a commission is paid but it is less than the amount that would be charged by a NYSE member firm.

The *fourth market* is the direct exchange of securities between buyer and seller without the assistance of a broker. Since there are no reporting requirements for these transactions, and because confidentiality is valued by fourth-market participants, details on trading are scarce. Transactions are usually arranged by some individual or organization; Robert Brandt & Co. and Donald J. Tomaso Associates are two of these firms. An arranger's fixed annual fee, generally in the $10,000 range, or the charge for any individual order, is considerably smaller than corresponding brokerage fees. A financial institution will inform an arranger of its desire to buy or sell a block of stock. This expression of interest is stored until another institution expresses one on the other side. The arranger then negotiates price and exchanges securities without disclosing the identity of either party to the other. A popular fourth-market system is *Instinet*, a computer service of the Institutional Networks Corporation. Subscribers, with anonymity provided by code, enter requirements on a computer terminal; any interested subscriber can negotiate and complete the transaction in response. *Instinet* provides subscribers with a summary of all transactions at the end of every day. Aside from lower transaction costs, fourth-market block trading frequently results in more efficient pricing than would have resulted if the transaction had been executed through a specialist or a broker–dealer. The growth of this market, which appears assured unless it is constrained by future regulations, provides competitive stimulus to organized security exchanges.

Broker Services

The security broker is obligated ethically and by law to safeguard investors' financial interests. Brokers are compensated for services provided with commissions which are charged on transactions. Although the terms "broker" and "dealer" are sometimes used synonymously, and in a broad sense a security dealer is anyone in the securities industry, the term dealer more accurately refers to persons who trade for their own account. Dealers receive no commission; they profit from the difference between purchase and selling prices, as do other investors. Many firms act in the capacity of both dealer and broker and, when this is the case, the firm should specify its role in every customer transaction. Most brokerage firms are members of one or more exchanges, permitting them to execute customers' orders on the floor of the exchange. Others restrict operations to over-the-counter trading and they execute orders for listed securities on the third market or through a correspondent member broker. In the latter case the member firm "discounts" or "gives up" a portion of its normal charges and the two firms share the commission which is charged to the investor.

BROKERAGE RECORDS AND FEES. In arranging and executing customer orders, the broker provides a trade confirmation for each transaction which identifies all pertinent dates, prices, and charges. If the investor desires, the broker will retain the securities and credit all dividend and interest payments to the investor's account; this is referred to as a *street account*. The investor will receive a monthly statement and a year-end summary report for income

Table 2.4
Representative Commission Schedule—1976

100-Share Orders and Odd Lots

Money Involved in the Order	*% × Money Involved*	*plus*	*Round-Lot Fee*	*or*	*Odd-Lot Fee*
$ 100– 799	2.376		$ 7.60		$ 5.23
800–2499	1.544		14.26		11.88
2500–4999	1.069		26.14		23.76
5000 and above	none		80.73		80.73

Minimum Commission $25.00

100-Share Multiple Orders

Money Involved in the Order	*% × Money Involved*	*Plus*
$ 100– 2,499	1.544	$ 14.26
2,500– 4,999	1.069	26.14
5,000– 19,999	1.118	27.32
20,000– 29,999	.745	101.84
30,000–299,999	.497	176.36

Plus:

On orders involving *$5000 and less:*
$7.13 per 100-share lot to ten round lots
$4.75 per 100-share lot over the tenth round lot

On orders involving *more than $5000:*
$7.45 per 100-share lot to ten round lots
$4.97 per 100-share lot over the tenth round lot

Minimum commission $25.00

Maximum commission $80.73 per 100 shares

Note: In no case shall the commission per 100-share lot on a 100-share multiple order exceed the 100-share order commission.

tax purposes. The street account saves the investor considerable time and effort in physical handling and record keeping.

Transaction costs (commissions) are determined on a competitive basis; this is a recent innovation which began May 1, 1975. Until that date commissions were standardized by a fixed minimum commission schedule established by the NYSE. While competitive commissions have lowered costs on large orders, the overall impact on small transactions is not yet clear. Initially a few brokerage firms increased their rates while some smaller firms, dealing largely in the third market, lowered them considerably. Table 2.4 summarizes the commission schedule of a typical brokerage

Table 2.5
Example of Stock Transfer Taxes

	New York State: Tax Paid by Seller[a]	
Share Price	*N.Y. Resident Tax*	*Non-resident Tax*
Less than \$5	1.250¢	0.625¢
\$5 but less than \$10	2.500	1.250
\$10 but less than \$20	3.250	1.875
\$20 or more	5.000	2.500

Note: Maximum tax on single transaction is \$350. A $2\frac{1}{2}$¢/share tax is placed on transfers which are not sales. No tax on sales or transfer of rights or warrants. SEC fee—transactions on any registered exchange: 1 cent for each \$500 or fraction thereof of money involved. Security transactions are not currently subject to other federal taxes.

[a] Effective August 15, 1975, a 25 percent surcharge was added to the above rates and a new bond tax of 25¢ per 1000 par value to a \$250 per transaction maximum was begun. Effective August 1, 1978 this surcharge is eliminated. The tax itself is scheduled to be phased out through October, 1981.

firm in 1976. The percentage rates for small transactions are very close to the rates established by the former fixed minimum schedule. The fees reported in Table 2.4 do not reflect a broker's willingness to negotiate charges for large transactions. Additionally, charges are only one-half the stated rate for any day trade where the customer buys and sells a security during the same trading day.

Security transactions are subject to other fees. A tax on security sales is imposed by the State of New York with the primary burden shouldered by AMEX and NYSE transactions. It is paid by the seller according to the rate schedule shown in Table 2.5. In response to a 25 percent tax surcharge introduced in August of 1975, Weeden & Co. moved their selling operations from New York City to Jersey City, N.J. This removed the tax burden from over-the-counter and third-market transactions and it is expected to save Weeden & Co. \$1,000,000 per year in taxes related to dealer (selling) activities.[11] Other segments of the securities industry, including the national exchanges, also threatened to relocate because of rising transfer taxes. As a result, late in 1977 New York's state legislature voted to phase out the city stock transfer tax with its total elimination by October, 1981. A number of other state and local governments impose personal property, transfer, or other "nuisance" taxes on security ownership; they often purchase information on dividends and interest income from the Internal Revenue Service to assist in tax collection. The Securities and Exchange Commission charges a fee of 1 cent for each \$500 of value of securities which are sold.

[11] "Weeden to Move Trading to Jersey City from New York; Stock-Tax Boosts Cited," *The Wall Street Journal*, September 18, 1975.

To illustrate transaction costs, assume that an investor sells 100 shares of Union Airline stock at $40 per share. From the schedules of Tables 2.4 and 2.5, costs would be:

Commission on sale [.01069(4000) + 26.14]	$68.90
New York tax (nonresident) on sale, 1.25[.025(100)] =	3.13
SEC fee [(4000 ÷ 500)(.05)] =	.40
Total transaction costs	$72.43

ORDERS. Customer orders which are received by brokers are classified as market orders, limit orders, or stop orders. A *market order* instructs the broker to buy or sell at the prevailing market price. A *limit order* places restrictions on the execution price and it may never be exercised. Limit orders must have a stipulated period of time in which they remain valid; the most common periods are one day or "good until canceled" (GTC), which is usually treated as an open order for a six-month period. Some investors routinely place limit orders slightly below the market price for a stock they wish to purchase or slightly above for a stock they wish to sell. If the investment decision is a sound one, this practice adds little to return and it raises the possibility of missing an execution entirely; the use of limit orders is questionable unless an investor is unique in the ability to predict short-run price changes.

The third type of order is a *stop order* which is used to protect a gain or to minimize a loss. The stop order becomes a market order when a transaction takes place at or beyond the specified limit price. Assume that an investor purchased a stock at $50 and protected it with a GTC stop order at $45; if the price of the stock subsequently falls below that limit, the stop order will become a market order to be executed at the best possible price. If the stock traded slightly above the stop order limit at the close of a day but adverse news concerning the firm became known during the evening, it could open well below $45 and the price received would be less than the specified limit. Stop orders provide some degree of protection but they provide no guarantee; in some cases, where price adjusts rapidly, stop orders can be ignored by the specialist.

SHORT SALES. An investor who expects the price of a security to decrease may profit by selling shares short.[12] A *short sale* is the sale of stock which has been borrowed from a third party. The difference between the current selling price and the cost of replacing borrowed stock, less transaction costs, is the profit or loss from the short sale. Third parties are willing to lend securities because they, and not the short seller, receive the proceeds as

[12] Alternatively, an investor may use stock options for the same purpose. Chapter 12 discusses these alternatives which, because of greater leverage and favorable tax treatment, are generally superior to short selling.

collateral. Since the lender has the use of funds, no interest is charged. Brokers borrow stock for their customers from other customers or brokers.

OTHER BROKER SERVICES. Broker services also include investment advice and the granting of credit to qualified investors. Most firms provide free literature ranging from general information and tax guides to in-depth studies of individual industries and firms. The larger firms have extensive research facilities while smaller ones often arrange to publish recommendations provided by a larger brokerage firm or a private advisory service under their own name. Since commissions became competitive, some brokerage firms have "unbundled" their information services; advice which had been provided without charge is sold separately on a subscription basis. Merrill Lynch, for example, began charging customers for ten separate and allied services on the day that competitive brokerage fees were adopted (May 1, 1975). Although brokerage firms provide an important source of investment information, they are not an acceptable substitute for an investor's individual and comprehensive analysis. Recent studies by Lawrence Shepard and Clinton Bidwell suggest that typical brokerage information has very little value to individual investors.[13] Finally, brokerage firms provide a source of credit for the partial financing of security transactions. Trading on credit, which is known as margin trading, is discussed in the next section where regulatory provisions which govern margin accounts are discussed.

Capital Market Regulation

The regulation of capital markets has the dual purpose of (1) protecting the individual investor from fraud, manipulation, and misinformation and (2) protecting the public interest in the broader sense of maintaining free and open markets which are not destabilizing to other economic activity. Regulation of security transactions is enforced by state and federal governments and, through self-regulation, by exchanges and trade associations. The first security regulations were imposed on the issue of new securities; since the market crash of 1929, regulation of secondary markets has grown significantly in scope and prominence.

PRIMARY MARKET REGULATION

At first the regulation of new issues was the sole responsibility of state governments. State regulatory statutes, known as "blue sky" laws following an early and colorful judicial opinion, have been in effect since 1911. Today,

[13] Clinton M. Bidwell III, "How Good is Institutional Brokerage Research?" *Journal of Portfolio Management* (Winter 1977), pp. 26–31. In the same issue, Lawrence Shepard, "How Good is Investment Advice for Individuals?", pp. 32–36.

some form of regulation exists in all states except Nevada. State laws, which vary considerably, have provisions concerning registration, licensing, and fraudulent activities. Licensing applies to all security dealers within a state. Registration may apply to security dealers or to individual issues of new securities. These statutes are preventive in nature and designed to discourage illegal and unethical conduct; fraud statutes provide for the prosecution of offenders. State laws are limited to intrastate transactions and enforcement is generally lacking due to low budgetary appropriations.

Federal regulation began with the Securities Act of 1933. Its main purpose was to insure full and proper disclosure of all material information except an opinion as to the investment value of the new security. The 1933 act requires filing of a registration statement which details relevant information including financial statements. In addition to registration requirements, it also provides legal remedies against false and fraudulent statements concerning the issue of new securities. A recent court case prosecuted under the Securities Act of 1933 strengthened it by finding that members of the securities industry are liable for damages if it is determined that they did not exercise "due diligence" in investigating the statements and accounts of the firm.[14] The interpretation of due diligence is open to judicial determination on an individual basis but it is clear that an intention to misrepresent need not be established by plaintiff investors seeking damages.

When a corporation (or its investment banker) files a registration statement with the Securities and Exchange Commission, at least 20 days must pass before the issue is approved. If the SEC raises no objections within that period the securities can be issued. A portion of the registration statement containing detailed information is known as the *prospectus*; it must be provided to each buyer on or before delivery of securities. Prior to the 20-day waiting period, a preliminary version of the prospectus is usually circulated. The fact that it has not yet been approved by the SEC is printed in red in a statement on the cover; for this reason the preliminary prospectus is called a "red herring."

EXEMPTIONS. When the value of an initial offering is less than $500,000, registration requirements are less strict. These securities are frequently referred to as Reg A issues because limited registration is specified in Regulation A of the SEC act. Exemptions exist for government securities and issues by banks, nonprofit organizations, and railroads. The act also exempts

[14] *Escott* v. *Bar Chris Construction Company* (1961). The SEC has become very active in applying security regulations to accountants, bankers, and lawyers. In 1971 the SEC charged a public accounting firm with improperly certifying a financial statement of Utilities Leasing Company and again in 1972 as a co-conspirator in the offering of securities by Four Seasons Nursing Centers of America. Early in 1972 the SEC named two prestigious security law firms as defendants in a complaint issued against National Student Marketing Corporation. See "A Bid To Hold Lawyers Accountable to Public Stuns, Angers Firms," *The Wall Street Journal*, February 15, 1972. Also see T. W. Dunfee, and N. Gleim, "Criminal Liability of Accountants: Sources and Policies," *American Business Law Journal*, Spring 1971, pp. 1–20.

securities issued in reorganization, issues sold entirely within one state, and securities sold directly to a limited number of private buyers. This latter type is known as *letter stock* and restricted conditions for resale are imposed on first buyers. Letter stock will be discussed in more detail in Chapter 10.

SECONDARY MARKET REGULATION

The most important piece of legislation directed at the securities industry is the Securities Exchange Act of 1934. It extended disclosure provisions of the Securities Act of 1933 to secondary markets and it established the Securities and Exchange Commission in its present form. The act, supplemented by other legislation, provides for the regulation of credit and the registration of exchanges, brokers, and securities.

CREDIT REGULATION. A major factor in the severity of the stock market crash of 1929–1932, and the depression which followed, was the pyramiding of credit on security transactions. In 1929, there were 1,500,000 credit (margin) accounts; in many cases 90 percent of the purchase price of securities had been borrowed. Some brokers considered unrealized capital gains as additional equity and then allowed investors to extend borrowing on additional purchases on that basis. The collapse of security prices resulted in panic liquidation by investors and lenders including a large number of commercial banks. To prevent this in the future, the Security Exchange Acts of 1933 and 1934 authorized the Federal Reserve Board to regulate credit in security markets. As a result, Federal Reserve Regulations T and U were introduced.

Regulation T establishes the minimum percentage of collateral a broker may accept to cover the purchase or short sale of stock. It has ranged from 50 to 80 percent in recent years. The minimum investment initially required (I), after transaction costs, can be determined by:

$$I = xV \tag{2.1}$$

where x is the current Regulation T margin level and V is the market value of the securities involved. The maximum debit balance (D) provided by a broker is the difference between market value and the cash required to settle the transaction:

$$D = V - I = (1 - x)V \tag{2.2}$$

Assume that an investor purchased securities valued at \$10,000 with 65 percent margin; invested capital would be

$$I = .65(\$10{,}000) = \$6500$$

plus transaction costs. The loan from the broker would be:

$$D = \$10{,}000 - \$6500 = \$3500$$

or

$$D = (1 - .65)(\$10{,}000) = \$3500$$

Interest on the debit balance would accrue at 1 to 1.5 percentage points above the prime bank lending rate which is the brokers' usual source of funds for their margin customers.

Major exchanges also require a minimum cash investment of $2000 and a *maintenance margin* of at least 25 percent on outstanding purchases.[15] Brokers are free to require even higher maintenance margins or to establish other requirements for customers' accounts. If an investor's equity falls below the level needed to maintain the maintenance margin, the broker will issue a margin call requesting at least enough new money to restore that level. It will be restored by selling securities from an account if the investor does not respond to the margin call. Margin (m) in an account at any time can be determined by:

$$m = \frac{V - D}{V} \tag{2.3}$$

Continuing the preceding example, if the value of the shares decreased from $10,000 to $8000, margin would be:

$$m = \frac{8000 - 3500}{8000} = .56, \text{ or 56 percent}$$

By specifying the desired margin level in Equation 2.3, and rearranging, the minimum level of market value [V(min)] can be determined as:

$$V(\min) = \frac{D}{1 - m} \tag{2.4}$$

With a 25 percent margin V(min) would be:

$$V(\min) = \frac{\$3500}{1 - .25} = \$4667$$

If the value of the shares fell below $4667 the account would be under margined and a margin call would be issued.

The combination of a high initial margin and a low maintenance margin is designed to reduce the probability of widespread liquidation of securities. Although the account in the preceding example would not receive a margin call until the market value of collateral shares fell below $4667, additional credit purchases would not be allowed whenever the market value was less than $10,000. If the market value increased to levels

[15] The NYSE maintenance margin on short sales is 30 percent. Losses on short sales occur when security prices rise and Equation 2.2 is no longer appropriate. Instead, the margin level on a short sale can be approximated by applying: $m = [(V + I)/V] - 1.0$. For a short sale on $10,000 of stock with a $6500 cash investment, margin is $[(10{,}000 + 6{,}500)/10{,}000] - 1.0$, or 65 percent. Should the stock rise in value to $12,000, margin drops to $[(12{,}000 + 6{,}500)/12{,}000] - 1.0$, or 54 percent.

above $10,000, unrealized profits could be used as collateral for additional purchases or they could be withdrawn as cash, subject to any limitations which the broker established.

Regulation U extends the same initial margin requirements to commercial banks that Regulation T imposes upon broker accounts. Bank loans with securities pledged as collateral cannot exceed the amount which could be borrowed through a margin account. Until recently there were a number of loopholes in these regulations. An important one was the exclusion of stocks which are traded over-the-counter. In 1962 it was estimated that $8.6 billion of some $9.6 billion in bank credit extended was secured by over-the-counter stocks which were not subject to Regulation U. Beginning in 1968 certain over-the-counter stocks were made subject to margin requirements; by April of 1978 the list had grown to 1128 of the most active over-the-counter stocks. Another loophole existed for convertible securities. Although many convertible issues were traded primarily for their value as common stock, unregulated margins were as low as 10 percent. In 1968 the Federal Reserve Board extended margin requirements to convertible issues. At the same time they adopted Regulation G which applies to security credit extended by lenders other than brokers, dealers, or banks.

Margin requirements of the Federal Reserve Board are applied only at the time securities are purchased. If the margin level is changed, it is not retroactive; the new level applies only to new margin purchases. Investors trading on margin accept additional risk in an effort to increase potential return. Return is magnified by a factor equal to the reciprocal of the initial margin requirement for fully margined accounts; for a margin level of 65 percent the magnification factor would be 1/.65 or 1.54. If a stock increased in market value by 10 percent, a fully margined position would produce a return of $10(1.54) = 15.4$ percent, less margin interest costs. Both losses and gains are magnified and the investor is obligated to pay interest charges on the debit balance in either case.

EXCHANGE, BROKER, AND SECURITY REGULATION. The Securities Exchange Act provides for federal regulation of security exchanges; as an extreme measure the SEC is empowered to close an exchange. Exchanges must register with the SEC and then must conduct their affairs in an exemplary manner. Each exchange must regulate its membership by establishing and enforcing its own set of rules and regulations. Although the original act did not apply to brokers and dealers, amendments and supporting legislation have brought them under SEC jurisdiction. Amendments in 1936 required the registration of brokers; the Maloney Act of 1938, discussed previously, established a self-regulatory mechanism among brokers.

The direct regulation of securities is designed to provide full and complete information to investors and to prevent fraud and price manipulation activities. When securities are traded in the secondary markets the firm in question must file an audited annual report (10-K) with the SEC. An unaudited semiannual report (9-K) and a special report disclosing every factor of major importance to the firm (8-K) are also required. In 1964 these reporting requirements were extended to firms with consolidated assets in excess of $1 million.

To further discourage the withholding of information, or the publication of false information, the Securities Exchange Act restricts insider activities. Corporate officials who own more than 10 percent of a firm's stock must report all transactions on a monthly basis; these insider reports are then compiled and made public. Officers cannot engage in short selling of their firm's stock and profits realized on securities which were held for less than six months must be returned to the firm. These regulations and their stringent enforcement have discouraged insiders from taking advantage of any potential information advantage.

Direct manipulation of security prices by insiders or outsiders, through monopoly buying power or the use of false information, is prohibited. To insure that shareholders have a balanced view of management operations, proxy solicitation must meet stated requirements and be approved by the SEC before distribution.

Trends in Capital Market Operations

Capital markets are an integral and integrated segment of our national economic system. Accordingly, they must be resilient, adaptive, and innovative in response to changing economic and social conditions. Severe pressures have been exerted upon financial markets during the past decade. Among the more significant of these are major technological and communications advances, inflation and high interest rates, unusually volatile levels of security prices and trading volumes, concentration of money management, and shifts in regulatory priorities. As a result, financial markets are currently undergoing changes which, measured by historical standards, are both extensive and rapid. Changes are very evident in market-making procedures, the structure and nature of brokerage services, institutional trading, and regulation. A major unresolved issue is the role and power which each segment of the financial community will exercise in the evolving national market system for securities.

Strains in financial market operation began in the mid-1960s when an unexpected surge in trading volume created severe "back office" problems in processing orders. These problems accumulated to the point where many brokerage firms faltered, including such major firms as Goodbody and Company, and the NYSE and AMEX were forced to close on Wednesdays during the latter part of 1968. Implementation of modern data-processing techniques, many of which were recommended by the congressional *Security Industry Study*, significantly improved market operations by 1970.[16]

[16] United States Senate, *Securities Industry Study*, Report of the Subcommittee on Commerce and Finance, 92nd Congress, August 23, 1972, and Committee Print, 93d Congress, Februrary 1973.

THE SECURITY INVESTOR PROTECTION CORPORATION. Following the failure of Ira Haupt & Co. in 1963, the NYSE established a voluntary fund supported by its membership to reimburse customers and to restore investor confidence. Because of concern that it would prove to be inadequate, Congress adopted the proposal of a joint industry–SEC task force and created the Security Investor Protection Corporation (SIPC).[17] The proposal became law at the end of 1970 as an amendment to the Securities Exchange Act of 1934.

The SIPC provided a threefold service for investors:

1. It established a contingency fund to reimburse customers in the event of bankruptcy of a brokerage firm. The fund is supported by assessing brokers in an amount not to exceed $\frac{1}{2}$ of 1 percent of each firm's gross revenues.
2. It authorized the SEC to provide up to $1 billion in emergency loans with money obtained from the U.S. Treasury.
3. It required all exchanges and trade associations to notify the SEC if any affiliated firm appeared to be in financial difficulty.

An investor's brokerage account in cash and securities is fully guaranteed up to $50,000 and a proposal to raise this level is under consideration. Initially, some problems occurred with false and fraudulent claims but SIPC is now functioning smoothly and provides a valuable service to both investors and the financial community.

A NATIONAL MARKET SYSTEM

The structure and organization of a national market system remained undefined by the late 1970s, but there was general agreement that some type of centralized exchange would be introduced in the near future. The establishment of a national system was provided for in the Security Acts Amendments of 1975. This legislation was designed to clarify and enhance the ability of the SEC to support development of a national market system, to remove barriers to competition, and to increase the agency's authority with respect to self-regulatory organizations in the securities industry. By the time the 1975 legislation was enacted, major segments of the industry had already identified key elements of a centralized system, and differences in viewpoints had already narrowed considerably.

One view of a National Market System (NMS) was proposed by Merrill Lynch.[18] The Merrill Lynch plan is representative in many ways of views expressed on Wall Street, in Congress, and at the SEC with respect to integration of security markets. All actively traded stocks which are listed on exchanges or traded over-the-counter would be included. All transactions in an NMS security except those privately conducted between two individuals in the "fourth market" would be required to be executed through NMS.

[17] The proposal was very similar to an earlier proposal entitled the Federal Broker-Dealer Incorporation Act.

[18] *Proposal for a National Market System,* Merrill Lynch Pierce Fenner & Smith, originally presented before the Securities and Exchange Commission by Donald T. Regan, chairman and chief executive officer of Merrill Lynch, October 16, 1975.

The active "third-market" trading of listed securities on an over-the-counter basis would be eliminated.

Brokerage firms participating in NMS would have full and equal market access and they would be subject to equal regulation. Firms would be registered broker–dealers under the Securities Exchange Act of 1934 and they would be allowed to affiliate with a nonbank financial institution or a foreign entity. The rationale advanced for allowing any firm to make a market in any security is that it would result in extensive competition and a true auction market where securities are sold to the highest bidder. The

Figure 2.2
Typical Order Processing Under A Proposed National Market System*

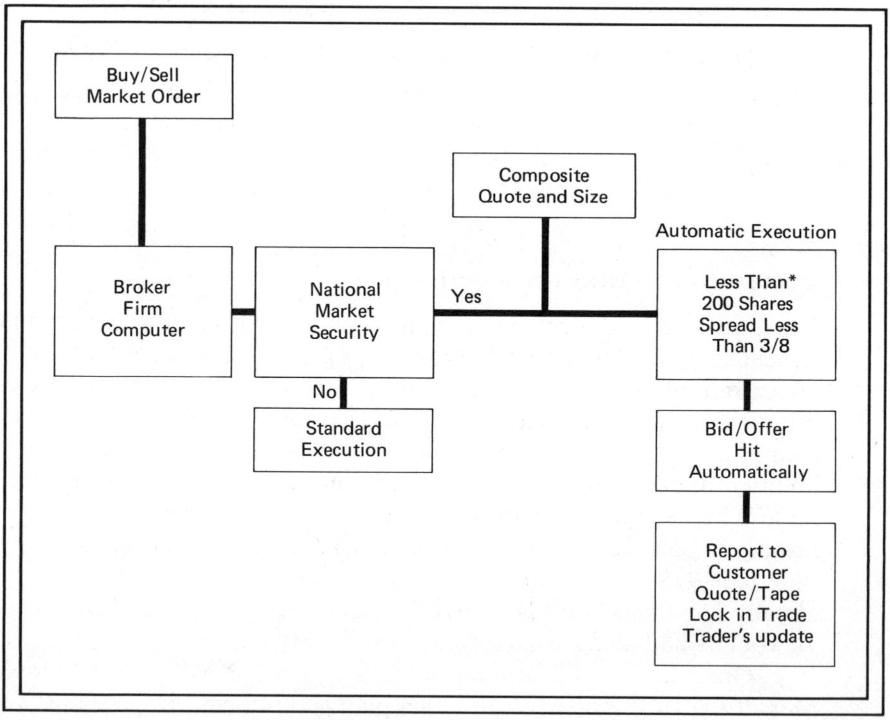

Source: Proposal for a National Market System, Merrill Lynch Pierce Fenner & Smith, Inc., October 16, 1975.

* Minimum quotation size might vary, depending on the liquidity of the particular stock. Securities eligible for trading in the NMS could be grouped into categories based on their liquidity (as measured by total capitalization, number of shares outstanding, number of shareholders, trading volume, etc.). In the most liquid category, market makers would have to make their quotations good for a minimum of at least, say, 500 shares; in the least liquid category, quotations would have to be good for at least one round lot. Stocks would be able to move from one category to another periodically as their trading characteristics changed. A graduated system of minimum quotation sizes such as that described would make it possible to execute a 500 share order of an active stock at a single price.

specialist system of exclusive market making with floor brokerage monopoly and information advantage would be eliminated.

The elimination or modification of the specialists' role is the most controversial aspect of any NMS plan of the type proposed by Merrill Lynch. The specialist system has worked well in the past but technological advances and increased work loads have reduced its efficiency with respect to available alternatives. For these reasons the specialist system seems likely to be replaced by an electronic auction market of the type described in the next paragraph. It is not a completely revolutionary development. A nonelectronic auction market has operated effectively in organized commodity markets since the late 1800s and the NASDAQ system for over-the-counter stocks, which began in 1971, is also similar in principle.

The central feature of the Merrill Lynch plan is an electronic processing and communications system capable of receiving, validating, sorting, ordering, displaying, canceling, processing, and reporting a variety of security transaction elements including orders, limit orders, quotations, and "feelers of interest" from all members of the NMS. The system would automatically establish price and time priorities and it would give precedence to public orders over member orders arriving at the same time and price. Most small orders for actively traded securities with a modest bid-ask spread would be processed immediately and automatically as outlined in Figure 2.2. Larger orders and cases where the bid-ask spread is larger than a specified size would be processed through an electronic auction that attempts to improve terms for the buyer or seller. In the case of block transactions an electronic "standing in crowd" routine would initiate direct broker (trader) involvement in the execution process.

RECENT DEVELOPMENTS TOWARD A NATIONAL MARKET SYSTEM. Substantial progress has been recorded in the development of a national market system. Its advantages and disadvantages have been debated on Wall Street and in academic circles since the late 1960s.[19] The Securities and Exchange Commission has openly favored some type of national market system and in March of 1975 an SEC advisory panel recommended consolidation of the nation's 13 stock exchanges into a single National Security Exchange.[20] Notable features of the plan were (1) the market would have a competitive

[19] Articles by Seymour Smidt, Fischer Black, Guthrie Baker, James Davant, and Donald Farrar in three successive issues of the *Financial Analysts Journal* (July–August, September–October, and November–December 1971) summarize divergent viewpoints. Another summary of viewpoints is present in "Outlook for the Securities Industry," *Journal of Financial and Quantitative Analysis* (Supplement to March 1972). Also see Donald E. Farrar, "The Coming Reform on Wall Street," *Harvard Business Review*, September–October 1972, pp. 108–117 and Morris Mendelson, "Issue of Stock Market Reform," *Wharton Quarterly*, Fall 1971, pp. 33–40.

[20] "Central Market is Recommended by SEC Panel," *The Wall Street Journal*, March 10, 1975. Previous progress on the SEC study was noted in *The Wall Street Journal*, March 30, 1973, and August 26, 1971.

specialist mechanism and (2) the exchange would be regulated by a board dominated by public representatives. The New York Stock Exchange generally favors a plan outlined by William McChesney Martin, former chairman of the Federal Reserve Board and former NYSE president.[21] *The Martin Plan* recommends the development of a national auction market by merging national and regional (but not over-the-counter) exchanges. Control of the new market would be exercised by NYSE members through a board of directors restructured to include public representation through directors elected by the exchange membership. Competition from the third market would not be permitted but a limited degree of competition among specialists would be allowed under the Martin Plan.

Many elements of a centralized market system, including clearance and settlement procedures, were in at least limited operation by 1976. Nevertheless, the Securities and Exchange Commission displayed increasing impatience with the securities industry for failure to establish a national market more rapidly. In January of 1978, for example, the SEC ordered the industry to define the basic market structure by September 30, 1978; although that date was expressed more accurately as a target date than a firm deadline, it seemed clear that regulatory authorities would press for early adoption of a centralized system. The major elements supported by the SEC were threefold:

1. A national quotation system for bid and ask prices for those securities selected for national trading. A foundation for this already exists in the Intermarket Trading System, which began pilot operation in 1978 for NYSE, AMEX, and several regional exchanges. If this system were expanded to include the OTC market, it would serve the purpose suggested by the SEC.
2. A market linkage and order routing system for prompt execution at the best offering price in any market for any nationally quoted security. The SEC pressed especially hard for immediate adoption of this key market element. At the same time, the threatened disallowance of Rule 390 was delayed until at least September 30, 1978.
3. A central file to protect customers' (but not broker-dealers') stock limit orders placed above or below the current market price. Market orders would continue to be processed conventionally. This computerized file, while falling far short of a complete electronic trading system, would replace the specialists limit order book for customers and it would significantly alter the specialist function of maintaining a continuous and orderly market.

DEVELOPMENTS IN OTHER FINANCIAL MARKETS

The movement toward centralized secondary markets has been accompanied by the rapid growth and increasing centralization of markets dealing in other types of financial claims. The most important of these developments

[21] William McChesney Martin, *The Securities Markets: A Report with Recommendations*, for the Board of Governors, NYSE, August 5, 1971. Reprinted in Commerce Clearing House, *Federal Security Law Reporter* p. 78184 (August 1971) and *The New York Times*, August 7, 1971, p. 52.

are the centralization of security option markets in calls and puts and the expansion of commodity futures markets into the areas of foreign exchange, bonds, and mortgage futures.[22] The two largest option markets, the American Stock Exchange and the Chicago Board Options Exchange, have jointly created the Options Clearing Corporation to clear and process trades on either exchange. In addition, the National Association of Securities Dealers is in the process of standardizing trading in unlisted options.[23]

The Securities and Exchange Commission delayed the approval of trading in listed stock options because of the possible impact of expanded option trading on existing debt and equity markets. Available evidence suggests that benefits derived from an expanded and centralized options market outweigh potential costs. A special study conducted by Robert R. Nathan Associates concluded that an organized option market was clearly in the public interest and that no social costs of any consequence could reasonably be anticipated.[24] Despite this study and the initial success of the market, SEC approval has been only tentative.[25] Ironically, the overwhelming acceptance of these markets by investors has contributed to regulatory caution. Permanent approval of central options trading, which seems assured, raises the prospect of combining and centralizing *all* financial markets. In view of difficulties encountered in developing a centralized secondary market system, and with limited experience with organized options markets, a careful and cautious approach is not unreasonable.

Summary

This chapter described important elements of the capital market system; primary markets, secondary markets, broker–dealer activities, and market regulation were reviewed in detail. Trends in capital market operations were also identified from a mid-1970s perspective. Principles of security analysis and portfolio management cannot be mastered without a clear understanding of the market environment in which transactions are executed. At this time that is a very difficult task because traditional institutions and operations are in the process of rapid and significant change. For that reason the chapter initially focused on existing organizations and functions. Topical issues were then introduced in an effort to convey an impression of the

[22] The nature of these claims and their markets are discussed in greater detail in Chapters 11 and 12. It is interesting to note that in recent years the dollar value of transactions on the largest futures market, the Chicago Board of Trade, has exceeded the value of transactions on the New York Stock Exchange.

[23] "NASD Board Asks Standardized Markets for Trading Options in Unlisted Issues," *The Wall Street Journal*, October 3, 1975.

[24] Robert R. Nathan Associates, Inc., *Public Policy Aspects of a Futures Type Market in Options on Securities*, Vols. I and II, November 1969.

[25] "SEC Options Hearing Will Open On Jan. 29: Chicago Fights Rivals," *The Wall Street Journal*, November 15, 1973.

transitory nature of financial markets. A complete and thorough understanding of the market environment is impossible unless continuing developments are monitored regularly in the financial press.

The next two chapters provide an introduction to elements of the investment process. Chapter 3 contains an analysis of rate of return components and Chapter 4 introduces concepts and terminology which are common to all types of investment analysis and management.

Questions and Problems

1. What are the similarities and differences between the function of an investment banker and the function of a stock exchange?
2. What has been the basic mission of the Securities and Exchange Commission? Comment on how you sense that mission may be changing.
3. An investor purchased stock for $12,000 on full margin when the Federal Reserve Board Regulation T margin level was 50 percent. Subsequently, the value of the stock decreased to $8000 and the Regulation T margin level later increased to 65 percent.
   a. At the time of the initial purchase, how much money did the investor deposit with his broker?
   b. As a result of the decline in market value to $8000 (assuming a 50 percent margin), what action, if any, needs to be taken?
   c. What impact does the increase in margin level to 65 percent have on your answer to (b)?
   d. Given your answers to (b) and (c), what additional investment would be needed to purchase another $8000 worth of shares?
4. What are the basic causes and directions of change affecting secondary security markets in the late seventies?

Selected References

FUNCTIONS OF THE CAPITAL MARKET SYSTEM

Baumol, W. J., *The Stock Market and Economic Efficiency* (New York: Fordham University Press, 1965).

Friend, Irwin, "The Economic Consequences of the Stock Market," *American Economic Review* 62, no. 2 (May 1972): 212–219.

Henning, C. N., W. Pigott, and R. H. Scott, *Financial Markets and the Economy* (Englewood Cliffs, N.J.: Prentice-Hall, 1975).

Institutional Investor Study Report of the Securities and Exchange Commission Supplementary Volume 2, 92d Congress, 1st Session—House Document No. 92–64, part 6, March 10, 1971.

"Individuals and the Corporate Equity Market," (a symposium) *Journal of Contemporary Business* 3, no. 1 (Winter 1974).

Murray, Roger, "The Securities Industry," text of the first annual Buttonwood Lecture (New York City, December 1972, published under joint sponsorship by Columbia University and the New York Stock Exchange).

Report of the Special Study of the Securities Markets of the Securities and Exchange Commission. Securities and Exchange Commission (Washington, D.C.: Government Printing Office, 1962).

Van Horne, James C., *Function and Analysis of Capital Market Rates* (Englewood Cliffs, N.J.: Prentice-Hall, 1970).

PRIMARY AND SECONDARY MARKETS

Brown, J. M., "Post-Offering Experience of Companies Going Public," *Journal of Business* 43, no. 1 (January 1970): 10–18.

Curran, Ward S., "Some Thoughts on the Stock Exchange Specialist," *Quarterly Review of Economics and Business*, Spring 1965, pp. 55–62.

Fenerstein, Donald M., "Toward a National System of Securities Exchanges: The Third and Fourth Markets," *Financial Analysts Journal* 28, no. 4 (July–August 1972): 57–60.

Furst, R. W., "Does Listing Increase the Market Price of Common Stocks?" *Journal of Business* 43, no. 2 (April 1970): 174–180.

Loll, L. M., and J. C. Buckley, *The Over-the-Counter Securities Market*, 3d ed. (Englewood Cliffs, N.J.: Prentice-Hall, 1973).

Niederhoffer, V., and M. F. Osborne, "Market Making and Reversal on the Stock Exchange," *Journal of the American Statistical Association* 61 (December 1966): 897–916.

Robbins, Sidney, *The Securities Markets: Operations and Issues* (New York: Free Press, 1966).

Santomero, A. M., "Economic Effects of the NASDAQ," *Journal of Financial and Quantitative Analysis* 9, no. 1 (January 1974): 13–24.

Schaefer, Jeffrey M., and Adolphe J. Warner, "Concentration Trends and Competition in the Securities Industry," *Financial Analysts Journal*, November/December 1977, pp. 29–34.

Tinic, S. M., and R. R. West, "Competition and the Pricing of Dealer Service in the OTC Market," *Journal of Financial and Quantitative Analysis* 7, no. 2 (June 1972): 1707–1728.

BROKER SERVICES

Basi, Bart A., "The Responsibility of the Broker-Dealer to the Investing Public," *American Business Law Journal* 13, no. 3 (Winter 1976): 371–384.

Bidwell III, Clinton M., "How Good is Institutional Brokerage Research?" *Journal of Portfolio Management* (Winter 1977), pp. 26–31.

Boudreaux, Kenneth J., "Competitive Rates and Market Efficiency," *Financial Analysts Journal*, March–April 1975, pp. 18–24.

Engel, L., *How To Buy Stocks*, 5th ed. (New York: Bantam Books, 1972).

Friend, I., and M. Blume, "Competitive Commissions on the NYSE," *Journal of Finance* 28, no. 4 (September 1973): 795–820.

Securities Industry Study, Committee on Banking, Housing, and Urban Affairs (92nd Congress, 2d Session, Committee Print).

West, R. R., and S. M. Tinic, "Minimum Commission Rates on New York Stock Exchange Transactions," *Bell Journal of Economics*, Autumn 1971, pp. 577–605.

CAPITAL MARKET REGULATION

A New Regulatory Framework, The President's Advisory Council on Executive Organization, January 1971.

Benston, George, "Required Disclosure and the Stock Market," *American Economic Review*, March 1973.

———, "The Value of the SEC's Accounting Disclosure Requirements," *Accounting Review*, July 1969, pp. 515–532.

Corley, Robert T., "'Blue Sky' Takes Many Forms," *American Business Law Journal* 8, no. 1 (Spring 1970): 53–63.

Dunfee, T. W., and I. N. Gleim, "Criminal Liability of Accountants: Sources and Policies," *American Business Law Journal* 9, no. 1 (Spring 1971): 1–20.

Friend, Irwin, "Broad Implications of the SEC Special Study," *Journal of Finance*, May 1966.

Largay III, J. A., "100% Margins: Combating Speculation in Individual Security Issues," *Journal of Finance* 27, no. 4 (September 1973): 973–986.

Moore, Thomas G., "Stock Market Margin Requirements," *Journal of Political Economy* 74, no. 2 (April 1966): 158–167.

Singhui, S. S., "Disclosure to Whom? Annual Financial Reports to Stockholders and to the Securities and Exchange Commission," *Journal of Business* 41, no. 3 (July 1968): 347–351.

TRENDS IN CAPITAL MARKET OPERATIONS

Farrar, Donald E., "The Coming Reform on Wall Street," *Harvard Business Review*, September–October 1972, p. 108.

Farrar, Donald E., "Toward a Central Market System: Wall Street's Slow Retreat into the Future," *Journal of Financial and Quantitative Analysis* 9, no. 5 (November 1974): 815–827.

Martin, Jr., W. M., "The Securities Markets, A Report with Recommendations," reprinted in Commerce Clearing House, *Federal Security Law Reporter* (August 1971), p. 78184.

"Outlook for the Security Industry," *Journal of Financial and Quantitative Analysis* 7, no. 2 Supplement (March 1972).

Proposal for a National Market System, Merrill Lynch, October 16, 1975.

Robbins, S. M., "Some Reflections on the Central Market," text of the second annual Buttonwood Lecture (New York City, December 1972, published under joint sponsorship by Columbia University and the New York Stock Exchange).

Securities and Exchange Commission. *The Future Structure of the Securities Market* (Statement), Washington, D.C., February 2, 1972, and *White Paper on the Structure of a Central Market System*, March 30, 1973.

Chapter 3
Return on Investment

Security analysis and portfolio management depend upon basic concepts and relationships which must be mastered before the evaluation of stocks, bonds, or other securities can be considered. These critical elements are defined and described in Chapters 3 and 4. This chapter focuses on the problem of measuring rate of return on investment. Rate of return, which is also referred to as yield, is commonly used to specify the outcome which is expected to be realized from the purchase of any particular security. It is also the most important measure of performance for evaluating the success or failure of past portfolio decisions. Chapter 4 describes other investment elements; particular emphasis is placed there on the nature and measurement of risk.

Rate of return is examined in the first section of this chapter. Yield is widely used in economics, finance, and accounting and many of its properties and characteristics may already be familiar. Nevertheless, for the sake of completeness, elementary concepts will be reviewed first and more difficult topics will then be introduced and developed from that basic foundation. In the process a general analytical model will be defined and specified; this model will be applied in later chapters to the analysis and valuation of common stocks, bonds, options, future contracts, and other securities.

The second section of the chapter discusses the problem of measuring return on investment for securities in the aggregate. Market performance indexes are analyzed in detail and properties of the more familiar ones are then compared and contrasted.

There are two appendixes at the end of the chapter. The first describes and illustrates an efficient methodology for calculating security yield by trial and error. The second is an arithmetic proof that security yield is independent of any assumption as to reinvestment of interim proceeds; this is an important factor in distinguishing between security yield and portfolio yield and it is discussed, without proof, in the main part of the chapter.

Rate of Return

Rate of return has several dimensions which must be specified if its meaning is to be clear. They include the calendar interval for which return is measured, the correspondence of that calendar interval with the time period for which rate of return is defined, the compounding of return from period to period, and the reinvestment of interim returns realized periodically within the interval. Because of these different elements there are many kinds of return on investment which should be differentiated:

1. Single-period and multiple-period rate of return.
2. Nominal and effective rate of return.
3. Arithmetic mean and geometric mean rate of return.
4. Security internal rate of return and net present value.
5. Security and portfolio rate of return.

The relationship among these several concepts is traced in Figure 3.1. The discussion which follows is based upon that diagram and numerical values given there are developed in the text to demonstrate each concept arithmetically.

PERIODIC RATE OF RETURN

Rate of return is a concept which must be defined for some specific time period if it is to have any clear meaning. If an investment of \$100 earns interest of \$3 over a 3-month period, the rate of return is 3 percent. If another investment of \$100 yields \$3 over a 12-month period, rate of return is again 3 percent but the two measures are obviously unrelated. Rate of return cannot be evaluated unless the time period to which it refers is either specified or clearly implied. When the period is not specified it is customary to assume that yield refers to return on investment on an annual basis. In the example given above the first investment earned a *quarterly* rate of return of 3 percent;

Figure 3.1
Calendar Period Return on Investment

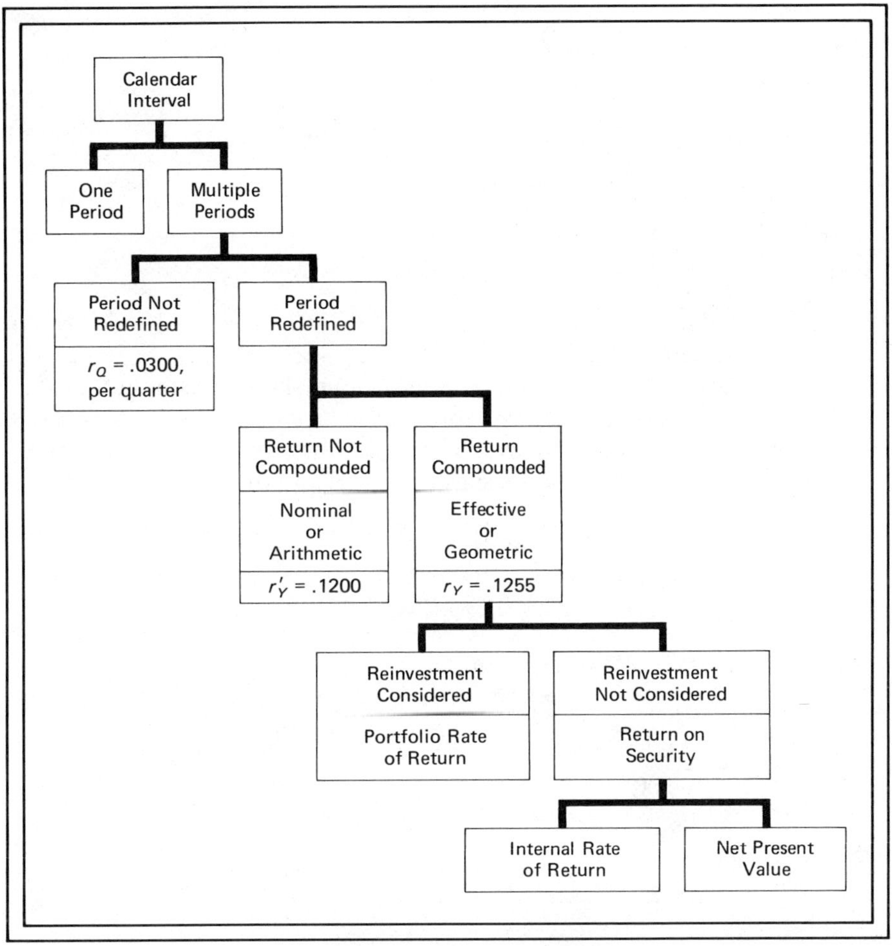

the second investment yielded 3 percent, or 3 percent *annually*, with both descriptions conventionally taken to mean the same thing.

Return on investment will be earned during a calendar interval which may or may not be the same as the time period used to specify rate of return. When they are the same, yield is a *one-period* rate of return and the relationships which exist among investment variables are easily defined. *Return on investment* is the excess cash flow recovered from an investment after that investment has been recovered. If C_0 dollars are used to purchase a security at the beginning of a period and C_1 dollars are recovered at the end of the period, return on investment R is defined:

$$R = C_1 - C_0 \tag{3.1}$$

Return on investment is an absolute measure; *rate of return* r is the corresponding relative measure:

$$r = \frac{R}{C_0} = \frac{C_1 - C_0}{C_0} \tag{3.2}$$

Another important relationship, *return relative* $(1 + r)$, is the ratio of cash recovered to cash invested:

$$1 + r = \frac{C_1}{C_0} = \frac{C_0 + R}{C_0} = \frac{C_0}{C_0} + \frac{R}{C_0} = 1 + r \tag{3.3}$$

Return relative is the sum of recovered investment C_0/C_0 and rate of return on investment R/C_0.

Assume that someone purchases one share of common stock today for \$100; at the end of three months a dividend of \$1 is received and the stock is then sold for \$102. Quarterly rate of return and quarterly return relative can then be calculated for security price P and dividend D:

$$\begin{aligned} R &= C_1 - C_0 = (P_1 + D_1) - P_0 \\ &= (102.00 + 1.00) - 100.00 \\ &= 3.00 \end{aligned}$$

$$\begin{aligned} r &= \frac{R}{C_0} = \frac{(P_1 + D_1) - P_0}{P_0} \\ &= \frac{3.00}{100.00} \\ &= .0300 \end{aligned}$$

$$\begin{aligned} 1 + r &= \frac{C_1}{C_0} = \frac{P_1 + D_1}{P_0} \\ &= \frac{103.00}{100.00} \\ &= 1.0300 \end{aligned}$$

In this example the *realized* rate of return was 3 percent per quarter. If the stock had not been sold at the end of the period, quarterly yield would still be 3 percent but it would be partly *unrealized.* In the absence of brokerage costs and taxes there is no difference between the two measures and realization can be ignored when *security* rate of return is calculated.[1] *Portfolio* yield, on the other hand, is very sensitive to the pattern of realized flows;

[1] Brokerage costs and taxes are ignored in this chapter in order to focus on rate of return elements; they will be considered later when security analysis is introduced.

this will be demonstrated later in this chapter. Since realization can be ignored at this point, one-period rate of return can be generalized for an investment in common stock for any time period t:

$$r_t = \frac{P_t + D_t - P_{t-1}}{P_{t-1}} \tag{3.4}$$

and

$$1 + r_t = \frac{P_t + D_t}{P_{t-1}}$$

MULTI-PERIOD COMPOUNDING

Return on investment may be earned during a calendar interval which is different from the time period used to define rate of return. In that case yield can be described in one of several ways depending on whether or not the rate of return period is redefined; if it is redefined it must be determined whether or not period returns are *compounded.* This can be illustrated by considering a security with the following dividend and price performance:

End of Quarter	*Quarterly Dividend*	*End-of-Quarter Price*	r_Q
0	$	$100.00	
1	0.00	103.00	.0300
2	0.00	106.09	.0300
3	0.00	109.27	.0300
4	0.00	112.55	.0300

If this security is purchased at the end of any three-month period and it is then sold at the end of the next period, quarterly rate of return r_Q, from Equation 3.4, is 3 percent. It then follows that an investor who purchased this security for $100.00 and sold it for $112.55 at the end of the fourth quarter must have realized a 3 percent per quarter rate of return throughout the entire year.

In this example rate of return could be redefined as an annual yield on either a *nominal* or an *effective* basis. Nominal rate of return is calculated by multiplying the period rate of return by the number of periods m in the calendar interval. In this case there are four periods (quarters) in the interval and nominal yearly rate of return r_Y' is 12 percent:

$$\begin{aligned} r_Y' &= mr_Q \\ &= (4)(.0300) \\ &= .1200 \end{aligned}$$

Nominal yield is a defective measure because it ignores the compounding of return within the measurement interval. A yearly rate of return of 12 percent on an investment of \$100.00 implies a terminal value of \$112.00 instead of the \$112.55 realized in the example.

Effective yield specifically recognizes the compounding of period return relatives. In this example effective yearly rate of return r_Y is calculated from quarterly values:[2]

$$\begin{aligned} 1 + r_Y &= (1 + r_Q)(1 + r_Q)(1 + r_Q)(1 + r_Q) \\ &= (1 + r_Q)^m = (1 + r_Q)^4 \\ &= (1.0300)^4 \\ &= 1.1255 \\ r_Y &= .1255 \end{aligned}$$

This relationship is easily generalized. When return relatives are compounded m times per year for t number of years, effective annual yield is

$$(1 + r_Y) = \left(1 + \frac{r_Y'}{m}\right)^{mt} \tag{3.5}$$

In the example given,

$$\begin{aligned} 1 + r_Y &= \left(1 + \frac{.12}{4}\right)^{4 \times 1} \\ &= (1.0300)^4 \\ &= 1.1255 \end{aligned}$$

Compounding is an important concept which is often misinterpreted or misunderstood. It is best described as an *averaging* mechanism which equates rates of return when they are defined for different time periods. In terms of the preceding numerical example, a yield of 3 percent per quarter, compounded quarterly, is equal to a yield of 12.55 percent per year, com-

[2] Effective rate of return can be defined for any period; it need not be annual. For example, if a semiannual yield is desired nominal return is then 6 percent ($2 \times .03$) and effective rate of return r_S is 6.09 percent:

$$\begin{aligned} (1 + r_S) &= \left(1 + \frac{.06}{2}\right)^{2 \times 1} \\ &= 1.0609 \end{aligned}$$

Effective semiannual yield can be converted to effective annual yield; since there are two six-month periods in each year,

$$\begin{aligned} (1 + r_Y) &= (1 + r_S)^{2 \times 1} \\ &= (1.0609)^2 \\ &= 1.1255 \end{aligned}$$

pounded annually. But equivalence exists only in the averaging sense; returns which are measured over different time periods cannot be compared for decision purposes unless the yield from reinvestment is given. A security which yields 3 percent over a three-month period should not be compared with another that yields 12 percent over a full year unless something is known about the rate of return from reinvestment during the nine months after the first investment is liquidated. The first security returns 12.55 percent on an annual basis while the second one returns a lesser 12.00 percent; nevertheless, the correct choice between the two depends on the return realized from investing the proceeds from the first investment over the remaining nine months in the year.

The importance of reinvestment in a decision context has led many people to believe, erroneously, that compounding implies the reinvestment of periodic cash flows at the period rate of return. The fallacy in that statement is subtle but it is very important in distinguishing between the security valuation models which are available to investment analysts. Compounding is a general concept which applies equally to rate of return for one security or rate of return for a portfolio of two or more securities. When compounding is applied to a single security, reinvestment has no relevance; when it is applied to a portfolio, reinvestment is very relevant but there is no necessary reason why the rate of return on reinvestment should be any particular value.

The problem, and its solution, can be illustrated by adjusting the dividend and price performance which were assumed for the security in the preceding numerical analysis:

End of Quarter	*Quarterly Dividend*	*End-of-Quarter Price*	r_Q
0	$	$100.00	
1	1.00	102.00	.0300
2	1.00	104.06	.0300
3	1.00	106.18	.0300
4	1.00	108.37	.0300

From Equation 3.4, quarterly rate of return is again 3 percent for each of the four quarters; from Equation 3.5, effective annual rate of return should therefore be 12.55 percent, as it was in the preceding example. But the two cases differ in one important respect: in the first case there were no dividends and return on investment was realized entirely from capital gain; in this example return consists of both periodic dividends and capital gain. As a result, terminal value at the end of the year will depend upon the rate of return realized from the reinvestment of quarterly dividends. If dividends are reinvested to yield 3 percent per quarter, terminal value will be $112.55;

if dividends are not reinvested, terminal value will fall to $112.37. With values rounded to the nearest penny:

Reinvested at 3 Percent

		1	2	3	4	
1st qtr. dividend	1.00		(1.03)	(1.03)	(1.03) =	1.09
2nd qtr. dividend	1.00			(1.03)	(1.03) =	1.06
3rd qtr. dividend	1.00				(1.03) =	1.03
4th qtr. dividend	1.00				=	1.00
Year end price						108.37
Terminal value						112.55

No Reinvestment

		1	2	3	4	
1st qtr. dividend	1.00		(1.00)	(1.00)	(1.00) =	1.00
2nd qtr. dividend	1.00			(1.00)	(1.00) =	1.00
3rd qtr. dividend	1.00				(1.00) =	1.00
4th qtr. dividend	1.00				=	1.00
Year end price						108.37
						112.37

For an investment of $100.00, a 12.55 percent annual return suggests a terminal value of $112.55. It therefore appears that equivalence between the 3 percent quarterly yield and the 12.55 percent annual yield for the security occurs only when dividends are reinvested at the 3 percent quarterly rate of return. Without reinvestment annual yield decreases to 12.37 percent. But that conclusion is unwarranted because it confuses security rate of return and portfolio rate of return.

Terminal values which were calculated under the two different reinvestment assumptions are values generated by *four* investments: the original security and reinvestment of dividends received at the end of the first, second, and third quarters. Rate of return on the first security is 3 percent per quarter or 12.55 percent annually, whatever the pattern of reinvestment. Portfolio rate of return is a weighted average of all four yields. When all four investments yield 3 percent quarterly, portfolio yield is also 3 percent and terminal value is $112.55. But when dividends are not reinvested, the 12.55 percent yield on the first investment is diluted by the zero yield on the other three and yearly portfolio rate of return decreases to 12.37 percent.

Compounding is an averaging mechanism which is independent of any particular reinvestment assumption. It allows an analyst to compare yields which are measured over different time intervals but that comparison cannot be used as the basis for choosing one security rather than another. Security selection depends instead on the expected portfolio rate of return;

portfolio yield, in turn, depends upon the assumed rate of return on reinvestment which may or may not be the yield for any one of the securities in the portfolio.

INTERNAL RATE OF RETURN

When an investment generates cash flow over a series of years, rate of return is usually described by some type of average yearly value. If annual rates of return are known from year to year, two different averages can be calculated: *arithmetic mean* yield and *geometric mean* yield. The arithmetic mean and geometric mean are simple extensions, respectively, of nominal and effective (compounded) rate of return.

Arithmetic mean return relative $(1 + \bar{r}_a)$ is defined for N number of years, where $Y = 1, 2, \ldots, N$:

$$(1 + \bar{r}_a) = \frac{1}{N} \sum_{Y=1}^{N} (1 + r_Y) \tag{3.6}$$

The arithmetic mean can be illustrated for a firm which pays no dividend and has the prices listed below; the arithmetic mean return relative in this case is 1.0500 and the arithmetic average rate of return is 5 percent.

Year	*Price*	$(1 + r_Y)$	r_Y
0	100.00		
1	105.00	1.0500	.0500
2	94.50	0.9000	−.1000
3	113.40	1.2000	.2000
Total (∑)		3.1500	.1500
Mean		1.0500	.0500

The formula for the geometric mean return relative $(1 + \bar{r}_g)$ is a simple modification of the compound rate of return definition of Equation 3.5. With the geometric mean, however, annual rate of return may differ from year to year; in addition, return is compounded backward in time, not forward, and the exponent is therefore a fraction:

$$(1 + \bar{r}_g) = [(1 + r_1)(1 + r_2), \ldots, (1 + r_N)]^{1/N}$$

$$= \left[\prod_{Y=1}^{N} (1 + r_Y)\right]^{1/N} \tag{3.7}$$

In the example given above, the geometric average return relative is 1.0428 and geometric mean rate of return is 4.28 percent:

$$\begin{aligned}(1 + \bar{r}_g) &= [(1 + r_1)(1 + r_2)(1 + r_3)]^{1/3} \\ &= [(1.05)(0.90)(1.20)]^{1/3} \\ &= [1.1340]^{1/3} \\ &= 1.0428\end{aligned}$$

In order to calculate the geometric mean it is necessary to solve for the Nth root of the product of N return relatives. This is easily accomplished when one of the new generation of hand calculators with an exponential key (y^x) is available. Otherwise logarithms can be used because the geometric mean is the antilog of the mean logarithm of return relatives:[3]

Log 1.05	=	0.021189
Log 0.90	=	−0.045758
Log 1.20	=	0.079182
Total		0.054613
Average		0.018204
Antilog		1.0428

Average annual yield can be measured by the arithmetic mean but the geometric mean, which recognizes compounding, is clearly superior. This is easily demonstrated by considering an investment of $10.00 which increases in value to $20.00 at the end of one year only to fall back to $10.00 at the end of the second year. In that case annual rates of return, respectively, are 100 percent and −50 percent and return relatives are 2.00 and .50.

	Arithmetic Mean	*Geometric Mean*
Return relative, 1st year	2.0000	2.0000
Return relative, 2nd year	.5000	.5000
Sum, $\sum$	2.5000	
Mean	1.2500	
Product, $\prod$		1.0000
Square root $(1/N = 1/2)$		1.0000
Rate of return	.2500	.0000

The arithmetic mean implies that the investment has earned a sizable return while the geometric mean correctly indicates that wealth has not changed.

[3] Common logarithms are contained in Table A.5 located at the back of the text. The text focused on logarithms to emphasize their relationship to the geometric mean return. The example can be solved easily by using Table A.1 (also at the back of the text) which contains values for the expression $(1 + r)^n$ for different values of r and n. Reading across the three-period row, values surrounding 1.134 are located:

.0450	1.1412	1.1412
.0400	1.1249	
	0.0163	
		1.1340
		0.0072

Interpolating,

$$
\begin{aligned}
(.0072/.0163) \times .005 &= -.0022 \\
& \; 1.0450 \\
& \; 1.0428
\end{aligned}
$$

In most situations where return from investment is received over a number of years, annual rate of return is unknown from year to year. In that event geometric mean yield is more difficult to calculate. This can be demonstrated by considering an investment of \$2561.98 which returns \$1000.00 after one year and \$2000.00 after two years. Unlike the example used previously, value at the end of the first year is not given and yearly rates of return r_1 and r_2 cannot be calculated. Accordingly, Equation 3.7 cannot be used to calculate geometric mean rate of return.

The problem can be placed in perspective by defining it in terms of the time-value discounting mechanism:

$$2561.98 = \frac{1000.00}{(1 + r_1)} + \frac{2000.00}{(1 + r_1)(1 + r_2)}$$

Any $r_1 - r_2$ combination which satisfies the equation might be called the yearly rate of return for each of the two years, respectively. In fact, however, there are an unlimited set of values which meet that requirement. The equation is satisfied, to cite one example, when r_1 is .0800 and r_2 is .1319; it is also satisfied, however, when r_1 is .1500 and r_2 is .0276, or when r_1 is .1000 and r_2 is .1000, or when one of an almost infinite set of $r_1 - r_2$ values is selected. This occurs because investment recovery is realized over a two-year period and the concept of annual rates of return, from year to year, actually has no relevance. Nevertheless, the two-year return can be expressed as a yearly geometric (compounded) mean yield. In the example given above a unique solution exists for some constant average value r where $r = r_1 = r_2$: r is then equal to 10 percent.[4] When a geometric average yield in the discounting mechanism is defined in this way, it is called the *internal rate of return.*

Formally, the internal rate of return is defined as the discount rate r which satisfies Equation 3.8 for investment C_0 and investment recoveries C_t, $t = 1, 2, \ldots, N$:

$$0 = -C_0 + \frac{C_1}{(1 + r)^1} + \frac{C_2}{(1 + r)^2} + \cdots + \frac{C_N}{(1 + r)^N} \tag{3.8}$$

For the numerical example used in the preceding section to illustrate the meaning of compound rate of return:

$$0 = -100.00 + \frac{1.00}{(1 + r)^1} + \frac{1.00}{(1 + r)^2} + \frac{1.00}{(1 + r)^3} + \frac{1.00 + 108.37}{(1 + r)^4}$$

$$r = .0300$$

The internal rate of return in this case, 3 percent, can be solved only by trial and error for reasons to be explained shortly.

[4] In fact there are two values of r which will satisfy the equation. This technical point, and its implications for investment analysis, will be discussed at a later point in the chapter.

The geometric mean internal rate of return is a critical concept in security and portfolio selection. *Equation 3.8 is the general valuation model which will be applied in forthcoming chapters to the analysis of common and preferred stocks, bonds, mortgages, options, warrants, and futures contracts.* Accordingly, the properties of the internal rate of return should be carefully analyzed before security analysis is introduced. First, however, it is helpful to introduce an alternative valuation model which is preferred by many security analysts.

INTRINSIC VALUE

If the internal rate of return formula of Equation 3.8 is adjusted slightly, *net present value* of an investment can be calculated. Specifically, net present value results when an investor's required rate of return k is substituted for r in the discounting mechanism; k is determined by the individual investor's attitude toward the trade-off between risk and expected rate of return. Formally, net present value (NPV) is defined:

$$\text{NPV} = -C_0 + \frac{C_1}{(1+k)^1} + \frac{C_2}{(1+k)^2} + \cdots + \frac{C_N}{(1+k)^N} \tag{3.9}$$

If a share of stock which is priced at \$36.30 today pays an annual dividend of \$1.50 at the end of the next three years, and if the stock is then sold for \$50.00 by an investor who requires an annual rate of return of 10 percent, net present value of the investment today is \$5.00:[5]

$$\begin{aligned}\text{NPV} &= -36.30 + \frac{1.50}{(1.10)^1} + \frac{1.50}{(1.10)^2} + \frac{1.50 + 50.00}{(1.10)^3} \\ &= 5.00\end{aligned}$$

The present value of the discounted inflows (benefits) in Equation 3.9 is referred to as *intrinsic value.* In the example given above intrinsic value is \$41.30 and, because the stock sells for the lesser value of \$36.30, the security is "undervalued" to that particular investor. When the market price of a share of common stock is equal to its intrinsic value, net present value is zero and required rate of return k is equal to internal rate of return r. Risk preference differs from person to person and any given intrinsic value is relevant only for an investor with the specified yield k.

[5] Net present value is calculated from Table A.2 (at back of text) which contains the present value of \$1.00 received n periods later at interest rate r and Table A.4 which contains the present value of \$1.00 received each period for n periods at interest rate r. For a more complete explanation turn to the text's appendix, "Compound Interest Relationships," and Tables A.1–A.5 which follow that appendix. In this case,

From Table A.4, two periods at .1000,	1.50(1.7355) =	2.60
From Table A.2, period three at .1000,	51.50(0.7513) =	38.70
		41.30

Internal rate of return and intrinsic value formulations are alternative valuation models which an investor can use in selecting among different investment opportunities. Under the internal rate of return a security should be purchased if rate of return r exceeds desired yield k. Under the intrinsic value rule a security should be purchased if the intrinsic value exceeds cost, that is, if net present value is positive. If only one security is being evaluated both models will provide the same accept-reject recommendation. For two mutually exclusive securities, however, the choice may not be clear. This can be shown by comparing Equations 3.8 and 3.9 graphically.

Figure 3.2 traces net present value for an investment of \$36.30 which yields returns over three years, respectively, of \$1.50, \$1.50, and \$51.50 at discount rates from 0 through 15 percent. Net present value is plotted along the vertical axis and discount rates are measured along the horizontal axis. At a zero discount rate the net present value is the sum of undiscounted flows of \$ − 36.30, \$1.50, \$1.50, and \$51.50. At a 10 percent required rate of return net present value is \$5.00, as calculated previously. As the discount rate increases, from .0000 through .1000 to higher values, the present value of future cash flows decreases until at some point it is equal to zero. At that point, 15 percent in this case, the discount rate is the internal rate of return defined in Equation 3.8. For the single security which is being evaluated, internal rate of return r (.1500) exceeds k (.1000) and net present value (\$5.00) is positive; thus both valuation rules recommend purchase of the security. Whenever one security is analyzed the internal rate of return model and the intrinsic value model will be consistent in that sense.

Figure 3.2
Net Present Value

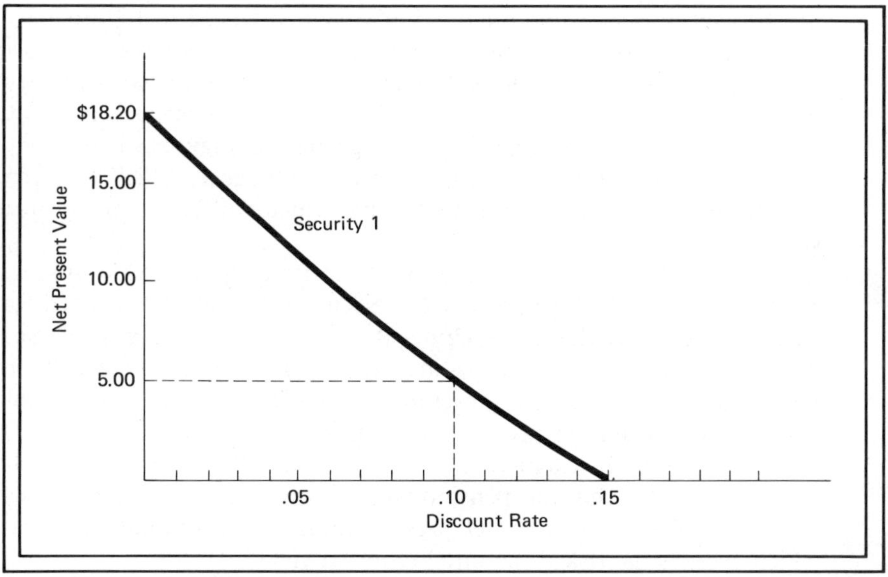

Figure 3.3
Net Present Value

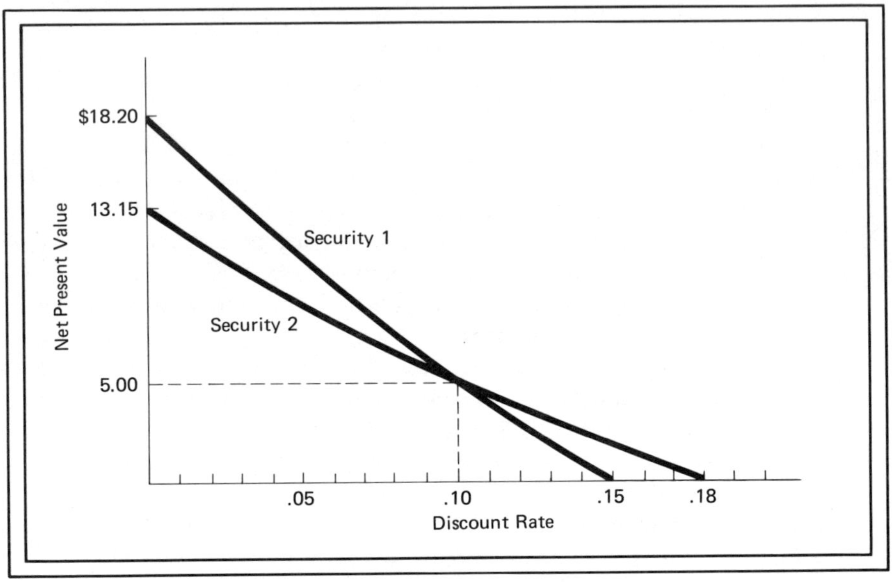

When more than one security is evaluated the two models may be in conflict. This can be illustrated by considering a second stock which currently sells for $3.63 per share; an investment in ten shares will return no dividends over the next three years but it is expected that stock will be disposed of throughout the period with proceeds, respectively, of $18.90, $15.45, and $15.10. Net present value for this investment is traced in Figure 3.3 under the label "Security 2"; the net present value of the stock which was graphed in Figure 3.2 is also shown as "Security 1." Net present value for Security 2 is $13.15 at a 0 discount rate and $5.00 at a 10 percent yield; the internal rate of return is 18 percent. The two graphs in Figure 3.3 intersect at a discount rate of 10 percent; this point of indifference, which is referred to as the *Fisher rate*, is an important value which will be examined in detail shortly.

Under the net present value rule, Security 1 is preferred for all required rates of return below 10 percent but Security 2 would be selected for any desired yield above that level. Under the internal rate of return rule Security 2, with a yield of 18 percent, would always be preferred to Security 1. The two valuation models are therefore in conflict when these two mutually exclusive opportunities are evaluated. In practice most investment opportunities are mutually exclusive in the limited sense that no investor, including the largest mutual fund or pension trust, can possibly acquire every security which promises a positive net present value or an internal rate of return which exceeds the risk-discounted required yield.

Internal rate of return and intrinsic value are analytical models which are both conceptually defensible. Both are derived from geometric mean yield because net present value employs a compound average required rate of return while the internal rate of return is a compounded mean yield, as demonstrated earlier. For this reason the two models should be examined in greater detail to provide the analyst with guidelines for choosing between them in any given application.

SECURITY VALUATION MODELS

The security valuation models of Equations 3.8 and 3.9 differ in several important respects. In part those differences arise because of certain properties and characteristics of the internal rate of return. The mathematics of the yield equation (Equation 3.8) need not be developed rigorously but mastery of the internal rate of return requires that mathematical properties should at least be recognized.

The internal rate of return was defined earlier as *the* yield which satisfies Equation 3.8. In the general N-period case, however, there are in fact N values of r where the present values of outflows and inflows are equated. Algebraically, Equation 3.8 is an Nth degree polynomial with N roots or solutions; roots may be positive or negative and they may be real or imaginary but the number of solutions will be the same as the value of the largest exponent (N) in the equation.

In the case of an example used previously where an investment of \$2561.98 generated returns of \$1000.00 and \$2000.00 over each of the next two years, the internal rate of return was said to be 10 percent. Actually, a *loss* of -170.9678 percent also satisfies the internal yield equation; with return relatives $(1 + r)$ of 1.1000 and -0.709678:[6]

$$\begin{array}{lr} 1000.00/(1.1000)^1 = & 909.09 \\ 2000.00/(1.1000)^2 = & 1652.89 \\ \hline & 2561.98 \end{array} \qquad \begin{array}{lr} 1000.00/(-0.709678)^1 = & -1409.09 \\ 2000.00/(-0.709678)^2 = & 3971.07 \\ \hline & 2561.98 \end{array}$$

[6] Since this is a second-degree or quadratic equation, the two roots can be solved by recalling the quadratic formula:

$$x = \frac{-B \pm \sqrt{B^2 - 4AC}}{2A}$$

for

$$-2561.98 + 1000.00(1 + r)^{-1} + 2000.00(1 + r)^{-2} = 0$$

$$-2561.98(1 + r)^2 + 1000.00(1 + r)^1 + 2000.00 = 0$$

Substituting $(1 + r) = x$ in the quadratic equation,

$$A = -2561.98$$
$$B = 1000.00$$
$$C = 2000.00$$

and the return relative roots are $x = 1.1000$ and $x = -0.7097$.

In this example there are two solutions to Equation 3.8 and the choice of one of them, 10.00 percent, appears to be arbitrary. But this is not the case, for two reasons. First, the solution to the internal rate of return model is given in terms of return relative $(1 + r)$ instead of yield r. A negative return relative is unlikely because it measures a loss which exceeds the original investment and that rarely happens with securities.[7] Similarly, imaginary roots have no economic interpretation because they are expressed in terms of the square root $\sqrt{-1.00}$. For these reasons, and assuming that there is only one such solution, the internal rate of return is defined as the *positive real root* of Equation 3.8. Second, the positive real root is a measure which is compatible with the measure used for portfolio rate of return; this will be illustrated shortly.

The major differences between internal rate of return and intrinsic value arise because yield is defined as one of a set of N values which equate cash flows in the polynomial discounting mechanism. These differences involve (1) computational difficulty, (2) uniqueness of the yield definition, and (3) future value maximization.

COMPUTATIONAL DIFFICULTY. In general the internal rate of return must be solved by *trial and error* because it is one of N solutions to Equation 3.8. In the two-period case the quadratic formula can be used and formulas also exist for third- and fourth-degree equations, although they are very complicated. When N is greater than 4, no algebraic formula exists and trial and error must be used. In contrast, net present value can be solved rather easily and intrinsic value therefore enjoys a computational advantage over internal yield. But that advantage is not sufficiently large to warrant preference for net present value on that basis alone. First, and most importantly, relevance, and not arithmetic facility, is the proper focus for selecting between two alternative models. Second, trial and error calculation is far less bothersome than it may appear to be at first.

Published yield tables are available for many investment situations and yield calculation can often be avoided entirely. Bond yield can be determined, for example, from tables which specify yield for a wide variety of prices, bond interest rates, and maturities. Moreover, hand calculators with programmed financial routines are available at a fairly modest cost. In effect these calculators are "electronic" yield tables capable of solving a wide variety of problems. In any situation where published or preprogrammed yield tables are not appropriate, routines exist for calculating the internal rate of return quickly and efficiently; Appendix A following this chapter demonstrates trial and error solution for problems involving both constant and nonconstant cash flows. Finally, most computer installations have "canned" routines which solve for internal yield in practically any application. A computer may not

[7] For common stock, for example, liability is limited to the amount invested unless the shares were issued below par or stated legal value. A loss of 100 percent is the typical limiting case and that is very unusual.

be available to an individual investor but a professional analyst will certainly have access to one. Although the internal rate of return is arithmetically awkward, it can be solved with tools which are currently available and the issue of computational difficulty is basically trivial.

MULTIPLE RATES OF RETURN. A potentially more serious problem with Equation 3.8 is the possibility that there may be *more* than one positive real root. In that case the internal rate of return would be ambiguous. The necessary but insufficient mathematical condition for multiple roots is multiple change in the sign of successive cash flows. This can be illustrated for the following two-period investments:

Case	*Period 0 Investment*	*Period 1 Cash Flow*	*Period 2 Cash Flow*	*Change in Sign*	*Root 1*	*Root 2*
1	−50	+ 25	+ 33	1	1.10	−0.60
2	−50	−100	+150	1	1.00	−3.00
3	−50	+150	−100	2	1.00	2.00

Case 1 involves only one change in sign, from negative to positive in the 0–1 interval, and there can be only one positive real root. In case 1, therefore, the internal rate of return is 10.00 percent. Case 2 has a different pattern of flows but there is only one change of sign again, from period 1 to period 2, and there is only one internal rate of return: 0.00 percent. But in case 3 there are two changes of sign, from negative to positive to negative, and two positive real roots are therefore possible. In fact both roots are positive and neither rate of return, 0 percent or 100 percent, can be taken as the conventionally defined internal yield.

If multiple rates of return are likely to occur in any given application, internal yield cannot be used as the basis for valuation. In business finance, for example, many authors consider the problem to be sufficiently serious to preclude use of Equation 3.8 in the capital-budgeting process. In security analysis, however, multiple rates of return are very unlikely. Multiple change in sign requires a negative cash flow beyond the original cost of a security in a sufficiently large amount to bend the present value function of Figure 3.2 so that it crosses the horizontal axis at least twice. Liability is limited for most security investments and change of sign is not possible in those cases. In situations where it is possible, it is unlikely that the negative flow will be large enough to generate multiple roots.[8] For these reasons multiple rates of return are not a serious concern in security analysis.

FUTURE VALUE MAXIMIZATION. Neither computational difficulty nor the multiple-yield problem is sufficiently serious in security analysis to reject

[8] One possible situation is the case of a total loss from an uninsured mortgage but simulations were unsuccessful in generating multiple rates even in this case. See Anthony J. Curley and Jack M. Guttentag, "The Yield on Insured Residential Mortgages," *Explorations in Economic Research*, Summer 1974, p. 159, fn. 7.

Equation 3.8 for valuation purposes. A more relevant basis for choosing between intrinsic value and the internal rate of return is the impact of the chosen model on the process of investors' wealth maximization. Wealth can be measured by either the present value or the future value of an investor's portfolio. When required rate of return k is a constant over time, and there is no realistic basis for assuming a variable k, present value maximization will also maximize future value. The discussion which follows will focus on future value for convenience.

Future value maximization is a difficult concept because it involves an assumption as to the rate of return which can be realized from recovered cash flows which are reinvested from period to period.[9] It also requires an assumption as to the availability of borrowed funds for partially financing the portfolio. If an unlimited amount of money can be borrowed at some fixed interest rate, intrinsic value should be used because that model will maximize future value under those circumstances. But the amount of funds that can be borrowed is limited by regulatory authorities and market conditions and unlimited leverage is therefore an uninteresting case. The impact of borrowing on portfolio rate of return will be analyzed in later chapters when portfolio selection techniques are discussed.

Reinvestment is a more pressing issue because it directly affects both the rate of return and the relative contribution to profit of every security in a portfolio. It is often claimed that Equation 3.8 implicitly assumes reinvestment at the internal rate of return but the fallacy in that statement, similar to the one discussed earlier when compounding was analyzed, is confusion between security yield and portfolio yield. Appendix B to this chapter examines and exposes the reinvestment fallacy. The internal rate of return involves no assumption, implicit or explicit, concerning the reinvestment of proceeds generated by the purchase of any individual security. At the same time, portfolio rate of return, and future value maximization, are highly dependent on the assumed yield from reinvestment.

Portfolio rate of return $\bar{r}$ is a weighted average of the rates of return of all securities in the portfolio. Portfolio weights are the investment in each security relative to total investment. For a portfolio consisting of P securities where each security has a yield of r_i and a weight of x_i, $i = 1, 2, \ldots, P$:

$$\bar{r} = \sum_{i=1}^{P} x_i r_i \tag{3.10}$$

If \$3000.00 is invested in Security 1 to yield 10.00 percent and \$7000.00 is invested in Security 2 to yield 20.00 percent, then x_1 is .30, x_2 is .70, and portfolio rate of return is 17.00 percent:[10]

[9] For an analysis of the reinvestment problem see Carlton L. Dudley, Jr., "A Note on Reinvestment Assumptions in Choosing Between Net Present Value and Internal Rate of Return," *Journal of Finance*, September 1972, pp. 907–915.

[10] In dollar terms, security 1 returns \$300 and security 2 returns \$1400. The total \$1700 return is 17 percent of the \$10,000 invested.

$$\bar{r} = \sum_{i=1}^{2} x_i r_i = x_1 r_1 + x_2 r_2$$
$$= (.30)(.1000) + (.70)(.2000)$$
$$= .1700$$

Portfolio yield can be calculated from Equation 3.10 if security yields r_i and weights x_i are known. Internal rate of return r_i can be calculated from Equation 3.8 but weight x_i presents a slightly more difficult problem. The cash flow recovered from any particular investment consists of the return of the amount invested plus any income earned on that principal value. In the case of an investment which is recovered entirely within one period, return *of* investment is easily distinguished from return *on* investment. If $1000.00 returns $1200.00 one year later, cash flow clearly consists of:

Return of investment (principal)	$1000.00
Return on investment (income)	200.00
	$1200.00

For a multiperiod investment, on the other hand, cash flow "stream splitting" is less obvious. In the case of an example used previously where an investment of $36.30 yielded $18.90, $15.45, and $15.10 during subsequent years, allocation of the three cash flows among principal and income cannot be accomplished merely by observation.

Allocation of multiperiod flows is necessary because the portfolio weights of Equation 3.10 are calculated from then-remaining unrecovered investment in every period. Portfolio yield cannot be computed unless the flows can be separated into principal and income components. Table 3.1 illustrates a simple method for doing this. First, the flows which are known are entered in the appropriate columns and yield is calculated from Equation

Table 3.1
Cash Flow Allocation

	(1)	(2)	(3)	(4)	(5)
			(1) × (2)		(4) − (3)
Year	Internal Yield	Unrecovered Investment	Return on Investment	Cash Flow	Recovered Investment
1	.1800[b]	36.30[a]	6.53	18.90[a]	12.37
2	.1800[b]	23.93	4.31	15.45[a]	11.14
3	.1800[b]	12.79	2.31	15.10[a]	12.79

[a] Values entered in table before flows are allocated and entered.
[b] Calculated by trial and error from Equation 3.8.

3.8 and then entered in column 1. Next, return on investment is calculated from the product of columns 1 and 2; for the first year it is \$6.53, (.1800 × \$36.30). Recovered investment, \$12.37 for the first year, is the difference between gross cash flow and income. Finally, unrecovered investment at the beginning of the second year is calculated from the preceding balance (\$23.93 = \$36.30 – \$12.37) and the process is then repeated for every year. The values in the second column of the table, \$36.30, \$23.93, and \$12.79, are the investment values to be used for the portfolio weights of Equation 3.10. This is proven in Appendix B of this chapter.

Portfolio weights were illustrated with the methodology of Table 3.1 for two reasons. First, an arithmetic example was selected in order to provide insight as to the meaning of "stream splitting" as it applies to the allocation of cash flow between recovered principal and interest. Second, the general format of Table 3.1 will be used in Chapter 7 as a basic device for interpreting the meaning of data generated by financial accountants; for that reason it is helpful to introduce it here where return on investment is first explored in detail. But it should be pointed out that unrecovered investment can also be calculated directly from a variant of Equation 3.8 as the present value of then-remaining cash flows, discounted at the internal rate of return. In the example of Table 3.1, unrecovered investment at the beginning of the second period is:

$$
\begin{aligned}
I_2 &= \frac{C_2}{(1+r)^1} + \frac{C_3}{(1+r)^2} \\
&= \frac{15.45}{(1.18)^1} + \frac{15.10}{(1.18)^2} \\
&= 23.93
\end{aligned}
$$

With x_i and r_i defined and illustrated, the relationship between portfolio yield and future value can be formulated. For one security which costs C_0 dollars, with cash recoveries reinvested through period N, cost and future value are linked by compound portfolio yield:

$$FV_N = C_0\left[\prod_{t=1}^{N}(1+\bar{r}_t)\right] = C_0\left[\prod_{t=1}^{N}\left(1+\sum_{i=1}^{P}x_i r_i\right)\right] \tag{3.11}$$

Equation 3.11 is a simplification of the portfolio process where securities are bought and sold periodically without identification of any specific source of funds. It is a useful abstraction, however, because it highlights the importance of reinvestment.

Appendix B contains an extended arithmetic illustration of Equation 3.11. But an important issue can be resolved directly from the equation, without resort to the appendix demonstration: the strategy of selecting securities with the highest r_i values is unlikely to maximize future value because portfolio yield depends on x_i weights as well as r_i yields. Portfolio weights, in turn, are calculated from periodic unrecovered investment which

Table 3.2
Portfolio Future Value

Rate of Return on Reinvestment		
8 Percent	*10 Percent*	*12 Percent*
	Security 1	
$1.50(1.08)^2 =$ 1.75	$1.50(1.10)^2 =$ 1.82	$1.50(1.12)^2 =$ 1.88
$1.50(1.08)^1 =$ 1.62	$1.50(1.10)^1 =$ 1.65	$1.50(1.12)^1 =$ 1.68
$51.50(1.08)^0 =$ 51.50	$51.50(1.10)^0 =$ 51.50	$51.50(1.12)^0 =$ 51.50
Total 54.87	54.97	55.06
	Security 2	
$18.90(1.08)^2 =$ 22.04	$18.90(1.10)^2 =$ 22.87	$18.90(1.12)^2 =$ 23.71
$15.45(1.08)^1 =$ 16.69	$15.45(1.10)^1 =$ 17.00	$15.45(1.12)^1 =$ 17.30
$15.10(1.08)^0 =$ 15.10	$15.10(1.10)^0 =$ 15.10	$15.10(1.12)^0 =$ 15.10
Total 53.83	54.97	56.11

is determined by the pattern of cash flows, as shown in Table 3.1. Accordingly, the internal rate of return model of Equation 3.8, and the intrinsic value model of Equation 3.9 by similar reasoning, should not be applied on an individual security-by-security basis. Security evaluation is only an input to portfolio analysis where the portfolio includes assets generated by previous investments. The choice between intrinsic value and internal yield in any given case, in the absence of unlimited borrowing capacity, is therefore reduced to the question of the return realized from reinvestment.

This can be demonstrated in the case of the two mutually exclusive securities which were analyzed in Figure 3.3. Security 1, with a cost of $36.30, generated cash flows over three succeeding years of $1.50, $1.50, and $51.50; Security 2, with the same cost, realized respective flows of $18.90, $15.45, and $15.10. Table 3.2 shows future value for both investments under assumed reinvestment rates of 8.00, 10.00, and 12.00 percent. When reinvestment realizes anything less than 10.00 percent, Security 1 is preferred; above 10.00 percent Security 2 is preferred. At 10.00 percent, which was referred to earlier as the *Fisher rate*,[11] an investor would be indifferent as to which security was purchased.

Referring again to Figure 3.3, the Fisher rate is the discount rate where the two present value functions intersect. Future value of the *portfolio* is maximized by selecting the security with the larger present value when flows are discounted at the *rate of return on reinvestment*. If reinvestment yield is less than the Fisher rate, Security 1 should be purchased. If required rate of

[11] Named after the noted economist Irving Fisher. See Armen A. Alchian, "The Rate of Interest, Fisher's Rate of Return over Costs and Keynes' Internal Rate of Return," *American Economic Review*, December 1955, pp. 938–942.

return k is also less than the Fisher rate, the intrinsic value Equation 3.9 will properly select Security 1; if k is greater, however, intrinsic value and internal yield will both lead to the wrong decision. If the rate of return on reinvestment is greater than the Fisher rate, the internal rate of return equation (Equation 3.8) will be correct; the intrinsic value model may or may not be correct, depending upon the value of k. It should be emphasized that these conclusions would have to be modified if the investor can partially finance the portfolio with borrowed funds. In that case the Fisher rate would have to be adjusted upwards but the general conclusion as to the importance of reinvestment would not be affected.

INTRINSIC VALUE AND INTERNAL YIELD. The preceding analysis introduced two security valuation models and demonstrated that neither one of them necessarily achieves wealth maximization unless yield from reinvestment is recognized. In practice future investment opportunities can only be estimated and that is a hazardous basis for selecting one model or the other for general purposes of security analysis. For purposes of consistency this text uses the internal rate of return equation (Equation 3.8) throughout. This choice was made for the following reasons:

1. In practice the internal rate of return is widely used. Bond yield, mortgage yield, and preferred stock yield, for example, are all measured by internal yield in the investment community.
2. The internal rate of return is compatible with the one-period portfolio selection model which is considered in detail beginning with Chapter 14. Security analysis and portfolio analysis are easily integrated when the former is measured by Equation 3.8.

Investment Indexes

Rate of return on investment was introduced and analyzed in the first section of this chapter. Rate of return is a measure of investment performance but it is difficult to interpret unless some standard measure is available for purposes of comparison. In addition, the behavior of security markets is of general interest to business executives, government officials, economists, and investors because capital market performance is an important indicator of economic activity. A number of aggregate performance indexes are therefore calculated and published regularly.

This section examines the properties and characteristics of some widely followed market indexes. Index properties are discussed generally to emphasize the fact that different indexes may give conflicting signals of market behavior. Following the discussion of general index properties, the most important averages will be examined in detail.

Market indexes differ in part because of statistical and analytical problems which will be discussed in this section. But major differences also evolved purely through historical accident. Limited data availability, together with data-processing inadequacy, retarded index development until very recently.[12] The Dow Jones industrial average (DJI) is a case in point. DJI is a continuous index of stock prices dating back to 1896. The original index averaged the prices of 12 securities; the number was increased to 20 in 1916 and to the present 30 in 1928. Occasionally the composition has had to be changed as one of the firms was merged or otherwise delisted but the number of firms has not changed in 50 years. Otherwise, continuity of the series would be disturbed. The number of DJI firms, viewed in this light, undoubtedly reflects the severe difficulties involved in data collection and averaging in the late nineteenth century when the index was introduced. In contrast, the more recent and comprehensive NYSE index is based on the entire population of some 1900 firms; values are calculated hourly. In the absence of sophisticated computer equipment this would have been impossible even a few years ago, no less the nineteenth or early twentieth century.

The vestige of nineteenth century information deficiency is found today in the Dow Jones "30" which nonetheless continues to be one of the most popular and widely recognized of all common stock indexes. Modern data technology is exercising an increasingly significant impact on the design of new measures of market behavior. But the relative merits of newer and older measures remain unsettled and both types are regularly reported in the financial press. Moreover, advancing technology promises added innovation which may someday provide integrated measures which are now lacking across the many capital markets. Viewed from this perspective, the statistical properties of indexes assume added significance.

INDEX CHARACTERISTICS

An index number is a value relative to some base value; it is a measure of the relative change over time in some variable. The construction of an index involves (1) identification of the variable to be measured, (2) selection of the mathematical formulation by which the index is calculated, and (3) definition of the data base to be used.

INDEX VARIABLE.[13] Capital market indexes are designed to measure market performance over time. For common stocks performance can be defined in terms of price behavior or rate of return behavior. The two definitions differ because of the exclusion or inclusion of dividends; this is clear from the rate of return definition of Equation 3.4. For any extended time period the difference between a price index and a rate of return index is likely to be very large because price relatives ignore the effect of dividend compounding. In

[12] Data deficiency continues to be a severe problem in some areas today. Real estate investment is an obvious case. Problems with respect to performance measures in this market are discussed in Paul F. Wendt and Sui N. Wong, "Investment Performance: Common Stocks Versus Apartment Houses," *Journal of Finance*, December 1965, pp. 633–646.

[13] A careful analysis of the merits of alternative definitions is found in Lawrence Fisher, "Some New Stock-Market Indexes," *Journal of Business*, January 1966 Supplement, pp. 192–194.

any specific application the relevance of either price or rate of return depends on the end use intended. In general, however, based upon the preceding discussion of investment yield, price indexes are inferior to rate of return indexes. Unfortunately, all common stock averages which are published daily are price indexes. They may be useful measures of short-run performance but they are biased values over longer time periods.

Indexes are also prepared for government bonds, corporate bonds, preferred stocks, and mortgages. Yield on these instruments is difficult to average because of variations in coupon and dividend rates, maturity, quality, and other factors which must be classified. These problems will be discussed in detail in Chapter 5.

The index variable can be measured in either *absolute* or *relative* terms. Interestingly, the American Stock Exchange Index has been both. When it was first introduced in 1966 the AMEX index was an absolute measure of average price. On April 30, 1973, for example, the index value of $23.49 was an unweighted average of closing share prices of all the securities traded on the exchange. But in September of that year the index was converted to aggregate value, price weighted by outstanding shares, and the September 3, 1973, value was assigned an index value of 100. Values published daily can be interpreted on that basis. On April 30, 1974, for example, the AMEX average of approximately 90 measured an average loss of 10.00 percent in the nine-month interval since the previous September. On that same day, the Standard and Poor's "500" average was also 90 but that index has a 1941–43 base of 10; this implies an average return of approximately 7.00 percent during the 32-year period.[14]

MATHEMATICAL FORMULATION. When the index variable has been identified, a specific formula for calculating the average must be selected. This involves several choices. First, the average can be an arithmetic mean or a geometric mean. Although the latter is conceptually superior, as demonstrated earlier, it makes little practical difference in the case of a price index because most price indexes are calculated at least daily. A performance index, based upon rate of return, should be averaged geometrically.

Price index *weighting* is a more important issue. Early formulations, including the DJI, are an unweighted average.[15] More recent indexes typically weight share price by the number of shares outstanding, which transforms a price index into a market value index. Despite the increasing popularity of market value indexes, however, there is no obviously correct

[14] Centered on 1942, for a base value of 10, r can be approximated: $10(1 + r)^{32} = 90$ and $r = .0711$.

[15] Butler and Decker point out that an unweighted price index serves to weight an index nonetheless because the influence of any firm on an index is a function of market price. Each time a stock is split its influence on the index average is reduced. See Hartman L. Butler, Jr., and Martin G. Decker, "A Security Check on the Dow Jones Industrial Average," in *Readings in Financial Analysis and Investment Management*, ed. Eugene M. Lerner (Homewood, Ill.: Irwin, 1963), pp. 84–96.

general solution to the weighting problem. Relevance depends upon the intended end use which varies with portfolio mix for any individual investor.

DATA BASE. Stock indexes are very sensitive to the data base which is used for measuring average value. Representation, consistency, and stability of the measurement unit should be considered when data are selected. Representation is important when an index is based upon sample values for a population of securities. When sample size was limited historically by data constraints, a great deal of attention was directed to industry classification in an attempt to achieve a representative sample. The current trend, which is influenced by the state of data processing technology, is to use the population, instead of a sample, for index purposes. But there is no necessary reason to believe that any population of securities is representative for any individual investor.

Consistency implies stability in the selection of firms for the index and stability in the variable which is used to measure performance. With sample-based indexes, as in the case of DJI, the firms included in the averaging process are fairly consistent from period to period. For population-based indexes, in contrast, frequent adjustments are necessary because of the listing and delisting of corporations. Stock splits and stock dividends are another potentially serious problem because they affect both the share price and the number of shares outstanding. Market value indexes are automatically adjusted for splits and stock dividends but unweighted indexes should be adjusted regularly, by rather complicated procedures, if consistency is to be preserved.

Market indexes are based on the assumption of a fixed monetary unit; they are not adjusted for changes in the general price level. In view of the rate of inflation which has occurred recently, the real rate of return on investment is obscured. A 20-point change in the DJI in the mid-1970s, for example, has a far different interpretation than did the same change in the early 1950s. No price-adjusted index is currently available; this is an area where future research efforts may profitably be directed.

Index numbers have analytical and empirical properties which tend to obscure underlying trends which they are designed to measure. Market indexes are significantly correlated over extended periods of time but there is plausible evidence of short-run deviation among the many indexes which are available.[16] For this reason an investor should be familiar with the

[16] During 1977 there was a great deal of controversy over which sector of the market provided the best measure of market trend. Analysts debated the difference between popular averages and what some people described as the "real market." During 1977 the Dow Jones Industrial average decreased by close to 17 percent, the S&P "500" index decreased by 12 percent, and the NYSE composite index decreased by 9 percent; during the same period the NASDAQ OTC composite index increased by 7 percent and the AMEX index increased by 16 percent. Under the circumstances it is very difficult to describe market performance for 1977. For a discussion of the problem see Fisher, "Some New Stock Market Indexes" and Anthony Gaubis, "Which Is the Best Stock Average From a Practical Viewpoint?" in Eugene M. Lerner, ed., *Readings in Financial Analysis and Investment Management*, pp. 103–111.

properties and peculiarities of any index used as a point of reference. The characteristics of some familiar indexes are therefore reviewed in the following sections.

DOW JONES AVERAGES

Dow Jones price averages are calculated for (1) 30 industrial firms, (2) 20 transportation companies, and (3) 15 utilities; (4) a composite average for all 65 companies is also available. Prices are averaged for large companies which are considered to have "blue chip" investment quality. Averages are "unweighted" but they are very sensitive to the price of firms which are included in the sample; a stock selling for \$100.00 per share has ten times the influence of another which sells for \$10.00 per share. In the summer of 1977, to cite one example, one stock (DuPont) accounted for almost 10 percent of the value of the Dow Jones "30"; together with three others (AT&T, General Motors, and Proctor and Gamble), approximately 30 percent of the average value was accounted for by four firms. Dow Jones averages are characterized by sensitivity to the price of a small number of firms.

Another important feature is the "divisor" which is used to maintain consistency in the averages. Originally the divisor was the number of stocks in the average; prices were summed and divided by that number. But stock splits and some stock dividends created a problem. Until 1928 they were recognized by adjusting price; after a 2 for 1 split, for example, a firm's price would be doubled before prices were averaged. Since 1928 the divisor instead has been adjusted. Following a split a proportionate price is substituted and a new divisor is calculated which results in the same presplit value. Thereafter the new divisor is used. Small stock dividends and stock rights are ignored in the calculation. Algebraically, for a divisor d and stock price p_i, $i = 1, 2, \ldots, 30$, the Dow Jones "30" is calculated:

$$\text{DJI}(30) = \frac{\sum_{i=1}^{30} p_i}{d} \tag{3.12}$$

To interpret a Dow Jones index the divisor must be considered.[17] On July 28, 1977, when the divisor was 1.443, 30 Dow Jones industrials closed down by 19.75. This was an aggregate loss for all securities of \$28.50 (19.75 × 1.443) and an average loss of \$0.95 per share (28.50/30). The aggregate closing value that day of 888.43 represents an unadjusted sum of \$1282.00 for the 30 securities in the industrial list. Similar adjustments are necessary for the other three Dow Jones averages.

[17] Divisors are published daily in *The Wall Street Journal.*

STANDARD & POOR'S INDEXES

Another popular group of measures are Standard & Poor's (S&P) indexes for (1) 400 industrials, (2) 20 transportation, (3) 40 utilities, (4) 40 financials, and (5) a composite of the other three, the Standard & Poor's "500" index. They are sample-based indexes but they include a larger number of firms and they represent a larger percentage of total market value than those used for Dow Jones averages. S&P indexes are weighted averages, with price weighted by outstanding shares, and a relatively small number of firms therefore exercise a disproportionate influence on index values. The impact of splits and stock dividends is automatically adjusted because market value is used but changes in the composition of the "500" are frequently necessary. Standard & Poor's indexes measure relative value for a defined 1941–1943 base value of 10; since 1962 they have been calculated hourly.

The "500" index was introduced in March of 1957. With the exception of Dow Jones data, very little information had been available on the behavior of stock prices until the late 1930s. In 1939 the Cowles Commission published monthly indexes of earnings, dividends, and common stock prices for approximately seventy industry groups over the period 1871–1938.[18] With the introduction of the Standard & Poor's "500," the Cowles data were merged, the 20-year gap (1938–1957) was filled, the base was adjusted to the 1941–1943 value of 10, and investors were provided with a comprehensive market history dating back to 1871. During the next ten years or so into the 1960s both Dow Jones averages and S&P indexes were calculated for increasingly narrower reporting intervals. With the development of the computer the stage was set for the introduction of comprehensive indexes for the population of securities on any organized exchange.

NEW YORK STOCK EXCHANGE INDEXES

On July 14, 1966, the NYSE introduced a comprehensive set of indexes based upon the closing price of all firms listed on the exchange. A composite index is calculated every half-hour during every trading day and four subgroup indexes—industrial, finance, transportation, and utility—are available hourly. The index is calculated from the aggregate market value of all listed firms after an adjustment to eliminate the effect of frequent listings and delistings. Share-weighted aggregate price is measured relative to a base value of 50 which represents total market value on December 31, 1965. Composite index values are available weekly from January 7, 1939, to May 28, 1964, and then daily thereafter. Subgroup indexes have been measured on a daily basis beginning with December 31, 1965.

[18] Alfred Cowles, III, et al., *Common Stock Indexes*, Cowles Commission for Research in Economics Monograph No. 3 (Bloomington, Ind.: Principia Press, 1939).

AMERICAN STOCK EXCHANGE INDEX

The American Stock Exchange has calculated a comprehensive index of closing prices for their population of listed companies since June of 1966. The original version was a price index but on September 3, 1973, when a base value of 100 was established, the index was converted to a market value measure for all stocks, warrants, and foreign securities. The AMEX index is the same as the NYSE index with respect to population-based values, share weights, and component consistency.

OVER-THE-COUNTER INDEXES

Date collection is a particularly difficult problem in the over-the-counter (OTC) market. Before the National Association of Security Dealers Automated Quotation System (NASDAQ) was introduced, price quotations were difficult and costly to acquire and a broad and representative OTC sample was not available. Until 1971 the National Quotation Bureau (a subsidiary of Commerce Clearing House) published the only index of over-the-counter prices for a sample of 35 common stocks. In view of differences among unlisted firms with respect to both size and industry, the relevance and representation of this index was highly questionable.

In February of 1971 NASD launched the automated NASDAQ system, leading one observer to comment that OTC had changed from "over-the-counter" to "over-the-computer." Shortly thereafter, in May of 1971, NASD began to publish seven daily OTC indexes: composite, industrial, banks, insurance, transportation, utilities, and "other." These indexes are price averages relative to a February 5, 1971, base value of 100.

NASD indexes are the best available measures of OTC behavior but sampling and measurement problems continue to be severe. Quotations are available for the "national" OTC list on which the NASD indexes are based and for the "regional" list. But smaller firms are seldom quoted and all OTC securities are subject to the problem of nominal pricing. The diversity among firms in the OTC market and prices which may or may not be supported by actual transactions create index problems which have yet to be solved.

PERFORMANCE INDEXES

In addition to the price indexes discussed above, several performance indexes, which explicitly recognize dividends, have been proposed. While the relevance of price versus performance depends on the end use intended, dividend-adjusted measures are preferable in many respects. Unfortunately, performance indexes are not published in the financial press because they have not been generally accepted by investors.

The most widely recognized performance measure is the Fisher Index which was created at the Center for Research in Security Prices (CRSP) at the University of Chicago.[19] This is a somewhat complicated measure of the return relatives for all NYSE firms from January, 1926, to date. The index is a monthly measure of the rate of return for a balanced portfolio of NYSE stocks, with a December, 1960, base value of 100. The first published data included a composite index and 45 separate industry indexes, with industries defined by Securities and Exchange Commission classification. CRSP data for individual firms on a daily basis are now available commercially from the University of Chicago. Although the Fisher Index has not been adopted by practitioners, it has been used as the measure of market performance in a large number of studies which are published in academic journals.

Performance indexes have been suggested only recently and, aside from research applications, they are neither generally available nor generally acceptable in the investment community. This may change in the future. Among other things, new portfolio measures based upon rate of return, in lieu of price, have found increasing acceptance on the part of investors.[20] A performance index is the logical mechanism for linking market behavior with the performance of an investor's portfolio.

Summary

This chapter focused on some important rate of return dimensions. The discussion began with elementary definitions and then proceeded to an in-depth examination of two important investment criteria: net present value and internal rate of return. These two rules were compared and the latter, internal rate of return, was selected as the basic analytical tool for security analysis in this text.

The importance of reinvestment was stressed. In this context portfolio return was introduced and defined. Appendix B at the end of this chapter contains an extended arithmetic illustration of portfolio yield.

The second section of the chapter considered rate of return indexes in light of the variety of statistical conventions which govern index construction. Emphasis was directed to index properties and some of the more popular indexes were interpreted in terms of those properties.

This chapter discussed a number of important investment elements but others remain to be considered before specific analytical procedures

[19] The index was named for Professor Lawrence Fisher of the University of Chicago. See Fisher, "Some New Stock-Market Indexes." Another noteworthy proposal is the average investment performance index (AIPI) suggested in Kalman J. Cohen and Bruce P. Fitch, "The Average Investment Performance Index," *Management Science*, February 1966, pp. B195–215. AIPI is calculated on the basis of random portfolios which are sampled iteratively; index means are thereby extended to include an associated measure of dispersion, the AIPI standard deviation. Evaluation of the risk underlying the performance measure is therefore possible in the sense to be discussed in Chapter 4.

[20] The portfolio measures which are referred to are considered in detail beginning in Chapter 14.

can be introduced. The next chapter assumes that task. Following an introduction to some basic concepts, the discussion turns to the vexing problem of risk and the trade-off between risk and return which an investor faces.

Appendix A
Calculating the Internal Rate of Return

The internal rate of return must be calculated by trial and error and that can be a burdensome process. But the computation can be simplified when either of the following tools is available.

1. PRESENT VALUE TABLES. Table A.2 in the appendix located at the back of the text contains present value factors for a single sum payable in some future period and Table A.4 contains present value factors for a series of future payments. In the first section below the use of these tables to estimate the internal rate of return is illustrated.

2. ONE OF THE NEW GENERATION OF ELECTRONIC HAND CALCULATORS. Particularly useful is one of the "finance" calculators with present value functions. In the second section below, calculation of the internal rate of return is discussed under the most difficult circumstance possible where cash flows vary from period to period.

PRESENT VALUE TABLES

The easiest yield calculation is the one where an investment returns a single cash flow in some future period. Assume that a current investment of $1000.00 will purchase a tract of land which is expected to be worth $1621.52 five years later. In that case the internal rate of return equation is:

$$1000.00 = \frac{1621.52}{(1 + r)^5}$$

$$\frac{1}{(1 + r)^5} = \frac{1000.00}{1621.52}$$

$$= .6167$$

For each $1.00 of value five years from now, $0.6167 has been invested; .6167 is the present value factor. From Table A.2 (at back of text) reading across values for period 5,

	Rate of Return	*Present Value Factor*
	.1050	.6070
	.1000	.6209
Difference	.0050	.0139
Interpolating—		
	.1050	.6070
	?	.6167
Difference		.0097

.0097/.0139 = .6978
.6978 × .0050 = .0035
.1050 − .0035 = .1015

The internal rate of return is 10.15 percent, correct to four decimal places of accuracy. In this example Table A.2 was used to illustrate the present value table; Table A.1 for future value could have been used just as easily.

Next, assume that an investor purchases a mortgage which matures in 30 years, with annual payments of \$1835.54 which amortize the \$20,000.00 face value. The internal yield equation is:

$$20{,}000.00 - \sum_{t=1}^{30} \frac{1835.54}{(1+r)^t}$$

$$\sum_{t=1}^{30} \frac{1}{(1+r)^t} = \frac{20000.00}{1835.54}$$

$$= 10.8960$$

Table A.4 has present value factors for the summation term in the equation. Reading across the period row, for period 30:

	Rate of Return	*Present Value Factor*
	.0850	10.7468
	.0800	11.2578
Difference	.0050	−.5110
	.0850	10.7468
	?	10.8960
Difference		−.1492

.1492/.5110 = .2920
.2920 × .0050 = .0015
.0850 − .0015 = .0835

The internal rate of return of 8.35 percent is again accurate to four decimal places.

USING AN ELECTRONIC CALCULATOR

If a "finance" calculator is available, both of the preceding problems could be solved with a single operation. But if cash flows differ from period to period, several operations are still required. Table A.2 can be used when there are variable flows but the arithmetic operation can become very lengthy. Where trial and error is required there are a number of efficient algorithms which can be used to simplify the problem. One of the most efficient of these is the iterative process illustrated below; most "canned" computer programs employ this technique.

Figure 3A.1 shows present value at different discount rates for a hypothetical investment; present value is the curved line which intersects the horizontal axis at point *r*, the internal rate of return. Point *A* is the present value at a zero discount rate. If the slope of the present value function is known at point *A*, triangle *AOB* can be constructed. The slope of the present value function can be approximated arithmetically by calculating net present

Figure 3A.1
An Internal Rate of Return Algorithm

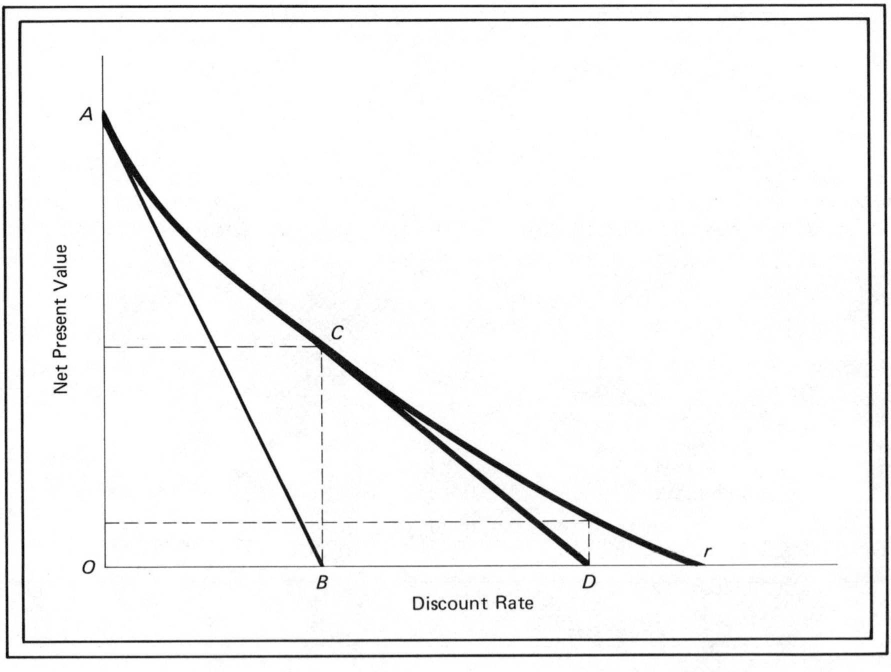

value at some discount rate which is very close to zero; by comparing this arithmetic value with net present value at 0 percent:

$$\text{slope} \approx \frac{\text{change in net present value}}{\text{change in discount rate}}$$

That is, the slope is calculated as the ratio of the "rise" to the "run"; it is an approximation because the function is not linear. Since the slope of triangle AOB equals

$$\text{slope}_{AOB} = \frac{AO}{OB}$$

then:

$$OB = \frac{AO}{\text{slope}_{AOB}}$$

Distance OB is a first approximation of the internal rate of return. By calculating present value at discount rate OB, which is a value of BC in Figure 3A.1, and at another rate which is close to OB, the process can then be repeated. Distance BD which was calculated in the second iteration is then added to OB and the sum, OD, is the second approximation. The iterations continue until present value is as close to zero as the analyst desires.

The method can be illustrated arithmetically for a 7 percent corporate bond which costs \$916.00; if the bond matures in ten years and interest is paid semiannually on the maturity value of \$1000.00, the internal rate of return equation is:

$$916.00 = \frac{35.00}{(1+r)^1} + \frac{35.00}{(1+r)^2} + \cdots + \frac{35.00}{(1+r)^{20}} + \frac{1000.00}{(1+r)^{20}}$$

$$= \sum_{t=1}^{20} \frac{35.00}{(1+r)^t} + \frac{1000.00}{(1+r)^{20}}$$

With semiannual interest payments, the ten-year maturity involves 20 periodic payments of \$35.00 which is calculated at half the nominal 7 percent rate. The internal rate of return will be a six-month yield.

Present value for this investment is the curved line of Figure 3A.2; only the first iteration is illustrated there because the initial approximation is very close to the correct value. The calculation is summarized in Table 3A.1 where a value which is accurate to five decimal places is solved in only three trials.

A hand calculator was used and a change of .000001 was chosen as an appropriate change in the discount rate for estimating slopes. On the first trial present value changed by .02 as the discount rate changed by .000001; thus the first slope which was calculated was 20,000. Present value at 0 percent is \$784.00; dividing this value by 20,000 results in the first approximation, .039200. This is accurate to two decimal places. Repeating the process gave

Figure 3A.2
Estimating the Internal Rate of Return

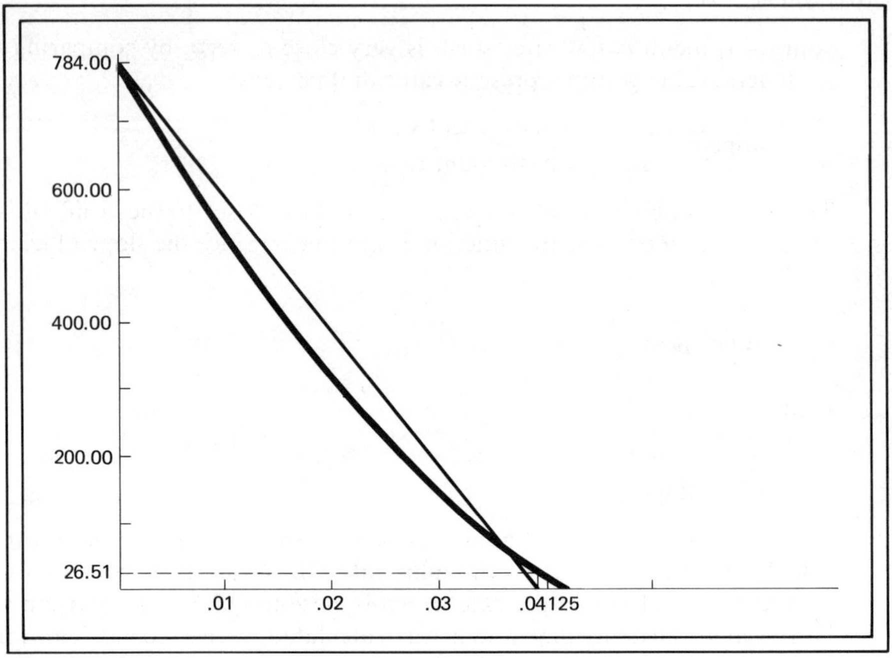

Table 3A.1
Iterative Calculation of Internal Rate of Return

Discount Rate	*Present Value*	*Slope (2)/.000001*	*Trial Value*	
(1)	*(2)*	*(3)*	*(2)/(3)*	
.000000	784.000000			
.000001	783.980000			
	.020000	20000.00	.039200	(1)
.039200	26.514142			
.039201	26.500966			
	.013176	13176.00	.002012	
			.041212	(2)
.041212	0.475744			
.041213	0.463035			
	.012709	12709.00	.000037	
			.041249	(3)
.041249	0.005634			

accuracy to three decimal places on the second trial and five places on the third. The third estimate was .04125; at that rate present value is approximately one-half of one cent; greater accuracy is unnecessary.

Annual rate of return is then found to be 8.42 percent:

$$(1 + r) = (1.04125)^2$$
$$= 1.0842$$

Appendix B
Reinvestment and Internal Yield

In the first section of this chapter Equation 3.11 defined the future value of an investment where cash recovery is reinvested periodically:

$$FV_N = C_0\left[\prod_{t=1}^{N} (1 + \bar{r}_t)\right] = C_0\left[\prod_{t=1}^{N}\left(1 + \sum_{i=1}^{P} (1 + x_i r_i)\right)\right] \tag{3.11}$$

This equation can be illustrated arithmetically with an example used in the chapter where an investment of \$36.30 returns \$18.90, \$15.45, and \$15.10, respectively, over each of the following three years. For purposes of this demonstration, it will be assumed that each periodic cash recovery is reinvested to yield 10.00 percent. In that case the following pattern of cash flows results for investment or reinvestment (−) and investment recovery (+):

	Year				*Annual Internal Rate of Return*
	0	*1*	*2*	*3*	
Investment	−36.30	+18.90	+15.45	+15.10	.1800
Reinvestment		−18.90		+22.87	.1000
Reinvestment			−15.45	+17.00	.1000
Total	−36.30	0.00	0.00	+54.97	

Portfolio future value at the end of the third year is \$54.97 and the average annual portfolio yield $\bar{r}$ is 14.83 percent:

$$\prod_{t=1}^{3} (1 + \bar{r}_t) = \frac{54.97}{36.30}$$
$$= 1.5143$$
$$\bar{r} = (1.5143)^{1/3} - 1.0$$
$$= .1483$$

Table 3B.1
Cash Flow Allocation

Year	Internal Yield	Unrecovered Investment	Return on Investment	Cash Flow	Recovered Investment
		(a) Original Investment			
1	.1800	36.30	6.53	18.90	12.37
2	.1800	23.93	4.31	15.45	11.14
3	.1800	12.79	2.31	15.10	12.79
					36.30
		(b) First Reinvestment			
2	.1000	18.90	1.89	0.00	(1.89)
3	.1000	20.79	2.08	22.87	20.79
					18.90
		(c) Second Reinvestment			
3	.1000	15.45	1.55	17.00	15.45
					15.45
		(a + b + c) Portfolio Total			
1		36.30	6.53	18.90	12.37
2		42.83	6.20	15.45	9.25
3		49.03	5.94	54.97	49.03

Table 3.1 illustrated a methodology for calculating the unrecovered investment for any security. The calculation of recovered investment RI was demonstrated arithmetically but the methodology can also be described, for cash flow C_t, internal rate of return r, and total unrecovered investment at the beginning of the period I_{t-1}:

$$RI_t = C_t - rI_{t-1} \tag{3B.1}$$

Unrecovered investment at the end of the period follows:

$$I_t = I_{t-1} - RI_t \tag{3B.2}$$

Table 3B.1 contains arithmetic values for each of these variables in the format used for Table 3.1. Values under the heading "Portfolio Total" are calculated by summing column values for each of the years. In the case of the first reinvestment, recovered investment is negative because there is no cash flow in the second year; the carrying value is increased by \$1.89 to reflect the unrealized 10.00 percent rate of return during that year.

Table 3B.2 employs the unrecovered investment values of Table 3B.1 to calculate portfolio weights x_{At}, x_{Bt}, and x_{Ct} for each of the three years,

Table 3B.2
Yearly Portfolio Weights

Year (t)	*Original Investment* (x_{At})	*First Reinvestment* (x_{Bt})	*Second Reinvestment* (x_{Ct})
1	36.30/36.30 (1.0000)		
2	23.93/42.83 (.5587)	18.90/42.83 (.4413)	
3	12.79/49.03 (.2609)	20.79/49.03 (.4240)	15.45/49.03 (.3151)

$t = 1, 2, 3$. Numerators are contained in the "Unrecovered Investment" column for each security for each year; denominators are entered in that column under "Portfolio Total."

Table 3B.3 summarizes the calculation of portfolio yield $\bar{r}_t$ for each of the three years; the arithmetic values are those defined in Equation 3.11. Compound portfolio return relative, derived from yearly values of 18.00, 14.47, and 12.09 percent, respectively, is 1.5141. This is the same as the value which was calculated directly from the initial cost of $36.30 and terminal value of $54.97, aside from a trivial rounding error. The average yearly portfolio yield is 14.83 percent again. Table 3B.3 clearly demonstrates how the internal rate of return of 18.00 percent is gradually diluted by the lesser reinvestment yield of 10.00 percent. As the original investment is recovered throughout the period, portfolio weight x_A falls and portfolio yield is increasingly influenced by the impact of weights x_B and x_C.

Table 3B.3
Portfolio Yield

Year (t)	*Original Investment* ($x_{At}r_{At}$)	*First Reinvestment* $+ (x_{Bt}r_{Bt})$	*Second Reinvestment* $+ (x_{Ct}r_{Ct})$	*Portfolio Total* $= (\bar{r}_t)$
1	(1.0000)(.18)			= 1.1800
2	(.5587)(.18)	+ (.4413)(.10)		= 1.1447
3	(.2609)[a](.18)[b]	+ (.4240)(.10)	+ (.3151)(.10)	= 1.1209
Three-year return relative:		(1.1800)(1.1447)(1.1209)		= 1.5141
Yearly portfolio mean, $\bar{r}$:		$(1.5141)^{1/3} - 1.0$		= .1483

[a] Security internal rate of return.
[b] Security portfolio weight.

Table 3B.3 also exposes the fallacy that the internal rate of return implicitly assumes reinvestment at that yield. The 18.00 percent *security* yield, which is contained in the first set of columns, will not change in Table 3B.3 if the rate of return on reinvestment is varied. Portfolio weights of .5587 and .2609 would be different, and *portfolio* yield would change, but the internal rate of return for the security would be unaffected.

Questions and Problems

1. Assume that a share of common stock is purchased on January 1 for $40.00 and sold on December 31 for $43.20.
   a. Calculate return on investment, rate of return, and return relative for the year.
   b. Assume instead that the stock is sold for $43.20 on June 30. Calculate the semi-annual rate of return, nominal annual return, and effective annual return.
   c. Assume that the stock was sold on December 31 for $43.30. Calculate the effective rate of return for both an annual and a quarterly period.
2. The following prices were observed for the shares of Bull Company and Bear Company over a three-year period:

Year	*Bull*	*Bear*
0	$100.00	$100.00
1	110.00	90.00
2	115.50	63.00
3	140.50	51.20

   a. Calculate the arithmetic mean and geometric mean annual rate of return for an investment in either security.
   b. In each case compare the two mean values. Does the difference appear to be systematic? If so, is there any apparent reason for the behavior you observed? Explain.
   c. Which of the two measures, if either, provides the most reasonable value for an average annual rate of return. Why?
3. Two investment opportunities, each of which will cost $2361.60, will generate the following cash flows:

Period	*A*	*B*
0	−2361.60	−2361.60
1	1000.00	0.00
2	1000.00	0.00
3	1000.00	0.00
4	1000.00	5765.50

   a. Calculate the internal rate of return for each project.
   b. Sketch the present value for each project. Will A ever be preferred to B? Explain.
   c. Calculate the Fisher rate for these securities and prove your calculation.
4. a. Assume that a corporate bond with an 8 percent coupon pays interest semi-annually on the maturity of $1000.00. If the bond matures in ten years and the rate of return required by investors to purchase the bond is a nominal 9 percent, prove that the bond will sell for $934.92. Ignore taxes and brokerage commissions.

b. What is the effective rate of return on this bond?
c. Assume the same conditions as (a) except that bondholders require an 8 percent nominal yield. What would the price of the bond be under these assumptions?
d. Is there a systematic relationship between bond yield and bond price? Explain.
e. It is sometimes said that the yields calculated in (a) and (c) above will be realized only if the bond is held to maturity. Otherwise, given variations in the market prices of bonds, some other rate of return will be realized. Is this argument correct? Explain.

5. Collect values for the four Dow Jones averages for the last five trading days from *The Wall Street Journal.* Interpret the numbers you collected in terms of implied dollar values in total and on average.
   a. Collect values for the same five days for the S&P "500" and the NYSE composite index and compare averages with the values you observed for the Dow Jones "65." Have all three measures tended to correspond in direction and magnitude? How can any differences you have observed be explained?
6. An investor makes the following purchases and sales:

Date	*Shares*	*Purchased*	*Sold*	*Yield*
1/1/75	100 A	1000.00		
1/1/76	30 A		360.00	.20
	5 B	360.00		
1/1/76	30 A		432.00	.20
	5 B		414.00	.15
	20 C	846.00		
1/1/78	40 A		691.20	.20
	20 C		1057.50	.25

a. Use the format of Table B3.1 to calculate project and portfolio rates of return for each of the three years in the interval from January 1, 1975 to January 1, 1978.
b. Recalculate both project and portfolio rates of return using Equation 3.8 for the latter.
c. Prove that the calculations in (a) and (b) can be reconciled.

Selected References

RATE OF RETURN

Alchian, Armen A., "The Rate of Interest, Fisher's Rate of Return over Costs and Keynes' Internal Rate of Return," *American Economic Review*, December 1955, pp. 938–942.

Ben-Sharar, Haim, and Marshall Sarnat, "Reinvestment and the Rate of Return on Common Stocks," *Journal of Finance*, December 1966, pp. 737–742.

Carlson, C. Robert, Michael L. Lawrence, and Donald H. Wort, "Clarification of the Reinvestment Assumption in Capital Analysis," *Journal of Business Research*, April 1974, pp. 201–208.

Dudley, Jr., Carlton L., "A Note on the Reinvestment Assumptions in Choosing Between Net Present Value and Internal Rate of Return," *Journal of Finance*, September 1972, pp. 907–915.

Latané, Henry A., "Criteria for Choosing Among Risky Ventures," *Journal of Political Economy*, April 1959, pp. 144–155.

Mao, James C. T., *Quantitative Analysis of Financial Decisions* (New York: McGraw-Hill, 1956).

Solomon, Ezra, "The Arithmetic of Capital-Budgeting Decisions," *Journal of Business*, April 1956, pp. 124–129
Teichroew, D., A. A. Robichek, and M. Montalbano, "Mathematical Analysis of Returns Under Certainty," *Management Science*, January 1955, pp. 395–403, and "An Analysis of Criteria for Investment and Financing Decisions Under Certainty," *Management Science*, November 1965, pp. 151–179.

INVESTMENT INDEXES

Cohen, Kalman J., and Bruce P. Fitch, "The Average Investment Performance Index," *Management Science*, February 1966, pp. B195–B215.
Fisher, Lawrence, "Some New Stock-Market Indexes," *Journal of Business*, January 1966 Supplement, pp. 191–225.
Latané, Henry A., D. L. Tuttle, and W. E. Young, "Market Indices," *Financial Analysts Journal*, September–October, 1971, pp. 75–85.
Lerner, Eugene M., ed., *Readings in Financial Analysis and Investment Management* (Homewood, Ill.: Irwin, 1963), pp. 84–96, 97–102, 103–110, 234–245, and 246–288.

Chapter 4
Investment Elements

Rate of return is a critical concept in security analysis and portfolio management. For this reason yield properties were introduced and illustrated arithmetically in Chapter 3. But other rate of return dimensions, most notably expectation and risk, must be considered before security analysis can be introduced. In addition, there are some other investment elements which affect the analytical process. This chapter examines these remaining items. They will be introduced and developed in the context of familiar principles of management to stress the managerial aspect of investment activity.

Investment Management

Investment is a managerial process. In accordance with the definition found in management texts, investment can be described as *planning*, *executing*, and *controlling* events to accomplish selected investment objectives. This may be accomplished informally, by an individual perhaps, or it may be a very formal process for a large mutual fund or investment trust. It is useful to assume formality where objectives are specified quantitatively in a statement of expected performance. Action is then taken to implement plans and,

Figure 4.1
Investment Management

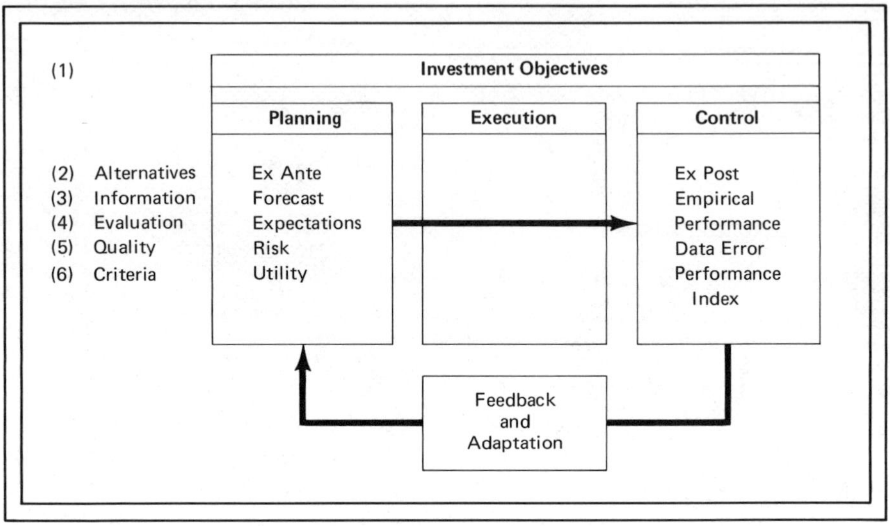

in the control phase, planned outcomes would be compared to actual outcomes in order to isolate, analyze, and correct observed variances. If corrective action is possible, it would be undertaken during the execution phase.

This is a dynamic or continuous process. Through time, as differences between planned and actual outcomes are observed, the investment manager is provided with feedback data which allow future plans to be adapted to meet objectives more realistically. In the process it is critical that objectives are clearly stated. These relationships are summarized in Figure 4.1.

Figure 4.1 describes elements which are common to any managerial system but investment differs from other activities in several important respects. One of these is the discretionary ability of the manager in achieving planned objectives. In the case of corporate management, for example, planning is quantified in the master budget and, through time, outcomes are monitored to isolate price and quantity variances.[1] Given observed variances between planned and actual outcomes, management can change pricing and production policies, to the extent allowed by demand and supply constraints, and unfavorable deviations can be controlled. Return on an investment in securities, in contrast, depends on capital market behavior which is influenced little, if at all, by the actions of any one investor. The investor must rely primarily on the quality of a number of subjective estimates which form the basis for the investment decision. Figure 4.1 identifies the subjective elements which are particularly important to the investment manager.

[1] Planning and control procedures are described in a number of financial management texts, including J. Fred Weston and Eugene F. Brigham, *Managerial Finance*, 4th ed. (New York: Holt, Rinehart and Winston, 1972), chaps. 2–5.

Figure 4.1 is organized in terms of the several procedures which are necessary in a rational decision process:

1. SPECIFY OBJECTIVES. The first procedure is selection of specific objectives which will guide planning-execution-control activities. Objectives are considered at length in the next section of this chapter.

2. IDENTIFY STRATEGIC ALTERNATIVES AVAILABLE TO THE MANAGER. In the planning stage alternatives are identified ex ante or before the fact; for control purposes alternatives which had previously been available are evaluated ex post or after the fact.[2] Ex post recognition of profitable opportunities which were previously available, by way of the feedback mechanism, results in more efficient ex ante planning. Planning is based upon estimated rates of return, together with the associated probability distributions which reflect uncertainty in those estimates. After the fact comparisons can be made between realized outcomes and the probability distributions which led to the selection of one portfolio from the set of alternatives which had been identified.

3. GATHER INFORMATION RELEVANT TO EACH ALTERNATIVE IDENTIFIED. Strategic alternatives cannot be evaluated without adequate information. For planning purposes ex ante information involves *forecasting* which is both a subjective and a difficult process. Past information has no relevance except to the extent that it can be extrapolated in forecasting future outcomes. Today's decisions will not alter past events; the future will be affected by current decisions which are based upon subjective and error-prone forecasts and predictions.

Empirical or historical data are used for control purposes. In this context ex post information is very relevant because an analysis of the variance between planned and realized outcomes gives insights as to the effectiveness of the investment management system. Isolated variances can be classified as controllable or uncontrollable. The former reflect planning deficiencies if ex ante data are properly measured, and future planning efforts can be improved on that basis. Uncontrollable variance is useful in assessing the risk involved in the management decision process.

4. EVALUATE THE IMPACT OF EACH STRATEGIC ALTERNATIVE. Strategies which have been identified are next evaluated with respect to selected objectives. For planning purposes *expectations* are involved. If an investment objective is specified in terms of rate of return, for example, the impact of each alternative will be expressed as an *expected rate of return*. Expectations are

[2] The relationship between ex ante and ex post measures is discussed in Peter O. Dietz, "Components of a Measurement Model: Rate of Return, Risk, and Timing," *Journal of Finance*, May 1968, pp. 267–275.

derived from information currently available; the reliability of expectations therefore depends on the reliability of both data and forecasting procedures.

Ex post evaluation is *performance* measurement. Realized rate of return, for example, can be calculated from observed empirical data. Performance should be measured for alternatives selected, but it should also be measured for strategies which had been available but were rejected in prior decision periods.

5. EVALUATE THE QUALITY OF EXPECTATIONS AND PERFORMANCE MEASURES. The procedures discussed above are clearly open to error. The reliability of ex ante evaluation, often referred to as risk or uncertainty, is important in any decision process but it is critical in the case of the investment decision. Expectation and risk cannot be separated.[3] With certain knowledge of the future, the investment decision would be a trivial problem. But under risk, because subjective and judgmental elements are involved, the problem is very complex. Risk is a very difficult and very important concept and it will be considered in depth in a later section of this chapter.

Empirical measures are also open to error but the impact is usually less severe than the impact of forecasting error. By and large, observed data are subject to conceptual error and/or error of observation. Conceptual error involves difficulty in defining relevant measures; the problem of defining a correct index of investment performance, discussed previously in Chapter 3, is one example of the problem of conceptual error. Error of observation may arise from missing data or it may reflect "poor calibration" of the measurement instrument. Accounting data are very susceptible to the latter. Accounting provides an important segment of the information required by the analyst; Chapter 7 is directed to an in-depth analysis of problems involving accounting data.

6. ESTABLISH CRITERIA FOR COMPARING ALTERNATIVES IDENTIFIED. The remaining step, prior to decision, is to establish criteria which allow differentiation among the several alternatives identified and evaluated. This too is a difficult process since objectives are interdependent and conflicting. For example, investors attempt to maximize expected return but they also try to minimize risk. Unfortunately there is a positive and significant correlation between risk and return.[4] By selecting an alternative promising higher expected return, higher risk must also be assumed. Decision criteria, then, must reconcile this trade-off (utility) between risk and return. With respect to planning the relevant object of choice is *expected utility*. But utility presents formidable operational problems and its measurability is a controversy

[3] See Alexander A. Robichek, "Risk and the Value of Securities," *Journal of Financial and Quantitative Analysis*, December 1969, pp. 513–538. Robichek argues that risk and valuation are inseparable, "two sides of the same coin."

[4] Supporting empirical evidence for this statement is found in a number of places including William F. Sharpe, "Risk Aversion in the Stock Market: Some Empirical Evidence," *Journal of Finance*, September 1965, pp. 416–422.

not yet settled among theorists and practitioners. Utility will be considered subsequently after risk has been studied.

From a control perspective, the criteria for comparison is some *index of performance*. The problem of rate of return indexes was treated in Chapter 3; combined risk-return indexes are referred to in Chapters 14 and 15 in the context of the *efficient set* portfolios introduced and developed there.

7. DECISION AMONG ALTERNATIVES. The final part of the process is to decide among alternatives identified and evaluated in earlier stages. Notwithstanding information imperfections and the subjectivity involved in analyzing expected outcomes, plans are finalized, actions are implemented, and the process is then monitored, adapted, and repeated through time.

In summary, investment has been viewed as a managerial process with emphasis placed on specific elements of the planning and control functions outlined in Figure 4.1. These elements provide the foundation for security and portfolio analysis and management. Each was defined or described relative to the analytical and decision processes underlying investment activity. Some, however, require more detailed consideration. Aside from investment indexes, treated in Chapter 3, these are: objectives, expectations, forecasting, risk, and utility. The problem of forecasting will be generalized and placed in perspective in Chapter 9 where the evaluation of common stock is illustrated. The remaining issues, largely involving planning, are the topic of the next four sections of this chapter. Objectives are studied to focus on operational criteria which guide the investment decision. Next, since criteria involve a distribution of expected outcomes, some elementary principles from business statistics are recalled and reviewed. Then, in the light of statistical description, risk is introduced and operational measures of expectation and risk are developed. Finally, the difficult problem of the meaning and usefulness of utility is explored.

Investment Objectives

Objectives structure the decision process. To be useful they must be both operational and relevant. Operationality implies clarity, feasibility, and a limited time horizon. Relevance implies focus on the correct object or objects of choice. In the discussion which follows operational characteristics are considered first. Next, objects of choice are described generally and theoretically to identify the types of decisions facing investors. Theoretical considerations are then narrowed and focused to develop objectives which, quantified, can serve as operational guides to the decision maker.

CLARITY

Investment objectives are too often defined in broad terms. A mutual fund, advertising in *The Wall Street Journal*, stated its objective as "... seeking possible growth of capital and income." Virtually any performance could be defended with respect to that goal. If expected return is the object of choice, the level of return should be specified; acceptable levels of risk should also be stated clearly. If current income is the objective, the level of income should be specified in measurable terms as, say, dividend yield. If "capital and income" are joint objectives, weights should be specified. It would be unreasonable to expect a fund to advertise quantified objectives, but for internal purposes objectives should be stated precisely and without ambiguity. Prospective investors should have objectives which are also precise and clear.

FEASIBILITY

Objectives must also be realistic. During the long "bull" market which existed after World War II many investors achieved unusually large annual rates of return. Expectations based on market performance over a relatively short time period were, for many investors, highly inflated thereafter.[5] On average, rate of return on investment is constrained by the rate of growth in the economy. Expected return greater than or less than that implied in aggregate growth will be accompanied by greater or lesser risk; accordingly, the relationship between return and risk must also be viewed realistically. There is no purpose in establishing goals which cannot be achieved. Investment management has no meaning in that case.

TIME DURATION

It is also important to specify a time horizon when objectives are established. There are two reasons for this. First, measures of performance are stated in discrete time units; planning and control procedures should be stated similarly. Second, objectives will vary over time as individual circumstances and preferences vary. Objectives are best stated for a limited duration beyond which, given review and reestablishment of policies, objectives should be reviewed and updated.

Given the operational characteristics cited, objectives must then focus on variables implied by the notion of an "economic person," one acting in accordance with laws of arithmetic and logic to maximize personal welfare.

[5] A comprehensive summary of rates of return on investment in NYSE common stock from January, 1926, through December, 1965, is contained in Lawrence Fisher and James H. Lorie, "Rates of Return on Investments in Common Stock: The Year-by-Year Record, 1926–65," *Journal of Business*, July 1968, pp. 291–316. According to values reported there post–World War II rates were large on average. For example, ignoring taxes and with dividend reinvestment assumed, annually compounded rate of return for the period December 1940–December 1965 was 16 percent. Similarly, for December 1950–December 1965 it was 14.5 percent and the average from December 1960–December 1965 was 15.9 percent. Annual rate of return for the one-year period December 1964–December 1965 was 28.3 percent. But over a much longer period, January 1926–December 1965, the average was 9.3 percent; from December 1935–December 1965 the mean value was 12.6 percent. Recognizing that these are compound rates, differences are very material.

THEORY OF CONSUMER CHOICE

Investment involves two decisions: (1) how much of current wealth to save (asset size) and (2) how to invest assets which are saved (asset mix). Both affect wealth maximization, both are implicit in the theory of choice, and together they introduce the important concepts of *time preference* and *risk preference.* These concepts can be illustrated for an investor with current resources or wealth which can be consumed currently for goods or services or can instead be saved and held as assets which will be available for future consumption. Assuming that savings can be invested at some risk-free rate of interest, these variables can be defined as follows:

W_0 = current wealth
C_0 = current consumption of goods and services
A_0 = current savings or assets
r_F = risk-free rate of return on investment

In the two-period case, current wealth must be allocated between consumption and savings:

$$W_0 = C_0 + A_0 \tag{4.1}$$

From savings at the end of the period C_1 dollars will be realized:

$$C_1 = A_0(1 + r_F) \tag{4.2}$$

and

$$A_0 = \frac{C_1}{(1 + r_F)}$$

Current wealth can then be redefined by inserting Equation 4.2 into Equation 4.1:

$$W_0 = C_0 + \frac{C_1}{(1 + r_F)} \tag{4.3}$$

If savings are invested in a different asset, one which is not risk-free, investors would demand some yield which is greater than r_F. For a risky yield $\tilde{r}$ future consumption will be uncertain $\tilde{C}_1$ and:

$$W_0 = C_0 + \frac{\tilde{C}_1}{(1 + \tilde{r})} \tag{4.4}$$

From Equation 4.3 or 4.4 consumption is shown to be the object of choice but the stream of consumption must be discounted to present value. In the general case, expanding from two periods to a life cycle of n years, where $t = 1, 2, \ldots, n$:

$$W_0 = C_0 + \frac{\tilde{C}_1}{(1 + \tilde{r})^1} + \frac{\tilde{C}_2}{(1 + \tilde{r})^2} + \cdots + \frac{\tilde{C}_n}{(1 + \tilde{r})^n} \tag{4.5}$$

Wealth depends on the percentage of current resources invested and the portfolio asset mix which determines risky yield $\tilde{r}$. The former reflects the savings decision and the latter the portfolio decision. The stream of consumption underlying wealth is augmented during productive years by salary payments which also increase future amounts available for savings. Given a stream of after-tax income, including pension benefits after retirement, the savings decision shifts consumption among the various years of the life cycle.[6] Present and future standards of living are thereby determined.

Under conditions of certainty the choice among current and future consumption, defined to be time preference, depends upon preference (utility) for current rather than future consumption; it also depends on investment opportunities which determine risk-free yield r_F. With uncertainty wealth also depends upon the portfolio choice where some level of risk is accepted in an effort to increase yield to the higher $\tilde{r}$ level. The choice of $\tilde{r}$ from the set of portfolio possibilities reflects an investor's attitude toward risk; this is called risk preference.

From theory, then, investment objectives include both the savings decision and the portfolio decision. Wealth results from the interaction of the two decisions through the stream of consumption discounted at a rate of return which reflects both time preference and risk preference. Wealth maximization is a theoretically sound objective which provides a basis for developing operational objectives. The savings decision probably exerts a greater influence on wealth than the portfolio decision but analytical problems in the choice of asset level are less difficult to cope with than problems involving asset selection.[7] For that reason it is appropriate to focus on the question of security selection.

Equation 4.5 identifies the elements of the portfolio decision. Wealth is a function of risk and return dimensions of discount rate $\tilde{r}$; it also requires that sufficient cash resources will be available in every period t to support consumption expenditures C_t. Three general objectives therefore appear:

1. Expected yield maximization.
2. Risk minimization.
3. Liquidity maintenance.

These are only a first approximation to an operational set of objectives. In any practical sense it may not be possible to maximize or minimize any quantifiable object of choice. But when any of the three is considered separately, operationality is not a serious difficulty. Securities can be ranked by

[6] Funds available for estate purposes are also determined by the savings decision, reflecting the bequest motive to provide for the family unit beyond an investor's lifetime. In this respect insurance premiums are a type of current expenditure which reduces risk and, depending on the type of insurance contract, may also augment savings.

[7] Savings A_0 invested for n periods at rate of return r accumulates to a value of $A_0(1 + r)^n$, assuming periodic compounding. Since r is a good deal less than the value 1 in return relative $(1 + r)$, it requires a good deal of time for portfolio contribution r to accumulate in value to savings contribution 1. For a stream of savings A_t, aggregate wealth may be more sensitive to the level of savings than to portfolio return. This is an empirical question, but evidence to support the view is found in Anthony J. Curley, "A Monte Carlo Experiment in Time-State Preference," *Proceedings, Midwest AIDS Meetings*, 1971.

expected rate of return, for example, with the greater yield preferred to the lesser in the case of mutually exclusive opportunities.[8] A "target" rate of return is clear and it can be stated in terms of a specific time horizon. It is also sufficiently specific to meet requirements of an investment control mechanism.

Separate risk and liquidity measures can be specified in the same manner. Thus operationality is not a severe problem. A far more serious difficulty arises because of interaction among the several objectives when they are considered jointly.

CONFLICTING OBJECTIVES

Unfortunately, the objectives implied in wealth maximization are in serious conflict. Simultaneous maximization of return and minimization of risk are not possible because a positive association exists between risk and return. The price attached to greater expected return is the acceptance of greater risk. Similarly, liquidity can be assured by holding all assets as cash but the price of that strategy is a zero monetary yield and, with inflation, a negative real rate of return.

The conflict among these objectives must be resolved in a probabilistic framework because both risk and return are probabilistic concepts. The next section reviews some basic concepts of probability to establish a foundation for the discussion of risk which then follows.

Probability

Security analysis uses probability because the objects of analytical focus, expected return and risk, are both defined as measures from a subjective probability distribution. For this reason security analysts should have a clear understanding of this important topic. This section reviews some basic elements of probability but the discussion is not intended to be comprehensive; standard statistical texts should be consulted for complete coverage. The purpose instead is twofold: (1) to establish some common definitions and notations which will be used frequently when security analysis is introduced, and (2) to focus on some aspects of probability which have particular importance to security analysts.

DEFINITIONS

When an experiment or event may result in a number of different outcomes, that set of outcomes is defined to be a sample space. For example, in the

[8] This statement assumes employment of an internal rate of return criterion. If net present value is used instead, alternatives would be ranked by net present value. The two decision rules were developed and analyzed in Chapter 3 and the reasons for selecting the IRR were set forth there.

case of an investment which must have one of two possible outcomes—the asset is lost entirely or its value will double—return relative is a sample space with two elements, 0.0000 and 2.0000. A *random variable* is a variable with numerical values assigned to each element of the sample space; in the example given above return relative is a random variable. *Probability* is the relative frequency of occurrence of any outcome for some random variable; it is the percentage of successes for an element given the total number of trials for which success or failure could be recorded. Probability may reflect belief based on observation of past experiments or it may be defined conceptually, as in the case of a "fair coin" which is properly balanced and cannot come to rest on its edge. Whatever the method of measurement or estimation, probability can be described in terms of a *probability distribution.* For any random variable a probability distribution exists; this is a function which identifies all possible values the variable can assume, together with the probability associated with each. Defined in this fashion the sum of all probabilities involved necessarily equals 1.

A random variable and its associated probability distribution may be either *discrete* or *continuous.* A discrete random variable can only assume one of a finite set of values in the relevant sample space. A continuous random variable can assume any value in the range defined by the sample space. In practice, the frequency of observed ex post data is discrete but analytical advantage often accrues from assumption of a continuous distribution. This point will be pursued shortly.

Discrete data can be analyzed by grouping observations into classes with midpoint values substituted for all values in any given class interval.

Figure 4.2
Rate of Return Histogram

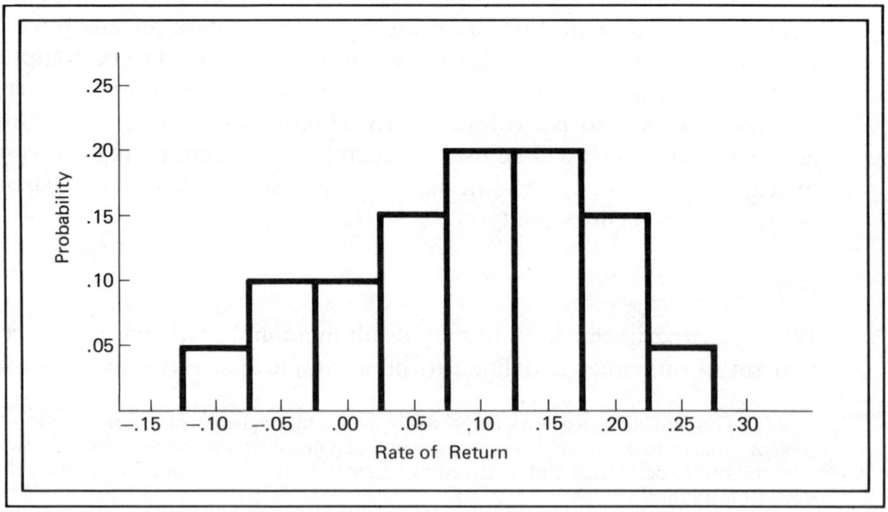

The number of observations in any class is a *frequency*. Combined, classes and frequencies constitute a *frequency distribution* which can be described either graphically or in tabular form. Figure 4.2 is a graphic description of the frequency distribution of rate of return for some hypothetical security; when presented in this fashion the frequency distribution is called a *histogram*.

Probability distributions may also be described by one of a set of analytical characteristics or *parameters*. This is true of empirical frequency distributions and subjective probability distributions alike. A *subjective probability distribution* consists of estimates of the probability of future outcomes. Subjective probabilities are usually based on historical frequency distributions but other quantitative and qualitative data will also affect estimates. An analyst, for example, may be willing to assign probabilities to next year's earnings per share of General Motors on the basis of observed past data, but the same analyst is less likely to rely as heavily on reported earnings of Penn Central. In any event, one or more parameters of a probability distribution are useful in describing it generally.

PARAMETERS OF A PROBABILITY DISTRIBUTION

1. EXPECTED VALUE. An important parameter is some average value or measure of central tendency. Several of these exist, including the mean, median, and mode, but the mean value is the one most commonly identified. In the case of a subjective probability distribution mean value is conventionally defined to be *expected value*. It is usually denoted by the *expected value operator*, $E(\ )$. For the random variable rate of return r, for example, expected rate of return would be $E(r)$.

Expected value is calculated in the same manner as any other mean value. Defining p_i probabilities as weights, and r_i as the possible set of i outcomes,

$$E(r) = \sum_{i=1}^{n} p_i r_i \tag{4.6}$$

Probabilities sum to 1 and expected value is therefore a weighted average of all probable r_i outcomes. Table 4.1, for example, contains probable outcomes derived from midpoints of rate of return class intervals graphed in Figure 4.2. Eight possible outcomes are identified in column 1; associated probabilities are given in column 2. From Equation 4.6, expected value is the sum of products $p_i r_i$, column 3 of the table. In this case expected value is 9 percent. Note that 9 percent is *not* one of the eight possible values defined; it is interpreted as a measure of the average return expected if samples were taken repeatedly from the distribution underlying columns 1 and 2. An investor facing that distribution over a number of time periods would expect, on average, to realize a periodic rate of return of 9 percent.

Table 4.1
Expected Return and Standard Deviation

	r_i	p_i	(1) × (2) $p_i r_i$	$r_i - E(r)$	(4) × (4) $[r_i - E(r)]^2$	(2) × (5) $p_i[r_i - E(r)]^2$
i	(1)	(2)	(3)	(4)	(5)	(6)
1	−.10	.05	−.0050	−.19	.0361	.001805
2	−.05	.10	−.0050	−.14	.0196	.001960
3	.00	.10	.0000	−.09	.0081	.000810
4	.05	.15	.0075	−.04	.0016	.000240
5	.10	.20	.0200	.01	.0001	.000020
6	.15	.20	.0300	.06	.0036	.000720
7	.20	.15	.0300	.11	.0121	.001815
8	.25	.05	.0125	.16	.0256	.001280
Total		1.00				
$E(r)$			.0900			
var(r)						.008650
$\sigma(r)$						.0930

2. STANDARD DEVIATION. A second important parameter is a measure of dispersion in the distribution. When expected value is defined as the measure of central tendency, standard deviation is generally accepted as the relevant measure of dispersion. The standard deviation is the square root of the variance.[9] Both are calculated in the usual manner:[10]

$$\text{Var}(r) = \sum_{i=1}^{n} p_i[r_i - E(r)]^2 \tag{4.7}$$

$$\sigma(r) = \sqrt{\text{var}(r)} \tag{4.8}$$

Referring again to Table 4.1, deviations from expected value, $r_i - E(r)$, are contained in column 4; these are the values in brackets in Equation 4.7. Deviations are squared in column 5 and then averaged in column 6, with probabilities of column 2 again serving as weights. Variance is the sum of these products; it is the weighted average of squared deviations from expected value. In this case variance var(r) equals 0.00865. Standard deviation $\sigma(r)$, 0.0930, is the square root of variance.

[9] In calculating variance, deviations from expected value, in column 4, are squared because the sum of products $p_i[r_i - E(r)]$ is zero. Standard deviation is then the square root of variance, the mean deviation from expected value.

[10] Variance is a special case of a more general statistic, the covariance. Covariance is a measure of critical importance to portfolio analysis. Without a complete understanding of covariance, portfolio cannot be evaluated; it will be developed and illustrated in Chapter 8 and it will be applied in Chapters 14 and 15.

Figure 4.3
Skewness

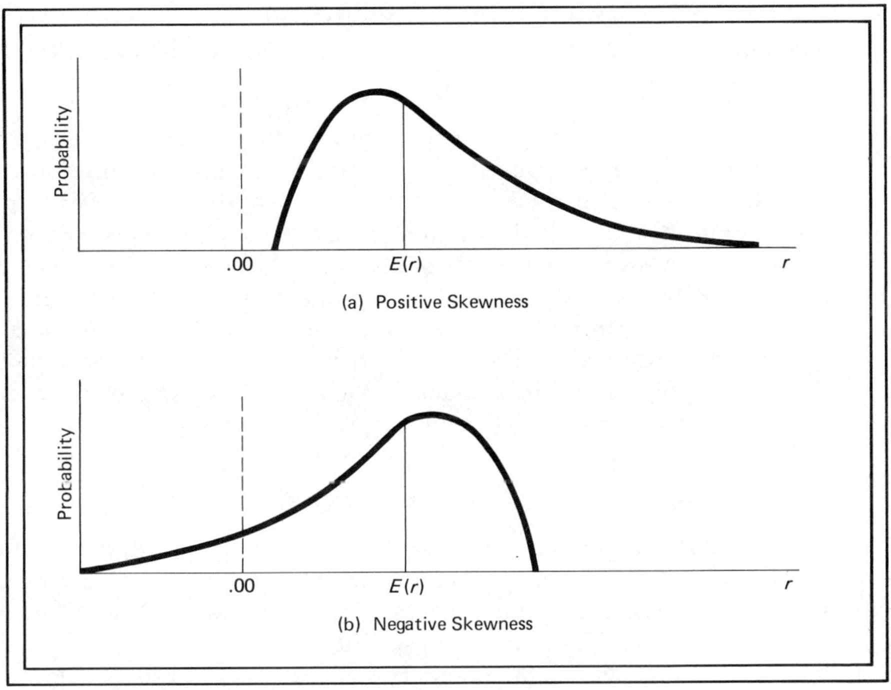

Applied to investments, expectation is defined as expected rate of return $E(r)$; risk is similarly defined as standard deviation $\sigma(r)$ *if* the probability distribution can be completely described by these two parameters. But additional parameters may be required to measure asymmetry and/or "peakedness" of the distribution.

3. SKEWNESS. A third parameter may also describe risk; *skewness* involves an asymmetric distribution. Figure 4.3 depicts two skewed distributions. Both have the same mean value and the same standard deviation but distribution a, skewed positively, would be attractive to investors since opportunity for very large gain exists.[11] Distribution b, on the other hand, is not desirable in view of the probability of significant loss it promises.

If rate of return behaves in the manner portrayed in Figure 4.3, risk will have to be defined in terms of both a dispersion parameter and a skewness parameter. In practice, given the current state of the art and the observed

[11] Investor preference for positive skewness is discussed in Fred D. Arditti, "Risk and the Required Rate of Return on Equity," *Journal of Finance*, March 1967, pp. 19–36. Also see Arditti, "Another Look at Mutual Fund Performance," *Journal of Financial and Quantitative Analysis*, June 1971, pp. 909–912.

empirical behavior of security rates of return, attention is typically limited to the first two parameters described. Future research may well prove it necessary to extend these measures to skewness;[12] at this time practical considerations limit operational criteria to expected value and standard deviation (or variance).

4. KURTOSIS. A fourth parameter, *kurtosis*, has recently assumed significance in the investments literature, but it requires only brief mention here. Kurtosis is a measure of the relative "peakedness" of a probability distribution. It is discussed in that part of the literature, currently on the frontier, which studies departures of observed rates of return from behavior implied by the well-known "normal probability distribution." But the extent and significance of these departures are less than clear, and analysts are seldom concerned with the problem in practice. An interpretation of the meaning of kurtosis is included in the appendix to this chapter which considers some important continuous probability distributions.

CONTINUOUS PROBABILITY DISTRIBUTIONS

To this point attention has been limited to discrete frequency distributions. By and large these are most useful when class intervals are very narrow. From a practical viewpoint, interval width depends on the number of observations available to the analyst. With only a few observations, wide intervals are dictated; as the number of observations increases data can be grouped into progressively narrower intervals. As interval width approaches zero, the distribution approaches a continuous distribution.

Continuous distributions are important to investment analysts. Some can be defined algebraically, allowing the analyst to estimate data by inserting observed values into algebraic equations. Of the problems facing any analyst, forecasting is probably the most vexing. But statistical tools which are derived from continuous probability distributions are very useful in reducing forecasting difficulty.

Of the continuous distributions available, two are especially important in the investments area: the *normal* distribution and the *log-normal* distribution. A third, the *stable Paretian* distribution, also deserves mention but the treatment afforded it need not be detailed here. All three of these are discussed in the appendix to this chapter.

This section has reviewed some important definitions and relationships with respect to probability which are of interest to investment analysts. Notation introduced here will be used throughout the text. More importantly, given the foundation established above, risk can be considered in detail.

[12] Blume found symmetry in his study of the distribution of returns on common stock; this is in conflict with Arditti's findings cited in footnote 11. While the issue is unsettled, data reported by Blume provide little justification for employing skewness pending more conclusive evidence to the contrary. See Marshall E. Blume, "Portfolio Theory: A Step Toward Its Practical Application," *Journal of Business*, April 1970, pp. 152–173.

Risk

Risk is a concept with both ex ante and ex post meaning. In the former context risk is a decision variable reflecting the probability of realizing unfavorable outcomes in the future as a result of a decision made currently. Ex post risk is historical: it refers to observed variation in outcomes during prior periods. While risk has relevance in either sense, its significance is greatest in a future context. The estimation and evaluation of future outcomes, based on current information, is the most difficult problem involved in security and portfolio analyses. For that reason the discussion which follows will generally be stated in terms of ex ante risk, although the definitions and measures considered most often are applicable to empirical data as well.

CERTAINTY, RISK, AND UNCERTAINTY

With respect to future outcomes, three states can be identified: certainty, risk, and uncertainty. Under *certainty*, all future outcomes are given with a probability of one. The evaluation of decision alternatives in this state is a trivial computational problem. It is also an uninteresting case since, death and taxes notwithstanding, nothing is known with certainty. It is often useful to assume certain knowledge when studying complex relationships, but in applying whatever is learned in the process, the assumption must be relaxed if decision models are to have any operational validity.

The second category, *risk*, refers to a situation in which future outcomes, together with their associated probabilities, are known. Risk is defined conceptually as dispersion in a subjective probability distribution. Operational measures of risk will be considered below.

The third state, *uncertainty*, refers to a situation in which at least some future outcomes and/or their associated probabilities are unknown. Uncertainty is the best description of the state of the world which investors face. It is also, unfortunately, almost impossible to deal with in practice. To attempt to define uncertainty with any rigor presents extremely complex and hazardous conceptual and mathematical problems. Moreover, given a rigorous statement, practical application proves to be elusive. For this reason the discussion which follows will ignore the difference between risk and uncertainty. It will be assumed that the distribution of expected returns, arrived at subjectively, adequately describes objective probability. No other assumption has pragmatic relevance. Moreover, the experienced analyst, profiting from the error-learning mechanism often called experience, should become progressively more skilled in estimating probabilities.

THE MEANING OF RISK

Risk, then, is defined as dispersion in the subjective distribution of probable outcomes. The reasoning behind that definition, and the relationship

Figure 4.4
Risk-Return Relationship

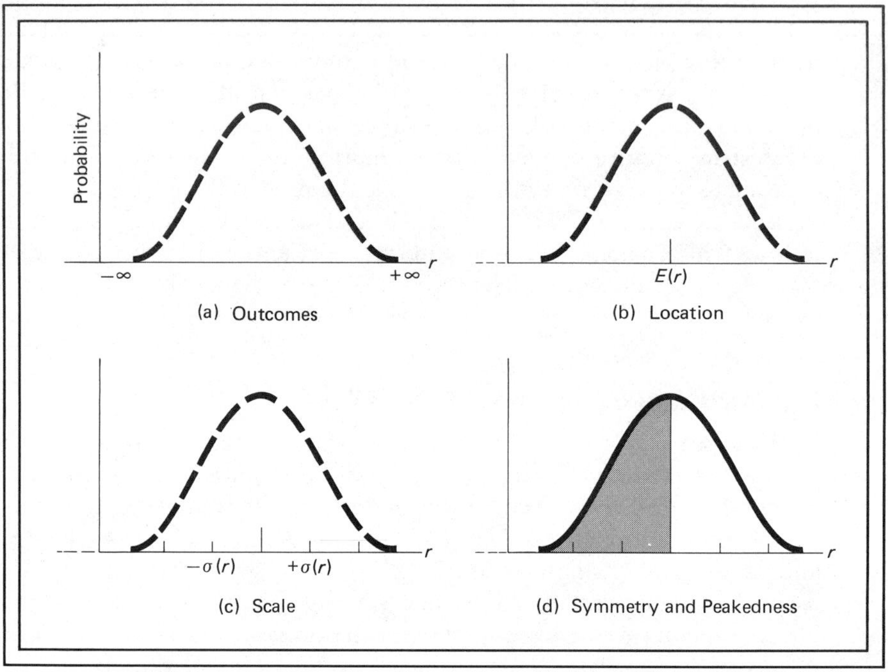

between risk and return, is illustrated in Figure 4.4. Part (a) depicts the infinite range of possible rates of return which might result from some investment but provides no information concerning outcomes represented by the broken-line distribution. The first step in identifying the distribution is to locate it on the line—this requires selection and estimation of a *location parameter*, a measure of central tendency. Part (b) assumes that expected value has been selected to be the location measure. At this point something is known about probable outcome; the distribution has been "located" in a general sense and the range of probable values has been somewhat delimited. In part (b), then, expected value $E(r)$ is defined as the appropriate measure of central tendency and the first step in specifying the distribution has been accomplished.

But the location parameter, by itself, is inadequate since the range of outcomes is poorly defined. The next step is to provide a numerical scale on the axis of possible outcomes. This *scale parameter*, given location parameter $E(r)$, provides some measure of dispersion for the random variable. A number of statistics are available but, following convention, the measure of dispersion associated with the mean or expected value is generally selected. This is the standard deviation, $\sigma(r)$; scale parameter $\sigma(r)$ is added in part (c) and yet more information concerning the distribution is now available. The greater the dispersion in $\sigma(r)$, the greater the risk of an unfavorable outcome *relative to return parameter* $E(r)$. It is in this sense that risk is defined as dispersion in a probability distribution and it is in this sense that standard deviation $\sigma(r)$ is typically selected as a defensible operational measure of risk.

Other parameters may also be specified.[13] Part (d) of Figure 4.4 assumes that two additional parameters, skewness and kurtosis, are specified; these four parameters then fully specify the probability distribution at issue. The distribution of probable outcomes, unknown in part (a), is now given and the investor is able to compare this distribution with those of other investment opportunities, balancing risk and return elements in choosing among alternative strategies.

To summarize, risk has been defined as dispersion in the subjective probability distribution of the random variable rate of return. While this provides an operational measure of absolute investment risk, it is also bothersome in at least one respect. The definition is symmetric—dispersion about expected value in either direction, positive or negative, is defined to be risk. But it makes little sense to tell an investor that a rate of return of 10 percent, say, can be expected, but the "risk" exists that a return of 20 percent might instead be realized. No investor would be unwilling to accept a "risk" of this type.

An alternative definition would calculate deviations from some given level of return, possibly expected value, only when that deviation is negative. In Figure 4.4(d), for example, only the shaded area to the left of expected value would be used in estimating risk. One such measure is the *semivariance*. Unfortunately, this statistic is difficult to interpret and it is neither generally accepted nor generally understood at this time.[14] Semivariance may yet come to general acceptance in the future because it has conceptual relevance and it is also closely related to the practical concept of "downside risk." Currently, semivariance is not used, it poses difficult mathematical and empirical problems, and it is a concept which cannot easily be made operational. For these reasons, variance (or standard deviation) is adopted here as the most useful measure of absolute risk available.

ABSOLUTE AND RELATIVE RISK MEASURES

To this point risk has been defined in terms of dispersion in a subjective probability distribution and, specifically, as the standard deviation of that distribution. But this is an *absolute* measure as contrasted with a *relative* measure; to be meaningful risk should be defined relative to its associated

[13] Fewer parameters may be sufficient. In the case of the normal distribution, for example, probabilities are fully specified by mean and variance.

[14] An excellent description of the semivariance is found in chap. 9 of Harry M. Markowitz, *Portfolio Selection*, Cowles Foundation Monograph No. 16 (New York: Wiley, 1959), pp. 188–201.

Table 4.2
Absolute and Relative Risk Measures

Investment	*Expected Value* $E(\tilde{r})$	*Standard Deviation* $\sigma(\tilde{r})$	*Coefficient of Variation*
A	0.10	0.01	0.10
B	0.10	0.02	0.20
C	0.20	0.02	0.10

level of expected return. The point is illustrated in Table 4.2 where expected rate of return and standard deviation are summarized for three probability distributions of rate of return.

Distributions A and B have the same expected rate of return but B has greater dispersion and thus greater risk in both absolute and relative terms. C, on the other hand, defining risk by the absolute measure $\sigma(\tilde{r})$, has the same risk as B. But the yield for C would have to fall by five standard deviations from expected value just to equal the mean yield for B. Investment B, clearly, is far more risky than C but that is not indicated by the standard deviation.

A better measure of risk results when the standard deviation is normalized by dividing it by expected value. This statistic is called the *coefficient of variation* (CV):

$$CV = \frac{\sigma(\tilde{r})}{E(\tilde{r})} \tag{4.9}$$

The coefficient of variation is given for all three investments in Table 4.2. It is a *relative* measure of dispersion because it is adjusted for the expected level of rate of return. In relative terms A and C are shown to be equally risky and both have less risk than B. This is illustrated graphically in Figure 4.5.

The slope of each line in Figure 4.5, the ratio of the "rise" to the "run," is the coefficient of variation $\sigma(\tilde{r})/E(\tilde{r})$. Whatever an investor's attitude toward risk and return may be, investment C will always be preferred to B because expected return is greater at the same level of risk. For similar reasons A is also preferred to B because it has less risk at the same level of expected yield. Preference between A and C is not evident from Figure 4.5; it can be resolved only on the basis of some assumption as to risk preference (utility) as discussed in the next section. For the moment it is evident that a reliable measure of risk must reflect the associated level of expected rate of return. The coefficient of variation is one such measure.

Another measure uses the concept of a "risk-free" rate of return. No investment is completely risk-free but the yield on an insured savings

Figure 4.5
Coefficient of Variation

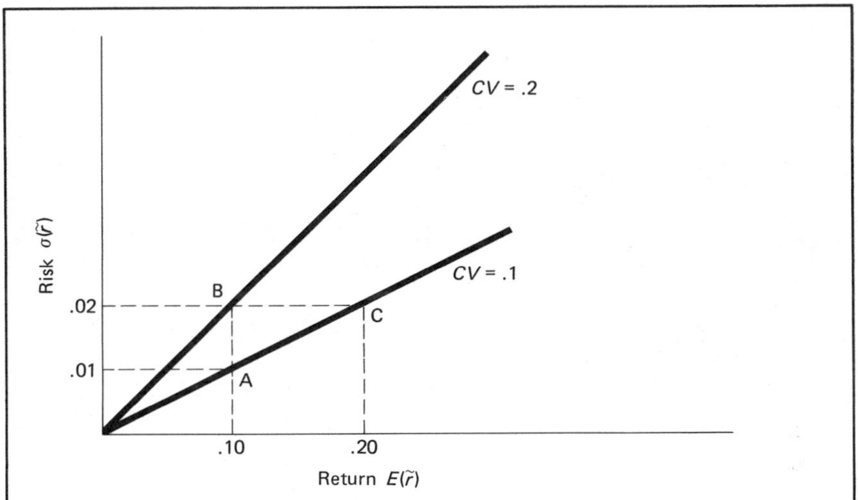

account or an investment in government securities is sufficiently certain to serve the purpose. Given a risk-free yield r_F and the expected yield on some risky security $E(\tilde{r}_i)$, the value $(r_i - r_F)$ is the excess return which is realized for accepting the risk attached to an investment in security i. Risk premium $\tilde{r}_i - r_F$ is the return to risk acceptance which, normalized by $\sigma(\tilde{r}_i)$, defines a risk premium coefficient of variation:

$$CV(i) = \frac{\sigma(\tilde{r}_i)}{E(\tilde{r}_i) - r_F} \tag{4.10}$$

This relationship is graphed in Figure 4.6 where the coefficient of variation has been adjusted to reflect a risk-free yield r_F. Unlike Figure 4.5 above, the axes have been reversed to show the more likely case where return is a function of risk; the slope of each line is therefore changed to the reciprocal of the coefficient of variation. The statistical relationship of Figure 4.5 is transformed into the portfolio relationship of Figure 4.6 but there is no substantive difference between the two graphs.

In Figure 4.6 the intercept on the vertical axis shifts to r_F to recognize existence of an asset with a positive rate of return at zero risk. Relative risk is still measured by the slope of the risk-return line, still the "rise" divided by the "run," but the vertical distance is now defined as the risk premium $E(\tilde{r}_i) - r_F$. This risk premium and the associated measure of risk $\sigma(\tilde{r}_i)$ are very important concepts which will be used when portfolio selection is considered in later chapters.

Figure 4.6
Risk Premium Coefficient of Variation

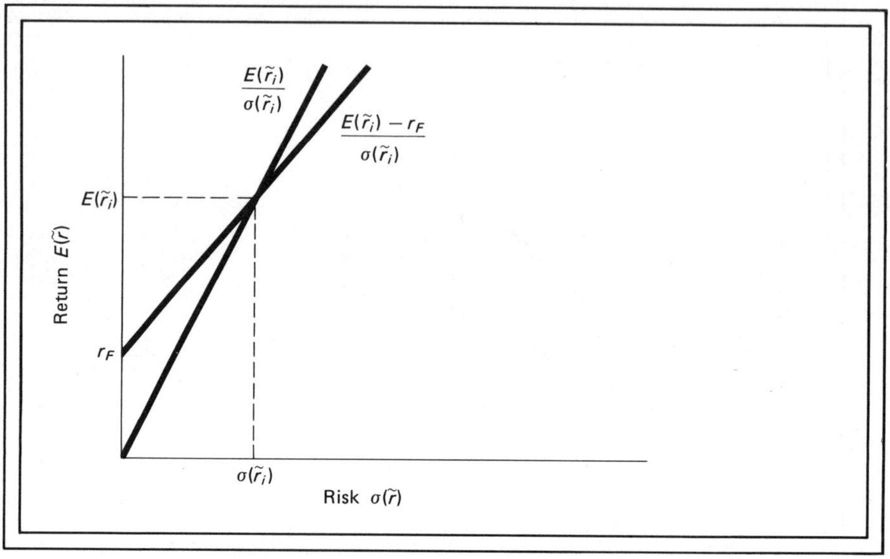

AN OPERATIONAL MEASURE OF RISK

The preceding discussion identified the standard deviation (variance) of a subjective probability distribution of rate of return as a conceptually valid measure of investment risk. The coefficient of variation, a relative risk concept, was shown to be preferable to an absolute measure. The coefficient of variation is also an operationally valid risk measure, for three reasons:

1. It relates risk and expected return in the sense described and portrayed in Figure 4.4.
2. It provides a measure which is valid for both security analysis and portfolio analysis. The integration of these two important topics is therefore feasible.
3. It is a definition that is compatible with statistical tools which are critical in security analysis.

Analysis requires forecasting; the end product of this process is a subjective probability distribution estimated by extrapolating empirical data. Familiar statistical techniques, applied to that data, generate parameters of the distribution including, at least, expected value and standard deviation.[15] Thus the analytical methods employed by analysts generate measures of risk and return which are both conceptually defensible and operational. The resolution of the trade-off between risk and return is the only remaining impediment to operationality; this is discussed in the next and final section of this chapter.

[15] Regression analysis provides an important illustration. By inserting estimated values for independent variables, given estimates of regression parameters generated from the ordinary least-squares technique, a distribution of values for the dependent variable can be generated.

Investors' Utility

To this point, beginning with the theory of choice and then focusing on the portfolio decision, investors' objectives have been discussed in terms of rate of return on investment. But rate of return is a random variable with at least two important dimensions: expected value (return) and standard deviation (risk). More of the former and less of the latter would normally be preferred but this is not possible because there is a positive association between the two. That is, the price attached to seeking greater expected return is the assumption of greater risk.

Choice among alternative risk-return combinations, in any given instance, will depend on attitudes of the individual investor; these are often defined in terms of that investor's *utility function.* The point can be illustrated by referring again to Figure 4.5. Investment opportunities A and C are clearly preferable to B, but choice between A and C is not evident in the figure. An investor who prefers opportunity C would have to be willing to accept the higher level of risk (0.02) to achieve the higher level of expected return (0.20). A more conservative investor might settle for the lesser expected return (0.10) at lesser risk (0.01). To settle this problem of choice, attitude toward risk-return trade-off, or utility, must be specified. This is a difficult conceptual problem and a far more difficult operational one.

EXPECTED VALUE VERSUS EXPECTED UTILITY

The earliest notions of rational behavior assumed *expected value maximization* as the correct object of choice.[16] This later changed to assumption of *expected utility maximization.* The reasoning here is that the "pleasure" attaching to utility and the "pain" attaching to disutility are not symmetrical. That is, it hurts somewhat more to lose a wager of \$100 than it pleases to win the same sum. To illustrate, assume that some wager depending on the toss of a fair coin will result in payment of some monetary amount, \$X. Expected value can be calculated from Equation 4.6 for a 50 percent probability of success (p):

$$\begin{aligned} E(X) &= p(X) + (1 - p)(-X) \\ &= 0.5(X) + 0.5(-X) \\ &= 0 \end{aligned} \qquad (4.11)$$

On the basis of expected value an investor would be indifferent to the wager. If X were equal to 1 cent, say, or \$1, this might be true. But if X were \$1000, how many people would accept the wager? If it were possible to numerically specify the pleasure arising from winning the sum, $U(X)$, and

[16] Early history of utility theory is traced, from 1776 through 1915, by Stigler. See George Stigler, "The Development of Utility Theory," *Journal of Political Economy*, August 1950, pp. 307–327, and October 1950, pp. 373–396.

the displeasure of losing it, $U(-X)$, the problem could be resolved. Denominating utility in "utils," assume 1000 utils of satisfaction from winning \$1000 and -2000 utils of dissatisfaction from losing that sum. Expected utility $E(U)$ can now be calculated in a manner similar to expected value:

$$\begin{aligned} E(U) &= p[U(1000)] + (1 - p)[U(-1000)] \\ &= 0.5(1000) + 0.5(-2000) \\ &= -500 \end{aligned} \tag{4.12}$$

In this example utility is not symmetrical, as monetary gain and loss is, and the person in question would reject the wager because expected utility is negative (-500).

If pleasure and pain, or satisfaction and dissatisfaction, could somehow be easily measured in "utils," the choice among risk-return alternatives could easily be resolved. But the measurement of utility is a problem yet to be resolved; at the same time it must be resolved because expected utility, and not expected value, is the correct object of choice. The point will be pursued shortly; first, however, it is necessary to consider patterns of behavior more carefully.

UTILITY OF WEALTH

Underlying the discussion in the preceding section was the assumption that utility values (utils) can be assigned to different levels of wealth. A graphic portrayal of the numerical example presented there is contained in Figure 4.7. Utility function U provides measures of utility for various levels of

Figure 4.7
Utility of Wealth

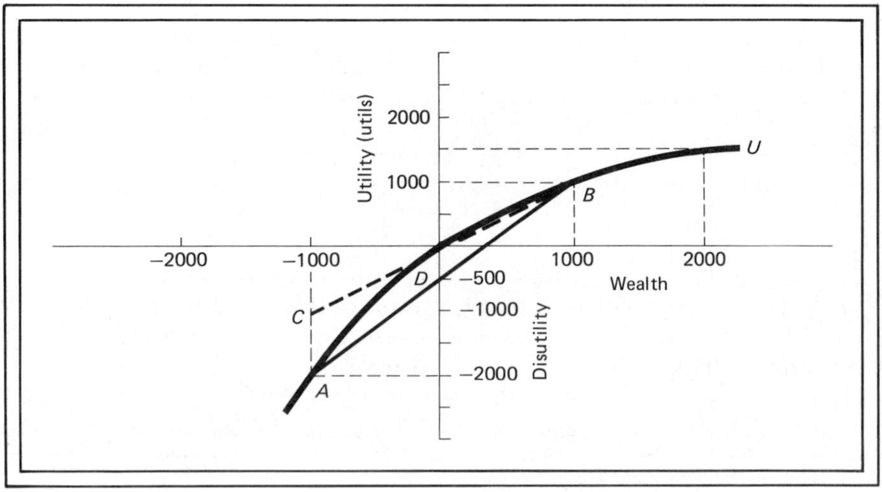

wealth.[17] The unfavorable outcome (−1000), at point A, has negative utils of −2000; the favorable outcome (1000), at point B, has a positive util value of 1000. The expected value of the wager, calculated in Equation 4.11, is zero; for that value expected utility, measured along line AB, is −500 utils (point D). Notice that *expected utility* is negative here but *utility* of zero wealth is zero; the former reflects the risk impacted in the possible loss of $1000. Thus less utility attaches to the *uncertain* prospect of zero expected wealth than to the *certain* prospect of that same zero wealth. Expected utility would equal expected wealth along the broken line CB. If CB were the utility function, and not curve ABU, mathematical expectation of utility and wealth would coincide. For that to be the case, the disutility of the possible loss of $1000 would have to be −1000 and attitude toward gain and loss would be symmetrical. It is this lack of symmetry, as noted previously, which establishes the relevance of expected utility and the irrelevance of expected wealth.

Marginal utility is defined by the slope of the utility function and its change is the rate of change in the slope. Figure 4.7 portrays positive but *diminishing marginal utility* since the slope is positive but concave downward.[18] Diminishing marginal utility implies that each increment to wealth provides successively smaller increments to utility. Wealth of $1000, for example, provides 1000 utils of satisfaction but doubling wealth to $2000 increases utility by only half that amount to 1500 utils. There is no necessary reason, however, why the curve need be concave downward nor, for that matter, why it must assume only one shape for the entire set of possible wealth outcomes.[19]

Figure 4.8 portrays three different attitudes toward risk.[20] The first, (a), is concave downward with *risk-aversion* implied by the diminishing marginal utility pictured there and in Figure 4.7. In this case, for an uncertain prospect, expected utility is less than expected value for any random wealth

[17] Treatment in the literature sometimes refers to the utility of money, or income, or wealth. This discussion focuses on wealth in the sense of an income (consumption) stream discounted to present value as in Equation 4.5.

[18] Mathematically, the slope of the utility function is the first derivative and the second derivative is the rate of change in the slope. Expressing utility curve U of Figure 4.7 as a function of wealth W, $U = f(W)$, then $dU/dW > 0$, and $d^2U/dW^2 < 0$. The slope of the utility function is marginal utility since it measures the ratio of change in utility to change in wealth. Figure 4.7, then, portrays positive but diminishing marginal utility since the first derivative is positive and the second derivative is negative.

[19] A utility function that is concave downward in one area, which implies risk aversion, and concave upward in another, implying risk-seeking behavior, would provide a rational explanation of behavior of a consumer who both purchases insurance and gambles. See Milton Friedman and Leonard J. Savage, "The Utility Analysis of Choices Involving Risk," *Journal of Political Economy*, August 1948, pp. 279–304, and Harry Markowitz, "The Utility of Wealth," *Journal of Political Economy*, April 1952, pp. 151–158.

[20] The first derivative is positive for all three utility functions in Figure 4.8; all three show positive marginal utility. But second derivatives for parts (a), (b), and (c), respectively, are negative, zero, and positive. This implies (a) diminishing, (b) constant, and (c) increasing marginal utility.

Figure 4.8
Attitudes Toward Risk

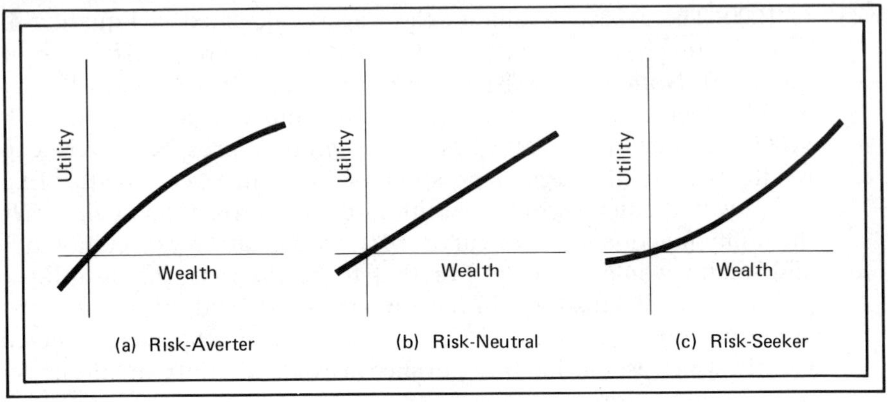

outcome. Figure 4.8(b) depicts *risk-neutrality.* The linearity of the utility function there implies indifference to risk; expected utility is equal everywhere to the expected monetary outcome. In part (c), *risk-seeking* behavior is pictured. An investor with a utility function of this type would be willing to pay to accept risk; successive increments to wealth provide successively larger increments to utility. Part (c) can be described as increasing marginal utility.

Figure 4.8(c) suggests a gambler, one willing to pay a premium to accept a wager with zero expected value. This contrasts with the behavior implied in (a) where risk-averters would be willing to pay to avoid risk, as in the case of purchase of an insurance contract. From an investments perspective, risk-seeking behavior probably has no relevance. Gamblers certainly exist, but part of the satisfaction of gambling undoubtedly rests in the game per se, and not merely in monetary outcome of the game. Risk-neutrality is more likely the limiting case, and risk-aversion the general one, since an investment strategy which finds merit in negative expected value is a highly questionable objective.

One other property of a utility function requires comment before the question of measurability can be considered. This is the arbitrariness or uniqueness of the numbers used to measure utility; these may be classified as *ordinal* or *cardinal.* Table 4.3 illustrates the difference in the two measures. For the six outcomes listed, four sets of values are contained in columns A, B, C, and D. All four sets indicate preference for outcome 6 over 5, for 5 over 4, and so forth, according to numerical util values contained in the table. All four sets provide the same *ranking* of prospects. But the *intensity* of ranking implied in column B differs from that implied in columns A, C, and D.

Since all four sets provide the same ordering of prospects they are said to be *monotone transformations* of each other. That is, for purposes of

Table 4.3
Utility of Random Outcomes (utils)

Outcome	*Monetary Outcome*	*Utility Measure A*	*Utility Measure B*	*Utility Measure C*	*Utility Measure D*
1	$ 0	0	5	10	0
2	1000	11	20	21	22
3	2000	20	21	30	40
4	3000	28	40	38	56
5	4000	34	80	44	68
6	5000	38	90	48	76

indicating order of preference, any measure will provide the correct choice; in this sense each set of numbers is a transformation of the other. But the comparison between A and B, say, stops there; between outcome values of $3000 and $4000, for example, A indicates a modest increase in utility but B indicates a very large increase. If utility can be described only by either A or B, specific values employed are arbitrary and utility is *ordinal.* Increasing or decreasing marginal utility has no relevance in this situation.

Columns A and C, in contrast, are said to be *linear transformations*; C is the same as A except that a constant, 10, has been added to C. It is in this sense that the transformation is linear. Column A and C values are graphed in Figure 4.9; both describe unique utility *except for origin.* That is,

Figure 4.9
Cardinal Utility Functions

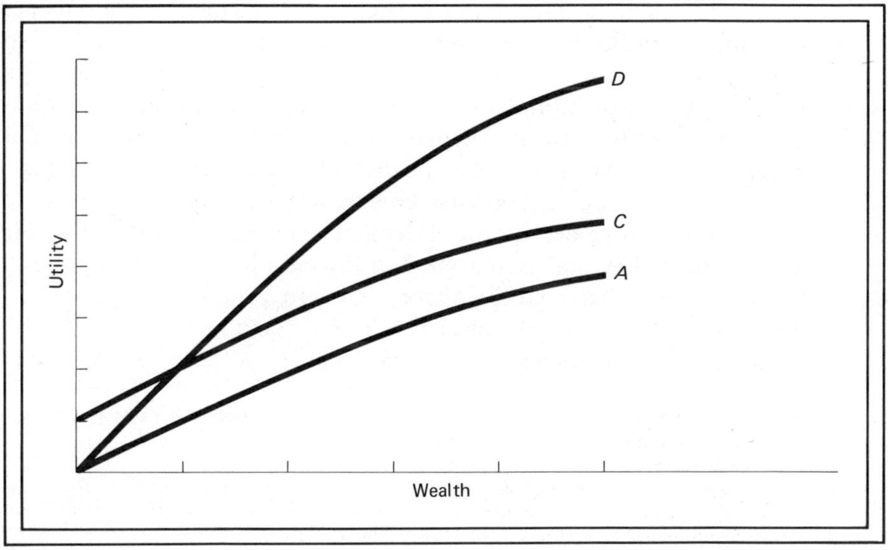

if each value of C is decreased by 10, A and C will be identical; they differ only with respect to the origin selected on the vertical axis. Similarly, A and D are unique *except for scale.* That is, if each value for D is divided by 2 (if the scale on the vertical axis is halved), A and D would be identical. Thus A, C, and D all are the same utility function except for origin and scale. In this situation, one defined as *cardinal utility*, increasing and decreasing marginal utility are both relevant and measurable.

To summarize, cardinal utility values are unique except for origin and scale. This is analogous to measurement of altitude from the earth's surface; it too is unique up to two constants—origin, such as sea level, and the unit of scale, such as the meter.[21] Given those constants altitude can be uniquely and accurately measured if instruments are properly calibrated. But the measurement of cardinal utility, reversing the analogy, is a far less certain prospect.

MEASURING UTILITY

Utility theory has developed over the last two centuries; it has been considered by virtually all leading economists from the time of Adam Smith, through Ricardo and the classicists, to the modern period. But it was not until the 1870s that utility began to be generally accepted in economics. Economists of that era, including Jevons, Menger, and Walras, accepted utility somewhat casually in deriving demand curve relationships; they were, at the same time, rather vague as to its measurement.[22]

Measurable utility was suggested by Jeremy Bentham as early as 1782, but the problem was largely ignored until the beginning of this century when Fisher examined it carefully and then rejected it. Among other leading economists of that time, Pareto emphatically denied the uniqueness and relevance of utility functions. His position was supported by Johnson and Slutsky, among others. Others of that general period, including Wickstead, Wicksell, Edgeworth, and Pigou, did not reject measurability largely from a desire to apply it to problems of welfare economics. Measurability was never denied by Marshall, perhaps the outstanding economist of his period.

Among modern theorists, Gustav Cassel was the first to reject a utility approach to derivation of demand functions; he attacked notions of measurable value, that is, marginal utility, and his views were followed and supported by others. Utility theory fell into general disrepute during the first half of the twentieth century, where it remained until rescued by von Neumann and Morgenstern in 1953. The hypothesis of expected utility

[21] A number of writers have suggested similar analogies. This one was used in Jacob Marshak, "Rational Behavior, Uncertain Prospects, and Measurable Utility," *Econometrica*, April 1950, pp. 111–141.

[22] Actually, Jevons had denied that utility can be measured but then, with what Stigler described as "gallant inconsistency," he proceeded to devise a way to measure it in monetary terms. See Stigler, "Development of Utility Theory," p. 317.

maximization dates back at least to 1738 when Daniel Bernoulli proposed the celebrated "St. Petersburg paradox."[23] But it had generally been rejected because belief in diminishing marginal utility was in conflict with observed behavior, as in the case of gambling. Moreover, with certainty, ordinal utility is sufficient to rationalize riskless choice. But certainty is uninteresting and von Neumann and Morgenstern provided an axiomatic treatment of choice under conditions of risk.[24]

They proposed measurable utility to a linear transformation, reintroducing increasing and decreasing marginal utility in the process. With added support from others, most notably Freidman and Savage, Marshak, and Markowitz, cardinal utility received new emphasis and vitality.[25] Rational behavior is defined axiomatically and, based on those axioms, numerical values can be assigned to utility by the process of *revealed preference*. An origin and scale are selected and a person is then given a choice among a set of hypothetical lotteries with various monetary outcomes and associated probabilities. Since the subject is assumed to choose among uncertain prospects according to expected utility, the utility function is derived from experimental outcomes. Given the utility function, choice among risky alternatives can be evaluated.

If revealed preference provides an accurate estimate of the cardinal utility function, the trade-off between investment risk and return can be resolved. Unfortunately, the issue remains to be settled. Empirical tests are inconclusive and, indeed, they are subject to severe methodological difficulty.[26] Answers provided to the lottery experiment are subject to bias

[23] The "St. Petersburg Paradox" involves a game in which a fair coin is tossed until such time as a predetermined outcome, say, "tails," occurs. If tails results on the first toss, the player wins $1; on the second try, $2; on the third $4; then $8, and so forth. The problem is the value someone would be willing to pay to play this game.

Expected value of the game if played until a tail appears is *infinite*; this can be seen from Equation 4.6. For a fair coin, probability of tails on the first trial is $\frac{1}{2}$, on the second, $\frac{1}{4}$, then $\frac{1}{8}$, etc. Thus the mathematical expectation is:

$$\begin{aligned} E &= \tfrac{1}{2}(1) + \tfrac{1}{4}(2) + \tfrac{1}{8}(4) + \cdots \\ &= \tfrac{1}{2} + \tfrac{1}{2} + \tfrac{1}{2} + \cdots \\ &= \infty \end{aligned}$$

But while mathematical expectation is infinite, few persons would be willing to pay more than a modest sum to play the game.

The Bernoulli paradox has important implications for investment in growth stocks. See David Durand, "Growth Stocks and the St. Petersburg Paradox," *Journal of Finance*, September 1957, pp. 348–363.

[24] John von Neumann and Oskar Morgenstern, *Theory of Games and Economic Behavior* (New Jersey: Princeton University Press, 1953).

[25] See Friedman and Savage, "Utility Analysis of Choices Involving Risk"; Markowitz, "Utility of Wealth"; and Marshak, "Rational Behavior, Uncertain Prospects, Measurable Utility."

[26] There is little empirical evidence available on this question, and the evidence which does exist is not conclusive. See Frederick Mosteller and Philip Nogee, "An Empirical Measurement of Utility," *Journal of Political Economy*, October 1951, pp. 371–404, and Martin Weitzmann, "Utility Analysis and Group Behavior: An Empirical Study," *Journal of Political Economy*, February 1965, pp. 18–26.

because (1) they involve hypothetical situations, (2) investment opportunities may be poorly represented, and (3) individual tastes may vary over time.

It is tempting to ignore utility because of these measurement problems, but that substitutes a known irrelevance (expected value) for an unknown relevance (expected utility) and it is an unsatisfactory solution. At the same time, the revealed preference technique described above is not clearly defensible from an operational perspective. Under the circumstances an intermediate position will be adopted here. Security and portfolio risk-return measures will be developed as the end product of analysis under the assumption that an investor facing these combinations can, on the basis of expected utility, choose among them. In effect this is a variant of revealed preference, with choice among estimated outcomes for actual strategies at a particular point in time. While this is less than wholly satisfactory, it does address the three elements of bias detailed above and it is an operational approach. Pending refinement of the technique of revealed preference, it appears to be the only viable alternative available to investment managers.

Summary

Chapters 3 and 4 have set the foundation for security analysis and portfolio management. Rate of return was introduced and developed in terms of both expected value and standard deviation—operational measures of risk and return which underlie investors' decisions. These concepts were considered in a managerial context with emphasis placed on important elements and definitions which are an integral part of the investment process. Utility was briefly reviewed and, in light of bothersome dimensions yet to be resolved, a pragmatic approach to expected utility maximization was proposed. It is less than fully satisfactory but, given the current state of the art, it is viewed here as the most realistic approach possible at this time.

The basic analytical model was defined in Chapter 3:

$$C_0 = \frac{C_1}{(1+r)^1} + \frac{C_2}{(1+r)^2} + \cdots + \frac{C_{n-1}}{(1+r)^{n-1}} + \frac{C_n}{(1+r)^n} \qquad [(3.8)]$$

Analytical chapters which follow are directed to the problem of identifying and estimating cash flows C_t which determine r for different investment opportunities. Since future cash flows are uncertain, they exist in terms of a subjective probability distribution. Viewing numerators of Equation 3.8 in this sense implies a *distribution of* r as the logical *output* of security analysis procedures; this is the *input* required, in part, for portfolio analysis.

Chapter 5 begins the process of examining individual investment opportunities. Securities considered there include bonds, preferred stock, and mortgages; these are the so-called fixed income securities where estimation of flows C_t, while difficult, is far less complex than in the case of other opportunities.

Appendix
Continuous Distributions

Of the distributions defined in statistics, three are of particular significance to investment analysts. These are the normal, log-normal, and stable Paretian distributions. While rigorous coverage of these three is not intended here, they will be surveyed in order to provide a basic description of what they are and why they are important.

NORMAL DISTRIBUTION

The most familiar distribution in statistics is the *normal* or *Gaussian* distribution. This is the familiar "bell curve" known to students of most disciplines and it is the keystone of classical statistics. It is a two-parameter symmetric distribution; given mean and variance, probabilities are fully described. A table of values for the normal distribution is provided in all standard statistical texts.

The normal distribution has many applications in investment analysis. Among the most important is multiple regression analysis, a technique which assumes that regression residuals are normally distributed about the regression line. Estimates derived from regression analysis provide point estimates of future values, and, from regression residuals, the distribution about those point estimates. This technique will be considered in depth in Chapter 8.

The normal distribution may also provide an acceptable definition for a number of variables of interest to analysts. In some given instance, as in the distribution of some important macroeconomic variable, the distribution may be well defined by the normal distribution. One variable of interest, however, is poorly described by normality: empirical evidence suggests that the distribution of security rates of return are closer to the log-normal than to the normal distribution.[27]

LOG-NORMAL DISTRIBUTION

In one sense the *log-normal distribution* is merely a subset of the normal; it is a distribution in which the underlying variable is transformed logarithmically. That is, for some random variable Y, where $Y = \log X$, Y is distributed normally. When applied to return relative $(1 + r)$, where $X = (1 + r)$, negative values of X are undefined. Moreover, the underlying X value will be positively skewed with skewness increasing as the variance of Y increases. If a variable of interest assumes this general shape, it may be possible to use

[27] Breen and Savage provide evidence that security returns are not distributed normally; the log-normal is found to be better but still questionable. William Breen and James Savage, "Portfolio Distributions and Tests of Security Selection Models," *Journal of Finance*, December 1968, pp. 805–819.

Figure 4A.1
Observed Deviation from Normal Behavior

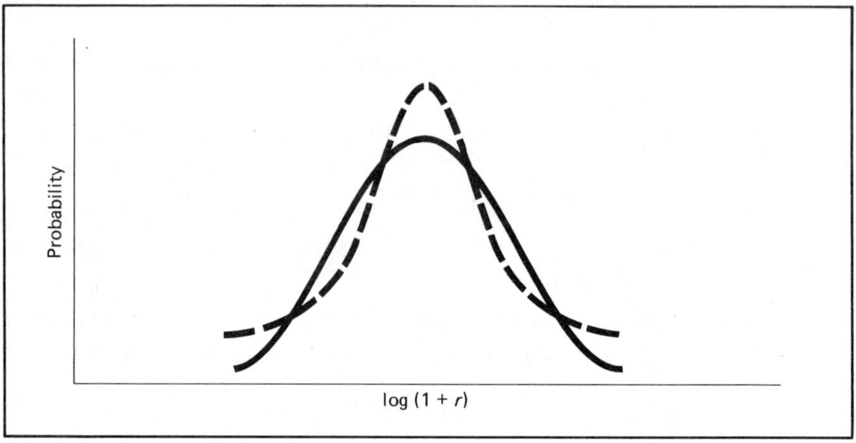

the properties of the normal distribution even in this case where the variable is not normal. This is accomplished by changing all values to logarithms.

There are important conceptual reasons for using the logarithms of return relatives when observing the behavior of security prices. First, as shown in Chapter 3, the antilog of the mean of logarithms is the geometric mean value. This was shown to be the most relevant measure of multiperiod return. Second, it can be shown that logarithms approximate percentage changes in the range of ± 15 percent. This provides a measure of relative change which is important in a number of applications.[28]

The relevance or nonrelevance of the log-normal distribution is an empirical question. Research studies suggest it is not a wholly satisfactory specification of return relatives because empirical distributions have taller peaks and greater probability in the "tails" (leptokurtosis) than the normal distribution allows. The situation is portrayed in Figure 4A.1. Relative frequencies imply greater probability of an extreme outcome and thus greater risk. Several explanations have been advanced to rationalize this observed behavior. One is the argument of *nonstationarity*; that is, the distribution may be log-normal at every *point in time* but mean and variance may change *over time*. This could account for the frequencies observed from a time series but the proposition is difficult to test and the point cannot be resolved.[29] A second argument advanced is that the distribution is not log-normal. The next section considers this viewpoint.

[28] See Eugene F. Fama, "The Behavior of Stock-Market Prices," *Journal of Business*, January 1965, pp. 45–46.

[29] Many of these difficulties are noted by I. G. Morgan, "Stock Prices and Heteroscedasticity," *The Journal of Business* (October 1976), pp. 496–508. Morgan concludes that non-stationarity is an important part of the problem but that it is incomplete as an explanation of departure from normality.

STABLE PARETIAN DISTRIBUTION

Benoit Mandlebrot, observing extreme values in the tails of empirical distributions, advanced the proposition that they were of a class he referred to as *stable Paretian*.[30] This is a particularly complex and difficult distribution which has little operational relevance at this time for the analyst. For this reason it is included here with a very limited objective: to recognize that an issue exists which, should it be resolved subsequently, will require close attention by practitioners.

A stable Paretian distribution has four parameters. These measure (1) location, (2) scale, (3) skewness, and (4) probability in the extreme tails (kurtosis). The fourth parameter is called the *characteristic exponent* and it is conventionally denoted by the Greek letter alpha (α); it can assume any value in the range $0 < \alpha \leq 2$. When $\alpha = 2$ the distribution is normal; thus the normal is one of the family of stable Paretian distributions. But as α assumes values less than 2, variance is undefined and probability in the tails increases. Since empirical studies have found larger tail values, it is plausible to argue the validity of this family of distributions for investment returns. Moreover, impressive evidence has been accumulated to suggest that values of α fall in an approximate range between 1.7 and 1.9, short of the required Gaussian value of 2. Unfortunately, the significance of values close to, but less than, 2 is difficult to assess.

If it is true, as the evidence suggests, that rates of return on securities are stable Paretian distributed, analysts will find it necessary to become more familiar with the distribution and its implications for investment risk and return. To further complicate matters, some researchers suggest that the student *t*-distribution is a closer approximation of the behavior of security returns than either normal, log normal, or stable Paretian.[31]

Questions and Problems

1. Growth Fund invests only in common stocks; it has advertised, as its planned objective, realization of an annual rate of return of 9 percent, on average. During this last year realized rate of return was 7 percent. Can you conclude that the fund's management has performed inefficiently this year? Why or why not? Would your answer differ if the fund had realized 12 percent? Why or why not?
2. You are considering purchase of shares in the mutual fund described in question 1 above. In your opinion, what would be a fair annual rate of return to expect the fund to earn over some extended period of time? Would your answer differ if you were:
   a. A recent college graduate just embarking on a career pursuit?
   b. A successful executive at middle age with children in college?
   c. A recently retired professional with moderate retirement income?

[30] Benoit Mandlebrot, "The Variation of Certain Speculative Prices," *Journal of Business*, October 1963, pp. 394–419. Also see Fama, "Behavior of Stock Market Prices," pp. 34–105.

[31] Peter D. Praetz, "The Distribution of Share Prices Changes," *The Journal of Business* (January 1972), pp. 49–55. Also worth noting is Robert C. Blattberg and Nicholas J. Gonedes, "A Comparison of the Stable and Student Distribution as Statistical Models for Stock Prices," *The Journal of Business* (April 1974), pp. 244–280; Praetz, "Comment" and Blattberg and Gonedes, "Reply," *Journal of Business* (January 1977), pp. 76–79.

3. An investor with current resources of $1000 decides to spend $800 and save the other $200. Savings can currently be invested, totally without risk, to yield 6 percent.
   a. Assume that the investor decides to purchase the risk-free asset for one year, after which time it will return a total of $212. What is the value of the investor's total wealth?
   b. Assume that a different asset is available which promises $230 at the end of the year but which also carries the risk that loss will be incurred. If the investor is indifferent between this risky asset and the risk-free asset of part (a), what is the present value of current wealth? What is implied in your answer to this question and the question in part (a)?
   c. Assume that the risky asset of part (b) has a 50 percent probability of returning $230 at the end of the year and a 50 percent probability of returning $194. Would you prefer this investment or the risk-free investment? Explain.
4. You have determined the following subjective probability distribution for rate of return on investment:

Probability	*Outcome*
0.02	−0.20
0.03	−0.15
0.04	−0.10
0.05	−0.05
0.10	0.00
0.15	0.05
0.20	0.10
0.20	0.15
0.10	0.20
0.10	0.25
0.01	0.30

   a. Calculate expected rate of return, variance, standard deviation, and the coefficient of variation.
   b. Compare this distribution to the one contained in Table 4.1. Which one promises the greater expected return? The greater risk? Which of the two would be preferred if you could invest only in one or the other?
   c. Without attempting involved calculations, which of the two opportunities appears to have the greater "downside risk"? Would this alter your answer to part (b) above? Explain.
5. You are attempting to select one of the five investment opportunities summarized below; they are mutually exclusive—you can purchase only one of the securities with summarized expected return and standard deviation. Given the information supplied, can you at least partially determine a rational choice? Explain. What other information, if any, is needed to solve the problem?

	$E(r)$	$\sigma(r)$
A	0.10	0.10
B	0.10	0.20
C	0.20	0.20
D	0.25	0.25
E	0.30	0.25

Selected References

INVESTMENT MANAGEMENT AND INVESTMENT OBJECTIVES

Bauman, W. Scott, "Evaluation of Prospective Investment Performance," *Journal of Finance*, May 1968, pp. 276–295.

Dietz, Peter O., "Components of a Measurement Model: Rate of Return, Risk, and Timing," *Journal of Finance*, May 1968, pp. 267–275.

Henderson, James M., and Richard E. Quandt, *Microeconomic Theory: A Mathematical Approach* (New York: McGraw Hill, 1958).

Katona, George, and John B. Lansing, "The Wealth of the Wealthy," *Review of Economics and Statistics*, February 1964, pp. 1–13.

Lorie, James H., and Mary T. Hamilton, *The Stock Market: Theories and Evidence* (Homewood, Ill.: Irwin, 1973), chaps. 13–15.

PROBABILITY AND RISK

Arditti, Fred D., "Risk and the Required Rate of Return on Equity," *Journal of Finance*, March 1967, pp. 19–36.

Florence, P. Sargant, "The Reward for Risk-Bearing by Shareholders in Large Companies," *Journal of Industrial Economics*, March 1957, pp. 81–111.

Francis, Jack Clark, "Skewness and Investors' Decisions," *Journal of Financial and Quantitative Analysis*, March 1975, pp. 163–172.

Friend, Irwin, and Douglas Vickers, "Portfolio Selection and Investment Performance," *Journal of Finance*, September 1965, pp. 391–415.

Hayes, Douglas A., "The Multi-Dimensional Aspects of Risk," *Journal of Portfolio Management*, Summer 1976, pp. 23–28.

Hirshleifer, Jack, "Risk, the Discount Rate, and Investment Decisions," *American Economic Review*, May 1961, pp. 112–120.

Logue, Dennis E., "Are Stock Markets Becoming Riskier?" *Journal of Portfolio Management*, Spring 1976, pp. 13–19.

Markowitz, Harry M., *Portfolio Selection*, Cowles Foundation Monograph No. 16 (New York: Wiley, 1959), chaps. 3, 4, and 9.

Robichek, Alexander A., "Risk and the Value of Securities," *Journal of Financial and Quantitative Analysis*, December 1969, pp. 513–538.

Ryan, J. M., and A. O. Gardner, "The Measurement of Dynamic Risk," *Southern Economic Journal*, January 1965, pp. 207–214.

INVESTORS' UTILITY

Alchian, Armen A., "The Meaning of Utility Measurement," *American Economic Review*, March 1953, pp. 26–50.

Arrow, Kenneth J., "Utilities, Attitudes, Choices: A Review Note," *Econometrica*, January 1958, pp. 1–23.

Debreu, Gerard, *Theory of Value: An Axiomatic Analysis of Economic Equilibrium*, Cowles Foundation Monograph No. 17 (New York: Wiley, 1959).

Freidman, Milton, and Leonard J. Savage, "The Utility Analysis of Choices Involving Risk," *Journal of Political Economy*, August 1948, pp. 279–304.

Handa, Jagdish, "Risk, Probabilities, and a New Theory of Cardinal Utility," *Journal of Political Economy* 85 (February 1977), pp. 97–122.

Markowitz, Harry, "The Utility of Wealth," *Journal of Political Economy*, April 1952, pp. 151–158.

Marshak, Jacob, "Rational Behavior, Uncertain Prospects, and Measurable Utility," *Econometrica*, April 1950, pp. 111–141.

Pratt, John W., "Risk Aversion in the Small and in the Large," *Econometrica*, January–April 1964, pp. 122–136.

Stigler, George, "The Development of Utility Theory," *Journal of Political Economy*, August 1950, pp. 307–327 and October 1950, pp. 373–396.

Von Neumann, John, and Oskar Morgenstern, *Theory of Games and Economic Behavior*, 3d ed. (New Jersey: Princeton University Press, 1953).

CONTINUOUS DISTRIBUTIONS

Aitchison, John, and J. A. C. Brown, *The Lognormal Distribution* (New York: Cambridge University Press, 1957).

Blume, Marshall E., "Portfolio Theory: A Step Toward Its Practical Application," *Journal of Business*, April 1970, pp. 152–173.

Fama, Eugene F., "The Behavior of Stock-Market Prices," *Journal of Business*, January 1965, pp. 34–105.

———, "Risk, Return, and Equilibrium," *Journal of Political Economy*, January–February 1971, pp. 30–55.

——— and Richard Roll, "Some Properties of Symmetric Stable Distributions," *Journal of the American Statistical Association*, September 1968, pp. 817–836.

Mandlebrot, Benoit, "The Variation of Certain Speculative Prices," *Journal of Business*, October 1963, pp. 394–419.

Chapter 5

Bonds, Mortgages, and Preferred Stock

This chapter examines the determinants of yield (internal rate of return) for a number of investments which are generally referred to as fixed income securities. These include U. S. government obligations, state and local bonds, corporate bonds, mortgage commitments, and preferred stock. Securities which are convertible into common stock are discussed separately, in Chapter 11, when the discussion of common stock analysis has been completed.

The first section of the chapter contains a description of the determinants of yield. Yield is defined and illustrated and risk is discussed in detail. The second section examines interest rates both conceptually and empirically. The relationship between yield and maturity is studied, and published "quality ratings" are examined and evaluated. Interest rate forecasting is also discussed. The remaining sections review specific features of bonds, mortgages, and preferred stocks which influence the decision to invest in fixed income securities. The chapter appendix examines the term structure of interest rates both conceptually and empirically.

Elements of Yield

YIELD CALCULATION

Yield can be introduced by considering a bond which is issued under conditions of certainty. In that case, bond yield depends upon its current price

P_0, periodic coupon (interest) payment I_t, the number of periods n to maturity, and maturity value P_n. Yield is formalized by redefining the general analytical model of Equation 3.8 to include all of these elements; yield is the discount rate y which satisfies:

$$P_0 = \sum_{t=1}^{n} \frac{I_t}{(1+y)^t} + \frac{P_n}{(1+y)^n} \tag{5.1}$$

To illustrate, assume that an 8 percent corporate bond, which can be purchased for \$875.39, will mature in ten years. With very few exceptions, corporate bond interest is paid semiannually and par (maturity) value is \$1000.00. In that case there will be 20 payments of \$40.00 each as well as a terminal payment of \$1000.00. Equation 5.1 for yield becomes:

$$875.39 = 40.00 \sum_{t=1}^{20} (1+y)^{-t} + 1000.00(1+y)^{-20}$$

From Tables A.2 and A.4 located at the back of the text, yield is shown to be 5 percent per semiannual period:

Present value of coupon payments	40.00(12.4622) =	498.49
Present value of principal payment	1000.00(0.3769) =	376.90
		875.39

Compound annual rate of return is 10.25 percent:

$$(1.05)(1.05) - 1.0 = 1.1025 - 1.0 = 0.1025$$

Equation 5.1 was solved by trial and error and in the case of a real bond this is both tedious and time-consuming. In addition, the formula must be adjusted to recognize the interim period from the date the bond is purchased to the date of the first coupon payment. As a result the calculation becomes even more complicated. Fortunately, there are other alternatives for determining or estimating bond yield.

1. BOND TABLES AND CALCULATORS. Published bond tables are available which contain yield for a large variety of prices, interest rates, and remaining time to maturity, with time defined in three-month intervals.[1] They are similar in principle to the present value tables in the appendix at the back of the text because values were developed by solving Equation 5.1 for a large number of combinations of variables P_0, I_t, and n. Published tables were used extensively until very recently when hand calculators were developed with bond price and yield functions. Calculators provide values quickly and accurately and published tables are rapidly becoming obsolete.

[1] Bond tables are available from the Boston Financial Publishing Company.

2. YIELD APPROXIMATION. Yield can be approximated as the ratio of average interest payment to average investment. Periodic interest is defined as the sum of interest payment I_t and periodic amortization of bond discount or premium; average investment is the mid-value between current price P_0 and terminal value P_n. Yield approximation y' is then defined:

$$y \approx y' = \frac{\text{interest expense}}{\text{average investment}} = \frac{I_t + (1/n)(P_n - P_0)}{(P_0 + P_n)/2} \tag{5.2}$$

For the preceding example,

$$y' = \frac{40.00 + (1/20)(1000.00 - 875.39)}{(1000.00 + 875.39)/2}$$

$$= \frac{46.23}{937.70}$$

$$= 0.0493$$

Semiannual yield approximation here is inaccurate by only 7 basis points.[2] Inaccuracy results because capital gain or loss $(P_n - P_0)$ is amortized by use of an arithmetic mean $(1/n)$ in lieu of the geometric mean implied in Equation 5.1. Nonetheless, the method defined by Equation 5.2 is often an accurate approximation of actual yield and, in any event, it is an excellent starting point for trial-and-error calculation.

The calculation of bond yield is a mechanical process when the values of P_0, P_n, I_t, and n are known with certainty. But certainty has no relevance because there is no assurance that estimated cash flows will in fact be realized. Uncertainty causes yield to vary for any single security over time and for different securities at any given point in time.

RISK PREMIUMS

Figure 5.1 traces the level of interest rates during 1968–1975 for newly issued utility bonds, long-term U.S. government bonds, high-grade (Aaa) municipal bonds, seasoned high-grade and medium-grade (Baa) corporate bonds, and mortgage commitments on new homes which are insured by the Federal Housing Authority (FHA). Similarities in the six series are obvious but differences are also very evident. Variations in yield among the several series reflect risk differentials which are perceived by investors.[3] In the case of corporate bonds, for example, Baa yields always exceed Aaa yields; Aaa corporate yields, in turn, are greater than the yields on U.S. government

[2] A basis point is a hundredth of 1 percent; 100 basis points is equal to 1 percent.

[3] An important exception involves the yield on state and local issues. Municipal yields are significantly lower than any of the other five series because interest payments on municipal bonds are not taxed under the Internal Revenue Code. State and local bond yields are measured on an after-tax basis while the other five series are measured on a before-tax basis. The impact of taxes on yield will be developed in detail later in this chapter.

Figure 5.1
Long-Term Interest Rates (monthly averages)

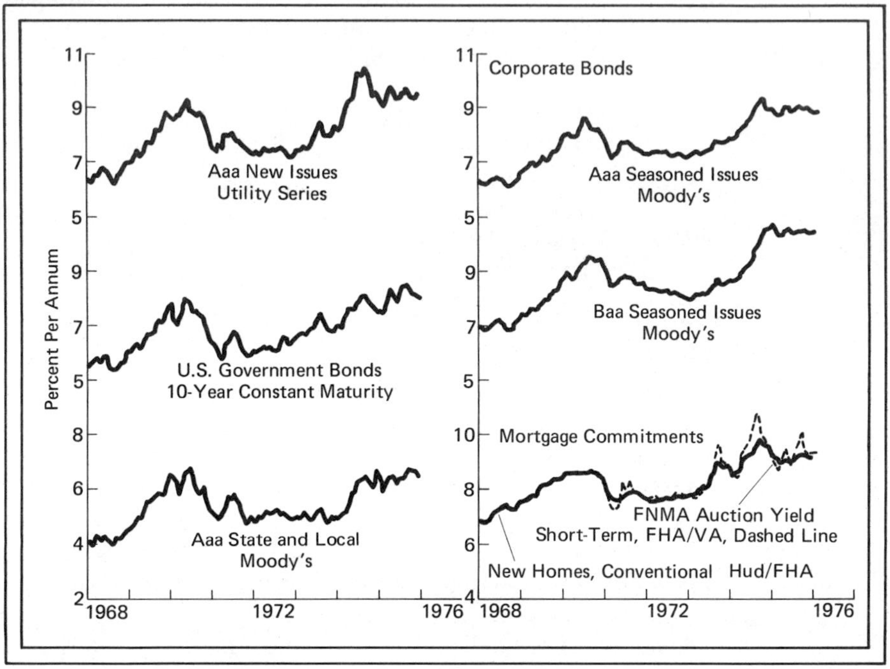

Source: Board of Governors of the Federal Reserve System.

securities. This suggests that investors demand a risk premium to offset expected default losses.[4] Other types of risk are also implied in the yield differentials which can be observed in Figure 5.1.

If all elements of risk are denoted as R, bond yield y can be conceptualized as follows:

$$y = i + R \tag{5.3}$$

Variable i is a "pure" rate of interest—a discount rate which induces an investor to forgo current consumption in return for a larger stream of future consumption. R is an aggregate risk premium which compensates the investor for the uncertainty involved in future cash flows.

Equation 5.5 is an adequate representation of bond yield but the components of R must be identified if the formula is to have any operational value. These are (1) exchange rate risk, (2) marketability or liquidity risk, (3) inflation or purchasing power risk, (4) default risk, and (5) interest rate risk.

[4] Baa securities are assumed to have greater default risk than Aaa and U.S. government obligations are assumed to be free of this type of risk. Default risk and quality ratings will be discussed in detail shortly.

EXCHANGE RATE RISK. Exchange rate risk applies to investments which are denominated in foreign currencies. Revaluation of the domestic monetary unit with respect to other currencies will result in gain or loss for investors who own foreign securities. Foreign bonds are not an important part of most portfolios and exchange rate risk is not a serious problem for most U.S. investors. Nonetheless, some currencies have appreciated or depreciated significantly since the floating exchange rate system was adopted in 1973. As a result, exchange rate risk has increased for international investors.

MARKETABILITY RISK. Marketability or liquidity risk arises when there is no ready market for an otherwise valuable security. Market value implies that there is a willing buyer available to purchase an asset from a willing seller at some bargained "fair" value. An investor with pressing liquidity problems may find it necessary to sell an asset for a lesser value than would be realized if it were possible to delay until a willing buyer appeared. Real estate is especially vulnerable to marketability risk while U.S. government obligations, for all practical purposes, are free of it. Lower grade corporate and municipal bonds, which are not actively traded, are also open to serious marketability risk.

It is impractical to attempt to measure liquidity risk directly. Instead, the trade-off between profitability and liquidity must be recognized when investment goals are established. A portfolio manager can provide for unexpected liquidity pressures by including some highly marketable securities among the assets which are held.

INFLATION RISK. Inflation risk can be demonstrated by distinguishing between real and monetary rates of return. A \$100.00 Series E U.S. Savings Bond which was purchased in May of 1969 for \$75.00 could have been redeemed in May of 1975 for \$98.64. *Monetary yield y* is 4.67 percent for that investment:

$$75.00 = \frac{98.64}{(1 + y)^6}, \qquad y = 0.0467$$

In May of 1969 the Consumer Price Index (CPI), where 1967 = 100, was 109.0; in May of 1975 the CPI was 159.3. In terms of constant purchasing power, the 1975 value of \$98.64 reduces to \$67.49 in 1969 dollars:

$$(98.64)\,\frac{109.0}{159.3} = 67.49$$

The *real yield x* is not 4.67 percent; it is a *loss* of 1.74 percent:

$$75.00 = \frac{67.49}{(1 + x)^6}, \qquad x = -0.0174$$

If investors correctly anticipated the 1969–1975 inflation rate, they would have either spent the \$75.00 or searched for another investment which compensated for inflation risk. To illustrate, assume that an alternative investment existed which was identical to the savings bond in every respect except that market supply and demand factors determined its price. If investors required a real rate of return of 3 percent to induce them to save, the alternative security would be priced at \$56.52:

$$P_0 = \frac{67.49}{(1.03)^6} = 67.49(0.8375)$$
$$= 56.52$$

Although real rate of return x is 3 percent, nominal yield y is 9.73 percent:

$$56.52 = \frac{98.64}{(1 + y)^6}, \qquad y = 0.0973$$

Real and nominal yields are linked through inflation risk premium R_I:

$$y = x + R_I$$
$$= 0.03 + 0.0673 = 0.0973 \qquad (5.4)$$

Equation 5.4 is a simplistic definition of inflation risk. Economic theory has not yet established any precise specification for the relationship among the variables defined there. Nonetheless, the equation does provide insights which are useful in explaining the pattern of increasing interest rates graphed in Figure 5.1.

Gibson studied the relationship between nominal rate of interest and price level expectations.[5] Observed yields on U.S. government obligations were studied in order to avoid the problem of default risk. Expectational data were constructed from a survey of the opinions of leading economists conducted semiannually by financial columnist Joseph Livingston. Gibson tested the hypothesized relationship

$$y = \alpha + \beta P^* \qquad (5.5)$$

where y is the nominal yield on government securities, P^* is the expected rate of price change, and α and β are coefficients of the two-variable linear regression model.[6]

Equation 5.5 tests the relationship among observed nominal interest rates and price level expectations.[7] Assuming no change in the real rate of interest during the period studied, a β value of 1 would imply that a 1 percent change in the expected rate of inflation would result in a 1 percent

[5] William E. Gibson, "Interest Rates and Inflationary Expectations: New Evidence," *American Economic Review*, December 1972, pp. 854–865.

[6] The linear regression model is described in detail in an appendix to Chapter 8. A basic familiarity with regression, on the level of an introductory statistics course, is sufficient background for this discussion.

[7] The reliability and accuracy of price level expectations will be discussed subsequently when interest rate forecasting is considered.

change in the nominal rate of interest. Gibson's study supports the argument that nominal interest rates reflect informed opinions as to future price level movements. For short-term obligations β estimates were strikingly close to 1 and they decreased as the remaining time to maturity increased. This is reasonable because the influence of short run expectations should decrease as the term to maturity increases and because expectations become more uncertain as the time horizon expands.

DEFAULT RISK. The yield formula of Equation 5.1 assumes that the investor actually receives interest payments I_t and maturity value P_n. But default may occur and investors will adjust the yield they require to reflect expected loss from default. This can be shown by changing the example that was used to illustrate Equation 5.1 so that a portfolio of 1000 bonds, issued in groups of 50 by 20 different firms, is purchased at a price of \$875,388. With an 8 percent coupon yielding 5 percent semiannually over ten remaining years to maturity, cash flows are therefore increased by a thousandfold over the earlier example:

$$875{,}388 = 40{,}000 \sum_{t=1}^{20} (1 + y)^{-t} + 1{,}000{,}000(1 + y)^{-20}, \qquad y = 0.05$$

If all promised payments are received the semiannual portfolio yield of 5.00 percent is the same as the yield for each of the individual bonds;[8] for this reason y is often referred to as the *promised yield.* If default occurs cash flows will decrease and yield will fall accordingly. Bondholders normally recover some part of any defaulted interest or principal payment but it is convenient here to assume that no recovery occurs. If one firm defaults on its 50 bonds after the tenth payment and another defaults after the nineteenth payment, with resulting losses of \$2,000.00 per period in interest and \$50,000.00 in maturity value in both cases, semiannual yield will decrease to 4.56 percent:

PV at 0.0456 of interest payments, \$36,000 for 20 periods	\$465,778
2,000 for 19 periods	25,058
2,000 for 10 periods	15,778
PV at 0.0456 of principal payment, 900,000 in period 20	368,774
	\$875,388

No one would purchase the bonds in question, at that price, if it were known that they would be defaulted. The bonds which defaulted in the nineteenth year realize a loss of 1.38 percent and those with a ten-year

[8] Portfolio yield, as it is used here, does not adjust for reinvestment in order to focus on the group of bonds as if they were a single security. The correct definition of portfolio yield, with reinvestment, was provided in Chapter 3.

default result in a loss of 12.18 percent.[9] But assume that it was known that 2 of the 20 issues would default, in precisely the pattern specified, but those specific securities could not be identified. If investors required a rate of return of 5 percent per semiannual period, the price they would be willing to pay for the entire portfolio would fall to \$827,463:

PV at 5 percent, 20 periods,	\$ 36,000 (12.4622)	\$448,639
, 19 periods,	2,000 (12.0853)	24,171
, 10 periods,	2,000 (7.7217)	15,443
PV at 5 percent, 20 periods later,	900,000 (0.3769)	339,210
		\$827,463

In this case *expected yield*, compounded semiannually, would be 10.25 percent but *promised yield* would be 11.18 percent:

$$827{,}463 = 40{,}000 \sum_{t=1}^{20} (1 + y)^{-t} + 1{,}000{,}000(1 + y)^{-20}, \qquad y = 0.0544,$$

and

$$(1.0544)(1.0544) = 1.1118$$

The difference between expected yield of 10.25 percent and promised yield of 11.18 percent, 93 basis points, is the default premium for this portfolio of bonds.

Default risk must be estimated and the estimation cannot be precise. It is impossible to predict the default of some part of a portfolio at some specified time, as the preceding example suggested. In practical terms default probability cannot be calculated with accuracy for any individual security. Instead, risk premiums are determined by market forces and they are quantified by grouping securities with similar risk characteristics so that "quality"—classified average yields can be calculated. Aaa and Baa corporate yields of Figure 5.1 are an example of this procedure. Quality ratings will be discussed in detail later, after this introduction to the concept of risk has been concluded.

INTEREST RATE RISK. Interest rate risk refers to the possibility that capital loss will result because of an increase in the level of interest rates; this is the major risk element for most investment grade debt securities. It can be

[9] The approximation of Equation 5.2 is accurate in the case of the bond defaulted in the nineteenth year but not for the one defaulted after ten years. For the former,

$$Y \approx \frac{40.00 + (1/19)(0.0 - 875.39)}{875.39/2}$$

$$\approx -.0139$$

When the same procedure is applied to the other defaulted bond, estimated yield is -10.86 percent, an error of 132 basis points.

Table 5.1
Bond Prices

	Annual Coupon Rate			
	8 Percent		10 Percent	
	Annual Market Yield		Annual Market Yield	
Maturity	*8 Percent*	*9 Percent*	*10 Percent*	*9 Percent*
1	\$1000.00	\$990.64	\$1000.00	\$1009.36
5	1000.00	960.44	1000.00	1039.57
10	1000.00	934.96	1000.00	1065.04
20	1000.00	907.99	1000.00	1092.01

illustrated by observing the impact of a change in interest rates on bonds with different coupon rates and maturities. For this purpose it will be assumed that four 8 percent coupon bonds, with maturities of 1, 5, 10, and 20 years, are purchased today at par. For purposes of comparison, yields will also be calculated for 10 percent bonds with the same maturities. Table 5.1 summarizes bond prices for all eight securities under the assumption that current yield levels of 8 and 10 percent, respectively, suddenly change to 9 percent. Calculations follow the methodology illustrated previously; for the ten-year, 8 percent bond, for example:

	8 Percent Yield	*9 Percent Yield*
PV of interest payments	40.00(13.5903) = 543.61	40.00(13.0079) = 520.32
PV of maturity value	1000.00(0.4564) = 456.39	1000.00(0.4146) = 414.64
	1000.00	934.96

Table 5.1 illustrates the relationship which exists among bond yield, price, and maturity. Price is inversely related to yield. As yield increases (decreases), price decreases (increases), with the magnitude of change positively related to maturity. For the 8 percent bond, a 1 percent increase in market yield caused a \$9.36 decrease in price for the 1-year maturity (\$1000.00 – \$990.64) and a \$92.01 decrease for the 20-year maturity (\$1000.00 – \$907.99).

The relationships illustrated in Table 5.1 are generalized in Figure 5.2 which extends the example over the entire range of maturities to 50 years; Figure 5.2 also graphs prices for the 8 percent bond at 7 percent and 10 percent market yields. From the price behavior pictured there:[10]

[10] The mathematics underlying Figure 5.2 are contained in Burton Malkiel, "Expectations, Bond Prices, and the Term Structure of Interest Rates," *Quarterly Journal of Economics*, May 1962, pp. 197–218.

Figure 5.2
Bond Prices, Yield, and Maturity

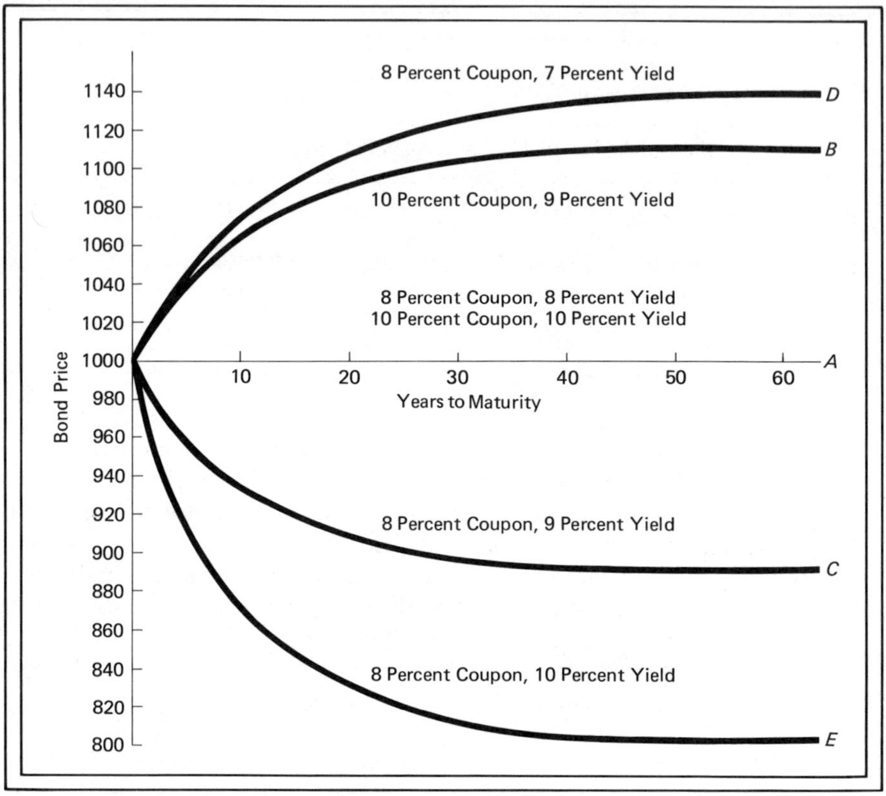

1. Bond prices move inversely to bond yields. When the coupon rate and market yield are equal, bond price is \$1000.00, along the horizontal axis *A*. As yield changes, bond price changes in the opposite direction.
2. For any given change in yield, bond price changes at a decreasing rate as maturity lengthens. This can be observed from the behavior of curves *B*, *C*, *D*, and *E* of Figure 5.2.
3. For any given market yield, price behavior is symmetric with respect to coupon rates; curves *B* and *C* with a 9 percent market yield and coupon rates of 10 and 8 percent, respectively, are mirror images. Low coupon bonds are more sensitive to a given change in yield than higher coupon bonds ($D - A > B - A$).
4. In contrast to (3), price behavior is asymmetric with respect to market yield, with the impact of a change in yield inversely related to the level of yield. For the 8 percent interest rates of curves *D*, *A*, *C*, and *E*, for example, the impact of a 1 percent change in yield is greatest from 7 to 8 percent ($D - A$), then from 8 to 9 percent ($A - C$), and it is smallest for a change from 9 to 10 percent ($C - E$).

Although bond prices may change in either direction, interest rate risk normally refers to the probability of *capital loss*. As shown above, potential

Table 5.2
Quality Ratings

Moody's		Standard & Poor's	
	Corporate Bonds		
Aaa	Best quality	AAA	Highest grade
Aa	High quality	AA	High grade
A	Upper medium grade	A	Upper medium grade
Baa	Medium grade	BBB	Medium grade
Ba	Speculative elements	BB	Lower medium grade
B	Desirable characteristics lacking	B	Speculative
Caa	Poor standing, possible default	CCC-CC	Outright speculative
Ca	Highly speculative, often in default	C	Income bonds
C	Lowest rated, poor	DDD-D	In default
	Preferred Stocks		
aaa	Top quality	AAA	Prime
aa	High grade	AA	High grade
a	Upper medium grade	A	Sound
baa	Lower medium grade	BBB	Medium grade
ba	Speculative elements	BB	Lower grade
b	Desirable characteristics lacking	B	Speculative
caa	Probably in arrears	C	Nonpaying

loss increases as the period to maturity increases and low coupon bonds are more sensitive to a given change in market yield than higher coupon bonds. The relationship among these variables is very important to bond managers. Interest rate risk is particularly relevant when market yields are relatively low and the prospect of a more restrictive monetary policy is suggested by current economic conditions.

Interest Rate Variations

QUALITY RATINGS

It is difficult, if not impossible, to measure default risk directly. For this reason investment rating services publish discrete "quality" ratings which provide their opinion as to the relative safety of corporate bonds, municipal bonds, and preferred stocks. Ratings are provided by Moody's Investors Services and Standard & Poor's.[11] Table 5.2 illustrates abbreviated rating categories for corporate bonds and preferred stocks; more complete descriptions can be found in services published by each of the firms.[12] Moody's and Standard & Poor's rating descriptions are roughly similar with respect to

[11] Moody's and Standard & Poor's also provide ratings for private placements, commercial paper, and debt issued by foreign governments. Another source, Fitch Investors Service, also publishes ratings and they are best known for their bank ratings.

[12] Quality classifications within rating categories (+ or −) are also commonly provided.

the higher grade categories but they differ for the lower grades. Although the firms operate independently, ratings for any particular security usually coincide. In 1975 Moody's rated 692 corporate issues and 1253 municipal issues while Standard & Poor's rated 470 corporates and 1440 municipals.[13] Revenues are realized from fees charged to firms and municipalities and from subscriptions to their several publications.

Securities are rated within discrete classifications but this does not imply homogeneity of default risk among issues with the same rating. Assume that all outstanding securities could be ranked with respect to default risk; by establishing cutoff points these securities could then be grouped by quality classes Aaa, Aa, and so on. But the most risky security in class Aaa would be more similar to the least risky security in class Aa than it would be to others in the higher Aaa category. Moreover, risk cannot be evaluated and ordered in that fashion; if that were possible quality ratings would be unnecessary. Instead, evaluation is a subjective process and ratings must be interpreted as a professional opinion concerning the relative safety of any particular security.

On average yield tends to vary inversely by rating category, with the lowest yields observed for "high-grade" investments and the highest yields observed for "low-grade" investments. Yields for individual securities will differ from yields for other issues in the same rating category, for reasons discussed above. Figure 5.1 suggests a yield differential ranging from 50 to 100 basis points, on average, between Aaa and Baa ratings during the period 1968–1976. At times yield differences can be even larger; during 1976, for example, the yield differential between adjacent Aa and A categories ranged from 25 to 100 basis points for newly issued securities.

Default risk for any given security may change over time and ratings will be upgraded or downgraded periodically as circumstances dictate. The number of rating changes increased dramatically during the 1970s with better than 750 reclassifications in 1974 in contrast to approximately 200 changes in 1969. But existing evidence suggests that reclassification is anticipated by the market, with security prices responding accordingly; thus there is little reason to believe that a strategy of portfolio adjustment based upon announced changes will be profitable. This is plausible because the bond market is dominated by large institutions with information-processing capacity which provides an opportunity to evaluate trends in risk determinants before they reach a sufficient magnitude to justify a rating change.

Quality ratings are determined subjectively on the basis of both qualitative and quantitative factors relating to the probability of default. These factors include the following:

1. LEVEL AND STABILITY OF EARNINGS. Risk is minimized when the issuer is able to generate sufficient funds internally to satisfy contractual obliga-

[13] *The Wall Street Journal*, October 26, 1976, p. 37.

tions. The probability of default is small when the stream of earnings is large enough and stable enough to support the stream of interest and principal payments. For this reason quality ratings tend to increase as earnings increase and earnings variability decreases.

While there are many measures of profitability, the most important, in this respect, is the earnings coverage ratio. For debt coverage this is defined as the ratio of earnings before interest and taxes (EBIT) to interest expense. For preferred stock, because dividends are not tax deductible, dividends are divided by the complement of the tax rate $(1 - t_x)$ to place them on the same basis as tax deductible interest. Rules of thumb are often used to specify minimum coverage ratios within industry groups and these minimums are defined differently for average years and "poor" years. Although it is difficult to evaluate the relevance of rules of thumb, interest coverage ranging from 5 to 7 is usually required for industrial corporations with high-grade ratings. Coverage ratios focus on relative profitability and adoption of a range of values adjusts for earnings instability.

2. LIQUIDITY. Default occurs when the issuer of a security is unable to meet current commitments, including debt service requirements. For this reason default risk decreases as liquidity increases. Quality ratings tend to improve as liquidity increases and risk classification tends to be positively correlated with the current ratio, acid test ratio, receivables turnover, and other familiar measures of current solvency.

3. FINANCIAL LEVERAGE. Financial leverage refers to the proportion of assets financed by debt relative to the proportion financed by common stock. As financial leverage increases, a given earnings stream must support increasingly larger commitments for debt servicing. Thus default risk increases as leverage increases. For this reason leverage ratios are inversely related to quality ratings and an increase in the debt-equity ratio, for example, may lead to a decrease in the quality rating for any security in question.

4. CONTRACTUAL PROVISIONS. The indenture (contract) which establishes the legal relationship among issuer and borrowers may contain provisions which affect the security's quality rating. Some indentures require that the issuer establish a *sinking fund* through periodic deposits of cash prior to maturity; at maturity sinking fund assets are available to satisfy the obligation to repay the principal amount borrowed. The existence of a sinking fund is generally considered to reduce the risk of default and this should favorably influence a security's quality rating.[14]

[14] Cash which is deposited in a sinking fund is unavailable for general corporate purposes. Since sinking fund assets typically consist of low-risk securities with relatively low rates of return, long-run profitability is thereby adversely affected. Because the stream of profits supports debt service payments, it can be argued that a sinking fund requirement *increases* default risk in the long run.

At times one debt issue will rank behind other unsecured issues of the same firm with respect to claims against assets in the event of liquidation. Holders of these *subordinated* bonds would receive settlement in default only in the event that all other secured and unsecured creditors were paid their full claim. Quality ratings for subordinated bonds are typically low, usually less than the Baa group which is generally defined as the lowest category of "investment grade" bonds.

The factors listed above, and others which rating agencies may use, can be measured quantitatively. For this reason there have been a number of attempts to explain bond ratings with statistical models.[15] Pinches and Mingo, for example, were successful in correctly classifying the quality rating for 70 percent of a sample of 132 bonds with a model employing six explanatory variables: (1) number of years of consecutive cash dividends (stability), (2) size of the issue (marketability), (3) five-year average coverage ratio, (4) five-year average debt to net worth ratio (leverage), (5) ratio of income to assets (profitability), and (6) a dummy statistical variable with a value of zero or one to measure whether the issue is or is not subordinated.[16] Other studies used similar specifications. Together they provide impressive empirical evidence which supports the relevance of the rating determinants discussed above.

Although statistical models have been successful in *explaining* rating determinants, it is not clear that they can be used for *predicting* bond ratings. First, long-run forecasting requires a stability over time in statistical values which has not been observed. Predictive models must be revised and updated regularly and their relevance for other than short-run forecasting becomes very questionable.[17] Second, it is known that rating agencies rely on interviews and other factors which cannot be specified quantitatively. Third, predictive models perform worst in the case of adjacent rating categories. It is easier to distinguish between Aaa and Baa than it is to distinguish between A and Baa when models are applied to individual securities. The

[15] The earliest study of this type was Lawrence Fisher, "Determinants of Risk Premiums on Corporate Bonds," *Journal of Political Economy*, June 1959, pp. 217–237. Also see James O. Horrigan, "The Determination of Long-Term Credit Standing with Financial Ratios," *Empirical Research in Accounting: Selected Studies*, 1966; Supplement to *Journal of Accounting Research* (1966): 44–62; Thomas F. Pogue and Robert M. Soldofsky, "What's in a Bond Rating," *Journal of Financial and Quantitative Analysis*, June 1969, pp. 201–228; Richard R. West, "An Alternative Approach to Predicting Corporate Bond Ratings," *Journal of Accounting Research*, Spring 1970, pp. 118–127.

[16] George E. Pinches and Kent A. Mingo, "A Multivariate Analysis of Industrial Bond Ratings," *Journal of Finance*, March 1973, pp. 1–18.

[17] George E. Pinches, Kent A. Mingo, and J. Kent Caruthers, "The Stability of Financial Patterns in Industrial Organizations," *Journal of Finance*, May 1973, pp. 389–396, and James S. Ang and K. A. Patel, "Bond Rating Methods: Comparison and Validation," *Journal of Finance*, May 1975, pp. 631–640. Pinches and Singleton argued that the bond rating lag is more extensive; they found that changes in the financial and operating conditions of firms are fully realized by stock market investors from 6 to 18 months before bond ratings are changed by the rating agency. Thus rating changes are not an important signal to investors. George Pinches and J. C. Singleton. "The Adjustment of Stock Prices to Bond Rating Changes," *Journal of Finance*, March 1978, pp. 29–44.

latter comparison, of course, is the critical one for the portfolio manager. Finally, a predictive model is most useful when it can be applied in forecasting a *change* in rating as contrasted to the *level* of that rating. To this time formal statistical models have been relatively unsuccessful in predicting rating changes.

Statistical models cannot be applied mechanically to the forecasting of bond ratings or rating changes. But this does not minimize the contribution of the many studies which have isolated rating determinants. Analysts studying trends in those variables, relative to trends in other firms within industry groupings, subjectively identify securities which are candidates for a rating change. For electric utilities, for example, quantitative factors are evaluated in the light of regulatory environment and the adequacy of fuel supplies. In this fashion bond portfolios are adjusted and prices respond in anticipation of rating changes which are likely to occur subsequently.

Published quality ratings are generally believed to be very accurate but there is little evidence available to settle the question one way or the other. Safety is a long-run concept and accuracy can be evaluated only by observing defaults over an extended time period. Hickman studied default records for corporate issues from 1900 to 1943 and his results suggest that rating services were highly accurate during that period.[18] The number of defaults which have occurred since the end of World War II is not large enough to evaluate rating accuracy currently.

Quality ratings are subjective and their accuracy cannot be proven or disproven. At the same time, ratings affect the yields on existing securities and they have an important impact on the ability of an issuer to raise new funds in the debt market. As a result, rating agencies have been subjected to increasing criticism in both the investment community and in Congress. When Moody's lowered the rating for New York State Municipal Assistance Corporation (MAC) bonds from A to B in May of 1976, prices of MAC bonds fell sharply. MAC threatened to sue Moody's, a threat which never materialized, and a bill was subsequently introduced in Congress which would allow the Securities and Exchange Commission to order reclassification whenever it believed a rating to be incorrect. This particular legislation was never enacted but the threat of congressional intervention remains and it is likely to remain until such time as the accuracy of quality ratings can be firmly established or rejected.

YIELD AND MATURITY

Yield varies with risk but it also varies with the length of time until maturity. Bonds which are similar in every respect except the date on which they mature may have significantly different market yields. This is illustrated in Figure 5.3 where yields for U.S. Treasury obligations on May 29, 1975, are

[18] W. Braddock Hickman, *Corporate Bond Quality and Investor Experience* (New York: National Bureau of Economic Research, 1958), p. 10.

Figure 5.3
Yield on U.S. Government Securities (May 29, 1975)

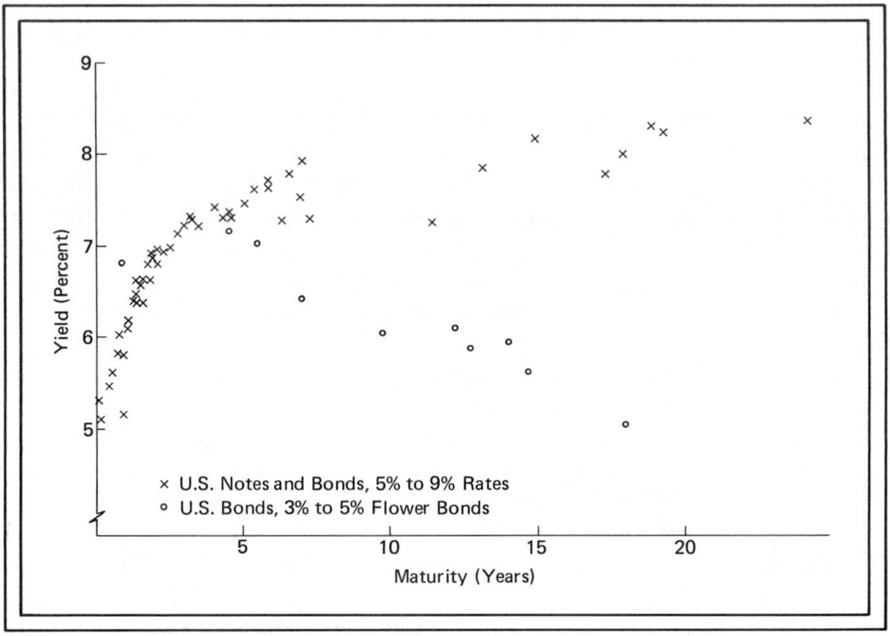

plotted against maturity. Except for some so-called "flower bonds" which are redeemable at par for estate tax purposes, the pattern of yields tends to increase as maturity lengthens. (Flower bonds will be described more fully later in the chapter.)

The upward-sloping yield curve of Figure 5.3 is the most common pattern observed although negative slopes and "humped" patterns occur from time to time. In part the behavior of yields reflects interest rate risk but the relationship between yield and maturity is more complicated than that. It has been studied theoretically and empirically and these studies are usually classified under the general expression "the term structure of interest rates." Theories which have been advanced to explain the type of yield variation traced in Figure 5.3 are examined in detail in the appendix to this chapter.

INTEREST RATE FORECASTING

Interest rate forecasting is an integral element in bond portfolio management. It is a difficult problem which cannot be resolved through the mechanical application of any "magic formula." Instead, analysts must evaluate the impact and interaction of macroeconomic forces in assessing probable

Figure 5.4
Consumer Price Index and Aaa Corporate Yield

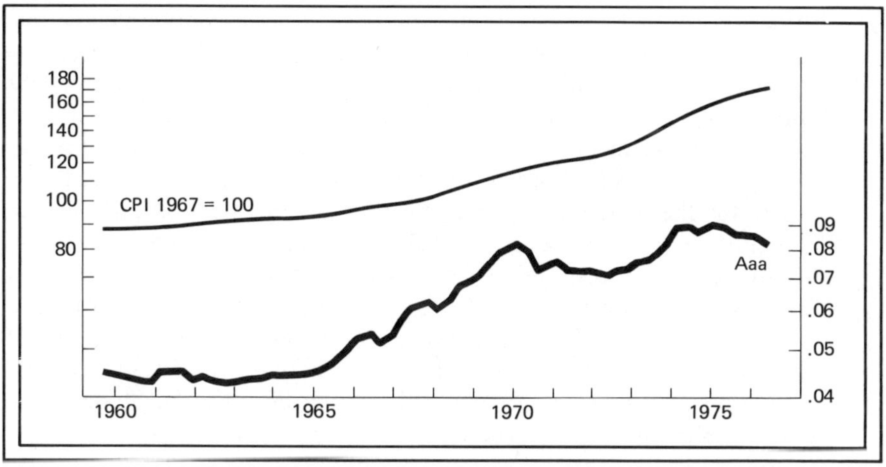

changes in interest rates. An accurate forecast typically involves an estimate of the *direction* of change and possibly a rough approximation of the *magnitude* of change; precise forecasts have proven to be elusive. Major determinants include (1) the rate of inflation, (2) the level of business activity, and (3) the rate of change in the money supply. Interrelationships among these variables are too complex to be developed here satisfactorily but basic relationships can be summarized.

RATE OF INFLATION. One of the most critical determinants of the monetary rate of interest is the expectations of investors as to the rate of inflation. Figure 5.4 traces the consumer price index and the quarterly average yield on Aaa corporate bonds from 1960 through 1976. Association between the two series is evident even with casual inspection. Bond yields moved from approximately 4.5 percent in 1965 to a peak of almost 9 percent in 1974; during the same period the consumer price index rose from 95 to 150, an annual average increase of 5.2 percent.

The relationship that exists among nominal interest rates and the rate of inflation has been demonstrated in a number of papers, including the work of Gibson which was discussed earlier when inflation risk was introduced.[19] Analysts who expect an increase in the rate of inflation will also expect interest rates to rise. It is very possible that the *real* rate of interest has changed little since the 1950s; most of the increase in nominal rates observed since then can probably be attributed to price level changes.

[19] A recent paper studies the rate of interest as a predictor for the rate of inflation. See E. Fama, "Short-Term Interest Rates as Predictors of Inflation," *American Economic Review*, June 1975, pp. 269–282.

BUSINESS ACTIVITY. Figure 5.4 traces an upward trend for interest rates since 1966, but cyclical variations about that trend are also evident. The business cycle affects the rate of savings and the rate of demand for funds. In periods of prosperity economic activity increases and added demand for money results in higher interest rates; during recession, as activity decreases, lessened credit demand depresses interest rates. In this fashion the behavior of the economy affects the level of interest rates.

Some analysts have attempted to forecast interest rates by forecasting aggregate sources and uses of funds. "Flow of funds" data, which are published by the Federal Reserve, provide a starting point for forecasting monetary supply and demand in all financial sectors. Imbalance in any sector suggests a corresponding change in interest rates; if excess demand is forecast for the mortgage sector, for example, an increase in mortgage yield is implied. Flow of funds analysis became very popular in the 1950s but analysts currently view it as only one of a number of tools available for predicting interest rates. In part this results because the model requires a number of comprehensive sectoral projections which are themselves subject to forecasting error. It also requires assumptions as to Federal Reserve policy in adjusting the money supply as well as U.S. Treasury policy in financing government deficits. In 1975, for example, federal, state, and local governments accounted for better than half of the total new funds raised in financial markets in the United States; this was in sharp contrast to 1973 and 1974 when government required only 20 and 25 percent, respectively. Error in forecasting government deficits and assumptions as to debt management and fiscal policy can result in serious error in sectoral flow of funds forecasts.

The interrelationship among macroeconomic variables has also been analyzed with complex computer programs consisting of hundreds of equations which attempt to model the economy.[20] These aggregate models have been fairly successful in predicting the *level* of short-run and long-run interest rates. Some forecasts are available by subscription at a price which is relatively inexpensive in view of the cost of constructing, maintaining, and operating the program. Macroeconomic models will be considered in greater detail in Chapter 9.

MONEY SUPPLY. Monetary policy influences both the level and the term structure of interest rates. For example, during the 1974–1975 recession the Federal Reserve System increased the money supply through open market operations and by reducing the discount rate which banks pay to borrow from the Federal Reserve. By supplying reserves to banks, downward pressure was exerted on the federal funds rate and this pressure was then transmitted to other short-term rates. Thus the immediate effect of expansionary

[20] Among the models which have been followed widely are the Federal Reserve Board–MIT model, the Brookings–Social Science Research model, and the University of Pennsylvania Wharton EFA model.

monetary policy was a decrease in short-term interest rates; the federal funds rate, which had been as high as 13.5 percent during the summer of 1974, had fallen to 7 percent during the first part of 1975. But monetary growth, if it is excessive, will increase inflationary expectations, exerting upward pressure on long-term interest rates in the process. Monetary supply and demand clearly impacts on the level of interest rates but the mechanism is complicated and any precise formulation of the relationship remains elusive. There is persuasive evidence to support the argument that the major determinant of long-term interest rates is the expected rate of inflation.

Bonds

Bonds are debt instruments which provide a contractual obligation on the part of the borrower to repay the face value together with a stream of interest payments, during the period to maturity or retirement. Bonds are owned by private pension funds, life insurance companies, fire and casualty companies, mutual funds, households, personal trusts, and nonprofit organizations. These fixed income securities have grown increasingly attractive recently as stock market volatility has encouraged both individual and institutional investors to seek the relatively safer return they promise. According to Federal Reserve flow of funds data, for example, pension funds invested $2.3 billion in common stocks and $4.7 billion in bonds in 1974; in 1972 funds had sold bonds in order to buy common stocks. Similar increases were observed for insurance companies and even for the household sector which became a net buyer of bonds in 1975, reversing a sales pattern which had existed for an extended number of years.

Bonds are issued by the United States government and several of its agencies, by state and local governments and foreign governments, and by private corporations.

U.S. GOVERNMENT SECURITIES

The major portion of the national debt is financed with marketable U.S. Treasury bills, certificates of indebtedness, notes, and bonds. Treasury securities are virtually free of default risk but they are subject to both inflation risk and interest rate risk. Interest payments are taxed as ordinary income but the difference between cost and selling price (or maturity value) is taxed under capital gains provisions of the Internal Revenue Code; interest received from treasury securities is not subject to state or local income taxes. New issues can be purchased through any of the Federal Reserve's 12 banks or 24 branches; small orders (*noncompetitive tenders*) will be sold at an average price determined after competitive bids are received. Outstanding issues can be acquired through a commercial bank or brokerage firm.

TREASURY BILLS. Treasury bills are highly liquid short-term obligations originally issued with maturities of 13, 26, or 52 weeks. Bills are issued and traded on a discount basis; income is the difference between purchase price and maturity value. A 13-week "T-bill" with a face value of $10,000 will yield a quarterly return of 2.04 percent if it is issued at 98 (200/9800 = 0.0204). Treasury bills are usually issued weekly.

TREASURY NOTES. Treasury notes are interest-bearing obligations originally issued for maturities ranging from one to seven years. Face value has varied from $1,000 to $10,000, depending on conditions in the mortgage industry. In August of 1974, for example, an offering of a 9 percent, $1,000 note received a heavy response from individual investors. During that same month the outflow of funds from savings institutions reached a record monthly level of $837 million and the treasury restored the $10,000 minimum one month later. In October of 1974 the $1,000 denomination was restored despite severe criticism from mortgage bankers.

CERTIFICATES OF INDEBTEDNESS. These are a less familiar obligation with characteristics representing a compromise between bills and notes. Maturity is usually 12 months or so but the securities are issued with a par value and they carry fixed interest rates.

TREASURY BONDS. Treasury bonds are long-term obligations, ranging in maturity up to 40 years, with fixed interest payments during the interval. They are backed by the United States government and they are considered to be risk-free in the sense of default risk. Treasury bonds are often described as if they shared homogeneous features, but differences in coupon rate, maturity, call provision, and estate tax treatment require that the details of each issue be studied separately. Some treasury bonds are callable prior to maturity; yields for these bonds are calculated to first call date rather than to maturity.[21] Complete descriptions of bond features can be found in published services available in most libraries.

A limited number of bonds maturing at different intervals through November of 1998 are redeemable at par plus accrued interest for estate tax purposes, whatever their acquisition price. The tax advantage of these "flower bonds" was reduced by the Tax Reform Act of 1976 and future issues are prohibited by law. Nevertheless, yields on flower bonds, with low coupon rates ranging from 3.25 to 4.50 percent, have deviated markedly from yields for other long-term treasury bonds.

FEDERAL AGENCY SECURITIES. Certain federal agencies issue bonds which are not technically guaranteed by the United States government. These agencies include the Central Bank for Cooperatives, Federal Home Loan Banks, Federal Intermediate Credit Bank, Federal Land Banks, Federal National

[21] The call provision, and the disadvantage it carries for investors, will be considered later when corporate bonds are discussed.

Mortgage Association (Fannie Mae), Government National Mortgage Association (Ginnie Mae), and the Postal Service. Yields on these securities tend to exceed yields on long-term treasury bonds although coupon and maturity differences make it difficult to specify differentials precisely. Moreover, default seems to be a remote possibility since the federal government is unlikely politically or economically to allow it to occur.

MUNICIPAL BONDS

Municipal bonds refer to a large variety of obligations issued by state and local governments and their agencies, authorities, municipal corporations, and colleges and universities. Interest on municipal securities is exempt from federal income tax and they are attractive investments for institutions and individuals in a high tax bracket.[22] Municipal default risk is especially difficult to evaluate because of generally inadequate disclosure of accounting information and the uncertainties involved in political decisions which affect municipal financing.

CLASSIFICATION. Municipal bonds are usually classified as either (1) *general obligation* or (2) *revenue*; in 1976, 64 percent of all outstanding municipal bonds were of the general variety. General obligation bonds are backed by the promise of a government unit with the authority to raise necessary funds by taxing property and income. Analysts sometimes evaluate risk for this type of municipal security by calculating debt–assessed value, per capita debt, and debt service–operating expense ratios. Unfortunately, comparative standards are difficult to specify. There is normally little relationship between assessed and market value, for example, and per capita debt varies widely by geographical location. In the final analysis, security exists in the ability and willingness of municipal officers to generate needed funds and this implies that each issue must be analyzed separately in light of trends in revenue and expense streams.

Revenue bonds are secured by the revenue generated from the specific properties financed by those securities. They have been widely used in the construction of roads, public utilities, sewage systems, and other works managed by municipal authorities. Analysts usually evaluate project coverage ratios although minimum standards are generally lower than corporate standards. Again, it is very difficult to select a yardstick against which coverage ratios can be evaluated.

TAXATION. Interest on municipal debt is exempt from federal income tax but capital gains and losses are not. For an investor in the 20 percent tax

[22] Under the doctrine of reciprocal immunity, which dates back to the time of President George Washington, interest on government securities is similarly exempt from state and local taxes. State and local authorities may tax interest payments on the obligations of other state and local government units.

bracket, a current yield of 7.2 percent on municipal bonds is equivalent to a current yield of 9 percent on taxable bonds; similarly, an investor in the 60 percent bracket is indifferent between a 3.6 percent municipal yield and a 9 percent taxable yield. The equalizing tax rate for current corporate y_c and municipal yield y_m, assuming the same risk, is:[23]

$$\begin{aligned} T_m &= \frac{y_c - y_m}{y_c} \\ &= \frac{0.09 - 0.036}{0.09} \\ &= 0.60 \end{aligned} \tag{5.6}$$

The spread between current municipal yield and comparable corporate yield increases as the effective tax bracket of investors increases.

Yield to maturity includes, in addition to current yield, the capital gain or loss which is realized when the security is either sold or surrendered at maturity. Capital gains on municipal securities are taxable under provisions of the Internal Revenue Code. For this reason, low coupon–deep discount municipal bonds are at a relative tax disadvantage when compared to higher coupon municipals which are priced closer to par value. This relative disadvantage is partially offset because capital gains are deferred until the period in which the gain is realized. Nonetheless, the municipal bond tax advantage implied by Equation 5.6 is limited when capital gain is a significant part of yield-to-maturity.

DEFAULT RISK. Municipal obligations are subject to default risk which is often difficult to evaluate. According to one source, 435 defaults occurred between 1940 and 1969; during the 1930s it was estimated that 15 percent of outstanding municipal debt was defaulted.[24] The severe financial difficulties encountered by New York City, which have received widespread attention since 1975, decreased investors' confidence in the safety of municipal securities and temporarily depressed prices broadly and generally in that market.

Municipal default risk is more difficult to analyze than corporate default risk. In the first place, government accounting procedures are far less standardized than corporate procedures. Actual cash expenditures may be matched against accrued revenue anticipations; federal grants may be commingled with other funds; current expenditures may be financed through long-term obligations, as occurred in New York; and substantial unfunded pension commitments need not be reflected in municipal accounts. Moreover, intensive disclosure is not required by the Securities and Exchange

[23] See Edward Shapiro, "The Absolute Level of Bond Yields and the Corporate-Municipal Differential," *Nebraska Journal of Economics and Business*, Summer 1970, pp. 3–13.

[24] Estimated by MGIC Indemnity Corporation, as reported by *The Wall Street Journal*, June 23, 1975, p. 16.

Table 5.3
Purchasers of New Municipal Issues (percentage)

	1965–1970	*1974–1975*
Commercial banks	64	26
Property and casualty insurance companies	11	15
Individuals	24	50
Others	1	9
	100	100

Source: Rodney Johnson, "A Fresh Look at the Municipal Bond Market," *Business Review*, Federal Reserve Bank of Philadelphia, July–August 1976, p. 12.

Commission, as it is in the corporate sector, and the process of obtaining available information is often very costly. Legislation was introduced in December 1977, to extend disclosure requirements to municipal securities; data will probably be more available in the future.

Default ratings are available for a number of municipal issues but accounting and disclosure deficiencies hamper professional analysts as well as individual investors. In the case of New York City bonds, for example, ratings were not downgraded immediately in response to widespread adverse publicity concerning the city's financial difficulties in 1975.[25] Municipal bond insurance is available for some issues and some individual portfolios; the yield on insured portfolios is reduced by the cost of insurance which varies with such factors as credit rating and coupon level.[26]

INVESTORS. The new-issues municipal market was dominated by commercial banks until very recently when individual investors, including trusts and nonprofit institutions, assumed that role. The increased availability of tax shelters for commercial banks, particularly the growth of tax-sheltered leasing arrangements, reduced their motivation to acquire municipal obligations. As shown in Table 5.3, banks, which had accounted for almost two-thirds of the activity during 1965–1970, accounted for only 26 percent during 1974–1975. The market share for property and casualty companies has varied with conditions in the stock market but it has been relatively stable over an extended time period. Individual investors have become the major force in the primary municipal market; yields on municipal securities

[25] See Rodney Johnson, "A Fresh Look at the Municipal Bond Market," *Business Review*, Federal Reserve Bank of Philadelphia, July–August 1976, pp. 18–20.

[26] Municipal bond guarantee insurance is offered in limited circumstances by federal and state governments and by a number of private carriers. The Mutual Bond Insurance Corporation, a consortium formed by four insurers in 1973, offers limited coverage to certain municipalities excluding most large city issues. Coverage is also available from MGIC Indemnity Corporation; in addition, MGIC provides selective coverage for individual portfolios in minimum amounts of $50,000.

have increased since 1962 (see Figure 5.1) partly in response to the decreased demand on the part of banks and the need to attract individuals with lower marginal tax rates.

Individual investors have also dominated the secondary municipal market recently, largely because of "tax swaps." A tax swap is a transaction in which a bond is sold at a substantial loss and the proceeds are used to purchase another bond which differs from the first by coupon rate, maturity, and/or the issuing municipality. Realized losses are then used to offset an investor's realized capital gains, resulting in a substantial tax savings after brokerage costs. During late 1975, for example, it was estimated that tax swaps accounted for 60 to 70 percent of the volume of trades in the secondary municipal market.

CORPORATE BONDS

Corporate bonds were a major source of external financing for firms during the 1970s although a large number of issues were privately placed, primarily through direct sale to life insurance companies. In 1976 38.9 percent of the approximately $40 billion of new corporate debt issues were privately placed as compared to 25.2 percent in 1975.[27] The legal document which sets forth all conditions of any bond offering is the *indenture agreement.* Public offerings generally involve a large number of bondholders and the responsibility for enforcing the terms of the indenture agreement therefore rests with a *bond trustee.* The trustee is usually a commercial bank which was selected by the issuing corporation. The trustee makes interest and principal payments directly from the corporate account and maintains a record of all bondholders. Almost all recently issued U.S. corporate bonds are registered to the owners and payments are remitted directly when they are due. Some older bearer bonds are still outstanding, however, and, as the name suggests, there is no record of ownership and they are subject to the risk of loss or theft.

The most important characteristics of corporate yields have been detailed previously: yield varies with coupon rate and maturity (term structure) and with default risk (quality ratings). Other characteristics also affect corporate bond yields.

CALL PROVISION. Some bonds may be called by the issuing corporation at prices determined at the time the bonds were issued. If current yields are substantially lower than the interest rate on outstanding bonds, it is profitable for a corporation to refund the issue by calling in the outstanding bonds, financing the transaction with the proceeds from a new issue at the lower current yield. Thus the call provision is disadvantageous to investors because of the potential loss involved in reinvesting proceeds from a called

[27] Securities and Exchange Commission, *Statistical Bulletin* 36, no. 3, (March 1977): 23.

issue at reduced yield levels. In effect, the call price is a ceiling value which limits price increases arising from falling interest rates. Investors will require a call premium to compensate for call risk. Twenty-five basis points is sometimes used as a rule-of-thumb measure for this risk but the premium is difficult to measure and it varies from time to time as bond market conditions change. It is customary to calculate yield-to-first-call date, in lieu of yield-to-maturity, particularly when current yields are high relative to historical values.

During periods of tight money, as in 1969–1972, corporations provided deferred call provisions to attract investors' savings. This is a binding promise not to call an issue within some specified period, typically five to ten years. Securities issued during 1969–1972 at unusually high yields are especially subject to call risk because falling interest rates anytime during the next few years will be a strong inducement to corporations to refund outstanding debt.

SECURITY. Some bonds are secured by specific assets which are pledged to protect promised principal and interest payments. Although collateral is attractive to investors, it probably affects yield only modestly since proceeds under bankruptcy are seldom more than a small fraction of the defaulted value. The best protection for an investor is the continued solvency and liquidity of the firm; the unsecured bonds of a stable and successful corporation are less risky than the secured bonds of a financially distressed company.

A *mortgage bond* is an issue secured by a lien on buildings or other real property. Some mortgage bonds have an *after-acquired clause* which pledges property acquired after the mortgage was issued. *Second mortgage bonds* have claims against property which are effective after first mortgage bondholders have been satisfied. *Collateral trust bonds* are secured by bonds and stocks issued by other corporations; for the most part collateral trust bonds are issued by holding companies. *Equipment trust certificates* are secured by railroad and airline equipment in what is essentially a lease transaction; title passes from the leasing trustee to the corporation after a number of fixed payments have provided for interest and amortization of the principal balance.

Debenture bonds are obligations without specific collateral which are backed by the general credit of the corporation. *Subordinated debentures* have claims in liquidation which will be discharged only after claims of debenture holders have been satisfied; because of the risk implied, these securities typically have low quality ratings and B is not unusual for a subordinated debenture. Another category, income bonds, will be discussed when preferred stock is considered.

Bonds are also classified by the manner of their retirement. *Sinking fund bonds* provide for periodic payments to a fund, administered by a trustee, where the fund is used to retire bonds through exercise of the call provision, open market purchase, or satisfaction at maturity. *Serial bonds* are divided into groups or series, with each series maturing at a different time; for example, one-tenth of a serial issue may mature during each of the last 10 years of a 20-year bond.

Mortgages

Mortgages on residential and commercial property have become an important investment opportunity for institutions and individual investors. Qualified residential loans may be insured by the Federal Housing Authority (FHA) or the Veterans Administration (VA); a noninsured loan is called a *conventional* mortgage. Insured mortgages are free of default risk, except for some legal and accounting costs, but they are subject to the potentially severe inflation risk associated with a 20- to 30-year fixed commitment. For this reason, proposals for a *variable rate mortgage* have become very numerous recently; this is a mortgage where monthly payments rise or fall as interest rates rise or fall. Some form of variable payment mortgage seems certain to be introduced in the near future.[28] Finally, the introduction of *mortgage-backed bonds*, obligations where mortgages are pooled and the issuer passes through principal and interest payments to bondholders, has increased the availability of mortgage investments to private investors.

YIELD AND VALUE

The yield on an individual mortgage y_p depends upon its contract rate r, maturity n, the period in which it is prepaid p, all expressed as monthly values, and the number of discount points d, expressed as a percentage. Discount points are a device used by lenders to increase mortgage yield to some value in excess of the contract rate. When a mortgage is issued at 2 points, for example, 98 percent of the face value of the mortgage is loaned but 100 percent is repaid through constant monthly payments which provide interest and amortize principal over the life of the loan to maturity. In the absence of discount points, yield equals the contract rate; as the discount increases, yield increases accordingly.

The mortgage yield equation is a simple variant of the general analytical model of Equation 3.8. For each dollar loaned,

$$1 - d = \frac{R}{(1 + y_p)^1} + \frac{R}{(1 + y_p)^2} + \cdots + \frac{R}{(1 + y_p)^n} + \frac{B_p}{(1 + y_p)^n} \tag{5.7}$$

where R is the monthly payment and B_p is the outstanding balance when the loan is prepaid after p months. Using compound interest relationships dis-

[28] Throughout 1976, the 4000 federally chartered savings and loan associations were prohibited from issuing variable-rate mortgages but growing pressure for this type of contract suggested a change in these regulations. Four associations chartered by the State of California adopted variable rate plans early in 1975.

cussed in the present value appendix at the back of the book, the equation can be restated:[29]

$$1 - d = \frac{r}{1 - (1 + r)^n} \sum_{t=1}^{p} (1 + y_p)^{-t} + \frac{1 - (1 + r)^{-(n-p)}}{1 - (1 + r)^{-n}} (1 + y_p)^{-p} \qquad (5.8)$$

Equation 5.8 may seem formidable at first, but careful inspection shows that the first term on the right-hand side is the present value of the stream of monthly payments and the second term is the present value of the outstanding balance at prepayment. More importantly, yield is expressed in terms of four variables of which three (contract rate, maturity, and discount points) are known and fixed when the loan is originated. In the case of FHA- and VA-insured loans, yield is then a function of the one remaining variable, the prepayment period.

These relationships are illustrated in Figure 5.5 in the case of a 30-year, 8.5 percent mortgage issued at either 2 or 12 discount points; annual yield shown there is compounded from monthly yields calculated by trial and error from Equation 5.8. The relationship among discount points, prepayment period, and yield is very important because yield is clearly sensitive to the other two. The prepayment period is unknown at the time the mortgage is originated and it must be estimated. Many lenders use the rule of thumb that average prepayment occurs at 40 percent of maturity; a 30-year mortgage, for example, will be assumed to be prepaid after 12 years. Given this estimate, yield y_p can also be estimated.

The relationship between yield and prepayment period is obviously nonlinear and the use of an average prepayment period biases the estimate of yield. A mortgage which is prepaid five years less than the average lifetime has a greater positive impact on yield than the negative impact when it is prepaid five years later than average. This results because of the compound interest effect of realizing capital gain on a discounted loan; as the prepayment period increases, the impact of discount points decreases at a decreasing rate. A conceptually correct methodology which adjusts for the entire distribution of termination probabilities was developed by Curley and Guttentag but their empirical tests suggest that the bias in the rule-of-thumb methodology has been very modest.[30] For this reason, and pending the development of a more accurate model for forecasting prepayment, mortgage yield can be estimated with the average life assumption.

Mortgage value can be calculated by reversing the process of Equations 5.7 and 5.8; desired yield y_p is inserted in the equation and price $(1 - d)$

[29] The derivation of Equation 5.8 can be found in Anthony J. Curley and Jack M. Guttentag, "The Yield on Insured Residential Mortgages," *Explorations in Economic Research*, Summer 1974, pp. 116–117.

[30] Curley and Guttentag, "Yield on Insured Residential Mortgages."

Figure 5.5
Effective Yield on a 30-Year, 8.5 percent Mortgage

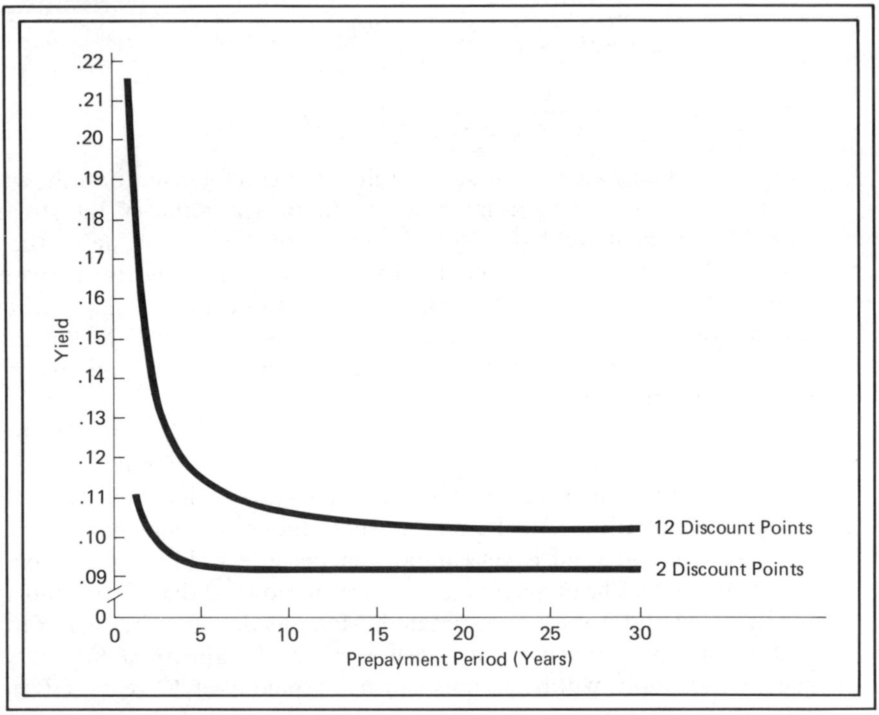

Source: A. J. Curley and Jack Guttentag, "The Yield on Insured Residential Mortgages," *Explorations in Economic Research* 1, no. 1 (Summer 1974): 119. Reprinted by permission of the National Bureau of Economic Research.

is then solved. The difficulty introduced by use of an average prepayment period is present again but, unlike yield estimation, value is very sensitive to variation in prepayment probability.[31] Unfortunately, a satisfactory predictive model for mortgage prepayments has yet to be developed and tested. An efficient and operational mortgage value model is the focus of continuing research. In the interim, crude estimates based upon Equation 5.7 continue to be used for that purpose.

MORTGAGE-BACKED BONDS

The efforts of the federal government to increase the flow of funds to the mortgage sector has increased the availability of mortgage investments for institutions and individuals. The Federal National Mortgage Association,

[31] See Anthony J. Curley and Jack M. Guttentag, "Value and Yield Risk on Outstanding Insured Residential Mortgages," *Journal of Finance*, May 1977, pp. 403–412.

commonly referred to as Fannie Mae (FNMA), is a government-sponsored private corporation which issues bonds and uses the proceeds to purchase FHA- and VA-insured mortgages. Since 1970, FNMA has also been allowed to buy conventional mortgages. FNMA acts as a "market maker" in the secondary mortgage market, buying and selling mortgages to smooth cyclical trends. FNMA bonds, available through most brokerage firms and relatively free of default risk, have yields which are somewhat higher than U.S. Treasury obligations.

With the expanded scope of FNMA operations in 1970, a new agency, the Government National Mortgage Association or Ginnie Mae (GNMA), was formed to increase residential financing through FHA- and VA-insured loans and to promote a number of other government programs. GNMA purchases mortgages from lenders who have financed home purchases. Mortgages are then grouped by similar characteristics, most importantly by the interest rate, and groups are either sold individually or they are used to back a security where interest and principal payments are "passed through" to investors. GNMA pass-through securities are available from brokers in $25,000 minimum amounts at an interest rate one-half percent below the pool contract rate. Shares are backed by insured mortgages and they are free of default risk. In effect, investors own a share of a portfolio of insured mortgages and they receive interest, principal, and prepayment proceeds monthly. Because of prepayments, yield must be estimated in the manner described above for single mortgages.

The Federal Home Loan Mortgage Corporation or Freddie Mac (FHLMC) was also created in 1970 to protect the competitive position of the savings and loan industry. FHLMC uses the proceeds of its own bond issues to purchase insured or conventional mortgages from savings and loan associations. In September of 1975, California Federal Savings and Loan Association issued $50 million in mortgage-backed bonds, similar in many respects to federal agency pass-through securities. This type of bond has not become common because of limitations imposed by the size of most savings and loan institutions, but it is an indication of the growing importance of mortgage-backed securities.

Preferred Stock

Preferred stock, unpopular for many years, has become increasingly attractive to investors recently. Historically, corporations have issued bonds instead of preferred stock because of the high cost of dividends in comparison to tax deductible interest. By the early 1970s, however, firms, burdened with excessive debt–equity ratios and faced with depressed stock prices, returned to preferred stock in record numbers. Investors were attracted by the high level of yields required to insure successful offerings and by the relative safety of a preferred dividend stream. In addition, preferred stock is usually issued in smaller denominations than the \$1000 principal value of bonds; this has made it easier for small investors to purchase preferred stock.

PROVISIONS

Preferred stock is similar to bonds in the sense of a promised stream of income (dividend) payments and it is similar to common stock because most issues entitle investors to vote at stockholder meetings. The preferred dividend is not guaranteed; it is paid only after it has been declared by the board of directors. Nonetheless, dividends on common stock cannot be paid until preferred dividends have been declared and, in any event, no corporation is likely to pass a preferred dividend unless it faces severe financial difficulty. Most outstanding preferred stock has the *cumulative feature* which prohibits common dividends when any current or past preferred dividends are in arrears. The return to preferred stockholders is usually limited to the preference rate; residual income is allocated to common stockholders unless the preferred stock carries the *participating feature*. Dividends on preferred stock are taxable to individual investors, after an exemption of \$100, but 85 percent of dividend income is nontaxable for corporate investors.

Unlike corporate bonds, preferred stock has no maturity date. Nonetheless, most issues include some provision for retirement. Most carry a *call feature* which allows retirement at some stated call price which may or may not decrease over time. Some issues provide for a sinking fund which allows for a planned and orderly retirement of the issue.

Current yield for preferred stock is the ratio of the preferred dividend to the current market price. Preferred stock is usually priced on the basis of current yield but when there is a call provision, yield should be calculated to the first-call date. This is accomplished by employing Equation 5.1, substituting periodic dividend D_t for interest payment I_t and call price P_c for maturity value P_n. For preferred stock yield y_c,

$$P_0 = \sum_{t=1}^{c} \frac{D_t}{(1 + y_c)^t} + \frac{P_c}{(1 + y_c)^c} \tag{5.9}$$

INCOME BONDS

Income bonds are unsecured obligations which are a hybrid security with some features similar to debenture bonds and others which resemble preferred stock. Interest on income bonds must be paid only when it is earned currently although most of these securities contain the cumulative feature. Claims are senior to both common stock and preferred stock.

Most outstanding income bonds have been issued as a condition to corporate reorganization under financial distress. For this reason they are considered to be very risky and they have not been popular with investors. Interestingly, however, interest expense is deductible for tax purposes and it is surprising that there has been so little effort expended to promote the issuance of income bonds since they combine advantageous features of both preferred stock and bonded debt.[32]

Summary

This chapter discussed the elements which determine yield on bonds, mortgages, and preferred stock. Major emphasis was directed to the meaning and evaluation of risk. The problem of interest rate forecasting was also discussed. The chapter concluded with a description of specific features of bonds, mortgages, and preferred stock. The term structure of interest rates is discussed in the chapter appendix.

The analysis of fixed income securities is a challenging problem but common stock analysis is yet more formidable. The next four chapters focus on common equity return. Chapter 6 provides an introduction in general terms and Chapters 7 and 8 expand upon elements of the equity model. Chapter 9 is a case illustration which demonstrates the process for an actual firm.

Appendix
Term Structure of Interest Rates

A number of theories have been advanced to explain the relationship between yield and maturity. These include (1) the unbiased expectations theory, (2) the liquidity preference theory, and (3) the market segmentation theory. In order to place this controversy in perspective, it is necessary to examine the arithmetic of multiperiod interest rates.

SPOT AND FORWARD RATES. An interest rate is classified as a spot rate, which is the current market quotation, or as a forward rate, which is the market quotation at some future date. Assume that the yield on U.S. Treasury notes maturing in one year is 8 percent today but the yield on one-year notes, two years from now, will be 7 percent; in that case the one-year spot rate is 8 percent and the one-year forward rate, measured two years forward, is 7 percent. These relationships can be simplified by defining spot rates $R(m)$ and forward rates $r(m)_t$ for obligations maturing in period m with forward

[32] See Sidney Robbins, *An Objective Look at Income Bonds* (Envision Press, 1974), revised from an article which originally appeared in the *Harvard Business Review*.

rates measured t periods later. With this notation, the preceding example can be formulated:

$$R(1) = 0.08$$
$$r(1)_2 = 0.07$$

Interest rates can also be classified as short-term or long-term, with long-term rates compounded from short-term spot and forward rates. Under conditions of certainty, these relationships are simply arithmetic definitions.

To illustrate, assume that it is known that interest rates for one-year notes, which are currently 6 percent, will increase to 8 percent one year later and to 10 percent two years from now. In that case, and ignoring taxes and brokerage costs for the moment, an investor would be indifferent between investing in one-year maturity loans over each of the next three years or investing in a three-year maturity loan today with a spot rate of 7.99 percent. This is true, under the assumptions given, because:

$$\begin{aligned} [1 + R(1)][1 + r(1)_1][1 + r(1)_2] &= [1 + R(3)]^3 \\ (1.06)(1.08)(1.10) = 1.2593 &= (1.0799)^3 \end{aligned} \tag{5A.1}$$

In either case, future value after three years is the same.

The investor would also be indifferent if the pattern of one-year maturity yields were reversed. For one-year maturity loans, a spot rate of 10 percent and forward rates one and two years later of 8 and 6 percent, respectively, also yield an annual average of 7.99 percent:

$$(1.10)(1.08)(1.06) = 1.2593 = (1.0799)^3$$

In both of the examples cited, investors would be indifferent between a series of one-year investments and a single investment with a three-year maturity. But the two cases differ in one very important respect: in the first case, graphed in Figure 5A.1(a), interest rates increased over time while in the second, in Figure 5A.1(b), interest rates decreased over time.

Figure 5A.1(c) summarizes the impact of these different assumptions by tracing yield levels with respect to maturity. In the case of falling one-year rates the term structure is negatively sloped while with rising rates it is positively sloped. Under the assumptions of certainty and the absence of brokerage costs and taxes, the future level of interest rates could be solved by observing current spot rates for different maturities and by calculating forward rates implied by those spot rates. Spot rates $R(1) = 0.06$ and $R(2) = 0.07$ would imply a one-year forward rate of 8.01 percent:

$$\begin{aligned} [1 + R(1)][1 + r(1)_1] &= [1 + R(2)]^2 \\ (1.06)[1 + r(1)_1] &= (1.07)^2 = 1.1449 \\ r(1)_1 &= .0801 \end{aligned}$$

Figure 5A.1
Interest Rate Movements

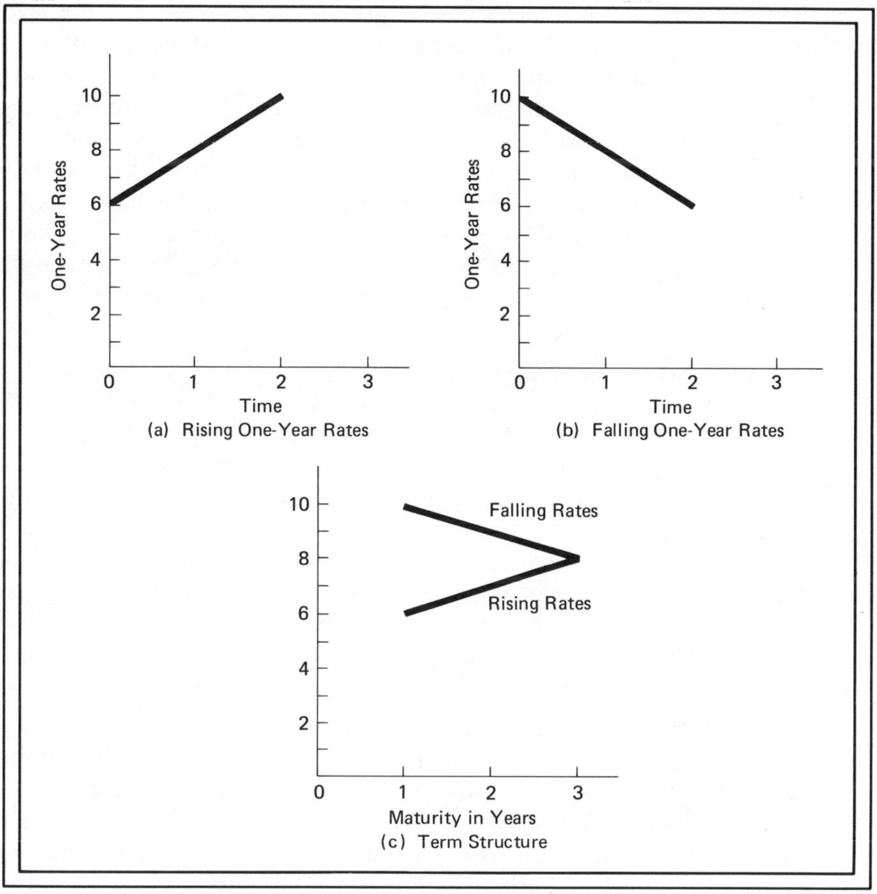

In practice, with uncertainty, this is not possible, and it is necessary to make behavioral assumptions as to the manner in which investors evaluate securities with different maturities. This has resulted in differing theories with respect to the term structure.

EXPECTATIONS THEORY. Under the unbiased expectations theory the observed term structure reflects investors' expectations as to the level of interest rates in the future. Long-term rates are viewed as a geometric average of short-term spot and (estimated) forward rates. If investors expected short-term rates to behave in the fashion portrayed in Figure 5A.1(a) or (b), for example, the related term structure portrayed in Figure 5A.1(c) would result.

This does not mean that specific short-term forward rates must be estimated. Instead, rational investors would adjust the term structure of their bond portfolios in accordance with expectations as to future levels of interest rates. If interest rates are expected to be constant over time, and if the ten-year spot rate exceeds the one-year spot rate, investors would purchase bonds with a ten-year maturity. As a result, profit-maximizing activities of rational investors will increase the price of ten-year bonds, reducing the ten-year spot rate in the process. In this fashion equilibrium rates would be restored.[33] This process is called *arbitrage.* If it is an accurate description of investors' behavior, the term structure reflects interest rate expectations. If interest rates are expected to rise, for example, the term structure will be positively sloped, as demonstrated in Figure 5A.1.

LIQUIDITY PREFERENCE THEORY. An alternative theory argues that the risk attaching to long-term bonds exceeds the risk for short-term bonds. Expectations are subject to uncertainty and the impact of a given change in interest rates increases as term-to-maturity increases, as demonstrated previously in Figure 5.2. Moreover, some argue that it is easier to forecast short-run outcomes than long-run outcomes. Accordingly, advocates of the liquidity preference theory argue that investors prefer shorter term maturities, other things equal, and will demand a yield premium to acquire long-term bonds. For this reason, long-term yields should tend, on average, to exceed yields determined by investors' expectations.

MARKET SEGMENTATION THEORY. A third theory is based upon the argument that the market for bonds is highly segmented with the result that short-term securities are a poor substitute for long-term securities. Short-term securities, which have relatively stable principal value in the face of interest rate fluctuations, would be preferred by industrial corporations, commercial banks, and others with pressing liquidity requirements. Institutions with long-run cash flow commitments, in contrast, would prefer investments with a long-run contractual stream of payments; life insurance companies and pension plans would be included under this category. According to the segmentation theory, interest rates on bonds with different maturities would be determined independently by market conditions in each of the several market segments. This implies that the arbitrage mechanism underlying the expectations theory would be operative, at best, within market segments.

EMPIRICAL EVIDENCE. The term structure controversy has motivated a number of empirical studies of the relationship between yield-to-maturity and

[33] If risk-neutral investors believe that an increase or decrease in yield is equi-probable, they would prefer long-term bonds because, as demonstrated earlier in Figure 5.2, the probable capital gain $(D - A)$ exceeds the probable capital loss $(A - C)$.

Figure 5A.2
Term Structure to Maturity

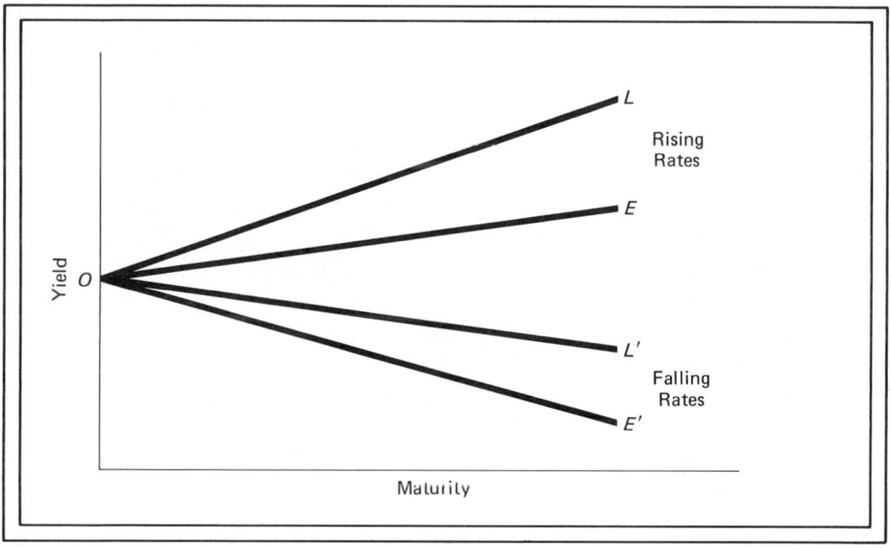

term-to-maturity.[34] Unfortunately, evidence is available which supports all three theories and it is not possible to distinguish among them clearly and decisively. There are two possible reasons for this.

First, the most accurate description of investors' behavior is probably a combination of the several theories, particularly the expectations and liquidity preference hypotheses. Figure 5A.2 describes this relationship. In the case where an expected increase in interest rates results in term structure *OE* under the expectations theory, investors would require yields along *OL* because of uncertainty. Similarly, liquidity risk premium *L'E'* would result in spot rates along *OL'* in the case of an expected decrease in interest rates. If the term structure described by Figure 5A.2 is correct, empirical tests will provide support for both theories because yields could be observed along *OL* or *OL'*, but not along *OE* or *OE'*. In addition, long-term bond prices have proven to be more volatile than short-term bond prices and the most typical term structure observed is upward-sloping. But there have been times when the term structure was "humped," with medium term yields exceeding those for both shorter and longer maturities. This could result from the

[34] Some of the more important papers are listed in the Bibliography at the end of this chapter. Theoretical and empirical studies are reviewed, among other places, in Thomas F. Cargill and Robert A. Meyer, "A Spectral Approach to Estimating the Distributed Lag Relationship Between Long and Short Term Interest Rates," *International Economic Review*, June 1972, pp. 223–238, and L. G. Telser, "A Critique of Some Recent Empirical Research in the Explanation of the Term Structure of Interest Rates," *Journal of Political Economy*, August 1967 Supplement, pp. 546–561.

temporary activity of institutions in segmented markets during times of economic disequilibrium.

A second reason why the term structure controversy has not been resolved involves a concept known as *duration.*[35] Term-to-maturity focuses on payment of the principal sum but the return to investors also includes a stream of payments; as a result, average term-to-maturity varies as the contract rate varies. The term structure, unadjusted, implies a zero coupon rate. Yield is a complicated average of yields over the entire life of a bond and averaging distorts the shape of the yield curve for longer maturity obligations. Unfortunately, the relationship between duration and maturity is very complicated and it has yet to be resolved satisfactorily. For this reason empirical studies relating yield and maturity are still open to serious difficulty.

MEASURING THE YIELD CURVE. Notwithstanding the duration problem, yield does vary with maturity and attempts have been made to estimate the yield curve empirically. This is accomplished by fitting a curve to observed yields of the type plotted in Figure 5.3. Yield is the dependent variable and one of several transformations of maturity becomes the independent variable; for example, studies have tested maturity m, its inverse $1/m$, its logarithm $\log m$, and its square m^2.[36] Given an adequate fit, yield-to-maturity for missing maturities can then be read from the yield curve. But no single specification has proven to be consistently superior to others and no combination of specifications is adequate from period to period. The best statistical fit for the values plotted in Figure 5.3, for example, explains only 42 percent of observed variation in yield. As a result, the yield curve for that data can probably be best described by a curve which is hand-fitted.

Although the yield term structure cannot yet be satisfactorily explained, theoretically or statistically, variation in the yield curve from period to period is of critical concern to bond portfolio managers. As a result, research efforts continue to be directed to this important relationship.

Questions and Problems

1. A 9 percent coupon bond matures on July 1, 1990. The current price, on July 1, 1975, is 92.316; that is, the bond sells at 92.316 percent of face value, or $923.16. What is the effective annual yield-to-maturity?

[35] Duration was first recognized in F. R. Macauley, *The Movement of Interest Rates, Bond Yields and Stock Yields in the United States Since 1856* (New York: National Bureau of Economic Research, 1938). It is treated rigorously in Lawrence Fisher and Roman Weil, "Return to Bondholders from Naive and Optimal Strategies," *Journal of Business*, October 1971, pp. 408–432. Empirical difficulties provided by the duration problem are reviewed in J. Huston McCulloch, "Measuring the Term Structure of Interest Rates," *Journal of Business*, January 1971, pp. 19–31. As stated in the text, volatility in bond prices increases as the term-to-maturity increases, but there are cases, when bonds sell at deep discounts, where the opposite behavior can be observed. This probably is due to the problem of duration. See Michael H. Hopewell and George G. Kaufman, "Bond Price Volatility and Term to Maturity: A Generalized Respecification," *American Economic Review*, September 1973, pp. 749–753.

[36] Kalman J. Cohen, Robert L. Kramer, and W. Howard Waugh, "Regression Yield Curves for U.S. Government Securities," *Management Science*, December 1966, pp. B168–175.

2. On January 1, 1976, a bond with a 10.4 percent coupon which matures on December 31, 1976, sold for par to yield 10.4 percent. If a relevant price index was 100.0 on January 1, 1976, 104.0 on June 30, 1976, and 105.2 on December 31, 1976, and if coupon payments were remitted on June 30 and December 31, what was the nominal yield and the real yield?
3. Each of the eight bonds listed below suffered capital losses when the level of market yields suddenly increased by 1 percent. Classify losses by maturity, coupon rate, and market yield:

	Coupon Rate (%)	*Maturity (Years)*	*Original Market Yield (%)*	*New Market Yield (%)*
A	6	10	7	8
B	6	20	7	8
C	7	10	7	8
D	7	20	7	8
E	6	10	8	9
F	6	20	8	9
G	7	10	8	9
H	7	20	8	9

4. Assume that the interest rate for obligations of the U.S. government which mature in one year is currently 6 percent but will change over the next four years, respectively, to 7.5, 8.0, 7.0, and 6.5 percent.
   a. If investors expect that pattern to occur, and under the expectations hypothesis, what is the current spot rate for five-year maturity bonds? Would investors be indifferent among investments with a one-, two-, three-, four-, or five-year maturity? Explain. What type of yield curve does that pattern of one-year rates imply?
   b. Assuming the same pattern of expected one-year forward rates, what would be the probable spot rate for five-year bonds with respect to the value calculated in (a) above? Would your conclusion as to the shape of the term structure remain the same? Explain.
5. An XYZ Corporation bond which matures in ten years pays 8 percent interest semiannually; it is priced at $934.92 to yield simple interest of 9 percent annually. Another XYZ bond, which also matures in ten years, pays 6 percent interest; at a price of $804.84 it also yields 9 percent. Would you be indifferent between these two securities if you were certain that you would want to hold them for the entire ten-year period? Explain.

Selected References

YIELD AND INTEREST RATE VARIATIONS

Ang, James S., and K. A. Patel, "Bond Rating Methods: Comparison and Validation," *Journal of Finance*, May 1975, pp. 631–640.

Cargill, Thomas F., and Robert A. Meyer, "A Spectral Approach to Estimating the Distributed Lag Relationship Between Long and Short Term Interest Rates," *International Economic Review*, June 1972, pp. 223–228.

Carleton, Willard T., and Ian A. Cooper, "Estimation and Uses of the Term Structure of Interest Rates," *The Journal of Finance* 31 (September 1976), pp. 1067–1083.

Cohen, Kalman J., Robert L. Kramer, and W. Howard Waugh, "Regression Yield Curves for U.S. Government Securities," *Management Science*, December 1966, pp. B168–175.

Fama, Eugene F., "Inflation Uncertainty and Expected Returns on Treasury Bills," *Journal of Political Economy* 84 (June 1976), pp. 427–448.

Fama, Eugene F., "Short Term Interest Rates as Predictors of Inflation," *American Economic Review*, June 1975, pp. 269–282.

Fisher, Lawrence, and Roman Weil, "Return to Bondholders from Naive and Optimal Strategies," *Journal of Business*, October 1971, pp. 408–432.

Gibson, William E., "Interest Rates and Inflationary Expectations: New Evidence," *American Economic Review*, December 1972, pp. 854–865.

Grier, Paul, and Steven Katz, "The Differential Effects of Bond Rating Changes Among Industrial and Public Utility Bonds by Maturity," *Journal of Business* 49:2 (April 1976), pp. 226–239.

Hickman, W. Braddock, *Corporate Bond Quality and Investor Experience* (New York: National Bureau of Economic Research, 1958).

Homer, Sidney, "The Historical Evolution of Today's Bond Market," *Explorations in Economic Research*, Summer 1975, pp. 378–389.

Homer, Sidney, and Martin Liebowitz, *Inside the Yield Book*, 5 Vol., (New York: Salomon Bros., 1970–1972).

Hopewell, Michael H., and George G. Kaufman, "Bond Price Volatility and Term to Maturity: A Generalized Respecification," *American Economic Review*, September 1973, pp. 749–753.

Macauley, F. R., *The Movement of Interest Rates, Bond Yields and Stock Yields in the United States Since 1856* (New York: National Bureau of Economic Research, 1938).

Malkiel, Burton, "Expectations, Bond Prices, and the Term Structure of Interest Rates," *Quarterly Journal of Economics*, May 1962, pp. 197–218.

McCulloch, J. Huston, "Measuring the Term Structure of Interest Rates," *Journal of Business*, January 1971, pp. 19–31.

Modigliani, Franco, and Richard Sutch, "Debt Management and the Term Structure of Interest Rates: An Empirical Analysis of Recent Experience," *Journal of Political Economy*, August 1967 Supplement, pp. 569–589.

Pinches, George E., and Kent A. Mingo, "A Multivariate Analysis of Industrial Bond Ratings," *Journal of Finance*, March 1973, pp. 1–18.

Pinches, George, and J. C. Singleton, "The Adjustment of Stock Prices to Bond Rating Changes," *Journal of Finance*, 33 (March 1978), pp. 29–44.

Pogue, Thomas F., and Robert M. Soldofsky, "What's in a Bond Rating," *Journal of Financial and Quantitative Analysis*, June 1969, pp. 201–228.

Telser, L. G., "A Critique of Some Recent Empirical Research in the Explanation of the Term Structure of Interest Rates," *Journal of Political Economy*, August 1967 Supplement, pp. 546–561.

BONDS, MORTGAGES, AND PREFERRED STOCK

Curley, Anthony J., and Jack M. Guttentag, "The Yield on Insured Residential Mortgages," *Explorations in Economic Research*, Summer 1974, pp. 114–161.

Fischer, Donald E., and Glenn A. Wilt, Jr., "Non-Convertible Preferred Stock as a Financing Instrument, 1950–1965," *Journal of Finance*, September 1968, pp. 611–624.

Jen, Frank C., and James E. Wert, "The Effect of Call Risk on Corporate Bond Yields," *Journal of Finance*, December 1967, pp. 637–652.

Joehnk, Michael D., and James F. Nielsen, "Return and Risk Characteristics of Speculative Grade Bonds," *Quarterly Review of Economics and Business*, Spring 1975, pp. 27–46.

Johnson, Rodney, "A Fresh Look at the Municipal Bond Market," *Business Review*, Federal Reserve Bank of Philadelphia, July–August 1976, pp. 18–20.

Michel, Allen J., "Municipal Bond Ratings: A Discriminant Analysis Approach," *Journal of Financial and Quantitative Analysis*, November 1977, pp. 587–598.

Pye, Gordon, "The Value of the Call Option on a Bond," *Journal of Political Economy*, March 1966, pp. 200–205.

Rogalski, Richard J., "Bond Yields or Random Walks?" *Decision Sciences*, October 1975, pp. 688–699.

Schaefer, Stephen M., "The Problem With Redemption Yields," *Financial Analysts Journal*, July–August 1977, pp. 29–35.

Shapiro, Edward, "The Absolute Levels of Bond Yields and the Corporate-Municipal Difference," *Nebraska Journal of Economics and Business*, Summer 1970, pp. 3–13.

Chapter 6
Common Stock Analysis

Introduction

Security analysis is an imperfect art and that imperfection is especially apparent in common stock analysis. An experienced analyst combines quantitative techniques, qualitative insight, and a good deal of professional judgment in arriving at an investment recommendation. Only the first of these can be considered formally, but it is a very imposing problem. Analytical forecasts are subject to statistical and data deficiencies and they are also open to difficulty because unexpected events alter expected return on investment. While conclusive evidence concerning predictive accuracy is not available, evidence which does exist suggests that the art of forecasting is still at an early stage of development.[1] It does not, however, imply the irrelevance of security analysis, for three reasons:

[1] Forecasting is discussed in general in Chapter 9. Specific evidence as to the accuracy of estimates provided by *security analysts* is not numerous, in part because analysts' data are not generally available in sufficient detail to be statistically significant. Fragmentary evidence provided by Cragg and Malkiel, which they warn is based on a very small sample, implies that analysts' predictions of long-run growth in corporate earnings are no better than those based naively on past growth rates. See John G. Cragg and Burton G. Malkiel, "The Consensus and Accuracy of Some Predictions of the Growth of Corporate Earnings," *Journal of Finance*, March 1968, pp. 67–84. An extension of the Cragg and Malkiel study by R. Malcolm Richards suggests that analysts are reasonably accurate in making short run earnings forecasts and that there is a lack of variation in forecasts among different analysts. R. Malcolm Richards, "Analysts Performance and the Accuracy of Corporate Earnings Forecasts," *The Journal of Business*, July 1976, pp. 350–357.

1. INFORMED DECISION MAKING. As discussed in Chapter 4, the rational decision process involves evaluation of all available information, qualitative and quantitative, which impacts on the probable outcome of that decision. The greater the reliability and accuracy of data, whether empirical or forecast, the greater the probability that a correct decision will be made. It is better to employ imperfect information than to decide on the basis of no information at all. Given careful analytical procedure, systematic bias from misleading information should not occur.

The point can be illustrated by considering the popular MONOPOLY® real estate board game which is familiar to persons of all ages. While most players are content to roll dice, counting on luck to acquire favored properties and to establish color groups, strategies exist for maximizing probable success.[2] Rents are not proportional to acquisition prices, for example, and rates of return vary widely among available properties. In addition, the probability of landing on alternate squares varies because of special instructions arising when tokens fall by chance on particular places on the board. As shown in Figure 6.1 for example, the orange color group (New York, Tennessee, and St. James) has a greater probability of producing rents than any other set of development properties. Knowledge of these probabilities and recognition of specific rates of return will increase the expertise of any player. While many might prefer to ignore them when playing for entertainment, a player risking actual wealth would not; the same point applies to investors who face the far greater difficulty of quantifying expected return on investment.

2. EVALUATION OF RISK. Forecasting deficiencies are also important in deriving estimates of the riskiness involved in any investment decision. With perfect forecasting the investment problem would be trivial; it is the existence of risk, as discussed in Chapter 4, which provides challenge to both analysts and investors.[3] In the time sequence of investment decisions, actual outcomes can be compared to the *distribution* of planned outcomes and the validity of predictive techniques can be assessed through feedback and adaptation. In this process of planning and control the concept of risk becomes operational.

3. EVOLUTION OF THE ART. Finally, it is important to recognize that analytical techniques are still at a relatively early stage of development with major innovations and advances having been realized only very recently.

[2] See Maxine Brady, *The Monopoly Book: Strategy and Tactics of the World's Most Popular Game* (New York: McKay, 1974).

[3] Standard forecasting techniques provide methods for assessing a distribution of values for a given random variable. In regression analysis, for example, the standard error of estimate allows the analyst to place confidence limits about any conditional point estimate for the dependent variable to be forecast. In the standard two-variable model, $Y = \alpha + \beta X + \varepsilon$, where α and β are parameters to be estimated and ε is a disturbance term with zero expectation and variance $\sigma_\varepsilon{}^2$, confidence limits about point estimate Y can be based on the standard error of estimate $\hat{\sigma}_\varepsilon$.

Figure 6.1
Probability of Landing on Alternative Squares (ranked in descending order)

This is partly a legacy of the depression period of the 1930s and partly a response to the lengthy bull market which followed World War II. Advancements in computer technology are yet more instrumental because sophisticated analytical techniques could not be developed and applied where the mechanical calculator was the only computational device available.[4] Early approaches to common stock valuation typically involved a

[4] In an article published in 1964 Herzog pointed out that the (then) existing lack of information on investment yields arose from computational difficulties. As set forth in Chapter 3, yield is an internal rate of return which can be solved, in general, only by trial and error. Herzog demonstrated a pilot technique in which performance was calculated for a small sample of bonds, preferred stocks, and common stocks. The technique he used is the one illustrated in the appendix to Chapter 3 of this text. See John P. Herzog, "Investor Experience in Corporate Securities: A New Technique for Measurement," *Journal of Finance*, March 1964, pp. 46–62.

stream of dividends or earnings, with an associated growth rate, and/or a terminal price for the security in question.[5] A model based on these variables was traced by Durand as early as the turn of the century (1901).[6] Nonetheless, developments in security analysis lagged for several decades until common stock became increasingly favored in the period approaching the market crash of 1929. In 1931, in the midst of the Great Depression, Samuel Guild introduced the specific security valuation model to be developed here in published tables relating growth rates and yields; it was, in words quoted by Soldofsky, "the worst possible time in the century for the publication of such a book."[7] Guild's work went unheralded as interest in growth stocks waned, awaiting rescue in the post–World War II period of renewed economic expansion.

Security analysis, based on "fundamental" valuation factors, found renewed emphasis throughout the 1950s and 1960s. Fundamental analysis focuses on growth in earnings and dividends, price-earnings ratios, and other underlying determinants of common stock value.[8] During this period increasing attention was also directed to the development and refinement of mathematical models which explore relationships among valuation elements. The next section reviews some of these studies.

Elements of Value

VALUATION MODELS

A model is an abstraction of reality used to study relationships and gather insights when reality is too complex to deal with in any practical sense. Model aircraft, for example, are observed in wind tunnels to simulate and study aerodynamic properties. Similarly, algebraic models can be used to specify

[5] For a detailed analysis of the development of security valuation models see Robert M. Soldofsky, "A Note on the History of Bond Tables and Stock Valuation Models," *Journal of Finance*, March 1966, especially pp. 106–111.

[6] The reference by Durand was to Ralph Todhunter, "The Institute of Actuaries Textbook on Compound Interest and Annuities Certain" (1901); revised by R. C. Simmonds and T. P. Thompson (New York: Cambridge University Press, 1937). See David Durand, *Bank Stock Prices and the Bank Capital Problem* (New York: NBER, 1958), p. 44. Valuation models, including the one cited by Durand, will be used in the next section of this chapter to identify variables which are inputs to security valuation models.

[7] Samuel Eliot Guild, *Stock Growth and Discount Tables* (Boston, Mass.: Financial Publishing Company, 1931). The quotation in the text was by an official of the publishing company to Professor Soldofsky. See Soldofsky, "Note on History of Bond Tables," p. 109.

[8] The search for valuation techniques was given strong impetus by the now classic work of J. B. Williams, *The Theory of Investment Value* (Cambridge, Mass.: Harvard University Press, 1938). During the post–World War II period a popular text by Graham, Dodd, and Cottle became the "bible" for security analysts. B. Graham, D. Dodd, and S. Cottle, *Security Analysis*, 4th ed. (New York: McGraw-Hill, 1962). The influence of Graham and Dodd's safety-first valuation principles is still evident. For example see Anatol W. Bigus, "Managing Portfolios with Graham & Dodd," *Journal of Portfolio Management* (Spring 1977), pp. 58–62.

economic relationships. Equation 6.1 is a model of the price of a share of common stock:[9]

$$P_0 = \frac{D_0}{k - g}, \quad \text{where } k > g \tag{6.1}$$

and

P_0 = price of the security in time period 0 (now)
D_0 = dividend currently paid periodically to shareholders
k = rate of return required by investors for that stock
g = periodic rate of growth in dividends

According to Equation 6.1 price P_0 is positively related to dividend D_0 and growth rate g and inversely related to required rate of return k. Moreover, yield k must exceed growth rate g or price would be negative ($g > k$) or infinite ($g = k$).

Whatever the merits of Equation 6.1 in any other respect, these relationships seem to be reasonable. Price should increase with an increase in either dividend or growth and it should fall as yield k increases because a lower price for a given dividend stream will result in a larger rate of return. If Equation 6.1 is accepted as an adequate abstraction of reality, rate of return can be modeled also:

$$k = \frac{D_0}{P_0} + g, \qquad k > g \tag{6.2}$$

Equation 6.2 appeals to common sense because rate of return is described in terms of the two components of common stock yield: dividend yield

[9] Equations 6.1 and 6.2 are familiar statements of a popular model which was developed, refined, and tested by Myron Gordon. It is also the basic model attributed to Todhunter by Durand, as noted in footnote 6 above. See Myron Gordon, *The Investment, Financing, and Valuation of the Corporation* (Homewood, Ill.: Irwin, 1962). The Gordon model, in its simplest form, defines the value of an equity-financed firm as the present value of an infinite stream of dividends discounted at yield k:

$$P_0 = \sum_{t=0}^{\infty} \frac{D_t}{(l + k)^t}$$

If the current dividend D_0 grows at a constant rate g,

$$D_t = D_0(1 + g)^t \quad \text{and} \quad P_0 = \sum_{t=0}^{\infty} \frac{D_0(1 + g)^t}{(1 + k)^t}$$

For this form of discrete compounding, or if continuous compounding is assumed,

$$P_0 = \int_0^{\infty} D_0 e^{-t(k-g)}\, dt$$

and also assuming $k > g$, price can be solved to the expression of Equation 6.1:

$$P_0 = \frac{D_0}{k - g}$$

D_0/P_0 and capital gain or loss g. Nevertheless, naive acceptance of this or any other model is hazardous.

The underlying assumptions of a model must be both understood and accepted if conclusions derived from that model are to be accepted. For example, Equations 6.1 and 6.2 assume that a constant proportion of income will be retained each period and a constant yield will be realized on those retained earnings; since external financing is also assumed away, this implies a constant growth rate as well.[10] This may be a poor abstraction of reality for a firm which pays no dividend or engages in debt financing.

A mathematical model has underlying assumptions which must depart from reality, in the strict sense, since otherwise it *is* reality. The problem is one of assessing the acceptability of these departures in terms of their impact on model conclusions. When underlying assumptions are not acceptable, it may be possible to adjust variables, add equations, or impose constraints; but in this process models soon become mathematically intractable. If defined relationships are totally unacceptable, there are but two alternatives. The first is to ignore assumptions entirely and test model relationships empirically, if that is possible. Unfortunately, experimental deficiencies sometimes preclude satisfactory testing of models and in that case there is only one remaining alternative, and that is to ignore the model entirely.

Valuation models, aside from the extreme situation of the second alternative above, are very useful to corporate financial managers, to students of finance, and to security analysts. Security valuation models generally focus on (1) earnings and dividends, (2) capital structure, and/or (3) equity capitalization rates (price-earnings ratios). Price-earnings ratios will be examined in Chapter 8; the other elements are considered next.

EARNINGS AND DIVIDENDS

An obvious determinant of a firm's value is its stream of earnings or, alternately, dividends. Two important issues are involved here. The first is the question of investor preference for income in the form of either dividends or capital gains. The problem is unresolved but it is important to analysts since preference for one or the other would influence estimates of security value. A second important and related issue is the relationship between rate of growth in earnings (or dividends) and the value of common stock.

[10] In the Gordon model financing is assumed away and periodic investment I_t is financed completely with funds retained from operations. Under this assumption, and defining a constant proportion of retained income b, where income is Y, $b = [(Y_t - D_t)/Y_t]$. The proportion of income which is available for reinvestment is bY_t. If this sum is invested to yield the firm a constant average internal rate of return r, increment to income in period $t + 1$ is rbY_t dollars and period $t + 1$ income is $Y_{t+1} = Y_t + rbY_t = Y_t(1 + rb)$. For a firm growing at a constant periodic rate g, $Y_{t+1} = Y_t(1 + g)$, for all t, and growth rate g is equal to the product rb. Thus the model is relevant for (1) a pure equity firm, (2) with constant yield r and (3) constant retention rate b; (2) and (3) imply a constant g.

DIVIDENDS VERSUS CAPITAL GAINS. A firm's income may be defined as earnings, in an accounting sense, or as operating cash flows; the difference between these two definitions will be examined in Chapter 8. For the moment it is sufficient to consider a stream of flows which the shareholder receives either (1) as cash dividends are declared or (2) as capital gains, where foregone dividends are reflected thereafter in market price. Theoretical models have attempted to determine if the dividend decision, the allocation between current and future return, affects the value of the firm. These range from idealized economic models under certainty to analyses based upon generalized uncertainty.[11] While theoretical treatments provide no operational solution to the problem, they do serve to highlight potential differences between income received as dividends and income received as capital gains.

In theory one can argue the irrelevance of the dividend decision. Assume that an investment of $100 in shares of XYZ Corporation increases in value to $110 during some time period. If a $10 dividend is distributed to shareholders, price of the stock will decrease to $100 and the investor will have realized a 10 percent rate of return. But if the dividend is not declared, the stockholder could sell one-eleventh of the shares, for $10, again realizing 10 percent in current income and $100 in end-of-period security value. It may then be argued that there is no difference between either form of income realization.

In practice, however, there are differences. In the first place, dividends are taxed to investors at a different rate than capital gains are taxed. Second, in order to realize capital gains, shares must be liquidated and this involves brokerage commission and transfer taxes.[12] Third, some argue that a dividend declaration has an information effect in the sense that management announces its expectations of future prospects by its dividend behavior. By influencing shareholder expectations, value would also be influenced. Another point advanced is that dividend payments resolve uncertainty; capital gains promised in the future become certain when received currently. Moreover, some shareholders may depend on dividends for maintaining current consumption; this class of investors, including retired persons, may be unwilling to subject current needs to the ebb and flow of short-run market price movements.

On balance the debate concerning dividends versus capital gains has yet to be settled; research has failed to provide clear statistical evidence

[11] At one extreme, under conditions of perfect capital markets, rational behavior, and certainty, Miller and Modigliani demonstrated the irrelevance of the dividend decision. Merton Miller and Franco Modigliani, "Divided Policy, Growth, and the Valuation of Shares," *Journal of Business*, October 1961, pp. 411–433. On the other extreme Lintner argued that dividend policy is not value neutral except under very rigid assumptions as to certainty and capital market behavior. John Lintner, "Dividends, Earnings, Leverage, Stock Prices and the Supply of Capital to Corporations," *Review of Economics and Statistics*, August 1962, pp. 243–269. A penetrating analysis of the dividend problem and the role of dividends is found in James E. Walter, "Dividend Policy: Its Influence on the Value of the Enterprise," *Journal of Finance*, May 1963, pp. 280–291.

[12] Tax treatment and transaction costs are considered in the next section of this chapter.

supporting one hypothesis or the other.[13] A number of major corporations have approached the problem by offering their shareholders the option of reinvesting dividends in additional stock, with banks providing "brokerage" service at commission rates well below the level charged by brokers. Since the program was first introduced in 1968 by the First National City Bank of New York, it has grown rapidly to the point where more than two hundred major firms were participating by late 1972.[14]

While the problem of dividends versus capital gains has yet to be resolved, and perhaps cannot be, it must be considered in developing analytical techniques. The evaluation model introduced in this chapter will provide for taxes and transaction costs and it will recognize the risk impacted in variability in market performance. Other points cited above cannot be addressed directly. In the final analysis the question depends on investors' behavior. Normative valuation models take the viewpoint of financial managers who seek optimal dividend policy given their perception of stockholder preference. In practice it may be more reasonable to assume that investors observe managerial behavior, acquiring those types of securities which meet their dividend–capital gain preference. If this is true it would be a *change* in dividend policy, and not dividend policy per se, which would exercise the greatest influence on security value.[15]

GROWTH. A second important dimension of earnings and dividends is the growth rate in either stream of values. This is one of the most critical of investment elements and one of the most difficult to isolate and evaluate. To pursue the question it is necessary to consider the *magnitude*, *stability*, and *duration* of growth. For the moment the distinction between earnings and dividends will again be deferred and the discussion will focus on the stream of dividend payments. In this case the value of a share of common

[13] Evidence supporting the significance of dividend payout behavior will be discussed in Chapter 8. A number of studies attempt to resolve the question by testing the regression equation $P_{it} = a + bD_{it} + cR_{it} + e_{it}$, where P_{it} is price per share of security i in time period t; D_{it} is dividends per share; R_{it} is retained earnings; and e_{it} is the random disturbance term. By gathering sample data for a given industry for some given time period, regression coefficients b and c can be estimated by the ordinary least-squares method. A finding that $b > c$ would imply preference for dividends over retained earnings.

But Friend and Puckett have shown that data deficiencies and statistical bias render conclusions drawn from this test at least suspect, if not in fact in serious error. See Irwin Friend and Marshall Puckett, "Dividends and Stock Prices," *American Economic Review*, September 1964, pp. 656–682.

[14] "More Companies Offer Stockholders a Chance to Reinvest Dividends," *The Wall Street Journal*, December 4, 1972, p. 1. Some firms provide the service directly, without the assistance of banking institutions.

[15] The relative stability of corporate dividends and the reluctance of corporate managers to reduce dividends provides support for this proposition. For a more detailed analysis of dividend policy see John Lintner, "Distribution of Incomes of Corporations Among Dividends, Retained Earnings, and Taxes," *American Economic Review*, May 1956, pp. 97–113; J. A. Brittain, *Corporate Dividend Policy* (Washington, D.C.: Brookings Institute, 1966); and Eugene Fama and Harvey Babiak, "Dividend Policy: An Empirical Analysis," *Journal of the American Statistical Association*, December 1968, pp. 1132–1161.

stock can be defined as the discounted present value of that dividend stream:[16]

$$P_0 = \sum_{t=1}^{\infty} \frac{D_t}{(1+k)^t} \tag{6.3}$$

Variable definitions are the same as those used in Equations 6.1 and 6.2, for time periods t, $t = 1, 2, \ldots$. The importance of growth can be demonstrated by distinguishing three cases in which the magnitude and duration of growth vary.

1. *Single-period duration, variable growth.* The most general situation is one in which growth rate varies period by period. Defining periodic growth rate g_t, for periods $t = 1, 2, \ldots$, dividend in any period t can be linked to period 0 dividend, D_0,

$$D_t = D_0(1+g_1)(1+g_2)\cdots(1+g_{t-1})(1+g_t)$$

To illustrate, assume that a current dividend of \$2.00 per share will grow over the next four years, respectively, by 6, 8, 10, and 7 percent. The fourth-year dividend, D_4, will be \$2.69:

$$\begin{aligned}
D_1 &= 2.00(1.06) &&= 2.12\\
D_2 &= 2.00(1.06)(1.08) &&= 2.29\\
D_3 &= 2.00(1.06)(1.08)(1.10) &&= 2.52\\
D_4 &= 2.00(1.06)(1.08)(1.10)(1.07) &&= 2.69
\end{aligned}$$

In this case price per share is defined:

$$P_0 = \frac{D_0(1+g_1)}{(1+k)} + \frac{D_0(1+g_1)(1+g_2)}{(1+k)^2} + \cdots \tag{6.4}$$

In Equation 6.4 each periodic growth rate of *magnitude* g_t has a one-period *duration.* It is the most general definition, and the most realistic, but it is also the most difficult to analyze and the least tractable mathematically. The security model introduced later in this chapter can be adapted to this type of growth pattern, but for present purposes it is convenient to consider the case where any given growth magnitude has greater than single-period duration.

2. *Infinite duration, constant growth.* This situation lies at the other extreme; growth is defined perpetually at some constant rate g. In this case price per share is defined:

$$P_0 = \sum_{t=1}^{\infty} \frac{D_0(1+g)^t}{(1+k)^t} \tag{6.5}$$

[16] In the discussion in this section it is assumed that an investor purchasing a security in period 0 will receive the first dividend at the end of the period, in period 1. Period 0 dividend D_0 is defined as the level of dividend per share which forms a base for growth through any period defined. This assumption simplifies mathematical derivation for the infinite period–constant growth case described.

Table 6.1
Dividend Multipliers for Constant Growth Dividend Model

$k - g$	*Value of \$1.00 Dividend*
0.01	100.0000
0.02	50.0000
0.03	33.0000
0.04	25.0000
0.05	20.0000
0.06	16.6667
0.07	14.2857
0.08	12.5000
0.09	11.1111
0.10	10.0000
0.11	9.0909
0.12	8.3333
0.13	7.6923
0.14	7.1429
0.15	6.6667

Equation 6.5 solves to Equation 6.1:[17]

$$P_0 = \frac{D_0}{k - g}, \qquad k > g \qquad [(6.1)]$$

For each dollar of current dividend D_0, price P_0 is the reciprocal of the difference between yield k and growth rate g; Table 6.1 provides these capitalized values for a \$1.00 dividend at $(k - g)$ values ranging from 0.01 through 0.15. To illustrate its use, assume that a firm which currently pays a dividend of \$3.00 per share has an *expected* constant growth rate of 7 percent per year; assume also that investors assessing the riskiness of that firm require a 12 percent rate of return to be willing to purchase the company's stock. From Equation 6.1 and Table 6.1, price per share would be \$60.00:

$$P_0 = 3.00\frac{1}{0.05}$$

$$= 3.00(20.0000)$$

$$= 60.00$$

Table 6.1 provides a first approximation of the importance of growth in determining value of a share of stock. *Dividend multipliers* reported there, $1/(k - g)$, decrease as $k - g$ increases, but at a decreasing rate. While value and growth are positively associated, it is the relationship between yield k

[17] See footnotes 9 and 16 above.

Table 6.2
Variable Growth Dividend Multipliers
($g^* = 0.15$; $g = 0.07$; $k = 0.12$)

Duration of Abnormal Growth	*Present Value of Abnormal Growth (1)*	*Present Value of Normal Growth (2)*	*Total (1) + (2)*
0	—	20.0000	20.0000
1	1.0268	21.9732	23.0000
2	2.0811	22.5618	24.6429
3	3.1636	23.1661	26.3297
4	4.2751	23.7866	28.0617
5	5.4164	24.4238	29.8402
6	6.5883	25.0780	31.6663
7	7.7916	25.7497	33.5413
8	9.0270	26.4394	35.4664
9	10.2956	27.1476	37.4432
10	11.5982	27.8748	39.4730

and growth rate g, and not merely growth, which determines the value of each dollar of dividends. If it is assumed that high-growth firms are also high-risk firms, it is possible that $k - g$ may be large, notwithstanding a high value of g. In other words, there is no difference in the dividend multiplier for a firm with a required yield of 15 percent and a growth rate of 10 percent and another firm with yield and growth rate, respectively, of 9 and 4 percent. Both would be valued at a multiple of 20 times dividend per share. Although it is hazardous to generalize from Table 6.1 values, it can be observed that both the *magnitude* and *stability* of growth are important valuation elements.

3. *Two-level variable growth.* An infinite set of growth patterns can be defined which fall between the extreme cases of (1) totally variable and (2) constant growth discussed above.[18] One of special interest is the case where growth occurs at a greater than "normal" level for a limited period of time after which it returns to some average level experienced by other firms in the industry or the economy. In this instance, for abnormal growth rate g^* with n period duration, and for normal growth g thereafter,

$$P_0 = \sum_{t=1}^{n} \frac{D_0(1 + g^*)^t}{(1 + k)^t} + \sum_{t=n+1}^{\infty} \frac{D_n(1 + g)^{t-n}}{(1 + k)^t} \tag{6.6}$$

To illustrate, assume that a firm with a current dividend of \$1.00 per share will grow at 15 percent per year for 3 years; thereafter growth will return to a normal rate of 7 percent. The value of the firm, assuming a 12 percent rate of return required by investors, is \$26.33. From Equation 6.6:

[18] Mao examined various growth patterns beginning with exponential growth, followed by constant growth, then by declining growth; thereafter the firm only replaces equipment as needed. See James C. T. Mao, "The Valuation of Growth Stocks: The Investment Opportunities Approach," *Journal of Finance*, March 1966, pp. 95–102.

Year	*Dividend*		× *Present Value Factor*	*Value*
1	$[1.00(1.15)^1 = 1.1500]$		$\times [(1.12)^{-1} = 0.8929] =$	1.0268
2	$[1.00(1.15)^2 = 1.3225]$		$\times [(1.12)^{-2} = 0.7972] =$	1.0543
3	$[1.00(1.15)^3 = 1.5209]$		$\times [(1.12)^{-3} = 0.7118] =$	1.0825
$4 \rightarrow \infty$	$1.00(1.15)^3(1.07) =$	1.6273		
	$\dfrac{1}{k-g} = \dfrac{1}{0.12 - 0.07} =$	20	$\times [(1.12)^{-3} = 0.7118] =$	23.1662
		32.5460		26.3298

Calculation for the first three years is straightforward. From the fourth year on, since growth thereafter is constant, value is calculated as in case 2 above—with a capitalized value of dividend D_4 (\$1.6273) providing a value *at that time* of \$32.5460. It is then necessary to calculate the present value of that sum at 12 percent: $\$32.5460/(1.12)^3 = \$23.1662$.

Table 6.2 contains values for the abnormal growth situation for durations of 0 through 10 years.[19] The table places the importance of *duration* of growth in sharp focus. In the example given, the existence of abnormal growth for a five-year period increases value per dollar of dividend from \$20.00 to \$29.84, approximately a 50 percent increase. For a ten-year duration, value almost doubles. The specific numbers involved are arbitrary and illustrative, but the principle involved is clear. Whatever the pattern of growth for an individual firm, value is sensitive to (1) growth rate magnitude, (2) growth rate stability, and (3) growth rate duration. Growth patterns will be reconsidered in Chapter 9 when security analysis will be illustrated in the case example presented there.

CAPITAL STRUCTURE

The value of common stock is also affected by the degree of financial leverage applied to a firm's stream of operating income.[20] Financial leverage refers to the employment of nonequity funds to finance a portion of the

[19] The values for Table 6.2 can be derived as in the example in the text, but it is easier to simplify Equation 6.6 for that purpose. Since both terms of Equation 6.6 are geometric progressions, it can be shown that for each \$1 dividend,

$$\text{present value of abnormal growth} = \sum_{t=1}^{n} \frac{(1+g^*)^t}{(1+k)^t}$$

$$= (1+g^*)\left[\frac{1 - \left(\dfrac{1+g^*}{1+k}\right)^n}{k - g^*}\right]$$

$$\text{present value of normal growth} = \sum_{t=n+1}^{\infty} \frac{D_n(1+g)^{t-n}}{(1+k)^t}$$

$$= \frac{(1+g^*)^n(1+g)}{(k-g)(1+k)^n}$$

These equations were used to calculate values for Table 6.2; most values needed can be found in Tables A.1 and A.2 at the back of the text.

[20] Financial leverage is sometimes referred to as "trading on equity."

firm's assets; equity refers here to shareholder claims against assets. Aggregate assets contribute to the generation of the aggregate stream of cash flows providing income to both debt and equity investors. If a firm realizes a rate of return on assets which exceeds the cost of nonequity funds, excess return accrues to common stockholders. Thus the rate of return on equity exceeds the rate of return on assets, having been "levered" upward by debt financing. The process is symmetrical. If rate of return on assets is less than the cost of nonequity funds, shareholders' equity yield will be less than asset yield. The greater the degree of financial leverage, the greater the expected return on equity and the greater the dispersion in that expected return. In this manner financial leverage affects common stock value through both risk and return elements.

The relationship between nonequity and equity sources of funds is referred to as *capital structure*. Assume that management of a firm is able to earn some level of income Y independent of the firm's capital structure; that is, however the firm is financed, Y dollars are earned on assets A, and rate of return on assets is defined to be Y/A. Assume also that the capital structure consists of both debt L and equity S claims; interest I is paid to debt holders from gross return Y with the residual, or net income NI, accruing to common stockholders. For purposes of this illustration it is further assumed that the cost of debt capital I/L is constant, whatever the firm's capital structure. Under these assumptions, and with defined relationships

$$A = L + S \tag{6.7}$$

$$Y = I + NI \tag{6.8}$$

rate of return on assets Y/A and rate of return on equity NI/S are related as follows:[21]

$$\frac{NI}{S} = \frac{Y}{A} + \left(\frac{Y}{A} - \frac{I}{L}\right)\frac{L}{S} \tag{6.9}$$

[21] Students of financial management will recognize Equation 6.9 as a "book" or accounting version of the well-known Modigliani and Miller capital structure "Proposition II" where values are given as market values. See Franco Modigliani and Merton Miller, "The Cost of Capital, Corporation Finance, and the Theory of Investment," *American Economic Review*, June 1958, pp. 261–297.

To derive the relationship, Equation 6.8 can be rearranged and divided by S: $NI/S = Y/S - I/S$. Multiplying both terms on the right side of the equation by 1 (A/A and L/L, respectively),

$$\frac{NI}{S} = \frac{Y}{A}\left(\frac{A}{S}\right) - \frac{I}{L}\left(\frac{L}{S}\right)$$

and since $A = S + L$,

$$\frac{NI}{S} = \frac{Y}{A}\left(\frac{S}{S}\right) + \frac{Y}{A}\left(\frac{L}{S}\right) - \frac{I}{L}\left(\frac{L}{S}\right)$$

$$\frac{NI}{S} = \frac{Y}{A} + \left(\frac{Y}{A} - \frac{I}{L}\right)\frac{L}{S}$$

Equation 6.9 shows that equity yield NI/S consists of return on assets Y/A plus or minus the gain or loss from financial leverage. That gain or loss depends upon the differential between rate of return on assets and the cost of nonequity funds, $Y/A - I/L$, and the magnitude of financial leverage measured by the debt-equity ratio L/S.

Table 6.3 provides the basis for an arithmetic interpretation of Equation 6.9. It assumes a firm with periodic income of $1 million based on a $10 million investment in assets. The cost of debt funds is 6 percent and three financing plans are analyzed: (1) all-equity financing; (2) 28.57 percent debt and 71.43 percent equity; and (3) 50 percent debt and 50 percent equity. Under plan 2, for example,

$$\frac{NI}{S} = \frac{Y}{A} + \left(\frac{Y}{A} - \frac{I}{L}\right)\frac{L}{S}$$

$$= \frac{1{,}000{,}000}{10{,}000{,}000} + \left(\frac{1{,}000{,}000}{10{,}000{,}000} - \frac{171{,}420}{2{,}857{,}000}\right)\frac{2{,}857{,}000}{7{,}143{,}000}$$

$$= 0.10 + (0.10 - 0.06)0.40 = 0.116$$

Under plan 2 financial leverage increased rate of return on equity by 1.6 percent over the 10 percent rate of return on assets. From Table 6.3, case 1 equity yield is the unlevered 10 percent and case 3 levered return is 14 percent.

Table 6.3
Rate of Return Under Alternative Financing Plans

		Case 1	*Case 2*	*Case 3*
		All Equity	*28.57% L* *71.43% S*	*50% L* *50% S*
Total income to firm	Y[a]	1,000,000	1,000,000	1,000,000
Assets	A	10,000,000	10,000,000	10,000,000
Asset yield	Y/A	0.100	0.100	0.100
Range		−0.10–0.30	−0.10–0.30	−0.10–0.30
Interest paid	I	0	171,420	300,000
Debt	L	0	2,857,000	5,000,000
Cost of debt capital	I/L	—	0.060	0.060
Range (constant)		—	—	—
Income to shareholders	NI	1,000,000	828,580	700,000
Equity	S	10,000,000	7,143,000	5,000,000
Equity yield	NI/S	0.100	0.116	0.140
Range		−0.10–0.30	−0.164–0.396	−0.26–0.54
Debt-equity ratio	L/S	0.0	.40	1.0
Outstanding shares	N[b]	1,000,000	714,300	500,000

[a] Defined net of a 40 percent tax rate.
[b] These values are presented for later use, in Figure 6.3.

With a constant cost of debt capital and a variable asset yield, equity rate of return also varies. The break-even point is 6 percent; when Y/A is greater than 6 percent stockholders benefit from leverage whereas Y/A values below 6 percent have a negative impact on equity yield. The degree of gain or loss depends upon the magnitude of leverage as measured by the debt-equity ratio. The debt-equity ratio is widely accepted as a measure of financial risk. These relationships are shown graphically in Figure 6.2.

The relationship between asset yield and equity yield is represented by straight lines rotating about the 6 percent break-even point. Above 6 percent, as leverage increases, rate of return on equity also increases at all levels of asset yield. But dispersion increases as well. Assume that yield on assets can be any value in the range $-0.10 \leq Y/A \leq 0.30$; also assume a mean value of 10 percent. In unlevered case 1, mean asset yield and mean equity yield are both 10 percent and possible values for each fall within the same range of -10 to 30 percent. But as leverage is introduced, in cases 2 and 3, mean return on equity increases to 11.6 and 14.0 percent, respectively,

Figure 6.2
Effect of Financial Leverage on Equity Rate of Return

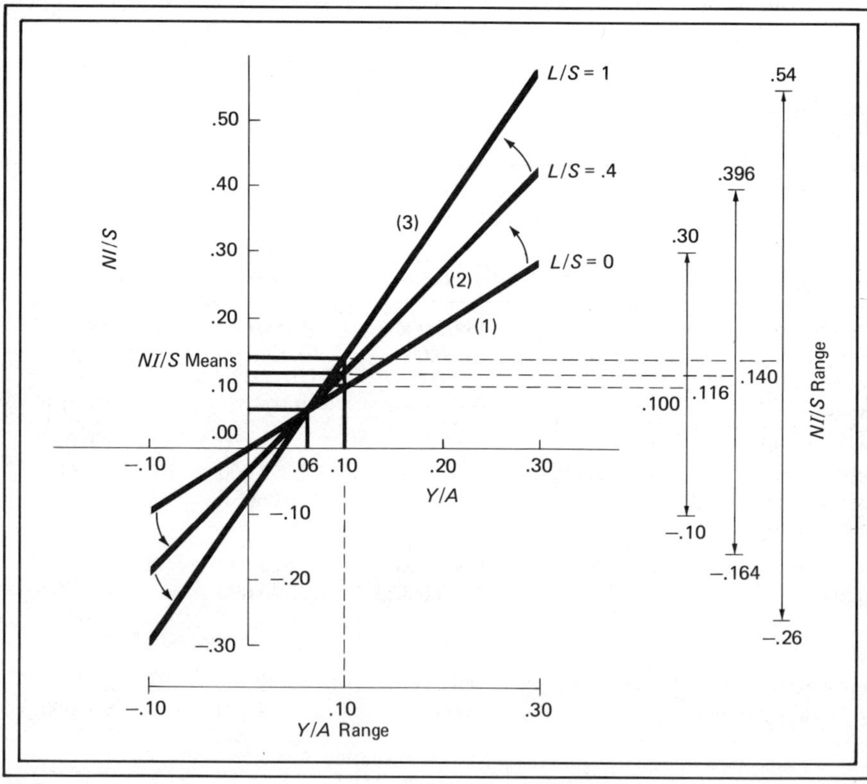

and dispersion increases also, to a range of $-16.4 \leq NI/S \leq 39.6$ for case 2 and $-26.0 \leq NI/S \leq 54.0$ for case 3. The overall impact on common stock value depends on the trade-off between the positive influence of greater expected return and the negative influence of greater dispersion in return. In addition, the cost of debt capital probably increases as leverage increases; this possibility, assumed away here, would further dilute any positive advantage accruing from financial leverage.

The preceding discussion has demonstrated the impact of financial leverage on equity yield. But the stock price effect is not clear because of the change in both risk and return. One possible approach is to separate the earnings per share effect (EPS) from the price/earnings multiple m effect. Since price is the product of EPS and m, separation provides a basis for evaluating the capital structure effect. Impact on m will be considered in Chapter 8; impact on earnings per share can be considered in terms of the relationship between earnings before interest and taxes (EBIT) and earnings per share (EPS).

Earnings per share is defined as aggregate earnings after interest, taxes, and preferred dividends, divided by the number of shares of common stock outstanding. For interest before taxes of I, tax rate t_x, preferred dividends DP, and outstanding shares N:

$$\text{EPS} = \frac{(\text{EBIT} - I)(1 - t_x) - DP}{N} \tag{6.10}$$

EPS and EBIT are variables which can be related either in tabular form or graphically. The relationship can be illustrated with the values from Table 6.3 if a tax rate of 40 percent is assumed. In that case the after-tax cost of capital of 6 percent will be equivalent to a before-tax cost of 10 percent and interest for the three cases, respectively, will be \$0, \$287,500, and \$500,000. For case 2, for example, Equation 6.10 becomes:

$$\text{EPS} = \frac{(\text{EBIT} - 285{,}700)(1 - 0.40)}{714{,}300}$$

$$\text{EPS} = \frac{(0.60)\text{EBIT} - 171{,}420}{714{,}300}$$

For any given EBIT value, EPS can be solved. This relationship is graphed in Figure 6.3; case 1 and case 3 values are also presented there.[22]

At an EBIT of \$1 million, earnings per share under all three financing plans would be \$0.60; this is demonstrated in Table 6.4.[23] At an EBIT level

[22] Figure 6.3 assumes symmetric treatment of gains and losses for tax purposes. That is, it is assumed that the firm will receive tax rebates if losses are incurred through tax carryback procedures. If losses are not tax-shielded, EBIT-EPS lines will bend at values where EPS is zero, and negative EPS will be larger than those levels depicted in the figure.

[23] In practice, alternate financing plans will not intersect at a common point; it occurs here because of the assumption of a constant rate of interest and proportional change in the number of shares outstanding as the debt-equity ratio varies.

Figure 6.3
EBIT-EPS Relationship

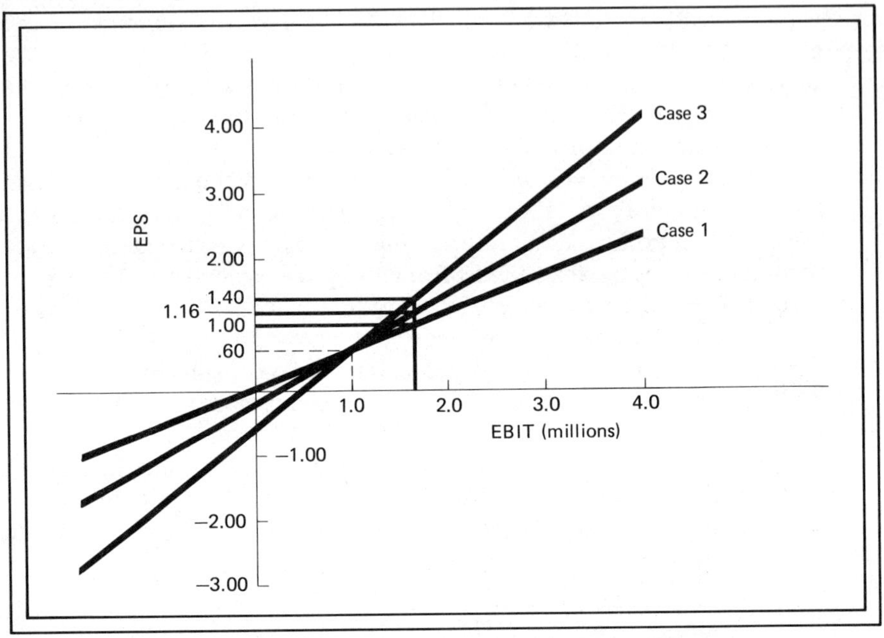

of $1.67 million, EPS for the three plans, respectively, would be $1.00, $1.16, and $1.40; this corresponds to the mean return on assets of 10 percent in Figure 6.2.

With EBIT–EPS analysis, forecast operating income can be transformed into forecast earnings per share and the risk which is impacted in financial leverage can be observed as shown in Figure 6.3. Given an estimate of the applicable price-earnings ratio, one corresponding to the level of risk

Table 6.4
EBIT–EPS Relationship
(for EBIT = $1,000,000)

	Case 1	*Case 2*	*Case 3*
EBIT	1,000,000	1,000,000	1,000,000
Less interest	0	287,500	500,000
Earnings before tax	1,000,000	712,500	500,000
Tax, at 40 percent	400,000	285,000	200,000
Earnings after tax	600,000	427,500	300,000
Shares outstanding	1,000,000	714,300	500,000
EPS	0.60	0.60	0.60

implied by the capital structure, the impact of financial leverage can be estimated. This approach will be demonstrated later in this chapter when the security evaluation model is introduced and illustrated.

RISK

A third important determinant of value, partially discussed in the preceding section, is risk. Risk was defined in Chapter 4 as dispersion in a subjective probability distribution; the relative measure of risk suggested there was the coefficient of variation, the standard deviation of a distribution divided by its expected value (Equation 4.9). This is a general definition with two important applications in valuation models:

1. BUSINESS RISK. Business risk is defined as dispersion in the distribution of after-tax *operating income*, independent of a firm's capital structure. That is, however the firm is financed, the gross earnings stream will vary due to variation in demand and supply factors underlying the stream of operating revenues and expenses.

2. FINANCIAL RISK. Financial risk, discussed in the preceding section, is defined as dispersion in the distribution of after-tax *net income*, and it is dependent on both the level of business risk and the firm's capital structure. Financial risk is variability in earnings accruing to common shareholders, given the variability in operating income.

If a firm's capital structure includes both debt and equity, return to shareholders will be variable but return to bondholders is fixed by contract. Aside from situations of bankruptcy, the absolute measure of dispersion is therefore the same for operating income and net income; relative measures, however, will differ because expected operating income exceeds expected net income. It is in this sense that financial risk is defined as relative dispersion in net income, given the relative dispersion in operating income. The point can be demonstrated arithmetically.[24]

Referring again to the numerical example given in Table 6.3 and Figure 6.1, assume that value ranges given there represent three standard deviations to either side of mean values. Table 6.5 summarizes business risk and financial risk measures under this assumption for each of the three financing plans

[24] The point can also be demonstrated statistically. Recalling the definition of operating income $\tilde{Y}$ and net income $\tilde{N}I$ both of which are random variables, and for constant interest payment I, $\tilde{N}I = \tilde{Y} - I$. Expected value and variance are calculated, $E(NI) = E(Y) - I$ and $\text{var}(NI) = \text{var}(Y) - I = \text{var}(Y)$. For financial risk $\sigma_{NI}/E(NI)$ and business risk $\sigma_y/E(Y)$, $\sigma_{NI}/E(NI) = \sigma_Y/E(NI) > \sigma_Y/E(Y)$.

For a firm partially financed by preferred stock, the preferred dividend, technically, is also a random variable because dividends can be passed on preferred stock. For practical purposes, however, no firm can long afford to maintain dividend arrearages, and it is convenient to consider preferred dividends as equivalent to interest payments for this purpose.

Table 6.5
Business Risk and Financial Risk

	Business Risk	*Financial Risk*		
		Case 1	*Case 2*	*Case 3*
(1) Standard deviation[a]	0.0667	0.0667	0.0933	0.1333
(2) Expected value	0.1000	0.1000	0.1160	0.1400
(3) Risk: coefficient of variation (1)/(2)	0.6667	0.6667	0.8046	0.9524

[a] From the range of values of Table 6.3, divided by 6 standard deviations.

outlined.[25] For case 1, where there is no external financing, business risk and financial risk are equal; both are measured at 0.6667. As leverage increases, in cases 2 and 3, business risk remains constant but financial risk increases to respective values of 0.8046 and 0.9524. Table 6.5 illustrates the positive association between leverage and *financial risk* and it also underscores the significance of *business risk* even for the pure equity firm. Both dimensions of risk are a significant influence on common stock value.

TAXES AND TRANSACTION COSTS

A brief word is in order concerning taxes and transaction costs since both affect equity yields. Portfolio implications and tax planning will be considered in Chapter 18; this discussion will be limited to the impact of taxes on the security valuation model. Investment income, whether dividends or capital gains, is probably taxed by both local and state governments but since those tax regulations vary so widely, the discussion will be limited to federal tax regulations.

TAX ON DIVIDENDS. Under regulations in effect at the time of this writing, each individual taxpayer may exclude up to $100 of dividends received from most domestic corporations. The exclusion applies to individuals; a husband and wife filing jointly where one has dividends of, say, $200 and the other $50 are only entitled to exclude $150. Abstracting from other considerations entirely, it would be advantageous to have shares either held jointly or redistributed within the family unit. Dividend income beyond the excluded level is taxed at ordinary income tax rates.

[25] As set forth here, both business risk and financial risk are defined in terms of rate of return variability. It is also possible to define them absolutely, without dividing through by assets and equity. The definition was adopted here to maintain consistency with the rate of return approach underlying the development of material in this text.

CAPITAL GAINS AND LOSSES. Capital gains and losses are accorded special treatment under federal tax regulations. Securities held one year or less are defined as short-term holdings; beyond a year it is a long-term holding. Long-term gains and losses are taxed at one-half the ordinary tax rate with a maximum 25 percent rate on the first $50,000 long-term gain and a maximum of 35 percent on long-term gains in excess of $50,000. Short-term gains and losses are taxed at the ordinary rate. In the case of a net long-term gain exceeding net short-term loss, the net gain (long-term gain less short-term loss) is taxed at one-half the ordinary tax rate. Capital loss deductibility is limited to $3000 in any year, but losses not deductible currently may be carried over to the next year.

TRANSACTION COSTS. Security transactions are subject to brokerage costs and to fees and taxes imposed by the Securities and Exchange Commission and the state of New York (and Florida, where applicable). The SEC fee is 1 cent per each $500 in value of shares sold; the New York State tax varies among residents and nonresidents. On May 1, 1975, brokerage commission schedules became competitive and this element of transaction cost, by far the largest, varies from broker to broker. An investor should investigate commission schedules as part of the process of selecting or changing brokers.

INDUSTRY AND SIZE EFFECTS

Valuation models have been used in this chapter to identify basic elements of common stock value. In the process the major variables required for constructing a security valuation model have been isolated and it is now possible to synthesize them in terms of an operational analytical technique. Before proceeding to that, however, some comment is in order as to the possible effect of (1) industry classification and (2) size of the firm on a firm's equity value. Neither of these is a valuation element per se; they are instead surrogate variables which may or may not influence underlying determinants of value.

INDUSTRY EFFECT. Industry classification implies that firms in an industry share a number of common characteristics which impact on value. While all firms in an economy are affected by changes in fiscal policy or the level of interest rates, firms in an industry are related in terms of demand for their product, fixed and variable factors of production, concentration, barriers to entry, and other factors which influence determinants of value. For this reason, "fundamental" security analysis has long focused on the notion that evaluation procedures proceed sequentially from the economy to the industry, and then to the firm, in that order. This view was stated emphatically in 1939 by Mead and Grodinsky: "Beside the selection of the industry, other considerations of investment are unimportant." It was restated more recently, in less extreme terms, by Reilly.[26] Given post–World War II emphasis on growth, it was logical to attempt to identify growth industries, selecting the best individual stock thereafter from firms classified as part of that industry. But the viability of this approach, and the significance of the "industry effect," remains an unresolved issue.

Empirical evidence on the question is inconclusive. In a study that is often cited, King found a significant association between market returns to a firm's shareholders and returns to other shareholders in the same industry; Brown and Ball found very similar results by associating a firm's average earnings with the average earnings of firms in the same industry.[27] Other studies supporting the industry effect include those of Fisher and Hall, Latané and Tuttle, and Williams and Goodman.[28] But contradictory evidence is provided by, among others, Breen, Farrar, and Joy.[29]

The issue cannot be settled here. In theory the argument that an industry effect should exist is persuasive; it seems logical to assume that firms which share common economic factors will also share common valuation factors. Yet evidence to the contrary is bothersome. In this respect it is interesting to note that the King study, cited above, found that firm–industry association has weakened over time. In view of the intensity of the merger movement witnessed in the last several decades, it is entirely possible that the industry effect was and is significant but that many firms can no longer be classified as part of any identifiable industry.[30] In this case the economy-industry-firm analytical sequence would apply to some firms but not to

[26] E. S. Mead and Julius Grodinsky, *The Ebb and Flow of Investment Values* (New York: Appleton-Century-Crofts, 1939); Frank Reilly, "The Misdirected Emphasis on Security Evaluation," *Financial Analysts Journal*, January–February 1973, pp. 54–60.

[27] King's study found that approximately half the variability in a security's market return was explained by changes affecting the entire market while about 10 percent additional variability was explained by an industry effect. Brown and Ball's study of earnings provided similar findings: some 35 to 40 percent of the variability in annual earnings of the firms sampled was associated with variability of earnings averaged over time while another 10 to 15 percent was associated with variability in the industry average. Benjamin King, "Market and Industry Factor in Stock Price Behavior," *Journal of Business*, January 1966, Part II, pp. 151–152, and Philip Brown and Ray Ball, Some Preliminary Findings on the Association Between the Earnings of a Firm, Its Industry, and the Economy, *Empirical Research in Accounting: Selected Studies*, 1967; Supplement to *Journal of Accounting Research* (1967), pp. 55–77.

[28] I. N. Fisher and G. R. Hall, "Risk and Corporate Rate of Return," *Quarterly Journal of Economics*, February 1969, pp. 79–92; H. Latané and D. Tuttle, "Industry Analysis Framework for Forming Probability Beliefs," *Financial Analysts Journal*, July–August 1968, pp. 51–61; W. H. Williams and M. L. Goodman, "A Statistical Grouping of Corporations by Their Financial Characteristics," *Journal of Financial and Quantitative Analysis*, September 1971, pp. 1095–1104.

[29] W. Breen, "Low Price-Earnings Ratios and Industry Relatives," *Financial Analysts Journal*, July–August 1968, pp. 125–127; Donald Farrar, *The Investment Decision Under Uncertainty* (Englewood Cliffs, N.J.: Prentice-Hall, 1962); O. Maurice Joy, "A Simulation Test of the Industry Analysis Hypothesis," *Journal of Business Research*, October 1974, pp. 373–384.

[30] Walter's case study of Hercules Powder illustrates the point. Sales for that firm, aside from a variety of chemical industry classifications, included paper, plastics, rubber, mining, food, construction, and "miscellaneous" products. See James E. Walter, *Dividend Policy and Enterprise Value* (Belmont, Calif.: Wadsworth, 1967).

others and the analyst would have to select forecasting techniques based upon observed empirical relationships on a firm-by-firm basis.

SIZE EFFECT. Size has also been cited as a possible determinant of value in the sense that size may be related to the level and variability of a firm's earnings stream. A large firm may be able to enjoy scale efficiencies which a smaller firm cannot realize, and a large firm may have access to debt and equity funds not available to a smaller firm. Moreover, as Baumol has argued, large firms can compete in all venture situations available to small firms but large firms can also invest where the scale of operations excludes smaller companies.[31] In theory, then, a relationship between size and profitability can be argued.

As in the case of the industry effect, empirical evidence as to the relationship between size and profitability is inconclusive. There is evidence which suggests than an inverse relationship exists between profitability and size but only with regard to relatively modest scales of operation; beyond that level, some $5 to 10 million perhaps, no significant association is evident.[32] Stekler found evidence of an inverse relationship between *variability* in profit rates and size.[33] These studies imply that large firms operate at lower risk-return levels than smaller firms, but they also provide no support for theoretical arguments which have been advanced. Supporting evidence is presented by Hall and Weiss; in a careful study of profit determinants they found that size does tend to generate high rates of profit partly from capital financing barriers and, to a lesser degree, from concentration.[34]

For the most part, size need not be considered directly by the analyst since advantages or disadvantages accruing from size will probably be reflected in empirical data which form the basis for analysts' predictions. Nonetheless, analysts should be sensitive to situations in which size may directly impact on security value. Wippern, to cite one example, found a generally significant association between a firm's price-earnings ratio and its size.[35]

[31] W. J. Baumol, *Business Behavior, Value, and Growth* (New York: MacMillan, 1959), p. 33. Studies of the relationship between size and capital availability are not numerous but one study found no evidence that an equity financing gap exists for small firms. Hans R. Stoll and Anthony J. Curley, "Small Business and the New Issues Market for Equities," *Journal of Financial and Quantitative Analysis*, September 1970, pp. 309–322.

[32] See H. O. Stekler, *Profitability and Size of Firm* (Berkeley: University of California Institute of Business and Economic Research, 1963), and G. Stigler, *Capital and Rates of Return in Manufacturing Industries* (N.J.: Princeton, University Press, 1963). Wittnebert studied the same problem and he found a trend toward this inverse relationship based on performance of a sample of firms for the period 1956–1968. Fred R. Wittnebert, "Bigness Versus Profitability," *Harvard Business Review*, January–February 1970, pp. 158–165.

[33] H. O. Stekler, "The Variability of Profitability with Size of Firm, 1947–58," *Journal of the American Statistical Association*, December 1964, pp. 1183–1193.

[34] Marshall Hall and Leonard Weiss, "Firm Size and Profitability," *Review of Economics and Statistics*, August 1967, pp. 319–331.

[35] J. F. Wippern, "Financial Structure and the Value of the Firm," *Journal of Finance*, December 1966, pp. 615–633.

Security Analysis Model

With valuation elements now identified, the security analysis model can be introduced and developed. A hypothetical firm will be used to illustrate the process; illustrations presented in Chapter 9 will demonstrate the analysis under more realistic conditions. It will be assumed that accounting values are precise and accurate and require no adjustment; Chapter 7 will consider accounting measurements in detail. Finally, it will be assumed that the price-earnings ratio is given; this important variable is discussed in Chapter 8. The analysis begins by assuming that forecasts are determined under conditions of certainty; this restrictive assumption will then be relaxed and risk will be introduced.

CERTAINTY

INVESTMENT HORIZON. The value of a share of common stock was previously defined as the discounted present value of an infinite dividend stream. Equation 6.3, restated for yield r rather than k, is:

$$P_0 = \sum_{t=1}^{\infty} D_t(1 + r)^{-t}$$

Notice that Equation 6.3 is insensitive to the initial period defined. It could be stated in terms of price three periods later:

$$P_3 = \sum_{t=4}^{\infty} D_t(1 + r)^{-t} \tag{6.11}$$

Equation 6.3 is an *infinite horizon* model; it is also the basis for a *finite horizon* model. For a three-year holding period, with the value of dividends thereafter defined by Equation 6.11,

$$P_0 = \frac{D_1}{(1 + r)^1} + \frac{D_2}{(1 + r)^2} + \frac{D_3}{(1 + r)^3} + \frac{P_3}{(1 + r)^3} \tag{6.12}$$

Generalizing,

$$P_0 = \sum_{t=1}^{n} D_t(1 + r)^{-t} + P_n(1 + r)^{-n} \tag{6.13}$$

Equation 6.13 is the security analysis model. Value is the discounted present value of dividend stream D_t and terminal price P_n. An investor would select an appropriate holding period n; given values for current price P_0, dividends D_t, and terminal value P_n, rate of return is the discount rate r equating those values in the model of Equation 6.13. Determination of holding period n is a portfolio revision question which will be considered at a later time. For purposes of this illustration, a three-year period will be selected, as in Equation 6.12.

OPERATING FLOWS. The next step is to forecast values for both dividends and earnings per share. Underlying these forecasts are estimates of (1) the flow of operating income, (2) the stock of assets required to support that level of income, and (3) the financing decision which provides funds to purchase needed assets. Tables 6.6(a) through 6.6(d) contain financial data for a hypothetical firm.[36] Data reported in Table 6.6(a) are beginning values at the time the security is analyzed. Income statement data refer to the immediately preceding year and the balance sheet values are those at the beginning of the current year. In the balance sheet, current liabilities are deducted from current assets for the purpose of reporting net working capital among the assets. This convention, which is followed by a number of firms when they prepare their annual reports to stockholders, focuses attention on the flow of funds through the enterprise; the balance sheet entry "Total liabilities and equity" therefore excludes current liabilities. Numbers in parentheses at the extreme right in Tables 6.6(b) through 6.6(d) refer to analytical stages in which values are inserted in the table for years 1, 2, and 3.

1. *Growth in sales.* The first step, and one of the most critical in any analysis, is to estimate the rate of growth in sales. In this case sales are assumed to grow at a fixed rate of 8 percent per year; values for each of the three years then appear in Table 6.6(b). These are, respectively, \$8,640,000, \$9,331,200, and \$10,077,696.

2. *Cost-volume relationship.* Operating costs are estimated next. For this purpose costs are classified as either *variable* or *fixed.* Variable costs are determined by the level of output; as output changes aggregate variable cost will also change. For this illustration variable costs are assumed to be 30 percent of dollar sales throughout the period. Period-fixed costs are those which are unrelated to the volume of output. A one-year lease to rent an automobile, once the decision is made and the contract is signed, is an example of a period-fixed cost. In this case-period fixed cost is assumed to increase at the rate of 5 percent per year over the three-year period. Values for variable and period-fixed costs are then entered as projected values in Table 6.6(b).

3. *Required assets.* A growing level of sales implies a stream of investment which results, in turn, in an increase in the level of required assets. In this case it is assumed that each dollar of sales requires an investment of 25 cents in net working capital (current assets less current liabilities) and an investment of \$2.50 in fixed assets. Depreciation is defined on a straight-line basis at the rate of 5 percent of cost per year. Depreciation is another type of fixed cost; unlike period-fixed cost it involves an allocation of current expenditure to subsequent periods where income is generated as a result

[36] The income statement provided in Tables 6.6(a) through 6.6(d) is not organized in the usual accounting format. In lieu of line items and descriptions, for example, cost of sales, selling expense, etc., expenses are summarized functionally in terms of fixed and variable expenses. The reason for adopting this format is analytical; otherwise projection of the stream of expenses is exceedingly difficult.

Table 6.6(a)
Projected Financial Statements

	Year			
	Given	Projected		
	0	1	2	3
Income Statement				
Sales	8,000,000			
Variable costs	2,400,000			
Remainder	5,600,000			
Period fixed costs	1,940,000			
Remainder	3,660,000			
Depreciation	1,000,000			
Earnings before interest and taxes	2,660,000			
Interest expense	160,000			
Earnings before taxes	2,500,000			
Income taxes	1,000.000			
Net income	1,500,000			
Dividend on common stock	900,000			
Increased in retained earnings	600,000			
Common shares outstanding	1,000,000			
Earning per share	1.50			
Dividends per share	.90			
Balance Sheet				
Net working capital	2,000,000			
Plant and equipment				
Cost	20,000,000			
Accumulated depreciation	(12,000,000)			
Net	8,000,000			
Total assets	10,000,000			
8 percent bonds	2,000,000			
Equity				
Common stock, $5 stated value	5,000,000			
Retained earnings	3,000,000			
Total equity	8,000,000			
Total liabilities and equity	10,000,000			

Table 6.6(b)
Projected Financial Statements

	Year				
	Given	Projected			
	0	1	2	3	
Income Statement					
Sales	8,000,000	8,640,000	9,331,200	10,077,696	(1)
Variable costs	2,400,000	2,592,000	2,799,360	3,023,309	(2)
Remainder	5,600,000	6,048,000	6,531,840	7,054,387	
Period fixed costs	1,940,000	2,037,000	2,138,850	2,245,793	(2)
Remainder	3,660,000	4,011,000	4,392,990	4,808,594	
Depreciation	1,000,000				
Earnings before interest and taxes	2,660,000				
Interest expense	160,000				
Earnings before taxes	2,500,000				
Income taxes	1,000,000				
Net income	1,500,000				
Dividend on common stock	900,000				
Increased in retained earnings	600,000				
Common shares outstanding	1,000,000				
Earnings per share	1.50				
Dividends per share	.90				
Balance Sheet					
Net working capital	2,000,000				
Plant and equipment					
Cost	20,000,000				
Accumulated depreciation	(12,000,000)				
Net	8,000,000				
Total assets	10,000,000				
8 percent bonds	2,000,000				
Equity					
Common stock, $5 stated value	5,000,000				
Retained earnings	3,000,000				
Total equity	8,000,000				
Total liabilities and equity	10,000,000				

Table 6.6(c)
Projected Financial Statements

	Year				
		Projected			
	Given 0	1	2	3	
Income Statement					
Sales	8,000,000	8,640,000	9,331,200	10,077,696	(1)
Variable costs	2,400,000	2,592,000	2,799,360	3,023,309	(2)
Remainder	5,600,000	6,048,000	6,531,840	7,054,387	
Period fixed costs	1,940,000	2,037,000	2,138,850	2,245,793	(2)
Remainder	3,660,000	4,011,000	4,392,990	4,808,594	
Depreciation	1,000,000	1,080,000	1,166,400	1,259,712	(2)
Earnings before interest and taxes	2,660,000	2,931,000	3,226,590	3,548,882	
Interest expense	160,000				
Earnings before taxes	2,500,000				
Income taxes	1,000,000				
Net income	1,500,000				
Dividend on common stock	900,000				
Increase in retained earnings	600,000				
Common shares outstanding	1,000,000				
Earnings per share	1.50				
Dividends per share	.90				
Balance Sheet					
Net working capital	2,000,000	2,160,000	2,332,800	2,519,424	(3)
Plant and equipment					
Cost	20,000,000	21,600,000	23,328,000	25,194,240	(3)
Accumulated depreciation	(12,000,000)	(13,080,000)	(14,246,400)	(15,506,112)	(3)
Net	8,000,000	8,520,000	9,081,600	9,688,128	(3)
Total assets	10,000,000	10,680,000	11,414,400	12,207,552	
8 percent bonds	2,000,000				
Equity					
Common stock, $5 stated value	5,000,000				
Retained earnings	3,000,000				
Total equity	8,000,000				
Total liabilities and equity	10,000,000				

Table 6.6 (d)
Projected Financial Statements

	Year				
	Given	*Projected*			
	0	*1*	*2*	*3*	
Income Statement					
Sales	8,000,000	8,640,000	9,331,200	10,077,696	(1)
Variable costs	2,400,000	2,592,000	2,799,360	3,023,309	(2)
Remainder	5,600,000	6,048,000	6,531,840	7,054,387	
Period fixed costs	1,940,000	2,037,000	2,138,850	2,245,793	(2)
Remainder	3,660,000	4,011,000	4,392,990	4,808,594	
Depreciation	1,000,000	1,080,000	1,166,400	1,259,712	(3)
Earnings before interest and taxes	2,660,000	2,931,000	3,226,590	3,548,882	
Interest expense	160,000	161,220	161,115	159,476	(4)
Earnings before taxes	2,500,000	2,769,780	3,065,475	3,389,406	
Income taxes	1,000,000	1,107,913	1,226,190	1,355,762	(4)
Net income	1,500,000	1,661,867	1,839,285	2,033,644	(4)
Dividend on common stock	900,000	997,120	1,103,571	1,220,186	(4)
Increase in retained earnings	600,000	664,747	735,714	813,458	(4)
Common shares outstanding	1,000,000	1,000,000	1,000,000	1,000,000	(4)
Earnings per share	1.50	1.66	1.84	2.03	(4)
Dividends per share	.90	1.00	1.10	1.22	(4)
Balance Sheet					
Net working capital	2,000,000	2,160,000	2,332,800	2,519,424	(3)
Plant and equipment					
Cost	20,000,000	21,600,000	23,328,000	25,194,240	(3)
Accumulated depreciation	(12,000,000)	(13,080,000)	(14,246,400)	(15,506,112)	(3)
Net	8,000,000	8,520,000	9,081,600	9,688,128	(3)
Total assets	10,000,000	10,680,000	11,414,400	12,207,552	
8 percent bonds	2,000,000	2,015,253	2,013,939	1,993,453	(4)
Equity					
Common stock, $5 stated value	5,000,000	5,000,000	5,000,000	5,000,000	(4)
Retained earnings	3,000,000	3,664,747	4,400,461	5,213,919	(4)
Total equity	8,000,000	8,664,747	9,400,461	10,213,919	
Total liabilities and equity	10,000,000	10,680,000	11,414,400	12,207,372	

of previous investment. Income statement and balance sheet entries arising from assumptions of this section are reflected in Table 6.6(c).

4. *Financing.* The final step in the process concerns the financing of assets acquired under step 3 above. In order to keep this presentation simple, it is assumed that the firm finances internally to whatever extent is possible given a dividend payout ratio of 60 percent of annual earnings. Any imbalance in the source and use of funds will be adjusted by issuing additional bonds at an 8 percent cost of capital or by retiring existing 8 percent bonds. The firm is assumed to avoid additional equity financing; outstanding common stock will be held constant during the period at a level of 1 million shares.

Financing involves computational circularity since funds provided by operations are dependent on interest expense which, in turn, depends on the level of outstanding debt. Thus funds provided internally and externally must be determined simultaneously. But this is not a difficult problem in this case because it involves simple arithmetic calculations.[37] From Tables 6.6(a) through 6.6(d) or Equation 6.10, without preferred stock, it is apparent that retained earnings depend on earnings before interest and taxes EBIT, interest expense I, tax rate t_x, and earnings retention rate b:

$$\text{earnings retained} = [(\text{EBIT} - I)(1 - t_x)](b) \tag{6.14}$$

In period 0, for example,

$$\begin{aligned}\text{earnings retained} &= [(2{,}660{,}000 - 160{,}000)(0.6)](0.4)\\ &= [2{,}500{,}000(0.6)](0.4)\\ &= 600{,}000\end{aligned}$$

Funds provided by operations consist of earnings retained plus all noncash items charged against earnings; in this case the only noncash expense is depreciation d. Total funds provided consist of funds provided by operations plus funds provided by new debt ΔL; funds provided must be equal to funds employed to purchase assets ΔA. With the interest rate on new and old debt i assumed to be 8 percent, two simultaneous equations result:

$$\Delta A = [(\text{EBIT} - I)(1 - t_x)](b) + d + \Delta L \tag{6.15}$$

$$I = (i)(L + \Delta L) \tag{6.16}$$

Substituting Equation 6.16 into 6.15 and simplifying,

$$\Delta L = \frac{\Delta A - [(\text{EBIT} - iL)(1 - t_x)] - d}{1 - [(i)(1 - t_x)(b)]} \tag{6.17}$$

[37] In this example the debt-equity ratio is allowed to vary. If a debt-equity ratio is specified, outstanding shares will also vary. This would require the solution of more than two simultaneous equations and that is unnecessary for purposes of this illustration. For a simultaneous equation approach see James M. Warren and John P. Shelton, "A Simultaneous Equation Approach to Financial Planning," *Journal of Finance*, December 1971, pp. 1123–1142.

Table 6.7
Projected Source and Use of Funds

	1	*2*	*3*
Funds provided by operations			
Net income retained	664,747	735,714	813,458
Noncash expense, depreciation	1,080,000	1,166,400	1,259,712
Total	1,744,747	1,902,114	2,073,170
Assets required			
Working capital	160,000	172,800	186,624
Plant and equipment	1,600,000	1,728,000	1,866,240
Total	1,760,000	1,900,800	2,052,684
Deficiency (excess)	15,253	(1,314)	(20,486)
Funds provided by bonds	15,253	(1,314)	(20,486)

For periods 1 through 3, respectively, debt issued (+) or retired (−) is easily calculated; computations are proven in Table 6.7 where sources and uses of funds are reconciled.

$$\text{Year 1: } \Delta L = \frac{1{,}760{,}000 - [(2{,}931{,}000 - 160{,}000)(0.6)(0.4)] - 1{,}080{,}000}{1 - [(0.08)(0.6)(0.4)]}$$

$$= \frac{14{,}960}{0.9808}$$

$$= 15{,}253$$

$$\text{Year 2: } \Delta L = \frac{1{,}900{,}800 - [(3{,}226{,}590 - 161{,}220)(0.6)(0.4)] - 1{,}166{,}400}{1 - [(0.08)(0.6)(0.4)]}$$

$$= \frac{-1289}{0.9808}$$

$$= -1314$$

$$\text{Year 3: } \Delta L = \frac{2{,}052{,}684 - [(3{,}548{,}882 - 161{,}115)(0.6)(0.4)] - 1{,}259{,}712}{1 - [(0.08)(0.6)(0.4)]}$$

$$= \frac{-20{,}092}{0.9808}$$

$$= -20{,}486$$

Under the financing plan outlined, debt is issued in the first year and retired in both the second and third years. Given the solution to the financing plan set forth, projected income statements and balance sheets can be completed; this is demonstrated in Table 6.6(d). Other than the current price of the stock P_0 and the price-earnings ratio at the end of the third year, all values required for completing Equation 6.13 for valuation are now available.

TERMINAL VALUE. Third-year terminal value depends on earnings per share, \$2.03 from Table 6.6(d), and the capitalization factor or price-earnings ratio applied to that number. If a price-earnings multiple of 20 is assumed at the end of year 3, terminal value will be \$40.60 (20 × 2.03). If the current price P_0 is found to be \$30.00, all necessary values are available to calculate rate of return.

RATE OF RETURN. Abstracting from taxes and transaction costs momentarily, rate of return is the internal rate of return which equates projected flows:

$$30.00 = \frac{1.00}{(1+r)^1} + \frac{1.10}{(1+r)^2} + \frac{1.22}{(1+r)^3} + \frac{40.60}{(1+r)^3}$$

It is easily shown that r is approximately equal to 14 percent (13.94 percent).

With taxes and transaction costs the evaluation model of Equation 6.13 must be adjusted. Assume that securities can be either purchased or sold at some percentage c of value, that the investor's personal tax rate, ignoring the dividend exclusion, is t_p percent of taxable income, and that the rate for capital gains is $t_p/2$. Under these conditions the evaluation model of Equation 6.13 becomes:

$$P_0(1+c) = \sum_{t=1}^{n} \frac{D_t(1-t_p)}{(1+r)^t} + \frac{P_n(1-c) - (t_p/2)[P_n(1-c) - P_0(1+c)]}{(1+r)^n} \tag{6.18}$$

To illustrate, assume a brokerage commission of 2 percent and a personal tax rate of 40 percent. Then,

$$P_0(1+c) = 30.00(1.02) = 30.60$$

$$P_3(1-c) = 40.60(0.98) = 39.79$$

$$30.60 = \frac{1.00(0.6)}{(1+r)^1} + \frac{1.10(0.6)}{(1+r)^2} + \frac{1.22(0.6)}{(1+r)^3} + \frac{39.79 - 0.2[39.79 - 30.60]}{(1+r)^3}$$

$$= \frac{0.60}{(1+r)^1} + \frac{0.66}{(1+r)^2} + \frac{0.732}{(1+r)^3} + \frac{37.952}{(1+r)^3}$$

Adjusted for taxes and transaction costs, rate of return is now approximately 7 percent.[38] An investor requiring an after-tax yield of, say, 6 percent would find the security attractive.

[38] To four decimal places, r is equal to .0708.

INTRINSIC VALUE. The security analysis model of Equation 6.18 can be adapted to a present value or an intrinsic value approach by defining discount rate k as the investor's required rate of return, solving then for the present value of future cash flows. Assuming a required after-tax rate of 6 percent, for example,

$$\begin{aligned} 0.600(1.06)^{-1} &= 0.600(0.9434) = 0.5660 \\ 0.660(1.06)^{-2} &= 0.660(0.8900) = 0.5874 \\ 0.732(1.06)^{-3} &= 0.732(0.8396) = 0.6146 \\ 37.952(1.06)^{-3} &= 37.952(0.8396) = \underline{31.8645} \\ & \qquad\qquad\qquad\qquad\;\; 33.6325 \end{aligned}$$

Since intrinsic value of 33.63 exceeds cost of 30.60, the investor would be willing to purchase the security. It should be noted here that intrinsic value depends in part on the investor's tax rate; *intrinsic value changes, accordingly, from investor to investor*, and the use of the term *intrinsic* should not be interpreted literally.

ADJUSTMENT FOR RISK

ELEMENTS. To this point certainty has been assumed in the discussion of the security analysis models of Equations 6.13 and 6.18. Aside from net current price $P_0(1 + c)$, however, model variables are *random variables* represented by subjective probability distributions with, at least, expected values and standard deviations. Variables subject to risk are fivefold: (1) dividends, (2) terminal period earnings per share, (3) terminal period price–earnings multiple, (4) income tax rate, and (5) terminal period transaction costs. Variability in any of these factors, no less all of them, generates variability in both rate of return and intrinsic value. For practical purposes taxes and transaction costs should probably be treated as constants until information to the contrary is recognized; at that time all securities in a portfolio should be reevaluated. But dispersion in the other variables is too significant to ignore and distributions for each should be estimated. The difficulty involved in this depends on the relationship existing among model variables. The easiest case to deal with is one where variables are *independent* of each other; *dependence* is far more vexing a problem.

INDEPENDENCE AMONG VARIABLES. As a first approximation, and to illustrate the process, reconsider the evaluation procedure outlined in Tables 6.6(a) through 6.6(d). As before, retain all assumptions but one: assume that rate of growth in sales is a random variable with outcomes and associated probabilities given in Table 6.8. Under those assumptions dividends and terminal price were recalculated[39] and, for a current price of \$30.00, ignoring tax and transaction costs for simplicity, rates of return were calculated for

[39] Calculations are not given here since each is merely a replication of the illustration provided in the preceding section.

Table 6.8
Rate of Return Distribution with Variable Growth Rate for Sales

I. Rates of Return

Growth Rate	Probability	D_1	D_2	D_3	P_3	Rate of Return
0.06	0.25	0.98	1.06	1.14	38.20	0.1163
0.08	0.50	1.00	1.10	1.22	40.60	0.1394
0.10	0.25	1.02	1.15	1.30	43.20	0.1632

II. Distribution

i	r_i	p_i	$p_i r_i$	$r_i - E(r)$	$[r_i - E(r)]^2$	$p_i[r_i - E(r)]^2$
1	0.1163	0.25	0.0291	−0.0233	0.000543	0.000136
2	0.1394	0.50	0.0697	−0.0002	0.000000	0.000000
3	0.1632	0.25	0.0408	0.0236	0.000557	0.000139
Total		1.00				
$E(r)$			0.1396			
var(r)						0.000275
$\sigma(r)$						0.0166

each of the three growth rates defined. These calculations are summarized in part I of Table 6.8. In part II the rate of return distribution is calculated by way of the format of Table 4.1, from Chapter 4. Expected rate of return is found to be 13.96 percent with a standard deviation of 1.66 percent.

To complicate the process, assume that the price-earnings ratio is also a random variable with outcomes and probabilities as follows:

Outcome	Probability
8	0.05
12	0.05
16	0.20
20	0.60
24	0.05
28	0.05
	1.00

Assume also that growth rate and the price-earnings ratio are independent of each other.[40] Under these circumstances there are now 18 possible outcomes (3 × 6) with 18 associated probabilities. These are summarized in

[40] This is a highly unrealistic assumption, but it has been drawn to illustrate the notion of variability in the distribution of rate of return. The relationship between growth and price-earnings ratio will be considered in Chapter 8.

Table 6.9
Rate of Return Distribution with Variable Growth and Variable Price-Earnings Ratio

Growth Rate	Price-Earnings	Probability	= p	D_1	D_2	$D_3 + P_3$	Internal Rate of Return
	8	.25 × .05	.0125	.98	1.06	16.42	−.1564
	12	.25 × .05	.0125	.98	1.06	24.06	−.0471
.06	16	.25 × .20	.0500	.98	1.06	31.70	.0412
	20	.25 × .60	.1500	.98	1.06	39.34	.1163
	24	.25 × .05	.0125	.98	1.06	46.98	.1825
	28	.25 × .05	.0125	.98	1.06	54.62	.2418
	8	.50 × .05	.0250	1.00	1.10	17.46	−.1390
	12	.50 × .05	.0250	1.00	1.10	25.58	−.0275
.08	16	.50 × .20	.1000	1.00	1.10	33.70	.0625
	20	.50 × .60	.3000	1.00	1.10	41.82	.1394
	24	.50 × .05	.0250	1.00	1.10	49.94	.2068
	28	.50 × .05	.0250	1.00	1.10	58.06	.2673
	8	.25 × .05	.0125	1.02	1.15	18.58	.1209
	12	.25 × .05	.0125	1.02	1.15	27.22	−.0072
.10	16	.25 × .20	.0500	1.02	1.15	35.86	.0849
	20	.25 × .60	.1500	1.02	1.15	44.50	.1632
	24	.25 × .05	.0125	1.02	1.15	53.14	.2320
	28	.25 × .05	.0125	1.02	1.15	61.78	.2938
						$E(r)$	.1117
						$\text{var}(r)$	.0070
						$\sigma(r)$	.0837

Table 6.9. Internal rates of return were calculated for each in the same manner illustrated above and, again employing the methodology of Table 6.8, part II, expected rate of return and standard deviation were found to be, respectively, 11.17 percent and 8.37 percent.

It should be fairly evident, even at this stage, that the introduction of further variability will increasingly complicate the process and, in any practical sense, it will soon become necessary to perform necessary arithmetic by computer. This was the approach employed by analysts of the First National City Bank in their pioneering study of the copper industry in 1967.[41] As shown in Figure 6.4, supply-demand elements in the copper industry were used to forecast copper consumption by way of the multiple regression technique. Earnings were then forecast probabilistically with excellent near-term accuracy; to be effective this simulation technique must be repeated sequentially as new information is received, in the sense described earlier in Chapter 4 of this text.

[41] John A. Olsen and Terry A. Blaney, "Forecasting by Probabilities: The Copper Industry," *Financial Analysts Journal*, March–April 1968, pp. 36–40.

Figure 6.4

Probabilistic Analysis of the Copper Industry

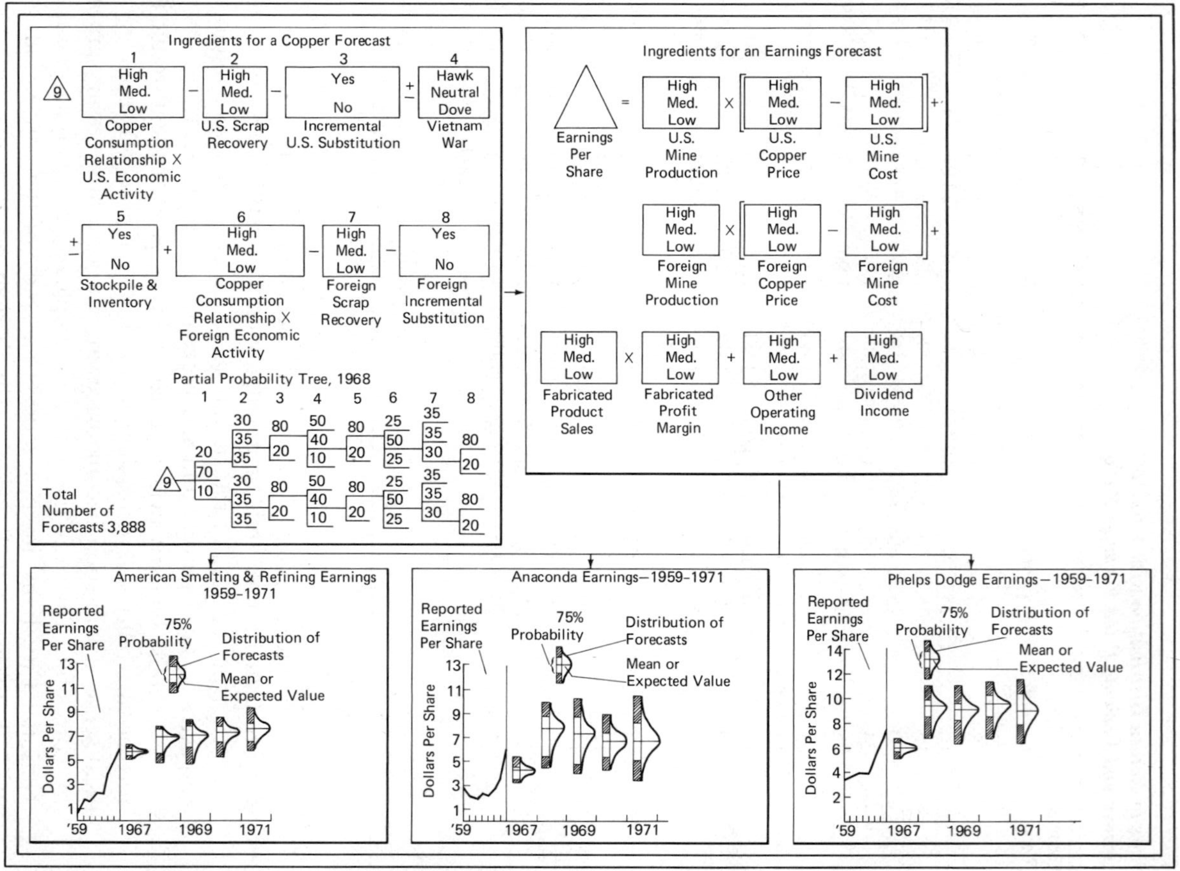

Source: I. A. Olsen and T. A. Blaney, "Forecasting by Probabilities: the Copper

INTERDEPENDENCE AMONG VARIABLES. The preceding examples assumed independence among random variables. Where dependence exists, forecasting is yet more difficult because patterns of association among variables must be specified for the estimated distribution to have relevance. Under these circumstances, because of the number of variables involved, computer analysis cannot be avoided.[42] Once programmed, however, and subject to feedback and adaptation as forecast outcomes are compared to actual outcomes, the computer provides the analyst with a powerful tool. Computer models are likely to be employed with increasing frequency in the foreseeable future, particularly in view of the need to evaluate risk.[43]

INTRINSIC VALUE ADJUSTMENT. Although the main emphasis here is directed to rate of return, intrinsic value provides an alternative investment criterion which should also be adjusted for risk. There are two possible approaches in this regard: (1) a formal one in which the distribution of intrinsic value is defined and calculated and (2) an informal approach using either a *risk-adjusted discount rate* or a *certainty equivalent.* The first approach is analytically formidable since it becomes necessary to specify interdependencies among variables over time to derive formulas for mean and standard deviation of intrinsic value.[44] It is possible to adjust the simulation technique described above, employing a risk-free rate of return for each iteration of the simulation model. In this manner a distribution of intrinsic value, in lieu of a distribution of internal rate of return, is the model output. As before, the adequacy of this distribution depends on the adequacy of interrelationships specified in the simulation model.

An alternative approach is to select a discount rate which reflects the investor's attitude toward the risk impacted in each cash flow element of the intrinsic value model. Since risk may vary from flow to flow, discount rates may also vary for each term in the present value model. Dispersion in the stream of dividends, for example, is probably less than dispersion in terminal price. This suggests a basic difficulty with this approach: identifying relevant discount rate or rates. Moreover, it proves to be difficult from a portfolio viewpoint where one of the necessary inputs is the distribution of rates of return of included securities.

[42] The process has been illustrated by Hertz. Although his study focused on the business investment problem and not on security analysis, the procedures are very similar. David B. Hertz, "Risk Analysis in Capital Investment," *Harvard Business Review*, January–February 1964, pp. 95–106.

[43] Computer models which provide for a distribution of values include those suggested by Ahlers, Eiteman, and Whittal. David M. Ahlers, "SEM: A Security Analysis Model," in *Analytical Methods in Banking*, ed. Kalman J. Cohen and Frederick S. Hammer (Homewood, Ill.: Irwin, 1966); David K. Eiteman, "A Computer Program for Common Stock Valuation," *Financial Analysts Journal*, July–August 1968, pp. 107–111; David Whittall, "A Simulation Model for Estimating Earnings," *Financial Analysts Journal*, November–December 1968, pp. 115–118.

[44] For an analysis of the problem of dependence see Frederick S. Hillier, "The Derivation of Probabilistic Information for the Evaluation of Risky Investments," *Management Science*, April 1963, pp. 443–457.

The remaining approach would have the investor select a certain value for which indifference exists among risky return and receipt of that selected value with certainty. Assume that an investor would be indifferent between \$0.90 with certainty and an uncertain \$1.00 of either dividends or terminal price. Then the 0.90 certainty equivalent would be substituted for each uncertain 1.00 in deriving flows for the purpose of calculating intrinsic value. As in the case of the risk-adjusted discount rate, estimation of certainty equivalents, together with portfolio considerations, poses difficulty for the analyst attempting to employ this technique.

Summary

In this chapter elements of security analysis were explored. Determinants of value were considered first; these were earnings and dividends, with growth emphasized, and risk. Particular emphasis was placed on the meaning and estimation of financial risk. Industry, size, transaction costs, and taxes were also considered.

With value elements identified, the security analysis model was introduced and illustrated with hypothetical examples. Finally, risk was analyzed in the context of a distribution of internal rates of return.

The next task is to add realism to the model introduced here. To do this it is necessary to carefully examine the relevance and accuracy of accounting measurements since these data are critical inputs to the evaluative system. Chapter 7 is devoted to this issue. In succeeding chapters price-earnings ratios will be analyzed (Chapter 8) and forecasting will be considered in detail (Chapter 9). Chapter 9 will also summarize the overall methodology with a case study of security analysis.

Questions and Problems

1. Which of the following has the greatest value?
   a. A current dividend of \$2.50 per share, growing at 4 percent per year, if the required rate of return is 8 percent.
   b. A current dividend of \$3.00 per share, growing at 10 percent per year, if the required rate of return is 16 percent.
   c. A dividend of \$5.00 per share per year to be received at the end of each of the next ten years, with \$8.00 per share to be received thereafter each year forever, with a required rate of return of 10 percent.
2. Calculate the impact on each \$1 of dividends if a firm has an "abnormal" growth rate of 12 percent, a normal growth rate of 8 percent, and a required rate of return of 10 percent where abnormal growth is realized for 0, 5, 10, and 20 years.
3. A firm with \$50 million in assets is financed by \$10 million in 8 percent first-mortgage bonds and \$40 million of common stock. Four million common shares are outstanding. Expected before-tax operating return on assets is \$10 million, but management estimates that that value could be as low as \$5 million or as high as \$15 million. The firm is considering the issue of an additional \$15 million in 10 percent debenture

bonds; proceeds would be used to acquire the firm's common stock in the open market at an average price of $15 per share. The firm's tax rate is 40 percent.

a. Calculate the expected after-tax rate of return on equity at the lowest, average, and highest levels of before-tax operating income under both the current and the proposed financing plans, and identify that part of equity yield arising from financial leverage.

b. Calculate earnings per share at all three levels, minimum, average, and maximum, under both financing plans. What is the EPS break-even level of EBIT?

c. Which plan seems preferable? Explain.

4. Table 6.8 of the text provides dividends and terminal prices for the firm illustrated in that section under the assumption that growth in sales is 6 percent in one case and 10 percent in another.

a. Prove the values reported by following the methodology of Tables 6.6(a) through 6.6(d).

b. What relationship exists among rates of growth in (1) sales, (2) EBIT, and (3) EPS? What causes variation in these values? Explain.

c. What is the effect of rate of growth on book measures of the capital structure?

5. Assume that an investment of $30 in a security which promises no dividend will generate an EPS, at the end of one period, of $2 with a 30 percent probability or $3 with a 70 percent probability; price-earnings ratio, which is independent of earnings per share, will be 10 with a 20 percent probability, 15 with 40 percent probability, or 20 with a 40 percent probability. Calculate the expected value and standard deviation of the distribution of rate of return for this security. Ignore personal taxes and transaction costs.

Selected References

ELEMENTS OF VALUE

Baxter, Nevins D., "Leverage, Risk of Ruin and the Cost of Capital," *Journal of Finance*, September 1967, pp. 395–403.

Bigus, Anatol W., "Managing Portfolios with Graham & Dodd," *Journal of Portfolio Management*, Spring 1977, pp. 58–62.

Black, Fischer, "The Dividend Puzzle," *Journal of Portfolio Management*, Winter 1976, pp. 5–8.

Brigham, Eugene F., and Myron J. Gordon, "Leverage, Dividend Policy, and the Cost of Capital," *Journal of Finance*, March 1968, pp. 85–103.

Brown, Philip, and Ray Ball, "Some Preliminary Findings on the Association Between the Earnings of a Firm, Its Industry, and the Economy," *Empirical Research in Accounting: Selected Studies, 1967*; Supplement to *Journal of Accounting Research* (1967): 55–77.

Cragg, John G., and Burton G. Malkiel, "The Consensus and Accuracy of Some Predictions of the Growth of Corporate Earnings," *Journal of Finance*, March 1968, pp. 67–84.

Friend, Irwin, and Marshall Puckett, "Dividends and Stock Prices," *American Economic Review*, September 1964, pp. 656–682.

Gordon, Myron, *The Investment, Financing and Valuation of the Corporation* (Homewood, Ill.: Irwin, 1962).

Hall, Marshall, and Leonard Weiss, "Firm Size and Profitability," *Review of Economics and Statistics*, August 1967, pp. 319–331.

Joy, O. Maurice, "A Simulation Test of the Industry Analysis Hypothesis," *Journal of Business Research*, October 1974, pp. 373–384.

King, Benjamin, "Market and Industry Factor in Stock Price Behavior," *Journal of Business*, January 1966, part II, pp. 139–190.

Latane, H., and D. Tuttle, "Industry Analysis Framework for Forming Probability Beliefs," *Financial Analysts Journal*, July–August 1968, pp. 51–61.

Lintner, John, "Distribution of Incomes of Corporations Among Dividends, Retained Earnings, and Taxes," *American Economic Review*, May 1956, pp. 97–113.

———, "Dividends, Earnings, Leverage, Stock Prices and the Supply of Capital to Corporations," *Review of Economics and Statistics*, August 1962, pp. 243–269.

Litzenberger, Robert H., and O. Maurice Joy, "Further Evidence on the Persistence of Corporate Profitability Rates," *Western Economic Journal*, June 1970, pp. 209–212.

Mao, James C. T., "The Valuation of Growth Stocks: The Investment Opportunities Approach," *Journal of Finance*, March 1966, pp. 95–102.

Miller, Merton, and Franco Modigliani, "Dividend Policy, Growth, and the Valuation of Shares," *Journal of Business*, October 1961, pp. 411–433.

Modigliani, Franco, and Merton Miller, "The Cost of Capital, Corporation Finance, and the Theory of Investment," *American Economic Review*, June 1958, pp. 261–297.

Reilly, Frank, "The Misdirected Emphasis on Security Evaluation," *Financial Analysts Journal*, January–February 1973, pp. 54–60.

Richards, R. Malcolm, "Analysts Performance and the Accuracy of Corporate Earnings Forecasts," *Journal of Business* 49:3 (July 1976), pp. 350–357.

Staubus, George J., "Earnings Periods for Common Share Analysis," *Journal of Business*, October 1968, pp. 472–476.

Stekler, H. O., *Profitability and Size of Firm* (Berkeley: University of California Institute of Business and Economic Research, 1963).

———, "The Variability of Profitability with Size of Firm, 1947–1958," *Journal of the American Statistical Association*, December 1964, pp. 1183–1193.

Walter, James E., "Dividend Policy: Its Influence on the Value of the Enterprise," *Journal of Finance*, May 1963, pp. 280–291.

———, *Dividend Policy and Enterprise Value* (Belmont, Calif.: Wadsworth Publishing Co., Inc., 1967).

SECURITY ANALYSIS MODEL

Ahlers, David M., "SEM: A Security Analysis Model," in Kalman J. Cohen and Frederick S, Hammer, eds., *Analytical Methods in Banking* (Homewood, Ill.: Irwin, 1966).

Churchman, C. West, "An Analysis of the Concept of Simulation," in Austin C. Hoggatt and Frederick E. Balderston, eds., *Symposium on Simulation Models: Methodology and Applications to the Behavioral Sciences* (Cincinnati: South-Western, 1963).

Cohen, Kalman J., and Richard M. Cyert, "Computer Models in Dynamic Economics," *Quarterly Journal of Economics*, February 1961, pp. 112–127.

Eiteman, David K., "A Computer Program for Common Stock Valuation," *Financial Analysts Journal*, July–August 1968, pp. 107–111.

Hertz, David B., "Risk Analysis in Capital Investment," *Harvard Business Review*, January–February 1964, pp. 95–106.

Hillier, Frederick S., "The Derivation of Probabilistic Information for the Evaluation of Risky Investments," *Management Science*, April 1963, pp. 443–457.

Olsen, John A., and Terry A. Blaney, "Forecasting by Probabilities: The Copper Industry," *Financial Analysts Journal*, March–April 1968, pp. 36–40.

Orcutt, Guy H., "Simulation of Economic Systems," *American Economic Review*, December 1960, pp. 893–907.

Shubik, Martin, "Simulation of the Industry and the Firm," *American Economic Review*, December 1960, pp. 908–919.

Soldofsky, Robert M., "A Note on the History of Bond Tables and Stock Valuation Models," *Journal of Finance*, March 1966, pp. 103–111.

Warren, James M., and John P. Shelton, "A Simultaneous Equation Approach to Financial Planning," *Journal of Finance*, December 1971, pp. 1123–1142.

Whittall, David, "A Simulation Model for Estimating Earnings," *Financial Analysts Journal*, November–December 1968, pp. 115–118.

Williams, J. B., *The Theory of Investment Value* (Cambridge, Mass.: Harvard University Press, 1938).

Chapter 7
Accounting Data

Introduction

Security analysis involves the processing of information generated and reported by financial accountants. The analyst, accordingly, should be completely familiar with detailed procedures of accountancy. That implies formal training beyond any level possible here. At the same time, the reliability and accuracy of accounting data cannot be completely ignored. For this reason accounting procedures will be surveyed in this chapter but the discussion will be focused from an analyst's perspective; accounting will be explored with respect to its impact on the valuation process.

The first and most obvious question to consider is whether or not any relationship should or does exist among accounting measures and security prices. Accounting provides ex post historical values which quantitatively summarize *past* events; security prices, as detailed in Chapter 6, depend upon *future* events. The record of the past is useless to the analyst per se; it is valuable only to the extent that past performance can be extrapolated in predicting future outcomes. The issue, then, reduces to whether or not the market reacts positively to accounting information. Since accounting provides the only internally generated record of a firm's performance, security analysis would be meaningless if investors failed to respond to accounting data.

To resolve the question it may be considered both theoretically and empirically. Nicholas Dopuch provides a convincing theoretical argument to support the relevance of accounting data: assuming a relatively efficient capital market, investors will react to new information, including accounting information, in an unbiased manner. The performance of a firm over time will either verify or refute the validity of accounting values. Investors will not respond indefinitely to irrelevant information.[1] This does not imply that reported values are necessarily accepted at face value. It argues instead that accounting data, which can be adjusted to meet analytical needs, are proven to be relevant if they are associated with observed market behavior. Thus relevance is an empirical question. Moreover, empirical evidence supports the proposition that accounting and market values are indeed related with differences arising from accounting diversity recognized by investors. Evidence supporting this view has been provided by a number of authors including Ball and Brown; Beaver, Kettler, and Scholes; Gonedes; Martin; Mlynarczyk; and O'Donnell.[2]

Given the relevance of accounting data, and the prospect that reported values may have to be adjusted for purposes of security analysis, it is then worthwhile to consider accountancy in some detail. To proceed, the familiar process of double-entry accounting will be reviewed briefly to provide a foundation for the discussion which follows. The problem of procedural diversity and its impact on security analysis will then be pursued. The evolution and development of accounting principles will also be considered to place the problem of diversity in topical context. With this background established, accounting rate of return will be compared to the internal rate of return which is the basis of security analysis. Finally, current controversies in accounting will be inventoried and examined with respect to their concurrence with, or departure from, internal rate of return elements.

Double-Entry Accounting

The core of double-entry accounting is the historical cost convention. Under historical cost, accounting is an ex post system of recording, summarizing,

[1] Nicholas Dopuch, "Discussion of an Empirical Test of the Relevance of Accounting Information for Investment Decisions," *Empirical Research in Accounting: Selected Studies*, 1971: Supplement to *Journal of Accounting Research* (1971): 32–40.

[2] Ray Ball and Philip Brown, "An Empirical Evaluation of Accounting Income Numbers," *Journal of Accounting Research*, Autumn 1968, pp. 159–178; W. Beaver, P. Kettler, and M. Scholes, "The Association Between Market Determined and Accounting Determined Risk Measures," *Accounting Review*, October 1970, pp. 654–682; N. Gonedes, "Efficient Capital Markets and External Accounting," *Accounting Review*, January 1972, pp. 11–21; Alvin Martin, "An Empirical Test of the Relevance of Accounting Information for Investment Decisions," *Empirical Research in Accounting: Selected Studies, 1971*; Supplement to *Journal of Accounting Research* (1971): 1–31; Francis A. Mlynarczyk, "An Empirical Study of Accounting Methods and Stock Prices," *Empirical Research in Accounting: Selected Studies, 1969*; Supplement to *Journal of Accounting Research* (1969): 63–89; J. L. O'Donnell, "Relationships Between Reported Earnings and Stock Prices in the Electric Utility Industry," *Accounting Review*, January 1965, pp. 549–553. Martin's paper contains an extended bibliography in Table 1, pp. 22–24.

and reporting the cumulative effect of transactions at values determined, with but a few exceptions, on the basis of original bargained cost. Transactions are recorded and traced over time in terms of their effect on assets, liabilities, and equity. Assets represent property rights, both tangible and intangible; liabilities and equity are claims against assets on the part of creditors and owners, respectively. Changes in ownership equity arising from income (revenue less expense) are summarized in temporary profit and loss accounts. These subsidiary accounts, together with the dividend account tracing distribution of income to owners, are closed to equity periodically.

The mechanics of double-entry accounting involve two offsetting classes of balances: debits and credits. In a number of countries, including the United States, accountants record debits on the left side and credits on the right side of books, records, and reports. Aside from some offsetting or "contra" accounts, cumulative debit balances remaining after closing of accounts are assets; liability and equity similarly are cumulative credit balances. The flow of debits and credits are recorded, traced, and reported periodically in accordance with two processes: the *transaction mechanic* and the *period reporting mechanic.*

TRANSACTION MECHANIC

Accounting records and summarizes the aggregate monetary effect of business transactions, with monetary measurement generally fixed in terms of the money unit relevant at the time of the transaction.[3] Transactions result in a flow of funds through the enterprise. In this context "funds" may be defined narrowly as cash or it may be defined more broadly to include all elements of working capital. For example, under the latter definition, also known as the accrual basis, sale of merchandise on account is a transaction; under the narrower definition no transaction would be recognized until the customer remits a cash payment. Accounting, except for some isolated instances, employs the accrual basis.

Transactions may be classified in six general categories with the following effect on assets, liabilities, and equity:

1. *Debt or equity financing.* Creditors or owners provide funds to the firm, increasing assets and (either) liabilities or equity.
2. *Sale of assets.* The firm disposes of existing assets, typically investments or fixed assets. Assets decrease in an amount equal to the book value of converted assets and assets increase by an amount equal to proceeds from the sale; equity decreases (increases) in an amount equal to the loss (gain) on the sale. Loss or gain is the difference between book value and proceeds.
3. *Operations.* Operations involve revenue, which increases both assets and equity, and expense, which decreases both assets and equity. Income is the residual of revenue after expense has been deducted. (Operating transactions

[3] The use of constant historical dollar values in lieu of price level adjusted values is a topic of controversy currently. This problem will be considered in the last section of this chapter.

may affect other accounts temporarily. An expense transacted on account, for example, temporarily increases liabilities but the long run effect is a decrease in assets.)

4. *Debt or equity retirement* (partial or full liquidation). Funds no longer required by the firm are returned to creditors or owners. Liabilities or equity decrease with a corresponding decrease in assets.
5. *Purchase of assets* (*expansion*). Funds provided by creditors or owners are invested in working capital, tangible or intangible assets, or securities. This results in a simultaneous increase in one asset and decrease in another (cash). (As in the case of category 4 above there may be a temporary increase in a liability in lieu of a decrease in assets.)
6. *Distribution of income.* Funds generated by operations are used to provide return on investment to those who originally provided funds: creditors (interest) and owners (dividends). This results in decreases in both assets and equity.

Figure 7.1 traces these six categories of transactions by debit and credit entries. Debit entries reflect an increase in assets and/or a decrease in liabilities or equity; credit entries involve a decrease in assets and/or an increase in liabilities or equity. The simultaneous recording of debits and credits for each transaction is known as *double-entry accounting.* For each transaction increases and decreases in assets, liabilities, and equity must offset; that is, debits must equal credits. Similarly, aggregate balances must be equal and the familiar accounting equation therefore results:

$$\text{assets} = \text{liabilities} + \text{equity} \tag{7.1}$$

Figure 7.1
Transaction Mechanic (sources and uses of funds)

Transaction	Sources		Uses		Transaction
	Debit	Credit	Debit	Credit	
1. Debt or equity financing					4. Debt or equity retirement
a. Creditors	+ Assets	+ Liabilities	− Liabilities	− Assets	a. Creditors
b. Owners	+ Assets	+ Equity	− Equity	− Assets	b. Owners
2. Sale of assets			+ Assets	− Assets	5. Purchase of assets
a. At loss	− Assets	− Equity			
b. At gain	+ Assets	+ Equity			6. Distribution of income
3. Income earned from operations			− Equity	− Assets	a. Interest
			− Equity	− Assets	b. Dividends
a. Revenue	+ Assets	+ Equity			
b. Expense	− Assets	− Equity			

Table 7.1
Neverfail Electric Shoelace Company Comparative Balance Sheet as at December 31, 19x0 and 19x1

	19x1	*19x0*		*19x1*	*19x0*
Current assets			Current liabilities		
Cash	$ 100	$ 300	Bank loans	$ 100	$
Accounts receivable	500	300	Accounts payable	200	250
Inventory	530	500	Accrued expense	360	300
Prepaid insurance	20	20	Total	$ 660	$ 550
Total	$1150	$1120	Long-term liability		
Investments, at cost			Bonds payable	$1000	—
Securities	$ 800	$ 800	Deferred taxes	$ 500	$ 200
Cash surrender value,			Owners' equity		
life insurance	50	40	Common stock	$ 100	$ 100
Total	$ 850	$ 840	Excess over par	900	900
Plant and equipment			Total	$1000	$1000
Cost	$4000	$2000	Retained earnings	1340	910
Accumulated depreciation	1700	1400	Total equity	$2340	$1910
Total	$2300	$ 600			
Deferred expense	$ 200	$ 100			
Total assets	$4500	$2660	Total liabilities and equity	$4500	$2660

The cumulative result of transactions on asset, liability, and equity accounts, the numerical equivalent of Equation 7.1, is summarized in the *balance sheet* or *position statement.* A hypothetical balance sheet is illustrated in Table 7.1. For analytical purposes changes in equity during each reporting period are recorded in temporary "profit and loss" accounts; these are transferred (closed) to equity at the end of the period.[4] Profit and loss accounts include revenue, a credit entry which increases equity, and expense, a debit entry which decreases equity. The difference between revenue and expense is accounting income. Since income is closed periodically to equity, the equity account "retained earnings" represents the aggregate earnings of the firm, net of earnings distributed to owners (dividends), since the time the firm was founded. Table 7.2 contains a combined *statement of income and retained earnings* which reconciles retained earnings values reported in Table 7.1. A complete set of financial statements includes balance sheet, income statement, and, since 1971, a statement of source and use of funds;

[4] A 12-month period, either the calendar year or some selected fiscal year, is the usual accounting period. Some firms prefer to end each accounting period on the same day of the week; these firms use a 52–53-week period.

Table 7.2
Neverfail Electric Shoelace Company
Statement of Income and Retained Earnings
for the Year Ended December 31, 19x1

Retained earnings, January 1, 19x1			$ 910
Income for the year			
Sales		5200	
Cost of sales[a]			
Beginning inventory	500		
Purchases	2200		
Total	2700		
Ending inventory	530	2170	
Gross profit		3030	
Other expense[a]			
Salaries	1200		
Marketing expense	300		
Insurance	310		
Research and development	200	2010	
Operating income		1020	
Interest expense		40	
Income before taxes		980	
Estimated income tax		490	
Net income			490
Total			1400
Dividends on common stock			60
Retained earnings, December 31,19x1			$1340

[a] Includes depreciation of 300.

the latter statement summarizes the flow of funds during the period in a format generally compatible with categories listed in Figure 7.1.[5] The funds statement will be considered in detail at a later time.

The transaction mechanic involves (1) *recognition* that an accounting event has occurred, (2) *measurement* of monetary value to be assigned to that event, and (3) double-entry *classification* of values as outlined in Figure 7.1. With transactions so recorded it would be a simple matter to complete the accounting cycle if all costs and benefits were fully realized within a single accounting period. Unfortunately, a number of transactions involve costs and benefits which influence accounting classifications over a number of

[5] The Accounting Principles Board of the American Institute of Certified Public Accountants recommended inclusion of a funds statement in 1971, and they recommended that it be called the "Statement of Change in Financial Position," "Reporting Changes in Financial Position," *Opinions of the Accounting Principles Board No. 19* (New York: AICPA, 1971).

accounting periods. Thus a second mechanism becomes a necessary component of the accounting process.

PERIOD REPORTING MECHANIC

Accounting reports reflect the cumulative impact of financial and operating transactions. To be useful to the decision maker, whether management, regulators, investors, or any other class of users, reports should be prepared with sufficient frequency to allow corrective adjustments in the decision process. For most applications accounting reports are required at least annually; for many purposes greater frequency is desirable. Publicly owned corporations, for example, typically provide summary reports at least quarterly.

But this convention, the period reporting mechanic, creates serious difficulty for accountants because some transactions are incomplete at the time period reports are prepared. It then becomes necessary to establish rules for measuring revenues and expenses during that period. Revenue recognition is usually guided by the *realization principle* that revenue must be earned before it is recorded in the accounts. This requires that the earnings process be substantially completed and evidenced by a transaction. Thus unrealized capital gains, to cite one example, are typically excluded from income. Expense recognition is guided by the *matching principle* where expenses are directly associated with revenues they generate, to the degree possible. When this is not possible it becomes necessary to *allocate* historical costs among periods in some systematic fashion. Of all the difficulties accountants face, cost allocation is probably the most severe.

Depreciation accounting illustrates the problem. Assume that a firm purchases machinery for $10,000 which proves to have a productive life of ten years; after ten years the equipment is useless with scrap value just equal to the cost of disposal. The cost of this investment for the ten-year interval is clearly $10,000. But the cost for any reporting period during that interval is not clear and some assumption is required to allocate total cost among each of the ten years. Values assigned to income, assets, and equity will depend on the particular assumption that the accountant uses. Since firms face a stream of investment through time, accounting values must be recognized as estimates subject to allocational error. Moreover, the problem is not peculiar to fixed-asset accounting; it exists for inventory, pension costs, purchased "goodwill," investments, intangibles, and a host of other transactions requiring judgment in the allocation of values among the various transactions in each individual reporting period.

Figure 7.2 portrays the period reporting mechanic. Given a beginning balance sheet for some period t, transactions occurring during the period from t to $t + 1$ are recorded and classified in asset, liability, and equity accounts, the latter including revenue, expense, and dividends. Values classified when a transaction occurs are reclassified during the interval as sub-

Figure 7.2
Period Reporting Mechanic

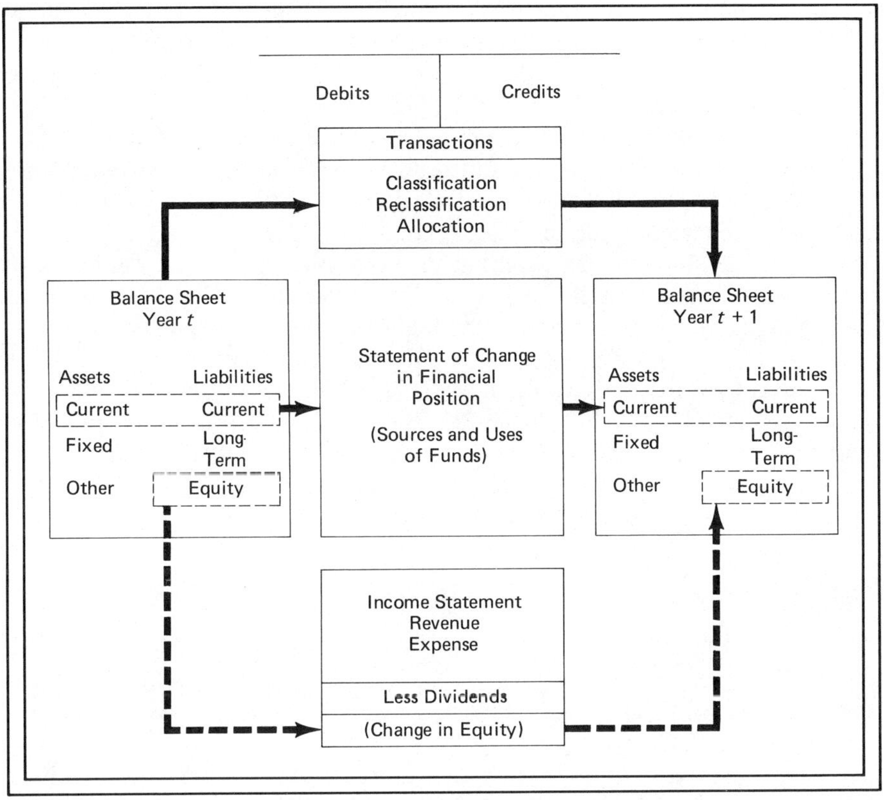

sequent events require. At the end of the period events with a multiperiod impact are allocated among accounts and the ending balance sheet, for period $t + 1$, is calculated. Change in equity during the period is isolated in profit and loss accounts, given period-allocation assumptions. A period income statement can then be prepared. Analysis of working capital, current assets net of current liabilities, provides measures of the source and use of funds reported in the statement of change in financial position. The process is then repeated through time, for periods $t + 2$, $t + 3$, and so on. The balance sheets and income statement of Tables 7.1 and 7.2 provide an arithmetic illustration of this process.

Since period values depend on allocational procedures, and since accounting principles allow a variety of different procedures, accounting values are not unique and diverse outcomes can be reported without violating generally accepted accounting principles. The relevant point is that accounting diversity provides serious difficulty for security analysts; the next section of this chapter explores this problem in greater detail.

Diversity in Accounting Values

Accounting is an inexact art and analysts can seldom rely on unadjusted data in estimating the investment value of any given firm. Balance sheet value, for example, is "value" in a very special sense. Owners' equity reported in the balance sheet of Table 7.1, \$1910 in year 19x0 and \$2340 in year 19x1, is not realizable value at either balance sheet date. It is, from the transaction and period reporting mechanics, a residual historical value which may vary widely because of procedural slack permissible under current "generally accepted accounting principles" (GAAP).

To illustrate, assume that the accountant preparing Tables 7.1 and 7.2 had selected the straight-line depreciation method and the last in, first out (LIFO) inventory valuation method. Assume also that accelerated depreciation would have amounted to \$600 and that the first in, first out (FIFO) inventory method would have resulted in beginning and ending values, respectively, of \$800 and \$900. By changing depreciation and inventory assumptions, variations permissible under GAAP, there are four (2 × 2) different numbers which could have been used to represent income before taxes; values vary from \$680 to \$1050:

	Inventory	
Depreciation	*LIFO*	*FIFO*
Straight line	980	1050
Accelerated	680	750

Balance sheet values for inventory, plant and equipment, and retained earnings would differ as well. Under these circumstances it is clear that reported values are indeed values in a special sense.

If diversity results in material differences in reported outcomes, analytical procedures will be adversely affected. Specifically, comparability will be obscured for one firm throughout a time series and for a cross section of firms at any point in time. Diversity also provides an opportunity for management to manipulate values reported to shareholders. Finally, diversity obscures underlying relationships which are the basis for predicting future outcomes. The basic issue then is the significance of variations allowable under GAAP; the relevant questions are the potential *extent* of diversity and the degree to which principles of *consistency* and *materiality* mitigate its impact.

EXTENT

The potential impact of accounting diversity is very serious. Based on then-existing accounting principles, and following the logic of depreciation and inventory permutations outlined above, R. J. Chambers estimated that there are more than 30,000,000 possible combinations of accounting methods which can be applied under GAAP![6] Now it is unlikely that all principles apply to any single firm, and some procedural variants will certainly generate immaterial differences. Professor Chambers's estimate is therefore exaggerated both in extent and in impact. But the thrust of his argument remains highly relevant—any reasonable estimate of allowable variations is still an extremely large number.

CONSISTENCY

The consistency principle is often advanced in defense of contemporary accounting principles. By applying the same method period after period, it is argued, comparability among reported outcomes is maintained. Under the LIFO method, for example, the most distant inventory costs are retained in the balance sheet while the most recent costs are matched against revenue in the process of calculating income. Period income thus tends to reflect costs at current price levels consistently and the impact of inventory valuation difficulties is mitigated.

But the consistency defense should be evaluated cautiously. The point at issue is relevance. In the case of inventory pricing LIFO results in progressively more distant balance sheet values even when the rate of inflation is modest. Thus the balance sheet loses relevance and comparability, and analyses based on the balance sheet become increasingly more hazardous. Analysts seek relevant measures; the consistent application of irrelevance is a questionable defense. The point was made clearly by Chambers: "One may lie, or talk nonsense, consistently; is consistency then a virtue?"[7]

Finally, consistency fails to address the problem of comparisons among firms. This is a question of serious concern to analysts. On balance, from the analysts viewpoint, consistency fails to solve the problem of accounting diversity.

MATERIALITY

Another argument sometimes advanced is materiality: methodological variation may generate immaterial differences in reported accounting values. At face value the point cannot be disputed; if differences are not material they provide no difficulty for the analyst. On balance, however, the argument is misleading. Aside from the question of defining materiality, the relevant question should be reversed: are material differences possible under

[6] See R. J. Chambers, "A Matter of Principle," *Accounting Review*, July 1966, pp. 443–457, and Paul Grady, "Inventory of Generally Accepted Accounting Principles in the United State of America," *Accounting Review*, January 1965, pp. 21–30. At the time he wrote the paper, Mr. Grady was director of accounting research for the American Institute of Certified Public Accountants.

[7] Chambers, "A Matter of Principle," p. 451.

procedural diversity? This cannot be addressed analytically; it is an empirical question.

Existing evidence suggests that the impact of diversity is indeed significant. The steel industry is a case in point. In 1968, faced with declining profits, firms in the industry changed from accelerated depreciation to straight-line depreciation in an effort to bolster reported income. The immediate effect of this change can be illustrated by examining the impact on one firm, Inland Steel Company. As disclosed in Inland's 1968 *Annual Report*, income would have been $62.6 million, or $3.43 per share, under accelerated depreciation. Under straight-line depreciation income increased by 28 percent to $79.2 million or $4.38 per share. However materiality is defined, an increase of $0.95 per share, solely from a change in accounting procedure, is clearly significant.

To summarize, methodological diversity may result in materially different reported accounting values and those differences are not adequately mitigated, from an analyst's viewpoint, by consistent application of any subset of accounting procedures. Diversity also creates an opportunity to manipulate accounting values. While accidental diversity is of concern to analysts, purposeful manipulation is far more serious since it implies an attempt to influence security prices. While manipulation poses no moral or legal issue if changes are fully disclosed, investors and analysts should be alert to the practice. The problem is particularly acute since evidence exists that managements do in fact attempt to picture accounting data in a favorable light. These efforts can be classified as (1) income maximization, (2) income smoothing, and (3) the "Big Bath" syndrome.

INCOME MAXIMIZATION

One hypothesis concerning managerial behavior is the strategy of income maximization: management will choose accounting procedures which tend to result in the largest possible stream of reported income. A number of motives can be cited to rationalize this policy. First, unless investors recognize and properly capitalize manipulated income, inflated earnings will result in inflated security prices. Aside from maintaining harmonious shareholder relationships, which tends to increase executive security, direct compensation can accrue to managers by way of the exercise of stock options. Nonpecuniary motivation may also be involved in terms of job satisfaction and the maintenance of executive reputation.

Depreciation policy in the steel industry is one example of (reported) income maximization policy. In this respect it is important to note that the change, and its impact, were fully disclosed in annual reports. In some instances, in fact, it was even emphasized. Inland Steel, for example, included the "increase" in earnings in the "Highlights" section of its 1968 *Annual Report*. Other examples of income-maximizing strategy are abundant; they include policies with respect to deferral of promotion and advertising costs[8] and the recording of mergers and business combinations,[9] among others.

INCOME SMOOTHING

An alternative hypothesis, income smoothing, is more subtle: managers would select among discretionary accounting procedures in a manner which tends to minimize variability in reported income from period to period. In the process stabilized income replaces maximized income as the object of managerial choice. Underlying the hypothesis is the assumption that investors dislike income variability; a stable income series would then be capitalized at a higher price-earnings multiple than a variable series.[10] Aside from any benefits accruing from security price behavior, this strategy can be rationalized in terms of executive compensation. Notwithstanding the income-averaging provision of the Internal Revenue Code, an executive whose compensation is based upon reported income may find a tax advantage in a stable income series, given progressive personal income tax rates.

Income smoothing strategy was suggested by Hepworth in 1953; it was revived by Gordon in 1964 and Monson and Downs in 1965.[11] During the late 1960s it received considerable attention in the academic literature and a number of papers were published which reported results of empirical tests of the hypothesis. Nonetheless, despite the existence of some evidence supporting the hypothesis, the issue has yet to be resolved empirically.[12]

[8] Michael Schiff, "Accounting Tactics and the Theory of the Firm," *Journal of Accounting Research*, Spring 1966, pp. 62–67.

[9] Ronald M. Copeland and Joseph F. Wodjak, "Income Manipulation and the Purchase-Pooling Choice," *Journal of Accounting Research*, Autumn 1969, pp. 188–195.

[10] The relationship between income variability and price-earnings multiple will be considered in Chapter 8.

[11] S. R. Hepworth, "Smoothing Periodic Income," *Accounting Review*, January 1953; M. J. Gordon, "Postulates, Principles and Research in Accounting," *Accounting Review*, April 1964, pp. 261–262; R. J. Monson and A. Downs, "A Theory of Large Managerial Firms," *Journal of Political Economy*, June 1965, pp. 221–236.

[12] Evidence supporting the smoothing hypothesis is found in Paul E. Dascher and Robert E. Malcolm, "A Note on Income Smoothing in the Chemical Industry," and Gary E. White, "Discretionary Accounting Decisions and Income Normalization," both in *Journal of Accounting Research*, Autumn 1970, pp. 273–295 and 260–273, respectively. Inconclusive evidence was reported by M. J. Gordon, B. N. Horwitz, and P. T. Meyers, "Accounting Measurements and Normal Growth in the Firm," in *Research in Accounting Measurement*, ed. R. K. Jaedicke, Y. Ijiri, and O. Nielson (New York: American Accounting Association, 1966), pp. 221–231; N. Dopuch and D. F. Drake, "The Effect of Alternative Accounting Rules for Nonsubsidiary Investments," *Empirical Research in Accounting: Selected Studies, 1966*; Supplement to *Journal of Accounting Research* (1966): 192–219; and R. M. Copeland and R. L. Licastro, "A Note on Income Smoothing," *Accounting Review*, July 1968, pp. 540–545. In addition, Cushing provided evidence which suggests that managers consciously choose reporting periods in which to implement accounting changes in a manner designed to impact favorably on current earnings per share. Whether this is classified as manipulation or smoothing, the question of *timing* appears to be recognized. See Barry E. Cushing, "An Empirical Study of Changes in Accounting Policy," *Journal of Accounting Research*, Autumn 1969, pp. 196–203.

The absence of convincing evidence may imply that managers cannot or do not smooth or it may reflect statistical difficulties in isolating smoothing behavior. The *long-run* impact of diverse accounting procedures is difficult to specify analytically and managers may be unable to identify effective procedures. Moreover, assuming that the strategy is attempted, the smoothing *objective* may vary; it may be aggregate earnings, earnings per share, or rate of return. By smoothing one series, another may become highly variable. Finally, the design of experiments to test the hypothesis rigorously is subject to severe statistical and definitional problems.[13] Since smoothing behavior has yet to be proven or disproven, analysts should remain alert to the possibility when observing and evaluating dispersion in an accounting time series.

THE "BIG BATH" SYNDROME

A third strategy is related to income smoothing. Often referred to as the "Big Bath," it consists of recognizing special write-offs, write-downs, and other losses during some year in which reported values are otherwise unfavorable. The rationale, according to the argument, is to recognize all bad news at one time, clearing the accounts for more favorable outcomes in the future. Since "extra-ordinary" items may involve operating costs not allocated previously, criticism of this practice has been especially severe.

In 1973, for example, the H. J. Heinz Company announced a $25 million write-off reflecting discontinuance of some foreign operations together with farming operations of a subsidiary in Oregon. Although the item was classified as extraordinary, the costs involved food production and the write-off received critical attention in the financial press.[14] Criticism was yet more widespread when Gulf Oil Corporation announced that a *1973* loss of $25 million arising from devaluation of the dollar would be reflected in *1972* operations; 1972 values were already depressed and a $250 million loss reflecting withdrawal from certain markets had already been announced.[15] This case is particularly interesting since Gulf apparently agreed to restate prior earnings on the recommendation of their auditors.

Until 1966 extraordinary losses could be hidden from the less astute observer by charging them directly to retained earnings. Accounting Principles Board (APB) Opinion No. 9, effective January 1, 1966, attempted to remedy the situation by requiring the inclusion of extraordinary items in the calculation of net income. But the opinion was largely ineffective and

[13] See Ronald M. Copeland, "Income Smoothing," *Empirical Research in Accounting: Selected Studies, 1968*; Supplement to *Journal of Accounting Research* (1968): 101–121.

[14] John H. Allan, "An 'Extraordinary' Fog Envelops Accounting," *The New York Times*, Financial Section, January 14, 1973, pp. 1 and 7. Other firms cited in the article included Indian Head, American Can Company, Amerada Hess Corporation, National Cash Register Company, RCA Corporation, and Boise Cascade Corporation.

[15] "Accountants Assail Gulf's Restatement of Its 1972 Results," *The Wall Street Journal*, February 22, 1973.

the APB was forced to draft a new opinion in 1973 which attempted to further clarify reporting practices for unusual gains and losses; currency revaluations and disposal of segments of a business were classified as non-extraordinary items.[16] The effectiveness of current disclosure requirements remains to be tested and, in any event, they cannot be addressed to the problem of currently assessing, period by period, the impact of poor managerial decisions. Whatever the method of classification and disclosure, costs relating to these activities too often remain locked into accounts until washed away in the "Big Bath."

In summary, procedural diversity under GAAP provides opportunities to portray events favorably and it is not surprising to observe managerial behavior which takes advantage of those opportunities. But the effect of diversity, whether by accident or by design, is to decrease the relevance of the accounting data base.[17] This is a serious problem for security analysts partly because of the increased complexity of accounting variants and partly because accounting procedures are not stationary. Familiarity with existing procedures is inadequate; abandoned procedures remain relevant as long as affected data are part of the analyst's time series of data. In addition changes must be monitored as they occur.

The accounting profession has been subjected to severe criticism recently and the process by which accounting principles are established and refined may itself be in a process of change. For this reason, and to provide a perspective for evaluating contemporary problems, the next section reviews the development of accounting practice.

Accounting Principles and Practice

Accounting evolved from and adapted to the structure and organization of the business community it served. More recently it has responded to other stimuli and principles are currently developed in both public and private sectors. But emphasis has been directed to specific problems of accounting for complex transactions and no conceptual foundation has yet been identified which is acceptable to any major segment of the accounting profession. As a result no framework currently exists for evaluating procedural variants and the accounting diversity discussed previously results.

The earliest form of record keeping was narrative. But with the growth and expansion of trade, and its extension beyond national borders, need emerged for more orderly and compressed records. Single-entry columnar journals evolved; they gave way in turn to double-entry systems because

[16] "Reporting the Results of Operations," *Opinions of the Accounting Principles Board, No. 9* (New York: AICPA, 1966), and "Reporting the Results of Operations," *Opinions of the Accounting Principles Board, No. 30* (New York: AICPA, 1973).

[17] For a particularly critical review of accounting and accounting practice, see Abraham J. Brilloff, *Unaccountable Accounting* (New York: Harper & Row, 1972).

joint ventures made it necessary to segregate ownership interests in business assets. Double-entry accounting was commonly used by Italian merchants and bankers of the fifteenth century. Bookkeeping procedures, transmitted through generations of master-apprentice record keepers, spread rapidly following publication of the first treatise on the subject in 1494. Thereafter, and throughout the period of industrialization, accounting procedures responded to increasingly complex needs arising from industrialization. With the introduction of the corporation, with separation of ownership and control, the balance sheet grew in importance as a statement of legal claims against corporate assets.

The late nineteenth century saw the organization of professional accounting associations which would, subsequently, exercise significant influence on the development of accounting principles. Corporate reporting created the need for external and independent verification of financial statements. External auditors or "public accountants" were of sufficient numbers by 1887 to organize the American Institute of Certified Public Accountants, or AICPA (originally the American Institute of Accountants). A second group, consisting largely of accounting educators, was formed in 1918; it has been known as the American Accounting Association, or AAA, since 1935. AICPA and AAA, together with other professional associations in the United States and abroad, provide a continuing forum for exposure and debate of controversies in accounting.

EXTERNAL STIMULI

Other forces influenced the development of accounting procedures. Introduction of the corporate income tax in 1913 greatly increased the need to establish detailed records. The provisions of subsequent Internal Revenue Codes, and their amendments, have significantly affected accounting practice. The inventory valuation method adopted for tax purposes, for example, must also be adopted for book purposes. In order to minimize taxable income it is necessary to adopt procedures which also tend to minimize reported income. The dilemma this provides managers is evidenced by the significant number of firms which changed inventory pricing policy during late 1974 and early 1975 in an effort to offset decreasing liquidity and the effects of "double-digit" inflation.[18]

The stock market crash of 1929, together with the severe depression which followed, had a profound impact on accountancy. In the first place, with new emphasis on income in lieu of property rights, focus began to shift from the balance sheet to the income statement. In the process historical cost allocation became prominent. The AICPA, in cooperation with the

[18] "More Companies Alter Accounting Methods to Neutralize Inflation," *The Wall Street Journal*, October 7, 1974, pp. 1 and 9, and "Earnings Head Lower as Economy Slows Up, Firms Switch to LIFO," *The Wall Street Journal*, January 3, 1975, pp. 1 and 10.

New York Stock Exchange and complemented by activities of the AAA, moved to establish detailed procedures designed to "fairly represent" the results of periodic operations. Historical cost became firmly established and, to many, the balance sheet diminished to a residual position of debits and credits remaining after "closing the books."

Another important factor was the establishment of regulatory authority. The Securities and Exchange Commission (SEC) was founded to regulate the securities industry and to improve reporting practices. Accounting, once the exclusive domain of the private sector, became firmly established in the public sector also. Since that time regulatory influence has increased and relationships among public and private authorities have sometimes become tenuous and strained.

In 1972, for example, the Federal Power Commission required natural gas pipeline companies to adopt a liberalized treatment of exploration costs at a time when AICPA authorities were moving to prohibit that particular treatment. In August of 1973 the SEC issued regulations concerning merger accounting which reinstated a procedure previously discarded by AICPA authorities. Faced with vigorous protests from accountants, and a law suit filed by one of the larger public accounting firms, the SEC relented two months later and suspended the order; on the same day, however, it adopted a proposal concerning lease accounting which was widely opposed in the accounting community. In November of 1971 the accounting profession was stunned when Congress, in reestablishing the investment credit, specifically *legislated* that no firm could be required to adopt any one of several methods of accounting for the credit in reports filed with any federal agency, *including the SEC*. Until that time accounting for the investment credit had been an issue on which influential AICPA members were keenly divided. Recent years have witnessed increased conflict among authorities in the public and private sectors.[19]

ROLE OF THE AICPA

As the AICPA grew in prominence its procedural instrument was the Committee on Accounting Procedure (CAP). Significantly, CAP was established to resolve specific problems as they arose; it was never intended to develop a consistent foundation from which a body of defensible principles could be constructed. From 1939 through 1958 CAP published 51 *Accounting Research Bulletins. Bulletin No. 43* (1953) was a codification and summary of the first 42 releases; it was, in its time, an authoritative statement of generally

[19] One recognized authority, Charles T. Horngren, argues that principles are established in the public sector, by the SEC, with AICPA serving in the role of a buffer which insulates the SEC from public criticism. Professor Horngren served as a member of the AICPA Accounting Principles Board. See Charles T. Horngren, "Accounting Principles: Private or Public Sector?" *Journal of Accountancy*, May 1972, pp. 37–41.

accepted principles.[20] Numerous currently accepted principles are still to be found there. In general, compatibility existed among CAP and SEC releases.

But by the late 1950s the authority and influence of CAP, and AICPA, were diminishing. Faced with increased procedural diversity and lacking an integrated conceptual foundation, a new program was adopted in 1959 in an effort to restore the AICPA's position of prominence.[21] The effort was two-pronged: an Accounting Research Division and an Accounting Principles Board (APB) were formed. Research, it was assumed, would provide answers to both foundational and pragmatic problems. An Accounting Research Series (ARS), tested by exposure and comment, would provide input to deliberations of the APB. The board, consisting of accountants with national reputations, would then issue opinions carrying sufficient authority to insure general acceptance. Enforcement machinery was not provided; given research and the prestige of the APB, authoritative support was expected to result from persuasion in lieu of compulsion.

The effort failed on both counts. Early research studies were widely viewed as overly abstract and they exercised little impact on APB efforts.[22] Emphasis in research shifted from conceptual issues to pragmatic questions; Accounting Research Study No. 7, for example, provided an inventory of accepted principles but there was no attempt to provide a basis for their acceptance.[23] Intellectual authority, in lieu of professional authority, remained elusive.

APB fared no better and it was unable to establish authority by persuasion even among its own membership. An early opinion which required deferred accounting for the investment credit proved to be disastrous because it was not accepted by a substantial minority of the board; when the SEC then announced their view that authoritative support existed for both positions, APB was forced to retreat and to issue a compromise opinion.[24]

[20] "Restatement and Revision of Accounting Research Bulletins," *Accounting Research Bulletin No. 43* (New York: AICPA, 1953).

[21] The spirit and tone of criticism which had been directed to the accounting profession was captured by Harvard Professor Robert Anthony: "The argument that accounting principles may end up eventually being prescribed by the SEC rests on two propositions:

1. If the American Institute of Certified Public Accountants fails in its present program for developing accounting principles, the Securities and Exchange Commission will act to develop those principles.
2. The AICPA effort is likely to fail."

See Robert N. Anthony, "Showdown on Accounting Principles," *Harvard Business Review*, May–June 1963, p. 99.

[22] Maurice Moonitz, *The Basic Postulates of Accounting*, Accounting Research Study No. 1 (New York: AICPA, 1961), and Robert T. Sprouse and Maurice Moonitz, *A Tentative Set of Broad Accounting Principles for Business Enterprises*, Accounting Research Study No. 3 (New York: AICPA, 1967).

[23] Paul Grady, *Inventory of Generally Accepted Accounting Principles for Business Enterprises*, Accounting Research Study No. 7 (New York: AICPA, 1967).

[24] See Robert K. Mautz, "Accounting Principles—How Can They Be Made More Authoritative?" *CPA Journal*, March 1973, pp. 186–187.

At this critical point the investment credit, later to be the focus of congressional action, rendered enforcement by persuasion null and void. Fairly or unfairly, dissatisfaction with APB increased; during this time opinions continued to focus on specific problems in the absence of any consistent foundation.[25] Efforts to bolster the prestige of APB failed amid accusations of conflict of interest, pressure from industry lobbyists, and an increasingly active SEC.

In the spring of 1970 AICPA tried again to reestablish its authority by forming two study groups. The first, chaired by former SEC Commissioner Francis M. Wheat, was established to examine *procedures* for developing accounting principles. The second, chaired by Robert M. Trueblood, focused on the *objectives* of financial reporting.

The Wheat study resulted in creation of the Financial Accounting Standards Board (FASB) in May of 1972. Membership consists of seven full-time members drawn from public accounting, university, government, and corporate backgrounds. It is backed by an advisory council which includes business and government accountants, security analysts, bankers, and accounting educators. With full-time members free of charges of vested interests, and with extensive public exposure of draft statements, FASB hopes to succeed where CAP and APB failed.[26]

The fate of FASB will be resolved only in time but the prospect for success remains worrisome. By late 1973, less than 6 months after staffing had been completed, severe criticism of the board had surfaced in the press. Impatience was also displayed by the SEC despite positions of public support provided by commission authorities. Congressional concern with the FASB and the accounting profession became very evident in 1977 and 1978. A subcommittee chaired by the late Senator Lee Metcalf recommended that all aspects of the FASB should be opened to public view, that its organization should be expanded, and that its work pace should be accelerated. The Metcalf report also expressed concern with public accounting practices with respect to competition, advertising, and the placement of staff with clients. A house subcommittee chaired by John E. Moss in 1978 expressed similar concern with self-regulation in the public accounting profession and the competitive effect of the AICPA division of firms, adopted in 1977, into two

[25] The Accounting Principles Board attempted to define a general framework for accounting principles in 1970. Drawing on other work, including *A Statement of Basic Accounting Theory* (Evanston, Ill.: American Accounting Association, 1966), they defined the accounting environment and conventions underlying contemporary practice. Nonetheless the search for a sound foundation continues. See "Basic Concepts and Accounting Principles Underlying Financial Statements of Business Enterprises," *Statements of the Accounting Principles Board, No. 4* (New York: AICPA, 1970).

[26] Efforts to establish international accounting standards may influence principles adopted in the United States. The International Accounting Standards Committee, formed in June of 1973, includes representatives from 22 countries. IASC issued the first standard, requiring disclosure of accounting policies, in January of 1975. Standards relating to depreciation, currency translation, inflation accounting, and other important controversies in accounting were scheduled for release at intervals throughout July of 1977.

groups, one consisting of SEC registrants and the other consisting of private companies not registered with the SEC. Congressional pressure dilutes the prestige of the FASB and AICPA, and the possibility that establishment of accounting standards will be moved to the public sector cannot be dismissed.

The key element in the search for defensible accounting standards, whether they are determined in the public or the private sector, is agreement on a basic foundation for accountancy. Fortunately, the FASB accepted this very difficult challenge and issued a draft memorandum in 1978 which was designed to identify a conceptual framework for accounting. The FASB proposal reflects many of the principles set forth in the Trueblood Committee report.

The Trueblood Committee, the second of the two committees established in 1970, reported their findings in late 1973; this group analyzed the objectives of financial reporting.[27] While the committee's efforts appear to have exercised very little immediate impact on accounting procedures, its long-run impact may be very significant because questions of relevance and usefulness were attacked directly. Unusual emphasis was placed on service to users who compare, evaluate, and forecast the *cash* consequences of economic decisions. Recognizing that no single set of procedures can serve all users for all uses, the committee identified four possible valuation bases which could be defended for measuring assets and equity. These are (1) *exit value*, the amount currently realizable if liquidated, (2) *replacement value*, the amount required to replace assets and liabilities at current prices, (3) *historical value*, original cost adjusted for period allocations, and (4) *discounted present value* of expected future cash flows.[28]

The latter is a significant departure from current procedures. Although general acceptance seems unlikely in the foreseeable future it provides a basis for reconciling accounting values and analytical procedures. Moreover, as the next section illustrates, a discounted present value basis can also be reconciled with the historical cost basis.

Present Value Accounting

It would be ideal if accountants could provide exact measures of income, assets, and equity. In practice this is impossible partly because accounting serves many users and partly because measurement error cannot be completely avoided. From an analyst's viewpoint accounting measures are biased. Bias can be evaluated by comparing accounting rate of return (ARR) with the analyst's rate of return. The latter, defined and illustrated in Chapter 3, is the internal rate of return (IRR) model of Chapters 5 and 6.

ARR and IRR appear to be conceptually irreconcilable. ARR is the ratio of income to investment (assets or equity); values are measured on the

[27] AICPA Study Group, *Objectives of Financial Statements* (New York: AICPA, 1973).
[28] Ibid., pp. 41–43.

basis of costs allocated under the period reporting mechanic. If ARR is unbiased, underlying income and balance sheet values (assets and equity) must also be unbiased. IRR is measured on the basis of the discounted present value of a stream of future cash flows. On the surface then ARR and IRR seem to be totally unrelated. But this is not the case; procedures exist, fully within the spirit of the historical cost convention, which formally and mathematically equate ARR and IRR. This can be demonstrated by reconsidering (1) cost allocation under the period reporting mechanic and (2) cost measurement under the transaction mechanic.

PERIOD ALLOCATION: DEPRECIATION AND AMORTIZATION

Depreciation expense illustrates the period allocation problem. Depreciation is the periodic value assigned to capital recovery; properly defined it separates each period cash flow into (1) return *of* capital (expense) and (2) return *on* capital (income). This involves two operations. The first is the choice of a formulation which defines capital recovery and the second is the estimation of parameter(s) to be inserted in that formulation. Under straight-line depreciation, for an asset with a productive life of n years, the formulation is $1/n$. To estimate depreciation expense all that remains is estimation of parameter n. An asset with an estimated life of ten years, for example, will be depreciated each year at the rate of one-tenth of depreciable cost. Combining the two operations, the accuracy of periodic depreciation expense, together with period income and end-of-period asset value, depends on (1) relevance of the depreciation formula selected and (2) accuracy with which formula parameter(s) are forecast.

The former, by far, is the more critical of the two. Parameter estimates are open to unavoidable error whatever the depreciation formula selected. But an irrelevant formulation, whatever the degree of estimation error, provides an irrelevant measure of both income and assets; accounting rate of return calculated under this circumstance is necessarily biased. For this reason the relative merits of a number of different depreciation formulas have been a topic of controversy in the accounting literature for some time. Curiously, one formulation, one which reconciles ARR and IRR, has largely been ignored.

The proposal at issue would define asset value as the discounted present value of the unrecovered stream of cash flows at the time the asset is valued. Depreciation expense would be defined as the difference between ending and beginning of period value. This suggestion is certainly not new; similar proposals are found in Ladelle (1890), Fisher (1906), Hotelling (1925), and Canning (1929).[29] Nonetheless "present value depreciation" has never

[29] O. G. Ladelle, "The Calculation of Depreciation," *The Accountant*, November 1890; Irving Fisher, *The Nature of Capital and Income* (1906; reprinted ed., New York: Augustus M. Kelley, 1965); H. Hotelling, "A General Mathematical Theory of Depreciation," *Journal of the American Statistical Association*, September 1925, pp. 340–353; J. B. Canning, *The Economics of Accountancy* (New York: Ronald Press, 1929).

been generally accepted by practicing accountants. The basic reason for this is widespread acceptance of historical cost as the appropriate basis for recognizing accounting values. By recording assets at the discounted present value of future cash flows, historical cost is, with one exception, abandoned.

That exception, referred to here as *internal return depreciation*, occurs when the internal rate of return is the discount rate in the present value mechanism. By constraining aggregate depreciation to the cost of a project, the internal return model provides a depreciation method which is consistent with the historical cost convention. This is accomplished for periodic depreciation D_t, with previously defined values for project cost C_0, project inflows C_t, and internal rate of return r, by restating Equation 3.8 of Chapter 3:

$$C_0 = \sum_{t=1}^{n} C_t(1 + r)^{-t} = \sum_{t=1}^{n} D_t \tag{7.2}$$

Equation 7.2 can then be disaggregated to provide periodic depreciation D_t:[30]

$$D_t = C_t - rA_{t-1} \tag{7.3}$$

with beginning asset value A_{t-1}. Under the depreciation formulation of Equation 7.3 ARR equals IRR for any project, in the context of historical cost procedures, whatever the pattern of cash flows. This can be demonstrated arithmetically.

Assume that an investment of \$12,000 generates the cash flows summarized in Table 7.3; flows of \$4000, \$5000, and \$5632, respectively, generate an internal rate of return of 10 percent. The table contains values for income tax, cash flow, and depreciation expense for each of three years of useful life. Income tax is calculated under sum-of-the-years digits depreciation; rate of taxation is 50 percent and tax is symmetrical in the sense that a loss provides positive cash flow from tax carryback. Cash flow is the residual of revenue after expense and tax have been deducted; alternately it is the sum of depreciation and net income. Table 7.3 also summarizes depreciation expense under three formulations. Two of the methods, straight-line (SL) and sum-of-the-years digits (SYD), are allowable for both book and tax purposes. The third, internal return depreciation (IR), cannot currently be used for either book or tax purposes; it is calculated for each year on the basis of Equation 7.3.

Table 7.4 summarizes project rate of return under each of the three depreciation assumptions specified. "Flow-through" and "deferred" tax captions will be considered shortly; for the moment only the first three sections of the table are of interest. Table 7.4 is structured in the same format as Table 3.1 of Chapter 3; the latter table was used previously to demonstrate

[30] Algebraic proof is found in Anthony J. Curley and Charles G. Carpenter, "The Present Value Model and the Multi-Asset Problem: Comment," *Accounting Review*, October 1974, pp. 812–815.

Table 7.3
Income Tax, Cash Flow, and Depreciation

	Year 1	*Year 2*	*Year 3*
Income tax			
Revenue	$7,000	$14,000	$22,000
Expense	5,000	8,000	12,736
Net	$2,000	$ 6,000	$ 9,264
SYD depreciation	6,000	4,000	2,000
Taxable income (loss)	($4,000)	$ 2,000	$ 7,264
Tax (tax reduction), 50 percent	($2,000)	$ 1,000	$ 3,632
Cash flow			
Revenue less expense	$2,000	$ 6,000	$ 9,264
Less income tax	(2,000)	1,000	3,632
Cash flow	$4,000	$ 5,000	$ 5,632
Depreciation expense			
Internal return (IR)	$2,800	$ 4,080	$ 5,120
Straight-line (SL)	$4,000	$ 4,000	$ 4,000
Sum-of-the-years digits (SYD)	$6,000	$ 4,000	$ 2,000

the separation of cash flows into (1) investment recovery (depreciation) and (2) income under the internal rate of return mechanism.[31] Tables 3.1 and 7.4 provide a logical basis for linking ARR with IRR.

Table 7.4 clearly demonstrates that equivalence of ARR and IRR occurs only in the case where internal return depreciation is used. Other depreciation measures bias rate of return with the degree of bias increasing as depreciation "front loading" increases. That is, straight-line is less biased than accelerated depreciation. The direction of bias varies over time as the understatement of early years reverses and becomes overstatement in later years.

On a project basis the impact of conventional depreciation formulas is evident. It is less clear, however, for the firm as a whole. A firm consists of

[31] Table 3.1 and Table 7.4 are identical except for rearrangement of the columns and redefinition of some of the terms. The "Investment Recovery" of Table 3.1 is now defined in an accounting context as "Depreciation" and the "Internal Rate of Return" is now "Rate of Return." The latter demonstrates equivalence between ARR and IRR under internal return depreciation. "Investment" of Table 3.1 is redefined as "Asset Value" in Table 7.4 and "Return on Investment" is redefined as "Income" to correspond to the accounting terminology which is relevant when the general relationship of Table 3.1 is applied to the transaction analyzed in Table 7.3. The explanation of Table 3.1 values was originally developed arithmetically. But "Investment Recovery" of that illustration is more easily calculated by employing Equation 7.3; in that case Table 3.1 values would be:

$$D_1 = 18.90 - (.18)(36.30) = 12.37$$
$$D_2 = 15.45 - (.18)(23.93) = 11.14$$
$$D_3 = 15.10 - (.18)(12.79) = 12.79$$

Table 7.4
Project Rate of Return

(1) Year	(2) Cash Flow	(3) Depreciation	(4) Income	(5) Beginning Asset Value	(4)/(5) Rate of Return
		Flow-Through Tax			
		a. Internal Return Depreciation			
1	$4,000.00	$2,800.00	$1,200.00	$12,000.00	.1000
2	5,000.00	4,080.00	920.00	9,200.00	.1000
3	5,632.00	5,120.00	512.00	5,120.00	.1000
		b. Straight-Line Depreciation			
1	$4,000.00	$4,000.00	$ 0.00	$12,000.00	.0000
2	5,000.00	4,000.00	1,000.00	8,000.00	.1250
3	5,632.00	4,000.00	1,632.00	4,000.00	.4080
		c. Sum-of-the-Years Digits Depreciation			
1	$4,000.00	$6,000.00	($2,000.00)	$12,000.00	(.1667)
2	5,000.00	4,000.00	1,000.00	6,000.00	.1667
3	5,632.00	2,000.00	3,632.00	2,000.00	1.8160
		Deferred Tax			
		d. Internal Return Depreciation			
1	$3,000.00	$1,879.45	$1,120.55	$12,000.00	.0934
2	5,000.00	4,054.95	945.05	10,120.55	.0934
3	6,632.00	6,065.60	566.40	6,065.60	.0934
		e. Straight-Line Depreciation			
1	$3,000.00	$4,000.00	($1,000.00)	$12,000.00	(.0833)
2	5,000.00	4,000.00	1,000.00	8,000.00	.1250
3	6,632.00	4,000.00	2,632.00	4,000.00	.6580

a portfolio of projects and accounting rate of return depends on the particular mix of assets for any year in question. Bias exists but its direction and magnitude will vary from firm to firm at any point in time and from time to time for any given firm. This will be demonstrated shortly for some actual firms; first, however, it is necessary to consider the second major source of disparity between ARR and IRR.

PERIOD COST DETERMINATION

On occasion hypothetical flows are recorded which distort accounting rates of return. The most prominent and serious instance is the case where book income and taxable income are different. Under the Internal Revenue Code, for example, it is permissible to use different depreciation procedures for book and tax purposes; firms may choose to record depreciation on the straight-line basis for book purposes without losing the favorable treatment afforded by accelerated depreciation for tax purposes. In this case taxable income differs from before-tax book income. When this occurs accountants record income tax for book purposes at a hypothetical value to maintain consistency between rate of taxation and before-tax income on the income statement. Differences between actual tax and this hypothetical tax are deferred until some future time when, presumably, the tax-book differential reverses. This procedure is referred to as *deferred tax accounting;* if the actual tax were reported in the income statement it would be referred to as *flow-through accounting.*

Table 7.4 demonstrates the impact of tax deferral on the accounting rate of return. The cash flows in parts d and e are hypothetical values implied by the deferral of income tax. The statement of change in financial position would be based upon the actual tax liability but the income statement, which is used to calculate rate of return, implies the values reported in parts d and e.

Part d of Table 7.4 isolates the bias arising from the deferred tax procedure. From Table 7.5, SL depreciation is $2000 less than SYD depreciation

Table 7.5
Deferred Tax Accounting

	Year 1	*Year 2*	*Year 3*
Actual income tax[a]	$2000	$1000	$3632
Flow-through income			
Revenue less expense	$2000	$6000	$9264
SL depreciation	4000	$4000	4000
Before-tax income (loss)	($2000)	$2000	$5264
Income tax, actual	(2000)	1000	3632
Net income	$ 0	$1000	$1632
Actual Cash Flow[b]	$4000	$5000	$5632
Deferred tax income			
Revenue less expense	$2000	$6000	$9264
SL depreciation	4000	4000	4000
Before-tax income (loss)	($2000)	$2000	$5264
Income tax, hypothetical, at 50 percent	(1000)	1000	2632
Net income, hypothetical	($1000)	$1000	$2632
Income over (under) stated	($1000)	$ 0	$1000
Hypothetical cash flow[b]	$3000	$5000	$6632

[a] From Table 7.3, at 50 percent.
[b] Revenue less expense less income tax, or net income plus depreciation.

in the first year and $2000 more in the third year. At a tax rate of 50 percent, income would be understated by $1000 in the first year with a corresponding $1000 overstatement in the third year. Internal return depreciation was calculated on the basis of flows of $3000, $5000, and $6632, respectively; for an investment of $12,000 the internal rate of return would be approximately 9.34 percent. The net effect of tax deferral in this case is a downward bias because an actual flow of $1000 is shifted forward in time in the income statement.[32] Part e of the table demonstrates the combined bias caused by both tax deferral and straight-line depreciation.

ACCRUAL ACCOUNTING

ARR and IRR differ because of amortization procedures and hypothetical cash flows required under current accounting principles. Another potential source of difference is the accrual basis which recognizes revenue and expense in lieu of cash receipts and expenditures. Under the accrual basis, for example, accountants record sales on account; under an alternative basis, "cash flow" narrowly defined, sales would not be recorded until customers remit payments. Since the internal rate of return is a cash flow mechanism it may appear that equivalence between ARR and IRR requires abandonment of the accrual convention. But this is not the case.

Accrual accounting recognizes working capital as part of the firm's investment in assets; a sale on account increases accounts receivable. Together with other elements of working capital, this account is an investment with a zero explicit rate of return. The internal rate of return is also an explicit measure and inclusion of working capital in the ARR denominator, without impact on the income numerator, has the effect of properly reflecting working capital investment in the firm's weighted average internal rate of return. The point can be proven formally, but it is sufficient to note here that the accounting accrual basis is correct from an analyst's perspective.[33]

ADJUSTING ACCOUNTING DATA

Generally accepted accounting principles involve specific procedures which may obscure rate of return and its underlying income, asset, and equity

[32] Although deferred tax accounting is biased from a rate of return viewpoint, it is part of the set of current generally accepted accounting principles. Partial support was provided for deferral in 1953; APB Opinion No. 11, in 1967, then moved to extend the procedure in an effort to achieve uniformity. Accounting for the investment credit provides a similar problem but congressional action in 1971, commented upon previously, has prevented accountants from selecting any given procedure in that case. Tax deferral remains controversial and the debate on this issue seems likely to continue despite preference for deferral on the part of accounting authorities. See "Restatement and Revision of Accounting Research Bulletins," *Accounting Research Bulletin No. 43* (New York: AICPA, 1953), chap. 10, sec. B, and "Accounting for Income Taxes," *Opinions of the Accounting Principles Board, No. 11* (New York: AICPA, 1967).

[33] Formal proof is provided in Curley and Carpenter, "Present Value Model," p. 815.

values. It is possible to determine if a particular procedure creates bias by analyzing it in the framework of the internal rate of return mechanism. But recognition of bias is insufficient; what is relevant are both (1) the necessity and (2) the feasibility of adjusting data to conform to the definition of financial yield. The former can easily be addressed but the latter remains a serious problem for the analyst.

Adjustment is necessary when differences between reported values and unbiased values are material. In this context materiality is an empirical question. Figure 7.3 contains the time series of rates of return on equity for three NYSE corporations. It includes reported values (ROE) as well as values (ROE*) adjusted to reflect internal return depreciation and flow-through tax treatment.[34] Internal return depreciation estimates are necessarily crude since values were calculated solely on the basis of public information of the type available to security analysts. Nonetheless, measurement error appears to be modest and unbiased estimates are more accurate than reported ROE. The adjustment to reverse deferred tax treatment is a straightforward process.

Figure 7.3 implies that bias in unadjusted rates may indeed be significant. It is in the case of General Cable Corporation where the pattern of peaks and valleys generated conventionally makes it extremely difficult to evaluate the firm's performance. That pattern results because reported depreciation is insensitive to variation in cash flows; separation of flows into income and capital recovery is therefore incorrect and accounting income is a residual which varies as periodic flows vary. As a result, risk, measured by variability in the series, is grossly exaggerated; in addition, average rate of return becomes overly dependent on the interval selected for measuring it.

Inland Steel is another interesting case partly because trend is more evident in ROE* than in ROE and partly in view of the change in depreciation policy adopted in 1968 to improve reported income. In contrast, there is very little difference among ROE and ROE* values for the less capital-intensive Standard Brands Corporation. The three cases pictured in Figure 7.3 demonstrate that differences among reported values and adjusted values conform reasonably to expectations: bias increases as capital intensity increases because of depreciation policy and tax deferral procedures.

Although reported values are open to bias, there is no reason to believe that adjusted values will correlate with market behavior, at least in the short run, since investor expectations are generally formed on the basis of unadjusted values. For the long run, as periodic values are averaged, adjustment may uncover instances of undervaluation or overvaluation. Note, for example, the similarity in average rate of return ROE and ROE* for the entire 21-year interval for General Cable; long run behavior of ROE is

[34] A detailed discussion of the procedures used to calculate ROE and ROE* values is found in Anthony J. Curley, "Bias in Corporate Accounting Rates," paper presented at the annual meeting of the Financial Management Association, 1975.

Figure 7.3
Rate of Return on Equity

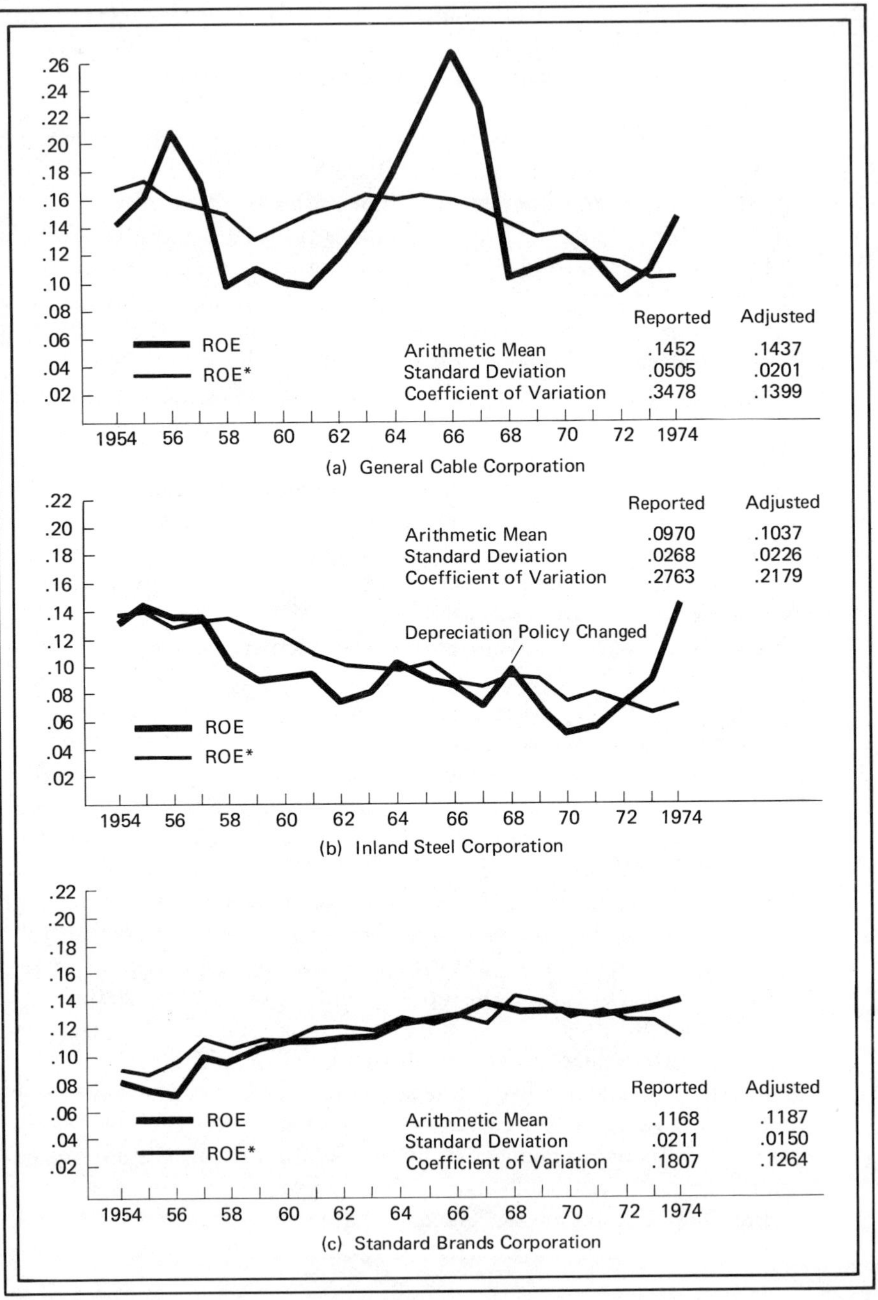

better approximated by ROE* for shorter intervals. On balance, adjustment of conventional accounting values seems both necessary and desirable; unfortunately, this may not be possible.

In the first place, analysts have access to the very limited data which are available publicly. Second, even if internal data were available, it would be extremely costly to attempt to reproduce and adjust the output of complex accounting systems in any detail. Thus the analyst faces a serious dilemma and judgment may have to be made on the basis of irrelevant or misleading data. Crude adjustments can be effected, as demonstrated in Figure 7.3. At worst this provides qualitative insight in the evaluation of quantitative forecasts; at best subjective probability distributions will more accurately represent objective probabilities. In any event, recognition of bias allows the analyst to avoid comparisons among firms which are not truly comparable. This implies that the analyst is able to interpret procedural diversity in the several areas of accounting practice which remain controversial.

Contemporary Issues in Accounting

Complex business operations result in complex procedures for recording business transactions. In many cases there is serious disagreement within the accounting community as to the propriety of one given procedure with respect to others. This section examines some of these contemporary controversies. Coverage is necessarily limited: an in-depth explanation of specific accounting procedures can be found in one of the several intermediate accounting texts which are available. The purpose here is simply to focus on important issues from an analyst's perspective.

AMORTIZATION PROCEDURES

Amortization procedures, including depreciation, were considered in detail in the preceding section. But some comment remains necessary for three specific types of long-term investment: land, research and development costs, and oil and gas exploration costs.

LAND. In one sense "depreciation" is an unfortunate term since it implies physical wear, tear, and deterioration. Land, which does not depreciate in that sense, is never amortized; it is carried at original cost until such time as it is sold. Viewed in terms of capital recovery, income is therefore misstated and, even with modest rates of inflation, assets are typically understated. An unbiased measure would be based upon Equation 7.3 for all estimated flows including terminal value. While this procedure is clearly subject to estimation error, rates of return calculated periodically would be free of serious conceptual bias. Undervaluation of land would probably be mitigated as well.[35]

RESEARCH AND DEVELOPMENT COSTS. Intangible investment in research and development (R&D) activity is expensed periodically under conventional accounting procedures. This is correct only when R&D expenditures contribute nothing to the generation of future cash flows; in that case there is little rationale for pursuing research. As demonstrated in the previous section, departures from internal return amortization will bias yield upward with the degree of bias increasing as depreciation front loading increases. Expensing is the maximum front loading procedure and firms which are research-intensive are open to serious upward bias. This is evidenced by the apparently extraordinary rates of return experienced recently by firms in the pharmaceutical industry; adjustment, in this case, is open to serious measurement error since both useful life and yield for R&D investment are very difficult to assess. Nonetheless, the analyst should clearly avoid comparisons among research-intensive and non-research-oriented companies.[36]

OIL AND GAS EXPLORATION COSTS. Accounting for oil and gas exploration costs continued to be one of the most controversial issues during the late 1970s. Two amortization procedures are possible. Under the first, "full cost" accounting, exploration and development costs are capitalized and amortized without regard to the success or failure of any particular venture. Most independent producers have employed full cost procedures because reported profits are maximized in the short run which, in the opinion of some people, increases the ability of these smaller firms to raise capital and compete for bids on lease properties. The second method, which major firms have adopted, capitalizes only "successful efforts" where exploration results in the discovery of new oil and gas reserves. Major oil companies generate a stream of revenue from previously developed fields which supports an ongoing exploration effort.

From a rate of return perspective the successful efforts methodology is correct because no future income stream is realized when exploration results in a dry hole. In 1975 Congress passed the Energy Policy and Conservation Act which, among other things, charged the SEC with establishing

[35] To illustrate, assume that land purchased as an investment for $1000.00 will sell for $17,449.40 30 years later. The internal rate of return on this investment is 10 percent. With zero cash flows in the interim periods and following amortization Equation 7.3, rate of return is correct when carrying value *increases* by 10 percent each year. Conventional procedures, relying on the realization rule, would generate 0 percent rates of return for the first 29 years; rate of return in year 30 would be 1645 percent! Land employed productively would have an increasing carrying value unless income generated periodically exceeded amortization charges.

[36] In view of the serious bias arising when R&D costs are expensed, it is particularly unfortunate that FASB requires this treatment. The board adopted this rule, effective January 1, 1975, possibly in response to difficulties outlined above when the "Big Bath" strategy was discussed.

uniform accounting practices for crude oil and natural gas producers by December of 1977; this legislation specifically authorized the SEC to rely upon relevant standards to be developed by the FASB. The FASB responded by issuing Statement No. 19, effective in December of 1978, which establishes the successful efforts method as the generally accepted principle for accounting for oil and gas exploration costs.[37]

The FASB position appears to be theoretically sound but the controversy has not been settled. In December of 1977 the Justice Department asked the SEC to delay adoption of the successful efforts method until the competitive effect of the FASB position could be determined. The Department of Energy, expressing concern with the potential impact on the balance of trade, entered the argument in 1978 by holding public hearings on the issue. In addition, several members of congress announced their intention to introduce legislation in 1978 which would prohibit acceptance of the FASB statement. Despite the congressional mandate contained in the 1975 energy act, accounting for oil and gas exploration costs continues to be a very difficult conceptual and political issue.

EARNINGS PER SHARE

Another important and unresolved issue involves the calculation of earnings per share. It is difficult because of contingent common stock represented by convertible securities, options, warrants, participating securities, and multiple-class common stock. Current practice requires that two values be reported.[38] The first, *primary earnings per share*, is calculated on the basis of average outstanding shares plus *common stock equivalents;* the latter value arbitrarily treats convertible debt as common stock when the straight bond yield at time of issue is $66\frac{2}{3}$ percent or less of the current prime interest rate. The second value is *fully diluted earnings per share;* it assumes that all contingencies which dilute earnings per share have been exercised.

What is really at issue is the value which investors capitalize. Contingencies create multiple classes of shareholders with different income streams depending on the course of future events. No single value represents the interests of any group and a simplifying assumption is required to calculate earnings per share. Since rational and informed investors are aware of the

[37] During 1969 and 1970 the APB and the SEC seemed to be moving against full-cost procedures by suggesting limitations on the definition of "cost centers" through which amortization is calculated. Some firms had selected all of North America as the relevant cost center. An APB proposal to limit the definition in 1971 was met by intense criticism and it was never implemented. At about the same time, in November of 1971, the Federal Power Commission ordered interstate pipeline companies to adopt full costing, placing themselves on a direct collision course with the SEC. Interestingly, the last two members named to the original FASB, Arthur Litke, chief accountant of the FPC, and Robert E. Mays, controller of the Exxon Corporation, had strongly opposing views on the question.

[38] "Earnings Per Share," *Opinions of the Accounting Principles Board, No. 15* (New York: AICPA, 1969).

dilutive effect arising from exercise of common stock contingencies, a tentative argument can be made for the fully diluted definition.[39]

INVESTMENTS AND BUSINESS COMBINATIONS

Accounting for investments and business combinations has also been controversial. Firms which acquire wholly owned subsidiaries prepare consolidated financial statements combining assets, liabilities, and equity, with intercompany transactions eliminated to avoid double counting. Consolidation views a parent firm and its subsidiaries as an economic entity and consolidated rate of return would be a correct measure if all segments of the enterprise otherwise account for operations with unbiased procedures. Consolidation provides no conceptual difficulty if acquisition values are properly recorded; recording acquisitions, on the other hand, does provide difficulty.

Firms may be acquired for cash or for common stock of the surviving company. In the former case values are usually recorded at cost with the difference between assignable book value and cost accounted for as acquired "goodwill"; this is often referred to as a "purchase." The major difficulty here is the problem of amortizing goodwill. In principle this is not a problem since the price paid for the firm can be associated with expected cash flows and all values can be amortized in accordance with Equation 7.3. But in practice this would be extremely difficult and goodwill amortization provides another source of bias in corporate rate of return. Bias would be greatest when goodwill is never amortized.

When firms are acquired in a stock-for-stock exchange the transaction is typically recorded as a "pooling-of-interest" with assets and liabilities of the acquired firm recorded at then-existing historical cost. Goodwill is not recognized and subsequent income statements are relieved of charges representing the difference between market value and book value of the acquired firm. This procedure tends to maximize the income stream and it has proven to be popular among acquiring managements. Nonetheless it can be defended on a rate of return basis since pooling implies the redistribution of interests among merging shareholder groups; unlike shareholders, the combined firm, in the aggregate, would measure values correctly if other transactions are recorded in accord with present value accounting procedures.

Investments which are not classified as business combinations might be accounted for in one of three ways. First, under the *cost* method, the asset would be carried at original cost and dividends would be credited to income. Second, under the *market* method, dividends and changes in market value both would be credited to income and asset value would be adjusted to current market value. Third, under the *equity* method, asset carrying value would be changed to reflect percentage ownership participation in

[39] The complexity of the problem can be illustrated by considering the convertible "preferred" stock issued by LTV; dividends were restricted to stock dividends and the conversion ratio was *variable* over time. As a result the dilutive effect was almost impossible to calculate.

the subsidiary's profit and loss and it would be decreased by the amount of any dividends received. Intercompany profits and losses would be eliminated. Equity is a compromise between cost and market methods and it has sometimes been referred to as "one-line" consolidation since subsidiary operations are restricted to investment and retained earnings accounts in the balance sheet.

Investment may be (1) a majority interest, (2) a minority interest with "significant influence," or (3) a minority interest without "significant influence" in the operation of the subsidiary. Under current accounting principles consolidated statements are considered the best procedure for reporting parent-subsidiary operations, including most majority interest situations. But when consolidation is not possible, and in cases where the parent does influence the subsidiary, the APB favored the equity method; in this respect significance was arbitrarily defined as ownership of 20 percent or more of the subsidiary's voting stock. With less than 20 percent interest the cost method is recommended.[40] From a rate of return perspective, with investment for an unspecified duration, market value would be the correct procedure although it is not generally allowable under current AICPA procedures.[41]

LEASE ACCOUNTING

Lease accounting has also been controversial[42] but the FASB has attempted to resolve the problem by setting forth new procedures effective January 1, 1977. Two different types of leases are recognized. A *capital lease* is a transaction where the asset is considered to be purchased by the lessee who financed the acquisition with rent payments; an *operating lease* is any other leasing agreement. FASB Statement No. 13 sets forth practical criteria for identifying a capital lease. If the capital leasing criteria are met, both the asset and the corresponding liability must be recorded by the lessee at the present value of the stream of rental payments. Operating leases are charged to expense on an accrual basis. Similar requirements exist for the lessee.

[40] "The Equity Method of Accounting for Investment in Common Stock," *Opinions of the Accounting Principles Board, No. 18* (New York: AICPA, 1971). Although the market value approach did have some support when Opinion No. 18 was considered, it was insufficient to receive general acceptance and the opinion concluded that further research was needed before use of the market value method was extended. The opinion does recommend that quoted market values be disclosed except for investment in common stock of subsidiaries. Disclosure aids the analyst who wishes to adjust values to a market basis.

[41] The same point can be made generally for any investment in securities including marketable securities and bonds.

[42] John H. Myers, *Reporting of Leases in Financial Statements*, Accounting Research Study No. 4 (New York: AICPA, 1962), and "Reporting of Leases in Financial Statements of the Lessee," *Opinions of the Accounting Principles Board, No. 5* (New York: AICPA, 1964). Lease accounting illustrates the lack of agreement among research and principles development efforts by the AICPA. Accounting Research Study No. 4, in 1962, suggested that the purchase method should be used for almost all lease agreements but Opinion No. 5, in 1964, recommended the procedure in a much smaller number of cases.

This new treatment required by the FASB results in an unbiased rate of return to the extent that published criteria are successful in differentiating between the two different lease transactions.

PRICE LEVEL ACCOUNTING

Accounting values are measured in original dollar costs. As a result the impact of price level changes is not shown in financial statements. Accounting procedures prohibit the addition of Canadian and U.S. dollars but 1945 dollars and 1975 dollars are added. The latter is as serious a distortion as the former would be and proposals for price-adjusted financial statements are heard increasingly. A FASB draft memorandum which would have required supplementary price-adjusted statements was withdrawn in 1976 following widespread opposition by corporations. The SEC now requires large corporations to report replacement costs for inventory and plant and equipment in 10-K filings but the validity of the values is open to serious question.[43]

To illustrate the problem, assume that a firm follows the practice of retailing inventory at values marked up by 5 percent over *current* cost; assume also that an item purchased one year ago for $1000 now costs $1100. Current selling price would then be $1155 and, in terms of the internal rate of return, yield would be 15.50 percent:

$$1000 = \frac{1155}{1.155}$$

In this case rate of return is a *monetary* yield; the *real* rate of return is 5 percent and the gain from inflation is 10 percent:

$$1000(1.05)(1.10) = 1155$$

Since management cannot control the rate of inflation, it would be very useful analytically if price level effects were available in financial statements; real and monetary performance could then be assessed. But general agree-

[43] Accounting Research Study No. 6 recommended that the effects of price level changes should be disclosed by supplementary statements. The Accounting Principles Board issued no *opinion* on the matter but it did issue a *statement* which supported the reporting of supplementary information; but APB concluded that price-adjusted information is not generally appropriate for reporting purposes. The AAA has suggested that both historical cost and current values be reported in separate columns in financial statements. "Reporting the Financial Effects of Price-Level Changes," *Accounting Research Study No. 6* (New York: AICPA, 1963); "Financial Statements Restated for General Price-Level Changes," *Statements of the Accounting Principles Board, No. 3* (New York: AICPA, 1969); *A Statement of Basic Accounting Theory* (Evanston, Ill.: American Accounting Association, 1966), pp. 30–31. Added support for price level disclosure was provided by the SEC in 1974 and the Institute of Chartered Accountants in 1973; the institute is the English equivalent of the AICPA.

Accounting for currency translation is a related issue which has become important since currencies were floated when the United States severed its currency linkage to gold in August of 1971. FABS Statement No. 8, which sets forth procedures for accounting for currency translation, has been severely criticized by firms.

ment on this issue remains distant and, in the event it were resolved, difficult problems remain with respect to specific procedures for adjusting accounts.[44]

DISCLOSURE

Given accounting diversity of the type detailed above, it seems evident that detailed disclosure is desirable in reported financial statements. In this respect both the AICPA and the SEC have moved to extend disclosure standards recently. Responding in part to pressure from security analysts, the APB in 1972 required detailed disclosure of significant accounting policies in preparing annual reports.[45] The SEC has also acted to improve reporting standards; since 1974, for example, shareholders may receive a copy of the detailed 10-K regulatory filing by requesting it from the corporate secretary. Disclosure does not solve the problem of accounting diversity, but it certainly mitigates it; the increased quality and quantity of data available to analysts and investors contribute importantly to increased efficiency in the evaluation process.

Forecasts of sales and profits is a special problem in disclosure; it has become one of the most controversial of recent issues. While the practice is currently prohibited by the SEC, commission authorities have been moving in that direction since early in 1972, and recommendations for publishing management forecasts were being actively pursued during 1978. SEC support has even been expressed for establishing guidelines for all forecasters, *including security analysts!* Standardization of forecasting techniques, and auditing standards for reviewing them, pose serious difficulties and proposals of this type have been received less than enthusiastically in accounting circles. Nonetheless, forecast data appear to be of serious concern at the SEC and efforts to extend disclosure standards in this area seem likely to intensify.

Summary

In this chapter accounting procedures were considered from the analyst's viewpoint. Following a brief review of the mechanics of double-entry accounting, the impact of procedural diversity on analytical procedures was examined. Forces leading to change in accounting theory and practice were reviewed in order to provide a foundation for interpreting those changes as they occur. Accounting procedures were formally compared to the accepted

[44] It is not clear, for example, if adjustments should be recorded by identifying specific current costs or by applying a price level index. In the latter case there are a number of indexes which might serve the intended purpose.

[45] "Disclosure of Accounting Policies," *Opinions of the Accounting Principles Board, No. 22* (New York: AICPA, 1972).

definition of financial yield and some of the major controversies in accounting were reviewed and interpreted in light of that definition.

While sources of bias can be identified by analysts, they cannot easily be evaluated since accounting records cannot be replicated externally in any detail. Crude adjustments are sometimes useful but accounting values must be recognized as data which are biased, sometimes seriously, and analytical procedures must be interpreted accordingly.

Chapter 6 began the process of examining security analysis procedures. This chapter reviewed one important dimension of that process in detail. In the next chapter another important element, the price-earnings ratio, will be considered. Problems arising from accounting diversity will be shown to be an important part of the problem of estimating price-earnings multiples.

Questions and Problems

1. The following balance sheet and income statement represent the financial condition of a firm at the end of its first year of operations. Depreciation of $10,000 calculated by the straight-line method was used for both book and tax purposes; if sum-of-the-years digits depreciation had been used, expense would have been $20,000. The tax rate is 50 percent.

Balance Sheet

Assets		
Current assets		$100,000
Fixed assets		
Cost	$150,000	
Accumulated depreciation	10,000	$140,000
Other assets		60,000
Total		$300,000
Liabilities and equity		
Current liabilities		
Tax payable	$ 20,000	
Other	80,000	$100,000
Equity		
Common stock	$180,000	
Retained earnings	20,000	$200,000
Total		$300,000

Income Statement

Revenue	$130,000
Operating charges and credits	80,000
Net	$ 50,000
Depreciation	10,000
Income before tax	$ 40,000
Income tax	20,000
Net income	$ 20,000

a. Calculate the impact on income, equity, and rate of return on equity of substituting sum-of-the-years digits depreciation for straight-line depreciation for *both* book and tax purposes. (Use end-of-year equity for calculating rate of return.)
b. Assume that the firm uses straight-line depreciation for book purposes and sum-of-the-years digits for tax purposes. Calculate income, equity, and rate of return on year-end equity under (1) deferred tax treatment and (2) flow-through tax treatment.
c. Compare rates of return calculated under (a) with those under (b). What is the net effect of using the deferred tax procedure? Based on the values you calculated, which tax accounting procedure is correct from a rate of return viewpoint?

2. The initial agenda of the newly formed Financial Accounting Standards Board in 1973 were the following:

   Accounting for foreign currency translation.
   Reporting data for segments of diversified companies.
   Criteria for determining materiality.
   Accounting for leases by lessors and lessees.
   Accounting for losses such as self-insurance reserves and catastrophe reserves.
   Accounting for research and development, start-up, and relocation costs.
   Broad guidelines and qualitative standards for financial reporting.

   a. How would you rank these items in order of importance to security analysts?
   b. If you were selecting this initial agenda, would you have chosen these issues? Would you substitute other problems for some or all of these? Explain.

3. Consider the following accounting policies:

   Purchase versus pooling of interests.
   LIFO versus FIFO inventory accounting.
   Accelerated versus straight-line depreciation.
   Full-cost versus expensing of oil and gas costs.
   Cost versus equity accounting for partially owned subsidiaries.
   Capitalization versus expensing of research costs.
   Flow-through versus deferred tax accounting.

   a. If you were in a position to select from among each of the seven variants listed without violating generally accepted accounting principles, and if you followed the strategy of *income maximization*, which method would you select in each instance?
   b. In general, and without detailing each of the seven items listed, would your answer to this question be the same if you wished to be a rate of return maximizer? Explain.

4. An investment in a project which costs \$16,000 will generate after-tax cash flows of \$3600, \$5760, \$6912, and \$10,368, respectively, over each of four years; internal rate of return on this project is 20 percent. Calculate accounting rate of return on the project for each of the four years of useful life by (1) the straight-line depreciation method and (2) the internal return depreciation method.

5. Refer to the data in problem 4 above. Assume that a firm has been organized today and has invested in that asset. One year from today the company purchases another of the same asset, at the same cost and generating the same stream of cash flows; the process is then repeated two years later and again three years later. After the investment three years from now, the firm will own four assets; at that point it reaches maximum size and thereafter it simply replaces worn-out assets, maintaining a "steady-state" size in which four assets are always owned and operated.
   a. If the firm is financed entirely by equity, so that assets always equal equity, what is the accounting rate of return for the firm during each of its first five years of operations under (1) straight-line depreciation and (2) internal return depreciation?

b. Compare income and asset values under each depreciation method during each of the first five years. What is the cause of bias under the straight-line method? Explain.

Selected References

DOUBLE-ENTRY ACCOUNTING

American Accounting Association, *A Statement of Basic Accounting Theory* (Evanston, Ill.: AAA, 1966).

Bierman, Jr., Harold, and Sidney Davidson, "The Income Concept—Value Increment or Earnings," *Accounting Review*, April 1969, pp. 239–246.

Buckley, John W., Paul Kircher, and Russell L. Mathews, "Methodology in Accounting Theory," *Accounting Review*, April 1968, pp. 274–283.

Edwards, Edgar O., and Philip W. Bell, *The Theory and Measurement of Business Income* (Berkeley: University of California Press, 1961).

Grady, Paul, "Inventory of Generally Accepted Accounting Principles in the United States of America," *Accounting Review*, January 1965, pp. 21–30.

Jensen, Robert E., "An Experimental Design for Study of Effects of Accounting Variations in Decision Making," *Journal of Accounting Research*, Autumn 1966, pp. 224–238.

Joy, O. Maurice, Robert H. Litzenberger, and Richard W. McEnally, "The Adjustment of Stock Prices to Announcements of Unanticipated Changes in Quarterly Earnings," *Journal of Accounting Research*, Autumn 1977, pp. 207–225.

Schattke, R. W., "An Analysis of Accounting Principles Board Statement No. 4," *Accounting Review*, April 1972, pp. 233–244.

DIVERSITY IN ACCOUNTING VALUES

Barefield, Russell M., and Eugene E. Comiskey, "The Smoothing Hypothesis: An Alternative Test," *Accounting Review*, April 1972, pp. 291–298.

Brilloff, Abraham J., *Unaccountable Accounting* (New York: Harper & Row, 1972).

Copeland, Ronald M., "Income Smoothing," *Empirical Research in Accounting, 1968*, Supplement to *Journal of Accounting Research* (1968): 101–121.

Gagnon, J., "Purchase-vs-Pooling," *Empirical Research in Accounting 1967*, Supplement to *Journal of Accounting Research* (1967): 187–204.

Monson, R. J., and A. Downs, "A Theory of Large Managerial Firms," *Journal of Political Economy*, June 1965, pp. 221–236.

O'Glove, Thornton, and Robert Olstein, "How Well Do Accountants Understand Materality?" *Journal of Portfolio Management*, Winter 1977, pp. 19–25.

Schiff, Michael, "Accounting Tactics and the Theory of the Firm," *Journal of Accounting Research*. Spring 1966, pp. 62–67.

White, Gary E., "Discretionary Accounting Decisions and Income Normalization," *Journal of Accounting Research*, Autumn 1970, pp. 260–273.

ACCOUNTING PRINCIPLES AND PRACTICE

Bradish, Richard D., "Corporate Reporting and the Financial Analyst," *Accounting Review*, October 1965, pp. 757–766.

Chambers, R. J., "A Matter of Principle," *Accounting Review*, July 1966, pp. 443–457.

Gordon, Myron J., "Postulates, Principles and Research in Accounting," *Accounting Review*, April 1964, pp. 251–263.

Horngren, Charles T., "Accounting Principles: Private or Public Sector?" *Journal of Accountancy*, May 1972, pp. 37–41.
Kemp, Patrick S., "The Authority of the Accounting Principles Board," *Accounting Review*, October 1965, pp. 782–787.
Mautz, Robert K., "Accounting Principles—How Can They Be Made More Authoritative?" *CPA Journal*, March 1973, pp. 185–192.
Stone, Willard E., "Antecedents of the Accounting Profession," *Accounting Review*, April 1969, pp. 284–291.
Vance, Lawrence L., "The Road to Reform of Accounting Principles," *Accounting Review*, October 1969, pp. 692–704.

PRESENT VALUE ACCOUNTING

Bierman, Jr., Harold, "A Further Study of Depreciation," *Accounting Review*, April 1966, pp. 271–274.
Burt, Oscar R., "A Unified Theory of Depreciation," *Journal of Accounting Research*, Spring 1972, pp. 28–57.
Fisher, Irving, *The Nature of Capital and Income* (1906; reprinted ed., New York: Augustus M. Kelley, 1965).
Johnson, Orace, "Two General Concepts of Depreciation," *Journal of Accounting Research*, Spring 1968, pp. 29–37.
Livingstone, John Leslie, and Gerald L. Salaman, "Relationship Between the Accounting and the Internal Rate of Return Measures: A Synthesis and an Analysis," *Journal of Accounting Research*, Autumn 1970, pp. 189–216.
Raby, William L., "Tax Allocation and Non-Historical Financial Statements," *Accounting Review*, January 1969, pp. 1–11.
Shwayder, Keith, "Expected and Unexpected Price Level Changes," *Accounting Review*, April 1971, pp. 306–319.
Stauffer, Thomas R., "The Measurement of Corporate Rate of Return: A Generalized Formulation," *Bell Journal of Economics and Management Science*, Autumn 1971, pp. 434–469.
Vatter, William J., "Income Models, Book Yield, and the Rate of Return," *Accounting Review*, October 1966, pp. 681–698.
Waugh, James B., "The Interperiod Allocation of Corporate Income Tax: A Proposal," *Accounting Review*, July 1968, pp. 535–539.

CONTEMPORARY ISSUES IN ACCOUNTING

Axelson, Kenneth S., "Needed: A Generally Accepted Method for Measuring Lease Commitments," *Financial Executive*, July 1971.
Brilloff, Abraham J., "Dirty Pooling," *Accounting Review*, July 1967, pp. 484–496.
Curry, Dudley W., "Opinion 15 vs a Comprehensive Financial Reporting Method for Convertible Debt," *Accounting Review*, July 1971, pp. 490–503.
Demski, Joel S., and Gerald A. Feltham, "Forecast Evaluation," *Accounting Review*, July 1972, pp. 533–548.
Drake, David F., and Nicholas Dopuch, "On the Case for Dichotomizing Income," *Journal of Accounting Research*, Autumn 1965, pp. 192–205.
Eigen, Martin M., "Is Pooling Really Necessary," *Accounting Review*, July 1965, pp. 536–540.
Frank, Werner G., and Jerry J. Weygandt, "Convertible Debt and Earnings Per Share: Pragmatism vs. Good Theory," *Accounting Review*, April 1970, pp. 280–289.
Knutson, Peter H., "Income Distribution: The Key to Earnings Per Share," *Accounting Review*, January, 1970, pp. 55–68.

Lauver, R. C. "The Case for Poolings," *Accounting Review*, January 1966, pp. 65–74.
O'Connor, Melvin C., and James C. Hamre, "Alternative Methods for Long-Term Investments," *Accounting Review*, April 1972, pp. 308–319.
Vatter, W. J., "Accounting for Leases," *Journal of Accounting Research*, Autumn 1966, pp. 133–148.

Chapter 8
Price-Earnings Multiple

The price-earnings ratio is one of the most critical and controversial of the many variables involved in security analysis. It is critical because difficult problems of definition and measurement may lead to serious error in estimating rate of return on equity investment. It is controversial because some analysts have suggested that stocks can be selected *solely* on the basis of the price-earnings ratio. These and other dimensions of the price-earnings multiple will be considered in this chapter.

The first section introduces the price-earnings ratio in the context of the valuation model set forth in Chapter 6; the controversy surrounding the "low price-earnings strategy" is also discussed there. The next section details problems of price-earnings definition and measurement. The third section considers probable determinants of the price-earnings ratio; empirical evidence supporting theoretical relationships is also reviewed. The last section of the chapter expands upon preceding material in considering forecasting procedures ranging from subjective estimation to application of statistical techniques.

Among the various statistical methods available to analysts, one of the most important is the regression technique. An understanding of this model is an important prerequisite to the understanding of material presented in this chapter and in a number of succeeding chapters as well.[1] For this reason regression is reviewed in an appendix to this chapter; the material presented there is an integral part of the text material. There is no attempt to develop the topic rigorously; formal training is required to accomplish that objective. Instead, regression is viewed from a user's perspective with emphasis on elements which are important in this chapter and elsewhere in the text.

Introduction

The meaning and significance of the price-earnings ratio can be introduced by recalling, from Chapter 6, the case of a firm with infinite duration constant growth. For such a firm current price P_0 was defined to be a function of current dividend D_0, required rate of return r, and growth rate g:

$$P_0 = \frac{D_0}{r - g} \qquad [(6.1)]$$

To further simplify the discussion, assume that the firm pays out all current earnings as dividends ($D_0 = E_0$) and also assume a zero growth rate ($g = 0$). In that case Equation 6.1 simplifies to Equation 8.1; current price P_0 is defined as the present value of a constant income stream, E_0, capitalized at rate of return r:

$$P_0 = \frac{E_0}{r} \qquad (8.1)$$

Dividing each side of the equation by E_0, the current price-earnings multiple m_0 is defined:

$$\frac{P_0}{E_0} = \frac{1}{r} = m_0 \qquad (8.2)$$

Thus price-earnings multiple m_0 is the reciprocal of equity capitalization rate r; if a 20 percent return is required, the appropriate earnings multiple would be 5.[2] In this case there is no difficulty in specifying or measuring m_0. But assumptions underlying Equation 8.2 are clearly unrealistic and when they are relaxed the price-earnings variable becomes far more difficult to define and analyze. Some of these difficulties were explored in detail in Chapter 6. Tables 6.1 and 6.2 demonstrated the impact of variations in the magnitude and duration of growth, respectively. Risk was also considered in Chapter 6; as uncertainty increases with respect to an earnings stream E_t, investors' demand for greater yield r will result in a smaller price-earnings multiple m_0.

[1] Regression is particularly important with respect to Chapters 9, 14, and 15.

[2] Under the assumptions given here, r is also the firm's cost of equity capital for financial management purposes. Under relaxed assumptions, cost of capital is more complex.

Equation 8.2 provides a simple description of the price-earnings ratio under very restrictive assumptions. As growth and risk elements are recognized, together with other variables which may impact on it, the price-earnings multiple tends to become very complex. In part this has led some analysts to focus on the price-earnings ratio per se, to the exclusion of other valuation elements, in selecting securities. Emphasis on m_0 reflects the *price-earnings multiplier effect* and its closely associated *low price-earnings strategy.*

MULTIPLIER EFFECT

Equation 8.2 is easily restated to show current price per share as the product of the price-earnings multiple and current earnings per share:

$$P_0 = m_0 E_0 \tag{8.3}$$

On the basis of Equation 8.3 price will respond, multiplicatively, to a change in either m_0 or E_0. But for some firms earnings per share tends to be rather stable when compared to variability in the price-earnings ratio. In other words, few firms are able to double earnings per share in the short run but there are instances in which the price-earnings ratio, as defined in Equation 8.3, has doubled in a limited time period. This leads some investors to concentrate on the earnings multiple in the hope of realizing significant short-run capital gains. But this can be hazardous, for a number of reasons.

First, Equation 8.3 implies that investors capitalize *current* earnings when the correct variable is the stream of *future* earnings purchased by current investment. Accordingly, price-earnings multiple m_0, as defined in Equation 8.3, is a proxy variable, unstructured, for investors' expectations as to future growth and risk prospects. It is far more reasonable to study risk and growth directly than to attempt to infer behavior from the current price-earnings ratio.

A second difficulty is practical. Evaluation of m_0 requires the selection of some standard for comparison, but no generally correct yardstick is obvious. A firm's current price-earnings ratio may be higher than the average for all other firms, for example, but it may also be lower than all other firms of similar risk-return attributes. Because there is no sound methodology for evaluating the price-earnings ratio, it is improbable that firms which promise substantial capital gains can be systematically identified in this manner.

Finally, there is no convincing empirical evidence which supports the multiplier strategy. In fact, one study suggests that the long-run multiplier effect is greatly overstated. Brigham and Pappas studied rates of return for 658 industrial and utility firms for the period 1946 through 1965.[3] They found that dividends accounted for 37.6 percent of realized returns over the period while capital gains accounted for the remaining 62.4 percent. But

[3] Eugene F. Brigham and James L. Pappas, "Rates of Return on Common Stock," *Journal of Business*, July 1969, pp. 302–316.

analysis of the capital gain segment revealed that 55.8 percent of return was attributable to growth in earnings while only 6.6 percent resulted from change in the price-earnings ratio.[4] This tends to support the argument that multiple m_0 of Equation 8.3 serves as a proxy variable for underlying valuation elements discussed in Chapter 6.

It is tempting to simply dismiss the price-earnings multiplier effect. But that fails to recognize the fact that some investors and institutions rely on it primarily for selecting securities. It also ignores evidence which suggests that low price-earnings firms may form a preferred subset for purposes of more rigorous security analysis.

THE "LOW PRICE-EARNINGS STRATEGY"

Ignoring conceptual and practical problems involved in identifying "low" price-earnings ratios momentarily, it is worthwhile to consider the conditions under which a low price-earnings ratio may occur.[5] Two hypotheses are possible:

1. The market correctly anticipates poor earnings performance; in this case the observed level of m_0 is justified.
2. The market erroneously anticipates future earnings. In this case the price of the firm's stock is undervalued and, as realized outcomes exceed expectations, price response will provide capital gain to investors who recognized the "low" price-earnings ratio.

To accept or reject either hypothesis is an empirical problem and existing evidence on the question is inconclusive. Nicholson, a proponent of the low price-earnings hypothesis, studied rates of return for a sample of securities for the period 1937 through 1962; he concluded that the strategy was successful in providing above average return during the period. In a more recent study covering the period April 1957 through March 1971, Basu concluded that portfolios comprised of low P/E stocks earned, on average, higher absolute and risk-adjusted rates of return.[6] Fluegel, on the other hand, provided statistically significant evidence to the contrary for a random selection of stocks with return measured over ten-year periods commencing between 1951 and 1955.[7]

An interesting study by Latané, Joy, and Jones used sort-rank analysis of earnings-price ratios to predict performance relative to the mean return

[4] Ibid., p. 309.

[5] The "low" price-earnings ratio controversy is reviewed in depth in Nicholas Molodovsky, "Recent Studies of P/E Ratios," *Financial Analysts Journal*, May–June 1967, pp. 101–108.

[6] S. Francis Nicholson, "Price Ratios in Relation to Investment Results," *Financial Analysts Journal*, January–February 1968, pp. 105–109 and S. Basu, "Investment Performance of Common Stocks in Relation to Their Price-Earnings Ratios: A Test of the Efficient Market Hypothesis," *Journal of Finance*, June 1977, pp. 663–681.

[7] Frederick K. Fluegel, "The Rate of Return on High and Low P/E Ratio Stocks," *Financial Analysts Journal*, November–December 1968, pp. 130–133.

an investor would receive on a portfolio of securities selected randomly.[8] Securities were ranked by their earnings-price ratios, measured on the basis of quarterly earnings; return on portfolios consisting of the ten highest and ten lowest ranks were compared to return measured by the Standard & Poor's "425" Index. The authors found that the earnings-price ratio was successful in identifying large "winners," but not large "losers," for the 1965–1968 period studied. Importantly, the earnings variable was lagged one quarter to predict price performance over the following six-month period; that is, E_{t-1}/P_t was used to forecast P_{t+2}/P_t. Thus the strategy tested used quarterly earnings *available to investors at the time a decision is made.*

Breen modified the price-earnings strategy by adding a growth-rate constraint; low price-earnings firms were limited to those which had realized a mean compound growth rate of 10 percent over the preceding five years.[9] He found that low price-earnings firms, filtered by growth-rate control, generally outperformed securities which were randomly selected. The Breen study is particularly important because it places the low price-earnings controversy in perspective. Undervaluation implies error in the expectation of risk, growth, and other underlying valuation elements. The price-earnings ratio should be analyzed relative to, and in conjunction with, these basic valuation factors.

While evidence concerning the low price-earnings hypothesis must still be regarded as inconclusive, it is strong enough to suggest that observed price-earnings multiples do provide useful information to analysts. Conceptually and empirically there seems to be little justification for using m_0 for purposes of security *selection*; nonetheless, the price-earnings ratio may prove to be a reasonable variable, among others, for purposes of *screening* securities prior to more intensive analysis. The problem of screening will be explored in detail in Chapter 13.

Measurement

The first step in analyzing a price-earnings ratio is to measure it over some particular time interval. This proves to be difficult because of serious operational problems in defining it. Unfortunately, there is no theoretically correct way of specifying the price-earnings ratio. Selection from among its many possible variants sometimes depends on the end-use intended; in other cases it depends on characteristics of the firm to be analyzed; in yet other cases it depends entirely on the judgment of the analyst. Moreover, while there

[8] Henry A. Latané, O. Maurice Joy, and Charles P. Jones, "Quarterly Data, Sort-Rank Routines, and Security Evaluation," *Journal of Business*, October 1970, pp. 427–438. In addition to the earnings-price variable, the authors also used an earnings-growth variable (E/E); they found the E/P ratio performed insignificantly better than the E/E ratio.

[9] William Breen, "Low Price-Earnings Ratios and Industry Relatives," *Financial Analysts Journal*, July–August 1968, pp. 125–127.

are several ways to define the price numerator, it is the earnings denominator which provides the greatest difficulty in measuring the price-earnings ratio in practice.

The numerator may be closing price at the end of the period but the more usual choice is the midpoint of the range between period high and low values. In the case of an unlisted security it is possible to use either the bid price or the ask price but the bid-ask midpoint is the more common choice. Problems involved with the earnings denominator include: (1) selection of a time interval, (2) seasonal adjustment, (3) earnings normalization, (4) leads and lags, and (5) the use of cash flow in lieu of earnings.

ANNUALIZED EARNINGS

Price-earnings ratios are calculated for some discrete time interval, for example, annually, quarterly, or monthly. Selection of the interval is constrained on one hand by usefulness of the price-earnings ratio and on the other by data availability. An extended time period obscures the behavior of security prices; annual price-earnings ratios, for example, fail to capture the impact of price movements during the year and they are of very limited value for most analytical purposes. For this reason it is preferable to calculate the price-earnings ratio for a smaller interval. But the typical reporting period for corporations is quarterly; while other values can be inferred by averaging quarterly data, they are values which have little impact on the price-earnings ratio. For practical purposes the three-month (or 13-week) interval is probably the minimum period for which earnings are available.[10] For these reasons the quarterly price-earnings ratio is the most common one used in practice.

Although the measurement interval may be quarterly, it is conventional to calculate the price-earnings ratio on the basis of yearly earnings. This requires that periodic earnings be annualized. To illustrate, consider the quarterly values contained in Table 8.1. Earnings per share could be changed to annual values by multiplying each of them by four, but that fails to recognize the obvious seasonal pattern in the series; without adjustment earnings calculated in this manner would be meaningless. One alternative is to sum the most recent four quarters as illustrated under the columnar heading "Four Quarter Moving Total." Other possibilities include seasonal adjustment and earnings normalization.

SEASONAL ADJUSTMENT

Seasonal variation refers to a cyclical pattern of behavior in a time series in which the cycle is completed within the calendar year with the basic pattern

[10] Recent efforts to provide audited quarterly statements have been unsuccessful partly because of the cost involved.

Table 8.1
Quarterly Earnings and Price Data

Year	Quarter	Earnings per Share	Four-Quarter Moving Total	Per Share Market Price
1971	1	1.98		96
	2	.78		106
	3	.48		98
	4	1.76	5.00	$97\frac{1}{2}$
1972	1	2.10	5.12	$98\frac{1}{2}$
	2	.80	5.14	$104\frac{3}{8}$
	3	.58	5.24	$106\frac{7}{8}$
	4	2.02	5.50	$115\frac{1}{4}$
1973	1	2.10	5.50	$87\frac{5}{8}$
	2	.75	5.45	78
	3	.56	5.43	79
	4	1.84	5.25	$67\frac{3}{4}$
1974	1	2.50	5.65	$73\frac{3}{8}$
	2	.78	5.68	$67\frac{1}{2}$
	3	.62	5.74	$59\frac{1}{4}$
	4	2.10	6.00	$43\frac{1}{8}$
1975	1	2.75	6.25	$66\frac{1}{2}$
	2	1.05	6.52	87
	3	.70	6.60	$87\frac{1}{4}$
	4	2.50	7.00	104

repeated year after year. Seasonal variation arises because of weather conditions, buying habits of consumers, and so on; when this occurs it is possible to adjust the series to eliminate the seasonal element. While there are several ways to accomplish this, a common one is the ratio-to-moving-average method illustrated in Table 8.2.

The first two columns repeat values from Table 8.1 but the four-quarter moving total has been shifted to more accurately center values with respect to earnings per share.[11] Moving totals of column 2 are divided by four to calculate moving average quarterly values of column 3. Next, original values of column 1 are divided by moving average values; this procedure removes trend and cyclical elements and only seasonal and random elements remain in the values in column 4. A seasonal index, summarized in column 5, is then calculated at the bottom of the table. Column 4 values are grouped

[11] To be completely centered the first four-quarter value would fall between the second and third quarters of 1971; the value corresponding to third-quarter earnings per share of 0.48 would then be 5.06, the midpoint between the first two moving totals. Centering also involves the problem of earnings leads and lags; these will be considered shortly.

Table 8.2
Deseasonalized Quarterly Earnings

		(1)	(2)	(3)	(4)	(5)	(6)
Year	Quarter	Earnings Per Share	Four-Quarter Moving Total[a]	Moving Average (1)/4.0	EPS as Percent of Moving Avg. (1)/(3) × 100	Seasonal Index	Deseasonalized EPS (1)/(5) × 100
1971	1	1.98				165.26	1.20
	2	.78				57.88	1.35
	3	.48	5.00	1.250	38.4	41.55	1.16
	4	1.76	5.12	1.280	137.5	135.31	1.30
1972	1	2.10	5.14	1.285	163.4	165.26	1.27
	2	.80	5.24	1.310	61.1	57.88	1.38
	3	.58	5.50	1.375	42.2	41.55	1.40
	4	2.02	5.50	1.375	146.9	135.31	1.49
1973	1	2.10	5.45	1.363	154.1	165.26	1.27
	2	.75	5.43	1.358	55.2	57.88	1.30
	3	.56	5.25	1.313	42.7	41.55	1.35
	4	1.84	5.65	1.413	130.3	135.31	1.36
1974	1	2.50	5.68	1.420	176.1	165.26	1.51
	2	.78	5.74	1.435	54.4	57.88	1.35
	3	.62	6.00	1.500	41.3	41.55	1.49
	4	2.10	6.25	1.563	134.4	135.31	1.55
1975	1	2.75	6.52	1.630	168.7	165.26	1.66
	2	1.05	6.60	1.650	63.6	57.88	1.81
	3	.70				41.55	1.68
	4	2.50				135.31	1.85

	Quarter 1	2	3	4	Total
1971			38.4	137.5	
1972	163.4	61.1	42.2	146.9	
1973	154.1	55.2	42.7	130.3	
1974	176.1	54.4	41.3	134.4	
1975	168.7	63.6			
Trimmed mean[b]	166.05	58.15	41.75	135.95	401.90
Index[c]	165.26	57.88	41.55	135.31	400.00

[a] Centered on the third of each four quarters.
[b] Smallest and largest values are eliminated.
[c] 400.00/401.90 × trimmed mean.

by quarters and averaged; a trimmed mean is calculated by eliminating extreme values to offset the effect of any serious random disturbance. These mean values, adjusted to a base value of 100, are the seasonal index. Earnings per share values are then divided by the index to construct the deseasonalized series of column 6. These quarterly values are easily converted to annual values by multiplying each of them by four.

NORMALIZED EARNINGS

Seasonally adjusted data are subject to trend variation and random disturbance.[12] The former is important to the analyst in predicting future values. But random elements tend to obscure underlying relationships; for that reason it is often desirable to adjust data to eliminate randomness. This process is defined as *normalizing* the series.

Earnings should usually be normalized when calculating the price-earnings ratio. This can be accomplished with moving averages or with trend analysis. The simple moving average values in column 2 of Table 8.1 are an example of the former; other methods exist for calculating more involved moving averages.[13] Trend can be analyzed with the ordinary least-squares method discussed in the appendix to this chapter. Trend values for moving total earnings per share data given in Table 8.2 were computed from Equation 8.4:[14]

$$\mathrm{EPS}_t = a + bt, \qquad t = 1, 2, \ldots, 19, 20 \tag{8.4}$$

EPS values were annualized for both observed and deseasonalized data; time values were transformed such that the first quarter of 1971 was set equal to a value of $t = 1$. The equations which resulted were, with values rounded:

$$\text{Original:} \quad \mathrm{EPS}_t = 4.77 + 0.09t, \qquad r^2 = 0.061 \tag{8.5}$$

$$\text{Deseasonalized:} \quad \mathrm{EPS}_t = 4.59 + 0.11t, \qquad r^2 = 0.715 \tag{8.6}$$

[12] The remaining component of the classical approach to time series analysis is cyclical variation. But cycles are a very complex question, both conceptually and statistically, and no generally satisfactory statistical model exists for isolating cyclical movement. For this reason the discussion here is limited to trend analysis.

[13] When moving averages are used, an exponentially weighted moving average generally provides the best empirical fit. A description of this technique, together with methods for estimating weights, is found in Robert G. Brown, *Smoothing, Forecasting and Prediction of Discrete Time Series* (Englewood Cliffs, N.J.: Prentice-Hall, 1962). A new and sophisticated approach is the Box-Jenkins method which combines the autoregressive and moving averages techniques. It appears to lead to superior forecasts but it is very technical and it has yet to be completely tested. This method, the autoregressive integrated moving average model, or ARIMA, is discussed in Vincent A. Mabert and Robert C. Radcliffe, "Forecasting—A Systematic Modeling Methodology," *Financial Management*, Autumn 1974, pp. 59–67.

[14] Trend could have been estimated from the semilogarithmic specification: $\log(\mathrm{EPS}_t) = a + bt$. In the case of the values given in Table 8.2 there is no appreciable difference between arithmetic and semilog formulations. In practice the latter often provides the better fit.

Table 8.3 contains original values and trend values for earnings per share for both observed and seasonally adjusted data. The table also contains price-earnings ratios calculated for each definition of earnings per share; prices are those given in Table 8.1. The price-earnings values in the table demonstrate the importance of normalization together with its interaction with seasonal adjustment. Price-earnings ratios calculated on the basis of observed quarterly earnings are clearly meaningless but it is difficult to distinguish among values calculated for the other three series. This is not surprising since the trend equation (Equation 8.4) also smooths seasonal variation. But Equation 8.5, which uses observed data, accounts for only 6.1 percent of the variability in earnings per share; this is statistically insignificant at the 10 percent confidence level. Equation 8.6, on the other hand, has an r^2 value of 0.715; this is significant at the 1 percent level. The standard error of estimate for Equation 8.6 can be used to estimate variability in earnings per share. Thus trend, combined with seasonal adjustment, provides measures of both risk and return elements.

Table 8.3
Normalized Price-Earnings Ratios (annualized earnings)

	Observed Data		Trend in Observed Data		Deseasonalized Data		Trend in Deseasonalized Data	
Period	EPS	P/E	EPS	P/E	EPS	P/E	EPS	P/E
1971 1	7.92	12.12	4.86	19.75	4.80	20.00	4.70	20.43
2	3.12	33.97	4.95	21.41	5.40	19.63	4.81	22.04
3	1.92	51.04	5.05	19.41	4.64	21.12	4.92	19.92
4	7.04	13.85	5.14	18.97	5.20	18.75	5.03	19.38
1972 1	8.40	11.73	5.23	18.83	5.08	19.39	5.14	19.16
2	3.20	32.62	5.33	19.58	5.52	18.91	5.25	19.88
3	2.32	46.07	5.42	19.72	5.60	19.08	5.36	19.94
4	8.08	14.26	5.52	20.88	5.96	19.34	5.47	21.07
1973 1	8.40	10.43	5.61	15.62	5.08	17.25	5.58	15.70
2	3.00	26.00	5.70	13.68	5.20	15.00	5.69	13.71
3	2.24	35.27	5.80	13.62	5.40	14.63	5.80	13.62
4	7.36	9.21	5.89	11.50	5.44	12.45	5.91	11.46
1974 1	10.00	7.34	5.98	12.27	6.04	12.15	6.02	12.19
2	3.12	21.63	6.08	11.10	5.40	12.50	6.13	11.01
3	2.48	23.89	6.17	9.60	5.96	9.94	6.24	9.50
4	8.40	5.13	6.27	6.88	6.20	6.96	6.35	6.79
1975 1	11.00	6.05	6.36	10.46	6.64	10.02	6.46	10.29
2	4.20	20.71	6.45	13.49	7.24	12.02	6.56	13.26
3	2.80	31.16	6.55	13.32	6.72	12.98	6.68	13.06
4	10.00	10.40	6.64	15.66	7.40	14.05	6.79	15.32

Price data source: Table 8.1.

Table 8.3 contains several sets of values for earnings per share and the price-earnings multiple. The relative superiority of any one of them cannot be proven because the correct measure depends on the definition of earnings which investors capitalize. That is not known; in fact, different investors may choose different definitions. Nonetheless, in the absence of convincing evidence to the contrary, the final set of values in Table 8.3, based on seasonally adjusted normalized earnings, is perhaps the most useful measure of the price-earnings ratio.

LEADS AND LAGS

Another price-earnings variant arises from the time interval used to measure price relative to the earnings interval. Let $t - 1$, t, and $t + 1$ represent, respectively, the past, the present, and the future; on a quarterly basis, for example, $t - 1$ would be the immediately preceding quarter. For a current price P_t, three price-earnings definitions are possible:

1. P_t/E_{t-1}.
2. P_t/E_{t+1}.
3. P_t/E_t.

The first of the three, P_t/E_{t-1}, may have predictive significance where current earnings could be used to forecast future market price; this is the variable used by Latané, Joy, and Jones in the paper cited in the preceding section of this chapter. The relevance of this formulation is largely empirical; if the lagged-earnings variable succeeds in providing a superior forecasting and/or screening measure it becomes very important because it uses information which is available at the time of the investment decision. Success in this regard should be tested and retested with outcomes evaluated in the judgment of the analyst.

The second measure, P_t/E_{t+1}, has theoretical significance since security value depends on future earnings rather than those of the past or the present. Assuming that the stream of future earnings can be measured by E_{t+1}, in the sense of an annuity, and assuming that investors have common expectations with respect to those earnings, P_t/E_{t+1} would be a theoretically correct measure. But it is an oversimplification to measure the earnings stream in this fashion and, moreover, investors' expectations are not homogeneous. As a result P_t/E_{t+1} has little practical relevance.

The other measure, P_t/E_t, is a compromise between the predictive and the theoretical. It is the most widely used of the three in practice and in research studies. But it is also a somewhat deceptive measure and it is important to recognize its limitations, especially in the case of a high-growth firm. Assume that a firm currently has annual earnings of \$1 per share but investors expect rapid growth to a level of \$5; also assume that, in the absence of growth, investors would require a 5 percent rate of return to invest in this firm. Ignoring growth stages between \$1 and \$5 momentarily,[15]

[15] See Table 6.2 of Chapter 6.

and assuming that the latter value is capitalized, current price per share would be \$100 based on a price-earnings ratio of 20.[16] But the current P_t/E_t is 100 (100/1); this is a biased measure of underlying capitalization factors.

The current earnings multiple, P_t/E_t, can be used only when risk, growth, and other valuation elements are accounted for in the process. This requires specification of the relationship among the price-earnings ratio and basic valuation factors. A number of studies have attempted to do this both theoretically and empirically; the next section of this chapter discusses some of these efforts. First, however, one remaining problem of measurement requires comment.

EARNINGS VERSUS CASH FLOW

The remaining measurement problem has been very controversial in the investment community. It involves the capitalization of cash flow, with a cash flow multiplier, in lieu of earnings and a price-earnings multiplier. To proceed it is necessary to define cash flow as it is used in this context; the rationale for using cash flow will then be introduced and evaluated.

CALCULATING CASH FLOW. In Chapter 7 accounting was described as the process of tracing the flow of funds through an enterprise. As indicated there, funds may be defined narrowly to include only cash and near-cash items or it may be defined more broadly to include all elements of operating working capital. But the analysis of present value accounting procedures demonstrated that the broad definition, based on accrual accounting procedures, is formally equivalent to the definition required for the internal rate of return mechanism. For this reason, cash flow will be defined as the flow of working capital in the discussion which follows; this is the definition commonly used by analysts although the term cash flow, and not working capital flow, tends to persist.

Analysts should be familiar with procedures for calculating cash flow despite the recent change which requires its disclosure in the annual report. In the first place, the statement of change in financial position was seldom reported before 1970 or 1971; cash flow data prior to that time must be calculated by the analyst. Second, and just as important, the analyst should understand the capacity and limitations of the data which are used.

Cash flow is calculated by analyzing changes in balance sheet accounts from one period to the next.[17] Define current assets CA, other assets OA, current liabilities CL, other liabilities L, and equity E; the familiar accounting balance sheet equation can then be restated:

$$CA + OA = CL + L + E \quad \text{and} \quad CA - CL = L + E - OA \tag{8.7}$$

[16] From Equation (8.2), 1/.05 = 20.

[17] The algebra of cash flow calculation is set forth in A. Wayne Corcoran and Ching-Wen Kwang, "A Set Theory Approach to Funds-Flow Analysis," *Journal of Accounting Research*, Autumn 1965, pp. 206–217, and Glenn L. Johnson, "Funds-Flow Equations," *Accounting Review*, July 1966, pp. 510–517.

Since Equation 8.7 holds for any time period, change in balance sheet values from period to period must also be equal. That is, denoting change in any account by Δ,

$$\Delta CA - \Delta CL = \Delta L + \Delta E - \Delta OA \tag{8.8}$$

The left-hand side of Equation 8.8 is aggregate cash flow; it can be analyzed by analyzing each term on the right-hand side of the equation. In this manner the sources and uses of funds can be isolated in terms of the six categories identified in Figure 7.1 of Chapter 7. One of those categories, funds provided by operations, is the definition of cash flow which is relevant for security analysis.

To illustrate, consider the balance sheet and income statement set forth previously in Tables 7.1 and 7.2 of Chapter 7. Table 8.4 restates the balance sheet in a format compatible with Equation 8.8. Changes in working capital and other accounts are classified as sources or uses of funds. A decrease in an asset or an increase in liabilities or equity is a source of funds;

Table 8.4
Analysis of Flow of Funds

			Change	
	19x1	*19x0*	*Source*	*Use*
Working capital				
Operating current assets	\$1150	\$1120		\$ 30
Operating current liabilities	560	550		(10)
Increase in working capital	\$ 590	\$ 570		\$ 20
Investments	\$ 850	\$ 840		\$ 10
Plant and equipment				
Cost	\$4000	\$2000		2000
Accumulated depreciation	(1700)	(1400)	\$ 300[a]	
Deferred assets	200	100		100
	\$3940	\$2110		
Bank loans	\$ 100		100	
Bonds payable	1000		1000	
Deferred taxes	500	\$ 200	300[a]	
Equity				
Common stock	1000	1000		
Retained earnings	1340	910	490[a]	60[b]
	\$3940	\$2110	\$2190	\$2170
Increase in working capital				20
			\$2190	\$2190

[a] Funds provided by operations.
[b] Dividends.

correspondingly, an increase in an asset or a decrease in liabilities or equity is a use of funds, as demonstrated previously in Figure 7.1. Balance sheet values in Table 8.4 were taken directly from the balance sheet of Table 7.1 except that operating current liabilities (accounts payable and accrued expense) are deducted from operating current assets to calculate net working capital. Change in retained earnings is segregated, in accordance with the income statement of Table 7.2, to separate the income source from the dividend use of funds.

Table 8.5 presents the statement of change in financial position for this hypothetical firm. Values were taken directly from worksheet Table 8.4; classification is straightforward except for noncash charges to income included under "funds provided by operations." In fact these charges, for depreciation and tax deferral, together with other noncash items, are the difference between the concepts of cash flow income and accounting income. Noncash entries clearly have no effect on cash flow but they do affect earnings under conventional accounting procedures. For this reason noncash charges (credits) must be added back to (subtracted from) income in calculating funds provided by operations.

Although a complete analysis of the sources and uses of funds requires a methodology similar to the one illustrated in Tables 8.4 and 8.5, cash

Table 8.5
Neverfail Electric Shoelace
Statement of Change in Financial Position
for the Year Ended December 31, 19x1

Source of funds		
Operations		
Net income		$ 490
Add noncash charges		
Depreciation		300
Deferred taxes		300
Funds provided by operations		$1090
Funds provided by financing		
Bank loans	$ 100	
Bonds payable	1000	1100
Total funds provided		$2190
Use of funds		
Dividends		$ 60
Purchase of assets		
Investments	$ 10	
Plant and equipment	2000	
Deferred assets	100	2110
Total use of funds		$2170
Increase in working capital		$ 20

flow, or funds provided by operations, is easily calculated with far less effort. It is sufficient for the analyst to review financial statements carefully to isolate noncash items; the cash flow computation is then easily accomplished as illustrated above. In this respect it should be emphasized that the two major adjustments will be: (1) depreciation, depletion, and other amortization charges; and (2) tax deferral charges or credits. These were the major differences between conventional accounting data and present value accounting data which were identified and discussed in Chapter 7.

CASH FLOW MULTIPLIERS. The relative advantages and disadvantages of substituting cash flow for earnings has been a topic of serious and unresolved debate in investment circles.[18] The basic argument in favor of cash flow arises because of problems caused by procedural diversity in accounting; aside from inventory valuation procedures cash flow is relatively invariant with respect to accounting methodology. In addition, cash flow is defended in terms of the internal rate of return model. In that mechanism, as demonstrated previously in Chapters 3 and 7, depreciation is reflected in the denominator of the discounted present value formulation; this leads some to conclude that gross flow (cash flow), and not net flow (earnings), is the proper variable to capitalize.

Cash flow opponents argue that gross flow is a poor definition of earnings since one major cost element, capital recovery (depreciation), is ignored in the process. The argument is persuasive, particularly since accounting earnings and discounted return can be reconciled by way of present value accounting procedures. Another valid objection to cash flow is practical: data are not generally available for less than annual intervals.

The pros and cons of cash flow versus earnings cannot be settled theoretically and the issue has yet to be resolved empirically. But if the price–cash flow variable is used it is still necessary to select one of several possible definitions of cash flow. These include: (1) unadjusted cash flow, (2) cash flow adjusted for capital expenditures, and (3) cash flow "earnings" modified on the basis of present value accounting. The first alternative is straightforward; it is the "funds provided by operations" of Table 8.5, adjusted to a per share basis. Under the second the stream of capital expenditures would be analyzed and normalized investment would be substituted for depreciation in calculating "cash flow earnings." The third possibility attacks the problem directly but the methodology is not widely known and it is unlikely to provide reliable values for the analyst. When cash flow is used in evaluating securities the unadjusted definition is the one most likely to be adopted although the other two possibilities appear to be superior in several respects.

[18] The theoretical significance of cash flow is set forth in Diran Bodenhorn, "A Cash-Flow Concept of Profit," *Journal of Finance*, March 1964, pp. 16–31. Also see Allan R. Drebin, "Cash-Flowitis: Malady or Syndrome," *Journal of Accounting Research*, Spring 1964, pp. 25–34, and L. S. Rosen and Don T. DeCoster, "Funds Statements: A Historical Perspective," *Accounting Review*, January 1969, pp. 124–136.

Price-Earnings Determinants

The first step in analyzing the price-earnings ratio is to specify its determinants. Because of its critical importance in the theory of equity valuation, extensive efforts have been directed to identifying and testing variables which may explain price-earnings variability. These efforts can generally be classified as (1) attempts to explain a firm's price-earnings ratio relative to "normal" price-earnings levels or (2) attempts to test price-earnings variability by application of statistical models, especially multiple regression.

RELATIVE PRICE-EARNINGS MULTIPLES

Models of the relative value of a firm's price-earnings ratio usually focus on the magnitude and duration of growth in earnings per share. Studies of this type include those of Holt (1962) and Malkiel (1963).[19] Holt analyzed the duration of above normal growth; for this purpose he assumed a finite period of abnormal growth after which the growth rate immediately returns to some "normal" level. This is the same assumption as the one underlying the variable growth multipliers of Table 6.2 of Chapter 6.

The Holt model is summarized in Equation 8.9:

$$\log\left(\frac{P_f/E_f}{P_m/E_m}\right) = t \log\left(\frac{1 + g_f + d_f}{1 + g_m + d_m}\right) \tag{8.9}$$

where

P = current share price
E = current earnings per share
g = growth rate in earnings per share
d = dividend yield, current dividend divided by market price
f = "abnormal" growth rate firm
m = firm of the same risk class as firm f
t = duration of abnormal growth rate for firm f

According to Equation 8.9, firm f will grow at some abnormal rate g_f for t years after which it will experience the more normal rate g_m. The dependent variable is t; values for the other variables can be observed or estimated from historical data. In illustrating the model, Holt used the Dow Jones index to represent firm m, the "normal" growth alternative. Equation 8.9 attempts to explain P_f/E_f relative to P_m/E_m through differences in growth rates and dividend yields. The relationship is linear in logarithms and it can easily be solved graphically or algebraically.

The model is limited in several respects, as Holt pointed out,[20] and it is not operational in the strict sense. But it does reinforce the importance

[19] Charles C. Holt, "The Influence of Growth Duration on Share Prices," *Journal of Finance*, September 1962, pp. 465–475, and Burton G. Malkiel, "Equity Yields, Growth, and the Structure of Share Prices," *American Economic Review*, December 1963, pp. 1004–1031.

[20] Most importantly, risk is ignored in the Holt model. Other difficulties include constancy of g and d during the abnormal growth period and the abrupt termination of excess growth which the model assumes.

of growth in terms discussed previously in Chapter 6. At the same time, it is obvious that there are other variables which also affect the price-earnings ratio; multivariate analysis has been used in an attempt to specify those variables.

MULTIVARIATE ANALYSIS

Multivariate analysis of the price-earnings ratio generally utilizes the least-squares regression model.[21] Most studies use cross-sectional regression although some are time series and others use pooled data combining cross section and time series. Among the major studies of this type are those of Benishay (1961), Whitbeck and Kisor (1963), Friend and Puckett (1964), Wippern (1966), Bower and Bower (1969), Malkiel and Cragg (1970), and Chung (1974).[22] These and other studies are often similar with respect to the variables selected but they usually differ in the empirical definitions employed to measure those variables.

VARIABLES. The price of a share of common stock is a function of the expected stream of earnings and its associated risk in the minds of investors. But expected earnings and risk cannot be measured precisely; for this reason *corrective* variables may be introduced to counteract measurement error in the *explanatory* variables (earnings and risk). Chung's study, for example, used growth in market price and dividend payout rate to "correct" earnings.[23] To illustrate the type of variables found in regression studies of the price-earnings ratio, Equation 8.10 summarizes the model tested by Bower and Bower:[24]

$$P/E = a + b_1(1 + g) + b_2\text{PAY} + b_3\text{MKT} + b_4\text{CON} + b_5\text{VAR} + b_6\text{FIR} \tag{8.10}$$

[21] This section assumes familiarity with the material contained in the appendix to this chapter.

[22] Haskel Benishay, "Variability in Earnings-Price Ratios of Corporate Equities," *American Economic Review*, March 1961, pp. 81–94; Volkert S. Whitbeck and Manown Kisor, Jr., "A New Tool in Investment Decision-Making," *Financial Analysts Journal*, May–June 1963, pp. 55–62; Irwin Friend and Marshall Puckett, "Dividends and Stock Prices," *American Economic Review*, September 1964, pp. 656–682; Ronald F. Wippern, "Financial Structure and the Value of the Firm," *Journal of Finance*, December 1966, pp. 615–633; Richard S. Bower and Dorothy H. Bower, "Risk and the Valuation of Common Stock," *Journal of Political Economy*, May–June 1969, pp. 349–362; B. G. Malkiel and J. G. Cragg, "Expectations and the Structure of Share Prices," *American Economic Review*, September 1970, pp. 601–617; and Peter S. Chung, "An Investigation of the Firm Effects Influence in the Analysis of Earnings to Price Ratios of Industrial Common Stocks," *Journal of Financial and Quantitative Analysis*, December 1974, pp. 1009–1029.

[23] Chung, ibid., pp. 1010–1015 and appendix II, pp. 1024–1027.

[24] Bower and Bower, "Risk and Valuation of Common Stock," pp. 351–356. All variables are measured in logarithms. This article is outstanding in developing and explaining each of the variables cited.

where

P/E = ratio of price to normalized earnings
g = estimated nonnormal growth in earnings
PAY = dividend payout ratio
MKT = measure of the stock's marketability based on the number of shares traded
CON = measure of conformity of the return on the security relative to return implied by the Dow Jones index
VAR = measure of price variability based on the high-low spread of the stock during the year
FIR = other characteristics peculiar to the particular firm[25]

Bower and Bower tested cross-sectional data for 100 stocks for each year 1960 through 1964 together with pooled observations for all years combined. Regression coefficients generally had the sign which theory suggests, most coefficients were statistically significant, and r^2 values exceeded 0.75 for all runs of the model. This is strong statistical support for this model; similar support exists for most of the other studies cited above.

The variables of Equation 8.10 are typical of those used in empirical studies of the price-earnings ratio. Differences which occur usually arise from the definition or measurement of one or more specific variables; this point will be considered shortly. On balance there is a good deal of similarity among the many studies of price-earnings behavior. Research, in the aggregate, has succeeded in narrowing the search for price-earnings determinants; it has also focused attention on two important dimensions of the problem. These are (1) the existence of a significant "firm effect" and (2) the advantage accruing from the use of expectational variables in lieu of historical variables.

FIRM EFFECT. The existence of a significant firm effect is evidenced in the previously cited work of Friend and Puckett, Bower and Bower, and Chung. In the Bower and Bower study, regression excluding the FIR variable explained between 30 and 40 percent of variability in cross-sectional and pooled data; when FIR was included the equation's explanatory power nearly doubled. In Chung's study, based on 1959–1968 data, r^2 values ranged from 0.45 to 0.62 in the absence of a firm effect variable; with the variable included, explanatory power increased to values between 0.87 and 0.95.

The firm effect variables used in these studies were derived from cross-sectional regressions excluding a firm effect; regression residuals for the year or years prior to the cross section year were used to measure the firm variable. This procedure may seem complex but it is easily explained. Consider the following equations:

$$Y = a + b_1X_1 + b_2X_2 + e \tag{8.11}$$

$$Y = a + b_1X_1 + \mu \tag{8.12}$$

[25] FIR turns out to be a critical variable in this and similar studies and it will be defined more carefully below.

Assume that Equation 8.11 is a correct statement of the relationship among variables Y, X_1, and X_2 but that Equation 8.12 is formulated and tested instead. In this case regression residual μ is not a random disturbance term; systematic behavior of missing variable X_2 obscures the underlying residual e.

In testing variable Y it would be preferable to use Equation 8.11 but specific identification of variable X_2 may not be possible; in the case of a firm effects variable, to this point in time, it is not. For this reason, and assuming a persistent impact of X_2 over time, prior μ values can be used to account for the missing variable. Although their specific measures differ, this is the general approach adopted by Bower and Bower and Chung:

$$Y_t = a + b_1 X_{1t} + b_2 \mu_{t-1} + e_t \tag{8.13}$$

The firm effects variable appears to be one of the most influential of the price-earnings ratio determinants. It is also one of the most bothersome since it has yet to be defined precisely. In the Malkiel and Cragg study the authors noted that the stock of Reynolds Tobacco Company always appeared to be underpriced according to their model; the reason advanced was the nonmodeled threat of government sanctions against tobacco firms.[26] Bower and Bower described the effect as characteristics including management resiliency and vulnerability to government action.[27] This sheds light on the nature of the firm effect but it does not and probably cannot aid in specifying the multitude of factors which differentiate one firm from another. In this sense an important determinant of a firm's price-earnings ratio remains unresolved and analysts lack a completely reliable model for predictive purposes.[28]

EXPECTATIONAL VARIABLES. Another major difficulty with empirical studies of the price-earnings ratio is the measurement of expectations of earnings and risk. Malkiel and Cragg attacked the problem directly by using expectational data gathered from 17 investment firms.[29] They tested a multiple regression model, similar to others discussed here, for 178 corporations for the years 1961 through 1965. Earnings and risk variables measured on the basis of available historical data explained approximately 50 percent of the variability in observed price-earnings ratios. But when analysts' expected data were introduced, explanatory power increased to approximately 75 percent. Regressions combining historical data and expectational data had r^2 values ranging from 0.78 to 0.84.

[26] Malkiel and Cragg, "Expectations and Structure of Share Prices," p. 616.

[27] Bower and Bower, "Risk and Valuation of Common Stock," p. 350.

[28] This is particularly true in light of Chung's observation that the relationship among regression residuals, u of Equation 8.12, weakens over time. See Chung, "Investigation of Firm Effects," pp. 1019–1021.

[29] Malkiel and Cragg, "Expectations and Structure of Share Prices." Data were collected from four brokerage houses, five banks, five mutual funds, two pension trusts, and one insurance company.

Malkiel and Cragg extended their work by considering implications of their findings for security analysis. They used the regression model to calculate a "normal" price-earnings ratio which could be compared with the observed price-earnings ratio; in this fashion "overvalued" or "undervalued" securities might be identified.[30] But they found it was not possible to profit systematically from this procedure with their model; among the reasons they offered to explain this was that the model overlooks important factors unique to individual companies—the firm effect discussed previously. The Malkiel–Cragg study is not conclusive, but predictive accuracy would certainly be improved if research succeeds in specifying the firm effect more precisely.

DEFINING AND MEASURING VARIABLES. The empirical search for price-earnings determinants has resulted in extensive experimentation with the definition and measurement of explanatory variables. Theory provides guidance in identifying independent variables but correct specification of those variables is an empirical problem which cannot otherwise be settled. The discussion in Chapter 6, for example, demonstrates the importance of financial risk but it does not distinguish among two common measures of that risk: the debt-equity ratio and the number of times fixed charges are covered by earnings.[31] It also fails to distinguish among alternative measures of debt, equity, and earnings. Although similar measures tend to be highly correlated, the precise specification of model variables is a problem best solved by experimentation.[32]

Research has succeeded in identifying major price-earnings determinants despite difficulties arising from persistence of the firm effects variable and the general lack of availability of expectational data. But identification of determinants is only the first step in the analytical process; the more difficult problem of forecasting remains.

Forecasting the Price-Earnings Ratio

The preceding discussion provides a basis for forecasting the price-earnings distribution for purposes of security analysis. But forecasting is a difficult process involving both subjective and objective elements. Techniques range from naive extrapolation of past values to statistical forecasts based on subjective/objective estimates of future values of explanatory variables.

[30] This is similar to an approach which will be discussed in the next section of this chapter.

[31] Of the papers cited earlier in this section, Benishay and Chung both used debt-equity variables while Wippern used a cash flow definition of earnings coverage. Bower and Bower, in contrast, model risk generally in terms of marketability, conformity with market behavior, price variability, and the firm effect.

[32] See the Malkiel and Cragg model, previously cited, for an excellent illustration of the specification and testing of alternative measures of explanatory variables.

SUBJECTIVE ESTIMATES

The simplest approach is the purely subjective one in which the analyst determines levels of expected value and variance on the basis of experience and judgment. Isolated from prior information this method would be overly arbitrary but subjective estimates derived on the basis of observed price-earnings multiples may be superior to other apparently more scientific forecasts. An ex post distribution is the point of departure; the time period selected should, when possible, describe market behavior and firm performance within the range of probable future outcomes. Given the observed distribution, and in light of the analyst's beliefs as to future growth and risk elements, the price-earnings distribution can be estimated subjectively.[33] This is a dynamic process in which an analyst's judgment benefits from an error-learning experience.

STATISTICAL PREDICTION

Statistical forecasts formalize the subjective process. For the most part these are applications of the multiple regression model in times series or in cross section. Widely quoted models are those of (1) Whitbeck and Kisor and (2) Ahlers; both studies combine statistical and subjective forecasting.

WHITBECK-KISOR MODEL.[34] Whitbeck and Kisor proposed a least-squares model for estimating a "theoretical" price-earnings ratio which could be compared with the actual price-earnings ratio at some given point in time. Both P/E values were computed on the basis of a normalized estimate of earnings. The theoretical value, $\widehat{P/E}$, was hypothesized to be a function of growth in earnings G, dividend payout rate D, and earnings instability σ, the latter variable measured by percentage deviation from trend in earnings.

$$PE_i = a + b_1 G_i + b_2 D_i + b_3 \sigma_i, \quad \text{for firm } i, \quad i = 1, 2, \ldots, 135 \tag{8.14}$$

Ex post data were used to derive G_i, D_i, and σ_i values for each of 135 firms on June 8, 1962; in the proposal derived values would be adjusted to conform to the analyst's subjective opinion of changing economic trends.

Cross-sectional multiple regression was then used to estimate model parameters for June 8, 1962:

$$PE_i = 8.2 + 1.5G_i + 6.7D_i - 0.2\sigma_i \tag{8.15}$$

[33] Robichek and Bogue analyzed the conditions under which the price earnings ratio may be expected to remain constant over time; this is the special case where growth rate and dividend payout are constant. Unless these conditions are met, in theory, the price-earnings multiple cannot have a normal level in the sense of a constant expected value. Alexander A. Robichek and Marcus C. Bogue, "A Note on the Behavior of Expected Price Earnings Ratios Over Time," *Journal of Finance*, June 1971, pp. 731–735.

[34] Volkert S. Whitbeck and Manown Kisor, Jr., "A New Tool in Investment Decision-Making," *Financial Analysts Journal*, May–June 1963, pp. 55–62.

Whitbeck and Kisor did not provide evidence as to the statistical significance of their model but the signs of regression coefficients are plausible with the price-earnings ratio positively associated with growth and dividend payout and negatively associated with earnings variability. Moreover, the variables specified in Equation 8.14 are similar to those tested successfully in other studies.

Whitbeck and Kisor intended the model for locating "undervalued" and "overvalued" securities. The ratio of theoretical P/E, from the regression model, to a firm's actual P/E provides a measure of relative valuation. With the same definition of earnings E employed in both numerator and denominator,

$$\frac{\widehat{P/E}}{P/E} = \frac{\hat{P}}{P} \tag{8.16}$$

Undervaluation is implied when the price ratio of Equation 8.16 is greater than one since theoretical price $\hat{P}$ is accordingly greater than current market price P.

The usefulness of the model for *selecting* among a group of securities is questionable, but it does illustrate a methodology for *forecasting* the price-earnings ratio. It is also somewhat limited in application. The regression model is a cross-sectional equation; if the expected holding period is extended it is strictly applicable only if model parameters are stationary. In practice, it may be necessary to add a variable to account for changes in the general level of market rates of return as economic conditions vary over time.

AHLERS MODEL.[35] The Ahlers model extends the work of Whitbeck and Kisor. The basic differences in the two studies are in the degree of theoretical soundness and statistical rigor. Ahlers employed exponentially weighted moving averages to normalize earnings and growth estimates; smoothing weights were varied from firm to firm to provide the best fit for each in minimizing forecasting error over the time period observed.[36] He also adjusted the multiple regression model of Equation 8.14 by transforming data to logarithmic values and by altering the explanatory variables; dividend yield was substituted for the payout rate and the coefficient of variation was used in lieu of the standard error to measure earnings variability. Ahlers also added an explanatory variable designed to measure persistence in market undervaluation or overvaluation of securities. Regression values were disclosed in detail.

[35] David M. Ahlers, "SEM: A Security Evaluation Model," in *Analytical Methods in Banking*, ed. Kalman J. Cohen and Frederick S. Hammer (Homewood, Ill.: Irwin, 1966), pp. 305–338.

[36] The moving average technique which Ahlers used was adapted from Peter R. Winters, "Forecasting Sales by Exponentially Weighted Moving Averages," *Management Science*, April 1960, pp. 324–342.

While Ahlers's model is more complex than the one proposed by Whitbeck and Kisor, it seems to provide the better technique for predictive purposes. At the same time, as Ahlers pointed out, the model represents only one step in solving problems involved in security analysis, including the forecasting of the price-earnings ratio. Until forecasting deficiencies are resolved, prediction of the price-earnings distribution will continue to be a severe analytical difficulty.

Summary

This chapter considered theoretical and practical aspects of defining and measuring the price-earnings ratio. Probable price-earnings determinants were identified and empirical studies of probable associations were surveyed. The important problem of forecasting was introduced in terms of two models which had been designed for practical application by investing institutions.

The concepts discussed in this chapter, together with Chapters 6 and 7, set forth a framework for evaluating common stock investment. But the most difficult part of the process remains—translating the model into an estimate of the distribution of rate of return. The next chapter considers this problem and a case demonstration is presented to illustrate the methodology and to emphasize both the merits and hazards of forecasting procedures.

Appendix
The Least-Squares Regression Model

This appendix considers the least-squares regression model. The discussion is not rigorous; that is not the objective. The purpose instead is twofold: (1) to review the basic elements of the model from a user's perspective and (2) to provide a common basis for discussing applications of regression in this chapter and in chapters which follow. The major portion of the appendix is contained in the first section where the two-variable linear model is examined. Other sections briefly consider statistical measures of association, transformation of variables, multivariate models, and the impact of various common errors in specifying and testing the model.

THE TWO-VARIABLE MODEL

The two-variable model can be formulized as

$$Y = a + bX \tag{8A.1}$$

where Y is the dependent variable, X is the independent variable, and a and b are constants. Equation 8A.1 is the formula for a straight line with intercept a on the Y axis and slope b. If any specific value of X is given, the corresponding value of Y is also given; for a value of X_1 (or X_2), Y assumes the value Y_1 (or Y_2). Variable Y is linearly related to X along line $Y = a + bX$, the loci of (X, Y) points. This is illustrated in Figure 8A.1.

According to Equation 8A.1 explanatory variable X completely describes the value of variable Y. But Y may also react to other influences. Consider value Y_3 in Figure 8A.1: it is determined by X_2, moving *along* line $Y = a + bX$, but it also depends on some other factor e which influences Y *around* the value $a + bX_2$. In this case Equation 8A.1 incorrectly specifies the determinants of variable Y and Equation 8A.2 is the correct formulation:

$$Y = a + bX + e \tag{8A.2}$$

Variability in Y is now explained by variability in X together with some other residual factor e. In the case of Equation 8A.1 all Y points would fall exactly on straight line $a + bX$; for Equation 8A.2, however, Y would be a scatter of points around that line. In this case, if X and Y are observed values drawn from some conditional probability distribution, constants a and b would be unknown and they would have to be estimated.

Residual factor e may be a number of things but it is convenient for the moment to assume that it represents completely random elements which cannot be predicted. In that case explanatory variable X cannot completely

Figure 8A.1
The Two-Variable Linear Model,
$Y = a + bX$

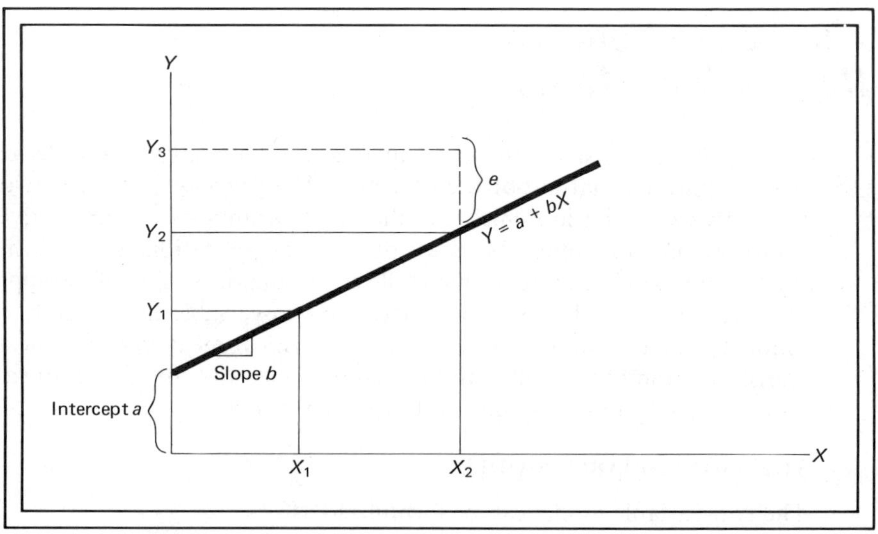

Figure 8A.2
The Two-Variable Linear Model,
$Y = \hat{a} + \hat{b}X + e$

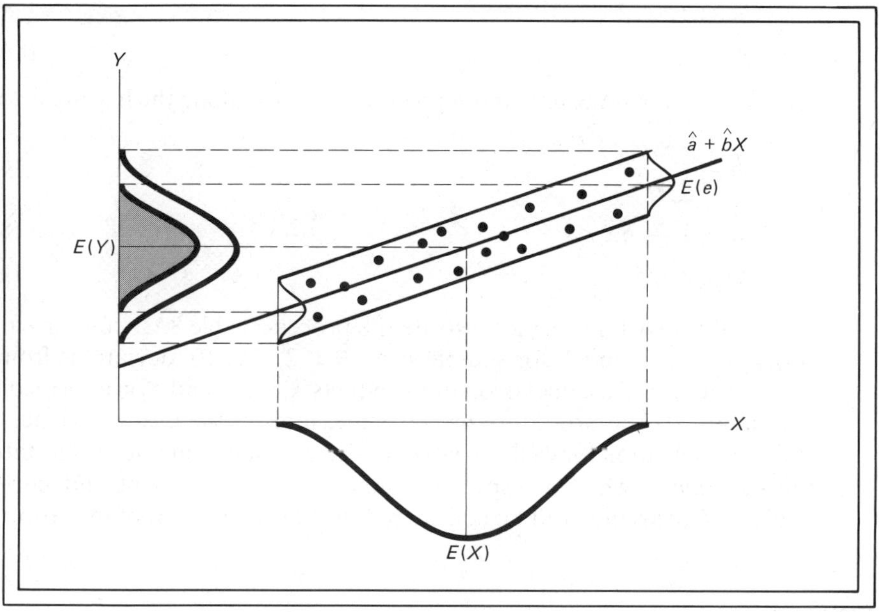

explain observed variability in dependent variable Y. Variability in Y along regression line $a + bX$ is referred to as *explained variance* while variability around the line is referred to as *unexplained variance.* This is illustrated in Figure 8A.2; Y, X, and e are portrayed as random variables with mean values $E(Y)$, $E(X)$, and $E(e)$. The variance in Y associated with variance in X, along the regression line, is implied by the shaded area within the distribution of Y. Distributions centered along the regression line represent the distribution for e. Variability in e generates added variability in Y, implied by the unshaded area in the distribution of Y.

The scatter of points in Figure 8A.2 represent sample observations drawn independently from distributions X and Y. Given only those observations, and the hypothesized relationship of Equation 8A.2, it is necessary to calculate intercept $\hat{a}$ and slope $\hat{b}$ which estimate true values a and b.

LEAST-SQUARES ESTIMATORS. Parameter estimates $\hat{a}$ and $\hat{b}$ can be calculated by the method of ordinary least squares. This involves passing a line through the observations such that the sum of positive and negative residuals, $\sum e$, is zero, and the sum of squared deviations, $\sum e^2$, is minimized. Standard formulas exist for estimating $\hat{a}$ and $\hat{b}$ to conform to those requirements. Data used may be observed sample values or the deviation of those values from their mean. The latter, defined in Equation 8A.3, are the most useful for purposes of this discussion:

$$x_i = X_i - \bar{X} \tag{8A.3a}$$

$$y_i = Y_i - \bar{Y} \tag{8A.3b}$$

Given Equation 8A.3, $\hat{a}$, $\hat{b}$, and regression values $\hat{Y}_i$ along the line are defined:

$$\hat{b} = \frac{\sum x_i y_i}{\sum x_i^2} \tag{8A.4}$$

$$\hat{a} = \bar{Y} - \hat{b}\bar{X} \tag{8A.5}$$

$$\hat{Y}_i = \hat{a} + \hat{b}X_i \tag{8A.6}$$

Tables 8A.1 and 8A.2 illustrate the process. Table 8A.1 contain sample observations X_i and Y_i for sample size $i = 1, 2, \ldots, 10$; deviations from the mean x_i and y_i are calculated, and products x_i^2, y_i^2, and $x_i y_i$ are calculated and summed. The procedure provides measures of the mean, variance, and standard deviation for each variable. It also provides a measure of a statistic, the *covariance*, which is especially important in investment and portfolio analysis. Covariance will be considered in the next section of this appendix.

Table 8A.1
Deviation in Observed Variables
(n = 10)

	i	X_i	$-\bar{X}$	$=x_i$	Y_i	$-\bar{Y}$	$=y_i$	x_i^2	y_i^2	$x_i y_i$
	1	190	150	40	43	35	8	1600	64	320
	2	150	150	0	36	35	1	0	1	0
	3	110	150	−40	30	35	−5	1600	25	200
	4	100	150	−50	24	35	−11	2500	121	550
	5	180	150	30	43	35	8	900	64	240
	6	160	150	10	36	35	1	100	1	10
	7	120	150	−30	29	35	−6	900	36	180
	8	160	150	10	34	35	−1	100	1	−10
	9	200	150	50	43	35	8	2500	64	400
	10	130	150	−20	32	35	−3	400	9	60
Sum:		1500		0	350		0			
		$\bar{X}$			$\bar{Y}$					
Mean: $\bar{X}$ and $\bar{Y}$		150			35					
Sum: $\sum x_i^2$, $\sum y_i^2$, and $\sum x_i y_i$								10600	386	1950
Variance: $\sum x_i^2/n$ and $\sum y_i^2/n$								1060	38.6	
Standard deviation: $\sqrt{\sum x_i^2/n}$ and $\sqrt{\sum y_i^2/n}$								32.5576	6.2129	
Covariance: $\sum x_i y_i/n$										195

Table 8A.2

Regression Values
(n = 10)

(A8.4) $\hat{b} = \sum_{i=1}^{10} x_i y_i \Big/ \sum_{i=1}^{10} x_i^2 = 1950/10{,}600 = 0.1840$

(A8.5) $\hat{a} = \bar{Y} - \hat{b}\bar{X} = 35 - (0.1840)(150) = 7.40$

(A8.6) $\hat{Y}_i = 7.40 + 0.1840X_i$

i	$\hat{Y}_i$ −	Y_i =	$\hat{e}_i$	$\hat{e}_i^2$
1	42.36	43.00	−0.64	0.4096
2	35.00	36.00	−1.00	1.0000
3	27.64	30.00	−2.36	5.5696
4	25.80	24.00	1.80	3.2400
5	40.52	43.00	−2.48	6.1504
6	36.84	36.00	0.84	0.7056
7	29.48	29.00	0.48	0.2304
8	36.84	34.00	2.84	8.0656
9	44.20	43.00	1.20	1.4400
10	31.32	32.00	−0.68	0.4624
Sum: $\sum\hat{e}_i$ and $\sum\hat{e}_i^2$			0.00	27.2736
Variance: $\sum\hat{e}_i^2/(n-2)$				3.4092
Standard deviation: $\sqrt{\sum\hat{e}_i^2/(n-2)}$				1.8464

Data source: Table 8A.1.

Coefficient estimates $\hat{a}$ and $\hat{b}$, together with $\hat{Y}_i$ values along the regression line, are calculated in Table 8A.2. Regression residuals are also calculated, as defined in Equation 8A.7; their sum, in the case of the arithmetic example, is shown to be zero.

$$\hat{e}_i = \hat{Y}_i - Y_i \qquad (8A.7)$$

Moreover, the sum of squared residuals, averaged, provides the standard error of estimate about the regression line:

$$\hat{\sigma}_e = \sqrt{\frac{\sum(\hat{Y}_i - Y_i)^2}{m-2}} = \sqrt{\frac{\sum\hat{e}_i^2}{m-2}} \qquad (8A.8)$$

In the numerical example the standard error of estimate is 1.846.

The least-squares method illustrated in Tables 8A.1 and 8A.2 is only one of several methods available for calculating parameter estimates $\hat{a}$, $\hat{b}$, and $\hat{\sigma}_e$. It is generally used because, under a set of assumptions concerning the probability distribution of e, it provides the "best linear unbiased estimator," which some refer to as BLUE. But if the assumptions concerning residual e are seriously violated the analyst cannot rely on estimates generated by the least-squares model. These assumptions, and their meaning, will be discussed in the last section of this appendix.

Aside from general assumptions regarding e, an important case in regression occurs when the probability distribution of the residual is *normally distributed.* In that event maximum-likelihood estimates are available and hypotheses concerning $\hat{a}$ and $\hat{b}$ can be tested. For hypothesis testing, the standard error of regression coefficient $\hat{b}$ is needed; this can be calculated:

$$\hat{\sigma}_b = \frac{\hat{\sigma}_e}{\sqrt{\sum x_i^2}} \tag{8A.9}$$

To illustrate, an important hypothesis to test is $b = 0$; if the slope of the regression model of Equation 8A.2 is zero, there is no relationship between variables X and Y. This hypothesis can be tested by applying the *student t* distribution found in elementary statistics texts. Specifically, for the null hypothesis $b = 0$,

$$\begin{aligned} t &= \frac{\hat{b} - b}{\hat{\sigma}_b} \\ &= \frac{\hat{b} - 0}{\hat{\sigma}_b} \end{aligned} \tag{8A.10}$$

Arithmetically, for values from Tables 8A.1 and 8A.2,

$$\hat{\sigma}_b = \frac{\hat{\sigma}_e}{\sqrt{\sum x_i^2}} = \frac{1.8464}{\sqrt{10{,}600}} = 0.0179$$

$$t = \frac{\hat{b} - 0}{\hat{\sigma}_b} = \frac{0.1840}{0.0179} = 10.279$$

From a table of the student t distribution, and for 8 degrees of freedom $(n - 2)$, the critical t value at the 1 percent significance level is 3.355. Since the t value exceeds the critical level, the hypothesis of no association, $b = 0$, is rejected.

Standard error $\hat{\sigma}_b$ and the t statistic are important to analysts in evaluating the significance of parameter estimates; most empirical studies will provide one value or the other and "canned" computer regression programs will generally include both as part of the printout. These statistics become even more important in the case of the multiple regression model discussed in a later section.

In summary, the least-squares regression model provides the analyst with a powerful tool when it is used properly and when its underlying assumptions are understood and tested. The remaining sections of this appendix consider measures of association in general together with practical problems involved in using regression.

STATISTICAL MEASURES OF ASSOCIATION

A familiar measure of association among variables is r, the *coefficient of correlation;* a related measure is r^2, the *coefficient of determination.* Formulas for both measures, together with arithmetic values based on Table 8.1 and 8.2 data, are given in Equations 8A.11 through 8A.13:

$$r^2 = 1 - \frac{\hat{\sigma}_e{}^2}{\sigma_y{}^2} = 1.0 - \frac{2.7274}{38.6000} = 0.929 \qquad (8A.11)$$

$$r = \frac{\sum x_i y_i}{n\sigma_x\sigma_y} = \frac{1950}{(10)(32.5576)(6.2129)} = 0.964 \qquad (8A.12)$$

$$r = \sqrt{r^2} = \sqrt{0.929} = 0.964 \qquad (8A.13)$$

From Equation 8A.11, r^2 is the percentage of total variability in Y explained by variability in X. Arithmetically this is almost 93 percent; unexplained variance, in $\hat{\sigma}_e{}^2$, is approximately 7 percent. r^2 must vary in the range between 0, which implies no association among X and Y, and 1, which implies perfect association. With r^2 values in the range between 0 and 1, correlation coefficient r must fall in the range from -1 to $+1$. With perfect association ($r^2 = 1$ or $r = \pm 1$) all Y observations would fall exactly on regression line $a + bX$ with either negative ($r = -1$) or positive ($r = +1$) slope; for $r = r^2 = 0$, the variables are not associated and line $a + bX + e$ has zero slope.

Since r and r^2 can be interpreted in terms of the regression equation, a relationship between r, r^2, and $\hat{b}$ is implied; this relationship is defined and evaluated arithmetically in Equation 8A.14:

$$r = \hat{b}\frac{\sigma_X}{\sigma_Y} = (0.1840)\frac{32.5576}{6.2129} = 0.964 \qquad (8A.14)$$

From Equation 8A.14, $r = 0$ clearly implies $b = 0$, in the sense of hypothesis testing discussed previously; for $r = 1$, similarly, $\hat{b}\sigma_X = \sigma_Y$ and Y observations will fall exactly on the regression line.

Covariance is also related to r and b; it measures the direction and magnitude of change in one random variable as another associated variable changes. For that reason it is critical to the concept of a diversified portfolio of securities where diversification is directed to reduction of risk in the aggregate; this point will be pursued in detail in Chapter 14. Covariance is sometimes symbolized as cov(X, Y), other times as $E(X, Y)$, and yet other times as σ_{XY}; it is defined and evaluated arithmetically in Equation 8A.15:

$$\sigma_{XY} = \frac{\sum x_i y_i}{n} = \frac{1950}{10} = 195 \qquad (8A.15)$$

The positive value of the covariance in Equation 8A.15, which results from the positive value of $\sum x_i y_i$, suggests that variables X and Y tend to change in the same direction. That is also implied in the positive values of r and $\hat{b}$:

from Equations 8A.15, 8A.12, and 8A.4 it is easily shown that:

$$\sigma_{XY} = r\sigma_X\sigma_Y = (0.964)(32.5576)(6.2129) = 195 \tag{8A.16}$$

$$\hat{b} = \frac{\sigma_{XY}}{\sigma_X{}^2} = \frac{\text{cov}(X, Y)}{\text{var}(X)} = \frac{195}{1060} = 0.1840 \tag{8A.17}$$

Thus four important measures of statistical association, r, r^2, $\hat{b}$, and σ_{XY} exist, and all are specifically interrelated. In investment analysis one or more of these may be used for some specific purpose but it is important to recognize that they are indeed related. In the case of the two-variable regression model, for example, significance may be judged at one time or another by r, r^2, or $\hat{b}$.

TRANSFORMATION OF VARIABLES

The two-variable model of Equation 8A.2 assumes a linear relationship between variables X and Y but the underlying association may instead be nonlinear. In that case it may be possible to specify the relationship properly by transforming one or more of the variables. Two common possibilities are (1) reciprocal transformation and (2) logarithmic transformation. Reciprocal transformation of independent variable X is defined in Equation 8A.18:

$$Y = a + b\left(\frac{1}{X}\right) + e \tag{8A.18}$$

As X increases, $1/X$ falls and it approaches zero as X grows very large. Thus Equation 8A.18 defines a relationship in which Y approaches intercept a, from above where $b > 0$ or from below where $b < 0$. This specification has proved to be useful in a number of studies.

Logarithmic transformation is more common in investments. In this case the dependent variable, the explanatory variable, or both, will be transformed by substituting logarithms of values for the original data. An important application of this specification for security analysts is illustrated in Equation 8A.19 where the dependent variable is earnings per share (EPS) and the explanatory variable is time (t):

$$\log \text{EPS}_t = a + bt + e_t, \qquad b = \log(1 + g) \tag{8A.19}$$

In Equation 8A.19 the antilog of $\hat{b}$ is estimated growth relative $(1 + \hat{g})$ which provides a least-squares estimate of EPS growth $\hat{g}$. This is particularly useful to analysts because of the importance of growth in the analytical process. Another important specification is double-log transformation; this has been used in a number of studies of security price behavior.

THE GENERAL LINEAR MODEL

A dependent variable Y may be a linear function of more than one independent variable as defined in Equation 8A.20:

$$Y = a + b_1X_1 + b_2X_2 + \cdots + b_kX_k + e \tag{8A.20}$$

Equation 8A.20, the general linear model, is an extension of the two-variable model of Equation 8A.2. Least squares again provides parameter estimates $\hat{a}$, $\hat{b}_1$, $\hat{b}_2, \ldots, \hat{b}_k$, and $\hat{\sigma}_e$ although the formulas are somewhat more complicated than those for the two-variable model. In practice computers are often used to calculate multiple regression coefficients. In the general linear model, with assumptions concerning residual e similar to those of the two-variable model, least-squares estimators are again unbiased (BLUE) and, if the distribution of e is normal, least-squares estimators are maximum-likelihood estimators. Finally, as in the case of the two-variable model, some or all of the variables may be transformed to better specify the relationship among dependent variable Y and the set of independent variables X.

With multiple regression, measures of association are similar to those for the two-variable model. The *coefficient of multiple correlation* r^2 measures the percentage of variance in dependent variable Y which is accounted for by the combined influence of explanatory variables $X_1, X_2, \ldots, X_k$ of Equation 8A.20. For individual variables association is measured by r_k, the *partial correlation coefficient*; r_1, for example, measures correlation between Y and X_1 when values of $X_2, \ldots, X_k$ are held constant in the multiple analysis. Standard errors $\hat{\sigma}_{b(k)}$ and related t_k values are also defined; these are very useful in testing the significance of individual explanatory variables. The combined significance of regression coefficients can be tested by the F ratio derived from multiple correlation coefficient r^2. Critical values of the F distribution are found in tables in elementary statistics texts:

$$F = \frac{r^2(n-k)}{(1-r^2)(k-1)} \tag{8A.21}$$

with $k - 1$ and $n - k$ degrees of freedom for k independent variables and n sample observations.

Standard computer programs provide most or all of the values needed to test significance of statistics $r^2, r_k, \hat{\sigma}_{b(k)}, t_k$, and F. More importantly, relationships should be logically consistent. A positive association can be expected, for example, between the price-earnings ratio and the growth rate in earnings; a negative $\hat{b}$ for growth should encourage the analyst to search for possible errors in variables or in the specification of the model.

ERRORS IN APPLYING THE MODEL

The regression model is based on assumptions which may or may not be true when applied to real data; if one or more of them is seriously violated, corrective action should be taken or the model will not be reliable. The problem of regression assumptions is lengthy and complex and it is often referred to as the study of *econometrics.* While detailed analysis is not possible here, it is useful to specify the more basic difficulties.

In the case of the two-variable model, two assumptions are relevant; both relate to disturbance term e. Equation 8A.22 assumes constant variance or *homoscedasticity*; that is,

$$\text{cov}(e_i e_j) = \sigma_e{}^2, \quad \text{for } i = j \tag{8A.22}$$

Equation 8A.22 is easily interpreted graphically from Figure 8A.2 where constant variance in the distribution of e is implied by the parallel lines representing confidence limits about line $\hat{a} + \hat{b}X$. When the variance of e is not constant, a condition defined as heteroscedasticity, the efficiency of the model may be lessened and, importantly, risk cannot be accurately estimated from standard error σ_e.

The other assumption is serial independence of successive disturbances; that is, residuals are assumed to be uncorrelated:

$$\text{cov}(e_i e_j) = 0, \quad \text{for } i \neq j \tag{8A.23}$$

If Equation 8A.23 is not true, disturbances are said to be *autocorrelated* and formulas for σ_b, t, and F are no longer valid. Moreover, the calculated $\hat{\sigma}_e$ is probably biased downward or underestimated. Autocorrelation can be a serious problem in time-series analysis where unspecified and unknown variables may remain in the residual; if these variables are associated through time, by trend or cycle, disturbance terms will be serially correlated.

Another common problem arises in the multiple regression model when independent variables are so closely associated that the influence of one cannot be separated from the others; this is referred to as *multicollinearity*. In this case $\hat{b}$ coefficients are not reliable for purposes of testing association among individual explanatory variables and the dependent variable. But for predictive purposes the model may still be reliable if the correlation existing among explanatory variables in the past continues in the future.

The errors discussed above are technical and techniques for correcting them, when possible, are often very complex. Another kind of error, which may be yet more serious, involves the data observed by the analyst. Sources of difficulty include sampling error and error in defining empirical variables. Model assumptions can be examined by observing the behavior of regression residuals, but the validity of dependent and independent variables, risk to cite one example, depends on the training and experience of the analyst.

Questions and Problems

1. Earnings per share for Trent, Inc. are given below for a 13-year period. Estimate the average growth rate and project EPS for 1977. It will be helpful to graph the values before proceeding.

1964	$10.00	1969	$16.11	1973	$23.58
1965	11.00	1970	17.72	1974	25.94
1966	12.10	1971	19.49	1975	28.53
1967	13.31	1972	21.44	1976	31.38
1968	14.64				

2. Calculate the price-earnings ratios for each of the 12 quarters listed below for TNE Corporation. EPS values are quarterly data and prices are the midpoint of quarterly highs and lows.

		EPS	*Price*			*EPS*	*Price*			*EPS*	*Price*
1972	1	1.00	$83.00	1973	1	1.20	$ 96.00	1974	1	1.40	$130.00
	2	2.10	93.00		2	2.40	116.00		2	2.90	96.00
	3	2.60	82.00		3	3.00	112.00		3	3.50	80.00
	4	1.50	92.00		4	1.80	116.00		4	2.10	60.00

3. During 1969 a "glamor" firm in the service industry sold at a current price-earnings ratio of almost 200; less than two years later the current multiple was slightly less than 10. What, if anything, can be inferred from these values with respect to investors' required rate of return for this security?
4. The following information was abstracted from the 1975 income statement and December 31, 1974 and 1975 balance sheets of Jerd Company:

	Income Statement	*Balance Sheet* 1974	*Balance Sheet* 1975
Accumulated depreciation		$1,730,000	$2,090,000
Current assets		1,433,000	1,561,000
Common stock		2,000,000	2,000,000
Deferred tax liability		124,000	185,000
Dividends	$112,000		
Earnings per share	5		
Fixed assets		5,200,000	5,800,000
Investments		616,000	627,000
Net income	576,000		
Retained earnings		3,289,000	3,753,000

No assets were disposed of during 1975. Calculate cash flow per share on the basis of (1) unadjusted cash flow and (2) cash flow adjusted for capital expenditures for the year 1975. Which of these two values is the better definition for investors to capitalize?

5. A firm which pays no dividend currently sells at a price-earnings multiple of 25. Average rate of growth in earnings for a market index is 6 percent per annum and the market dividend yield is 2 percent; P/E ratio for the market is 12.
   a. If the firm's earnings are growing at 25 percent per year, what is the expected duration of that growth according to the Holt model?
   b. If abnormal growth is expected to last for 7 years, what is the rate of abnormal growth according to the Holt model?

Selected References

INTRODUCTION

Basu, S., "Investment Performance of Common Stocks in Relation to Their Price-Earnings Ratios: A Test of the Efficient Market Hypothesis," *Journal of Finance*, June 1977, pp. 663–681.

Breen, William, "Low Price-Earnings Ratios and Industry Relatives," *Financial Analysts Journal*, July–August 1968, pp. 125–127.

Brigham, Eugene F., and James L. Pappas, "Rates of Return on Common Stock," *Journal of Business*, July 1969, pp. 302–316.

Christy, George A., "Economic Development, Investor Expectations, and the Trend of Stock Prices," *Western Economic Journal*, Summer 1964, pp. 209–232.

Fluegel, Frederick K., "The Rate of Return on High and Low P/E Ratio Stocks," *Financial Analysts Journal*, November–December 1968, pp. 130–133.

Latané, Henry A., O. Maurice Joy, and Charles P. Jones, "Quarterly Data, Sort-Rank Routines, and Security Evaluation," *Journal of Business*, October 1970, pp. 427–438.

Malkiel, Burton G., "Equity Yields, Growth, and the Structure of Share Prices," *American Economic Review*, December 1963, pp. 1004–1031.

Molodovsky, Nicholas, "Recent Studies of P/E Ratios," *Financial Analysts Journal*, May–June 1967, pp. 101–108.

______, "Stock Values and Stock Prices," *Financial Analysts Journal*, November–December 1968, pp. 134–148.

Nicholson, S. Francis, "Price Ratios in Relation to Investment Results," *Financial Analysts Journal*, January–February 1968, pp. 105–109.

MEASUREMENT

Bierman, Jr., Harold, and Sidney Davidson, "The Income Concept-Value Increment or Earnings Predictor," *Accounting Review*, April 1969, pp. 239–246.

Bodenhorn, Diran, "A Cash Flow Concept of Profit," *Journal of Finance*, March 1964, pp. 16–31.

Drebin, Allan R., "Cash-Flowitis: Malady or Syndrome," *Journal of Accounting Research*, Spring 1964, pp. 25–34.

Rosen, L. S., and Don T. DeCosta, "Funds Statements: A Historical Perspective," *Accounting Review*, January 1969, pp. 124–136.

Staubus, George J., "Alternative Asset Flow Concepts," *Accounting Review*, July 1966, pp. 397–412.

PRICE-EARNINGS DETERMINANTS

Benishay, Haskell, "Market Preferences for Characteristics of Common Stocks," *Economic Journal*, March 1973, pp. 173–191.

______, "Variability in Earnings-Price Ratios of Corporate Equities," *American Economic Review*, March 1961, pp. 81–94.

Bower, Richard S., and Dorothy H. Bower, "Risk and the Valuation of Common Stock," *Journal of Political Economy*, May–June 1969, pp. 349–362.

Chung, Peter S., "An Investigation of the Firms Effect Influence in the Analysis of Earnings to Price Ratios of Industrial Common Stocks," *Journal of Financial and Quantitative Analysis*, December 1974, pp. 1009–1029.

Friend, Irwin, "Equity Yields, Growth, and the Structure of Share Prices: Comment," *American Economic Review*, December 1964, pp. 1029–1035.

Friend, Irwin, and Marshall Puckett, "Dividends and Stock Prices," *American Economic Review*, September 1964, pp. 656–682.
Holt, Charles C., "The Influence of Growth Duration on Share Prices," *Journal of Finance*, September 1962, pp. 465–475.
Johnson, Harry L., and Eugene W. Lambert, Jr., "Supply and Demand Forces in the Equities Market: Fact and Fantasy," *Western Economic Journal*, Fall 1964, pp. 15–27.
Malkiel, B. G., and J. G. Cragg, "Expectations and the Structure of Share Prices," *American Economic Review*, September 1970, pp. 601–617.
Wippern, Ronald F., "Financial Structure and the Value of the Firm," *Journal of Finance*, December 1966, pp. 615–633.

FORECASTING THE PRICE-EARNINGS RATIO

Ahlers, David M., "SEM: A Security Evaluation Model" in Kalman J. Cohen and Frederick S. Hammer, eds., *Analytical Methods in Banking* (Homewood, Ill.: Irwin, 1966), pp. 305–338.
Mabert, Vincent A., and Robert C. Radcliffe, "Forecasting—A Systematic Modeling Methodology," *Financial Management*, Autumn 1974, pp. 59–67.
Robichek, Alexander A., and Marcus C. Bogue, "A Note on the Behavior of Expected Price/Earnings Ratios Over Time," *Journal of Finance*, June 1971, pp. 731–735.
Whitbeck, Volkert S., and Manown Kisor, Jr., "A New Tool in Investment Decision-Making," *Financial Analysts Journal*, May–June 1963, pp. 55–62.

Chapter 9
Forecasting

Principles of security analysis are meaningful only when they are applied to the evaluation of actual securities. The process involves forecasting of risk and return measures and it follows that the relevance and validity of forecasting procedures determine the relevance and validity of the overall analytical process. For this reason forecasting is described and illustrated in this chapter. The first section is a brief introduction designed to indicate what forecasting is and, of equal importance, what it is not. The next section introduces forecasting techniques. The remainder of the chapter consists of a case study which demonstrates the problems and, at times, the frustrations involved in operationalizing the security analysis model.

The Art of Forecasting

Forecasting is any combination of objective and subjective procedures designed to predict future events and outcomes. In economic applications, and in security analysis in particular, estimates are usually stated quantitatively. Unfortunately, numerical estimates, especially those based upon statistical models, too often imply an unrealistic degree of accuracy. Forecasts should be relevant and free of bias; they cannot be free of error. Moreover, forecasting techniques will differ from one application to another because of differences in objectives, data, interrelationships among variables, and other forecasting elements. Finally, prediction necessarily involves subjective factors which cannot be evaluated mechanically. For these reasons forecasting is best described as an imperfect art subject to the kinds of problems and difficulties which characterize other professional pursuits.

An understanding of forecasting error is important to analysts for several reasons. The first and most obvious is the need to limit error to the minimum level possible under existing predictive methodologies. A second reason is somewhat more subtle but just as important: forecasting error should not be confused with dispersion in a subjective probability distribution. That is, actual outcomes will vary from expected outcomes but differences should reflect risk and not forecasting errors which could have been avoided.

Bias occurs for a number of reasons:

USE OF AN INAPPROPRIATE OR IRRELEVANT MODEL. An important explanatory variable may be excluded, misdefined, or misspecified or an irrelevant variable may be selected. To illustrate, consider the problem of forecasting sales for a firm which prepares and markets baby food. Disposable personal income is correlated with baby food sales and it could be selected as an explanatory variable. But population is also related to sales and it is possible that population should be added to, or substituted for, the income variable. Precise specification is also important; in this case infant population would be a more reasonable choice than total population. In addition, significant factors may prove to be difficult to explain and/or evaluate. Brand preference is not easily explained and the impact of the "quality" of management is not easily evaluated. Finally, irrelevant factors should be avoided. No analyst would be willing to use the population of storks to predict baby food sales even if sample data suggested that the two variables were statistically correlated. The selection of an appropriate model depends upon the skills and judgment of the analyst; given a reasonable and logical specification, model variants can be tested empirically in arriving at the final one to be used in forecasting.

UNDUE RELIANCE ON ONE TECHNIQUE OR ONE SPECIFICATION. Forecasting is *not* a mechanical procedure in which a single technique is applied in all cases and at all points in time. Regression may prove to be successful in one aplication while a moving average scheme is found to be preferable in another. In yet another case it is possible that *no* statistical model will be correct. Instead, the analyst may be forced to arrive at an expected value in a completely subjective manner. Moreover, a successful model may lose relevance if it is not updated to reflect changes in underlying factors. A model which had been accurate for an undiversified firm may prove to be poorly suited to that same firm after it has become active in acquiring others. Variables which had been useful in explaining the level of costs may have little relevance if the firm changes from a labor-intensive to a capital-intensive production function. Forecasting is a continuous process; predictive models must be formulated and reformulated and model estimates must be evaluated and reevaluated regularly if that process is to be meaningful.

MEASUREMENT ERROR. Data which are stated quantitatively are subject to measurement error which may prove to be severe. Accounting data, discussed in Chapter 7, are a case in point. The analyst should do everything possible to restrict the level of error since otherwise forecast values become highly suspect. Data should be collected carefully and observations should be verified, when possible, against several sources. Observations should be analyzed for consistency and unusual values or "outliers" should be rechecked and verified. It is important to minimize error but it is also important to recognize that it cannot be eliminated entirely. Unavoidable error should be evaluated, to the extent possible, in estimating dispersion (risk) in the subjective probability distribution of outcomes.

In summary, forecasting should be recognized as an art combining statistical methodology with judgment and common sense. It is not a "crystal ball" operation, it is not a set of uniform techniques to be applied mechanically, and it is subject to prediction error. In the final analysis the judgment and skill of the analyst in reviewing and interpreting data provide the basis for successful forecasting.

Forecasting Techniques

Security analysis involves macroeconomic forecasts which deal with aggregate values (the economy) and microeconomic forecasts which deal with individual units (firms). Macroeconomic forecasting is a logical point of departure for security analysis because the behavior of the economy impacts on prospective outcomes for all firms within the economy. But economic performance affects far more than security price behavior. Forecasts are valuable to decision makers in government and private industry alike and, in fact, it is not unusual for security analysts to purchase macroeconomic predictions instead of generating them separately. In addition, economic forecasting involves very complex and difficult relationships. For these reasons it is useful to consider macroeconomic forecasting before microeconomic forecasting is introduced.

MACROECONOMIC FORECASTING

Macroeconomic forecasting includes a number of activities which can be classified as (1) analysis of *leading indicators*, (2) analysis of *foreshadowing*

Figure 9.1
Leading Indicator

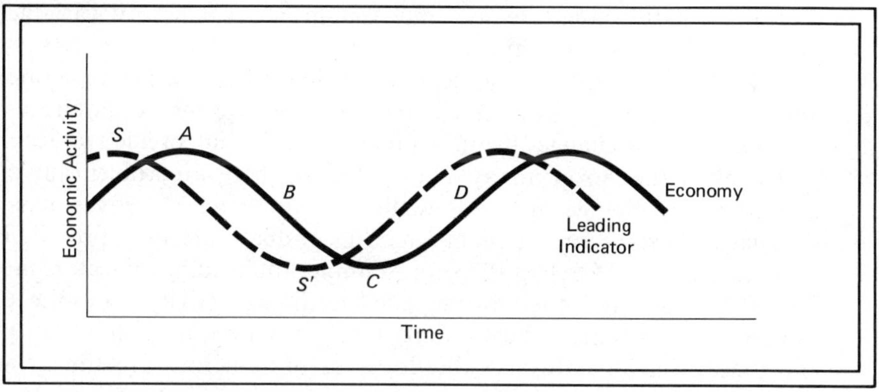

data, and (3) *statistical forecasting*; a fourth category consists of the averaging of other forecasts in a "consensus" of polled economists.

LEADING INDICATORS. Analysis of leading indicators consists of the study of time series of economic data which are believed to lead the economy in shifting from prosperity to recession and vice versa. Leading indicators are economic barometers which signal reversal in the trend of economic performance. Figure 9.1 illustrates the concept. The solid line represents economic activity from prosperity through reversal (*A*), recession (*B*), and recovery (*C*) to renewed prosperity (*D*). The broken line represents a series of observed data which lead the economy in time; observed cyclical changes *S* and *S′* predict subsequent changes in economic performance.

Leading indicators include (1) time series of the type pioneered by the National Bureau of Economic Research and (2) monetary indicators.[1] A large number of the former exist but attention usually centers on the following:

1. Average workweek
2. Building permits
3. Change in consumer-installment debt
4. Industrial materials prices
5. Initial claims for unemployment insurance
6. New durable-goods orders
7. Orders for plant and equipment
8. Ratio of price-to-unit labor costs
9. Stock prices

The Commerce Department reports values for these series monthly, when they are available, and a composite index is also provided for the same

[1] Coincident and leading indicators are available monthly in *Business Conditions Digest* published by the U.S. Department of Commerce.

interval. Monetary indicators reflect rates of change in the money supply; for predictive purposes they assume that the economy can be treated as if central bank decisions are the only significant explanatory variable for predicting economic activity.

Leading indicators have been somewhat successful in predicting the *direction* of change in economic activity but they are suspect in forecasting the *magnitude* of change. From a practical viewpoint predictive accuracy exists only in the short run, say six months, and there are problems involved in recognizing change in trends within that interval. Moreover, it is not unusual to observe situations in which individual indicators provide conflicting signals; in March of 1975, for example, four leading indicators moved favorably while the other five signaled declining activity.[2] Despite these shortcomings, leading indicators are widely reported in the financial press and their behavior influences the decisions of numerous investment managers. Proponents claim significant predictive consistency and leading indicators are an important element in macroeconomic forecasting.

FORESHADOWING DATA. A second approach to macroeconomic forecasting consists of surveys of the intentions of buyers of goods and services, especially industrial goods.[3] Anticipations provide an indicator of likely change in economic activity, particularly when they are used in conjunction with other forecasting techniques. Unfortunately, consumer goods and services are a major segment of economic activity and reliable estimates of consumers' intentions are difficult to accomplish. Moreover, there is no assurance that planned transactions will be realized. Nonetheless, anticipations provide an important measure of expectations and foreshadowing data are accepted as a valid indicator by a number of economists.

STATISTICAL FORECASTING. The most familiar macroeconomic forecasting approach, and probably the most controversial, involves formal statistical models which attempt to abstract economic activity by a system of simultaneous equations.[4] Models are constructed on the basis of economic theory and relationships among model variables are estimated and evaluated empirically, typically by application of the regression technique. Models are then used to predict economic behavior under a variety of assumptions with respect to fiscal and monetary policy, collective bargaining positions, "Third World" pricing of raw materials, and other forces which affect aggregate economic behavior.

Econometric models are complex; some consist of more than four hundred equations used to predict some four hundred economic variables.

[2] See "Key Barometer of the Economy Fell in March," *The Wall Street Journal*, April 29, 1975.

[3] See Franco Modigliani and Kalman J. Cohen, *The Role of Anticipations and Plans in Economic Behavior and Their Use in Economic Analysis and Forecasting* (Urbana: University of Illinois Bureau of Economic and Business Research, 1961).

[4] See B. G. Hickman, ed., *Econometric Models of Economic Behavior* (New York: National Bureau of Economic Research, 1971).

They are a formalized statement of economic relationships based upon advanced economic theory. Models are internally consistent in that complex interrelationships among variables are recognized. But abstraction of the economy is a monumentally difficult task and, moreover, it may be impossible to model important political and social events which influence the economy. For these reasons, together with the unavoidable error which characterizes any forecasting procedure, econometric models have not succeeded in providing accurate estimates of the timing and magnitude of economic cycles. As a result, and in the wake of serious forecasting error attributable to the unforeseen oil embargo of 1973, mathematical techniques have been subjected to severe criticism and skepticism.

Nonetheless, statistical models provide a structured and logical approach to forecasting and, despite the attention they receive when they fail notably, they have achieved measurable success in short-run economic prediction.[5] Econometrics is still an emerging art which profits from continuing research, and mathematical models will undoubtedly remain prominent in macroeconomic forecasting.

CONSENSUS FORECASTS. Some information services poll economists as to their opinion of the immediate economic outlook and they report their findings as a consensus forecast.[6] While there is no necessary reason to assume that average opinion is reliable, consensus forecasts do provide a measure of probable economic behavior in the view of leading professional economists. More importantly, they provide a basis for interpreting macroeconomic forecasting in general since consensus involves opinions based on different forecasting approaches. None of the techniques discussed above is demonstrably superior to any other. Instead they are complementary; econometric models seem to be more accurate, for example, when they employ foreshadowing data. Forecasts are most useful when they reflect a variety of predictive techniques; in the final analysis, as argued previously, forecasts should be evaluated in light of the judgment and experience of the analyst.[7]

MICROECONOMIC FORECASTING

Microeconomic forecasts are the end products of security analysis since they focus on earnings and capitalization factors which determine rate of return

[5] For evidence in this respect, and an assessment of the level of prediction error, see J. W. Elliott, "A Direct Comparison of Short-Run GNP Forecasting Models," *Journal of Business*, January 1973, pp. 33–60, and Nariman Behravesh, "Forecasting the Economy with Mathematical Models: Is It Worth the Effort?" *Business Review*, Federal Reserve Bank of Philadelphia, July–August 1975, pp. 15–25.

[6] The Federal Reserve Bank of Philadelphia has published this type of consensus annually since 1958.

[7] F. G. Adams and Vijaya G. Duggal, "Anticipations Variables in an Econometric Model: Performance of the Anticipations Versions of Wharton Mark III," *International Economic Review* (1974): 267–283.

on investment. Forecasting techniques for individual firms are similar in many respects to forecasting techniques for the aggregate economy and it is useful to consider microeconomic approaches within the same categories used to describe macroeconomic approaches.

LEADING INDICATORS. No current technique at the firm level is formally analogous to leading indicators at the aggregate level. It is possible that a time series can be located for a specific firm or group of firms which serves as a leading indicator; trends in used car sales, for example, may prove to lead trends in tire sales. But that type of relationship is more properly classified under statistical forecasting since no general technique exists which applies to all firms. A variant of the leading indicator technique consists of the ranking of firms and/or industries by various growth and yield measures in an attempt to uncover and isolate favorable changes in trends.[8] For the most part this is more properly described as a *coincident indicator* than a leading indicator and the technique is probably more relevant in the screening process than it is in security analysis.[9]

FORESHADOWING DATA. On the firm level foreshadowing data are the expectations of corporate officials with respect to new ventures, plant expansion, financing transactions, and other activities which affect corporate prospects. The most familiar foreshadowing data are forecasts of corporate profits. Anticipations are made available through (1) public releases and (2) private meetings, particularly with groups of security analysts. Securities and Exchange Commission disclosure rules require that information which is "material," including earnings, cannot be announced in private. But disclosure rules are difficult to enforce because materiality is difficult to define, trained analysts can draw inferences from apparently immaterial comments, and there may be a significant time gap between press release and public access to information.[10]

Publicly held firms may be required to disclose earnings forecasts in the foreseeable future. This is currently a very controversial issue with strong opposition voiced by organized exchanges and the accounting profession. Prediction is clearly an inexact art and a number of firms are reluctant to publish their forecasts.[11] The impact and significance of foreshadowing data received in private meetings cannot be assessed but "quasi-

[8] A variety of data of this type are available from DataScan published by Investors Management Sciences, a subsidiary of Standard & Poor's.

[9] Screening is discussed in Chapter 13.

[10] See "Analysts' Closed Talks With Firms Are Called Unfair by the Press," *The Wall Street Journal*, March 31, 1972.

[11] Existing empirical evidence suggests that published corporate forecasts are not highly accurate. See Bart A. Basi, Kenneth J. Carey, and Richard D. Twark, "A Comparison of the Accuracy of Corporate and Security Analysts' Forecasts of Earnings," *Accounting Review*, April 1976, pp. 244–254.

inside" information received by analysts certainly provides them with a relative advantage with respect to other investors.

STATISTICAL FORECASTING. Statistical forecasting is a major factor in security analysis but predictive models vary widely from analyst to analyst, from firm to firm, and from time to time. The variety of possible models makes it extremely difficult to assess the validity of statistical analysis and no public record exists to identify the more successful applications. Model variations exist with respect to a number of elements including (1) earnings disaggregation, (2) data grouping, and (3) statistical methodology.

1. *Earnings disaggregation.* Earnings forecasts are a major objective of security analysis. Predictive models may focus on aggregate earnings or they may predict sales, expenses, and other earnings components. The choice between the two alternatives depends upon the stability of interrelationships among components and the reaction of individual income statement items to explanatory factors. The case study which follows illustrates earnings disaggregation.

2. *Data grouping.* Forecasting accuracy may be increased when observed data are grouped into classes according to identifiable characteristics. The most obvious and familiar grouping is by industry, as defined by Commerce Department Standard Industrial Classification (SIC). Firms within a given industry have similar product-demand and cost structures, to some degree, and grouping by industry classification may be helpful in identifying important variables which are common to firms within that SIC category. In fact, traditional security analysis procedures began with industry analysis; firms within the industry were then ranked according to relative value. Industry classification is only one of the possible bases for homogeneous grouping; whatever the methodology, identification of groups with similar structural relationships is analytically valuable.[12]

3. *Statistical methodology.* A number of statistical techniques exist for predicting future outcomes by extrapolating observed data. Two of these, *regression analysis* and *exponentially weighted moving averages*, are the more common ones used in security analysis. The regression technique was discussed in the appendix to the preceding chapter; because of its relative familiarity it is used in the case illustration which follows. Exponentially weighted moving averages are a set of statistical formulations which modify a moving average by weighting the influence of current versus past data and by allowing for the influence of trend.[13] Although exponentially weighted

[12] Homogeneous grouping can be accomplished statistically. Elton and Gruber used principal components analysis to group firms for purposes of forecasting earnings per share. Forecasts based on these statistical "pseudoindustries" were generally superior to forecasts based on traditional industry classifications. Edwin J. Elton and Martin J. Gruber, "Improved Forecasting Through the Design of Homogeneous Groups," *Journal of Business*, October 1971, pp. 432–450.

[13] See Peter R. Winters, "Forecasting Sales By Exponentially Weighted Moving Averages," *Management Science*, April 1960, pp. 324–342.

moving averages are less familiar than regression analysis, there is some evidence which suggests that the former technique is superior to the latter.[14]

In summary, microeconomic security analysis consists of a number of procedures, largely quantitative and lacking uniformity, which attempt to forecast accurately earnings and earnings capitalization rates. The next section of this chapter provides a case study which is designed to illustrate that process.

Security Analysis: A Case Study

INTRODUCTION

The case study provided here is designed to demonstrate the process of security analysis. It is not a "cookbook" prescription for analytical procedures; calculations and conclusions are entirely illustrative. Some estimates are necessarily crude and there is no assurance that alternative procedures would not generate a more accurate forecast. The case demonstrates forecasting methodology and the estimation of forecasting error in assessing the risk associated with expected rate of return.

Forecasts were originally generated during early 1975 when 1974 corporate data were unavailable. Expected values were calculated as of April 1, 1974, on the basis of observed 1952–1973 data; 1974 data, which subsequently became available, were then used to evaluate forecasting error. This approach was adopted in an effort to simulate and illustrate the adaptive feedback procedure described in Chapter 4.

Data used in the study were limited to publicly available information. For the most part this consisted of values reported in SEC 10-K filings, supplemented where necessary by data reported in published services available in most libraries. An appendix to this chapter surveys representative sources of information for the type of analysis illustrated here.

General Cable Corporation was selected to illustrate the process for several reasons. First, the firm's operations are concentrated within a specific industry grouping; wire and cable and related equipment and accessories accounted for better than 90 percent of consolidated sales during the years 1970–1973. General Cable is included under SIC industry classification 3350, "Rolling and Drawing, Non-Ferrous Metals." This offered the prospect of increased forecasting accuracy by data grouping, as discussed previously. Second, a preliminary analysis of several groupings suggested that industry 3350 was among the most sensitive ones in reacting to changes in the business cycle. This provides a realistic challenge in forecasting, highlighting hazards that could not be demonstrated with values for an easily predictable firm. Third, General Cable financial statements are outstanding

[14] Edwin J. Elton and Martin J. Gruber, "Earnings Estimates and the Accuracy of Expectational Data," *Management Science*, April 1972, pp. B409–B424.

Figure 9.2
Earnings Per Share (before extraordinary items, adjusted for stock splits)

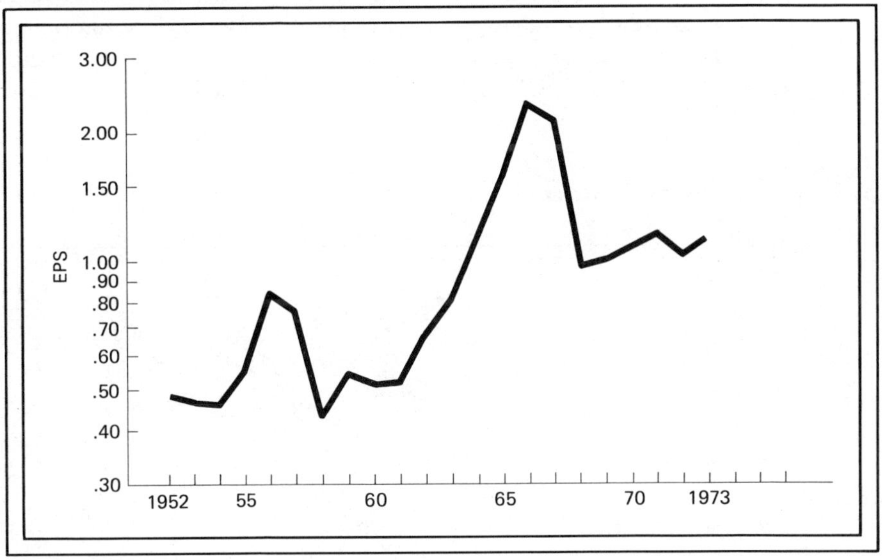

with respect to clarity and disclosure. The firm provided a statement of change in financial position in the mid-1960s, for example, long before they were required to under generally accepted reporting standards. Financial statements contain sufficient detail for analytical purposes over an extended period of time, which is not always the case, and footnote disclosures specify relevant accounting variants of the type discussed in Chapter 7.

In summary, the case study which follows is intended to demonstrate security analysis. Values reported are illustrative and there is no intention to represent them as investment values or as measures of the quality of management of the firm which is studied.

SALES AND EARNINGS

The first problem was to forecast earnings per share. Figure 9.2 traces earnings per share from 1952 through 1973; earnings are measured before extraordinary items and values were adjusted for stock splits in 1964 and 1966.[15] The vertical scale is logarithmic to reflect relative values. Observed values displayed sufficient variability to discourage any effort to forecast EPS directly. Instead, earnings components were studied individually in a disaggregated model.

[15] Earnings per share were not restated to retroactively adjust for the impact of mergers, partly because there were very few acquisitions during the period and partly because data were not easily accessible in the mergers which did occur. This should not have any material impact on forecast values.

SALES. Sales for the period 1952–1973 were tested against a large number of aggregate values in an effort to identify explanatory variables. Values were plotted by computer to reduce the number of variables to a manageable number. The most promising candidates identified were gross national product GNP, gross national product in constant dollars $GNPC$, the index of industrial production IIP, population POP, and time T. Regression analysis

Figure 9.3
Sales, Index of Industrial Production, and Time

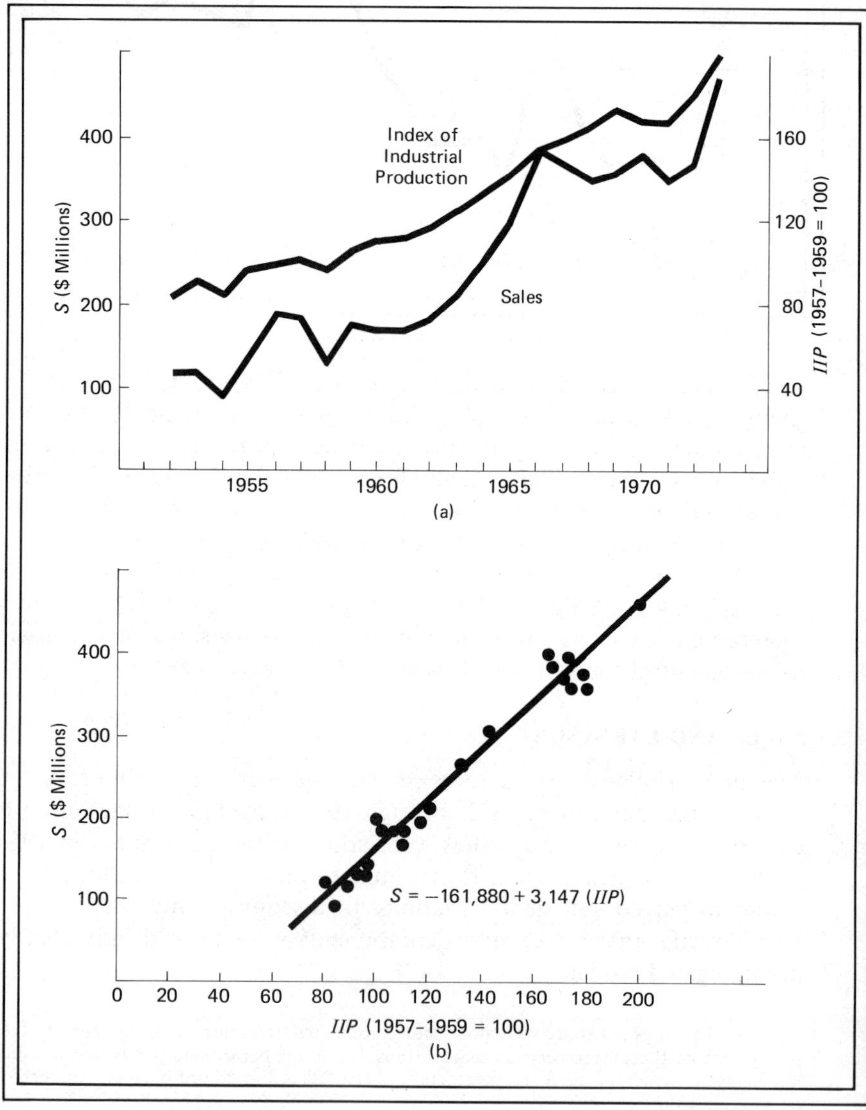

was used to study the relationship among these five variables and sales S. Explanatory variables were tested individually and in combination and variables were also tested directly and with reciprocal and logarithmic transformations.[16] Multiple regressions were found to have excessive multicollinearity and the search for an explanatory model was narrowed to three:

Dependent Variable	*Independent Variables*	*R^2, Adjusted for Degrees of Freedom*	*Standard Error (000)*
S	T and T^2	.894	40,484
S	$GNPC$	.935	29,210
S	IIP	.955	24,343

Based upon an analysis of regression residuals, to be discussed shortly, Equation 9.1 was selected; dollar values are measured in thousands (000):

$$S_T = -161{,}880 + 3{,}147(IIP_T) + e_{S,T}$$

t values	(8.05) (21.12)	
r^2, adj.		.955
Standard error $\sigma(e_S)$		24,343
Sample size, n		22
IIP, 1957–1959 = 100		

(9.1)

Figure 9.3(a) is a graph of the time series of both IIP and S; except for 1965 and 1966, similarity in the two series is evident. Figure 9.3(b) is a plot of S against IIP. A strong association is evidenced again; with the exception of a few values in the upper right corner, sales conform closely to conditional values along the regression line.

Under the assumptions of the regression model, residual e_S should be independent of both IIP and time and the variance of e_S should be constant (homoscedastic). These assumptions were tested with observed residuals from Equation 9.1. Figure 9.4(a) contains a plot of residuals against explanatory variable IIP. While no association is observed, the relationship was tested directly with Equation 9.2:

$$e_{S,T} = .1075 - .0019(IIP_T) \qquad (9.2)$$

t values	(0.0) (0.0)	
r^2, adj.		.000
Standard error		24,343

Empirical values for Equation 9.2 support the assumption that no relationship existed between IIP and e_S.

[16] This type of statistical "fishing" is justified because no obvious theoretical association exists to guide specification of the regression model. It is also an extremely simple and inexpensive computer operation.

Figure 9.4
Sales Regression Residuals, Index of Industrial Production, and Time

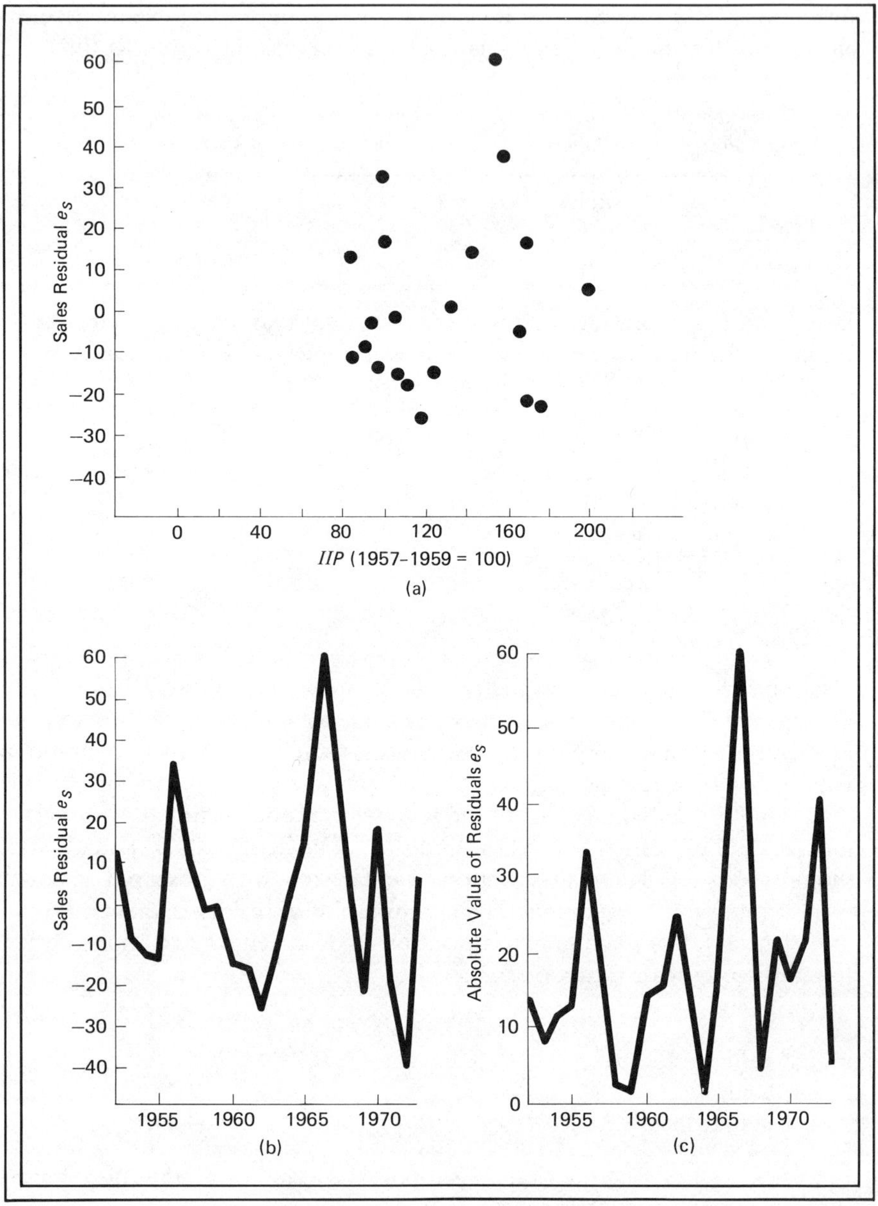

Figure 9.4(b) contains a plot of residuals against time. With independence the series should contain a greater number of reversals than Figure 9.4(b) portrays; that is, residuals appear to be somewhat more cyclical than an independent series should be. Equation 9.3 tests the relationship among successive residuals directly:[17]

$$e_{S,T} = -569.330 + .360(e_{S,T-1}) \tag{9.3}$$

t values	(0.11)	(1.74)	
r^2, adj.			.137
Standard error			22,998

Empirical values for Equation 9.3 indicate a statistical association at the 10 percent level. While this is not large, it is large enough to be worrisome. As a result, values were subjected to additional analysis which will be discussed at a later time when the question of risk is introduced.

The constancy of the variance of residuals was tested next. Figure 9.4(c) contains a plot of the absolute values of residuals against time. The plot of Figure 9.3(b) suggests that no trend existed in e_S but the existence of three larger than average values in 1966, 1967, and 1972 was worrisome. Absolute values of Figure 9.4(c) were regressed against time and the insignificant r^2 value of .066 was taken as evidence that heteroscedasticity was not a problem in this case.

In summary, explanatory Equation 9.1 seemed to perform well except for evidence of positive serial correlation to be explored subsequently. To forecast sales, a 1974 value was required for the index of industrial production. While there are a number of methods for accomplishing this, including consensus forecasts, the analysis was performed at a time when 1974 index of industrial production values were actually available. For this reason, to maintain the spirit of forecasting as if values were unavailable, *IIP* was regressed against time for the years 1952–1973 and Equation 9.4 was used to predict *IIP* for 1974:[18]

$$IIP_T = 81.6039 + 2.1511(T) + .1393(T^2) + e_{I,T} \tag{9.4}$$

r^2, adj.	.972
Standard error	5.839

Equation 9.4 provided a 1974 estimate of *IIP* of 204.7689; substituting this value in Equation 9.2 resulted in a point estimate for 1974 sales of $482,527,730.

[17] A more typical test for autocorrelation is the Durbin-Watson Statistic. See J. Johnston, *Econometric Methods* (New York: McGraw-Hill, 1963), p. 192.

[18] An analysis of residuals provided evidence that cyclical variations are not explained adequately by Equation 9.4. It is probable that an exponentially weighted moving average would be preferable to the trend equation but this was not attempted because the illustration relies entirely on the regression model.

Figure 9.5
Cost of Sales ($ million)

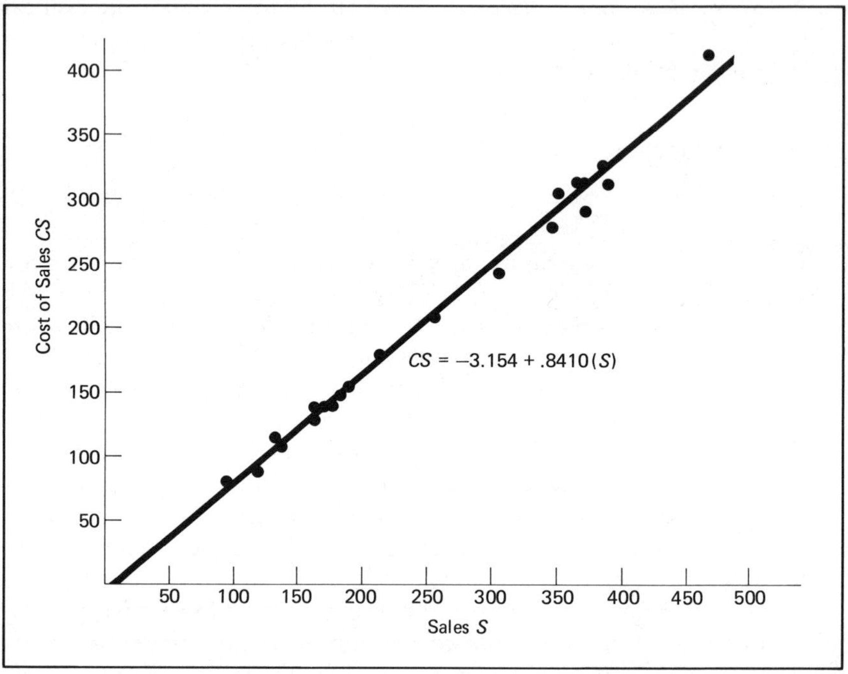

EXPENSE. Costs and expenses were separated into five categories on the basis of detail presented in income statements and each of these categories was forecast separately:

1. Cost of sales
2. General, selling, and administrative expense
3. Other income and expense
4. Taxes
5. Interest expense

Disaggregation is subject to unavoidable measurement error which is often difficult to evaluate. In 1972, for example, the firm reclassified state and local taxes from cost of sales to the tax category and insufficient data were publicly available to adjust the entire time series through 1952. This type of problem is common for analysts working entirely with publicly available information. Under these circumstances it is necessary to either (1) adjust data crudely or (2) ignore the problem with differences reflected in analytical residuals. In this particular case the adjustment is minor and the latter alternative was chosen; analysis of regression residuals suggests that the reclassification had no material impact on forecasting accuracy.[19]

[19] The adjustment amounts to only 0.3 percent of reclassified 1972 cost of sales but it was close to 10 percent of 1972 income taxes.

Nonetheless, this type of problem can be serious and analysts often encounter severe difficulty in adjusting time series data to a consistent basis.

Cost of sales *CS* and general, selling, and administrative expense *GSA* were regressed against sales with both original data and logarithmic transformations tested. There was no appreciable difference with respect to data transformation and original data were selected (000):

$$CS_T = -3154 + .8410(S_T) + e_{C,T}$$

t values	(0.90) (65.34)		
r^2, adj.		.995	(9.5)
Standard error		6764	
n		22	

$$GSA_T = -1347 + .0545(S_T) + e_{G,T}$$

t values	(1.05) (11.58)		
r^2, adj.		.864	
Standard error		2472	
n		22	
			(9.6)

Empirical values for Equations 9.5 and 9.6 are graphed in Figures 9.5 and 9.6, respectively. Cost of sales provides an excellent fit and general, selling, and administrative expense is highly satisfactory. (Note that both figures have the same scale for the horizontal axis but the scale of the vertical axis of Figure 9.6 is only one-tenth the scale of Figure 9.5.) Analysis of residuals

Figure 9.6
General, Selling, and Administrative Expense (\$ million)

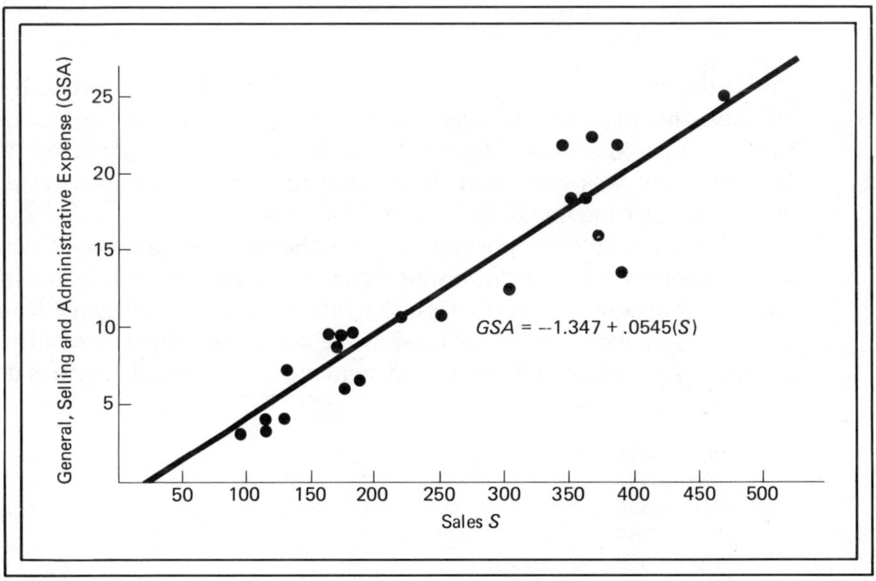

for both equations uncovered no difficulty with respect to residual variance or correlation among S and e_C or e_G values. Correlations among e_C and e_G and time were statistically insignificant at the 10 percent level but the behavior over time was similar in many respects to the behavior of sales residual e_S. For this reason, and despite empirical values which support the assumptions of the regression model, expense residuals will be considered in greater detail when risk analysis is introduced.

Substituting the sales point estimate of $482,527,730 into Equations 9.5 and 9.6 provided an estimated cost of sales of $402,651,820 and an estimated general, selling, and administrative expense of $24,950,760.

Reported "other income" included equity in earnings of associated foreign companies and dividends, interest, and miscellaneous items. Extraordinary items were reported separately and they were excluded from this analysis. Rigorous association between other income and the investments account was not possible, for two reasons. First, the company changed its policy of accounting for investment in several associated foreign companies to the equity method in 1970 and a consistent time series could not be constructed. Second, the company entered into a mutual stockholding relationship with British Insulated Callender's Cables Limited in 1970 which materially altered the relationship between investments and other income. Balances for these accounts during the years in question are shown below (000):

	Other Income	*December 31 Balance, Investments*	*Percentage*
December 31, 1969	1005	13,431	7.48
December 31, 1970	1594	16,784	9.50
December 31, 1971	4072	69,751	5.84
December 31, 1972	6527	73,081	8.93
December 31, 1973	9016	78,148	11.54

Under the circumstances, other income was forecast subjectively. By 1973 the investments account was increasing at the rate of approximately $4,000,000 per year and a 1974 value of $82,000,000 was predicted. Return on investment was estimated to increase to 13 percent which resulted in estimated other income of $10,660,000 for 1974.

General Cable Corporation follows the required practice of deferring tax differentials arising from timing differences between taxable income and accounting income. Nevertheless, the rate of taxation will vary from any "average" rate for a number of reasons including differing depreciation rates and the impact of foreign income tax regulations. Reported tax rates derived from income statements from 1969 through 1973 are shown below:

1969	.4871
1970	.4481
1971	.4316
1972	.3994
1973	.3573

Despite the obviously decreasing trend, reinforced by the accounting reclassification of 1972, a five-year average value was selected because effective tax rates are volatile and they react to factors which cannot be estimated externally. The average of the five values listed above, .4247, was used as the estimated rate of taxation for 1974.

The remaining item, interest expense, will be discussed after projected asset requirements and financing assumptions are considered. A summary of forecasted sales and earnings will be presented at that time.

ASSET REQUIREMENTS

The next major task was to estimate the level of assets required to support the predicted level of sales. For this purpose current liabilities were reclassified to exclude installments on long-term debt and specific short-term sources of funds; the remaining "operating" current liabilities were then deducted from current assets to calculate net operating working capital WC.[20] The ratios of working capital to sales and gross fixed assets FA to sales were then regressed against time to observe changes in relative asset requirements. For $T = 1$ in 1952;

$$(FA/S)_T = .4429 + .0019(T)$$

t values	(12.76)	(0.74)		(9.7)
r^2, adj.			.026	

$$(WC/S)_T = .1823 + .0020(T)$$

t values	(8.21)	(1.21)		(9.8)
r^2, adj.			.050	

Empirical values for Equations 9.7 and 9.8 disclose no trend in asset requirements relative to sales. Accordingly, regression constants (.4429 and .1823, respectively) provide one approach to forecasting 1974 asset values based upon the 1974 point estimate for sales.

An alternative approach proved to be superior. Historical values for both fixed assets and working capital were regressed against sales for the period 1952–1973 to observe the magnitude of response in asset requirements to variations in sales. All variables were transformed to logarithms to measure relative changes or "elasticities."

$$\log FA_T = -.2103 + .9743(\log S_T) + e_F$$

t values	(0.54)	(13.36)		(9.9)
r^2, adj.			.899	

$$\log WC_T = -.6952 + .9992(\log S_T) + e_W \qquad (9.10)$$

t values	(1.20)	(9.21)	
r^2, adj.			.809

[20] Assets classified under the caption "Deferred Charges" were also included in current assets for purposes of this analysis.

Statistical association is significant well beyond the 1 percent level for both equations and an analysis of regression residuals disclosed no significant departure from the assumptions of the regression model. As before, the behavior of regression residuals over time remained worrisome and the problem was again deferred until risk analysis could be introduced. It is interesting to note that regression coefficients for both equations (.9743 and .9992, respectively) are insignificantly different from the value of 1 which implies that asset requirements are unit elastic with respect to sales. On the basis of Equations 9.9 and 9.10, and the previously derived point estimate of sales of $482,527,730, 1974 gross fixed assets was estimated to be $212,400,610 and working capital was estimated to be $96,333,080.

An analysis of the ratio of accumulated depreciation to fixed assets disclosed that the relationship changed significantly from 1966 to 1967; thereafter it remained fairly constant, and the average value from 1967 through 1973, .4044, was used to forecast the 1974 ratio. On this basis accumulated depreciation for 1974 would be $85,894,810. Remaining assets included investments, discussed previously, and consolidated goodwill which reflects the excess of the cost of acquiring subsidiaries over their net equity value at the date of acquisition. The firm does not amortize existing goodwill and the 1973 value of $4,368,000 was selected as the forecast value for 1974.

DIVIDENDS

An analysis of corporate dividend policy suggested that management attempted to stabilize dividends despite the cyclical variation in earnings per share portrayed in Figure 9.2. Efforts to analyze dividend payout ratios were unsuccessful. Based upon stable dividends per share evidenced in 1967–1968, 1969–1970, and 1971–1972, it was assumed that 1974 dividends would be the same value as 1973. Dividends per share were forecast to be $0.575.

FINANCING

The next problem involved the financing of assets required to support the predicted level of sales. Funds flow statements were analyzed in order to gain insights concerning corporate financing policy; 1968–1973 values are contained in Table 9.1 in a format which is consistent with the structure described in Chapters 6 and 7. Data in Table 9.1 suggested that the firm was unlikely to resort to equity financing to support normal levels of asset expansion since the only major equity transaction in the six-year period involved the mutual stockholding agreement noted previously. On this basis shares outstanding in 1974 were forecast at the December 31, 1973, level: 14,269,186, net of treasury shares.

Table 9.1 data, with the support of underlying detail, also suggested that the firm was able to finance normal expansion internally, with short-

Table 9.1
Flow of Funds (000)

	1968	1969	1970	1971	1972	1973
Funds provided by operations	$20,018	$22,621	$21,839	$25,763	$20,467	$22,640
Less dividends	16,200	13,520	10,847	11,415	11,415	8,205
Operating excess (deficiency)	$ 3,818	$ 9,101	$10,992	$14,348	$ 9,052	$14,435
Funds required for asset expansion						
Fixed assets, net	$15,101	$ 6,443	$24,943	$11,082	$ 7,485	$ 8,590
Operating working capital	6,436	160	23,702	12,742	3,615	(24,297)
Investments and other	326	4,121	3,091	45,883	659	(674)
	$21,863	$10,724	$51,736	$69,707	$11,759	($16,381)
Less other proceeds[a]				(1,163)	147	(7,229)
	$21,863	$10,724	$51,736	$70,870	$11,612	($ 9,152)
New funds required	$18,045	$ 1,623	$40,744	$56,522	$ 2,560	($23,587)
Funds provided by financing						
Equity[b]	$ 345	$ 124	$ 328	$17,064		
Debt[c]	19,192	2,626	40,416	41,681	$25,382	$16,028
	$19,537	$ 2,750	$40,744	$58,745	$25,382	$16,028
Less retirement of claims						
Equity[b]	$ 1,492	$ 1,127				
Debt[c]				$ 2,223	$22,822	$39,615
	$ 1,492	$ 1,127		$ 2,223	$22,822	$39,615
Net funds provided	$18,045	$ 1,623	$40,744	$56,522	$ 2,560	($23,587)

[a] Including extraordinary items, net of tax.
[b] Including treasury stock transactions and stock option exercises.
[c] Including short-term debt and current portion of long-term debt in current liabilities.

to intermediate-term obligations used to moderate the effect of cyclical fluctuations. For this reason debt financing was forecast at interest costs relevant in 1973. The maturity structure of long-term debt was studied and a 1974 average interest rate of 9.41 percent was predicted.

PRO FORMA FINANCIAL STATEMENTS

All values needed to prepare estimated or pro forma financial statements are now available. Table 9.2 summarizes predicted values in the form of a condensed income statement and balance sheet. For analytical purposes deferred charges are included under the working capital caption and, consistent with the analysis of Chapter 7, deferred tax liability is included in retained earnings. Beginning equity values are inserted directly in the table.

Table 9.2
Pro-Forma Financial Statements (partial)

a. Condensed Balance Sheet
(000)

Assets		
Operating working capital		$ 96,333
Plant and equipment	212,401	
Less accumulated depreciation	85,895	126,506
Investments		82,000
Good will		4,368
Total		$309,207
Liabilities and equity		
Long and short term debt		$ X
Common stock, 14,269,186 shares		35,411
Retained earnings, beginning	143,170	
Add net income for the year	X	
Less dividends	(8,205)	X
Total		$309,207

b. Income Statement
(000)

Sales		$482,528
Cost of sales		402,652
Gross profit		79,876
General, selling, and administrative expense	24,951	
Other income	(10,660)	14,291
Earnings before interest and taxes		65,585
Interest expense, at .0941		X
Earnings before taxes		X
Income taxes, at .4247		X
Net income		$ X

Statements are complete with the exception of values for interest expense I, net income E, and long- and short-term debt L. These are easily calculated:

$$L + E = 309{,}207 - 35{,}411 - 143{,}170 + 8{,}205$$
$$= 138{,}831 \tag{9.11}$$

$$E = (65{,}585 - I)(1.0 - .4247)$$
$$= 37{,}731 - .5753I \tag{9.12}$$

$$I = .0941L \tag{9.13}$$

Substituting Equation 9.13 into 9.12, and 9.12 into 9.11, and simplifying,

$$L = 106{,}886$$

$$\begin{aligned} I &= (.0941)106{,}886 \\ &= 10{,}058 \end{aligned}$$

$$\begin{aligned} E &= 37{,}731 - (.5753)10{,}058 \\ &= 31{,}945 \end{aligned}$$

Financial statements can now be completed:

Long- and short-term debt		\$106,886
Common stock		35,411
Retained earnings, beginning	143,170	
Net income	31,945	
Dividends	(8,205)	166,910
Total		\$309,207

Earnings before interest and taxes	\$ 65,585
Interest expense	10,058
Earnings before taxes	55,527
Income tax, at .4247	23,582
Net income	\$ 31,945

Earnings per share can also be estimated from aggregate earnings E and the number of shares outstanding N:

$$\begin{aligned} E(\text{EPS}) &= E(E)/E(N) \\ &= 31{,}945/14{,}269.186 \\ &= 2.24 \end{aligned} \tag{9.14}$$

The remaining component of rate of return, the price-earnings ratio, will be discussed next.

PRICE-EARNINGS RATIO

Forecasting of the price-earnings ratio is probably the most formidable problem in security analysis. It is especially difficult in this case study because the analysis focuses on one firm in lieu of the group of firms which survive the screening process; *relative* price-earnings ratios are far more important than *absolute* values. In addition, the period selected for analysis was one of historically low P/E values and the market was characterized by great uncertainty. Under the circumstances no analyst could predict capitalization rates with any great degree of confidence. Forecast values were calculated without reference to actual 1974 outcomes but it was impossible to ignore the reality of the 1973–1974 bear market in preparing the study. The case therefore assumes that the analyst was bearish in evaluating the expected price-earnings ratio.

An attempt to simulate the large-scale cross-sectional model of the type discussed in Chapter 8 failed. Price, earnings, and cash flow data were collected for 31 firms in four SIC groupings for 1972 and 1973. Price-earnings ratios and price–cash flow ratios were then regressed against variables representing earnings growth, dividend payout, debt-equity, earnings variability, size, industry, and market conformity. But statistical measures were generally insignificant and analysis of cross-sectional residuals indicated that data for the two years could not be pooled. As a result, the firm effect discussed in Chapter 8 could not be measured; this is particularly important because the firm effect is the most important variable of any in empirical studies.

Table 9.3 summarizes high, low, and mean values among firms in the industry groups studied. Variability within each year is pronounced and the declining trend from 1972 to 1973 is evident. It is clear from the data contained in the table that no advantage resulted from grouping data and the price-earnings ratio of General Cable Corporation was therefore studied separately.

Table 9.3
Industry Capitalization Ratios
(number of firms in parentheses)

	1972		*1973*	
	Price-Earnings	*Price–Cash Flow*	*Price-Earnings*	*Price–Cash Flow*
Packaged foods (6)				
High	34.2	26.7	17.7	13.4
Low	15.8	4.0	5.0	2.2
Mean	24.8	14.5	13.8	3.8
Tire and rubber goods (9)				
High	16.8	5.9	9.9	4.1
Low	7.2	3.0	5.0	2.4
Mean	10.2	4.7	7.1	3.2
Industrial machinery (10)				
High	25.9	18.3	16.0	12.3
Low	9.4	4.5	4.9	3.8
Mean	16.6	11.8	10.9	7.8
Rolling and drawing, nonferrous metals (6)				
High	15.4	12.9	21.0	7.5
Low	12.8	5.6	6.3	2.6
Mean	14.0	8.8	9.7	4.1

Figure 9.7
Price-Earnings Ratio

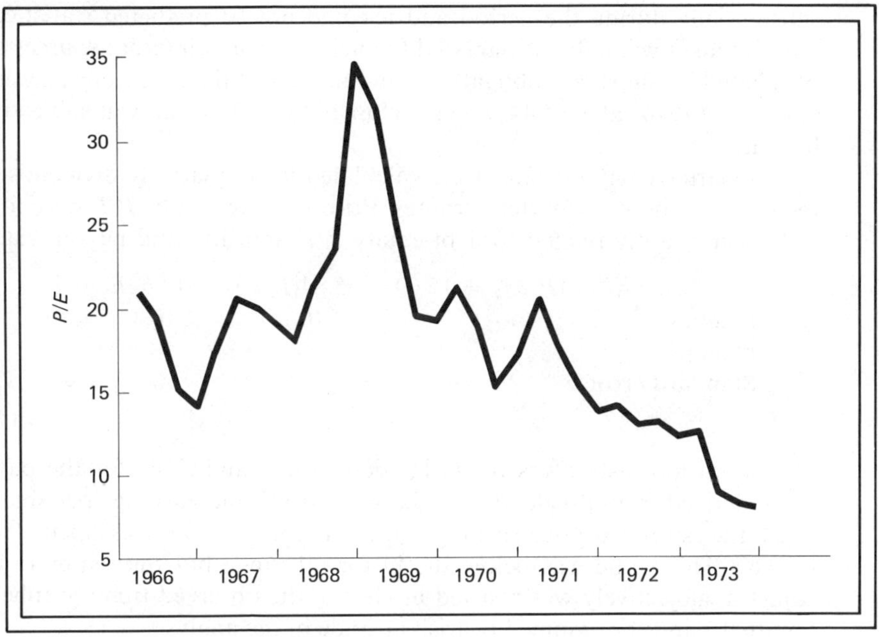

The case assumes that the analysis occurred on April 1, 1974, when 1973 accounting values were available. Quarterly earnings were collected and annualized by summing the most recent four quarter values. The midpoint of quarterly high and low values was then used to calculate price-earnings ratios from the first quarter of 1966 through the fourth quarter of 1973. Calculated values are graphed in Figure 9.7.

Earnings growth rates, debt-equity ratios, and dividend payout ratios were calculated for the same period. Growth rates were computed under a variety of definitions for both unadjusted and normalized earnings but no statistical association between growth and price-earnings was observed under any specification. This is bothersome because a significant relationship had been expected but growth rate was excluded from the analysis on empirical grounds.

Quarterly debt-equity ratios were calculated from moving averages of annual values. Debt was defined to include (1) only long-term debt and (2) both long- and short-term obligations. The first definition is the conventional one and a significant relationship was found between that debt-equity ratio and the price-earnings ratio. The second definition is more consistent with the analysis presented here but statistical association was considerably weaker and the conventional variable was used instead. This created difficulty in forecasting the debt-equity value for 1974 since the model described previously does not distinguish among long-term and short-term obligations. In addition the firm's long-term debt-equity ratio varied substantially during the period and it could not be predicted statistically. Since funds flow analysis suggested financing through internal sources supplemented by short-run obligations, and in view of the firm's debt maturity schedule, a 1974 value of .44, which is close to the 1973 value, was subjectively forecast.

Quarterly payout rates were calculated from quarterly dividends and the most recent four quarter earnings. Price-earnings ratios P/E were found to be significantly related to debt-equity L/V and dividend payout rate B:

$$(P/E)_T = 16.69 - \underset{(6.75)}{35.84}(L/V)_T + \underset{(6.42)}{14.62}B_T + e_P$$

t values	(6.75) (6.42)
r^2, adj.	.925
Standard error	2.587

(9.15)

With forecast values of .44 for debt-equity and .2568 for the payout ratio, derived from dividends per share of \$0.575 and earnings per share of \$2.24, the estimated price-earnings ratio for April 1, 1974, was calculated to be 4.67. This value was below the historical range but the temptation to adjust it subjectively was resisted in view of the observed trend graphed in Figure 9.7 and the assumed bearish attitude of the analyst.

EXPECTED RATE OF RETURN

General Cable Corporation shares closed at $9\frac{3}{8}$ on April 1, 1974. The expected price for those shares on March 31, 1975, is the product of expected earnings per share and expected price-earnings ratio, assuming independence between those two variables:

$$\begin{aligned} E(P) &= E(\text{EPS}) \times E(P/E) \\ &= 2.24 \times 4.67 \\ &= 10.461 \end{aligned} \tag{9.16}$$

With these values, together with the dividend estimate of \$0.575, expected rate of return $E(R)$ can be calculated for the one-year holding period:

$$\begin{aligned} E(R) &= \frac{E(P_{T+1}) - P_T + D_T}{P_T} \\ &= \frac{10.461 - 9.375 + .575}{9.375} \\ &= .1772 \end{aligned} \tag{9.17}$$

The next problem concerns the assessment of risk associated with this estimate of expected rate of return.

SUBJECTIVE RISK

The analysis of Chapter 2 demonstrated that the internal rate of return cannot be solved analytically; solution requires the application of trial and error procedures.[21] In addition, the model analyzed in this case study employs the product of two random variables in estimating expected price per share. The formula for the variance of the product of two random variables is extremely complex and it cannot be applied in security analysis in any practical sense.[22] For these reasons, and in view of the subjective elements which influence forecasting, simulation was used to estimate rate of return dispersion.

The simulation model can be illustrated by defining a normally distributed random variable, Z, with a mean of 0.0 and a standard deviation of 1.0. That is, if a large number of Z values were collected and analyzed the average value would be zero and the standard deviation would be unity. Any value which is multiplied repeatedly by Z would be transformed to a normal distribution with a mean of zero and a standard deviation equal to the original value. To demonstrate, recall sales Equation 9.1:[23]

$$S_T = -161{,}880 + 3{,}147(IIP_T) + e_{S,T}, \qquad \sigma(e_S) = 24{,}343 \qquad [(9.1)]$$

Regression residual e_S has an expected value of zero and a standard deviation of 24,343; if 24,343Z is calculated a large number of times, the distribution will also have a mean of zero and a standard deviation of 24,343. A distribution for S can therefore be generated by adding random values 24,343Z to the remaining terms in the equation.

This procedure would be unnecessary if the distribution of S were the only set of values required; the standard error around conditional regression values, 24,343, is known. But with a number of model variables which are subject to random disturbance, it is possible to estimate each separately, substituting values as described in the case of point estimates to calculate rate of return. By repeating the process a number of times, an estimated rate of return distribution results. This is the process used here to estimate risk. Because of the large number of calculations required for even a modest number of trials, the model was programmed and solved by computer; a "canned" routine was used to generate pseudo-random normal Z values.

Unfortunately, the procedure assumes independence among disturbance terms and it was previously observed that regression residuals appeared to react similarly with respect to economic variations. This is not

[21] The one-period rate of return demonstrated above is an exception to this statement.

[22] See George W. Bohrnstedt and Arthur S. Goldberger, "On the Exact Covariance of Products of Random Variables," *Journal of the American Statistical Association*, December 1969, pp. 1439–1442.

[23] For predictive purposes the standard error should be adjusted for values of the independent variable which are beyond the range of sample observations used to estimate regression coefficients. In this case, in view of the subjectivity of a number of equations in the model, and to avoid added complications, this adjustment was not included in the model. See J. Johnston, *Econometric Methods* (New York: McGraw-Hill, 1963).

Table 9.4
Correlations Among Regression Residuals

		IIP (e_I)	*S* (e_S)	*COS* (e_C)	*GSA* (e_G)	*FA* (e_F)	*WC* (e_W)
IIP	e_I	1.000					
S	e_S	.545[a]	1.000				
COS	e_C	−.084	−.516[a]	1.000			
GSA	e_G	−.765[a]	−.773[a]	.462[b]	1.000		
FA	e_F	−.780[a]	−.754[a]	.254	.813[a]	1.000	
WC	e_W	−.846[a]	−.591[a]	.148	.851[a]	.872[a]	1.000

[a] Significant at the 1 percent level.
[b] Significant at the 5 percent level.

surprising because firms can be expected to react to changing cyclical conditions which affect operations. Association was tested by correlating residuals for the index of industrial production e_I, sales e_S, cost of sales e_C, general, selling, and administrative expense e_G, fixed assets e_F, and working capital e_W. Results are reported in Table 9.4.

Correlations among residuals were far too significant to ignore and Equations 9.18 through 9.20 were used to account for common behavior among disturbance terms; fixed asset and working capital errors were not simulated because their logarithmic transformations are very sensitive to small changes.

$$e_{S,T} = .0027 + 2165.50(e_{I,T}) + u_{S,T},\ \sigma(u_S) = 20{,}413 \tag{9.18}$$

$$e_{C,T} = -.0343 - .1432(e_{S,T}) + u_{C,T},\ \sigma(u_C) = 5{,}796 \tag{9.19}$$

$$e_{G,T} = -.0075 - .0784(e_{S,T}) + u_{G,T},\ \sigma(u_G) = 1{,}570 \tag{9.20}$$

While the procedure may appear to be overly complicated, simulations are very sensitive to interrelationships among model variables and the purpose of the exercise can easily be thwarted unless elements are specified carefully. In this case association among remaining residuals u_T is insignificant and random Z values can be used for all other simulated error terms.

Predicted values for some variables were determined subjectively; in these cases disturbance terms were also estimated. A complete statement of the model is contained in an appendix to the chapter. The programmed version was solved by computer with 500 iterations. This resulted in the following rate of return distribution:

$$E(R) = .1772$$

$$\sigma(R) = .3250$$

The mean value is the same as the point estimate derived previously. The standard deviation is reasonable; within one standard deviation of the mean, rate of return would range between −.1478 and +.5022. In terms of price per share this translates to $7.41 and $13.50, respectively, and these values are credible for a security priced at $9.375 at the time of the analysis.

FORECASTING ERROR

Table 9.5 summarizes forecasting errors for key variables discussed in the case. Forecast values are compared with realized values and errors are reported numerically and as a percentage of actual value. Earnings per share was over-estimated by approximately 18 percent; this appears to be a serious error since EPS is a critical determinant of price. But an unforeseen event proved to be the major cause of the discrepancy. During 1974 the LIFO inventory method was extended to some types of materials previously accounted under the FIFO method in response to the impact of inflationary pressure on reported operating costs. The net effect was a decrease in earnings per share of approximately $0.25. Without this adjustment earnings per share would have been $2.15 which compares favorably with the forecast value of $2.24. In an efficient market security prices will not be affected by any change in accounting procedures and this may account in part for the 11 percent understatement of the price-earnings ratio. On balance forecast error is not severe with the realized rate of return of .1408 falling within .11 standard deviations of the expected value of .1772. With a beginning price of $9.375, a change in the ending price of $\frac{1}{8}$ or $0.125 will result in a 1 percent change in rate of return.

Table 9.5
Forecasting Error

	1974 Forecast Value	*1974 Actual Value*	*Error*	*Percentage Error*
Sales	$482,528	$518,690	−$36,162	−.0697
Cost of sales	402,652	443,617	−40,965	−.0923
General, selling, and administrative expense	24,951	28,748	−3,797	−.1321
Interest expense	10,058	9,743	315	.0323
Net income	31,945	27,068	4,877	.1802
Earnings per share	2.24	1.90	.34	.1789
Dividends per share	.575	.570	.005	.0088
Working capital	96,333	93,905	2,428	.0259
Plant and equipment	126,506	118,308	8,198	.0693
Total assets	309,207	295,819	13,388	.0453
Total liabilities	106,886	96,863	10,023	.1035
Equity	202,321	198,956	3,365	.0169
Price-earnings ratio	4.67	5.26	−0.59	−.1122
Price	10.461	10.125	.336	.0332
Rate of return	.1772	.1408	.0364	.2585

Forecast values are very sensitive to variations in the price-earnings ratio caused by changing capital market conditions. While that did not prove to be severe in this case study, the price-earnings model employed is less than satisfactory and it is probably the most vulnerable specification employed.

Summary

This chapter illustrated security analysis with a detailed examination of data for a real firm. The purpose of the analysis was to demonstrate forecasting procedures and to emphasize the importance of subjective elements at the same time. The use of a highly structured analytical model should not obscure the problems involved in changing market conditions, data inconsistencies, and unforeseen events.

The next chapter concludes the study of debt and equity securities by considering special situations in which basic elements of the analytical model are either omitted, unavailable, or irrelevant.

Appendix A
Security Analysis Model

The following is an algebraic listing of the model discussed in this chapter. Z values represent a standardized normally distributed random number which differs each time it is defined in any of the equations. Mnemonic notation is the same as that used in the chapter.

Part I: Establish Values for Risk Assessment

$IIP\ e_I$	$SE1 = 5.839Z$
$S\ e_S$	$SE2 = .0027 + 2165.5065(SE1) + 20413.2506Z$
$COS\ e_C$	$SE3 = -.0343 - .1432(SE2) + 5796.7313Z$
$GSA\ e_G$	$SE4 = -.0075 - .0784(SE2) + 1569.7005Z$
Other income	$SE5 = .0000$
Investments	$SE6 = .0000$
Tax rate	$SE7 = .0492Z$
$FA\ e_F$	$SE8 = .0000$
$WC\ e_W$	$SE9 = .0000$
Acc. depr.	$SE10 = .0133Z$
Other assets	$SE11 = .0000$
Dividends	$SE12 = .0000$
Interest rate	$SE13 = .0100$
L/V	$SE14 = .0300$
$P/E\ e_p$	$SE15 = .0000$

Part II: Calculate Values for Forecast Year T = 23

IIP	$IIP = 81.6039 + 2.1511T + .1393T^2 + SE1$
S	$S = -161{,}880 + 3{,}147(IIP) + SE2$
COS	$COS = -3154 + .8410S + SE3$
GSA	$GSA = -1347 + .0545S + SE4$
Investments	$IVS = 82{,}000 + SE5$
Other income	$OI = (.1300 + SE6)\mathrm{IV}S$
Tax rate	$TXR = .4247 + SE7$
FA	$\log(FA) = -.2103 + .9743 \log(S) + SE8$
	$FA = 10^{\log(FA)}$
Acc. depr.	$AD = (.4044 + SE10)FA$
WC	$\log(WC) = -.6952 + .9992 \log(S) + SE9$
	$WC = 10^{\log(WC)}$
Other assets	$OA = 4368 + SE11$
DPS	$\mathrm{DPS} = .575 + SE12$
Dividends	$DIV = 14269.186DPS$
Interest rate	$IRT = .0941 + SE13$
Common stock	$CS = 35{,}411$
Retained earnings	$RE = 143{,}170$
Required funds	$RF = WC + FA - AD + IVS + OA - CS - RE + DIV$
Operating earnings	$\mathrm{EBIT} = S - COS - GSA + OI$
	$ADJ = 1.0 - [(1.0 - TXR)(IRT)]$
Liabilities	$L = (RF - \mathrm{EBIT}(1.0 - TXR))/ADJ$
Interest expense	$I = (IRT)L$
Net income	$E = (\mathrm{EBIT} - I)(1.0 - TXR)$
EPS	$\mathrm{EPS} = E/14269.186$
Payout ratio	$B = \mathrm{DPS}/\mathrm{EPS}$
L/V	$L/V = .44 + SE14$
P/E	$P/E = 16.69 - 35.84(L/V) + 14.62B + SE15$
Price	$P = \mathrm{EPS}(P/E)$
Rate of return	$R = (P - 9.375 + \mathrm{DPS})/9.375$

Appendix B
Sources of Information for Security Analysis

I. Annuals

1. *Accounting Trends and Techniques*, American Institute of Certified Public Accountants. Annual.
2. *Agricultural Statistics*, U.S. Department of Agriculture. Annual.
3. *AMEX Databook*, American Stock Exchange. Every two years.
4. *Business Statistics; Statistical Supplement*, U.S. Office of Business Economics. A biennial supplement to the *Survey of Current Business.*
5. *Commodity Year Book*, Commodity Research Bureau. Annual.
6. *Investment Companies* (mutual and other types), Arthur Weisenberger. Annual.

7. *Key Business Ratios*, Dun & Bradstreet. Annual.
8. *Minerals Yearbook*, U.S. Bureau of Mines. Annual.
9. *Over-the-Counter NASDAQ Securities Handbook*, Review Publishing Company. Annual.
10. *Statistical Abstract of the United States*, U.S. Bureau of the Census. Annual.

II. Books

1. *Almanac of Business and Industrial Financial Ratios*, Leo Troy, 1972. Englewood Cliffs, N.J.: Prentice-Hall.
2. *Standard Industrial Classification Manual*, 1972. Washington: U.S. Office of Management and Budget.
3. *Statistical Services of the United States Government.* U.S. Bureau of the Budget Office of Statistical Standards.
4. *Statistics Sources*, Paul Wasserman, ed. Detroit: Gale.

III. Directories

1. *Directory of Companies Filing Annual Reports with the Securities and Exchange Commission.* U.S. Securities and Exchange Commission.
2. *Directory of Corporate Affiliations.* National Register Publishing Company.
3. *Fortune Double 500 Directory*, *Fortune* Magazine. Annual.
4. *Million Dollar Directory*, Dun & Bradstreet. Annual.
5. *Thomas' Register of American Manufacturers.* Annual.

IV. Indexes

1. *Business Periodicals Index*, H. W. Wilson Company. Monthly with quarterly and annual cumulations.
2. *F & S Index International*, Predicasts. Annual.
3. *Funk and Scott Index of Corporations and Industries*, Predicasts. Monthly with semiannual and annual cumulations.
4. *Predicasts.* Quarterly with annual cumulations.
5. *Public Affairs Information Service*, H. W. Wilson Company. Bi-weekly with quarterly and annual cumulations.
6. *Wall Street Journal Index*, Dow Jones. Monthly, with annual cumulations.

V. Services

1. *Bond Guide*, Standard & Poor's.
2. *Capital Changes Reporter*, Commerce Clearing House.
3. *Daily Stock Price Record, American Stock Exchange.* Quarterly.
4. *Daily Stock Price Record, New York Stock Exchange.* Quarterly.
5. *Daily Stock Price Record, Over-the-Counter.* Quarterly.
6. *Industry Surveys*, Standard & Poor's.
7. *Mergers and Acquisitions.* Quarterly.
8. *Moody's Bank & Finance Manual.* Annual with twice weekly updating.
9. *Moody's Bond Record.* Monthly.
10. *Moody's Bond Survey.* Weekly.
11. *Moody's Dividend Record.* Annual with monthly updates.
12. *Moody's Handbook of Common Stocks.* Quarterly.
13. *Moody's Industrial Manual.* Annual, with twice weekly updating.
14. *Moody's Municipal & Government Manual.* Annual, with twice weekly updating.

15. *Moody's OTC Industrial Manual.* Annual, with weekly updating.
16. *Moody's Public Utility Manual.* Annual, with twice weekly updating.
17. *Moody's Stock Survey.* Weekly.
18. *Moody's Transportation Manual.* Annual, with twice weekly updating.
19. *Outlook*, Standard & Poor's.
20. *Poor's Investment Advisory Survey*, Standard & Poor's.
21. *Security Owners Stock Guide*, Standard & Poor's.
22. *Standard Corporation Records*, Standard & Poor's.
23. *Trade and Securities: Statistics*, Standard & Poor's.
24. *Value Line Investment Survey*, Arnold Bernhard & Company. Weekly.

VI. Computer Readable Sources

1. *Compustat*, Investors Management Sciences.
2. *University of Chicago Return Relative File.*

Questions and Problems

1. "The entire process of security analysis can be computerized, with data inputs from computer tapes, as long as the analyst is careful in selecting statistical techniques," "Forecasting error is so hazardous that the best model for security analysis consists of the stock listings from *The Wall Street Journal* and a set of darts." Do you agree with either of these statements? Explain.

2. Assume that you are the analyst described in the case study contained in this chapter. Forecast expected rate of return for the two-year period beginning April 1, 1973. Use all 1974 values presented in the case and extrapolate them through 1975.

3. Examine values you calculated in problem 2 above for forecasting accuracy; evaluate the extent of error and, to the degree possible, determine the reason for errors observed.

4. Examine values you calculated in problem 2 for rate of return sensitivity. Which variables and/or specifications are most likely to have a serious impact on rate of return? Demonstrate your answer with values calculated in problem 2.

Selected References

FORECASTING ART AND FORECASTING TECHNIQUE

Basi, Bart, Kenneth Carey, and Richard Twark, "Accuracy of Corporate and Security Analysts' Forecasts," *Accounting Review*, April 1976, pp. 244–254.

Cairncross, Alec, "Economic Forecasting," *Economic Journal*, December 1969, pp. 797–812.

Elliott, J. W., "A Direct Comparison of Short-Run GNP Forecasting Models," *Journal of Business*, January 1973, pp. 33–60.

Hickman, B. G., ed., *Econometric Models of Economic Behavior* (New York: National Bureau of Economic Research, 1971).

Lewis, John P., "Short-Term General Business Conditions Forecasting: Some Comments on Method," *Journal of Business*, October 1962, pp. 343–356.

Modigliani, Franco, and Kalman J. Cohen, *The Role of Anticipations and Plans in Economic Behavior and Their Use in Economic Analysis and Forecasting* (Urbana: University of Illinois Bureau of Economic and Business Research, 1961).

Nelson, Charles R., "Rational Expectations and the Predictive Efficiency of Economic Models," *The Journal of Business* 48.3 (July 1975), pp. 331–343.

Umstead, David A., "Forecasting Stock Market Prices," *Journal of Finance* 32 (May 1977), pp. 427–441.

SECURITY ANALYSIS PROCEDURES

Elton, Edwin J., and Martin J. Gruber, "Earnings Estimates and the Accuracy of Expectational Data," *Management Science*, April 1972, pp. B409–424.

——— and Martin J. Gruber, "Improved Forecasting Through the Design of Homogeneous Groups," *Journal of Business*, October 1971, pp. 432–450.

Ibrahim, I. B., and T. Otsuki, "Forecasting GNP Components Using the Method of Box and Jenkins," *Southern Economic Journal*, January 1976, pp. 461–470.

Ijiri, Yuri, and Herbert A. Simon, "A Model of Business Firm Growth," *Econometrica*, April 1967, pp. 348–355.

Koot, Ronald S., and David A. Walker, "Short-Run Cost Functions of a Multi-Product Firm," *The Journal of Industrial Economics*, April 1970, pp. 118–128.

Lorek, Kenneth, Charles McDonald, and Dennis Patz, "A Comparative Examination of Management Forecasts and Box-Jenkins Forecasts of Earnings," *Accounting Review*, April 1976, pp. 321–330.

Winters, Peter, "Forecasting Sales by Exponentially Weighted Moving Averages," *Management Science*, April 1960, pp. 324–342.

Chapter 10

Other Valuation Elements

Chapters 5 through 9 described and illustrated the art of security analysis under normal circumstances where required information is available for processing in the manner described there. But there are special situations where the general analytical model is not completely applicable. In the case of an unseasoned firm which attempts to issue common stock for the first time, for example, accounting data are often unavailable for any extended period of time and security analysis of the type illustrated previously is not possible. In other cases the model must be adjusted to recognize special elements with respect to the type of security in question. Model adjustments are required for convertible securities and stock warrants, which are discussed in Chapter 11, and for stock options and futures contracts, which are discussed in Chapter 12. Other special analytical situations will be considered in this chapter.

Special situations arise because of (1) factors related to the individual firm or because of (2) structural or regulatory elements related to the operation of capital markets. The first section of this chapter is directed to firm-specific situations: new issues of common stock, mergers, and bankruptcy. The second section discusses the potential impact of market elements including the response to stock splits, exchange listing, and insider transactions.

Firm Structure Elements

Special analytical problems which arise for some particular firm at some particular point in time usually reflect an information deficiency of some type. This is true in the case of (1) unseasoned new issues, where historical financial data are typically inadequate, (2) mergers, where the combination of two earnings streams results in a third stream which is often difficult to evaluate, and (3) bankruptcy, where "going-concern" data are no longer relevant.

NEW ISSUES

New issues of common stock are classified as *seasoned*, where a publicly owned corporation issues additional shares, or *unseasoned*, where a firm offers common stock to the general public for the first time. For a seasoned new issue the model described in Chapters 6 through 9 remains relevant, with two added qualifications. First, the offering price will be somewhat lower than the current market price in order to achieve a successful offering; thus the offering price must be substituted for the market price when the expected rate of return is calculated. Second, and more important, the proceeds from the issue will affect the value of the firm, perhaps substantially.

A new issue of common stock has a twofold effect on value. On one hand, the number of outstanding shares will increase, depressing earnings per share in the process. At the same time proceeds can be either invested, which promises to increase earnings and earnings per share, or used to retire debt, thereby decreasing financial risk. The trade-off among these different elements determines the impact of new common stock on the value of the issuing firm. Unfortunately, the evaluation of this trade-off is necessarily subjective and somewhat crude for external analysts who have no access to detailed information concerning the application of proceeds from the new issue. In most cases the prospectus will provide a general statement of managerial intent in this respect but numerical forecasts are not made available. In any realistic sense, long-term projections can be adjusted only subjectively. In time, the effect of the new issue will be reflected in observed data and it will also be reflected in future projections based upon that data.

Any analytical shortcoming arising from the disposition of funds raised through a seasoned new issue is likely to be immaterial, particularly if equity financing is only one part of managerial actions with respect to expansion of the firm. Unseasoned new issues, in sharp contrast, provide a far more formidable analytical problem. In some cases historical data are virtually nonexistent and evaluation is replaced by speculation based upon assumed firm or industry prospects. Information availability varies with the size of the firm and with regulatory disclosure requirements; in this sense unseasoned new issues can be classified as follows:

1. *National or regional over-the-counter issues.* These are securities which are registered with the Securities and Exchange Commission in accordance with

normal disclosure requirements. Secondary market transactions occur in the over-the-counter market and bid-ask quotations are available from national or regional OTC listings.

2. *Regulation A issues.* Certain issues, which are restricted to a ceiling of $500,000, are exempted from full registration procedures, although some minimal data must be filed with the Securities and Exchange Commission. These "Reg A" issues provide financing for very small companies and bid-ask quotations are usually difficult to locate.
3. *Intrastate issues.* Some new issues are offered for sale only to residents of the state in which the firm transacts business. These securities are exempt from SEC requirements and they are registered with state authorities where regulatory provisions differ from state to state. Price quotations for intrastate issues are also difficult to find.

NATIONAL AND REGIONAL LISTINGS. In theory the equity evaluation model developed previously can be applied to unseasoned new issues; in practice this will prove to be difficult because financial accounting data provided in the prospectus are likely to be limited to a short period of time. If financial data are available for only one to five years, for example, statistical forecasting becomes extremely hazardous. This does not imply that the model should be abandoned because that would result in an arbitrary investment decision. But it does suggest two modifications of the analytical procedure which recognize forecasting uncertainty and taxes.

First, it is probably a good strategy to minimize the assumed holding period, limiting it initially to one year or less. Forecasting error is likely to be large for any new firm in a stage of high anticipated growth where the time series of financial data is limited. In addition, unseasoned new issues differ from other securities when they are subsequently traded in the secondary after-market. By definition, investors who purchase new issues in the primary market are in a short-term capital gain or capital loss position for the next 12 months. If the stock does poorly, investors will be motivated to sell the shares within a year to take advantage of the short-term capital loss; if it does well, they will be motivated to hold for at least one year to take advantage of the long-term capital gain. Timing becomes critical in the case of a new issue and the problem is especially important as the anniversary of the original flotation nears.

Second, particular attention should be directed to the question of risk. While this is always important in equity evaluation, it is particularly critical in the case of new issues. Given inadequate data, statistical estimates of dispersion are of doubtful reliability. For that reason it is useful to experiment with forecast values in order to evaluate the degree of error required to break even and/or result in a given loss. This type of sensitivity analysis is a simple but effective tool for assessing downside risk. In the case of an unseasoned firm where dividends are unlikely, and assuming a one-year holding period, expected rate of return depends upon the price-earnings ratio and earnings per share, together with any assumed relationship between them. These two variables can be changed systematically and the effect on rate of return can then be observed.

In addition to other elements which distinguish them from other securities, new issues are unique in the sense that a professional opinion is freely available as to the correct price in the primary market. This judgment is provided by the underwriter who establishes the offering price in negotiation with the issuing firm. The underwriter is in the best position to evaluate a new security, having access to both quantitative and qualitative factors relating to the firm's prospects. But there is also a potentially serious conflict of interests in the pricing procedure because underwriting profits depend upon acceptance of the issue in the primary market and subsequent performance of the security in the secondary after-market. Probable success in both respects increases as the offering price decreases; this had led many people to suspect that underwriters systematically underprice new issues.

In the underwriting process, three different prices are involved:

1. The *expected price* in the secondary market following a successful offering. It is the underwriter's responsibility to arrive at an unbiased estimate of this price, based upon all available information.
2. The *offering price* at which shares can be purchased.
3. The *net proceeds price* to the firm. This is the offering price, less flotation costs and the underwriting commission (spread).

Some people have argued that the underwriter should estimate initial secondary market price (1), and then establish offering price (2) at that level; given estimates of the risk involved, underwriting spread can then be negotiated and proceeds price (3) can be determined. To illustrate, assume the following per share values:

1. Estimated secondary market price, $12.00.
2. Offering price, $11.00.
3. Proceeds, net of 5 percent spread, $10.45.

Under the argument stated above, the $1.00 differential between $11.00 and $12.00 reflects a downward pricing bias on the part of the underwriter which is designed to increase the probability that the offering will be successful. Under this hypothesis, empirical findings of a positive offering price-secondary price differential is taken as evidence of systematic downward bias in new issue pricing.[1]

But the argument has several flaws. First, both the expected secondary market price and the offering price which will clear the primary market are *random variables* at the time the actual offering price is established. Accordingly, risk aversion on the part of the underwriter implies a positive offering price-secondary market price differential. Second, new issue investors should be compensated for the risk attached to bridging the primary and secondary markets. This also implies a positive differential. Third, systematic underpricing implies irrationality on the part of the issuing corporation which can

[1] See J. G. McDonald and A. K. Fisher, "New Issue Stock Pricing Behavior," *Journal of Finance*, March 1972, pp. 97–102; F. K. Reilly and K. Hatfield, "Investors Experience with New Stock Issues," *Financial Analysts Journal*, September–October 1969, pp. 73–80; and F. K. Reilly, "Further Evidence on Short-Run Results for New Issue Investors," *Journal of Financial and Quantitative Analysis*, January 1973, pp. 83–90.

select among underwriters in a highly competitive industry. Finally, there is no assurance that the secondary market price is correct, even when an efficient market is assumed, because of information deficiencies noted previously.

The underpricing hypothesis is difficult to test directly but one recent study which explicitly recognizes underwriting risk failed to support any systematic pattern of downward bias.[2] If anything, it implies a fairly efficient primary market although the empirical evidence presented is clearly far from conclusive. This is an important issue because of the problem which data deficiencies present in the evaluation of new equity shares. The underwriter's offering price established a point of reference for comparison with the analyst's estimate. Given an unbiased offering price, the new issue investor is in a better position to evaluate the unseasoned offering.

With respect to financial information which is contained in the prospectus, two additional points require comment. First, accounting data which are reported at or near the date of issue are usually unaudited. This has led to conflict among public accountants and underwriters because of potential liability in the event of fraudulent statements. Accountants are normally required to provide a written statement, usually called a *comfort letter*, under terms of the underwriting agreement. The comfort letter will typically refer to compliance with accounting requirements of the Securities and Exchange Act of 1933, inclusion of unaudited data in the registration statement, changes in financial data subsequent to the date of the latest included statements, and the independence of the accountants with respect to both the underwriter and the issuing firm. Underwriters applied severe pressure to force accountants to provide "negative assurance" as to events subsequent to the date of audited statements; they also pressed to have comfort letters reproduced in the prospectus. But the AICPA responded to these efforts by limiting the activities of auditors in both respects.[3] The analyst should be aware of possible quality defects of information provided in the prospectus.

The second point concerns the question of including managerial projections in the registration statement. In view of data deficiencies with respect to new issues, this would seem to be a useful proposal and the SEC seriously considered requiring it early in 1972. The proposal was opposed by the Securities Industry Association and, in one form or other, it was supported by officials of the Financial Analysts Federation. Eventually the SEC withdrew its support but that may have simply reflected the collapse of the "hot" new issues market in 1973–1975. New firms enjoyed widespread market acceptance during the "hot issues" markets of 1961–1962, 1968–1969, and 1970–1971; fast-food chains, bowling alleys, medical and related health services, and so-called sonics and tronics operations were especially

[2] Robert M. Bear and Anthony J. Curley, "Unseasoned Equity Financing," *Journal of Financial and Quantitative Analysis*, June 1975, pp. 311–325.

[3] See American Institute of Certified Public Accountants, Committee on Auditing Procedures, *Statement on Auditing Procedure No. 48: Letters for Underwriters*, October 1971.

popular. Investors' acceptance of new issues, and the potential impact of speculative activity, caused concern in the SEC which resulted in hearings on a number of proposals including the publication of budgeting and cash flow projections. But the new issues market became almost nonexistent by the mid-1970s because of depressed common stock values at that time. It is not unlikely that proposals for the disclosure of projected data will emerge again whenever the new issue market reappears.

REGULATION A ISSUES. Reg A issues provide financing for very small firms. After-market transactions are typically infrequent and Reg A investors accept a high degree of risk. There have been very few empirical studies of this market, presumably because of the difficulty involved in locating secondary market prices. The most comprehensive paper on Reg A performance was provided by Stoll and Curley who studied rates of return for 205 firms which went public in 1957, 1959, and 1963.[4] They found remarkable short-run performance, measured from the offering date to the first market transaction, but they also found longer run performance which was inferior to returns realized by larger firms. Reg A firms also had greater return variability, as would be expected. The data reported in this study are limited, as the authors point out, but the evidence suggests that investors fared poorly in the long run in view of the level of risk which they assumed.

INTRASTATE ISSUES. Intrastate issues also provide financing for small firms and after-markets are also typically inactive. In most cases shares are issued by management without the assistance of underwriters. Securities are registered with state authorities for sales to residents of that particular state. National and regional over-the-counter firms have the largest dollar volume of unseasoned new issues but the largest number of offerings are by intrastate firms. Studies of the intrastate market are infrequent, similar to Reg A issues, because market prices are generally unavailable. Some evidence was presented by Stizell but it is difficult to interpret because of the small number of firms where price data existed.[5] It is probable that rate of return patterns in the intrastate market are similar to patterns which exist in the Reg A market.

MERGERS AND ACQUISITIONS

Business combination is another special situation where the equity valuation model must be adjusted by the analyst. Adjustment is necessary only when there is some reasonable relationship between the acquiring firm and

[4] Hans R. Stoll and Anthony J. Curley, "Small Business and the New Issues Market for Equities," *Journal of Financial and Quantitative Analysis*, September 1970, pp. 309–322. Also see Burke A. Ferrari and D. Robert Papera, "Short Term Market Analysis of Selected Regulation A Issues, 1959–61," *Quarterly Review of Economics and Business*, Autumn 1974, pp. 47–53.

[5] Thomas E. Stitzel, "Investing in New Intrastate Issues of Common Stock," *Journal of Financial and Quantitative Analysis*, January 1970, pp. 697–706.

the acquired firm with respect to size; when a firm which is listed on the NYSE acquires a small, privately owned corporation, the impact on the market price of the parent company is likely to be negligible. This point will be developed more rigorously later in this section. Model adjustments will differ from one combination to another depending upon classification by type and by financing method.

CLASSIFICATION BY TYPE. There are several ways to classify mergers and acquisitions. The conventional approach is based upon similarity in product lines and economies of scale in the manufacture and distribution of products and services:

1. *Horizontal combination.* This is the merger of two companies which market identical or similar products. The net effect, assuming that antitrust provisions are not violated, is an increase in the market share of the surviving company, together with any economies realized in distribution costs.
2. *Vertical combination.* This is the merger of two firms which might otherwise be associated as buyer and seller. For example, if an automobile manufacturer merges with a steel company or a glass company, it would be classified as a vertical combination. The net effect is increased control of the supply of raw materials, together with any economies realized in an integrated production schedule.
3. *Conglomerate combination.* This is any combination which is not classified as horizontal or vertical. Conglomerate corporations merge firms from different industries with the presumed objective(s) of reducing risk or increasing return through a vigorous acquisition policy. Risk can be reduced through diversification, to a limited degree; diversifiable risk will be explored in depth in Chapter 14. Conglomerates substitute corporate diversification for diversification opportunities which are available to their shareholders. Since stockholders can adjust their portfolios more easily than conglomerates can dispose of subsidiaries, the rationale for conglomerate diversification is open to serious question. Conglomerates pursue increased return by applying the firm's managerial expertise or fund-raising advantages to smaller firms which they acquire.

Howell suggested an alternative classification.[6] Although his proposal was directed internally to the management and integration of acquisition strategy, it is very useful in detailing the type of adjustments necessary for modifying the analytical model in the case of mergers. The classifications suggested by Howell are (1) financial, (2) marketing, and (3) manufacturing.

Financial combinations occur when a company acquires a number of unrelated businesses with the basic intention of allowing them to operate autonomously. Under this classification there is no general association among parent and subsidiaries with respect to the markets served or the manufacture of products and services. In this case the analyst would adjust the model by aggregating the expected earnings streams of the merged companies and by adjusting the price-earnings ratio subjectively for any perceived decrease in risk.

[6] Robert A. Howell, "Plan to Integrate Your Acquisitions," *Harvard Business Review*, November–December 1970, pp. 66–76.

Marketing combinations occur when a firm selects a number of products and then searches for acquisitions within those market-related categories. In this case both financial and marketing advantages may be realized. Accordingly, in addition to aggregating earnings and adjusting the capitalization rate, forecasts should be modified to reflect any economies realized from increased market shares.

Manufacturing combinations extend the other two categories to situations where closely related operations are merged. The primary association between parent and subsidiary in this case is the production function; markets may or may not be related. In addition to any adjustments reflecting financial or marketing factors, analytical focus should be directed to the cost stream for purposes of forecasting cash flows.

Howell's classification identifies the variables to be adjusted in the case of a merger but the problem of numerical estimation remains. In addition, the adjustment will be affected by the manner in which the acquisition is financed.

CLASSIFICATION BY FINANCING. Mergers and acquisitions can be financed with common stock, convertible preferred stock, debt, cash, or stock warrants. Most transactions are tax-free exchanges involving the issue of voting shares—convertible preferred and common stock; taxable exchanges are financed through debt, cash, or warrants. The relative importance of each type of financing may vary from time to time but a study by Shad provides a reasonable estimate:[7]

Convertible preferred stock	46 percent
Common stock	31
Debt	19
Cash or warrants	4
	100 percent

When common stock is issued, the number of outstanding shares must be increased, decreasing earnings per share in the process. In the case of debt, after-tax interest expense must be subtracted from the cash flows. When a firm is purchased for cash, there is no direct capital structure effect but it may become necessary to reevaluate overall financing adequacy, as discussed previously in Chapter 6, since the acquisition applies funds that would have been available for other projects. In each case the earnings stream will also be augmented, offsetting these financing effects.

Convertible securities and warrants provide a somewhat more difficult problem. As detailed in Chapter 7, accountants provide a "dual presentation" of earnings per share which reflects the potential dilution of these hybrid securities. In general "primary" earnings per share is intended to

[7] John S. R. Shad, "The Financial Realities of Mergers," *Harvard Business Review*, November–December 1969, p. 133. The sample consisted of 65 announced mergers, some of which were never completed.

reflect the most probable dilution and "fully diluted" earnings per share reports the largest possible dilution. In the case of convertible preferred stock issued in a merger, it is possible to adjust the earnings numerator by subtracting the preferred dividend, or to adjust the denominator, on either a primary or fully diluted basis, by increasing the number of common shares. The central issue is the EPS definition which investors capitalize; because this is not known, and for reasons given in Chapter 7, the fully diluted definition seems to be the preferable one for convertibles and warrants issued in a business combination.

Summarizing to this point, the equity evaluation model must be adjusted in the case of a merger or acquisition to reflect (1) the increase in aggregate earnings which are acquired, (2) any additional earnings realized through marketing or manufacturing economies, (3) any change in the price-earnings ratio resulting from a change in risk, and (4) any change in the capital structure caused by the method of financing the acquisition. One additional element must still be considered before the merger-adjusted model is illustrated; this is a phenomenon which is sometimes referred to as *instantaneous merger profit*. It is an especially critical factor because failure to recognize its effect has apparently caused a number of investors to suffer serious losses because of inflated growth expectations for merger-active companies.

MERGED EARNINGS PER SHARE.[8] Merger profit was defined by Mead as an instantaneous increase in the earnings per share of an acquiring company which is caused solely by the merger.[9] It is unrelated and totally independent of operating efficiency, market power, risk reduction, or any other value element which occurs with the passage of time. Merger profit depends upon (1) a price-earnings differential which favors the acquiring firm and (2) the relative size of the two firms, measured by aggregate earnings. When a corporation acquires a number of other firms, each of which yields a merger profit, apparent growth and efficiency result even in the absence of real growth and efficiency. Mead hypothesized that the major cause of the conglomerate movement of the 1960s was the pursuit of merger profit. He also argued that the prospect for continued growth was severely limited because the number and size of annual acquisitions must increase at a compound rate just to maintain constant growth in earnings per share. Since this is not possible, conglomerate growth rates must fall, the price-earnings ratio which reacts to growth must also fall, and sharp price declines will result.

To illustrate, Table 10.1 summarizes the earnings per share effect of a common stock-for-common stock merger between two firms which are expected to contribute constant annual earnings to the combined firm. Both

[8] This section is adapted from Anthony J. Curley, "Conglomerate Earnings per Share," *Accounting Review*, July 1971, pp. 519–528.

[9] Walter J. Mead, "Instantaneous Merger Profit as a Conglomerate Merger Motive," *Western Economic Journal*, December 1969, pp. 295–306.

Table 10.1
Merger Profit

	Parent Firm (P)	*Acquired Firm (S)*	*Merged Firm (C)*
Constant annual earnings (*E*)	$ 4,000,000	$ 2,000,000	$6,000,000
Outstanding shares	3,000,000	3,000,000	
Premerger earnings per share	$ 1.33	$ .67	
Price-earnings multiple	10	5	
Premerger price per share	$ 13.33	$ 3.33	
Conversion ratio	1	4	
Total market value (*V*)	$40,000,000	$10,000,000	
Number of shares issued, $1P = 4S$		750,000	
Outstanding shares			3,750,000
Postmerger earnings per share			$ 1.60
Merger profit—EPS			20%
Assuming Postmerger Price-Earnings Ratio of 8.33			
Price per share			$ 13.33
Market value gain	$ 0	$ 0	
Assuming Postmerger Price-Earnings Ratio of 10.00			
Price per share			$ 16.00
Market value gain	$ 2.67	$ .67	
	20%	20%	

growth and synergism are assumed away. *Synergism* refers to the condition in which the value of the whole exceeds the sum of the value of the parts. In this case there are no marketing or manufacturing economies which generate a synergistic increase in aggregate earnings. Values are also given for the number of outstanding shares and the price-earnings ratio for both the acquiring parent company *P* and the prospective new subsidiary *S*. Given these values, earnings per share ($1.33 and $0.67), price per share ($13.33 and $3.33), and total market value ($40 million and $10 million) can be calculated for both *P* and *S*, respectively.

In the example given, it is assumed that any premium paid by the acquiring parent to induce the shareholders of the subsidiary firm to agree to the merger is included in the premerger price of $3.33 per share. On this basis a conversion ratio of one share of *P* for every four shares of *S* is implied (13.33/3.33). Accordingly, 750,000 shares will be issued by the parent and, with an aggregate 3,750,000 shares outstanding, postmerger earnings per share will be $1.60. This is an instantaneous *accounting* merger profit of 20 percent over the previous parent company level of $1.33. Despite the lack of growth in either firm's aggregate earnings, there is a 20 percent increase in earnings per share.

In the absence of growth, the acquired firm's price-earnings multiple of 5 suggests greater risk than the parent company which is capitalized at 10 times earnings. Ignoring any possible gain from diversification, the price-earnings ratio of the merged firm must be 8.33 if the combined firm is priced at the premerger value of \$13.33 per share.[10] The accounting merger profit would be exactly offset by a market merger loss and no gain or loss would accrue to either group of stockholders. But if the nature of merger profit is not understood, or cannot be isolated, merger profit may be realized in market terms. If the parent firm's premerger price-earnings ratio (10) continues after the merger, as shown in Table 10.1, shareholders would realize a 20 percent increase in market price. In that case instantaneous merger profit becomes very real.

Before 1968 accounting merger profit was almost impossible to identify. Since that time accountants are required to provide restated financial data on a proforma basis, reporting earnings per share *as if* the merged firms had always been combined. This is very useful because the restated series is free of the instantaneous effect. Nonetheless, an investor who monitors fundamental data for a particular firm, as reported in the financial press, can still be misled, especially in view of the infrequency of annual reports. In that case it is possible that the price-earnings ratio will *increase* in response to inflated expectations as to future growth. This is a plausible explanation for the temporary market success realized by a number of conglomerates during the late 1960s and early 1970s.

As stated previously, Mead argued that merger profit was limited by the size of the acquiring parent. This can be shown by defining the instantaneous growth effect:

$$G = \frac{(E_S/E_P) - (V_S/V_P)}{1 + (V_S/V_P)}, \tag{10.1}$$

where E is aggregate earnings and V is aggregate value for P and S prior to the merger. In the case of the example given in Table 10.1, with data expressed in millions of dollars,

$$\begin{aligned} G &= \frac{(2/4) - (10/40)}{1 + (10/40)} \\ &= \frac{.50 - .25}{1.25} \\ &= .20 \end{aligned}$$

Equation 10.1 clearly demonstrates how size limits merger profit: growth cannot exceed the ratio of aggregate earnings even if the shareholders of

[10] See Kermit D. Larson and Nicholas J. Gonedes, "Business Combinations: An Exchange Ratio Determination Model," *Accounting Review*, October 1969, pp. 720–728. In this case a postmerger price of \$13.33 results when earnings per share of \$1.60 is capitalized at an 8.33 multiple (1.60 × 8.33 = 13.33).

the acquired firm were willing to give it away. The earnings denominator, E_P, increases each time a firm is acquired; in order to maintain growth at any given level, successively larger firms would have to be acquired.

In the example given above, exaggerated values were used to highlight the merger profit effect. Company P, for example, acquired a firm which was half its size, measured by earnings. In practice this is unusual because large firms more often acquire far smaller ones. Nonetheless, mergers do occur among relatively large firms and when this happens the instantaneous effect must be isolated and adjusted.

EQUITY EVALUATION—MERGER SITUATION. The evaluation of a proposed merger is an extremely difficult task for company employees with access to detailed internal records. It is clearly far more difficult for an external security analyst who must resort to crude estimates of the effect of synergism and diversification on merged data. Nonetheless, the basic terms of an announced merger are known and the analytical problem is therefore a straightforward extension of the general analytical problem which was discussed in Chapters 6 through 9. Estimation error which is attributable solely to the merger will be immaterial unless both firms are of roughly comparable size. In that event sensitivity analysis can be used to evaluate the significance of synergistic and diversification effects.

In order to illustrate the process, it will be assumed that the firm which was analyzed in Chapter 6 announces an agreement, subject to shareholder approval, to acquire another firm in a common stock-for-common stock exchange. Relevant data for the parent company, which were generated in Chapter 6, are summarized in Table 10.2; corresponding data for the proposed subsidiary, which would have been developed in the same fashion, are also shown in the table. In addition, the following conditions apply:

1. The parent firm agrees to pay a premium of approximately 10 percent ($0.75 per share) to persuade the shareholders of the acquired firm to agree to the proposed plan. At a bargained price of $8.00 per share (7.25 + 0.75), the exchange ratio is 1 share of the parent company stock for 3.75 shares of the subsidiary's stock (30/8 = 3.75).
2. The subsidiary sells a product which the parent firm requires as an input to its production process. As a result the analyst estimates that earnings per share can be increased by 5 percent as a result of economies in the production function. It is also assumed that the combined price-earnings ratio will not be influenced by synergism or the impact of diversification on risk.
3. The parent firm will continue with its policy of a 60 percent payout ratio; an analysis of proforma source and use of funds over the next three years indicates that this is a viable financing policy.

Under these conditions, the merged firm can be evaluated. Table 10.3 summarizes the projected dividend stream. The calculation is straightforward and results in values for each of the three years, respectively, of $1.07, $1.19, and $1.33. Terminal value is also projected. With an estimated price-earnings multiple of 20 for the parent and 15 for the subsidiary if the

Table 10.2
Data for Proposed Merger

	Period (Year)			
	0	*1*	*2*	*3*
Parent				
Aggregate earnings	\$1,500,000	\$1,661,867	\$1,839,285	\$2,033,644
Outstanding shares	1,000,000	1,000,000	1,000,000	1,000,000
Earnings per share	\$ 1.50	\$ 1.66	\$ 1.84	\$ 2.03
Dividends per share	\$ .90	\$ 1.00	\$ 1.10	\$ 1.22
Terminal price-earnings ratio				20
Market price	\$ 30.00			\$ 40.60
Subsidiary				
Aggregate earnings	\$ 348,000	\$ 400,000	\$ 460,000	\$ 529,000
Outstanding shares	800,000	800,000	800,000	800,000
Earnings per share	\$ .43	\$ .50	\$ .58	\$ .67
Dividends per share	\$ .30	\$ .30	\$ .30	\$ .30
Terminal price-earnings ratio				15
Market price	\$ 7.25			\$ 10.05

Parent Rate of Return, Premerger

$$30.00 = \frac{1.00}{(1+r)} + \frac{1.10}{(1+r)^2} + \frac{1.22}{(1+r)^3} + \frac{40.60}{(1+r)^3};\ r = \underline{\underline{.139}}$$

Subsidiary Rate of Return, Premerger

$$7.25 = \frac{.30}{(1+r)} + \frac{.30}{(1+r)^2} + \frac{.30}{(1+r)^3} + \frac{10.05}{(1+r)^3};\ r = \underline{\underline{.152}}$$

firms did not merge, and in the absence of any diversification effect, the combined price-earnings ratio should be an average of the other two, weighted by earnings. This is the ratio of aggregate value to aggregate earnings.[11] In Table 10.3 the estimated price-earnings ratio for the combined firm is 19 and estimated terminal price is \$42.18. For a preannouncement parent firm value of \$30.00, expected rate of return increases from 13.9 percent to 15.6 percent; for a preannouncement subsidiary value of \$27.19 (7.25 × 3.75), expected rate of return increases from 15.2 percent to 19.6 percent. Following the announcement, the price of the subsidiary firm should approach the

[11] Define aggregate value V, aggregate earnings E, and price-earnings multiple m for parent P and subsidiary S. Then $V_P = m_P E_P$ and $V_S = m_S E_S$, and

$$\frac{V_P + V_S}{E_P + E_S} = \frac{m_P E_P + m_S E_S}{E_P + E_S} = m_P\left(\frac{E_P}{E_P + E_S}\right) + m_S\left(\frac{E_S}{E_P + E_S}\right)$$

Table 10.3
Rate of Return Analysis for Merged Firms

	Period (Annual) Dividends			*Terminal Price*
	1	*2*	*3*	
Earnings: Parent	$1,661,867	$1,839,285	$2,033,644	
Subsidiary	400,000	460,000	529,000	
	2,061,867	2,299,285	2,562,644	
Synergism factor	× 1.05	× 1.05	× 1.05	
Total	$2,164,960	$2,414,249	$2,690,776	
Shares: Parent	1,000,000	1,000,000	1,000,000	
Issued 800,000/3.75	213,333	213,333	213,333	
	1,213,333	1,213,333	1,213,333	
Earnings per share	$ 1.78	$ 1.99	$ 2.22	
Dividends, at 60 percent	$ 1.07	$ 1.19	$ 1.33	
Parent earnings				$ 2,033,644
Price-earnings				× 20
Terminal value				$40,672,880
Subsidiary earnings				$ 529,000
Price-earnings				× 15
Value				$ 7,935,000

Terminal price-earnings, $\dfrac{40{,}672{,}880 + 7{,}935{,}000}{2{,}033{,}644 + 529{,}000} = 18.97 \approx$ 19

Terminal price, $2.22 \times 19 =$ $ 42.18

Parent Rate of Return, Postmerger

$$30.00 = \frac{1.07}{(1+r)} + \frac{1.19}{(1+r)^2} + \frac{1.33}{(1+r)^3} + \frac{42.18}{(1+r)^3};\ r = .156$$

Subsidiary Rate of Return, Postmerger

$$27.19 = \frac{1.07}{(1+r)} + \frac{1.19}{(1+r)^2} + \frac{1.33}{(1+r)^3} + \frac{42.18}{(1+r)^3};\ r = .196$$

price of the parent company because of arbitrage; this point will be developed shortly. As the subsidiary price approaches $8.00 per share, expected rate of return will approach the parent company's 15.6 percent.

In this example the only necessary values beyond those generally required are the synergism factor and the price-earnings effect. Sensitivity to the former can be tested by removing the 5 percent value entirely from the calculations contained in Table 10.3. In that case the three-year dividend stream is reduced to \$1.02, \$1.14, and \$1.27 and expected rate of return for the parent company falls from 15.6 percent to 15.4 percent. Thus this particular model is fairly insensitive to assumed synergism. With respect to the price-earnings ratio, substitution of values of 21 and 17, respectively, results in expected rates of return of 19.3 percent and 11.6 percent; the calculation is clearly sensitive to the capitalization rate but to no greater degree than the sensitivity in the case of an unmerged firm.

In the example given, instantaneous merger profit is not an important factor; it amounts to only 1.54 percent on the basis of the bargained exchange value of \$8 per share.[12] This is not surprising because there is very little difference between the parent company's price-earnings ratio of 20 (30/1.50) and the subsidiary firm's ratio of 18.6 (8.00/.43) at the time of the announcement.

MERGER GAINS. The numerical example in the preceding section assumed that the acquiring company paid a premium to the shareholders of the acquired company to persuade them to agree to the exchange of shares. The existence of this type of inducement is widely acknowledged although estimates of the amount of the premium differ from one study to another.[13] This occurs because of differences with respect to the base date from which the gain is measured and because of market conditions during the interval from announcement to completion of the merger. A common rule of thumb suggests a 20 percent premium; this is supported by data reported in a study by Shad which was referred to earlier in this section:[14]

		Percentage Premium to Sellers	
Type of Financing	*Number*	*Median*	*Range*
Common stock	20	21	1–46
Convertible preferred	30	20	3–91
Cash, debt, warrants	14	22	3–87

The most rigorous study of merger gains was published by Halpern who estimated values for both the acquiring and the acquired firm.[15] He found that *dollar* gains were divided almost evenly between the two parties while

[12] With values denominated in millions of dollars, $E_S = .348$; $E_P = 1.500$; $V_S = 6.400$, with premium reflected; $V_P = 30.000$. From Equation 10.1, $G = [(.348/1.5) - (6.4/30.0)]/[1.0 + (6.4/30.0)] = (.2320 - .2133)/1.2133 = .0154$.

[13] Estimates of mean premiums paid to selling companies have ranged from 10 to 46 percent. See Paul J. Halpern, "Empirical Estimates of the Amount and Distribution of Gains to Companies in Mergers," *Journal of Business*, October 1973, pp. 554–575, table 1, p. 556.

[14] Shad, "Financial Realities of Mergers," pp. 134–136.

[15] Halpern, "Empirical Estimates." In this study firms are classified as "larger" or "smaller" rather than as parent and subsidiary although a close correspondence could normally be expected.

relative gains on an annualized basis averaged 6.4 percent for acquiring companies and 30.4 percent for acquired firms.

Acquisition can also be pursued directly with stockholders through a cash *tender offer* which is normally advertised in the financial press. The offer may or may not be made with the consent of management. In the case of an "unfriendly" attack, there are defensive tactics which reduce the probability of a successful offering. A tender premium is likely to be greater than a merger premium, particularly if the offeror attempts to bypass management, but there is very little published evidence in this respect. Examination of a sample of 1976 tender offers suggests an average premium in excess of 40 percent.

The tender offer presents a particularly difficult decision for the shareholder who is faced with the prospect of liquidating the investment or retaining the stock. In the latter case, in the event that the offeror succeeds in gaining control of the corporation, the long-run impact on the firm is a matter of speculation. For that reason, the Securities and Exchange Commission adopted expanded disclosure rules in July of 1977 requiring detail as to the offeror's source of funds, plans for the company, and any past dealings with the company. These rules apply to any offer for more than 5 percent of a company's shares.

MERGER ARBITRAGE. In the numerical example above, a merger was announced at a time when the acquiring firm sold for $30.00 per share while the acquired firm was priced at $7.25. With an exchange ratio of 3.75 to 1, the proposed subsidiary has a value of $8.00 per share *if* the merger occurs. The spread between the current price and the price as part of the merged firm presents an investment opportunity subject to the risk that the transaction will not be consummated. For this reason the price differential should decrease and, assuming that the $30.00 price is maintained, the price of the proposed subsidiary should approach $8.00. In the event that negotiations should collapse because of shareholder dissent, an unfavorable tax ruling by the Internal Revenue Service, intervention by the Justice Department, or some other reason, price would return to $7.25 and a loss would be realized. In any event, this is an investment decision which should be based upon careful evaluation of the parent firm. Otherwise, with capital funds locked into the hedged position, with transaction costs, and with the parent company subject to market risk in the short run, expected return is probably too small to offset the merger risk that the proposal will fail.

Short-run market risk can be hedged through arbitrage but most merger-hedge transactions are executed by a few brokerage firms which benefit from the small capital balances which an exchange requires of its members.[16] In the example given, the arbitrager, following a careful analysis

[16] Merger arbitrage is described and illustrated in Guy P. Wyser-Pratte, *Risk Arbitrage*, Institute of Finance Bulletin Nos. 74–75, New York University, May 1971.

of the probability that the merger will succeed, could purchase 375 shares of the proposed subsidiary for $2718.75. This long position would then be hedged by selling 100 shares of the parent short at $3000.00, with borrowed shares covering the short position. The spread of $281.25 (3,000.00 – 2,718.75) is the gross profit to be realized when shares are exchanged and the short position is cleared. The arbitrager will borrow the maximum possible amount to finance the long position, levering the return upward in the process.[17] Assuming that the merger occurs, rate of return will be sizable; if the talks collapse, on the other hand, serious loss will be realized. In either case rate of return is very sensitive to the period of time required to complete the transaction; unusual delay normally proves to be very costly.

BANKRUPTCY

The remaining firm-specific situation is corporate failure and bankruptcy. Failure encompasses a number of financial difficulties ranging from temporary insolvency through reorganization and liquidation. The probability of failure has too often been associated with small business operations but the collapse of Penn Central, W. T. Grant, and other large firms, and rumored difficulty encountered by still others, has recently increased investors' awareness in this respect. Since 1972 the SEC has identified corporations where the public accounting firm has given a qualified opinion because of reservations with respect to financial condition.

Two aspects of corporate failure are important to investors. In the first place, there is the question of the analysis and valuation of a company which is in serious financial difficulty. Second, there is the question of the predictability of failure. In many ways the second problem is more important than the first because recognition at an early stage can protect an investor from the severe losses which are certain to occur subsequently when failure becomes generally known.

In the case of extreme financial difficulty where creditor claims cannot be satisfied, settlement may occur on a voluntary basis or legal procedures may be invoked. In the latter case the court assumes responsibility for operation of the firm until it can be determined if survival is possible under a plan of reorganization of the capital structure. If reorganization is not viable, the company will be liquidated. In all these cases, in any realistic

[17] The New York Stock Exchange requires a 30 percent charge against capital (referred to as a "haircut") and a debt to capital ratio of 15 to 1 on the remainder of the long position. In this case $1784.17 (66 percent) of the $2718.75 could be borrowed:

Long position		2718.75
30 percent haircut	815.63	
15 to 1 ratio, (2718.75 – 815.63)/16	118.95	934.58
Borrowed capital		1784.17

sense, the "going-concern" model is no longer relevant. Under reorganization, debt and equity claims will be readjusted and the equity valuation model will no longer be appropriate until such time as normal operations are resumed. At that time historical data will be of doubtful relevance and the valuation problem will become similar in most respects to the new issues situation discussed earlier in this chapter. In the case of liquidation, exit values are relevant and these cannot be estimated externally. The book value of working capital is sometimes useful but book value in general is not. From the viewpoint of the equity investor, the issue is probably moot because very little will be realized upon liquidation after creditors have been paid.

A number of studies have been directed to the prediction of corporate failure.[18] Most of them focus on financial ratios which should provide an early warning of impending difficulty. In Figure 10.1, for example, mean ratios are shown for a sample of paired firms classified as "failed" and "nonfailed." Deterioration at least two years prior to failure is clearly evident for firms in the failed category; no such trend is found for the control group of nonfailed companies. The particular ratios shown in Figure 10.1 provide an accurate description of a company facing an increasingly dangerous problem with solvency: it has declining cash reserves; it generates an increasingly smaller flow of funds from operations; it borrows at an increasing rate to offset declining funds flow and curtailed credit; and, finally, it is unable to maintain the level of investment needed to continue normal operations.

The accounting ratios and measures which have been successfully related to instances of failure include the following, many of which are obviously interrelated or substitutes for others:

1. Profitability
   a. EBIT to total assets
   b. Net income to total assets
   c. Retained earnings to total assets
   d. Sales to total assets
2. Financial leverage
   a. Cash flow to total debt
   b. Debt to equity
   c. Debt to total assets
3. Liquidity
   a. Current ratio
   b. Working capital to total assets
4. Growth rate in total assets

[18] See William H. Beaver, "Financial Ratios as Predictors of Failure," *Empirical Research in Accounting: Selected Studies, 1966*, Supplement to *Journal of Accounting Research* (1966): 71–111; William H. Beaver, "Alternative Accounting Measures as Predictors of Failure," *Accounting Review*, January 1968, pp. 113–122; and Edward I. Altman, "Financial Ratios, Discriminant Analysis, and the Prediction of Corporate Bankruptcy," *Journal of Finance*, September 1968, pp. 589–609. An excellent summary of the literature is contained in Baruch Lev, *Financial Statement Analysis: A New Approach* (Englewood Cliffs, N.J.: Prentice-Hall, 1974), chap. 9, "The Prediction of Corporate Failure," pp. 133–151.

Figure 10.1
Selected Ratios (means)

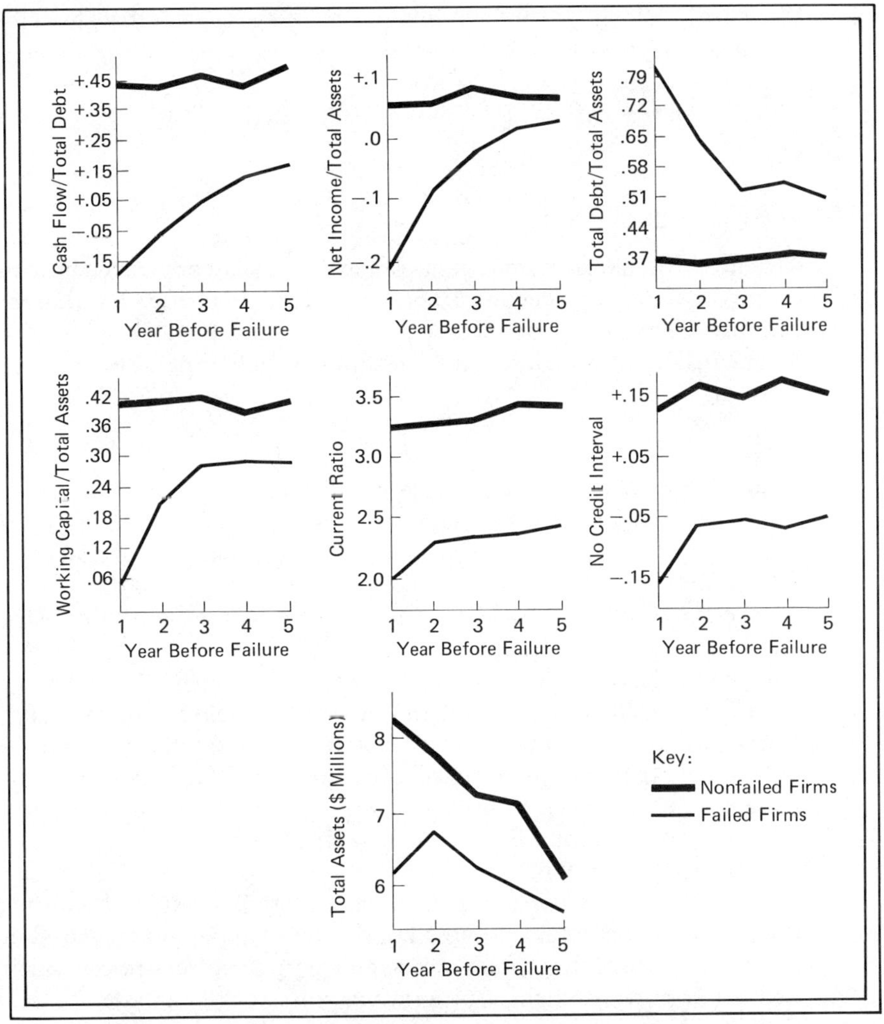

Source: W. H. Beaver, "Financial Ratios as Predictors of Failure," *Empirical Research in Accounting: Selected Studies, 1966*, p. 82.

Empirical studies have demonstrated that failed and nonfailed companies differ with respect to financial characteristics which can be measured. But this does not necessarily mean that any one of the several models can adequately *predict* failure.[19] Failure has been related to ratios but the more important issue is the use of ratios to forecast failure; this has yet to be

[19] See C. J. Johnson, "Ratio Analysis and the Prediction of Firm Failure," *Journal of Finance*, December 1970, p. 1168.

demonstrated. In addition, nonaccounting and qualitative elements should also be considered. Nonetheless, the contribution of the studies cited, and others as well, should not be minimized. They have provided impressive evidence that financial ratios deteriorate markedly well in advance of failure; accordingly, investors have been provided with a very useful tool for recognizing situations of potentially serious financial distress.

Market Response Elements

The price of a share of common stock may or may not be affected by a number of factors which are classified here, for want of a better term, as market response elements. These include market reaction to stock splits, exchange listing, insider transactions, and institutional trading patterns.

STOCK SPLITS

A stock split is an increase in the number of outstanding shares, usually through a proportional decrease in the par or stated value.[20] If 500,000 shares of a $10 par value stock sell for $80 per share, and the stock is then split 2 for 1, other things equal there would then be 1,000,000 shares of a $5 par value outstanding, each priced in the market at $40 per share. In theory a stock split provides no economic gain to the shareholder who remains in the same position relative to other stockholders after the new shares are issued. The aggregate market value should be the same although marketability of the shares may be improved. Nonetheless, some people have argued that the split itself will cause the price of the security to increase. Others have attempted to profit from a strategy of buying a security when a stock split is announced, on the assumption that the price will increase after the split takes effect.

Historically, stock splits have been most frequent in boom markets where security prices have soared but this trend apparently reversed in 1976 when a number of firms announced splits despite current prices which were well below previous highs. Corporations split stock in an attempt to attract individual investors who are seemingly discouraged from investing when share prices are too high.[21] When the composition of shareholders is broadened, the corporation is less sensitive to institutional transactions and it is less vulnerable to attack through a cash tender offer. Some corporations have announced splits as part of their marketing strategy: potential shareholders are viewed as prospective customers.

[20] Sometimes the capitalization is changed when a stock is split. For example, a $10 par value stock may be changed to no-par, no stated value at the time it is split.

[21] When a security sells for $80 per share, an investment of $8000 (plus transaction costs) is required to purchase a round lot. After a 4 for 1 split, only $2000 is required. Odd-lot commissions are slightly larger than commissions on round lots.

Figure 10.2
Stock Price Behavior (adjusted for market performance)

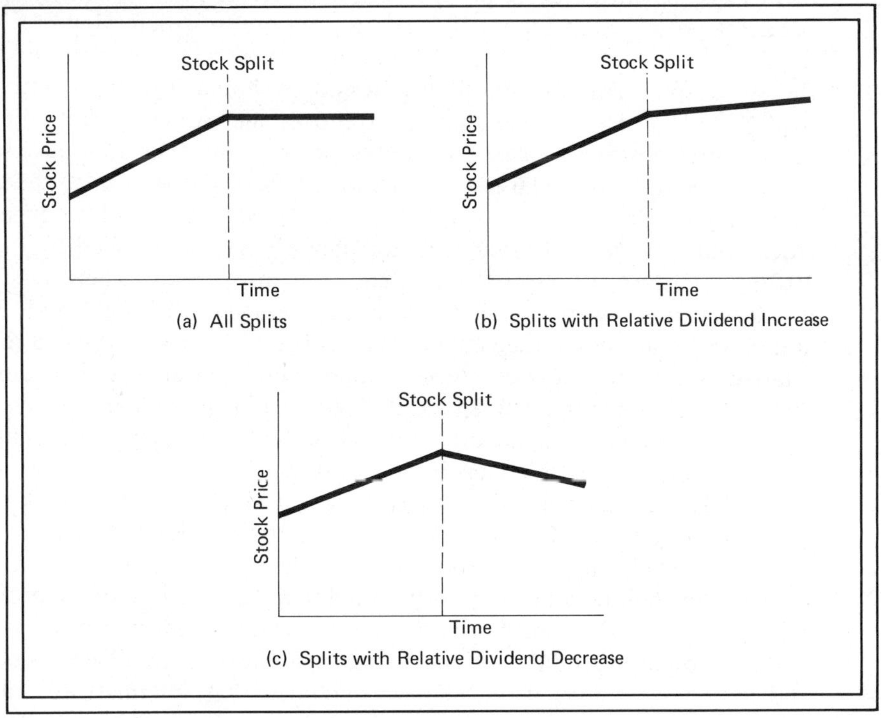

It is well known that market price tends to increase prior to the announcement of a stock split. This is shown in Figure 10.2(a) where the behavior of the price of a share of common stock, adjusted for general market performance, is represented both before and after a stock split is announced.[22] It is the preannouncement increase in price which suggests to some that anticipation of a split has a positive impact on value. But this overlooks the question of cause and effect. On one hand, price behavior may reflect the anticipation of a forthcoming split; on the other hand, however, price may react to underlying fundamental factors with the split no more than management's response to the increase in price.

When a stock split is announced it is not uncommon for an increase in dividends to be announced as well. Corporate managers are reluctant to

[22] Figure 10.2 is based upon empirical behavior observed by E. F. Fama, L. Fisher, M. C. Jensen, and R. Roll (FFJR), "The Adjustment of Stock Prices to New Information," *International Economic Review*, February 1969, pp. 1–21. In the FFJR study the horizontal axis is the cumulative average residual observed when the logarithm of return relative is regressed on a market index of performance. The behavior portrayed in Figure 10.7 is a simplification based upon their empirical work.

decrease dividends once they have been increased. For that reason the announcement of a dividend increase can be interpreted as evidence of management's assessment of future prospects. It is therefore possible that the price behavior portrayed in Figure 10.2(a) is a response to anticipation of a dividend increase. In that event there is no direct effect which is attributable to the stock split. This hypothesis was tested by Fama, Fisher, Jensen, and Roll (FFJR).[23] They found that the trend of increasing market-adjusted returns was positive at least 29 months prior to the split announcement; despite the fact that the largest returns were observed just prior to the split, this is far too long a time period to be explained in terms of an expected stock split. The general price behavior they observed is implied by Figure 10.2(a). FFJR then classified empirical data into groups where postsplit dividend changes were (1) greater than the average change for NYSE firms and (2) less than the average change. They observed market-adjusted return relatives for each of these categories and their data suggest behavior of the type shown in Figure 10.2(b) and 10.2(c). FFJR provide impressive evidence that fundamental factors, and not a stock split per se, account for the presplit behavior which has been observed.

FFJR also examined the return realized from purchasing a stock when a split is announced. They found no evidence to suggest that this will lead to systematically higher expected return although the monthly data they used, as they pointed out, are poorly suited to a complete test of the proposition. Hausman, West, and Largay tested the strategy with returns measured at the announcement date, the effective date, and over several periods before and after the effective date.[24] They concluded that systematically higher expected returns cannot be expected from the purchase of shares following the public announcement. But their data does suggest that knowledge of a forthcoming split, reached through information "leakage" or however, remains useful even if it is received as late as one month prior to announcement.

EXCHANGE LISTING

When the common stock of a corporation is listed on an organized exchange, shareholders benefit from increased marketability and the ready availability of a quoted market price. This raises the question of whether or not listing on the NYSE (or AMEX) results in a higher market price than the price that would have resulted if the security had been traded over-the-counter. It is difficult to construct a defensible economic rationale in support of a listing premium, but some financial writers have assumed that price does react favorably when shares are first listed.

[23] Ibid. Aside from the evidence provided with respect to stock splits, this is an extremely important paper in finance because it introduced a new empirical methodology which has since been used in hundreds of research efforts.

[24] W. H. Hausman, R. R. West, and J. A. Largay, "Stock Splits, Price Changes, and Trading Profits: A Synthesis," *Journal of Business*, January 1971, pp. 69–77.

One of the few studies which carefully examines the price impact of listing was published recently by Ying, Lewellen, Schlarbaum, and Lease.[25] These authors, using the methodology referred to in the preceding section where stock splits were discussed, provide evidence that listing does in fact influence security prices favorably. This effect is difficult to isolate because firms which meet the listing requirements described in Chapter 2 above have typically been successful with respect to growth and other fundamental valuation factors. Nonetheless, the price response observed in this study appears to be concentrated too closely to application and listing dates to be dismissed on the basis of that argument. The statistical evidence in this respect is not conclusive, and it cannot be assumed that systematic gains can be realized from a strategy of purchasing securities when listing applications are announced. At the same time, however, listing does appear to influence price favorably.

INSIDER TRADING

Corporate insiders have access to confidential information which affects the value of the firm before it is made public. In order to discourage the abuse of private information, Rule 10B-5 of the Securities Exchange Act of 1934 regulates trading in securities by corporate officers, directors, and beneficial owners, the latter referring to anyone who owns more than 10 percent of a company's outstanding stock. Over time the Securities and Exchange Commission has gradually extended the definition of an insider to anyone in a position to receive confidential information, including brokers and investment analysts. Under the law an insider who purchases and sells shares within six months is liable to the company for any profit which is realized. The courts have usually held that profits are recoverable without proof of intent to take advantage of private information and even when there is no proof of access to that information.

Ignoring situations where one specific piece of information is likely to affect market price seriously, insiders regularly trade in their own company's securities. Officers and directors are in a unique position to evaluate corporate prospects; their expectations, which can sometimes be inferred from their trading activity, is clearly of interest to analysts and investors. Inside transactions are reported to the Securities and Exchange Commission which then makes them public. Officers and directors are aware of the sensitivity of price to the transactions they execute and they will typically avoid unnecessary turnover. Nonetheless, there may be an opportunity to profit from an analysis of insider trading. While the evidence in this respect

[25] Louis K. W. Ying, Wilbur G. Lewellen, Gary G. Schlarbaum, and Ronald C. Lease, "Stock Exchange Listings and Securities Returns," *Journal of Financial and Quantitative Analysis*, September 1977, pp. 415–432. For an earlier paper which provides a different view see Richard W. Furst, "Does Listing Increase the Market Price of Common Stocks?" *Journal of Business*, April 1970, pp. 174–180.

is not conclusive, one study suggests that trading patterns can result in the occasional realization of unusual profit.[26] On balance, however, the prospect of any systematic pattern of excess return appears to be very limited.

LETTER STOCK

Insider transactions may be difficult to trace because they are often executed with unregistered shares, called *letter stock* or *Form 144 stock*, which a corporation issues privately. Corporations rarely disclose the number of shares of letter stock which are outstanding; they surface only when shareholders file Form 144 with the SEC in order to sell shares on the open market through a broker. By the time the SEC publishes the monthly summary of Form 144 filings, most of those shares have been sold. Shares of letter stock are usually issued to corporate officers and directors although institutional investors and others may acquire them in a private placement.

At one time the SEC ruled on every individual request to sell restricted shares unless they were registered for sale in a public offering. New regulations governing the sale of letter stock became effective on April 15, 1972. They require that shares must be fully paid for and owned for at least two years before they can be resold publicly; this rule was adopted in order to prevent firms from using letter stock to evade registration requirements. They also limit the number of shares that can be sold in any six-month period to either 1 percent of the number of shares outstanding or to the average weekly volume over a four-week period preceding the sale; this is designed to prohibit block sales which may depress the price of shares. Finally, they prohibit unusual solicitation of buyers and they require that adequate information concerning the corporation must be publicly available.

The potential impact of outstanding Form 144 stock is difficult to estimate but some indication of the widespread issue of unregistered shares was given during the period of market recovery early in 1975 when filings were received for more than 700 corporations.[27]

INSTITUTIONAL INVESTORS

The efficient market hypothesis will be explored in detail in Chapter 13. For the moment it can simply be noted that efficiency implies that the price of a security will change only in response to new information which alters risk-return expectations or because of a widespread change in investors' risk preferences. Security transactions alone would cause no price response because there would always be buyers and sellers who were willing to execute transactions at or near the equilibrium price. Market efficiency is an em-

[26] J. H. Lorie and Victor Niederhoffer, "Predictive and Statistical Properties of Insider Trading," *Journal of Law and Economics*, April 1968, pp. 35–53.

[27] See the "Heard on the Street" column, "Market Buoyancy Lures Unregistered Stock in Growing Amounts, SEC Filings Indicate," *The Wall Street Journal*, April 10, 1975.

pirical question which will be discussed at a later time. Nevertheless, there is little doubt that many members of the investment community are convinced that trading by large institutional investors does in fact influence the level of security prices.

The impact of supply and demand factors on the market price of common stock is a complex relationship but valuable insights are provided in two related papers published by Alan Kraus and Hans Stoll.[28] The first examines block transactions where a large number of shares are cleared in the normal course of business. Blocks were classified as those initiated by sellers, where the clearing price is less than the preblock price, and those initiated by buyers, where the block price is greater than the preceding price. Seller-initiated blocks were the more numerous in the sample; buyer-initiated blocks included a large number which were associated with mergers or acquisitions.

Kraus and Stoll observed the price behavior of securities involved in a block transaction and they attempted to distinguish between the information effect associated with market efficiency and the distribution effect associated with a limited number of sellers (or buyers) on one side of the market. Although their empirical results are difficult to interpret, as they are carefully detailed in the paper, the evidence provided does support the existence of a distribution effect for seller-initiated blocks. In the case of buyer-initiated blocks, price change apparently reflects adjustment to new information. On balance the empirical tests reported suggest an important institutional effect on price, at least in the short run, in block transactions.

The second paper studies the price impact of parallel trading where some group of investors are concentrated as either buyers or sellers. Parallel trading may reflect a variety of conditions ranging from chance behavior, through unintentional response, to a conscious decision to either "follow the leader" or to engage in manipulative activity. Based upon sample transactions for 229 institutions during 1968 and 1969, the evidence presented by Kraus and Stoll suggests that parallel trading, when it occurs, results from chance behavior. There is no implication of cooperative or collusive trading. On the other hand, when parallel trading does occur the authors found a positive relationship between trading and price behavior: parallel buying accompanied price increases and parallel selling accompanied price decreases. Observed price reversals in the following period suggest price response to the distribution effect. Taken together, the studies of block trading and parallel trading imply that institutional investors can exercise a significant influence on security prices in the short run.

[28] Alan Kraus and Hans Stoll, "Price Impacts of Block Trading on the New York Stock Exchange," *Journal of Finance*, June 1972, pp. 569–588, and "Parallel Trading by Institutional Investors," *Journal of Financial and Quantitative Analysis*, December 1972, pp. 2107–2138. Both studies were based upon research conducted as part of Securities Exchange Commission, *Institutional Investor Study Report of the Securities and Exchange Commission*, 92nd Congress, House Document No. 92–64 (Washington, D.C.: Government Printing Office, 1971).

Summary

This chapter considered some special extensions of the equity evaluation model. The first section focused on difficulties encountered when information is incomplete or unavailable. New issues of stock in the primary market were discussed and the hypothesis of systematic underpricing by underwriters was examined. Next, mergers and acquisitions were considered and special emphasis was directed to the questions of synergism and diversification. Bankruptcy was then discussed and the possibility of predicting corporate failure was reviewed.

The second section considered the impact of market elements on the price of a security. Market response to stock splits was analyzed and empirical studies were referenced which argue that a split, in the absence of other fundamental factors, is not a significant influence on share price. Other market elements which were reviewed were exchange listing, insider transactions, the regulation of unregistered stock, and the potential impact of institutional investors on share prices.

The next two chapters consider extensions of the analytical model from a different dimension. Convertible securities and warrants are analyzed in Chapter 11 and options and futures contracts are discussed in Chapter 12.

Questions and Problems

1. "Hundreds of corporate managers have decided to split the stock of their corporation; it follows, therefore, that some value must be realized from this activity and that value should be reflected in an increase in the market price per share." Evaluate this argument.
2. Assume that you wanted to test the hypothesis that new issue underwriters systematically establish prices which are too low in view of activity in the secondary market, particularly in periods of "hot new issues." How would you proceed?
3. It is widely assumed that portfolio adjustments by institutional investors have a significant effect on the market price of common stock. Why should this be true?
4. Westerly Corporation has annual earnings of \$500,000 with 1,000,000 shares outstanding; the price-earnings ratio is 30. Westerly has agreed to purchase Lightway Company in a stock-for-stock exchange at \$7.50 per share. Lightway has annual earnings of \$100,000, or \$1.00 per share, and it sells at a price-earnings multiple of 6. All values given are on an after-tax basis.
   a. What is the dollar amount and percentage of the premium offered to Lightway's shareholders to induce them to accept the offer? Does this value seem reasonable? Explain.
   b. What is the instantaneous merger profit in this case? Is the merger profit close to the maximum possible percentage in view of the premium paid? Explain.
   c. Assuming that the combined price-earnings ratio was unaffected by synergism, growth expectations, or any risk reduction through diversification, calculate the postmerger price-earnings ratio and price per share. Was this acquisition profitable for Westerly's shareholders? Explain.
5. In addition to the facts presented in the preceding problem, assume the following:
   a. Earnings growth for Westerly will be 7 percent and for Lightway it will be 12 percent. The earnings streams for the two operations are completely independent.

b. Westerly's dividend payout rate of 50 percent will continue whether the merger takes place or not.

c. Westerly's price-earnings ratio of 30 will be unchanged during the next year if merger negotiations should fail. If the merger succeeds, the market will increase the combined earnings multiple by 10 percent because of the perceived advantages of diversification. (1) Under the assumptions given, calculate the expected rate of return for the Westerly shareholders, using premerger price per share of $15 as the relevant price today. (2) Recalculate the rate of return to Westerly shareholders on the assumption that the merger did not take place. Was the merger profitable or not? Why? Explain carefully.

Selected References

FIRM STRUCTURE ELEMENTS

Altman, E. I., *Corporate Bankruptcy in America* (Lexington, Mass.: Heath, 1971).

Bear, Robert M., and Anthony J. Curley, "Unseasoned Equity Financing," *Journal of Financial and Quantitative Analysis*, June 1975, pp. 311–325.

Beaver, William H., "Financial Ratios as Predictors of Failure," *Empirical Research in Accounting: Selected Studies, 1966*, Supplement to *Journal of Accounting Research* (1966): 71–111.

Curley, Anthony J., "Conglomerate Earnings Per Share," *Accounting Review*, July 1971, pp. 519–528.

Ederington, Louis H., "The Yield Spread on New Issues of Corporate Bonds," *Journal of Finance*, December 1974, pp. 1531–1543.

Halpern, Paul J., "Empirical Estimates of the Amount and Distribution of Gains to Companies in Mergers," *Journal of Business*, October 1973, pp. 554–575.

Ibbotson, Roger G., and Jeffrey F. Jaffe, "'Hot Issue' Markets," *Journal of Finance*, September 1975, pp. 1027–1042.

Larson, Kermit D., and Nicholas J. Gonedes, "Business Combinations: An Exchange Ratio Determination Model," *Accounting Review*, October 1969, pp. 720–728.

McDonald, J. G., and A. K. Fisher, "New Issue Stock Pricing Behavior," *Journal of Finance*, March 1972, pp. 97–102.

Mead, Walter J., "Instantaneous Merger Profit as a Conglomerate Merger Motive," *Western Economic Journal*, December 1969, pp. 295–306.

Reilly, F. K., and K. Hatfield, "Investors Experience with New Stock Issues," *Financial Analysts Journal*, September–October 1969, pp. 73–80.

Shad, John S. R., "The Financial Realities of Mergers," *Harvard Business Review*, November–December 1969, pp. 133–146.

Stoll, Hans R., and Anthony J. Curley, "Small Business and the New Issues Market for Equities," *Journal of Financial and Quantitative Analysis*, September 1970, pp. 309–322.

MARKET RESPONSE ELEMENTS

Bar-Yosef, Sasson, and Lawrence D. Brown, "A Reexamination of Stock Splits Using Moving Betas," *Journal of Finance* 32 (September 1977), pp. 1069–1080.

Carey, Kenneth J., "Nonrandom Price Changes in Association with Trading in Large Blocks: Evidence of Market Efficiency in Behavior of Investor Returns," *The Journal of Business*, 50:4 October 1977, pp. 407–414.

Fama, E. F., L. Fisher, M. C. Jensen, and R. Roll, "The Adjustment of Stock Prices to New Information," *International Economic Review*, February 1969, pp. 1–21.

Friend, Irwin, Marshall Blume, and Jean Crockett, *Mutual Funds and Other Institutional Investors: A New Perspective* (New York: McGraw-Hill, 1970).

Hausman, W. H., R. R. West, and J. A. Largay, "Stock Splits, Price Changes, and Trading Profits: A Synthesis," *Journal of Business*, January 1971, pp. 69–77.

Johnson, Keith B., "Stock Splits and Price Change," *Journal of Finance*, December 1966, pp. 675–686.

Klemkosky, Robert C., "The Impact and Efficiency of Institutional Net Trading Imbalances," *Journal of Finance*, 32 (March 1977) pp. 79–86.

Kraus, Alan, and Hans Stoll, "Parallel Trading by Institutional Investors," *Journal of Financial and Quantitative Analysis*, December 1972, pp. 2107–2138.

______ and Hans Stoll, "Price Impacts of Block Trading on the New York Stock Exchange," *Journal of Finance*, June 1972, pp. 569–588.

Lev, Baruch, *Financial Statement Analysis: A New Approach* (Englewood Cliffs, N.J.: Prentice-Hall, 1974).

Lorie, James H., and Mary T. Hamilton, *The Stock Market: Theories and Evidence* (Homewood, Ill.: Irwin, 1973).

Rau, Randall K. C., "Resale of Restricted Securities Under SEC Rule 144," *Yale Law Journal*, July 1972, pp. 1574–1591.

Chapter 11

Convertible Securities and Warrants

This chapter considers the analysis of securities which are somewhat more complex than those discussed previously. These "hybrid" securities include convertible bonds, convertible preferred stock, and stock purchase warrants. Convertible securities are similar to other bonds and preferred stocks in the sense of a promised stream of interest or dividend payments, maturity or par value, and other features typical of those fixed-income securities. But they differ in one very important respect: convertible securities can be exchanged for common stock, at a predetermined exchange ratio, at the option of the investor. Similarly, warrants provide an opportunity to purchase common stock, at a predetermined exercise price, at the option of the investor. For this reason the value of convertibles and warrants depends, at least in part, on the expected value of underlying common shares. This chapter extends the analytical models of Chapters 5 through 9 to reflect the combination of value elements present in the case of hybrid securities.

The first section of the chapter examines convertible securities. Relevant features are defined and described and risk-return elements are analyzed. Valuation is discussed and the analytical model is adjusted to include the expected value of the convertible feature. The second section of the chapter considers the use and valuation of stock purchase warrants.

Convertible Securities

The investor in a convertible security has a fixed income claim in the form of interest payments, in the case of bonds, or promised dividends, in the case of preferred stock. At the same time, the conversion feature provides an opportunity to share in any appreciation in the price of the underlying common stock. The *conversion ratio* defines the number of common shares received for each preferred share or convertible bond. The product of the market price of the common stock and the conversion ratio gives the *conversion value.* When a convertible security is first issued, the difference between the market price of the convertible and conversion value of the common stock is referred to as the *conversion premium.* After issue, the conversion premium for bonds is generally referred to as the *premium over conversion value* to distinguish it from a second premium known as the *premium over bond value.* Premium over bond value is the difference between the market price of the convertible security and the estimated price of a bond similar in all respects except the conversion privilege. These definitions and relations are described algebraically in Table 11.1.

These features may be illustrated by the Del Monte Corporation convertible subordinated debenture $5\frac{1}{4}$s, issued March 1, 1969, and due March 1, 1994, with a conversion price of \$39 per share. Dividing the par value of the convertible (\$1000) by the conversion price provides the conversion ratio, \$1000/\$39 = 25.64. Upon conversion, cash would be paid in lieu of fractional shares. At the time this convertible security was issued, Del Monte's common stock was selling for \$33 per share. At that stock price, the conversion premium was \$1000 – (\$33 × 25.64) = \$153.85. For comparison with other convertible issues, the conversion premium is frequently expressed as a percentage of conversion value; in the case of Del Monte the original percentage conversion premium was 154/(1000 – 154) = 18 percent.

FEATURES OF CONVERTIBLES

Two important provisions of convertible securities are the terms of conversion and provision whereby the firm may call and retire outstanding issues. The conversion price of the convertible is always greater than the current market price of the stock at the time the convertible is issued. If a firm were to set the per share conversion price below the current market price, it would be, in effect, an issue of new stock at a discount. Existing stockholders would quite properly react negatively to such a practice. By setting the conversion price above the market price, a firm issues new stock indirectly and at a premium over the current market price. The terms of conversion, which are described in the indenture agreement along with all other terms and conditions of the issue, typically prohibit conversion for a period from six months to three years after issue. Long-term convertible bonds may also have a limit, generally ten years, on the time they are eligible for conversion;

Table 11.1
Common Expressions in Convertible Securities

Conversion ratio	$= F/P_c$
Conversion value	$= [F/P_c] \times P_m$
Premium over conversion value	$= V_m - [F/P_c] \times P_m$
Premium over bond value	$= V_m - V_B$

where

F = par (face) value of convertible issue
P_c = conversion price per share of common stock
P_m = current market price per share of common stock
V_m = current market value of the convertible security
V_B = estimated market value of convertible security without conversion privilege

approximately one-third of all convertible bonds carry this restriction. The conversion period is generally unlimited in the case of convertible preferred stock.

The conversion price may be set by the firm to increase at fixed dates in the future. A less common feature is to increase the conversion price as the actual percentage converted increases. Both of these stipulations induce the investor to convert when the market price of common stock is above the conversion price. A recent innovation is to issue securities with conversion prices dependent on future market prices. For example, Pan American World Airways convertible subordinated debenture $7\frac{1}{2}$s, issued January 17, 1973, and due January 15, 1998, became convertible into common stock after January 16, 1975, at a discount of 20 percent from the average price of the common stock in the ten-day period prior to commencement of the conversion period. This stipulation is subject to minimum and maximum conversion price constraints of \$7.00 and \$13.50 per share. Fortunately for the analyst, complexities have not proven to be popular with investors and variable conversion prices are very rare.

Convertible bond and preferred stock agreements provide for either a call price above par (face) value or a series of successively lower call prices as time passes. The call price feature allows the firm to redeem the issue at its discretion for what is usually a penalty cost of 3 to 10 percent above par value. Call provisions permit a firm to "force conversion" at any time provided that conversion value adequately exceeds call value. When this occurs, convertible security holders must exchange their securities for common stock or suffer a needless loss of investment value. Forced conversion is commonly attempted only when the conversion value is significantly above the call price and the issue has been outstanding for a period of five or more years. A firm that abuses the call provision by calling a convertible security shortly after issue or before its conversion value rises substantially above par value jeopardizes future convertible issues by alienating potential investors. The indenture agreement for most convertible issues also provides for a sinking fund, where an amount ranging from 3 to 10 percent of the issue is routinely redeemed at the stipulated call price each year, beginning five to ten years after issue. Call and sinking fund provisions add another element of uncertainty to the ownership of convertible securities.

SUPPLY OF CONVERTIBLES

Convertible securities, as previously noted, are perceived by the firm as a delayed common stock issue. Firms issue convertible bonds and preferred stock with the expectation that they will be converted into common stock sometime in the future. When converted, the firm is relieved of its fixed payment obligation and, in the case of bonds, no return of principal needs to be provided. Fixed interest or dividend payments are less than the amount that would be paid on the same security without the conversion privilege. In periods of tight money, convertibles may provide the only source of funds available at reasonable rates, even for the larger blue chip firms. The extent of convertible financing increases in periods where interest rates are rising and the spread between interest cost on straight debt and convertible debt is large.[1]

The dollar amount of convertible securities outstanding during October 1976, was $16.39 billion according to Standard & Poor's *Security Owner's Bond Guide.* Standard & Poor's survey covers about two-thirds of the total population of convertible bonds with the rest concentrated in very small and privately placed securities. Table 11.2 identifies the population of convertible bonds by industry, quality, and quantity, relative to new straight debt issues. During the late sixties through the early seventies, manufacturing firms accounted for the largest volume of new convertibles.

Convertible bonds usually have low quality ratings. According to the data in Table 11.2, 94 percent of all issues rated by Standard & Poor's had a classification of BBB or lower. This results, in part, because most convertible bonds are subordinated debentures with lower priority claims than other bondholders and mortgagers. According to Standard & Poor's, BBB rating "is bordering between definitely sound obligations and those where the speculative element begins to predominate." In the early- to mid-seventies, the volume of new convertible bonds relative to new straight debt fell sharply; the value of nonconvertible bond issues was steady to rising during this period. The sharp decrease in convertible issues resulted from the then depressed level of common stock prices. In most cases management believed that the conversion terms necessary for a successful issue were too generous to be of benefit to current stockholders and that the premiums which potential investors were willing to pay through lower interest rates were too small. Additionally, concern over possible defaults in municipal

[1] Robert R. McKenzie, "Convertible Debentures, 1956–1965," *Quarterly Review of Economics and Business*, Winter 1966, pp. 41–51.

Table 11.2

Summary Statistics of Convertible Bond Financing

By Industry[a]		*By Quantity*[b]			*By Quality*[c]	
Industry	*Total Proceeds 1966–1975 ($M)*	*Date*	*Total Issued ($M)*	*As Percentage of Straight Debt Issued*	*Grade*	*Number of Issues*
Manufacturing	10,531	1966	1,781	11.45	AAA	1
Mining	966	1967	4,409	20.08	AA	3
Utility	406	1968	2,947	16.95	A	20
Transportation	1,979	1969	3,927	21.40	BBB	72
Communication	647	1970	2,554	8.42	BB	126
Sales and consumer finance		1971	3,678	11.54	B	148
	80	1972	2,191	8.33	CCC and lower	57
Finance and real estate		1973	566	2.61	Not rated (and others)	163
	4,705	1974	482	1.53		
Commercial and other	4,560	1975	1,338	3.21		
Column total	23,874		23,873			

[a] Securities and Exchange Commission *Statistical Bulletin*, vol. 35, no. 9 (September 1976), p. 427.
[b] Ibid. and *Survey of Current Business* (various issues).
[c] Standard & Poor's *Security Owner's Bond Guide*, November 1976, pp. 177–XVI.

financing, real estate investment trusts, and other areas made investment bankers reluctant to bring speculative new issues to market. In the event of improved economic and market conditions during the late seventies, convertible securities should again increase in popularity.

EARNINGS ESTIMATION. The exchange of convertible bonds or preferred stocks for common stock may decrease the reported earnings per share of common stockholders. Assume that a firm issues $30 million of convertible debentures paying $6\frac{1}{2}$ percent interest. If the conversion price is $60 per share, total conversion will result in the issue of ($30 million/$60 per share) = 500,000 shares. If the firm has 1 million shares outstanding, no other debt, and expects before-tax earnings of $15 million at a time when the convertible is fully converted, the earnings per share reported immediately before and after conversion would be:

	Before Conversion	*After Conversion*
Earnings before interest and taxes	$15,000,000	$15,000,000
Interest expense (6 1/2 percent on $30 million)	1,950,000	
Before-tax profit	13,050,000	15,000,000
Taxes (total federal, state & local at 50 percent)	6,525,000	7,500,000
After-tax profit	$ 6,525,000	$ 7,500,000
Number of shares	1,000,000	1,500,000
Earnings per share	$6.525	$5.000

Per share earnings have been diluted by $1.53, or 23.4 percent, upon conversion of the debenture. The dilution is mitigated by the fact that interest payments are reduced; however, more income is exposed to taxes when interest payments are eliminated. This is not the case when convertible preferred stock is exchanged for common because preferred dividends are not deductible for tax purposes. More importantly, the proceeds of the convertible issue contributed to the level of earnings before interest and taxes; in the absence of funds provided by that issue, earnings per share would probably have been less than $5.00.

When convertible securities are outstanding, the calculation of earnings per share becomes a very difficult problem. The number of outstanding shares should be adjusted to include shares which will be issued in the future as a result of conversion. An adjustment should also be made to reflect the exercise of outstanding stock purchase warrants. Unfortunately, neither future conversions nor warrant purchases are known at any given time and it is necessary to make some assumption in this respect before calculating earnings per share. Accounting Principles Board Opinion No. 15 (1969) provides a very complicated set of procedures requiring "dual presentation" of EPS in which the most likely dilution is presented ("primary earnings per share") together with the most pessimistic estimate ("fully diluted earnings per share"). Convertibles and warrants which would *increase* earnings per share in any given year are classified as antidilutive and they are excluded entirely from the calculation for that year. Dilutive convertible securities are classified as common stock equivalents, for purposes of calculating primary EPS, if the market value *at time of issue* is judged to be derived largely from the underlying common shares; dilutive convertibles are always included for purposes of calculating fully diluted EPS. Dilutive warrants are included in both categories of the EPS dual presentation.

The complexity of the procedures required by APB Opinion No. 15 have resulted in confusion and controversy. The application of specific criteria set forth in the opinion can result in either the inclusion or exclusion of specific securities from year to year. As a result, a number of alternative procedures have been suggested but none have received general acceptance at this time.[2] In the interim, investors should be aware of the details and difficulties involved in reported earnings per share.

The investor in a convertible issue may face potential dilution of a different nature, although its occurrence would be rare. Dilution would occur if the firm declares a stock split or stock dividend which is smaller than those covered in the indenture agreement.[3] Assume that the indenture agreement calls for adjustment of the conversion price in the event of a stock split or stock dividend in excess of 8 percent. If the conversion price of a convertible debenture were $50 and the firm declared a 100 percent common stock dividend, the conversion price would become $25 and the investor's position would remain unchanged. But if the firm issued a 5 percent stock dividend, or a series of similar stock dividends, the debenture holder would suffer direct dilution of his or her investment by an equal percentage.

FORCED CONVERSION. When the common stock price increases sufficiently, a firm can force conversion by exercising the call provision on all or part of the issue. Investors in convertible issues with call provisions thus face the possibility of involuntary termination. Of 108 convertible debentures maturing after 1975 which were identified in Moody's Bond Survey of November 21, 1960, the number still listed had declined to 8 by mid-1970.[4] As shown in Table 11.3, half of all convertibles were called when the conversion value was 1.5 times the par value or higher. When an issue is fully or partially

[2] Werner G. Frank and Jerry J. Weygandt, "A Prediction Model for Convertible Debentures," *Journal of Accounting Research*, Spring 1971, pp. 116–126.

[3] Stanley A. Kaplan, "Piercing the Corporate Boilerplate: Antidilution Clauses in Convertible Securities," *University of Chicago Law Review*, Autumn 1965, pp. 1–30.

[4] J. E. Walter and A. V. Que, "The Valuation of Convertible Bonds," *Journal of Finance*, June 1973, pp. 713–732.

Table 11.3
Forced Conversion of 108 Convertible Issues

Ratio of Conversion Value to Par Value	*Number of Calls*[a]	*Percentage of Issues Called*
1.75 and over	68	20.5
1.50 to 1.75	30	30.0
1.10 to 1.50	103	25.1
1.00 to 1.10	42	14.3
Under 1.00	390	1.8

[a] Reflects the fact that most issues are only partially called at any one time. The large number of observations in the Under 1.00 category results from sinking fund calls.

Source: James E. Walter and Agustin V. Que, "The Valuation of Convertible Bonds," *Journal of Finance*, June 1973.

called, the firm sends a direct redemption notice to the owners of record. Interestingly, it has been estimated from the record of AT&T that from 0.1 to 3.8 percent of all convertibles are unconverted when called, resulting in a substantial loss of unrealized profits.[5] It is the investor's responsibility to initiate conversion when a convertible is called and the conversion value exceeds the redemption value.

When the market price of the common stock fails to rise above the conversion price within a reasonable period of time, outstanding convertibles are referred to as *overhanging issues.* Outstanding convertible issues may restrict a firm's ability to obtain additional capital. This can be especially serious for growth-oriented firms which frequently issue convertibles in connection with mergers and acquisitions.

THE PRICE OF CONVERSION

The value of the conversion privilege may be stated either in terms of a premium over bond (preferred) value or as a premium over conversion value. Unless investors believe that there is no chance that the common stock price will exceed the conversion price prior to expiration of the conversion privilege, the convertible security will sell at a premium with respect to the price of an otherwise similar bond or preferred stock without the conversion privilege. The higher the current market value of common stock relative to conversion value, the larger will be the premium over bond value. The straight bond or preferred stock value is commonly viewed as a "floor" value for the convertible security. This hypothetical straight debt value is not constant over time, because it varies inversely with market interest rates and it also shifts in

[5] A. B. Miller, "How To Call Your Convertibles," *Harvard Business Review*, May–June 1971, pp. 66–70.

response to changes in the overall riskiness of the firm. Downside protection offered by a convertible's floor value is greatest for firms with volatile common stock prices.

The nature of the relationship among these premiums can be observed by constructing a scatter diagram with premium over bond value on one axis and premium over conversion value on the other. Figure 11.1 demonstrates this relationship for a sample of convertible debentures of two different quality ratings. The curves identify an inverse relationship among the two premiums. When stock prices are far greater than conversion prices, premium over bond value is large because the convertible is priced on the basis of its stock equivalent. At these times investors pay little if any premium over conversion value since it would be lost if and when the firm forces conversion. Figure 11.1 demonstrates that higher quality convertibles have smaller premiums. This occurs because the common stock of high-quality firms enjoys greater market price stability and because of a possible tendency for these firms to force conversion at an early date.

Figure 11.1

Relationship Between Premium over Bond Value and Premium over Common Stock Value

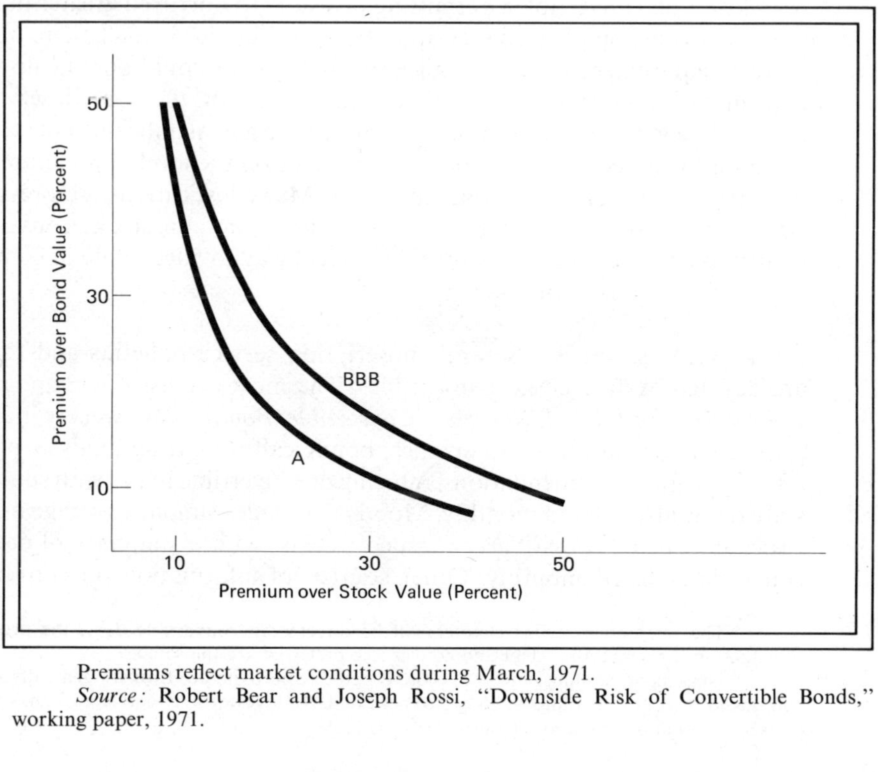

Premiums reflect market conditions during March, 1971.

Source: Robert Bear and Joseph Rossi, "Downside Risk of Convertible Bonds," working paper, 1971.

INVESTMENT ADVANTAGES OF CONVERTIBLES

The most attractive feature of convertible securities is that they permit investors to participate in corporate growth while maintaining a position which is protected against large losses, except in default.[6] Other features also affect the level of premiums which investors are willing to pay for convertible securities. One of these is the savings in transaction costs which results from purchasing a convertible instead of an equivalent amount of common stock. Under present negotiable rates, the commission on the purchase of 100 shares of stock selling for $50 per share ranges from $50 to $85; for a convertible bond for the same firm with an exercise price of $50, the commission on an equivalent amount of convertibles would be $30 to $45 (five bonds needed for 100 shares).[7] No transactions costs are incurred in the conversion process, which is accomplished by delivering the bond to the transfer agent designated by the firm in exchange for common shares. Another advantage is that the investor receives interest at the bond coupon rate from the purchase date to the date of sale or conversion. Interest payments are both larger and more stable than dividends on an equivalent amount of common stock.

Margin requirements for convertibles, as for common stock, are established by the Board of Governors of the Federal Reserve System. Currently no advantage exists because minimum margins for convertibles are equal to those for common stock. Historically, however, margin requirements have been lower on convertibles, permitting investors to borrow a greater portion of market value on pledged securities. Prior to March 11, 1968, there was no margin requirement on convertibles and individuals could borrow up to 90 percent of the convertible's market value. When the Federal Reserve announced new margin restrictions, an immediate and significant reduction in premiums resulted. A final important influence on the level of premiums has been the activity of institutional investors. Many institutions are prevented by law or corporate charter from purchasing common stock; convertible securities provide these investors with a legal way to participate in common stock price appreciation.

INFORMATION SOURCES. Several subscription service bulletins and reports are devoted exclusively to convertibles. The most extensive is Standard & Poor's *Standard Bond Reports—Convertible Bonds.* This weekly bulletin provides information on companies, bonds called, and an analysis of new offerings with recommendations. A listing of convertible issues with summary statistics is also offered monthly. Moody's provides similar coverage on new issues in *Moody's Bond Survey*, issued weekly, with a summary of data on convertibles listed monthly. Other sources of information on convertible

[6] The remainder of this chapter will be directed to convertible debt; the principles of valuation for convertible debt and convertible preferred are the same.

[7] Negotiable commissions make these figures approximate. Brokers generally charge commissions within the range of $6 to $10 per bond. An investor may find some banks willing to exercise bond orders at lower rates.

securities available on a subscription basis include Value Line's *Convertible Bond Service* and the R. H. M. *Convertible Bond Survey.*

VALUATION OF CONVERTIBLE SECURITIES

The valuation of a convertible bond is complicated because of its dual nature as partially debt and partially common stock. In addition, the conversion date may be determined by either the firm, assuming that conversion value exceeds the call price, or the investor; this increases the degree of uncertainty involved in the valuation process. Despite these complexities, however, the analysis of convertible securities can be structured in terms of the models developed previously for the evaluation of bonds and common stock.

BRIGHAM MODEL. Eugene Brigham developed a model of convertible value based upon conversion and straight bond values. The model is portrayed graphically in Figure 11.2. Recalling from Chapter 5 that ordinary bond value B_t at any time t is calculated by:

$$B_t = \sum_{t=1}^{n} \frac{I_t}{(1+y)^t} + \frac{B_n}{(1+y)^n}$$

for

B_t = market value of bond at time t
I_t = annual interest payments based on coupon rate and payment period
B_n = face value of bond at expiration date n periods from now
y = yield to maturity

Bond value depends upon the number of years to expiration, the anticipated movement in interest rates, and corporate risk. Brigham's model assumes no change in market interest rates or risk over time.[8] Conversion value depends upon investors' expectations of future stock value, which is stated in terms of the price of the stock when the convertible was issued, P_0, together with an assumed constant growth factor, g.

$$C_t = P_0\left(\frac{F}{P_c}\right)(1+g)^t \tag{11.1}$$

for

C_t = conversion value at time t
$\frac{F}{P_c}$ = conversion ratio (number of shares per convertible)

[8] This is true because B_t is a linear function of time to expiration. As portrayed in Figure 11.2, $B_t < F$ for all t prior to expiration date n; this implies a market yield-to-maturity which is higher than the coupon rate. But the assumption is illustrative and the model holds generally whatever the relationship of market rate to coupon rate.

Figure 11.2
Convertible Bond Valuation

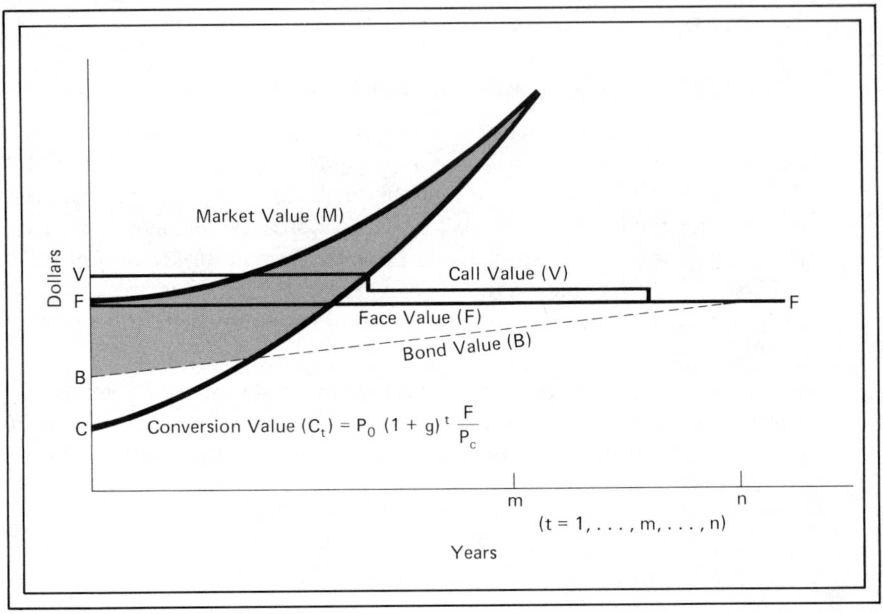

Source: Eugene F. Brigham, "An Analysis of Convertible Debentures: Theory and Empirical Evidence," *Journal of Finance*, March 1966, p. 37.

With a constant positive growth rate, conversion value rises over time. Call price, *V*, is shown in Figure 11.2 as decreasing in several steps. Line *BF* represents straight debt value which is the lower boundary, or floor, on the value of the convertible; ordinarily, the convertible should be valued at some higher market price, M_t. The shaded area represents the difference between market price and the greater of conversion or bond value. Thus the vertical distance in the shaded area measures the lesser of the premium over bond value or premium over conversion value. Typically, conversion value rises faster than market value, resulting in a decreasing premium over conversion value as time passes.

Market price of the convertible is portrayed by Brigham as intersecting conversion value at some time *m*, before the bond matures. Given any record of the firm's policy in calling convertibles, and its expected common stock growth rate, the investor can estimate the date of conversion *m*.[9] Defining *k* as the investor's required rate of return, the value of the convertible would then be determined by:

[9] See Eugene Brigham, "An Analysis of Convertible Debentures: Theory and Some Empirical Evidence," *Journal of Finance*, March 1966, pp. 35–54, for a more detailed development of the argument. Also see James C. Van Horne, *Financial Management and Policy*, 3d ed. (Prentice-Hall, 1974), pp. 373–375.

$$M = \sum_{t=1}^{m} \frac{I_t}{(1+k)^t} + \frac{C_m}{(1+k)^m} \tag{11.2}$$

for

M = present value of convertible
C_m = value of convertible when called[10]
k = investor's opportunity cost on investments of equal risk

The critical estimate in the Brigham model is the expected stock price at time m, which is determined by growth rate g. The difficulty of determining C_m and m, as well as the restrictive nature of some of the model's assumptions, have been noted by others.[11] Despite these limitations, however, the model is very useful in structuring the factors involved in the valuation of convertible securities.

BAUMOL-MALKIEL-QUANDT MODEL. In much the same manner as Professor Brigham, Baumol, Malkiel, and Quandt (hereafter BMQ) constructed a convertible valuation model which is dependent upon investors' expectations of future common stock prices.[12] At any given time, a convertible bond is worth the larger of either (1) its straight bond value plus the value of the conversion privilege or (2) its conversion value in common stock plus the insurance value of straight debt. Insurance value is the expected value of all instances where bond value is greater than conversion value. As the common stock price rises, and the expiration date nears, the probability that conversion value will be less than ordinary bond value becomes smaller and insurance value therefore approaches zero. This is consistent with the fact that premium over conversion value diminishes when conversion value becomes considerably greater than straight debt value. The value of the conversion privilege is the expected value of all instances where conversion value exceeds straight debt value. In this respect, Poensgen pointed out that straight bond plus conversion value and common stock plus insurance value are essentially equivalent valuation procedures.[13]

[10] The market value at the call date, M_m, equals conversion value C_m when g is large enough to make the conversion value exceed the face value prior to expiration. Otherwise, the call price determines market value and m equals the maturity date. The model assumes that the investor does not exercise before the call date, that there is no sinking fund, and that the conversion privilege does not expire prior to maturity.

[11] Van Horne, *Financial Management and Policy*, p. 391.

[12] W. J. Baumol, B. G. Malkiel, and R. E. Quandt, "The Valuation of Convertible Securities," *Quarterly Journal of Economics*, February 1966, pp. 48–59.

[13] O. H. Poensgen, "The Valuation of Convertible Bonds," Part 1, *Industrial Management Review*, Fall 1965, pp. 77–92. BMQ themselves noted this point in a footnote, ibid., pp. 55–56. In the same article, Poensgen argued that assuming a constant straight debt value would overstate (understate) the value of the conversion privilege if stock prices were positively (negatively) correlated. This is a logical argument, for when stock prices and bond prices move together there is less value in being able to switch from one to the other. Poensgen found no empirical correlation between bond and stock prices, which suggests that the BMQ formulation holds without modification.

The final form of the BMQ model is very similar to the Brigham model. Both view the value of a convertible as the present value of a stream of fixed payments and a terminal value which is dependent upon the expected stock price at that time. BMQ are vague as to the conversion date as well as the role, if any, which the firm plays in determining this date by exercising the call option. On the other hand, BMQ discussed the appropriate discount factor k in somewhat greater detail than Brigham did. They argue that this rate should be the yield to maturity if there is no premium over bond value; conversely, if there is no premium over conversion value, the investor's expected rate of return on equity is the proper discount factor. When the market value exceeds both the bond value and the conversion value, some rate between these two extremes would be appropriate.

CONVERTIBLE VALUATION MODEL

The Brigham and BMQ models are of limited usefulness in distinguishing among different convertible securities or in choosing between some particular common stock and a security which is convertible into shares of that same stock. Nonetheless, based upon the variables developed in those models, the convertible valuation model is a simple extension of the analytical models described in previous chapters. The major difficulty in using the convertible model arises because of the problem of estimating values for additional variables which are not relevant in the case of bonds, preferred stock, or common stock.

An approach to convertible bond valuation begins by recognizing that an investment in a convertible security is an indirect purchase of common stock. In the interim period from the date of purchase to the call date or conversion date, the investor receives a stream of interest payments in lieu of dividend payments (if any) together with an option to sell common at the conversion price. The premium over conversion value is the market's assessment of the value of the differential flows arising from purchase of the convertible instead of purchase of the underlying common shares. If the intrinsic value of the conversion privilege to an individual investor exceeds the market premium over conversion value, the convertible security represents a better opportunity than an equivalent purchase of common shares. For example, if a bond which sells for $1100 is convertible into 40 common shares which are quoted at $20 per share, the premium over conversion value is $300, [1100 − (20 × 40)]; if the intrinsic value of the conversion feature exceeds $300 for any particular investor, the convertible security should be purchased instead of 40 shares of common stock.

Unfortunately, the intrinsic value of the convertible feature is difficult to calculate, particularly because different discount rates may be relevant for each of the several flows involved. With respect to the interest-dividend differential, for example, the appropriate discount rate probably lies somewhere between the debt discount factor and the equity discount factor. In order to resolve the problem, it is necessary to specify the elements which determine the conversion premium.

VALUE ELEMENTS. Premium over conversion value depends upon benefits which reflect (1) safety resulting from the bond floor value, (2) transaction cost differentials, and (3) income stream differentials. The bond floor benefit can be viewed as a security option. Option valuation will be discussed in the next chapter but it can be noted here that the benefit arising from a floor value equals the present value of an option (put) which allows the investor to sell the conversion equivalent number of common shares for a price equal to the convertible par value at the time it matures. In practice the present value of such an option is likely to be small because similar protection can be obtained by entering a stop-loss order at the price which equates conversion value and straight debt value. For example, consider the case where a bond which is convertible into 50 shares of common stock sells for $1500 while the common stock sells for $28 per share. The convertible investor has a bond floor value—say, $1000—but the common stock investor does not. Nonetheless, the stock investor can enter a stop-sell order at $20 per share to protect a recovery value of $1000; the order can be placed for a modest cost.[14] For practical purposes, floor value protection is of little value when conversion value exceeds straight debt value; it is most valuable when conversion value is some amount in the range between debt value and par value.[15] For these reasons, the convertible valuation model defined below will exclude any benefit attributable to the floor value element.

Transaction cost and income stream differentials can be demonstrated by an example. For this purpose it will be assumed that a 6 percent bond which can be purchased for par value ($1,000) is convertible into 100 shares of common stock which are priced at $9.25 per share. A dividend per share of 12 cents per quarter is expected to remain unchanged into the foreseeable future; based upon fundamental analysis of the type described in Chapters 6 through 9, the price per share of common stock is expected to grow at an average rate of 7.2 percent per year. The brokerage commission is $5 per bond and $30 for 100 shares of stock; these rates are not expected to change materially in future periods.

In this case the transaction cost differential is $25 at the time of purchase of either the convertible bond or 100 shares of the stock. Assuming conversion and sale of the shares at some future time when the firm is able to force conversion, there is no terminal transaction cost differential because common

[14] A stop-sell order for the stock plus a simultaneous buy order for the bond would provide the stock investor with the same investment when and if the orders are executed.

[15] Several recent studies have suggested that investors recognize the limited value of the bond floor. Furthermore, if falling stock prices reflect an increasing likelihood of corporate insolvency, the bond floor value would also fall simultaneously. See R. L. Weil, Jr., J. E. Segall, and D. Green, Jr., "Premiums on Convertible Bonds," *Journal of Finance*, June 1968, pp. 445–463. Also see Weil, Segall, and Green, "Premiums on Convertible Bonds: Reply," *Journal of Finance*, December 1972, pp. 1163–1170.

stock commission rates are then relevant in either case. The interest-dividend differential based upon an investment in 100 shares of common stock is \$12 per year (\$60.00 – \$48.00) but it should be recognized that interest payments accrue daily and are paid semiannually while dividends are usually paid on a quarterly basis.

COMPARATIVE RATES OF RETURN. Continuing the example, comparative rates of return can be calculated for the two investment alternatives after the remaining variable, holding period m, has been estimated. The relevant period is the earlier of the date the bond matures or the date it is called, and estimation is therefore a difficult problem because most issues are called prior to maturity.[16] If the firm has established a consistent policy in this respect, the analyst's task is somewhat easier. Otherwise, the average behavior of firms might be used. Approximately half of the outstanding issues summarized previously in Table 11.3 were called by the time the conversion value was 1.5 times the par value; in the absence of better information, this value can be used to estimate the remaining period to forced conversion. Applying Equation 11.1 for a growth rate of 7.2 percent per annum:

$$1500 = 9.25(100)(1.072)^m$$

$$1.6216 = (1.072)^m$$

With the use of logarithms (or a hand calculator with present value functions),

$$m = \frac{\log 1.6216}{\log 1.072}$$

$$= 6.95 \approx 7$$

In this case the expected period to forced conversion is seven years.

The yield on an investment in common stock is a straightforward application of the security analysis model of Chapter 6. For 28 quarters (seven years), and adjusting the purchase price (\$925) and sale price (\$1500) of 100 shares by the common stock brokerage cost of \$30,

$$955 = \sum_{t=1}^{28} \frac{12}{(1 + r_s)^t} + \frac{1470}{(1 + r_s)^{28}} \tag{11.3}$$

$$\text{quarterly } r_s = .0259$$

$$\text{annual } r_s = .1077$$

The quarterly rate of return, 2.59 percent, was solved by applying the methodology described in Appendix 3A (Chapter 3); with quarterly compounding, the average annual rate is 10.77 percent.

[16] The investor's horizon may be shorter than this period. However, the premium at the end of the investor's horizon will depend on the income differential from that date through anticipated call or maturity, and these dates are therefore appropriate.

Yield on the convertible security, assuming conversion in seven years and a $5 purchase commission, is also a straightforward calculation; with semiannual compounding:

$$1005 = \sum_{t=1}^{14} \frac{30}{(1 + r_b)^t} + \frac{1470}{(1 + r_b)^{14}} \tag{11.4}$$

Semiannual $r_b = .0530$

annual $r_b = .1088$

Internal rate of return was again solved by application of the Chapter 3 methodology through use of Equation 3.8.

In the example given, expected yield on the convertible security (10.88 percent) exceeds expected yield on common stock (10.77 percent) by 11 basis points. But this does not necessarily indicate that the convertible is the preferable investment, for at least two reasons. First, the certainty of periodic payments is not the same in both cases. Bond interest payments are determined contractually but the dividend payment is a managerial decision subject to considerable uncertainty over any extended period of time. In the example given, a modest increase of 25 percent in the dividend stream, from 48 cents to 60 cents per share annually, would eliminate the interest-dividend differential. In view of the observed reluctance of firms to decrease dividends, common stock is probably the better choice in the particular example given above. In general, dividend rate variability must be evaluated in light of the actual differential between interest payments and expected dividend payments.

Second, the comparative analysis is very sensitive to the estimated period of forced conversion. Extending the previous example, assume that the *most likely* holding period is seven years, but the smallest is six and the longest is ten, based upon the analyst's projection of the distribution of common stock growth rates. Table 11.4 summarizes comparative annual yields under each of these assumptions, following the methodology of Equations 11.3 and 11.4. Preference for the convertible security clearly increases as the period to conversion increases. This is logical because the interest-dividend differential becomes more valuable as the holding period increases. In practice, judgment as to the merits of a convertible security relative to underlying

Table 11.4
Comparative Yields (annual compounding)

Annual Growth Rate	*Years to Conversion*	*Convertible Bond*	*Common Stock*
8.40%	6	11.86	11.91
7.15	7	10.88	10.78
4.95	10	9.13	8.78

Table 11.5
Margin Requirements (percentage of market value)

Period	*Margin Stocks (U, G, T)*[a]	*Margin Convertible (U, G, T)*	*Short Sales (T)*
11/6/63–3/10/68	70	—	70
3/11/68–6/7/68	70	50	70
6/8/68–5/5/70	80	60	80
5/6/70–12/3/71	65	50	65
12/6/71–11/22/72	55	50	55
11/24/72–1/2/74	65	50	65
1/3/74–	50	50	50

[a] Regulations T (brokers and dealers), U (banks), and G (others) are prescribed by the Board of Governors of the Federal Reserve System in accordance with the Securities Exchange Act of 1934. Regulation G and margin requirements for convertible bonds were adopted by the board effective March 11, 1968.

Source: Federal Reserve Bulletin, April 1977.

common shares cannot be exercised without a sensitivity analysis of the type illustrated in Table 11.4. Brennan and Schwartz argue that it is never optimal to convert an uncalled convertible bond except just prior to either a dividend date or an adverse change in conversion terms, or at maturity.[17]

The valuation elements discussed above are the major factors which affect the value of a convertible security. But other factors may also be important to investors at certain times; these include margin levels, tax liability, and risk characteristics. While their qualification is more subjective in nature, investors should be conscious of their role in valuation. The next paragraphs briefly describe these additional considerations.

MARGIN LEVELS AND TAXES. Margin requirements at the time of this writing are the same for convertibles and common stock. Historically, however, as shown in Table 11.5, margin levels were lower for convertibles than for common stock. The greater the difference between stock and convertible margin levels, and the greater the difference between borrowing rates and expected returns, the greater is the potential value of the margin differential for investors who are seeking leverage. When margin levels are equal, or when borrowing costs approach expected return which constrains borrowing in any event, margin differentials are not important.

Relative tax impact depends upon the investor's tax circumstances. For individuals, both interest and dividend income is fully taxable to all but tax-exempt investors, with the exception that the first $100 of dividends (up to

[17] Brennan, M. J., and E. S. Schwartz, "Convertible Bonds: Valuation and Optimal Strategies for Call and Conversion," *Journal of Finance*, December 1977, pp. 1699–1715.

$200 for married couples filing jointly) is exempt. For investors in high marginal tax brackets and for stocks with modest dividends, the interest-dividend differential resulting from convertible ownership poses a greater present value tax liability than the liability which accrues from directly owning the stock. For these investors, tax considerations reduce the relative attractiveness of convertible securities.

VARIABILITY. Even though a convertible security represents a delayed stock purchase, a difference in risk exists apart from the difference attributable to the respective income streams. When the premium over straight debt value is large, that is, when conversion value is high, a strong correspondence will be evident between changes in the value of the convertible and changes in the value of the common stock. But when conversion value is close to or below ordinary bond value, the relationship decreases because the convertible will be more sensitive to factors affecting interest rates and less sensitive to factors affecting stock prices directly. Investors with a portfolio of common stocks should favor a convertible security since its lower association with stock price movements would reduce the expected riskiness of all securities held when viewed as a group.[18] The reason for this expectation will be made more clear when portfolio management is discussed in Chapters 14 and 15.

Warrants

A stock purchase warrant is a corporate-issued negotiable certificate giving the bearer a contractual right to purchase the firm's common stock at a fixed price. Upon exercise, the investor exchanges the warrant plus cash equal to the exercise price in return for common stock. Popular in the 1920s, warrants fell from favor in the 1930s and they have only recently regained popularity among corporate issuers and investors. Warrants are most commonly issued with bonds as a "sweetener" to obtain lower interest rates and greater public acceptance of the bond offering. The investor receives both the bond and the warrants, which are generally detachable, allowing retention of one and sale of the other if so desired. In this sense an investor in a bond-plus-warrant package has a greater flexibility than an investor in convertibles.[19] Warrants may also be issued in connection with acquisitions and reorganizations or as partial compensation to underwriters in a new or

[18] J. E. Walter and A. V. Que, "Valuation of Convertible Bonds." They find that the average correlation between a sample of convertible prices and their related stock prices is .54. Their measure of market risk for convertibles averages two-thirds of the market risk of the corresponding common stock.

[19] Convertible debentures and bonds with warrants differ considerably with respect to the firm's capitalization. When an investor exercises a convertible, debt is exchanged for equity. The exercise of warrants results in the creation of new capital. See Van Horne, *Financial Management and Policy*, p. 381.

secondary issue of securities. Although it is rare, warrants may be issued without other securities to raise capital for the issuing firm.[20]

FEATURES OF WARRANTS

A warrant is an option to purchase stock. As a warrant holder, the investor has no equity rights in the firm, does not receive dividends, and does not have voting rights. The terms of the warrant are specified on the certificate. Provisions are made for the number of shares that can be purchased for each warrant, the exercise (purchase) price per share, and the expiration date of the warrant. Most warrants entitle the holder to purchase stock on a 1:1 ratio; that is, one share may be purchased per warrant. In the event of a stock split or a stock dividend, warrants are generally adjusted accordingly; investors should review these provisions carefully and should relate them to the observed behavior of the firm with respect to splits and stock dividends. Exercise price is always greater than current market price at the time the warrant is issued. This price may be fixed for the entire life of the warrant or (less commonly) it may be increased periodically. Expiration may be set for any date and, in a very few cases, warrants are perpetual; most warrants expire from five to ten years after they are issued.

Warrants are usually traded as over-the-counter securities but a modest number are traded on the NYSE and AMEX. When AT&T issued a \$1.57 billion bond-plus-warrant package in 1970, the New York Stock Exchange modified its listing requirements to allow trading of warrants. The AT&T offering expired in 1975 but by the end of 1974 a total of 66 warrants with a total market value of \$192 million were listed on the New York Stock Exchange.

THE RANGE OF WARRANT VALUES

Prices of warrants are subject to minimum and maximum limits. The minimum value of a warrant may be identified as:

$$\min(V_w) = \max \left| \begin{array}{ll} (P - P_e) \times N, & P > P_e \\ 0 \quad , & P \leq P_e \end{array} \right. \tag{11.5}$$

where

V_w = warrant value
P = current market price of the common stock
P_e = exercise price of the warrant
N = number of common shares per warrant: generally $N = 1$

[20] This may be a particularly attractive source of funds during inflationary periods. For a comprehensive survey on the value of warrants as a financing tool see S. Hayes, III, and H. Reiling, "Sophisticated Financing Tool: The Warrant," *Harvard Business Review*, January–February 1969, pp. 137–150.

Equation 11.5 states that a warrant will be worth *at least* the difference between the stock's market price and the warrant's exercise price; this will be the minimum value provided that the market price exceeds the exercise price. Arbitrage assures this minimum value because at any lower warrant price an investor could purchase and immediately exercise the warrant, realizing an instantaneous risk-free profit. For market prices equal to or lower than the exercise price, the minimum warrant value is zero. Generally, the actual market value of the warrant will be greater than the minimum value.

The maximum value of a warrant is:

$$\max(V_w) = P \times N \tag{11.6}$$

Maximum value is the value of the associated common stock; it will not be greater because the warrant offers no income potential beyond that provided by the growth of the common stock. Since warrant holders are not entitled to dividends, and because most warrants have finite lives, a warrant price at or near the maximum value is rare. Figure 11.3 describes these limits and it traces the price of a typical warrant over a wide range of common stock values, with all other factors held constant. The difference between the

Figure 11.3
Relation Between Maximum, Minimum, and Actual Warrant Value

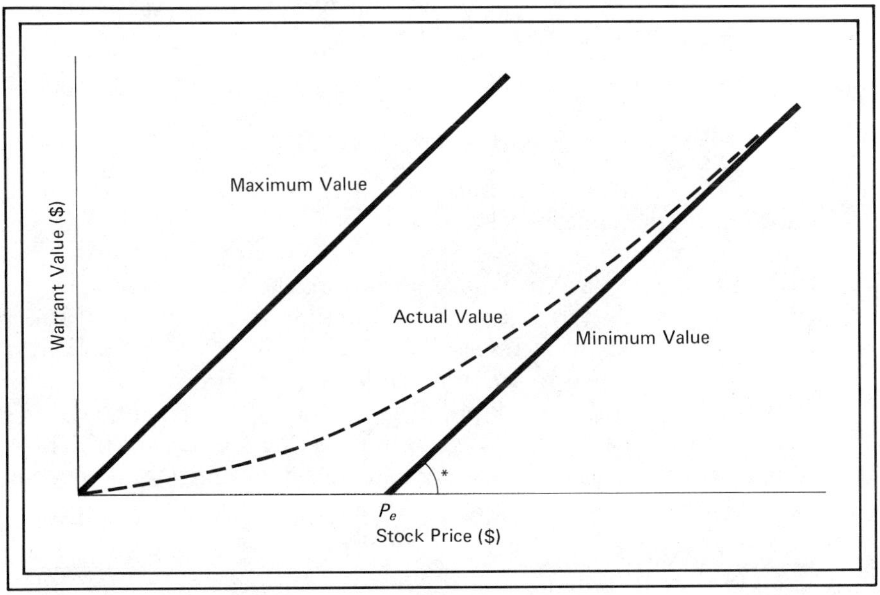

Slope depends on number of shares exchanged per warrant; if 1:1, slope = 45°.

actual price of a warrant and its minimum value is the premium over minimum value.

As the price of common stock rises above the exercise price of its associated warrant, the warrant approaches its minimum value. Thus premium over minimum value decreases and it ultimately vanishes as the price of the stock increases. In a recent study, John P. Shelton observed that this vanishing point occurs when stock price levels are about four times the exercise price of the warrant.[21] When the current stock price equals the exercise price, the warrant typically sells in the range of 25 to 55 percent of the price of the stock. The magnitude of the premium over minimum value for any given differential between stock price and exercise price depends on a number of interrelated factors. All these factors are inputs to the valuation process which determines the investor's expected rate of return. Time remaining to expiration, stock price volatility, and leverage provided by the warrant are the factors of primary importance. The following paragraphs will examine these elements more closely.

TIME REMAINING TO MATURITY. The value of a warrant and its premium over minimum value increase as the period remaining to expiration increases; that is, a warrant with five years to expiration is worth more than its four-year counterpart, and so forth. This results because growth potential and stock price volatility both increase with the passage of time. For a stock selling at $20 which has no dividends, and with an anticipated growth rate of 10 percent per year over the next five years, the expected stock price at the end of four and five years can be estimated by:

$$\hat{P}_4 = P_0(1 + \hat{g})^4 = 20(1 + .10)^4 = \$29.28$$

and

$$\hat{P}_5 = P_0(1 + \hat{g})^5 = 20(1 + .10)^5 = \$32.21$$

Since $\hat{P}_5 > \hat{P}_4$, a five-year warrant will be worth more than a four-year warrant with the same exercise price.

STOCK PRICE VOLATILITY. Unlike an investment in common stock, anticipated price volatility is a desirable feature for warrant holders. The more volatile the stock, other things equal, the more valuable the warrant is because loss is limited to the price of the warrant in the event of declining stock prices. For rising stock prices, in contrast, the warrant holder participates fully. Consider the case of a warrant expiring in one year which provides an option to purchase one share of common stock at $20. If it were known

[21] John P. Shelton, "The Relation of the Price of a Warrant to the Price of Its Associated Stock," *Financial Analysts Journal*, May–June 1967, pp. 144–146. Also S. T. Kassouf, "Warrant Price Behavior: 1945–1964," *Financial Analysts Journal*, January–February 1968, pp. 123–126. For the theoretical arguments see Paul A. Samuelson, "Rational Theory of Warrant Pricing," *Industrial Management Review*, Spring 1965, pp. 13–31.

with certainty that the stock price would be \$20 at the end of the year, the value of the warrant at expiration would be zero. But assume the following price expectations:

Probability	*Stock Price*	*Probability × Price*
$\frac{1}{3}$	\$15.00	\$ 5.00
$\frac{1}{3}$	20.00	6.67
$\frac{1}{3}$	25.00	8.33
		\$20.00

In this case the expected share price is also \$20, but the expected value of the warrant, since it cannot be less than zero, will be positive:

$$E(V_w) = \tfrac{1}{3}(0) + \tfrac{1}{3}(0) + \tfrac{1}{3}(\$25 - \$20)$$
$$= \$1.67$$

In both cases the expected stock price is \$20 but variability about that estimate results in a positive warrant value. If the stock price were more volatile, such that the investor perceived a $\frac{1}{3}$ probability of a \$10 price, a $\frac{1}{3}$ probability of a \$20 price, and a $\frac{1}{3}$ probability of a \$30 price, the warrant value would be \$3.34. Thus the value of a warrant increases, other things equal, with an increase in the dispersion of expected prices above the striking (exercise) price.

LEVERAGE. Warrants are a highly leveraged investment opportunity where leverage increases as the differential between exercise price and the current stock price increases. Unlike other leverage situations, warrants can be beneficial to investors in the event of either an increase or a decrease in the price of the underlying common stock. The nature and impact of leverage can be demonstrated by reconsidering a common stock selling at \$20 which has two warrants outstanding, identical in all respects except that one can be exchanged for a share of stock at an exercise price of \$15 and the other can be exchanged at \$25. Assuming that both are selling at a \$5 premium over minimum value, the price of the low-levered (\$15) warrant, by Equation 11.5, is (\$20 − \$15)(1) + \$5 = \$10; the price of the high-levered (\$25) warrant is (\$0)(1) + \$5 = \$5. If the stock price subsequently doubled, providing a 100 percent return to stockholders, the holder of the low-levered warrant would realize a \$15 profit [(\$40 − \$15)(1) − \$10];[22] since the warrant cost \$10, this is a rate of return of 150 percent. But with the same stock price movement, the buyer of the high-levered warrant would realize a profit of \$10, [(\$40 − \$25)(1) − \$5], which is a 200 percent return on a \$5 investment. On the other hand, if the stock fell by 50 percent to \$10, with little expectation that it would rise above \$15 prior to expiration, the low-levered warrant

[22] That is, (market price at exercise minus exercise price)(number of shares per warrant) minus price paid per warrant = profit.

would generate a $10 loss as opposed to a $5 loss for the high-levered warrant. The dollar return from the high-levered warrant would be less than the dollar return from the low-levered warrant only within the price range from $20 to $30.[23]

OTHER FACTORS AFFECTING WARRANT VALUE. In addition to duration of the option, stock price volatility, and leverage, several other factors may influence the value of a warrant. These include the opportunity cost of investment, the dividend policy of the firm, and the market in which the warrant is traded. Considering each in turn, the incentive to invest in warrants instead of common stock is greatest when alternative opportunities are numerous because purchase of a warrant represents a smaller dollar investment than the purchase of a corresponding number of common shares. On the other hand, because return on the warrant is limited to stock price appreciation, high dividend payments reduce the desirability of owning warrants relative to owning common stock. Finally, listing on a major exchange assures an investor of both liquidity and an immediate source of price information. Listed warrants therefore command smaller premiums over minimum value than unlisted warrants. The influence of listing, as well as the impact of other factors which were discussed, has been substantiated empirically as well as theoretically.

EVALUATION OF WARRANTS

The value which an investor places on a warrant depends on both the expected stock price and the investor's required rate of return. Assume for a moment that an investor envisions the distribution of future stock prices represented by Figure 11.4. The exercise price of the hypothetical warrant is denoted by P_e; P_{max} is the investor's estimate of the highest possible stock price up to the time the warrant expires. All previously unexercised warrants would necessarily be exercised on the expiration date, provided that the stock price then exceeds the exercise price. If the stock price at expiration is less than the exercise price, outstanding warrants become worthless. Thus the expected value of all possible outcomes having positive value, shown by the shaded area of Figure 11.4, is found by

$$E(V_w) = N \sum_{P_e}^{P_{max}} (P - P_e) f(P) \tag{11.7}$$

where $E(V_w)$ is the expected warrant value, P represents all possible stock prices in the range $P_e \leq P \leq P_{max}$, and $f(P)$ is the probability that price P will actually occur. The number of shares of stock available per warrant is given by N.

[23] On a rate of return basis, the low-levered warrant would be preferred to the high-levered warrant over the range of future stock prices between $15 and $35.

Figure 11.4
Expected Stock Price Distribution Given the Expiration Date of Warrant

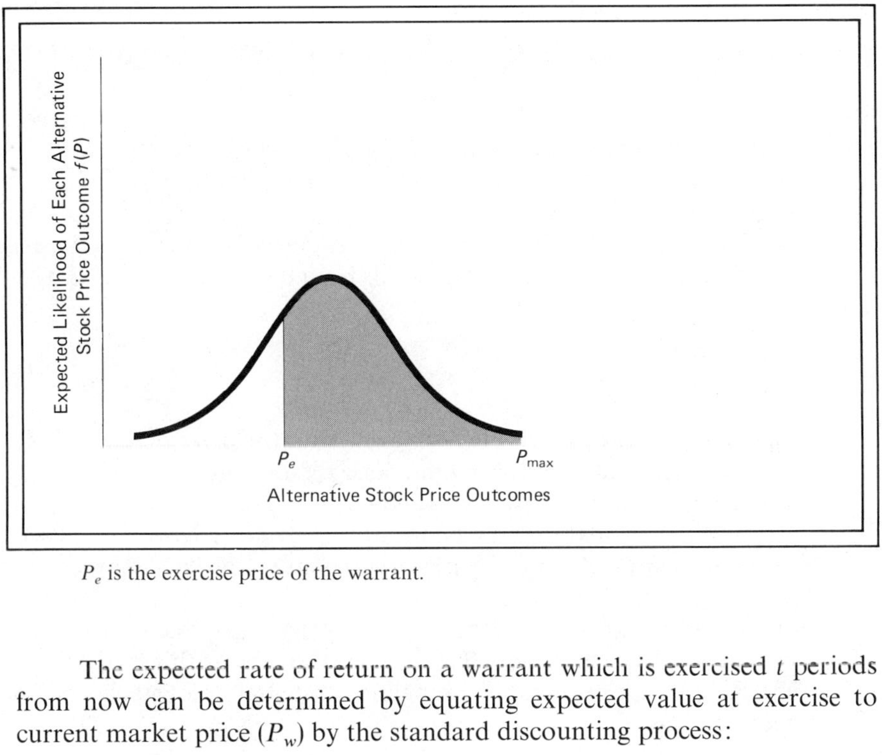

P_e is the exercise price of the warrant.

The expected rate of return on a warrant which is exercised t periods from now can be determined by equating expected value at exercise to current market price (P_w) by the standard discounting process:

$$P_w = \frac{E(V_w)}{(1 + r)^t} \tag{11.8}$$

Since no interim (dividend) payments are received, only the terminal value of the warrant must be considered. The relevant time horizon is generally taken to be the warrant's expiration date unless the investor has serious reason to believe that the warrant should be exercised sooner. Upon exercise, an investor realizes the minimum warrant value identified in Equation 11.5. Since warrants typically sell at a premium to minimum value, early exercise may result in a partial loss of investment.[24]

Under many circumstances a complete analysis of warrant value must incorporate taxes and transaction costs. This will be the case whenever alternative investments have significantly different tax rates and transaction costs. To receive expected warrant value $E(V_w)$ at its expiration date requires an investment amounting to the current market price of the warrant P_w

[24] This loss could be avoided by a strategy of selling instead of exercising the warrants combined with a market purchase of the common stock. However, this subjects the investor to two transaction charges, compared to none if the warrants are exercised.

plus transaction costs T.[25] The difference between $E(V_w)$ and $(P_w + T)$ is subject to income tax at some percentage rate t_x. For warrants held less than 12 months, tax liability is calculated at the investor's marginal rate; both warrants and stocks are taxed as capital gains when held in excess of 12 months. Allowing for transaction costs and taxes, Equation 11.7 becomes

$$E(V_w') = (1 - t_x)[E(V_w) - (P_w + T)] + P_w \tag{11.9}$$

The expanded first term on the right-hand side represents the net dollar return to investment while the remaining term represents the return of investment.

The period after tax rate of return r, implied by receiving an expected amount $E(V_w')$ at a future date t periods from the present, is found by solving as before:

$$P_w + T = \frac{E(V_w')}{(1 + r)^t} \qquad [(11.8a)]$$

Comparing implied rate of return r with the investor's required return determines the advisability of purchase; if the implied return equals or exceeds the required return, the warrant should be purchased.

Warrant valuation may be illustrated by considering the purchase of either 100 shares of XYZ Corporation or an equivalent number of shares through purchase of outstanding warrants. The stock is currently priced at \$30 per share and the 50 cent annual dividend is expected to remain unchanged in the near future. The warrants expire in three years, at which time the investor believes the probability distribution of stock prices is best represented as:

Probability	*Stock Price* (P)	
.10	\$20	
.10	25	
.20	30	
.25	35	$E(P) = f(P) \times P$
.15	40	
.10	45	$= \$34.75$
.10	50	

Each warrant, currently selling for \$3, may be exchanged for one share of XYZ stock at an exercise price of \$30. The investor expects to pay taxes at effective marginal rates of 30 percent on ordinary income and 15 percent on capital gains. Transaction costs are 2 percent of stock value and 5 percent of warrant value because of a sliding commission scale.

[25] Commissions on warrants are the same as commissions on common stock selling at the same price as the warrant. Since a warrant is exercised by presenting it directly to the firm or its transfer agent, no commission is incurred upon exercise. Total transaction costs on the indirect purchase of stock through warrants is therefore cheaper than direct stock purchase, provided that warrants are selling below their maximum theoretical value.

It will be assumed that the investor requires a 10 percent after-tax return on XYZ common stock. In determining a required return on warrants, the hypothetical investor notes that possible dollar gains, gross of tax and transaction costs, favor stock only by the amount of dividends. Possible dollar losses, on the other hand, are greater for the stock than the warrant, since loss on the warrant is limited to the purchase price. In percentage terms, however, possible gains or losses from warrant investment are both much larger because of the leverage provided. Considering different return possibilities and their relationship to other securities in the portfolio, differences in the level of invested capital, liquidity, and the availability of price quotations for the warrants, the investor is assumed to demand a warrant return of at least 15 percent in contrast to the 10 percent return required on the firm's common stock.

Recalling the basic common stock valuation model of Equation 6.18, the implied after-tax rate of return on XYZ stock, assuming sale in three years, and ignoring quarterly compounding for simplicity, is:

$$30.00(1.02) = \frac{.7(.50)}{(1+r)} + \frac{.7(.50)}{(1+r)^2} + \frac{.7(.50)}{(1+r)^3} + \frac{34.75(.98) - .15[34.75(.98) - 30.00(1.02)]}{(1+r)^3}$$

Solving for r provides $r = .0316$. The implied rate of return on the purchase of the warrants is (from Equation 11.8a)

$$P_w + T = \frac{E(V_w')}{(1+r)^t}$$

and since, by Equation 11.7,

$$E(V_w) = 1\left[\sum_{P=30}^{50} (P - 30)f(P)\right] = 4.75$$

Equation 11.8a becomes

$$3.00(1.05) = \frac{4.75(.95) - .15[4.75(.95) - 3.00(1.05)]}{(1+r)^3}$$

Solving again for r yields $r = .110$.

Since both implied returns are less than the respective required returns of 10 and 15 percent, they should be rejected. Given the investor's assumed circumstances and beliefs regarding future stock price performance, neither the warrant nor its associated stock is attractive at current market prices.

Summary

This chapter has reviewed the investment characteristics of corporate-issued convertible securities. At the date of issue, convertible bonds are essentially a fixed-income security with a conversion privilege, but both the issuing firm and investors typically regard this type of bond as a deferred equity issue. Traditional analysis treats a convertible as part debt and part equity. While this approach clearly identifies all features of convertibles, it falls short of providing an adequate basis for valuation. By viewing convertibles as deferred equity, all relevant features of fixed-income securities are captured and translated in terms compatible with the basic valuation model.

By attaching warrants to bond issues, firms are provided with an alternative source of equity capital. In some cases warrants represent a separate security unconnected with other financing instruments. In either case warrants are a distinct type of hybrid security. They are easier to analyze than convertible securities because their value is derived solely from characteristics of the common stock and they are not subject to forced conversion. This chapter discussed the range of a warrant price relative to an underlying stock price, and the normal behavior pattern within that range was also considered. Finally, the valuation process was examined; no fundamental difference exists between the warrant valuation model and models used to analyze other types of investments.

The next chapter discusses stock options and futures contracts. In many applications these investments involve low rather than high degrees of risk, and their valuation may proceed in a manner very similar to the processes developed in this and earlier chapters.

Questions and Problems

1. Why might an investor consider a convertible bond over either straight debt or the common stock of a firm?
2. Identify the critical factors in evaluating the worth of a convertible security and the degree of certainty which an investor may reasonably be expected to have about each.
3. During June 1975, ITT issued a 10 percent debenture due in the year 2000 and also an $8\frac{5}{8}$ convertible subordinated debenture due 2000 and convertible into common stock at a price of $25\frac{3}{8}$. Both issues are traded on the NYSE. On December 10, 1976, the debenture traded at $109\frac{3}{4}$ to yield 9.5 percent. The convertible debenture traded at $133\frac{3}{4}$ and the stock closed at $33\frac{5}{8}$.
   a. Assuming that there is no premium over conversion value, how many shares of stock would be expected in exchange for one bond? Is a zero premium over conversion value a fair assumption?
   b. Actually, the conversion value of the convertible issue may be calculated directly. Do so, and then determine what you think would happen to the market value of the convertible should the company announce its intention to call the issue at 107.
   c. What would be the likely trading range of the convertible should the stock price rise to \$50 per share or, alternatively, fall to \$20 per share?
4. Future Shock's $8\frac{1}{2}$ convertible debentures due ten years hence are currently selling for \$1220. The debentures may be exchanged for 50 shares of common stock at any time up to maturity. Commissions run \$10 per convertible and \$36 per 100 shares of stock. Current market price of the stock, which pays a \$0.50 per share annual dividend, is \$22. Based on company analysis, it appears reasonable to expect a common stock growth rate (without reinvestment) of 11 percent over the next five years,

with a lower rate around 8 percent thereafter. The current rate of interest on straight debt of like quality is 8 percent. Recently, Future Shock forced conversion of another convertible when it traded at 1.75 times its par value. Provide an estimate of the conversion date and the expected annual return to holding (a) the convertible and (b) the common stock up to the expected conversion date. Which appears to be the better buy?

5. In the above problem if the investor thought conversion (at 1.75 times its par value) could occur as soon as two years, but also believed that the stock could conceivably fall below the level where conversion is profitable and remain depressed for ten or more years, what then is the range of return possibilities for the convertible? What range is implied for the common stock?
6. Explain the nature of the relationship between expected stock price volatility and the market value of a warrant. Why is volatility "good" instead of "bad"?
7. What limits are there on the range of warrant prices? Explain why these limits exist.
8. During December 1975, the Occidental Petroleum warrant traded for 6 and the stock for $14\frac{3}{4}$. The warrant permits purchase of one share of stock at $16\frac{1}{4}$ until expiration on April 22, 1980.
   a. What return on Occidental Petroleum's stock would cause the warrant holder to just "break even" upon exercise?
   b. By December 1976, Occidental Petroleum's stock was selling for $22\frac{1}{2}$ and the warrant for $9\frac{3}{8}$. Calculate the one year price relative for each and comment on the results.
   c. Based on the 1975 and 1976 prices quoted above, what appears to have happened to investors' beliefs regarding Occidental Petroleum's common stock?

Selected References

CONVERTIBLE SECURITIES

Bacon, Peter W., and Edward L. Winn, Jr., "The Impact of Forced Conversion on Stock Prices," *Journal of Finance*, December 1969, pp. 871–874.

Baumol, William J., Burton G. Malkiel, and Richard E. Quandt, "The Valuation of Convertible Securities," *Quarterly Journal of Economics*, February 1966, pp. 48–59.

Brennan, M. J., and E. S. Schwartz, "Convertible Bonds: Valuation and Optimal Strategies for Call and Conversion," *Journal of Finance* 32:5 (December 1977), pp. 1699–1715.

Brigham, Eugene F., "An Analysis of Convertible Debentures: Theory and Some Empirical Evidence," *Journal of Finance*, March 1966, pp. 35–54.

Frank, Werner G., and Jerry J. Weygandt, "A Prediction Model for Convertible Debentures," *Journal of Accounting Research*, Spring 1971, pp. 116–126.

Ingersoll, Jonathan, "An Examination of Corporate Call Policies on Convertible Securities," *Journal of Finance* 32 (May 1977), pp. 463–478.

Jennings, Edward H., "An Estimate of Convertible Bond Premiums," *Journal of Financial and Quantitative Analysis*, January 1974, pp. 33–56. Also "Reply: An Estimate of Convertible Bond Premiums," *Journal of Financial and Quantitative Analysis*, June 1975, pp. 375–376.

Kaplan, Stanley A., "Piercing the Corporate Boilerplate: Antidilution Clauses in Convertible Securities," *University of Chicago Law Review*, Autumn 1965, pp. 1–30.

Liebowitz, Martin L., "Convertible Securities," *Financial Analysts Journal*, November–December 1974, pp. 57–67.

Miller, Alexander B., "How to Call Your Convertibles," *Harvard Business Review*, May–June 1971, pp. 66–70.

Pinches, George E., "Financing with Convertible Preferred Stocks, 1960–1967," *Journal of Finance*, March 1970, pp. 53–64.

Poensgen, Otto H., "The Valuation of Convertible Bonds," Parts I and II, *Industrial Management Review*, Fall 1965 and Spring 1966, pp. 77–92 and 83–98.

Soldofsky, Robert M., "Yield-Rate Performance of Convertible Securities," *Financial Analysts Journal*, March–April 1971, pp. 61–65.

Vinson, Charles E., "Pricing Practices in the Primary Convertible Bond Market," *Quarterly Review of Economics and Business*, Summer 1970, pp. 47–60.

Walter, James E., and Agustin V. Que, "The Valuation of Convertible Bonds," *Journal of Finance*, June 1973, pp. 713–732.

Weil, Jr., Roman L., Joel E. Segall, and David Green, Jr., "Premiums on Convertible Bonds," *Journal of Finance*, June 1968, pp. 445–463. Also "Premiums on Convertible Bonds: Reply," *Journal of Finance*, December 1972, pp. 1163–1170.

WARRANTS

Bierman, Jr., Harold J., "The Cost of Warrants," *Journal of Financial and Quantitative Analysis*, June 1973, pp. 499–504.

Hayes, III, Samuel L., and Henry B. Reiling, "Sophisticated Financing Tool: the Warrant," *Harvard Business Review*, January–February 1969, pp. 137–150.

Kassouf, Sheen T., "Warrant Price Behavior 1945–1964," *Financial Analysts Journal*, January–February 1968, pp. 123–126.

Merton, Robert C., "The Theory of Rational Option Pricing," *Bell Journal of Economics and Management Science*, Spring 1973, pp. 141–183.

Miller, Jerry D., "Effects of Longevity on Values of Stock Purchase Warrants," *Financial Analysts Journal*, November–December 1971, pp. 78–85.

Parkinson, Michael, "Empirical Warrant-Stock Relationships," *Journal of Business*, October 1972, pp. 563–569.

Rush, David F., and Ronald W. Melicher, "An Empirical Examination of Factors Which Influence Warrant Prices," *Journal of Finance*, December 1974, pp. 1449–1466.

Samuelson, Paul A., "Rational Theory of Warrant Pricing," *Industrial Management Review*, Spring 1965, pp. 13–31.

Shelton, John P., "The Relation of the Price of a Warrant to the Price of its Associated Stock," *Financial Analysts Journal*, May–June and July–August, 1967, pp. 143–151 and 88–99.

Stone, Bernell K., "Warrant Financing," *Journal of Financial and Quantitative Analysis*, March 1976, pp. 143–153.

Turov, Daniel, "Dividend Paying Stocks and Their Warrants," *Financial Analysts Journal*, March–April 1973, pp. 76–78.

Van Horne, James C., "Warrant Valuation in Relation to Volatility and Opportunity Costs," *Industrial Management Review*, Spring 1969, pp. 19–32.

Chapter 12
Forward Pricing

This is the second of two chapters devoted to the discussion of financial claims other than equity and debt. The previous chapter considered investments deriving value from the *firm's* obligation to convert them into common stock; this chapter deals with security options and commodity futures, two financial claims created in the market place by *investors*. The value of these claims depends upon the expected value of the underlying stock or commodity for which they may ultimately be exchanged. Each claim will be defined and its economic purpose and benefits will be identified. In addition, the similarities among these claims and equity ownership, and not their differences, will be stressed. Specifically, the basic principles of valuation will be used to provide a logical framework for analyzing the value of forward contracts.

In general a forward contract is an agreement between two parties to exchange some good, claim, or service at a specified place and later time for an agreed price. Forward pricing results through the establishment, at the time a contract is made, of the fixed price which determines the value of the contract at a later date. Warrants, convertible bonds, and convertible preferred stock, as well as security options, are examples of forward pricing.[1]

[1] Less formalized examples of forward pricing are commonplace; among these are magazine subscriptions and mail order services.

Warrants and convertibles are issued by firms which initiate option contracts in conjunction with new financing or financial reorganization. Security options and commodity futures originate in the private sector as secondary claims. In essence, these claims facilitate risk bearing by providing flexibility, diversification, liquidity, and risk transfer among segments of the investment community.

Examples of forward pricing have been found in the history of ancient Greece and Rome. The development of modern forward markets can be traced through European origins, beginning in Venice around the tenth century and developing into centralized markets by the fifteenth century. The history of forward pricing can also be traced in India and Asia. Futures trading is an open, competitive form of forward pricing with a central auction market which insures (1) a large number of buyers and sellers, (2) free entry and exit, (3) a standardized, homogeneous product, (4) full information to all participants, and (5) an exchange mechanism which assures investors of liquidity and which eliminates problems of legal recourse. Although forward trading had become quite sophisticated following the establishment of the Royal Exchange in London in 1570, modern futures trading actually evolved at the Chicago Board of Trade during the Civil War.

Today, futures trading is most commonly associated with primary commodities such as grains, livestock, and metals. In response to the recognized advantages which centralized auction markets provide in dealing with uncertainty, security options, mortgages, interest rates, foreign exchange futures, and commodity futures are now traded centrally on major exchanges. The first section of this chapter considers the operation of security option markets and option valuation. The second section provides a parallel presentation for commodity futures together with a brief discussion of other types of futures markets.

Security Options

Security options are agreements between two parties exchanging the right to buy or sell common stock at a later date for an agreed price. The agreed price is known as the *striking price.* The established striking price will be close to the market price in effect at the time the option agreement is reached. The buyer of the option pays the writer (seller) a premium for selling the option. The premium is a dollar amount which generally ranges between 5 and 30 percent of the market value of the underlying common stock.

The most common forms of security options are puts, calls, and straddles. A put gives the buyer the right to deliver (sell) to the writer a specified number of shares, generally 100, of a certain stock at any time on or before the expiration date of the option. The buyer of a put profits, and the writer loses, if the market value of the stock falls below the striking price by an amount exceeding the premium. A call provides the buyer with the opposite opportunity, the right to receive delivery of shares at any time within the option period at the striking price. The buyer of a call profits if the market value of the stock when the call is exercised exceeds the striking price by more than the premium. A straddle is a combination of a put and a call, giving the buyer the right to either receive or deliver stock at the exercise price. If the price of the stock fluctuates sufficiently, the buyer may exercise both the put and call portions of the straddle. Hybrid forms of security options are also occasionally available, but they represent a very small portion of all options traded.[2]

The life or duration of an option contract is one of three variables which influence investment value. Security options can be written for periods as short as 27 days but they are more commonly written for periods as long as one year. The trend in recent years has been toward options of longer duration. The other two variables are the striking price and the premium. The premium is the compensation the buyer pays to the writer for making the option available. The amount of the premium depends upon expectations of writers and buyers with regard to price behavior of the stock, the life of the option, and the relationship between the striking price and current market price.

Buyers and writers of security options face distributions of returns similar to those shown in Figure 12.1. Returns from buying options are subject to greater dispersion than returns from writing because only the premium is paid by buyers; writers must invest a larger proportion of capital as margin. Margin required of option writers, unlike stock margins, is simply a good faith cash deposit held by brokers to insure performance of the writer's obligations. Since premiums paid by buyers are smaller than the margins deposited by writers any given change in stock price has a greater impact on the buyer's return on invested capital. A writer's return is limited to the total amount of the premium received and this maximum is realized when the option expires without being exercised. Losses, on the other hand, are limited only by the maximum possible adverse price movement of the common stock within the option period. Buyers, in contrast, face possible outcomes ranging from total loss of premium to gains bounded only by the largest possible favorable stock price movement.[3] Slightly less than half of all outstanding options expire unexercised; approximately half of those which are exercised result in a loss for the buyer when the cost of the premium is considered.

[2] These are spreads, straps, and strips. A spread, which is similar to a straddle, consists of a separate put and call option on the same stock. The difference is that in a spread the striking price of the put is lower than the striking price of the call. A strap is a combination of two calls and one put, and a strip is a combination of two puts and one call. Each of these variations of of the standard security option accounts for less than one percent of all option contracts actually executed.

[3] The relationship between stock price changes and returns to investment strategies utilizing options in whole or in part is examined in the appendix to this chapter.

Figure 12.1
Return Distributions to Buying and Writing Options

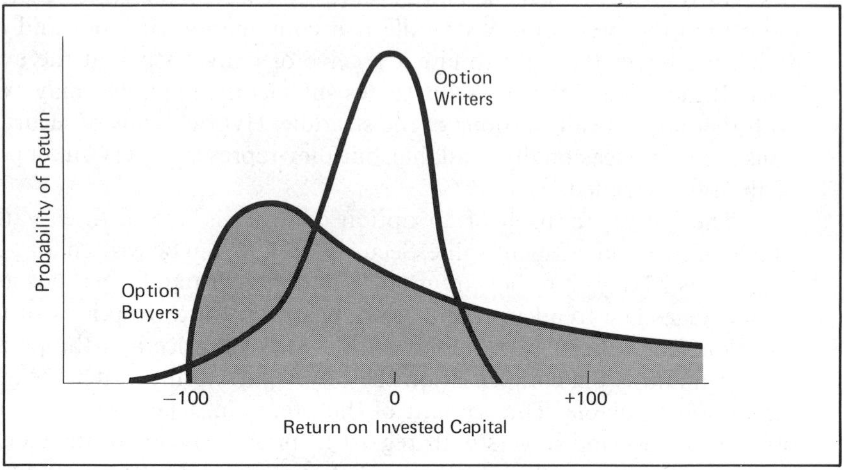

MECHANICS OF OPTION TRADING

Until recently all security option contracts were traded through a decentralized procedure similar to the purchase and sale of over-the-counter securities. In addition to buyers and writers, this option market requires several specialized activities which are provided by brokers. Some brokers deal in these services exclusively. Beginning in 1973, however, this "unlisted" market for security options was supplemented with the introduction of trading on major exchanges. A complete discussion of option exchanges will be provided shortly but one difference between listed and unlisted options should be noted at this point. The dollar value of dividends paid on stock during the option period is subtracted from the exercise value for unlisted options. If a broker-arranged unlisted put or call carries a striking price of $50.00 per share, and the stock pays a dividend of $0.50 per share, the striking price, in effect, is adjusted to $49.50. Thus dividends benefit the buyers of unlisted calls and the writers of unlisted puts. Listed options are not adjusted for dividends paid during the life of the option.

BROKERS AND DEALERS. For unlisted security options, trading is accomplished through brokers and dealers who specialize in option transactions. There are currently about two dozen of these firms and they are represented by their own trade organization, the Put and Call Dealers Association. They are financial intermediaries who bring together buyers and writers; in most cases, they will purchase an option from writers before they have located a buyer. Dealers are willing to make a market in any stock traded on the New York Stock Exchange. For intermediary services provided, the writer pays a commission that averages 12 percent of the gross premium paid by the buyer.

Two other intermediaries receive a portion of the premium paid by the buyer for an unlisted option. These are the buyer's broker and the writer's broker; each receives about 1 percent of the gross premium paid. The writer's broker, a New York Stock Exchange member firm, acts as the endorser. The endorser guarantees the writer's performance if the option should be exercised and handles the actual receipt or delivery of the stock on behalf of the writer. The endorser requires the writer either to provide a minimum of 30 percent cash margin, based on the market value of the stock, or to keep the optioned stock on deposit with the broker in case of a call. Either (1) a 25 percent cash margin or (2) maintenance of a short sale position is required in the case of a put.

PROFITABILITY OF OPTION TRADING

Numerous studies have attempted to measure the profitability of security option trading.[4] Unfortunately, some findings have been contradictory and possibly misleading. Two serious problems are common to most studies. First, the decentralized nature of option trading in the past prevented the development of a reliable data base. Second, security options have been considered separately from other investments and not as an integrated part of a total investment strategy.

Despite these shortcomings, some findings are of interest. First, writers appear to face a fair game, meaning that on average they break even before considering taxes; considering the potential tax and the portfolio advantages of options, writers' overall return is positive.. Also, writers appear to fare better with shorter duration options. A second observation is that options buyers generally face a negative before-tax expected return. Of the alternative types of options, puts have been the least rewarding to buyers. This is due in part to the role of dividends which are paid by the buyer of unlisted puts through the lowering of the striking price. Investors' reluctance against short selling together with difficulties involved in arranging short sales transactions have also been suggested as contributing factors to the poor performance of purchased puts. These conclusions result from studies of unlisted options prior to the opening of a centralized option market. Information and transaction costs are higher in unlisted markets and data scarcity and accuracy, as noted previously, are difficult problems. The impact of the

[4] Richard J. Kruizenga, "Profit Return from Purchasing Puts and Calls," in *The Random Character of Stock Market Prices*, ed. Paul H. Cootner (Cambridge, Mass.: M.I.T. Press, 1964), part IV, pp. 392–411. A. James Boness, "Some Evidence on the Profitability of Trading in Put and Call Options," ibid., pp. 475–496. Richard Katz, "The Profitability of Put and Call Option Writing," *Industrial Management Review*, Fall 1963, pp. 55–69.

centralized market structure on the pattern of option returns remains to be resolved.

A PORTFOLIO PERSPECTIVE. The observation of negative option returns, on average, would not necessarily imply a lack of rationality on the part of investors. Investors may believe that a small chance of a large gain more than compensates for a large chance of a small loss in terms of personal satisfaction. Alternatively, an investor may take an option position to hedge another type of investment. For example, an investor holding a stock for capital gains may be concerned with the probability that price will decrease in the short run; the purchase of a put would provide insurance against any price decline and failure to profit on the put would not mean that it failed to serve its purpose.

A comprehensive study by Malkiel and Quandt stressed the necessity of considering options in the context of the investor's total portfolio of securities.[5] By conducting an extensive series of computer simulations, each portraying a certain set of assumptions regarding market positions, actions, and preferences of the investor in conjunction with the price behavior characteristics of the underlying security, they studied the importance and role of options in a general market context. Malkiel and Quandt find that some form of option position is almost always desirable as part of an investment portfolio. This conclusion holds for all investor attitudes toward risk, investment decision criteria, and stock price distributions when transactions costs and taxes are fully considered.

OPTION EXCHANGES

Despite the general desirability of option trading, the volume of option transactions has historically been very small relative to the volume of stock transactions. Option volume averaged only 1 percent of New York Stock Exchange volume until recently. While a general lack of knowledge and legal restrictions against institutional trading account in part for the small volume of option trading, the basic impediment has been the absence of a central market place.[6] The first central market for options began on the Chicago Board of Trade, a major commodity futures exchange, in April of 1973; this market operates under the name of the Chicago Board Options Exchange (CBOE). Trading was initially limited to calls written on the most actively traded New York Stock Exchange securities such as American Telephone & Telegraph, RCA, and Xerox. A second market for listed call options

[5] B. G. Malkiel and R. Quandt, *Strategies and Rational Decisions in the Securities Option Market* (Cambridge, Mass.: M.I.T. Press, 1969).

[6] Some states do not allow certain financial institutions to engage in options trading. Others are restricted by their corporate charters or by the policy of management. Tax-exempt institutions are restricted by the Internal Revenue Service. The IRS considers premiums received to be taxable income which cannot exceed 10 percent of total income without jeopardizing the institution's tax-exempt status.

opened in January, 1975, on the American Stock Exchange and listings on several regional exchanges followed. In June of 1977 trading in puts began on CBOE and four other exchanges. While it is too early to judge the permanent acceptance of these markets, the centralized pricing mechanism and resale opportunity provided to both buyers and writers, as well as lower transaction and information costs, has greatly increased the use of options. CBOE trading volume in 1975 reached the level of 4–6 million per day, about 25 percent of the trading volume on the New York Stock Exchange. When the SEC approved the American Stock Exchange's request to trade call options, the cost of a seat on the exchange more than doubled.

CENTRALIZED MARKET OPERATION. A central market place simplifies and standardizes the option agreement. Options for a stock listed on an exchange come due at specific times throughout the year. A prospective buyer or seller (writer) selects the due date closest to the desired duration. An investor who wanted to write a six-month call on Upjohn early in April, for example, would take a short position (sell) in the October Upjohn call listed on the exchange. If the writer subsequently wanted to liquidate the position, an offsetting purchase would be made. The second transaction cancels the first, and the investor would be out of the market. The mechanism is the same for a buyer: an initial purchase is offset by a subsequent sale.

Every listed stock option has a fixed striking price.[7] Variation in the value of a listed option as the price of the underlying stock changes is reflected in the level of the quoted premium. As with stock prices, the latest premium indicates the price of the last transaction. Premium rises as the stock price increases and it falls as the stock price falls. Since listed options can be exchanged for the underlying common stock, arbitrage assures a proper parity between the levels of premiums and stock prices. An option exchange provides the advantage of professional floor traders who assure liquidity and fair pricing through arbitrage of any unwarranted differentials between option premiums and stock prices.

SECURITY OPTION VALUATION

Many interrelated factors influence the premium a buyer must pay relative to the value of the underlying stock. The most important factors are anticipated change in the price of the stock and the anticipated price variability during the option period. As the option period lengthens, the anticipated change in price and the variability of that estimate both increase. Similar to stock warrants, the greater the anticipated stock price variability, the more desirable the option contract is to the buyer. This occurs because a

[7] The striking price is changed periodically in accordance with major movements in the stock price. This keeps premiums for new option contracts within a reasonable trading range. Outstanding option contracts remain in effect at the original striking price but trading in these contracts may be done only for liquidation.

buyer is indifferent to the magnitude of change in the price of a stock when that change is contrary to expectation; in no case will the buyer lose more than the premium originally paid.

Additional factors are commonly believed to affect the level of option premiums. Options written on lower priced stocks are thought to command a higher percentage premium than options written on higher priced stocks under the assumption that option buyers prefer to commit only small dollar amounts of capital to any given transaction. High trading volume and a small number of shares outstanding are also believed to be beneficial to the buyer and options on such stocks are presumed to carry higher percentage premiums. High trading volume is believed to enhance predictability, making a stock more responsive to general market trends. A small supply of stock allegedly provides a larger price response to any given piece of new information affecting company operations.

Malkiel and Quandt formulated these beliefs into a testable hypothesis of relative option value.[8] Gathering information on a total of 167 three-month stock options written during 1964–1966, they performed a cross-sectional regression analysis of relative levels of option premiums. Their model for call premiums was

$$\frac{C}{P} = \underset{}{a_0} + \underset{(+)}{a_1 V} + \underset{(-)}{a_2 S_1} + \underset{(+)}{a_3 S_2} + \underset{(+)}{a_4 g} + \underset{(-)}{a_5 P} \tag{12.1}$$

where C is the call premium paid, P is the market price of the stock when the option is written, V is a measure of stock price variability, S_1 and S_2 are measures of the number of shares outstanding and share turnover, respectively, and g represents the anticipated growth rate in the price of the stock. Malkiel and Quandt's model consistently explained approximately 75 percent of the variability of option premiums. The most important independent variable was stock price variability. Over the three-year period all variables were statistically significant and they had the expected sign as indicated under the coefficients in Equation 12.1.

A MODEL FOR OPTION EVALUATION

The principles illustrated in Chapter 11 for valuing warrants apply to other forms of security options with only minor alterations. The model for warrant valuation was

$$E(V_w) = \sum_{P_e}^{P_{\max}} (P - P_e) f(P) \qquad [(11.7)]$$

[8] Malkiel and Quandt, *Strategies and Rational Decisions*, pp. 26–31.

where $E(V_w)$ is the expected warrant value, P represents all favorable stock price outcomes, and $f(P)$ is the probability that each favorable outcome P will occur. A favorable outcome is a stock price which is higher than warrant exercise price P_e.

CALLS. The duration of market-created options is generally shorter than the life of a warrant. Thus the factors to be considered by the investor emphasize short-run predictions but the format of the valuation model remains the same. For unlisted calls the model is

$$E(V_c) = 100 \sum_{P_e - D}^{P_{max}} (P + D - P_e) f(P) \tag{12.2}$$

The expected call value is $E(V_c)$. Since security options are transacted in units of 100 shares, per share price and dividends are multiplied by 100 in Equation 12.2. The option striking price is denoted by P_e and D represents per share dividends. Dividends are added for unlisted options because the striking price is adjusted by the value of any dividends paid. The model shows that a call has value if the market price of the stock exceeds the adjusted striking price $(P_e - D)$ at the time the option is exercised. No adjustment for dividends is made in the case of listed options. Thus the valuation of listed calls becomes:

$$E(V_c) = 100 \sum_{P_e}^{P_{max}} (P - P_e) f(P) \tag{12.2a}$$

These formulations are appropriate when the investor's time horizon equals the life of the option.[9]

The expected value of a call specified by Equation 12.2 does not consider the investor's tax circumstances t_x or transaction costs T and it does not identify the investor's status as a buyer or a writer. A call buyer invests an amount equaling the premium M plus transaction cost T. Tax liability is incurred on the portion of the value of the call which is profit to the investor as opposed to return of investment. A buyer's cash outflow is

$$I_B = M + T \tag{12.3}$$

and expected after-tax cash inflow is

$$E(V_c') = (1 - t_x)[E(V_c) - I_B] + I_B \tag{12.4}$$

[9] Since investors may select from alternative option durations, this assumption is made throughout. Listed options provide continuous resale opportunity prior to expiration. They will therefore carry a market premium above the value implied by Equation 12.2a owing to the potential for increased value between date of resale and expiration. This premium will decrease as expiration nears.

To qualify for capital gains, the buyer should sell an option held at least one year to a third party rather than exercise it personally. The Internal Revenue Service considers the profit on exercised options to be based on the holding period of the stock instead of the option. If the call is exercised rather than sold, the buyer would have to hold the stock for at least one year to qualify for the capital gains rate.

For a call, the expected period return would be found by solving

$$I_B = \frac{E(V_c)}{1 + r} \quad \text{for } r = \text{before-tax return} \tag{12.5}$$

and

$$I_B = \frac{E(V_c')}{1 + r'} \quad \text{for } r' = \text{after-tax return} \tag{12.5a}$$

If the expected rate r' is equal to or greater than the rate which the investor requires on an investment possessing the risk characteristics of the call, purchase is recommended.

Consider the situation of an investor contemplating the purchase of a listed call on AT&T which is being offered for a premium of $475; the current market price of AT&T is $54, and the call carries a striking price of $55. On this option, the investor is assumed to require an expected return of 20 percent after taxes. An assessment of AT&T has convinced the investor that future stock price outcomes are best estimated by the subjective probability distribution described by columns A through C in Table 12.1. From the calculations shown in Table 12.1, the expected value of the call is found to be $562.50. Assuming that the investor faces a 20 percent capital gains tax,

Table 12.1
Statistics for Call Valuation Example

(A) *Stock Price Interval* ($)	*(B)* *Average Price in Interval* ($)	*(C)* *Probability of Price* ($)	*(D)* *Call Value at Price* ($)	*(E)* *Expected Call Value* ($)
Below 55.00	—	.300	0.00	0.00
55.00–60.00	57.50	.300	250.00	75.00
60.00–65.00	62.50	.200	750.00	150.00
65.00–70.00	67.50	.100	1250.00	125.00
70.00–75.00	72.50	.050	1750.00	87.50
75.00–80.00	77.50	.025	2250.00	56.25
80.00–85.00	82.50	.025	2750.00	68.75
	Total	1.000		562.50

and assuming a \$30 transaction cost, the expected after-tax return is found by solving Equation 12.5a for r':

$$475.00 + 30.00 = \frac{(1 - .20)(562.50 - 505.00) + 505.00}{(1 + r')}$$

$$1 + r' = 1.091$$

The rate of return found to be approximately 9.1 percent is below the required rate and the call would not be purchased.

The writer of a call is also concerned with its expected value. The writer's required investment will differ from that of the buyer, as will the writer's circumstances and expectations, in all probability. Required rate of return will also differ, owing to both differences in risk characteristics of writing as opposed to buying and the writer's investment position and attitudes toward risk. While a buyer's loss on an individual transaction is limited to the premium paid, the call writer's potential loss is theoretically unlimited. On the other side, the writer's gain is limited to the amount of premium received.

Writing a call requires a larger investment than buying a call. Investment may be in the form of either cash or ownership of the underlying security if the call is hedged. The amount of investment required to write a call can be specified as

$$I_w = m(100P) + 100(P - P_s) + T - M' \qquad (12.6)$$

where m is the percentage margin supplied, P_s is the striking price, P is the current market price, and T represents all transaction costs associated with the position.[10] The amount of premium received by the writer, M', is the same as the premium paid for listed options. For unlisted options the premium received is less than the premium paid, with the difference reimbursing the intermediaries. Premiums received are subtracted from the amount of margin required at the time the option is written. The writer's

[10] Minimum rates for cash margin for writing calls is currently 35 percent and for writing puts it is 30 percent. The term $P - P_s$ in Equation 12.6 is referred to as the amount by which the option is "in the money" (or "out of the money" if the amount is negative). For example, if a call priced at \$50 per share is written for a \$6 premium on a stock selling at \$48 (\$2 out of the money) and transaction costs total \$60, required investment would be:

.35(100)(48)	=	1680
+ 100(48 − 50)	=	−200
+ 60	=	+60
− 600	=	−600
Total		940

Commonly a \$2000 or higher minimum deposit on any one account is imposed by the broker. If the writer should own or purchase the stock, it would substitute for a cash deposit. The margin rate in this case would be 100 percent.

return is determined by the difference between the premium received and the expected value of the call which the writer gives in exchange. Notationally this amount is

$$E(V_c'') = (1 - t_x)[M' - E(V_c) - T] + I_w \tag{12.7}$$

and, again, the rate of return which equates Equation 12.6 with 12.7 is found by solving Equation 12.8 for r.

$$I_w = \frac{(1 - t_x)[M' - E(V_c) - T] + (I_w - T)}{(1 + r)} \tag{12.8}$$

The desirability of writing an option depends upon future price expectations and the current composition of the investment portfolio. Assume that an investor in the 20 percent capital gains bracket, who owns no shares of AT&T currently, considers writing a listed option for that corporation for \$475.00. Unlike the buyer in the last example, this investor estimates the call to have an expected future value by expiration of \$387.50. With a 35 percent margin requirement and a transaction cost of \$30.00, the required investment would be

$$I_w = 5500(.35) + 30 - 475 = 1480$$

and the expected call value to writing is

$$E(V_c'') = .80[475.00 - 387.50 - 30.00] = 46.00$$

This very small profit represents only a 3.1 percent period return which may be inadequate. On the other hand, if the writer already owned 100 shares of AT&T, *writing hedged* may be a better strategy than either selling at the current market price or continuing to hold the shares unhedged. Writing an option on stock which is already owned changes both expected return and risk.

The relationship among return outcomes and stock price movements for various positions are traced in Figure 12.2. According to the figure, if AT&T's price fell by \$10 per share, stock ownership (i.e., buy stock) would produce an 18.5 percent loss (ignoring dividends). Buying the call would produce a total loss of 100 percent while writing would yield the largest possible gain, 32.1 percent. Writing hedged resulted in a 10.7 percent loss as the decrease in stock value exceeded the call premium received. By contrast, a \$10 per share gain in stock price would produce an 18.5 percent gain for shareholders, an 89.5 percent return for call buyers, a 28.7 percent loss for writers, and a maximum 9.6 percent gain for writers who hedge a purchase of stock.

PUTS. Buyers and writers of puts may utilize Equations 12.3 through 12.8, respectively, substituting the expected put value for the expected call value.

Figure 12.2
Possible Return Outcomes for the AT&T Call Option Example

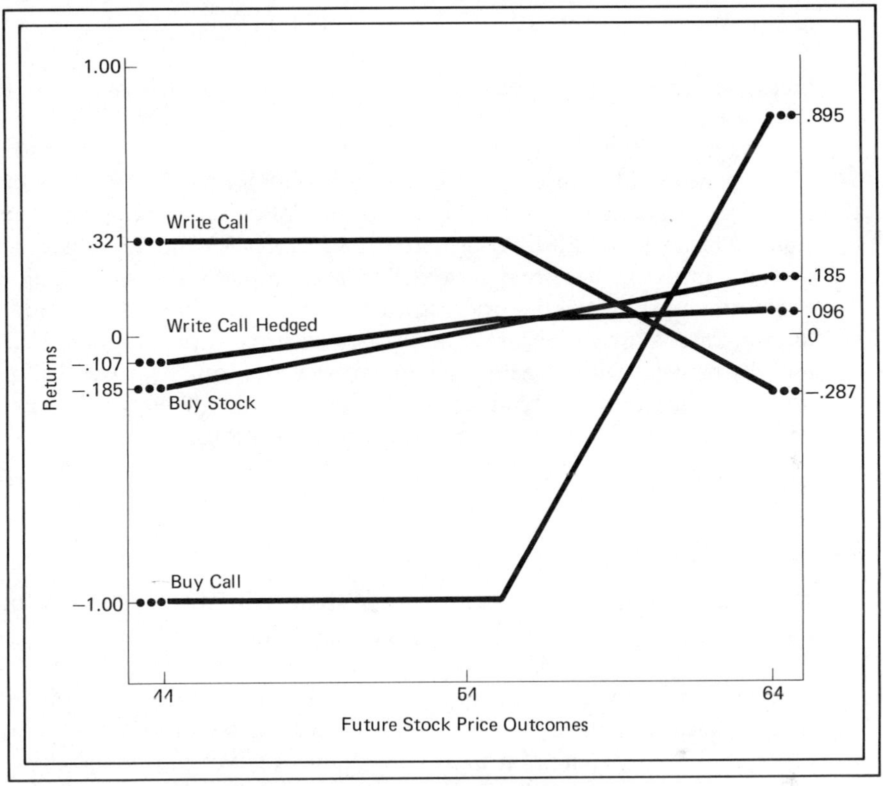

Returns presume a premium of \$475, a stock market price of \$54, call striking price of \$55, and an effective margin for writing unhedged calls of 35 percent. All returns are based on price and potential dividends, taxes, and transaction costs are ignored.

A put increases in value as stock prices fall; therefore, expected future value may be obtained by solving:

$$E(V_p) = 100 \sum_{0}^{P_s - D} (P_s - D - P) f(P) \tag{12.9}$$

for unlisted puts, and

$$E(V_p) = 100 \sum_{0}^{P_s} (P_s - P) f(P) \tag{12.9a}$$

for listed puts, for $E(V_p)$ which is the expected put value. All other variables are defined as in Equation 12.2. A put buyer's profit is theoretically more limited than a call buyer's because the stock price cannot fall by an amount greater than its current market price.

BLACK AND SCHOLES MODEL. To assist in option valuation and investment decision making, Black and Scholes developed and tested a formula for the theoretical value of an option.[11] Although their model is mathematically complex, it has received widespread attention in both academic and investment communities due to its generality and its practical implications. The model is general because it may be applied to all forms of contingent claims and it is consistent with other theories of capital market pricing and equilibrium, topics which will be considered in Chapters 13 and 15. It is practical because option values are determined from a limited set of identifiable variables: stock price, striking price, stock price variance, life of the option, and interest rate. With an accurate forecast of security variance, the model has initially proven useful in estimating proper levels of option prices. Empirical findings suggest a slight tendency for traders to overvalue low price variance options and to undervalue high price variance options.

Commodity Futures

Commodity futures contracts are formal standardized promises. The buyer, referred to as being "long" the contract, accepts an obligation to receive and the seller, referred to as being "short" the contract, receives the right to deliver a certain quantity and quality of a specified commodity. The settlement period, price, and place of delivery, as well as other details of the transaction, are specified in the standardized agreement. An increase in the price of a futures contract creates a profit for those who are long and a corresponding loss for those who are short. Since they are promises, buying or selling futures contracts does not involve the ownership or exchange of title to the specified commodity. This means that the number of futures contracts outstanding,

[11] Fisher Black and Myron Scholes, "The Valuation of Option Contracts and a Test of Market Efficiency," *Journal of Finance* 27, no. 2 (May 1972): 399–417, and "The Pricing of Options and Corporate Liabilities," *Journal of Political Economy*, May–June 1973, pp. 637–654. Using their notation, the option price model is $w = xN(d_1) - ce^{-rt^*} N(d_2)$ where w = per share option price; x = per share stock price; c = option striking price; r = short-term interest rate; t^* = duration of the option; $d_1 = [\ln(x/c) + (r + 1/2\sigma^2)t^*]/\sigma\sqrt{t}$; $d_2 = d_1 - \sigma\sqrt{t}$; $N(d)$ = value of the cumulative normal density function; and σ^2 = variance rate of the stock return. Their model has been generalized by Robert Merton, "Theory of Rational Option Pricing," *The Bell Journal of Economics and Management Science* 4, no. 1 (Spring 1973): 141–183, and their variance properties were tested by Henry Latané and Richard Rendleman, Jr., "Standard Deviations of Stock Price Ratios Implied in Option Prices," *Journal of Finance* 31, no. 2 (May 1976): 369–381.

Charts (Nomograms) based on the Black and Scholes option model which enable the investor to determine a fair value immediately for any option without computation are provided by Elroy Dimson, "Instant Option Valuation," *Financial Analysts Journal* (May/June 1977), pp. 62–69 and "Option Valuation Nomograms," *Financial Analysts Journal* (November/December 1977), pp. 71–74.

known as *open interest*, is determined through buying and selling in the marketplace.

MARKETS AND CONTRACTS

Futures trading occurs on exchanges which provide for liquid, continuous, and orderly trading. All trades are cleared through the exchange clearing house. In this process, the clearing house technically assumes the opposite side to both parties of a transaction, thereby removing any connection between the original buyer and seller. This assures all parties of full performance and the freedom to trade out of their position at will.

Ten futures markets are currently active in the United States, each trading a particular group of commodity futures. The structure of a futures exchange is similar to that of a security exchange. In each case, two exchanges dominate in size, with a number of smaller exchanges transacting less actively traded claims. The largest futures exchange is the Chicago Board of Trade, followed closely in size by the Chicago Mercantile Exchange. More than one hundred brokerage firms have clearing privileges on the Chicago Board of Trade. Member firms are referred to as futures commission merchants (FCMs). When an order is placed at a broker's office, it is transmitted to the floor of the exchange where it is delivered to the trader representing the futures commission merchant. The FCM, in turn, enters the commodity futures trading area, known as the pit, and executes the order by open outcry. All trading occurs during regular hours; this is 9:30 A.M. to 1:30 P.M. for most futures. Limit orders or orders specifying that the trade should be executed during the first or last minute of trading will be retained and executed, if possible.[12]

The principal commodity futures traded on the Board of Trade are wheat, corn, and soybeans. Livestock and related products, as well as futures in foreign exchange, are traded on the Chicago Mercantile Exchange. Details of these contracts are shown in Table 12.2. Other exchanges conduct futures trading in metals, fibers, and other agricultural products. Silver and gold futures are traded on several exchanges. The aggregate annual value of all futures traded during recent years has exceeded 30 million contracts valued in excess of $200 billion. The dollar value of all futures traded on the Chicago Board of Trade has approximately equaled or exceeded the value of all shares traded on the New York Stock Exchange in recent years.

Futures contracts specify the quantity of the commodity involved. Prices are quoted in units of measure; for example, one contract for any wheat future traded on the Chicago Board of Trade specifies 5000 bushels

[12] In futures, a limit order becomes a market order when a trade first occurs at the limit price. During periods of rapid price fluctuation, the price at which a limit order is ultimately executed may differ considerably from the limit price set by the trader. Limit orders therefore provide little protection from large losses during periods of great market uncertainty.

Table 12.2

Major U. S. Exchanges and Their Most Active Commodity Futures[a]
July 1970–June 1971

Exchange	*Major Commodities*	*Contract Size*	*Annual Volume of Trading (Contracts)*	*Number of Futures*	*Price Quoted In*	*Minimum Price Change*
Chicago Board of Trade	Wheat (soft)	5,000 bu	582	5	¢/bu	1/8¢/bu = $12.50/contract
	Corn	5,000 bu	2,734	5	¢/bu	1/8¢/bu = $12.50/contract
	Soybeans	5,000 bu	2,653	7	¢/bu	1/8¢/bu = $12.50/contract
	Soybean oil	60,000 lb	1,470	8	¢/lb	1/100¢/lb = $ 6.00/contract
	Soybean meal	100 tons	634	8	$/ton	$.05/ton = $ 5.00/contract
Chicago Mercantile Exchange	Cattle (live)	40,000 lb	606	6	$/cwt	$.025/cwt = $10.00/contract
	Pork bellies	36,000 lb	1,526	7	$/cwt	$.025/cwt = $ 9.00/contract
	Eggs (shell)	21,000 dz	524	12	¢/dz	.05¢/dz = $10.50/contract
New York Mercantile Exchange	Potatoes	50,000 lb	206	4	$/cwt	$.01/cwt = $ 5.00/contract
Kansas City Board of Trade	Wheat (hard)	5,000 bu	201	5	¢/bu	1/8¢/bu = $12.50/contract

Source: *Annual Summary of Commodity Futures Statistics*, 1970–71, USDA, Commodity Exchange Authority.
[a] Commodities regulated under the Commodity Exchange Act.

of #2 soft red winter wheat, and prices are quoted in cents and eighths of a cent per bushel. The dollar investment in a futures transaction is the deposit required by the broker to insure performance in the event of a price change which is adverse to the investor's position. This "good faith" deposit, referred to as margin, is generally 15 to 25 percent of the value of the underlying commodity.[13] Most large security brokers employ persons who hold membership on major commodity exchanges and the firm can therefore directly execute customers' orders.

Certain months are designated by the exchange as contract months for each commodity. For wheat, the months are March, May, July, September, and December. The life of a futures contract is most commonly 11 months and contracts are defined in terms of the last month of trading. Thus the May, 1978, wheat future began trading in June of 1977 and it expired five business days prior to the last day of May, 1978. A futures contract can be settled by delivery of the actual commodity only during the last contract month in accordance with procedures established by the exchange.[14] In practice only a small percentage of contracts are settled by delivery because of relatively higher transaction costs when compared to spot (cash) transactions in the cash market.[15]

Anyone buying or selling a futures contract can trade out of the investment at any time by placing an order for the opposite position in the same future with a broker. The second transaction offsets the first and the account is balanced in the broker's records. For example, an investor who sold a contract of May wheat and subsequently decided to close out the position would instruct the broker to purchase a contract of May wheat. The purchase offsets the prior sale and the investor is therefore out of the market. If the market price of May wheat had been $4.00 per bushel when the contract was originally sold and $4.08¼ per bushel when it was subsequently purchased, the investor would realize a loss of 8¼ cents per bushel or $412.50 on the 5000-bushel contract, exclusive of commission charges.

The price of a futures contract reflects the expected price of the cash commodity in the final month of the life of the future. Storage costs, weather, political conditions, and expectations with respect to specific supply and demand factors in ensuing months will cause prices for different futures months of the same commodity to differ.

[13] Minimum margin levels are established and administered by the commodity exchanges. Individual brokers may, and frequently do, require higher levels of margin from their customers. Gains or losses based on market quotations are credited daily to the investor's account. A minimum level of margin, generally 75 percent of the initial requirement, must be maintained at all times. Thus an investor faces the possibility of receiving margin calls in the case of a losing position.

[14] Delivery is at the option of the short position holder, who presents an approved warehouse receipt representing ownership to the clearing house of the exchange. The clearing house allocates the warehouse receipt to the oldest long-position holder in that future.

[15] Spot (or alternatively cash) transactions are contracts for immediate delivery. Actual spot transactions are conducted both on and, more frequently, off the futures exchange floor.

HEDGING

Commodity prices fluctuate far more than the price of services, manufactured goods, and most financial claims including common stocks and bonds. The uncertain nature of primary commodity prices can be both severe and widespread and the economic impact of these price changes places a burden on all levels of production and distribution. Uncertainty can impede economic growth and, in many cases, it can result in commodity storage and use patterns which are inconsistent with current market needs. Active futures markets mitigate these effects by transferring the uncertainty attached to ownership of primary commodities through a process known as *hedging*. Hedging is the establishment of a futures position to offset a commodity position taken for business purposes. The main objectives of hedging are risk reduction and an increased line of credit for the financing of inventories.

Hedging depends upon the tendency of cash and futures prices to move together through time. This positive association is assured by the fact that the futures contract may be settled by delivery of the cash commodity during the last month in which the future is traded. Futures prices can therefore be viewed as an expectation of the cash price at the time the futures contract matures. This relationship is called the *expectations hypothesis*, and it can be expressed as

$$F_0 = E(C_t) \tag{12.10}$$

where F_0 represents a futures price occurring at current time (0) for a contract maturing at later time (t); C_t is the cash price expected at time t.

When a position in a cash commodity is hedged by a futures position, the hedger is no longer concerned with changes in cash prices; an unfavorable change in the cash price will be offset by a favorable change in the futures position. The relationship between the cash price at the hedger's location and the price of the hedging future is called the *basis*. Because futures prices do not exactly correspond to cash prices, the basis changes over time. A comparison of the basis at the time a hedge is placed with an expected basis of zero at the time the futures contract matures (implied by Equation 12.10 after adjustment for any locational differences) provides the hedger with information on how the basis will change.

An example of a hedging transaction is provided in Table 12.3. The basis at the time the hedge is placed is 11 cents under the May future. The basis is 2 cents under the May future when the commodity is actually sold and the futures position is liquidated. This is the normal pattern for commodities which have a seasonal storage pattern. The narrowing of the basis reflects the cost of storing the commodity.[16] If the hedger had simply elected to store

[16] The exact amount of basis change is not known in advance and a hedged position does involve some risk. It should also be noted that part of the price of hedging is the sacrifice of an unusually large gain in any year in which a favorable movement in cash prices occurs.

Table 12.3
Hypothetical Hedging Transaction

Date	*Cash Account—Wheat Inventory*		*Futures Account*	
November 1	Bought 10,000 bu at $3.00/bu	$30,000	Sold two contracts May future at $3.11	$31,100
April 1	Sold 10,000 bu at $2.90/bu	29,000	Bought two contracts May future at $2.92	29,200
Gross profit or (loss)		($1,000)		$ 1,900
Costs:	Storage, insurance, interest on purchase price, etc., at $.015/bu/month for 5 months	$ 750	Commissions, interest on required margin	$ 100
Gain on account		($1,750)		$ 1,800

the grain, without an offsetting futures position, a loss of 10 cents per bushel before storage and financial costs would have occurred.

Most hedging situations require the sale of futures contracts to offset inventories. But some situations require going long the future, as in the case of an agreement to supply a commodity which is not owned at a later date for a fixed price. Some hedging requires a simultaneous long and short position in related commodity futures, as in the case of soybean processors who must be long soybean futures and short soybean oil and soybean meal futures to hedge their normal processing operations. This hedge is called "putting on a crush."

SPECULATION

Traders who are not classified as hedgers are usually called *speculators.* Speculators are characterized by the magnitude and type of their trading activity. Some invest in futures as part of an overall portfolio strategy. Others with sizable positions in futures are subject to direct regulatory surveillance and they are typically professional speculators who devote considerable time and effort to specialized risk-bearing activities. Many of this latter group have memberships on commodity exchanges and they trade directly for their own account. Some exchange members, referred to as *scalpers,* specialize in short-term transactions involving establishment and liquidation of futures positions within a single day. The activity of scalpers insures a liquid and continuous market for other traders.

SPREADING. Speculators typically purchase futures in anticipation of a rise in price or they sell futures in anticipation of a fall in price. Since hedging usually requires the sale of futures, most speculative transactions are purchases. An alternative form of speculation, *spreading*, involves a simultaneous long and short position in two related futures for either the same or different commodities. Spreading is similar to hedging but spreading involves the relationship between two futures while hedging involves a future and a spot commodity. The return from spreading depends upon the relative prices of two futures and it is insensitive to any absolute change in price levels. For example, if the current difference between a December corn future priced at 300 cents per bushel and a May future priced at 306 cents is thought to be too small, a speculator could spread by purchasing the May contract and selling the December contract. The investor profits when the price of the May contract rises relative to the price of the December contract, whatever the change in the level of prices. If the May price subsequently rises to 520 cents for example, and December to 510 cents, or for that matter if May falls to 150 cents and December to 140 cents, the spreader will realize a gross profit of 4 cents per bushel on the transaction. In both cases the gain on the profitable position exceeds the loss on the losing position by a 4-cent differential.

REGULATION OF FUTURES TRADING

Commodity futures are subject to dual regulatory control, by individual exchanges and by the Commodity Futures Trading Commission (CFTC). Exchanges audit the books and records of their members and they establish and enforce rules of ethical conduct. Acting through committees selected from their membership, exchanges establish margin, delivery, and other contract specifications. The CFTC enforces all provisions of the Futures and Forward Markets and Marketing Act, a law passed by Congress in 1974; this legislation replaced the Commodity Exchange Act of 1936 which, in turn, replaced the original Grain Futures Act of 1922. The 1922 and 1936 acts were more limited in scope and power than the 1974 legislation and they were enforced through an agency of the U.S. Department of Agriculture. The CFTC is patterned after the SEC: it is an independent federal commission with broad and flexible regulatory functions. The CFTC is structured along market lines, with separate departments for metals, agricultural products, foreign currency, and new markets. Each operates functionally in three major areas:

1. *Auditing.* Futures commission merchants are periodically audited to insure that all customers' margin funds are properly segregated from the broker's working capital. The act requires that margin deposits will be identified and protected in the event of failure of the brokerage firm.
2. *Trading and reporting.* Surveillance of economic and market operations is maintained to insure an orderly and fair market. Periodic reports are required

from commission merchants, hedgers, large position holders, and exchanges; these data are processed, compiled, and periodically published in statistical bulletins.

3. *Investigation.* All alleged violations of the act are fully investigated. When it appears to be justified, findings are formalized for legal proceedings. Violation of the act may result in the placement of civil and/or criminal charges.

SOURCES OF COMMODITY INFORMATION

Commodity and futures prices are influenced by factors related to commodity supply and demand. These include such specific elements as exports and inventories as well as general economic and credit conditions pertaining to the trading and operation of futures markets. Important new information affecting commodity value becomes available continuously, thereby affecting expectations and prices. Meaningful forecasting requires accurate and up-to-date information together with skilled interpretation of these data. Speculators and hedgers place great reliance on widely circulated news and statistical reports generated by government agencies and others. The principal sources of commodity information are the following:

GOVERNMENT REPORTS. The Commodity Futures Trading Commission (formerly the Commodity Exchange Authority) publishes numerous reports related to futures markets. These reports detail the volume of trading, open interest, and the quantity of positions classified as hedging and speculation. Other federal agencies, largely within the U.S. Department of Agriculture, publish reports on supply and demand conditions for commodities both domestically and abroad. The Economic Research Service, USDA, regularly publishes Situation Reports for all major commodities; these reports provide comprehensive coverage of all trends and factors which affect price. Other publications outline government agricultural programs.

TRADE PUBLICATIONS. For many commodities, such as soybeans and cattle, merchants' trade associations sponsor a tailored publication containing information affecting the price of that particular commodity.

COMMODITY RESEARCH FIRMS. There are a number of independent firms which also provide information for, or related to, commodity futures trading. The largest of these services is the Commodity Research Bureau in New York City. Some firms offer highly specialized services; for example, Doane Agricultural Services of St. Louis furnishes extended weather forecasts to its subscribers.

FINANCIAL NEWS SERVICES. The Commodity News Service provides broad-tape coverage of information concerning commodity prices. This up-to-the-minute wire service is similar to the Dow Jones Broadtape for securities which is commonly found in brokerage offices. Many financially oriented newspapers, including *The Wall Street Journal* and the *New York Journal of Commerce*, have regular sections which are devoted to commodity news.

COMMODITY INDEXES. Dow Jones provides two commodity indexes, one of cash commodity prices and the other of commodity futures prices. They are published frequently in *The Wall Street Journal* and other financial publications, and each index is based upon prices for the same 12 commodities. Each commodity in the cash index is weighted by a base period production value while volume of trading in the base period provides weights for the futures index. Unfortunately, changes in the relative importance of agricultural commodities since the indexes were introduced in 1937 have not been reflected by updating.[17] Thus the usefulness of these indexes as indicators of commodity value is very limited.

FUTURES CONTRACT VALUATION

Because futures may be settled by delivery on the first business day of the last month of trading, futures prices reflect expectations of the spot (cash) price at that date. This relationship was identified earlier in the chapter as the expectations hypothesis:

$$F_0 = E(C_t) \tag{12.10}$$

where t denotes the first day on which the future may be settled by delivery and 0 denotes the current date. In this form, the implied return to holding a futures contract over the interval $(0, t)$, long or short, is zero. This results from the fact that at time t the option to deliver the cash commodity against the future assures that future price F_t will equal cash price C_t. That is,

$$F_0 = E(C_t) = E(F_t)$$

If the futures price on all dates prior to time t equal the expected cash price at t, the expected difference between F_t and any earlier futures price is zero. Since returns are established by price differences, expected return is also zero.

RETURNS TO SPECULATORS. Lord Keynes and J. R. Hicks, among other economists, have argued that futures prices tend to rise as they near maturity. A small increase in futures prices would normally occur as the means whereby hedgers—who are short in the aggregate—reward speculators with a positive return for assuming the risk of uncertain commodity prices. Defining

[17] Only six of the twelve commodities carried in the indexes are currently major crops. Seven major commodities, including soybeans and livestock, are excluded, as are all metals. Interestingly, in 1975 the most actively traded futures were in silver which is not included among the index commodities.

this positive return as r, the expectations hypothesis would become

$$F_0(1 + r) = E(C_t) \tag{12.10a}$$

or, alternatively,

$$F_0 = \left(\frac{1}{1 + r}\right)E(C_t)$$

Keynes referred to this hypothesized tendency for futures price to rise as normal backwardation.

More recent studies of the actual behavior of futures prices have failed to find evidence of normal backwardation.[18] Futures prices appear to be unbiased expectations of cash prices as Equation 12.10 indicates. This implies that a policy of holding either a long or short contract until the future nears expiration will yield an expected return of zero, excluding transaction costs and taxes. Although the reasons for this return behavior are not clear, a number of potential influences on futures return can be identified:

1. Aggregate returns to futures positions may not be measured accurately. The changing number of outstanding contracts makes it exceedingly difficult to measure aggregate returns correctly. The problem is compounded by frequent changes in margin levels which directly affect the calculation of an accurate return.
2. Taxes are an important consideration for many investors. Futures trading provides an opportunity for converting ordinary income to capital gains and for deferring tax liabilities from current to distant years.
3. Futures are similar to options in the sense that they must be evaluated in relation to all other securities in an investor's portfolio. There is some evidence that futures prices move contrary to security prices.[19] While highly risky per se, futures might therefore significantly reduce the variability of a portfolio. For this potential benefit investors may be willing to accept a very low expected return.
4. Alternatively, futures provide an opportunity for large gains in short periods of time. Some individuals may be willing to accept the expectation of zero return for the small chance of a very large return.
5. Investors may systematically err in forecasting futures prices.

The first two of these factors imply that speculators do, on balance, realize positive returns; the last three suggest why they may not. Some additional evidence has recently been provided by Thomas Hieronymus. His study of the summary records of a major futures commission firm suggests that speculative transactions, on average, do not earn positive returns.[20] Hieronymus's findings support the notion that futures trading is a fairly

[18] Charles S. Rockwell, *Profits, Normal Backwardation and Forecasting in Commodity Futures* (Ph.D. Dissertation, The University of California at Berkeley, 1964). Also Katherine Dusak, "Futures Trading and Investor Returns: An Investigation of Commodity Market Risk Premiums," *Journal of Political Economy* 81 (November–December 1973): 1387–1406.

[19] A. Robichek, R. Cohn, and J. Pringle, "Returns on Alternative Investment Media and Implications for Portfolio Construction," *Journal of Business*, July 1972, pp. 427–443.

[20] Thomas A. Hieronymus, *Economics of Futures Trading* (New York: Commodity Research Bureau, 1971), esp. chap. 13.

even game among speculators; they also provide evidence that commissions are relatively expensive because of the short time during which futures positions are held. Statistics concerning size of position, regularity of trading, and profitability are of particular interest. Nearly half (49 percent) of all gains and losses on individual transactions were less than \$1000; investors who traded infrequently typically held small positions and then usually lost money. Regular traders as a group, in contrast, profited on a gross basis and then broke even after commissions. These results are consistent with the viewpoint that successful commodity futures trading demands a substantial commitment of skilled resources to the valuation process.

A VALUATION MODEL. The valuation of a futures contract requires two subjective inputs from the investor: (1) specification of a required rate of return and (2) expectations concerning cash and, thereby, futures prices at a later date. Thus a futures valuation model is directly analogous to the security valuation model discussed in preceding chapters. It is somewhat less complex in practice in the sense that the time horizon over which expectations are formed is short and relatively fixed.

Other inputs to the futures valuation process are usually known to the investor when a position is taken. These are the individual's tax status and the current levels of futures prices, margins, and transaction costs. In contrast with security transactions, transaction costs for liquidating a futures position are included in the brokerage fee at the time the position is taken. Depending on the commodity futures in question, brokerage fees range from \$30 to \$60 per contract traded. The investment required to take a one contract position in any future—long or short—equals the required margin plus transaction costs. Defining:

M_0 = margin required as commonly quoted per unit of commodity
N = number of units of commodity represented by one futures contract
T, t_x = total transaction costs and investor's marginal tax rate
r', r^* = investor's expected and required rates of return after taxes
F_0, F_t = futures price at current time 0 and maturity date t
C_t = price of the cash commodity at time t
V_f, V_f' = before- and after-tax value per contract

Purchase or sale of one futures contract requires an investment of

$$I = N \times M_0 + T \tag{12.11}$$

and its expected value at time t is either:

$$E(V_f)\begin{cases} E(V_{fB}) = N[E(F_t) - F_0] & \text{for an initial purchase } (B \text{ denotes buyer}) \\ E(V_{fS}) = N[F_0 - E(F_t)] & \text{for an initial sale } (S \text{ denotes seller}) \end{cases} \tag{12.12}$$

The expression $E(V_f)$ is a general one covering either buying or selling. Because time t occurs at or near the contract's maturity period, $E(C_t)$ can be substituted for $E(F_t)$.[21] The valuation process must therefore focus on problems of forecasting cash prices at the time the future expires. To complete the valuation model, the after-tax expected value of a futures position may be expressed as

$$E(V_f') = (1 - t_x)[E(V_f) - T] \tag{12.13}$$

and expected rate of return r' can be found by relating expected proceeds at liquidation with the initial investment:

$$I = \frac{E(V_f') + NM_0}{1 + r'} \tag{12.14}$$

A comparison between r' and r^*, the investor's required rate of return, determines the desirability of the investment. Equation 12.14 is the basic futures valuation model. It expresses the expectations formulation of Equation 12.10 from an individual's perspective and circumstances.[22] Consider the May wheat future selling on the first of February for 400 cents per bushel when a margin requirement of 40 cents per bushel is in effect. Transaction costs are assumed to be \$30 per contract. If an investor in the 30 percent marginal tax bracket expects the price of contract grade wheat to be 405 cents per bushel on May 1, the anticipated return from buying the May wheat future will be

$$5000(.40) + 30 = \frac{.7[5000(4.05 - 4.00) - 30] + 5000(.60)}{1 + r'}$$

Reducing,

$$2030 = \frac{2154}{1 + r'} \quad \text{and} \quad r' \cong .061$$

Since this is a three-month commitment, the implied annual return would be $(1.061)^4 - 1 = .267$. Assuming the investor requires less than this return, the future should be purchased.

The model is very sensitive to margin levels and taxes. Leverage is created by the large difference between the level of futures prices and the level of margin; for this reason margin levels are a prominent factor in the valuation process. Exchanges revise minimum margin levels periodically

[21] This presumes that the investor selects a future which nears maturity at the end of his or her investment horizon. If the investor's time horizon is shorter, some $\alpha < t$, then $E(F_\alpha)$ is not necessarily equal to $E(C_t)$ or $E(C_\alpha)$.

[22] To show this, assume a 100 percent margin and the absence of tax and transaction costs. Specifying the equations on a per commodity unit rather than contract basis, by dividing through by N, required investment becomes (Equation 12.11) $I/N = (N \cdot M_0 + T)/N = M_0 = F_0$, since $T = 0$, and the expected value at time t is, for an initial purchase (dividing Equation 12.12 by N), $\{N[E(C_t) - F_0] - T\}/N = [E(C_t) - F_0]$. Since $t_x = 0$, the total expected proceeds per unit is $[E(C_t) - F_0] + M_0 = E(C_t)$, since $M_0 = F_0$. Equating the expected proceeds to the investment, $F_0 = [1/(1 + r)]E(C_t)$, which is Equation 12.10. If an aggregate zero return is also assumed, this result becomes $F_0 = E(C_t)$, the original expectations hypothesis.

and quite frequently the magnitude of change is significant.[23] The tax treatment of commodity positions is a complex topic, requiring the investor to seek professional tax assistance in many cases. Generally, the Internal Revenue Code favors buying, as opposed to selling, futures contracts. Profits on long positions held six months or longer are taxed as capital gains but gains on short positions are taxed as ordinary income. Spreading positions in related (but not identical) futures have tax advantages under certain conditions.

ESTIMATING CASH COMMODITY PRICES

A meaningful evaluation of futures contracts requires an ability to forecast cash prices accurately. Cash prices are determined by complex interactions among a large number of factors; these factors can be classified into four basic categories:

1. *Factors affecting demand.* These include domestic consumption, exports, and the prices of complementary and substitute commodities.
2. *Factors affecting supply.* These include production, existing stocks, weather conditions, and governmental programs.
3. *Economic conditions.* These include industrial production, unemployment, inflation, and credit availability, as well as transportation and storage conditions.
4. *Futures market conditions.* These include levels of trading and open interest as well as market composition between hedgers and speculators.

Labys and Granger extensively tested the response of cash and futures prices to changes in variables derived from the factors listed above.[24] No single variable was able to explain adequately changes in cash commodity prices but combinations of two to five variables usually provided a good explanation. The types of information affecting futures prices, in order of importance, were found to be:

1. Weighted indexes of prices for complementary and substitute commodities.
2. Supply and demand factors.
3. Measures of the extent of hedging and speculative interest in the commodity future.
4. Measures of credit availability.

[23] Over the period 1947–1968, margins in wheat futures ranged from 6 to 102 cents per bushel. The average size of change was 5 cents and the average frequency of change was twice a year. Since 1968, both size and frequency of change have increased. An analysis of margins is found in Robert M. Bear, "Margin Levels and the Behavior of Futures Prices," *Journal of Financial and Quantitative Analysis* 7, no. 4 (September 1972): 1907–1930.

[24] Walter C. Labys and C. W. J. Granger, *Speculation, Hedging and Commodity Price Forecasts* (Lexington, Mass.: Heath, 1970). For example, their general model for cash soybeans is $\Delta C = .737 + 0.490X_1 + 0.2999X_2 + 0.0000756X_3 - 0.310X_4$, $R^2 = .60$. ΔC measures monthly differences in cash soybean prices, estimated over the interval from August, 1957, to June, 1966. The single most important variable, X_1, is a yield index measuring the value of soybean by-products; X_2 is the preceding month's cash price difference; X_3 is the amount of short futures positions classified as hedging; and X_4 measures soybean stocks. A detailed discussion of the variables affecting a particular commodity is found in Chapters 6 through 10.

The Labys and Granger study shows that commodity prices can be explained by identifiable market and economic conditions. Unfortunately, explanatory models often prove to have little value for purposes of forecasting. Many factors, including political conditions and pending legislation, are difficult to incorporate into econometric models but they assume major significance at certain times, dominating the impact of more stationary and identifiable variables. Successful futures analysis requires a sensitivity to all market, economic, political, and psychological influences which are relevant during the period under consideration.

FINANCE FUTURES

Increasing sophistication on the part of investors, business, and government in dealing effectively with uncertainty has led to increases in the level of futures trading and the development of new applications. In addition to the market for commodities, futures markets have recently been introduced in foreign exchange, insured mortgages, treasury bills, and bonds.

FOREIGN EXCHANGE. The Chicago Mercantile Exchange initiated trading in foreign exchange futures in 1972. This new market, designated as the International Monetary Market (IMM), has been very successful. Its success resulted from the widespread uncertainties in relative values of national currencies in the early 1970s as the world moved from a fixed to a flexible exchange rate system. An exchange rate is the price of a foreign currency valued in dollars which, when determined in a free market, contributes to the efficient allocation of resources. An economic objection to flexible exchange rates argues that constantly changing currency values increase the risk involved in international business transactions and serves as a restraint to trade. The ability to hedge international transactions on an active futures market counters this objection.

MORTGAGES AND TREASURY BILLS. Trading in mortgage futures began on the Chicago Board of Trade during October, 1975. Mortgage futures provide banks, mortgage bankers, savings and loan companies, and other financial institutions with hedging opportunities; at the same time, they offer speculative opportunities to investors who are interested in the movement of long-term interest rates. The unit of trading is $100,000 principal value of Ginnie Mae certificates carrying an 8 percent coupon. As described in Chapter 5, Ginnie Mae refers to the Government National Mortgage Association, a federally owned corporation within the Department of Housing and Urban Development. The agency guarantees payment of principle and interest on certificates issued by private mortgage lenders against specific pools of insured mortgages. Prices of Ginnie Mae futures are quoted as a percentage of par value. A price quotation of 95-14 means that the futures contract is valued at $95\frac{14}{32}$ percent of par or \$95,437.50. Prices of mortgage futures are closely associated with the value of other high-quality long-term debt, especially the more than \$140 billion of outstanding FHA–VA insured mortgages. In view of the volatility of mortgage and other interest rates recently, trading volume on this new futures market is expected to be large and it should provide a valuable service to the financial and investment community.[25]

Shortly after the introduction of mortgage futures, in January, 1976, trading began in treasury bill futures on the International Monetary Market of the Chicago Mercantile Exchange. This new market provides for hedging and speculation on short-term interest rate futures. The futures contract calls for delivery of \$1 million face value of three-month U.S. Treasury bills. Traders therefore anticipate yield on a three-month bill offered at the date corresponding to the expiration of the futures contract. Initial reaction to T-bill futures has been very favorable. Quotations for all these finance futures prices are reported in *The Wall Street Journal.*

Summary

This chapter has introduced security options and commodity futures, two important investments available to investors seeking expanded and complementary opportunities to stocks and bonds. The presentation began with basic definitions and a comparison of over-the-counter trading with trading on exchanges. A basic structure for determining option value was then introduced. This was shown to be a straightforward single-period rate of return model analogous to the model introduced in Chapter 5 for bonds and in Chapter 6 for common stocks.

Commodity futures contracts are formalized promises. The second half of the chapter emphasized this basic notion while developing a description and discussion of futures roughly paralleling the discussion of options. Futures valuation also involves a short-run estimation problem. Identifying the relevant factors and costs within the structure of the standard rate of return model is shown to provide a useful analytical technique consistent with the process applied to other financial claims. Leverage, however, adds considerable dispersion to estimates of expected returns.

The appendix considers the relationship between put and call premiums, a topic of specific interest to prospective option investors. The argument is developed in the appendix that percentage call premiums should exceed put premiums by the risk-free rate of interest.

[25] Richard L. Sandor, "Trading Mortgage Interest Rate Futures," *Federal Home Loan Bank Board Journal*, September 1975, pp. 2–8, and Neil A. Stevens, "A Mortgage Futures Market: Its Development, Uses, Benefits, and Costs," *Review* (Federal Reserve Bank of St. Louis) 58, no. 4 (April 1976): 12–19.

Appendix
The Relationship Between Put and Call Premiums

The relationship between put and call premiums is an issue which is related to option returns. Puts and calls may be interchanged by a process called conversion. Conversion provides an arbitrage mechanism that insures a parity between put and call premiums for the same stock. Profits resulting from arbitrage of puts into calls and profits resulting from arbitrage of calls into puts can be expressed in terms of cash flow as

$$G = C - \frac{100Mi}{1+i} - P \tag{12A.1}$$

$$H = P + \frac{100Mi}{1+i} - C \tag{12A.1a}$$

where G is the arbitrage profit of converting calls to puts and H is the arbitrage profit of converting puts into calls. The call premium is C, the put premium is P, and the per share market price of the underlying stock is M; i is the risk-free rate of interest, and $100Mi/(1 + i)$ is the present value of the cost of funds involved in the arbitrage operation discounted at the risk-free rate. In the first equation conversion involves writing a call to receive premium C while simultaneously buying the stock and writing a put. These latter activities incur costs of $100Mi/(1 + i)$ and P respectively. The difference between receipts and expenditures equals profit represented by G. The cash flows implied by Equation 12A.1 are, of course, a simplification of actual market conditions. Transaction costs and taxes are not considered. It is also assumed that because the transaction is risk-free no margin deposits are required and the arbitrager can borrow funds at the risk-free rate of interest. All these assumptions tend to make actual profits less than those reflected in G and H.

When the option market is in equilibrium no arbitrage opportunity will exist. In this case G will equal H and both will equal zero. That is, no profit opportunity exists for a riskless and costless transaction. All combinations of put and call premium levels that fall on line Z in Figure 12A.1 indicate an equilibrium where no arbitrage opportunities exist. Any point above this line, such as S, indicates levels where a positive profit G can be obtained by an investor who sells calls, writes puts, and hedges with stock purchases. Line Z is constructed in such a manner that the level of percentage call premiums always exceeds the level of percentage put premiums by an amount slightly less than the risk-free rate of interest. This result is obtained by substituting zero for either G or H in Equation 12A.1 or 12A.1a

Figure 12A.1
The Put-Call Parity

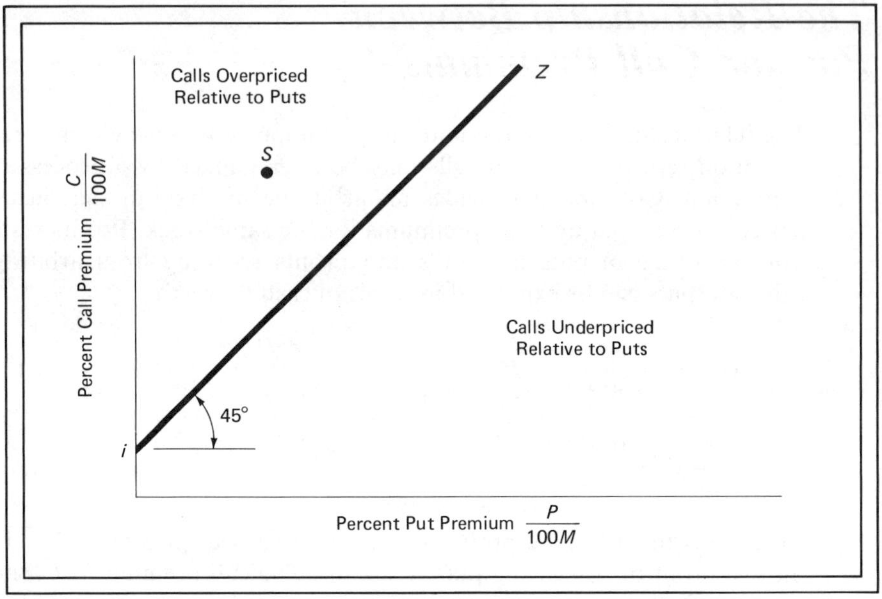

and dividing through by $100M$, providing

$$\frac{C}{100M} - \frac{P}{100M} = \frac{i}{1+i} \lessapprox i \tag{12A.2}$$

In other words, in a competitive option market percentage call premiums will exceed percentage put premiums by an amount slightly less than the risk-free rate of return.

The put and call parity for unlisted options has been identified and tested by Hans Stoll.[26] Using data submitted to the SEC by the Put and Call Dealers Association, Stoll finds support for the existence of the parity. Unlisted put and call options are closely related and arbitrage opportunities are limited. The unlisted market for options, despite high information and transaction costs, maintains a proper parity between levels of option premiums.

Questions and Problems

1. Explain the concept of forward pricing. What conditions need to be present to have a viable futures market?

[26] Hans R. Stoll, "The Relationship Between Put and Call Option Prices," *Journal of Finance*, December 1969, pp. 801–824.

2. The price of a share of Stagnation, Inc., is $50. The stock pays no dividends. You believe the range of possible stock prices six months hence will be:

Price/Share	*Probability*
$40	.15
45	.20
50	.30
55	.20
60	.15

Six-month treasury bills are priced to yield 4 percent to maturity and may be purchased in $1000 denominations. The price of a 190-day call with a striking price of $50 is $390, and a corresponding put costs $210. Commissions on the purchase *and* sale of 100 shares of stock total $130. What is the *relative* desirability of:
a. Purchase 100 shares of stock.
b. Purchase a call and five treasury bills.
c. Purchase a put and five treasury bills.
Prepare a graph showing all possible share prices on the horizontal axis and the returns to alternatives a, b, and c on the vertical axis. Are any of the three strategies clearly dominant or inferior?
3. What is the economic function of commodity futures contracts? How does the delivery procedure of futures contracts assure the proper functioning of these markets?
4. What is the expected holding period return to going long one contract (5000 bu) of the following grain futures and holding your position until first delivery day?

Future	*Margin*	*Commissions*	*Current Futures Price*	*Expected Cash Price—May 1*
May wheat	50¢/bu	$35/contract	$5.00	$4.90
May corn	30¢/bu	35/contract	4.00	4.20
May soybeans	80¢/bu	35/contract	6.00	6.40

Without additional information, is it possible to identify the relative desirability of these positions? Why or why not?
5. Explain carefully the differences between arbitraging, hedging, and spreading. Provide an example of each.
6. Explain how a call can be converted into a put. What implications does this have for the relationship between put and call option prices covering the same stock.

Selected References

SECURITY OPTIONS

Black, Fisher, "Fact and Fantasy in the Use of Options," *Financial Analysts Journal* 31, no. 4 (July–August 1975): 36–41+.

Black, Fisher and Myron Scholes, "The Valuation of Option Contracts and a Test of Market Efficiency," *Journal of Finance* 27, no. 2 (May 1972): 399–417.

———, "The Pricing of Options and Corporate Liabilities," *Journal of Political Economy* 81, no. 3 (May–June 1973): 637–654.

Clasing, Henry, *The Dow Jones–Irwin Guide to Put and Call Options* (Homewood, Ill.: Dow Jones–Irwin, 1975).

Cootner, Paul, ed., *The Random Character of Stock Market Prices* (Cambridge, Mass.: M.I.T. Press, 1964).

Galai, Dan, "Tests of Market Efficiency of the Chicago Board Options Exchange," *The Journal of Business*, April 1977, pp. 167–197.

Hettenhouse, George W., and Donald J. Puglisi, "Investor Experience with Put and Call Options," *Financial Analysts Journal* 31, no. 4 (July–August 1975): 53–58.

Katz, Richard, "The Profitability of Put and Call Option Writing," *Industrial Management Review*, Fall 1963, pp. 55–69.

Latané, Henry A., and Richard J. Rendleman, Jr., "Standard Deviations of Stock Price Ratios Implied in Option Prices," *Journal of Finance* 31, no. 2 (May 1976): 369–381.

Malkiel, Burton, and Richard Quandt, *Strategies and Rational Decisions in the Securities Option Market* (Cambridge, Mass.: M.I.T. Press, 1969).

Merton, Robert, "The Theory of Rational Option Pricing," *The Bell Journal of Economics and Management Science* 4, no. 1 (Spring 1973): 141–183.

Reback, Robert, "Risk and Return in Option Trading," *Financial Analysts Journal* 31, no. 4 (July–August 1975): 42–52.

Scholes, Myron, "Taxes and the Pricing of Options," *Journal of Finance* 31, no. 2 (May 1976): 319–332.

Stoll, Hans R., "The Relationship Between Put and Call Option Prices," *The Journal of Finance*, December 1969, pp. 801–824.

COMMODITY FUTURES

Bear, Robert M., "Margin Levels and the Behavior of Future Prices," *Journal of Financial and Quantitative Analysis*, September 1972, pp. 1907–1930.

Black, Fisher, "The Pricing of Commodity Contracts," *Journal of Financial Economics* 3 (1976): 167–179.

Dusak, Katherine, "Futures Trading and Investor Returns: An Investigation of Commodity Market Risk Premiums," *Journal of Political Economy* 81, no. 6 (November–December 1973): 1387–1406.

Hieronymus, Thomas A., *Economics of Futures Trading* (New York: Commodity Research Bureau, 1971).

Labys, Walter, and C. W. J. Granger, *Speculation, Hedging, and Commodity Price Forecasts* (Lexington, Mass.: Heath, 1970).

Peterson, Richard L., "Investor Preferences for Futures Straddler," *Journal of Financial and Quantitative Analysis*, March 1977, pp. 105–120.

Powers, Mark J., "Does Futures Trading Reduce Price Fluctuations in the Cash Markets?" *American Economic Review*, June 1970, pp. 460–464.

Robichek, Alexander, Richard Cohn, and John Pringle, "Returns on Alternative Investment Media and Implications for Portfolio Construction," *Journal of Business*, July 1972, pp. 427–443.

Schrock, Nicholas W., "The Theory of Asset Choice: Simultaneous Holding of Short and Long Positions in the Futures Market," *Journal of Political Economy*, (March–April 1971), pp. 270–293.

Stevenson, Richard A., and Robert M. Bear, "Commodity Futures: Trends or Random Walks," *Journal of Finance* 25, no. 1 (March 1970): 65–81.

Telser, Lester G., and Harlow N. Higinbotham, "Organized Futures Markets: Costs and Benefits," *Journal of Political Economy*, October 1977, pp. 969–1000.

Working, Holbrook, "New Concepts Concerning Futures Markets and Prices," *American Economic Review*, June 1962, pp. 431–459.

Chapter 13

Efficient Pricing and Security Screening

Investment management integrates a large set of diverse and individually complex activities. In addition to security analysis, these activities include security screening, portfolio construction, performance evaluation, and portfolio revision. This chapter will provide a link between the focus of prior chapters on individual securities and the focus of subsequent chapters on portfolio combinations. The topic of efficient pricing is concerned with how closely actual market prices measure true worth ("intrinsic value"). Security screening involves a search for procedures that will reduce the scope of security analysis to manageable proportions. The topics of efficiency and screening are important elements in the linkage of security analysis and portfolio management because both directly influence the inputs to and the results of investment activity. The first two sections consider the meaning and implications of pricing efficiency. The third section explores some techniques for reducing a large population of investments to a workable number which can be subjected to more intensive scrutiny. The chapter concludes with an appendix on technical analysis, an activity which remains popular on Wall Street despite its narrowly constrained and totally historical perspective.

Efficient Pricing of Securities

A security is properly priced when expected future return is commensurate with risk. Correct pricing is a necessary condition for allocational efficiency in the capital markets. A correct price is one which reflects a security's true value at the time of any transaction. When securities are properly priced the market is said to be in equilibrium. Because security prices are constantly changing, equilibrium exists only when price changes reflect changes in the underlying true value of every security. Although equilibrium values cannot be observed directly, it is possible to identify important properties of securities where prices behave as if they were properly priced. Capital market theory, which will be discussed in Chapter 15, is a body of knowledge which assumes that, on the whole, security prices approach equilibrium values. The performance evaluation techniques which will be discussed in Chapter 16 restate equilibrium concepts as standards and norms for evaluating the quality of security analysis and investment management. As a measure of performance, equilibrium standards are rigorous criteria in markets where most securities are indeed properly priced. Simply stated, in a highly efficient market a typical investor should expect to earn a fair return but not a superior (or inferior) one.

RANDOM WALK AND FAIRGAME MODELS

The concept and implications of market efficiency came into focus during the late 1950s and early 1960s through studies of what is commonly called the *random walk* hypothesis. Under this hypothesis stock price changes over any fixed interval of time are serially independent and normally distributed. At first random walk was merely an observation of the way prices appeared to behave. Later investigation provided an economic rationale for this observed behavior. The hypothesis can be stated formally as

$$P_{t+1} = bP_t + e_{t+1} \tag{13.1}$$

where P_{t+1} is the end of interval stock price, P_t is the corresponding beginning of interval price, b is a coefficient representing the long-run normal accumulation rate,[1] and e_{t+1} is a normally distributed error term with zero expected value. The expression algebraically defines the best unbiased estimate of price P_{t+1} as current price P_t adjusted for any long-run "drift" b appropriate to the particular security and time interval involved. Under these conditions, any deviation e_{t+1} of actual P_{t+1} from expected price bP_t is random and thus unpredictable in advance.

Random walk is an easily tested hypothesis. If the stock price in the next period is unpredictable, price changes should then be serially independent and they should have normal distribution properties. Results of extensive tests of securities, futures, and money markets over short intervals

[1] For example, if the interval of time is one month and the average historical rate of return r has been 1 percent per month, the coefficient b would be $(1 + r) = 1.01$.

of time including day to day, week to week, and month to month generally confirm the relevance of the random walk hypothesis.[2] Although the model appears to work reasonably well as a short-run description of security price changes, it is not a perfect description of price behavior. Generally, a low level of negative serial dependence is observed and the distribution of price changes is neither normally nor log normally distributed. But the observed departures from independence are so small that investors would have difficulty in profiting from them. Similarly, departures from a normal distribution occur because more observations than expected are grouped both near the center and in the tails of the distribution, with a lesser amount in the middle region on each side of the mean. A description of these distribution properties was provided in the appendix to Chapter 4. Again, no profitable strategies exist because of observed statistical departures from the random walk model.

Professional investors and academicians recognize that the random walk hypothesis, with its origin in the physical sciences,[3] is excessively and unrealistically restrictive. In an effort to correct and generalize the random walk model, faculty at the University of Chicago, under the leadership of Eugene Fama, popularized what is known today as the *fairgame model* where a properly priced security in an efficient market will behave such that over any and all intervals of time

$$E\{[P_{t+1} - E(P_{t+1}|\Phi_t)]|\Phi_t\} = 0 \tag{13.2}$$

The expression is not as formidable as it first appears to be. Starting within the brackets, $E(P_{t+1}|\Phi_t)$ represents the stock price which is expected at future date $t + 1$ where the expectation is based upon a specified information set Φ_t which is currently available at time t. The brackets enclose the difference between this expectation and stock price P_{t+1} which actually occurs at time $t + 1$. The outer braces signify that the expectation of this difference is zero, based upon the same set of information, when the security is properly priced. In other words, the fairgame hypothesis states that the difference between next period's actual price and the price expected currently by investors possessing a given set of information should be zero. If an investor is able consistently to use information represented by Φ to identify differences between actual and expected prices with a true value other than zero, the market has not fully discounted the particular information in question. This is the assumed case when an analyst identifies a security as being overvalued or undervalued.

[2] Eugene F. Fama, "The Behavior of Stock Market Prices," *Journal of Business*, January 1965, pp. 34–105; Arnold B. Larson, "Measurement of a Random Process in Futures Prices," *Food Research Institute Studies*, November 1960, pp. 313–324; Richard Roll, *The Behavior of Interest Rates: An Application of the Efficient Market Model to U.S. Treasury Bills* (New York: Basic Books, 1970).

[3] The random walk model was derived from Brownian motion theory which describes the behavior of an ensemble of molecular particles in statistical mechanics. M.F.M. Osborne, "Brownian Motion in the Stock Market," *Operations Research*, March–April, 1959, pp. 145–173.

The fairgame model is a more useful and realistic hypothesis of security price behavior than the random walk model. First, since it involves only expected prices, specific distributional properties of price changes are not required. The hypothesis is therefore consistent with price distributions which actually exist in the market place. Second, it does not assume, as random walk does, that risk is constant through time. Instead, the expectation of future price $E(P_{t+1}|\Phi_t)$ can be based on any level of risk which is perceived currently. If future risk is believed to be less than it has been in the past, expected price in the next period would involve a smaller adjustment of the current price than the change which was expected in past periods. The random walk model does not accommodate changing perceptions of risk or changing attitudes toward risk bearing. Instead, next period's price is expected to exceed the current price by a constant increment, thereby assuming away potential shifts in risk over time.

Although the fairgame model is commonly stated in terms of the price of a security, a more useful and convenient form is defined as a rate of return. The transition is straightforward because, for any given security or portfolio,

$$E(P_{t+1}|\Phi_t) = [1 + E(r_{t+1}|\Phi_t)] \times P_t \tag{13.3}$$

where P_{t+1} includes reinvestment of cash dividends and r_{t+1} is the one-period rate of return which is expected over time interval $(t, t + 1)$. Equation 13.3 equates the product of current price and the expected return relative to expected future price $E(P_{t+1})$. A notationally equivalent expression for the fairgame model defined in Equation 13.2, substituting rate of return for price, is

$$E\{[r_{t+1} - E(r_{t+1}|\Phi_t)]|\Phi_t\} = 0 \tag{13.4}$$

Equation 13.4 defines the sequence of differences between observed and expected rates of return as a fairgame with regard to information set Φ_t. In other words, the security or portfolio in question should yield a return commensurate with its level of risk.

INFORMATION SETS. The only information which is directly considered in the random walk model is the set of past and current prices. From this set, only the current price has any bearing on future prices. The fairgame model provides a more general perspective by the use of Φ to represent whatever set of information is assumed to be important in the forecasting process. The fairgame model is described in terms of three different levels of information which can usefully be identified:

1. *Weak-form information.* In this case only past price and volume information is available to the analyst. The weak-form information set is therefore roughly analogous to the information requirements of the random walk model. Weak-form information is more accurately described as price-volume information.
2. *Semistrong information.* Here all information which is publicly available and widely disseminated is considered in price and return expectations. This information includes all weak-form data plus knowledge of earnings, dividends,

public announcements by management, and other widely reported announcements. Semistrong information may more descriptively be called public information.

3. *Strong-form information.* The most comprehensive set of all, strong-form information includes everything of importance concerning the security in question. This would include knowledge of firm activities which have not yet been publicly reported, large buy or sell orders which are pending, private in-depth security analysis sold by advisory services on a limited subscription basis, pending government investigations, and all other activities with a potential impact on value which are not yet publicly known. Strong-form information may more descriptively be called private or inside information.

The main purpose of distinguishing among these different levels of information is to determine the degree to which security prices correctly reflect values. It may be true, for example, that price-volume information is effectively utilized in the formation of return expectations but other public information is not.[4] The next paragraphs consider the accuracy of the fairgame model as a description of actual security market conditions. Subsequent sections will deal with the fairgame model's implications for the traditional procedures of technical and fundamental security analysis.

ACCURACY OF FAIRGAME PRICING MODEL. The basic implication of the fairgame model is that an average investor cannot correctly expect an above normal return based on currently available information. Most studies of New York Stock Exchange securities tend to confirm this statement but the overall accuracy of the model remains to be proven conclusively. The fairgame model has been tested in markets other than the New York Stock Exchange only recently and the results of these applications have varied widely. Empirical testing of stock price behavior has taken three forms, each corresponding to one informational level of the fairgame model. Studies have tended to develop sequentially, moving from tests of weak-form efficiency to tests of strong-form efficiency. The next paragraphs will highlight the major methodologies and findings.

PRICE-VOLUME INFORMATION STUDIES

Studies of weak-form efficiency have evolved from, and in many cases were actually tests of, the random walk model. Both random walk and fairgame models imply that successive price changes will be independent. Typically, short-run price changes were tested for independence by means of serial correlation, run analysis, and filter techniques. Serial correlation measures the statistical relationship between price changes lagged with price changes one or more periods away. Unfortunately, interpretation of serial correlation measures is limited by the nonnormal characteristics of the distribution of

[4] It would not be possible to find the opposite, that weak-form conditions are violated but the semistrong form holds, because price-volume information is a subset of all public information. Similarly, public information is a subset of all possible information, both public and private.

security prices (and returns) because occasional large price changes dominate the observations and reduce confidence in the results obtained.

An alternative test is run analysis. A run is a series of like observations immediately followed and preceded by dissimilar observations. If a price increase of any size is designated by "+" and a decrease in price by "–" any pattern might be observed over time:

Hypothetical Stock		*Number of Runs*
A	+ + + + + – – – – –	2
B	+ – + – + – + – + –	10
C	– – + – + + + – – +	6

The pattern for stock A reflects continuing trends: if the price of the stock has been increasing (decreasing) it will probably continue to move up (or down). Stock B shows the opposite behavior, a tendency of price reversal from the preceding period. Stock A has very few runs but stock B has many. Stock C represents an unpredictable sequence, evidenced by a number of runs equal to the number expected by chance in a totally random series.[5] Since each observation is counted equally regardless of size, run analysis removes potential problems of nonnormality in identifying independence. However, run analysis is not a powerful test and, similar to serial correlation, results have stronger statistical than economic interpretation.

A final weak-form test is filter analysis. Filter analysis examines returns based upon mechanical trading rules of the following type: if the price of a stock increases by 10 percent, buy and hold until the stock decreases by 10 percent from its subsequent high. If stock prices move in trends, as stock A does in the example, this particular rule may produce better returns than a simple buy and hold investment policy. Because returns should be calculated net of transaction costs, filter tests have a direct economic interpretation. If a rule consistently works, price movements are not random and the security is improperly priced. But filter tests also have severe limitations. They truly require a "needle in the haystack" approach to specify the "right rule," and then the rule must have validity over a prolonged period of time.[6] Simulating numerous filter rules over very large data bases for stocks and futures has generally failed to identify any consistently profitable trends in prices. Most evidence suggests that short-run price and return behavior is

[5] Nonparametric statistical tests exist to test the significance of the number of runs observed in any series of consecutive prices or returns. See Jean Dickinson Gibbons, *Nonparametrical Methods for Quantitative Analysis* (New York: Holt, Rinehart and Winston, 1976), chap. 8.

[6] Jensen and Barrington have pointed out that it is possible to derive filter rules that appear to work for a finite series of truly independent returns. What is needed is a further demonstration that a rule will continue to work over other series as well. Michael Jensen and George Barrington, "Random Walks and Technical Theories: Some Additional Evidence," *Journal of Finance*, May 1970, pp. 469–482.

consistent with that expected in efficient markets according to the weak-form fairgame model.[7]

PUBLIC INFORMATION STUDIES

Past prices and returns are only one element of information which is available to the investment community. Other elements include past and current financial information as well as statements by management and others regarding future plans and operations. Tests of semistrong and strong-form efficiency are difficult to design because of the variety and lack of regularity of the information involved. Generally, studies of semistrong efficiency focus on one particular type of information, associating that information with stock price behavior. For example, as discussed in Chapter 10, Fama, Fisher, Jensen, and Roll studied the price impact of stock splits and they concluded that price behavior reflects the anticipation of dividend increases when stocks are split.[8] In another study, Ball and Brown examined the price impact of annual earnings announcements; they concluded that 85 to 90 percent of earnings information had been anticipated by the month the announcement was made.[9] These and other studies of firm-related information found that returns react to public announcements in a manner which is consistent with the fairgame model.

At an aggregate level, Victor Niederhoffer studied the reaction of security prices to world events which have potentially significant consequences.[10] Over the period 1950–1966, Niederhoffer found that the stock market reacted immediately to announcements of crisis proportions. Although reaction was rapid, some positive short-run price dependency was evident: large initial price decreases (increases) were more likely to be followed by other decreases (increases). This pattern is consistent with the observation that some investors react to major events immediately, while others pause to consider the situation before committing themselves. Within five days the market usually returned to normal trading conditions. Because major events occur over prolonged and irregular periods, it is doubtful that they could be exploited profitably unless the investor has advance private knowledge of those events. Overall, the majority of studies on how public announcements affect stock returns conclude that their results are consistent with the semistrong form of the fairgame model.

[7] A review of studies through 1969 has been provided by Eugene Fama, "Efficient Capital Markets," *Journal of Finance*, May 1970, pp. 383–417. Most subsequent studies have tested the fairgame model with more comprehensive information sets.

[8] Eugene Fama, Lawrence Fisher, Michael Jensen, and Richard Roll, "The Adjustment of Stock Prices to New Information," *International Economic Review*, February 1969, pp. 1–21.

[9] Ray Ball and Phillip Brown, "An Empirical Evaluation of Accounting Income Numbers," *Journal of Accounting Research*, Autumn 1968, pp. 159–178.

[10] Victor Niederhoffer, "The Analysis of World Events and Stock Prices," *Journal of Business*, April 1971, pp. 193–220.

PRIVATE INFORMATION STUDIES

Strong-form efficiency implies that all information is fully reflected in a stock's price at all times. If a market is strong-form efficient, no investor can expect abnormally high profits from the possession of inside information. One group of investors with a monopoly on inside information are the exchange specialists and studies have shown that they use this knowledge to obtain monopoly profits.[11] Corporate officers and directors are another group with access to inside information, and there is evidence which suggests that they determine buy-and-sell decisions on the basis of inside knowledge.[12] In contrast, studies of mutual fund returns have consistently found that fund managers have no special information advantage which allows them to earn consistently large returns for their customers.[13] The value of analysts' recommendations is less clear. The strongest interpretation of the efficient market hypothesis implies that professional recommendations are of no value. But in a study of major brokerage firms' recommendations and those carried in the "Heard on the Street" column of *The Wall Street Journal*, Lloyd-Davies and Canes concluded that analysts do provide inside information and that investors who use these services do receive something of value.[14] The question of which segments of the investment community possess useful "inside" information and what, if anything, should be done to eliminate insider advantage, given the overall costs and benefits of corrective regulation, are topics now being debated as part of the problem of restructuring the capital markets.

THE NATURE OF NEW INFORMATION

An investor faces many difficulties in relating information to security analysis. The first problem is one of recognizing just what constitutes information;

[11] A specialist has knowledge of the "book" of unfilled limit orders on the stock in question. Evidence on the trading activity of specialists is presented by Victor Niederhoffer and M. F. M. Osborne, "Market Making and Reversal on the Stock Exchange," *Journal of the American Statistical Association*, December 1966, pp. 897–916, and by the *Institutional Investor Study Report of the Securities and Exchange Commission*, Summary Volume, March 10, 1971.

[12] Joseph E. Finnerty, "Insiders' Activity and Inside Information: A Multivariate Analysis," *Journal of Financial and Quantitative Analysis*, June 1976, pp. 205–213.

[13] William Sharpe, "Mutual Fund Performance," *Journal of Business*, Special Supplement, January 1966, pp. 119–138; Jack L. Treynor, "How To Rate Management of Investment Funds," *Harvard Business Review*, January–February 1965, pp. 63–75; Michael Jensen, "The Performance of Mutual Funds in the Period 1945–1964," *Journal of Finance*, May 1968, pp. 389–416. Mutual fund performance is discussed in Chapter 18.

[14] Peter Lloyd-Davies and Michael Canes, "Stock Prices and the Publication of Second-Hand Information," *Journal of Business*, January 1978, pp. 43–56. Similar conclusions were reached by Lawrence Brown and Michael Rozeff, "The Superiority of Analyst Forecasts as Measure of Expectations: Evidence from Earnings," *Journal of Finance*, March 1978, pp. 1–16. The apparent inconsistency between the value of analysts' information and the performance of fund managers, who rely on analysts' services, might be explained by the fact that large investors with inside information cannot eliminate abnormal returns without creating undue concentration and, therefore, abnormal risk. At some point excess return becomes fair return for excess risk.

new information is any news which has problematical impact on a security's future value. For example, the reported loss of a large customer, a strike, a fire, or any similar event, may adversely affect the value of a firm. The threat of nationalization of a firm's foreign subsidiary would probably have a depressing effect on price even where the event did not, and may never, occur. Moreover, the complete absence of information may in itself be news which affects value. If a firm is engaged in merger or takeover proceedings which are perceived by stockholders as contrary to their best interests, an absence of news (that negotiations have broken off) as time passes increases the likelihood of merger and price should decrease accordingly.

Even when information is specific and certain, the interrelationship among a large number of events which are occurring simultaneously obscures the impact that each has on price behavior. One part of the problem is determining what information is relevant and to what extent it affects the value of the firm. Another part is determining whether the information has been anticipated and discounted and thus is not really "new." For these reasons, it is easy to see that the task of associating semistrong and strong-form information with security prices is a very difficult and imprecise process.

Investing in Efficient Markets

The knowledge that the financial market system results in effective and efficient security pricing serves as both a comfort and a challenge to investors. In a world of complete certainty and perfect pricing, security analysis would be meaningless; in an uncertain world, the need for forecasting and analysis is assured. With inefficient security pricing and an abundance of "inside information," security analysis would be trivial, but with market efficiency and minimal monopolistic information opportunities, it becomes far more difficult. The price of any security reflects a balance of individual forecasts by current and potential holders of that particular investment. The nature and complexity of forecasting implies that some persons will do better than others. For those able to predict more accurately and/or extend their predictions further into the future than the average investor, fundamental security analysis will provide greater than average rewards.

TECHNICAL ANALYSIS

Technical analysis is a forecasting technique which relies solely on past and current security prices and, in some cases, trading volumes. Fundamental security analysis is deliberately excluded and primary importance is placed on identifying and extrapolating price trends. The most popular tool of technical analysis is a chart of historical prices and volumes which extrapolates past activity into the future. Other approaches to technical analysis are more complex and they involve mechanistic trading rules which are often evaluated by computer. Whatever the specific technique, technical analysis requires the existence of identifiable and persistent trends in market values through time which provide an opportunity for above average return. Modestly efficient markets, described as price-volume efficient in the previous section, imply the absence of trends which can be identified solely on the basis of past prices and volumes: for this reason technical analysis should be rejected as a substitute for fundamental analysis. A proof of this point is contained in the next paragraph. Nonetheless, technical measures may reflect otherwise undetected information at an early stage and they may be of some value to the investment manager at the initial level of security screening. For this reason the basic mechanics of technical analysis and technical indicators are surveyed in the chapter appendix.

It is easily shown that technical analysis is in basic conflict with the assumption that capital markets price securities in at least a weak-form efficient manner. If all pertinent information resulting from past and current prices and trading volumes is indeed reflected in current price, trends cannot be predicted. A simple proof of this point has been offered by Eugene Fama.[15] Let $\alpha(\Phi_t)$ represent an overall trading strategy involving any number of stocks. This strategy can be identified notationally by the following expression:

$$\alpha(\Phi_t) = [\alpha_1(\Phi_t), \alpha_2(\Phi_t) \ldots \alpha_n(\Phi_t)] = \sum_{i=1}^{n} \alpha_i(\Phi_t) \tag{13.5}$$

The trading strategy results in the allocation of $\alpha_i (i = 1, \ldots, n)$ dollars which are available at time t to each of n stocks. Defining the information set Φ_t as containing only current and past price and volume levels, any trading plan $\alpha(\Phi_t)$ used to construct a portfolio from n stocks would of necessity be based on technical analysis. The total excess market value or portfolio differential return realized at any future time would be defined as

$$V_{t+1} = \sum_{i=1}^{n} \alpha_i(\Phi_t)[r_{it+1} - E(r_{it+1}|\Phi_t)] \tag{13.6}$$

For every security i that is properly valued, the expected excess return expressed by the bracketed term will be zero. This is the fairgame property defined in Equation 13.4. With efficient market pricing all expected excess returns are zero, and excess market value is also zero. Symbolically,

$$E(V_{t+1}) = \sum_{i=1}^{n} \alpha_i(\Phi_t)E\{[r_{it+1} - E(r_{it+1}|\Phi_t)]\Phi_t\} = 0 \tag{13.7}$$

which implies that efficient pricing is incompatible with technical analysis. With this in mind, the next section considers the relationship among technical analysis, fundamental analysis, and varying degrees of market efficiency.

[15] Eugene F. Fama, "Efficient Capital Markets: A Review of Theory and Empirical Work," *Journal of Finance*, May 1970, pp. 385–386.

COMPARING FUNDAMENTAL AND TECHNICAL ANALYSIS: A SUMMARY

Technical analysis differs in both focus and method from fundamental analysis. Technical analysis considers supply and demand forces indirectly through the behavior of price and volume statistics. The view is short-run, based on the belief that trading on the basis of recent short-run price behavior will provide greater returns than alternative strategies. In fact, technical analysts generally ignore fundamental factors, in order to avoid the "double counting" which is assumed to occur because fundamental considerations are already reflected in the price. The technical analyst believes that prices are influenced by both economic and psychological factors and that fundamental analysis, by concentrating on economic values, may be misleading. Fundamental analysts, on the other hand, would argue that all factors affecting value, both economic and psychological, are necessary and proper areas for forecasting. The anticipation of future events and their consequence is assumed to be more relevant to future returns than the pattern of past prices. Fundamental analysis evaluates all relevant factors which affect intrinsic value, a concept which technicians consider meaningless.

Although technical and fundamental analysis are viewed as being largely incompatible, some investment strategies attempt to reconcile the features of each approach. Burton G. Malkiel argued for an investment perspective which integrates the two viewpoints. From this integrated approach, he developed a set of rules which are designed for optimal security selection:[16]

Rule 1. Confine stock purchases to companies that appear to be able to sustain above average earnings growth for at least five years.

Rule 2. Never pay more for a stock than can reasonably be justified by a firm foundation of value.

Rule 3. It helps to buy stocks whose stories of anticipated growth are ones on which investors can build castles in the air.

Professor Malkiel's rules provide criteria for screening, economic analysis, and psychological analysis, respectively. Although technical analysis may be useful in identifying trends resulting from castle building, all three rules may be thought of as guidelines which are consistent with a strictly fundamentalist approach. Rule 3 is suggestive of an often-cited rationale for technical analysis: because so many investors use it, the market will reflect their expectations. But this notion of self-fulfilling prophecy is open to serious question because the techniques and interpretations of technical analysis differ widely and the overall impact of groups of technical traders may be largely offsetting.

A summary of the relationship between technical analysis, fundamental analysis, and various degrees of capital market efficiency is given in Figure 13.1. A third category, random selection, has been added to recognize the strategy of selecting investments by chance alone without prior

[16] Burton G. Malkiel, *A Random Walk Down Wall Street* (New York: Norton 1975), esp. pp. 113–116.

Figure 13.1
Levels of Market Efficiency and Approaches to Investment Analysis

	Inefficient	Weak-Form Efficient	Semistrong Form Efficient	Strong-Form Efficient
Technical Analysis	Best	Poor	Poor	Poor
Fundamental Analysis	Poor	Best	Good	Fair
Random Selection	Fair	Fair	Fair	Best

analysis of any kind. The classifications of *poor*, *fair*, *good*, and *best* suggest the potential which each methodology enjoys compared to other forms of security analysis in a given market environment. All classifications are approximate and they reflect both the benefits and the costs of each strategy. Fundamental analysis is more costly than random selection and somewhat greater returns are necessary with fundamental analysis to equal yields from random selection. The summary judgments expressed in Figure 13.1 refer to average outcomes in a market that is predominantly but not entirely efficient at each information level. In a market that is generally efficient, where there are at least a few mispriced securities, a competent analyst will achieve results which are superior to those realized under random selection. Technical analysis has value only under extremely inefficient market conditions; this may occur in small and decentralized markets (e.g., regional over-the-counter issues) but significant inefficiency is not consistent with available evidence on the operation of major marketplaces. Fundamental analysis loses relevance in an inefficient market setting because there is no reason to believe that prices will ultimately converge to the correct intrinsic value.

Fundamental Screening Procedures

INTRODUCTION

Screening is the reduction of a large number of potential investments to a manageable group of likely candidates for security analysis. With tens of thousands of publicly held firms, many of which have debt, preferred stock, and common stock outstanding, the need for screening is obvious. Unless some systematic procedure is adopted, security analysis would either be prohibitively expensive or it would be subject to the fortunes of any hit or miss operation. Fortunately, practical and relatively inexpensive procedures are available for this purpose. The strategy which is adopted will depend upon the objectives, perceptions, and resources of the investor together with recognition of the need for a diversified portfolio. One difficult but unresolved problem with most screening procedures is that they tend to identify a group of securities with common qualities and features. As the next few chapters will demonstrate, the risk-return dimensions of an investment portfolio can differ significantly from the same measures for its component securities. Focusing on similar securities can result in the selection of a less than optimal portfolio. By recognizing the value of diversity prior to screening, investors can resolve this dilemma by adopting flexible search and screening methods.

OBJECTIVES AND RESOURCES. The first step in screening investment opportunities is the decision to exclude assets which are inconsistent with the investor's risk and return objectives. Complex objectives can be defined in terms of the desired trade-off between stable income and safety of principal on one hand and the opportunity for substantial capital appreciation on the other.[17] Some investors may dismiss futures and options as being too speculative while others may rule out bonds, preferred stocks, and mortgages because of their level of expected return. The extent to which entire categories of investments must be arbitrarily excluded depends upon the availability of computational resources and financial information. For large institutions the ready availability of computerized data and software makes it feasible to screen large populations of securities. But for the small investor, armed only with a pocket calculator and the public library, some investment alternatives will be eliminated without the benefit of even an elementary screening procedure.

NAIVE DIVERSIFICATION. Diversification will be discussed in later chapters but the basic concept that concentration should be avoided must be recognized in the screening process. With some investment categories excluded, naive diversification implies that each remaining type should have some representation in the screened population. For example, assume that an investor has decided to purchase a portfolio of common stocks which are listed on the New York Stock Exchange;[18] in addition, diversity is to be assured by limiting investment to 10 percent in any one stock and 10 to 30 percent in any one of six general industry areas.[19] In this case the investor

[17] The adjustment of investor attitudes through time is discussed in Chapter 18.

[18] The idea of focusing only on Big Board stocks receives support from a study by Paul F. Jessup and Roger B. Upson, *Returns in Over-the-Counter Stock Markets* (Minneapolis: University of Minnesota Press, 1973). They find that over-the-counter common stocks have historically provided a lower average return per unit of risk than listed securities, with the deficiency being largest for smaller issues which are traded only on a regional basis. In contrast, Arthur Eubank, Jr., concludes that the performance of over-the-counter securities is as good as, if not superior to, listed securities. Arthur Eubank, Jr., "Risk/Return Contrasts: NYSE, AMEX, and OTC," *Journal of Portfolio Management*, Summer 1977, pp. 25–30.

[19] For example, the groupings might be (1) agricultural and mining, (2) sales and service, (3) manufacturing, (4) utility and transportation, (5) oils, and (6) finance. Industry classification is considered in greater detail in Chapter 15.

is likely to purchase between one and three stocks in each industry, depending on their prices, and if at least two firms are to be evaluated for each one which is finally selected, a logical screening objective would be to identify six potentially promising stocks in each industry.[20] For this investor, screening must reduce a population of approximately 1500 securities to 36 stocks, evenly divided among six general industry groupings. The two most popular criteria are relative strength and factor (ratio) analysis.

RELATIVE PERFORMANCE CRITERIA

Screening involves low-cost discrimination among a large population of potential investment opportunities. This is often accomplished with empirical data by identifying stocks with successful records and/or other desirable features. Moving averages or other measures of realized return on investment can be used as a point of reference; for example, all stocks exceeding some specified yield over the past five years might be identified. Return is positively related to risk and variability must therefore be considered because low-risk securities will otherwise be excluded. To continue the example, the rate of return requirement could be combined with some specified maximum level of dispersion. This dual requirement would yield a smaller and more balanced list of investment candidates. Another possible refinement would classify return according to dividend yield and capital appreciation with preset standards for each component according to the investor's objectives and risk preference.

Studies by Robert Levy suggest that favorable trends in return tend to persist for periods of time up to five years.[21] But persistent yield trends are contrary to the theory of efficient markets and random walks and Levy's findings have been challenged on that basis. Richard Brealey, for example, concluded that security markets are too efficient to permit the persistence of price trends except when they occur by chance alone; that claim continues to be disputed and the issue remains to be resolved.[22] It does appear that the persistence of trends in stock returns, if they exist at all, are too small to be profitable when transaction expenses are considered.

[20] For professional security analysts who are employed by large financial institutions, the screening problem is usually less difficult. Because a team approach is used, each analyst has responsibility for some specific industry or functional area. Narrow groupings may be further constrained by minimum firm size or other considerations.

[21] Robert Levy, "Random Walks: Reality or Myth," *Financial Analysts Journal*, November–December 1967, pp. 69–77; also "Reply," *Financial Analysts Journal*, January–February 1968, pp. 129–132; and "Relative Strength as a Criterion for Investment Selection," *Journal of Finance*, December 1967, pp. 595–610.

[22] Richard A. Brealey, *An Introduction to Risk and Return* (Cambridge, Mass.: M.I.T. Press, 1969), chap. 2. Also see F. E. James, Jr., "Monthly Moving Averages—An Effective Investment Tool?" *Journal of Financial and Quantitative Analysis*, September 1968, pp. 315–326, and Michael C. Jensen and George A. Bennington, "Random Walks and Technical Theories: Some Additional Evidence," *Journal of Finance*, May 1970, pp. 469–482. For a different view see Charles A. Akemann and Werner E. Keller, "Relative Strength Does Persist!" *Journal of Portfolio Management*, Fall 1977, pp. 38–45.

Since there is a positive relationship between a firm's income stream and the return to its shareholders the average rate of change in earnings can be used as a screening criterion. Unlike the case of historic price trends, there is no necessary conflict between earnings behavior and market efficiency because stock prices may change randomly regardless of earnings patterns. The persistence of earnings growth is also an unresolved question but, again unlike the case of price trends, the weight of evidence is slightly more favorable. Although Brealey finds little value in past earnings estimates, a more recent study by Latané, Jones, and Rieke found the concept of "unexpected earnings" to be a valid and useful means of identifying potentially superior investments.[23] As noted in Chapter 8, Basu suggests that there is a relationship between investment performance and price-earnings ratios; he found that portfolios consisting of low price to earnings stocks enjoyed greater absolute and risk-adjusted rates of return than high price to earnings stocks.[24] Growth of sales and growth of assets are two other common measures of performance. Although these variables have a greater tendency to persist over time, they are further removed and less strongly correlated with investor returns.

A statistic is useful only when there is some underlying reason for believing that observed performance will continue in the future. Screening by relative performance eliminates securities which have been less than outstanding in the past. For some rejected investments conditions will undoubtedly change, but failure to identify these potential opportunities is the cost of this type of screening. For investments which survive the screening process, security analysis will identify those cases where favorable trends are most likely to continue or possibly accelerate. For instance, the appearance of good growth over a period of several years may result from (1) accounting changes, (2) steadily increasing leverage and leasehold arrangements, (3) price increases and higher profit margins, (4) increasing production toward full capacity, or (5) a steady and proportionate growth of sales, assets, and profits. Security analysis will distinguish among these several possible reasons.

MULTIPLE FACTOR ANALYSIS

Multiple factor analysis views measures of relative strength as only one of several indications of investment quality. Many brokerage firms provide multiple factor guidelines for their customers. Dean Witter, for example,

[23] Richard A. Brealey, *Introduction to Risk and Return*, chaps. 7 and 8; H. A. Latané, C. P. Jones, and R. D. Rieke, "Quarterly Earnings Reports and Subsequent Six-Month Holding Period Returns," *Journal of Business Research*, April 1974, pp. 119–132. The earnings variable in the paper, SUE (Standard Unexpected Earnings), resulted from a prediction of quarterly earnings based on a regression of 20 previous quarterly earnings against 5 explanatory variables.

[24] S. Basu, "The Investment Performance of Common Stocks in Relation to Their Price-Earnings Ratios: A Test of the Efficient Market Hypothesis," *The Journal of Finance*, June 1977, pp. 663–682.

issues a quarterly report which screens 2800 listed and over-the-counter equities. Their screening variables and standards are:

1. A market price which is less than book value.
2. A price-earnings ratio below 10.0.
3. A dividend yield which is greater than 5 percent.
4. A dividend payout ratio which is less than 50 percent.
5. A current ratio which is higher than 2 to 1.
6. A debt equity ratio which does not exceed 40 percent.
7. Equity exceeding $25 million in value.

The Dean Witter report covers market conditions (items 1, 2, and 7), size and stability of income (items 3 and 4), and solvency (items 5 and 6). Because the minimum acceptable levels set by Dean Witter are high, only a limited number of stocks survive their screening process.[25]

A growth standard is conspicuously absent from this particular list. Because other criteria are very conservative, it is doubtful that any stock with exceptional growth potential would be on this list unless it was substantially underpriced. Identifying the appropriate screening ratios and their levels determines both the number and the characteristics of the screened securities. For income-seeking, risk-averse investors this particular screening device identifies a relevant population, but for investors with a different investment perspective, potentially promising opportunities are excluded and another screening standard should be selected.

A general screening procedure will survey the population of firms in each of the broad areas of productivity, liquidity, and financing. In addition to these firm-related quality standards, additional criteria may be added to reflect market values and the investor's current income requirements. Some of the more popular screening ratios are identified in Table 13.1. The variables which are listed there are representative of those used in practice; each investor must select measures which complement investment objectives, including some which may not be identified in the table. In some cases a financial aggregate is more appropriate than a ratio, as in the case of aggregate firm size. Some investors may believe that growth potential is too limited in firms which are already large.

Published sources of information provide data which are suitable for multiple factor analysis. The most comprehensive service, *Financial Dynamics*, is generated from COMPUSTAT data tapes. *Financial Dynamics* provides a continuously updated record of 111 annual financial ratios for major companies in over 100 industries, together with quarterly comparisons for a smaller number of key ratios, 12-month moving average comparisons, and annual industry comparisons. The *Financial Weekly*, a

[25] On their November 1976 report Dean Witter found 72 stocks which met the multiple criteria listed above. Dean Witter & Company, *Book Value Discount List*, November 1976, pp. 4 and 6.

Table 13.1
Screening Factors

Area	*Measures*	
	Firm-Related	
Productivity		
a. Profitability	Return on sales:	$\frac{\text{earnings before interest and taxes}}{\text{sales}}$
	Return on assets:	$\frac{\text{EBIT}}{\text{assets}}$
	Return on equity:	$\frac{\text{after-tax earnings}}{\text{shareholder equity}}$
	Cash flow:	$\frac{\text{after-tax earnings plus depreciation}}{\text{shares outstanding}}$
b. Efficiency	Asset turnover:	$\frac{\text{sales}}{\text{assets}}$
	Inventory turnover:	$\frac{\text{cost of goods sold}}{\text{average yearly inventory}}$
	Receivable turnover:	$\frac{\text{sales}}{\text{average accounts receivable}}$
Liquidity	Current ratio:	$\frac{\text{current assets}}{\text{current liabilities}}$
	Quick ratio:	$\frac{\text{current assets} - \text{inventory}}{\text{current liabilities}}$
	Liquidity ratio:	$\frac{\text{cash and marketable securities}}{\text{current liabilities}}$
Financing	Debt to equity:	$\frac{\text{liabilities}}{\text{net worth}}$
	Debt to asset:	$\frac{\text{total debt}}{\text{total assets}}$
	Times interest earned:	$\frac{\text{current interest}}{\text{EBIT}}$
	Market-Related	
Pricing	Price to earnings:	$\frac{\text{current price}}{\text{earnings}}$
	Book ratio:	$\frac{\text{book value}}{\text{market price}}$
Income	Payout ratio:	$\frac{\text{dividends}}{\text{earnings}}$
	Current yield:	$\frac{\text{dividends}}{\text{market price}}$
Marketability	Turnover:	$\frac{\text{annual volume}}{\text{shares outstanding}}$
	Institutional share:	$\frac{\text{institutionally held shares}}{\text{shares outstanding}}$

newspaper published by Media General Financial Services, provides numerous summaries, ratios, moving averages, and other useful financial data for 3400 stocks, bonds, commodities, options, and mutual funds. *Moody's Manuals* and *Value Line* are two other popular sources of information useful for screening purposes. *Value Line* provides a monthly ranking of investments in accordance with their own evaluation procedures. Fisher Black found that *Value Line*'s highest and lowest ranked securities proved in fact to be under- and overvalued, respectively.[26] A more limited set of data is available monthly in the *Standard & Poor's Stock Guide* and weekly in *Barron's*. In addition, many brokerage firms provide data in a format which is readily adaptable for screening. In their quarterly report, for example, Goldman Sachs ranks all S&P 500 stocks by size, price-earnings ratio, dividend yield, and percentage change in value.[27]

A multifactor screening program requires the flexibility which can be achieved by varying criteria according to specific industry or market conditions. A required price-earnings ratio below 10 may be suitable for utilities but it would probably exclude most of the securities in other industries. An investor should also consider interrelationships among selected screening factors. For example, growth firms tend to reinvest earnings and the choice of a high dividend yield will reduce the growth prospects of securities which survive the screening process. On balance the application of multiple factor screening requires an appreciation of the qualities which are excluded as well as those which are selected. The following section discusses other relevant considerations when large populations of securities are screened for further analysis.

MANAGEMENT OBJECTIVES

Performance measures should be supplemented, when possible, with a preliminary assessment of managerial expertise. This is not an especially difficult task; many business periodicals, including *The Wall Street Journal*, *Forbes*, and *Business Week*, routinely report information on the activity and viewpoints of leading business executives. Patterns of creditability can also be implied from introductory comments in quarterly and annual reports when they are compared to outcomes which are reported subsequently. A qualitative assessment of a firm's management provides an added dimension and depth to purely statistical measures.

Very few studies have attempted to compare management structure and investor returns. It appears from the limited evidence which is available that owner-controlled firms achieve higher profit rates and they are willing to take greater risks, with the greatest difference observed where the firm en-

[26] Fisher Black, "Yes Virginia, There Is Hope: Tests of the Value Line Ranking System," *Financial Analysts Journal* 29 (September–October 1974): 10–14.

[27] Goldman Sachs, *Analysis of Market Trends, Quarter Ended December 1976*.

Table 13.2
Shareholder and Management Concerns

	Shareholder	*Management*
Goal:	Maximize Satisfaction	Survival
Objectives:	Highest return at acceptable level of risk	a. Production b. Sales c. Market share d. Inventory e. Working capital f. Dividends g. Financing
Constraints:	a. Market conditions b. Interrelationships among investments c. Information, search, and transaction costs	a. Profits b. Funds available c. Regulation d. Management stability

joys some form of monopoly advantage.[28] In the only study which directly associates management orientation and stock market performance, Robert Masson has found that more effective management resulted in cases where executive pay was linked to shareholder interests through use of stock options or other special forms of compensation.[29]

The potential conflict between stockholder and managerial interests is a natural one arising from the fact that managers earn their livelihood and receive a wide and continuous sense of satisfaction from their positions. The concern of shareholders is both more narrow and less intense because any particular firm represents only one of at least several financial commitments. Table 13.2 highlights the major goals, objectives, and constraints of stockholders and managers. The differences highlighted in the table suggest that it is easy for management to lose sight of shareholder interests

[28] Owner-controlled is defined by the percentage of stock held by the largest shareholder. An arbitrarily selected dividing line is usually in the area of 20 percent: if at least one person holds 20 percent or more of the outstanding shares, the firm is classified as owner-controlled. By this standard Robert Larner found that in 1963, 169 of the then largest 200 nonfinancial firms were management-controlled, almost double the number that would have been so classified in 1929. Robert Larner, "Ownership and Control in the 200 Largest Nonfinancial Corporations, 1929 and 1963," *American Economic Review*, September 1966, pp. 777–787. Also R. Joseph Monsen, John Chiu, and David Cooley, "The Effect of Separation of Ownership and Control on the Performance of the Large Firm," *Quarterly Journal of Economics*, August 1968, pp. 435–442; Kenneth Boudreaux, "Managerialism and Risk-Return Performance," *Southern Economic Journal*, January 1971, pp. 366–372; and Ben Branch, "Corporate Objectives and Market Performance, *Financial Management*, Summer 1973, pp. 24–29.

[29] Robert Masson, "Executive Motivations, Earnings, and Consequent Equity Performance," *Journal of Political Economy*, November–December 1971, pp. 1278–1292.

Figure 13.2
A Model of Managerial Behavior

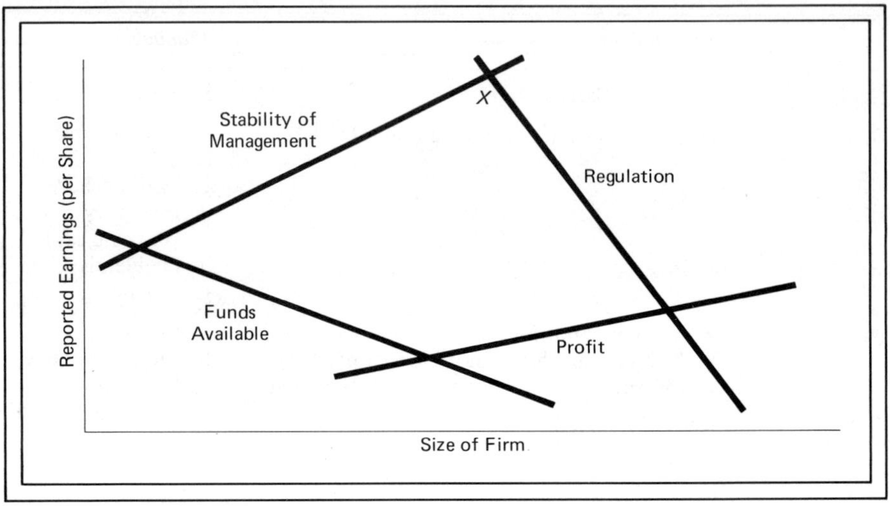

in the face of seemingly more pressing and immediate concerns. The question of growth, by expansion or merger, is a case in point; stockholder-oriented management will focus on earnings growth which is not necessarily synonymous with the expansion of sales and assets.

Figure 13.2 provides a graphic model of management orientation by focusing on the two attributes of earnings and size. Acceptable levels of earnings and firm size are identified as falling within the boundaries determined by the constraints of funds availability, profitability, regulation, and management stability. While all firms are subject to these constraints, a stockholder-oriented management will seek to operate near point X on Figure 13.2 where equity return is the greatest. Shareholders would also expect these constraints to be set at realistically high levels so that significant opportunities are not overlooked. A management group which fails to emphasize stockholder interests will be satisfied with operating results provided that they fall anywhere within the bounded area. Although this model is abstract, it may still prove to be useful to an investor. Point X would be difficult to determine for any firm but it is much less difficult to recognize circumstances which imply less profitable operation below that point. A record of unprofitable mergers or ineffectual cash management are two examples of suboptimal behavior.

Summary

This chapter bridges security and portfolio construction by considering two major issues which are relevant to both areas. The first is the question of the efficient discounting of information in the security markets. While there is little reason to believe that markets for real goods and services are necessarily efficient, there is ample theoretical and empirical evidence to support the belief that major financial markets are at least moderately efficient in pricing financial claims. This observation implies that a technical approach to security transactions, especially as a means of seeking short-run profitability, is of dubious value. Moreover, moderate levels of stock market efficiency place strong performance demands on the security analyst. To identify undervalued securities consistently, an analyst must develop superior insights and competence in evaluating financial data.

The second major element is security screening. Screening identifies the securities to be analyzed and it therefore determines the basic character of the investment portfolio. This can be accomplished by ranking a large number of investments by one or more readily determinable characteristics. Measures of market performance, ratios based on financial data, and assessment of management orientation are three complementary criteria which are available for use in screening. A problem with screening is that it tends to identify a sample of securities with similar traits; the next few chapters demonstrate that effective portfolio building requires a diversity of investments. However, the alternative to systematic screening is random selection, and this is even less appealing because it has no relationship to basic valuation factors and it is inconsistent with the concept of normative portfolio management.

The next chapter introduces portfolio building; emphasis shifts to a combination of investments based upon the inputs from individual security analysis.

Appendix
Technical Trading Procedures

Technical analysis encompasses a variety of procedures, many of which have several variations. This appendix surveys the most popular and well-known forms of technical analysis to provide a basic description of what they are and how they operate.

CHARTING. Charting is the most common tool of technical analysis. The technical analyst relies on two types of charts: bar charts and point and figure charts. Bar charts represent the range of stock prices over a prescribed period of time. In contrast, point and figure charts focus on the direction of major stock price movements without concern for calendar time. Each charting procedure is considered in the following paragraphs.

The purpose of bar charts is to identify patterns of price movements. They form a historical record of a security's past stock price behavior. Patterns observed from these records are identified as either reversals of past price movements or consolidations suggesting continuation of a long-run trend. Reversal patterns are alleged to result from underlying supply and demand conditions for the stock in question. With prices moving upward, an increasing number of investors would be willing to sell at higher prices and this selling activity would create a *resistance level.* Conversely, falling prices will at some point induce sufficient demand to provide a level of support. Resistance and support levels are identified by simple reversal patterns known as rounded tops or rounded bottoms, head and shoulder formulations, and triangle formulations. Each of these patterns is illustrated hypothetically in Figure 13A.1. The horizontal line is the key to a triangle formulation. If the top line is flat, a price rise is expected, and a falling price is implied if the bottom line is horizontal. Trading volume is commonly used as a confirming signal: heavy volume in the direction of the expected change is taken to mean that a new trend has begun.

Consolidation periods, or pauses, are periods of relatively stable prices following substantial upward or downward movements. Technicians believe that consolidation periods result from investors' reexamination of their investment positions. A move in either direction will then occur as a con-

Figure 13A.1
Resistance and Support Level Patterns

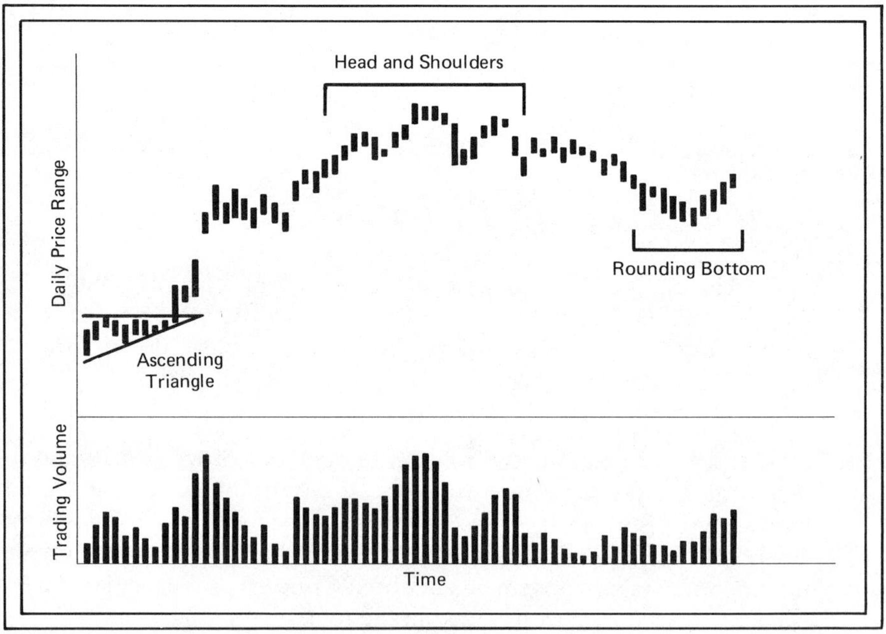

Figure 13A.2
Consolidation Patterns and Trend

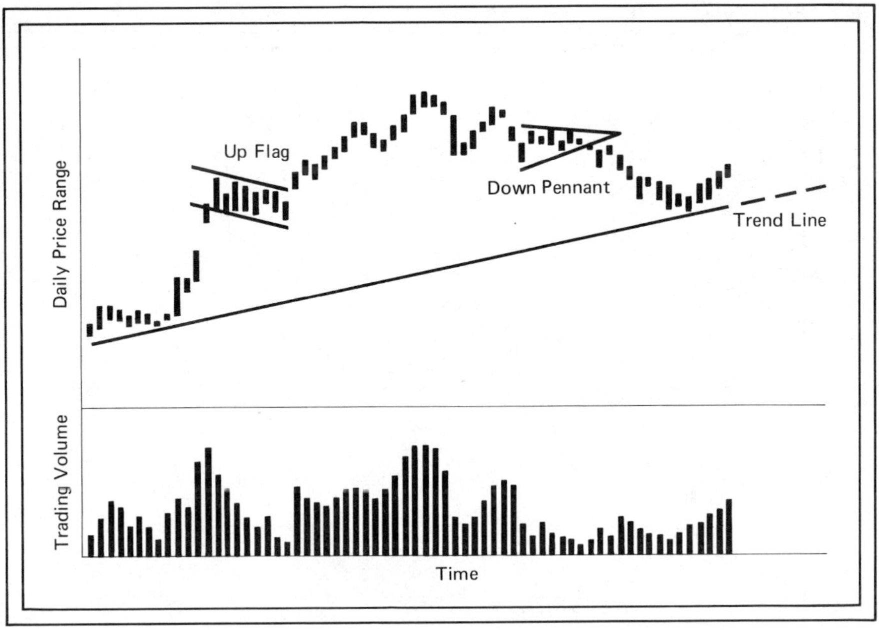

sensus of opinion emerges. The typical patterns, referred to as flags and pennants, identify minor drifts in prices accompanied by declining trading volume. The drift in price is believed to be contrary to the direction of the next major movement, as Figure 13A.2 illustrates with another hypothetical sequence. It is often difficult to distinguish between resistance and consolidation phases; for example, the down pennant of Figure 13A.2 and the descending triangle in Figure 13A.1 are indeed very similar, and their interpretation would probably vary among technical analysts. In this situation the trend in trading volume would be an additional factor to be considered. Heavy volume would suggest resistance; lighter volume would imply consolidation. Resistance and support levels are seen as forming major price trends around a long-run normal return while consolidation patterns are viewed as interim movements.

The concept and rationale of resistance and consolidation (support levels) which have become integrated into the techniques of bar charting had their beginnings in several 1900–1902 *Wall Street Journal* editorials by Charles H. Dow, founder of Dow Jones and Company. His investment principles were known as the Dow theory and they were expanded by William P. Hamilton, until his death in 1929, in further *Wall Street Journal* editorials. The Dow theory was concerned with the movement of the market as a whole, and not individual securities, and it was very popular during the 1920s and

Figure 13A.3
Point and Figure Chart for Levi-Strauss, July, 1975, to July, 1976.

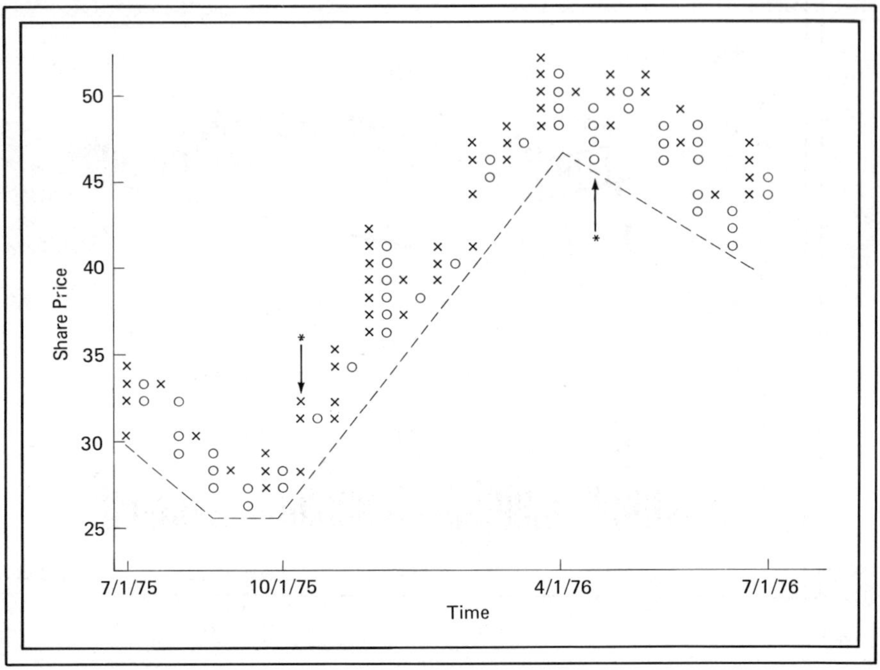

1930s.[30] In its pure form, the Dow theory retains few followers today because it has generally failed to be a leading indicator of future stock prices and it has not enabled investors to achieve superior investment performance.

Point and figure (p.f.) charts focus on major price movements, ignoring both minor price fluctuations and fixed intervals of time. Point and figure charts were especially popular in the early 1960s. They can be constructed on any square grid paper and they are similar to the one illustrated in Figure 13A.3. Figure 13A.3 is a point and figure chart for Levi-Strauss from July 1975 to July 1976. An X indicates that the stock has risen to the price level indicated; an O indicates that price has fallen to the level on the vertical scale. Every time price reverses direction a new column is started. Before constructing point and figure charts the technician must make four critical assumptions:

1. The observation interval; commonly daily or weekly closing prices are used.
2. The price range (vertical scale); \$1 per share for low-priced stocks and \$2 or

[30] Robert Rhea, *The Dow Theory* (Denver, Colo.: Daniel-Smith, 1932). A more recent summary of the Dow theory has been given by George W. Bishop, Jr., "Evolution of the Dow Theory," *Financial Analysts Journal*, September–October 1961, pp. 23–36.

$5 for higher priced issues are commonly used, but the scale should be influenced by the stock's historical volatility.

3. The evidence of trend (breakout either up or down); generally a trend is identified when successive lows and highs exhibit a movement from the recent range of trading.
4. The extent of trend (how far the move will go); a rule of thumb has been the number of columns of "congestion," where price has fluctuated without sign of trend, times the vertical scale. For example, if ten trendless columns of X's and O's precede a breakout when $1 intervals are being used, the stock price change is assumed to be $10 per share. No theoretical argument exists for this predictive technique.

The price behavior of Levi-Strauss demonstrates how point and figure analysis may be employed to diagnose price movements. An important aspect of point and figure analysis is the concept of congestion, mentioned in item 4 above. Congestion is a period of time when price drifts with no identifiable upward or downward trend. Periods of congestion are used to provide information about subsequent trends. Levi-Strauss, however, reversed value quickly during the 1975–1976 period, making it difficult to identify new trends or to predict the magnitude of change. Hypothetical trend lines and the points at which they might reasonably be identified are shown by broken lines and asterisks on Figure 13A.3.

FILTER ANALYSIS. Filter analysis is a procedure of systematically monitoring price patterns, often with computer assistance, which has become popular since the late 1960s. These methods employ price level filters combined with trading rules to determine when a stock should be purchased or sold. For example, one filter strategy might observe a security until it rises 10 percent from the initial observation. At this point, the stock would be purchased and held until it falls 10 percent from its subsequent high, at which point the position is liquidated and another sequence is started. The strategy could be expanded by permitting short sales whenever the stock falls by 10 percent, with a policy of covering when the stock rises 10 percent above its subsequent low. An infinite number of strategies can be developed by varying the size of the filter and/or the type of position taken when a trend is observed.

OTHER INDICATORS. In addition to filter analysis, other technical trading schemes have enjoyed occasional popularity. One of these is the odd-lot theory, which is based upon analysis of the odd-lot index, the ratio of odd-lot sales to odd-lot purchases. This theory assumes that small investors are usually wrong and an increase in the odd-lot index supposedly signals bullish market conditions or the end of a bear market. Since the odd-lot index is believed to be more accurate at forecasting market peaks than troughs,[31] a variant of the index, the ratio of odd-lot short sales to total odd-lot sales,

[31] Stanley Kaish, "Odd-Lot Profit and Loss Performance," *Financial Analysts Journal*, September–October 1969, pp. 83–89.

is sometimes used. A high odd-lot short sale index indicates a bottoming out of the market, again on the assumption that small investors do the wrong thing at the wrong time.

Another technical indicator of market support is the short interest ratio. The short interest ratio is the number of outstanding short sales divided by the average daily volume of trading over some recent period. The rationale for observing the short interest ratio is that short sales must be covered by future stock purchases. Unfortunately, studies of short interest suggest that this measure has little predictive ability.[32] The same observation can also be made for Barron's Confidence Index, another measure of market conditions; this index, which is published weekly in *Barron's*, is the ratio of an average high corporate bond yield to a lower grade corporate average. The confidence index is said to monitor the behavior of the professional investor. In a favorable investment period professionals are believed to buy low-quality bonds for higher yields, thereby lowering the premium of these yields relative to high-quality issues. In more uncertain times investors will seek higher grade debt, thereby increasing the interest rate differential between high- and low-quality bonds.

Questions and Problems

1. Explain what is meant by saying that the market behaves as a random walk. What is the relationship between random walk and efficient markets?
2. Explain the relationship between fundamental analysis and efficient markets. What is the relationship between technical analysis and efficient markets?
3. What is the role of new information in the pricing of securities? Explain how the concept of new information relates to the efficient market hypothesis.
4. Provide a brief outline of both the benefits and the costs of screening potential investments.
5. Why is the orientation of management a potentially important consideration in the screening process? How does one "judge" a firm's management?
6. Construct a point and figure chart for a hypothetical security by repeatedly flipping a coin and recording an X for heads (up movement) and an O for tails (down movement). Compare your results with a chart constructed from price movements of a stock of your own choosing.

Selected References

EFFICIENT PRICING OF SECURITIES

Black, Fisher, "Implications of the Random Walk Hypothesis for Portfolio Management," *Financial Analysts Journal*, March–April 1971, pp. 16–22.

Boudreaux, Kenneth J., "Competitive Rates and Market Efficiency," *Financial Analysts Journal*, March–April 1975, pp. 18–25.

Brealey, Richard A., *Security Prices in a Competitive Market* (Cambridge, Mass.: M.I.T. Press, 1971).

[32] Randall D. Smith, "Short Interest and Stock Market Prices," *Financial Analysts Journal*, November–December 1968, pp. 151–154.

Brown, Lawrence, and Michael Rozeff, "The Superiority of Analyst Forecasts as Measure of Expectations: Evidence from Earnings," *Journal of Finance*, March 1978, pp. 1–16.

Fama, Eugene F., "Efficient Capital Markets: A Review of Theory and Empirical Work," *Journal of Finance*, May 1970, pp. 383–417.

______, "Random Walks in Stock Market Prices," *Financial Analysts Journal*, September–October, 1965, pp. 55–59.

Fama, Eugene F., Lawrence Fisher, Michael Jensen, and Richard Roll, "The Adjustment of Stock Prices to New Information," *International Economic Review*, February 1969, pp. 1–21.

Fama, Eugene F., and Arthur B. Laffer, "Information and Capital Markets," *Journal of Business*, July 1971, pp. 289–298.

Gibbons, Jean Dickinson, *Nonparametrical Methods for Quantitative Analysis* (New York: Holt, Rinehart and Winston, 1976), chap. 8.

Lloyd-Davies, Peter, and Michael Canes, "Stock Prices and the Publication of Second-Hand Information," *Journal of Business*, January 1978, pp. 43–56.

Vasicek, Oldrich, and John A. McQuown, "The Efficient Market Model," *Financial Analysts Journal*, September–October 1972, pp. 71–84.

INVESTING IN EFFICIENT MARKETS

Arbit, Harold L., and James E. Rhodes, "Performance Goals in a Generally Efficient Market," *Journal of Portfolio Management*, Fall 1976, pp. 57–61.

Dann, Larry Y., David Mayers, and Robert J. Raab, Jr., "Trading Rules, Large Blocks and the Speed of Price Adjustment," *Journal of Financial Economics*, January 1977, pp. 3–22.

Jensen, Michael, and George Barrington, "Random Walks and Technical Theories: Some Additional Evidence," *Journal of Finance*, May 1970, pp. 469–482.

Malkiel, Burton G., *A Random Walk Down Wall Street* (New York: Norton, 1975).

Niederhoffer, Victor, "The Analysis of World Events and Stock Prices," *Journal of Business*, April 1971, pp. 193–220.

Pettit, R. Richardson, "Dividend Announcements, Security Performance, and Capital Market Efficiency," *Journal of Finance*, December 1972, pp. 993–1008.

Pinches, George E., "The Random Walk Hypothesis and Technical Analysis," *Financial Analysts Journal*, March–April 1970, pp. 104–110.

Roll, Richard, *The Behavior of Interest Rates: An Application of the Efficient Market Model to U.S. Treasury Bills* (New York: Basic Books, 1970).

Smidt, Seymour, "A New Look at the Random Walk Hypothesis," *Journal of Financial and Quantitative Analysis*, September 1968, pp. 235–261.

FUNDAMENTAL SCREENING PROCEDURES

Akemann, Charles A., and Werner E. Keller, "Relative Strength Does Persist!" *Journal of Portfolio Management*, Fall 1977, pp. 38–45.

Basu, S., "Investment Performance of Common Stocks in Relation to Their Price-Earnings Ratios: A Test of the Efficient Market Hypothesis," *Journal of Finance* 32 (June 1977): 663–682.

Black, Fisher, "Yes Virginia, There Is Hope: Tests of the Value Line Ranking System," *Financial Analysts Journal* 29 (September–October 1974): 10–14.

Boudreaux, Kenneth, "Managerialism and Risk-Return Performance," *Southern Economic Journal*, January 1971, pp. 366–372.

Branch, Ben, "Corporate Objectives and Market Performance," *Financial Management*, Summer 1973, pp. 24–29.

Brealey, Richard A., *An Introduction to Risk and Return* (Cambridge, Mass.: M.I.T. Press, 1969).

Eubank, Jr., Arthur, "Risk/Return Contrasts: NYSE, AMEX, and OTC," *Journal of Portfolio Management*, Summer 1977, pp. 25–30.

Grossman, S. J., and Stiglitz, J. E., "On Value Maximization and Alternative Objectives of the Firm," *Journal of Finance* 32 (May 1977): 389–402.

James, F. E., Jr., "Monthly Moving Averages—An Effective Investment Tool?" *Journal of Financial and Quantitative Analysis*, September 1968, pp. 315–326.

Jessup, Paul F., and Upson, Roger B., *Returns in Over-the-Counter Stock Markets* (Minneapolis: University of Minnesota Press, 1973).

Latané, Henry, C. P. Jones, and R. D. Rieke, "Quarterly Earnings Reports and Subsequent Six-Month Holding Period Returns," *Journal of Business Research* 2 (April 1974): 119–132.

Levy, Robert, "Random Walks: Reality or Myth," *Financial Analysts Journal*, November–December 1967, pp. 69–77.

______, "Relative Strength as a Criterion for Investment Selection," *Journal of Finance* 22 (December 1967): 595–610.

Masson, Robert, "Executive Motivations, Earnings, and Consequent Equity Performance," *Journal of Political Economy*, November–December 1971, pp. 1278–1292.

Ofer, Aharon R., "Investors' Expectations of Earnings Growth, Their Accuracy and Effects on the Structure of Realized Rates of Return," *Journal of Finance*, May 1975, pp. 509–523.

O'Hay, Charles F., and Charles T. Casazza, "A New Screen to Superior Stock Selection," *Journal of Portfolio Management*, Spring 1976, pp. 45–52.

Chapter 14

Diversification and Risk Reduction

This chapter is the first of three which extend the analytical process to include portfolio selection. The foundation for that analysis is provided here. Portfolio risk and return measures are contrasted with security risk and return measures and the concept of diversification is introduced and interpreted in that context. General criteria for portfolio selection are also developed. Principles of portfolio construction are then considered in Chapter 15 while Chapter 16 examines the important problem of portfolio evaluation and revision.

Security analysis focuses on risk and expected return; since portfolios are combinations of individual securities, portfolio analysis depends on those same two decision elements. But portfolio risk and return are more than a simple extension of those measures for individual securities and that fact has important consequences for investors. Specifically, portfolio expected return is a weighted average of the expected returns of individual securities but portfolio variance, in sharp contrast, can be *something less* than a weighted average of security variances. As a result, an investor can sometimes *reduce* portfolio risk by adding another security *with greater individual risk* than any other security in the portfolio! This seemingly curious result occurs because risk depends greatly on the *covariance* among returns of individual securities. This is a central theme in this chapter and it will be developed in detail shortly.

The first section of the chapter defines and illustrates portfolio expected return and risk measures; the relationship between covariance and efficient diversification is examined in depth. The second section considers the meaning of an "efficient set of portfolios" and data inputs which are necessary for the calculation of efficient portfolios are developed there. Next, investor utility functions are reconsidered briefly to establish a basis for portfolio selection and for the inclusion of lending and borrowing opportunities in the analysis. Long-run portfolio growth is then discussed and the chapter concludes with an exploration of the number of securities which are required for efficient diversification.

Rationale for Diversification

EXPECTED RETURN AND COVARIANCE

If a portfolio consists of m different securities, $j = 1, 2, \ldots, m$, with rates of return R_j, and if the percentage of wealth invested in each security is defined to be X_j, portfolio rate of return R_p is then defined:

$$R_p = X_1R_1 + X_2R_2 + \cdots + X_{m-1}R_{m-1} + X_mR_m$$

$$= \sum_{j=1}^{m} X_jR_j \tag{14.1}$$

Expected return and variance for weighted average R_p are also defined:

$$E(R_p) = \sum_{j=1}^{m} X_jE(R_j) \tag{14.2}$$

$$\text{var}(R_p) = \sum_{j=1}^{m} \sum_{k=1}^{m} X_jX_k\sigma_{jk} \tag{14.3}$$

In Equation 14.3 σ_{jk} is the covariance which was defined and described in Equation 8A.16 of the appendix to Chapter 8; for correlation coefficient r_{jk} and standard deviation σ_j, it was specified as:

$$\sigma_{jk} = r_{jk}\sigma_j\sigma_k \qquad [(8A.16)]$$

Covariance is a statistical measure of the relationship among expected outcomes for a set of random variables; in this case security rate of return is the random variable. If the information that the return on a security will be less than had been expected does not affect expectations as to return on a second security, the two returns are statistically independent;[1] that is, independent returns have zero covariance and zero correlation r_{jk}. If bearish new information concerning one security results in lowered expectations for a

[1] This is not the same as economic independence arising from the nature of the operations of the firms. In general, firms that are highly dependent economically (e.g., tire and auto manufacturers) provide shareholders with returns which are closely associated statistically. But the opposite need not hold: firms with unrelated operations may and generally do have some systematic association in the pattern of their returns to shareholders.

second security, covariance is positive. If the same information increases expectations for the second security, covariance would be negative. Finally, and most importantly, the covariance of a rate of return with itself is that rate's variance. Stated differently, variance is a special case of covariance; with perfect positive correlation,

$$\sigma_{jj} = r_{jj}\sigma_j\sigma_j = \sigma_j^2, \quad \text{for } r_{jj} = +1 \tag{14.4}$$

Table 14.1 contains an arithmetic illustration of Equations 14.2 and 14.3 for a two-security portfolio in which 30 percent of wealth is invested in security 1 and 70 percent of wealth is invested in security 2. Expected return for the example given is 11.20 percent and the variance (standard deviation) is 3.05 (17.46) percent. The typical portfolio model consists of risk-return formulas given in Equations 14.1 through 14.4 together with the following constraints:

$$0 \leq X_j \leq 1 \tag{14.5}$$

and

$$\sum_{j=1}^{m} X_j = 1 \tag{14.6}$$

which implies

$$\sum_{j=1}^{m}\sum_{k=1}^{m} X_jX_k = 1 \tag{14.7}$$

ble 14.1
rtfolio Expected Return and Variance
$_1 = .30$ and $X_2 = .70$)

	Return R_1	Deviation $D_1 = R_1 - E(R_1)$	D_1^2	Return R_2	Deviation $D_2 = R_2 - E(R_2)$	D_2^2	D_1D_2
	.00	−.07	.0049	−.15	−.28	.0784	.0196
	.15	.08	.0064	.50	.37	.1369	.0296
	−.10	−.17	.0289	.10	−.03	.0009	.0051
	.25	.18	.0324	.20	.07	.0049	.0126
	.05	−.02	.0004	.00	−.13	.0169	.0026
Σ	.35	.00	.0730	.65	.00	.2380	.0695
erage	.07		.0146	.13		.0476	.0139
	$E(R_1)$		σ_1^2	$E(R_2)$		σ_2^2	σ_{12}

$$(R_p) = X_1E(R_1) + X_2E(R_2)$$
$$= (.30)(.07) + (.70)(.13) = .0210 + .0910 = \underline{\underline{.1120}}$$

$$(R_p) = X_1^2\sigma_1^2 + X_1X_2\sigma_{12} + X_2^2\sigma_2^2 + X_2X_1\sigma_{21}$$
$$= (.3)^2(.0146) + (.3)(.7)(.0139) + (.7)^2(.0476) + (.7)(.3)(.0139)$$
$$= .0013 + .0029 + .0233 + .0029 = .0305; \sqrt{.0305} = \underline{\underline{.1746}}$$

Equation 14.5 prohibits short sales of securities, since X_j cannot be less than zero, and it also prohibits the purchase of securities on margin, since X_j cannot exceed a value of one.[2] Constraint 14.6 requires that an investor's wealth be fully committed to the portfolio; that is, all savings must be "invested." Equations 14.6 and 14.7 also specify that expected returns and variances of Equations 14.2 and 14.3 are *both* weighted averages, with weights X_j determined by the percentage of wealth invested in security j. While this may be obvious for the weighted average return of Equations 14.2 and 14.6, it is probably far less apparent for the weighted average covariance of Equations 14.3 and 14.7.

The portfolio variance of 3.05 percent which was calculated in Table 14.1 can be represented in a variance-covariance matrix:

$$\text{var}(R_p) = \begin{bmatrix} X_1{}^2\sigma_1{}^2 & X_1X_2\sigma_{12} \\ X_2X_1\sigma_{21} & X_2{}^2\sigma_2{}^2 \end{bmatrix}$$

$$= \begin{bmatrix} (.09)(.0146) & (.21)(.0139) \\ (.21)(.0139) & (.49)(.0476) \end{bmatrix} = .0305$$

In this format two important dimensions of portfolio variance, and portfolio risk, can be discerned. First, portfolio variance depends on included variances, along the matrix diagonal, and included covariances, in off-diagonal elements. In this particular example 58 percent weight is given to individual security variances (.09 + .49) and 42 percent weight is given to covariances (.21 + .21); portfolio variance is clearly a weighted average with the sum of weights equal to one. Second, covariances in the off-diagonal elements are symmetrical; that is, there is no difference between $X_1X_2\sigma_{12}$ and $X_2X_1\sigma_{21}$ values. The two-security variance can then be redefined as

$$\text{var}(R_p) = X_1{}^2\sigma_1{}^2 + 2X_1X_2\sigma_{12} + X_2{}^2\sigma_2{}^2 \tag{14.8}$$

Equation 14.8 will prove very useful in demonstrating the meaning of diversification in the next section of this chapter.

Figure 14.1 extends the matrix notation to other portfolios. In the two-security case, with equal investment in each security, variances and covariances each account for one-half of the total portfolio variance. In general, for any portfolio size, the relative significance of variance will be minimized when weights X_j are equal. In addition, variance tends to lose significance as the size of the portfolio increases. This is evident from a comparison of the two-, four-, and ten-security equal-percentage cases of Figure 14.1; in those cases covariance accounts, respectively, for 50, 75, and 90 percent of total portfolio variance. Clearly, for any moderately sized portfolio, it is average covariance, and not average variance, which largely determines portfolio risk. For this reason it is important to consider the impact of covariance more closely.

[2] The margin constraint will be relaxed in a later section of this chapter when borrowing and lending opportunities are introduced.

Figure 14.1
Variance-Covariance Matrix Weights

Two Securities

$X_1 = .3;\ X_2 = .7$

$$\begin{bmatrix} .09\sigma_1^2 & .21\sigma_{12} \\ .21\sigma_{21} & .49\sigma_2^2 \end{bmatrix}$$

Variances — .58
Covariances — .42

$X_1 = X_2 = .5$

$$\begin{bmatrix} .25\sigma_1^2 & .25\sigma_{12} \\ .25\sigma_{21} & .25\sigma_2^2 \end{bmatrix}$$

Variances — .50
Covariances — .50

Four Securities

$X_1 = X_2 = X_3 = X_4 = .25$

$$\begin{bmatrix} .0625\sigma_1^2 & .0625\sigma_{12} & .0625\sigma_{13} & .0625\sigma_{14} \\ .0625\sigma_{21} & .0625\sigma_2^2 & .0625\sigma_{23} & .0625\sigma_{24} \\ .0625\sigma_{31} & .0625\sigma_{32} & .0625\sigma_3^2 & .0625\sigma_{34} \\ .0625\sigma_{41} & .0625\sigma_{42} & .0625\sigma_{43} & .0625\sigma_4^2 \end{bmatrix}$$

Variances — .25
Covariances — .75

Ten Securities

$X_1 = X_2 = \cdots = X_9 = X_{10} = .10$

$$\begin{bmatrix} .01\sigma_1^2 & .01\sigma_{12} & \cdots & .01\sigma_{1,10} \\ .01\sigma_{21} & .01\sigma_2^2 & \cdots & .01\sigma_{2,10} \\ \vdots & \vdots & & \vdots \\ .01\sigma_{10,1} & .01\sigma_{10,2} & & .01\sigma_{10}^2 \end{bmatrix}$$

Variances — .10
Covariances — .90

THE TWO-SECURITY CASE

The relationship between diversification and risk reduction is most easily demonstrated in the two-security case. In that event expected return and standard deviation are defined:[3]

$$E(R_p) = X_1E(R_1) + X_2E(R_2) \tag{14.9}$$

$$\sigma_p = \sqrt{X_1^2\sigma_1^2 + 2X_1X_2\sigma_1\sigma_2r_{12} + X_2^2\sigma_2^2} \tag{14.10}$$

[3] Risk can be measured by either the variance or its square root, the standard deviation; for present purposes it is most convenient to use the standard deviation.

The importance of covariance can be observed by allowing correlation coefficient r_{12} to vary within its allowable range of ± 1.0. Table 14.2 contains $E(R_p)$ and σ_p values for assumed values of $E(R_i)$ and σ_i as X_1, X_2, and σ_{12} all vary.

When r_{12} is equal to $+1.0$, when the two securities are perfectly positively correlated, Equation 14.10 is a perfect square:

$$\begin{aligned}\sigma_p &= \sqrt{X_1{}^2\sigma_1{}^2 + 2X_1X_2\sigma_1\sigma_2 + X_2{}^2\sigma_2{}^2}, \qquad r_{12} = +1.0 \\ &= \sqrt{(X_1\sigma_1 + X_2\sigma_2)^2} \\ &= X_1\sigma_1 + X_2\sigma_2 \end{aligned} \tag{14.11}$$

In this case, from Equations 14.9 and 14.11, expected return and standard deviation are both linear in X; this can be observed from Table 14.2 data and it is portrayed graphically in Figure 14.2(a). Then, as the correlation coefficient decreases, and ignoring nondiversified portfolios where either X_1 or X_2 is equal to 1, risk σ_p also decreases but expected return $E(R_p)$ is unaffected. From Table 14.2, for example, with $X_1 = X_2 = .50$, expected return is always 8 percent but the standard deviation varies from 6 percent to 3 percent as r_{12} changes from $+1.0$ to -1.0.

As the correlation coefficient decreases the opportunity for risk-return trade-off becomes increasingly advantageous and selected levels of expected return can be achieved with increasingly lesser risk. This is illustrated in

Table 14.2
Portfolio Expected Return and Standard Deviation (for two securities)

$E(R_P) = X_1E(R_1) + X_2E(R_2)$

$\sigma_P = X_1{}^2\sigma_1{}^2 + 2X_1X_2r_{12}\sigma_1\sigma_2 + X_2{}^2\sigma_2{}^2$

$E(R_1) = .06 \quad \sigma_1 = .03 \quad \sigma_1{}^2 = .0009$

$E(R_2) = .10 \quad \sigma_2 = .09 \quad \sigma_2{}^2 = .0081$

		$r_{12} = +1.0$	$r_{12} = 0.0$	$r_{12} = -1.0$
$X_1 = 1.00$; $X_2 = .00$	$E(R_P)$	.0600	.0600	.0600
	σ_P	.0300	.0300	.0300
$X_1 = .75$; $X_2 = .25$	$E(R_P)$	.0700	.0700	.0700
	σ_P	.0450	.0318	.0000
$X_1 = .50$; $X_2 = .50$	$E(R_P)$	.0800	.0800	.0800
	σ_P	.0600	.0474	.0300
$X_1 = .25$; $X_2 = .75$	$E(R_P)$	.0900	.0900	.0900
	σ_P	.0750	.0679	.0600
$X_1 = .00$; $X_2 = 1.00$	$E(R_P)$	.1000	.1000	.1000
	σ_P	.0900	.0900	.0900

Figure 14.2
Portfolio Opportunities at Different Levels of Return Correlation

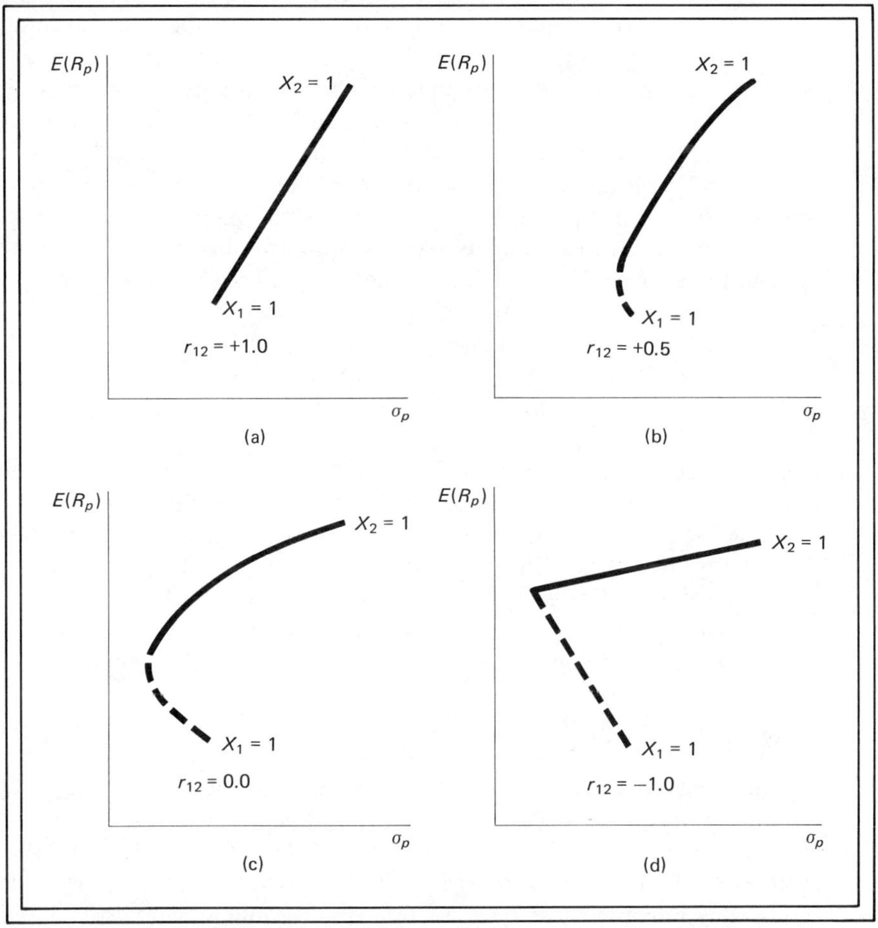

Figures 14.2(b) and 14.2(c); broken lines there represent inefficient portfolios where greater expected return can be achieved with the same risk by increasing the relative investment in security 2. Figure 14.2(d) portrays the extreme case of perfect negative correlation where risk can be totally eliminated by investing $\sigma_2/(\sigma_1 + \sigma_2)$ percentage of wealth in security 1.[4] In Table 14.2, for example, the standard deviation is 0.0 when X_1 is set equal to .75 (.09/.12). But perfect negative correlation is rare; it is only found in certain arbitrage situations including the simultaneous purchase and short sale of a

[4] This results because perfect negative correlation also results in a perfect square which solves to: $\sigma_P = X_1\sigma_1 - (1 - X_1)\sigma_2$. Setting this equal to zero, and solving for X_1, $X_1 = \sigma_2/(\sigma_1 + \sigma_2)$.

security traded in two different markets.[5] Moreover, any degree of negative correlation among security rates of return is very unusual and gains from diversification are more likely limited to cases of low but positive covariance.

Portfolio risk depends to a large degree upon the covariance among securities' expected rates of return. Risk tends to be minimized when average covariance is minimized, particularly where the number of securities in the portfolio is relatively large. Portfolios can be diversified, and covariance reduced, either formally or informally. One popular method of informal diversification is to limit investment to a small number of firms in any identifiable industry; this presumes significant positive correlation among returns to firms in the same industry. While this strategy is a useful rule of thumb, the portfolio problem is better approached formally. The next section of this chapter considers that problem in greater detail.

Portfolio Construction

Portfolio selection consists of two distinct processes, the first of which is identification of the *set* of efficient portfolios. A portfolio is efficient when it is expected to yield the highest return for the level of risk accepted. Efficient portfolios are discussed in this section of the chapter. The second process is selection of the *individual* portfolio, from among the set of efficient portfolios, which provides the greatest satisfaction to the investor. This utility-maximizing portfolio is considered in the next section of this chapter.

THE EFFICIENT FRONTIER

Assume that expected return is plotted against risk for every existing security, *and every possible combination* of existing securities, with each point located in the shaded area of Figure 14.3. All feasible portfolios are found in that space. Portfolio *I* is imaginary; if investors believed that risk-return outcome *I* was possible, the feasible set would expand to include point *I*.

Portfolios in the feasible set are either efficient or inefficient. An efficient portfolio is one that yields the highest expected return for any given level of risk or the least risk for any given level of expected return. Portfolio *E*, for example, is inefficient since it has the same risk, but a lower expected return, when compared with portfolio *D*; similarly, portfolios *E* and *F* have the same expected return but *F* has lesser risk than *E*. Following this logic, portfolios along efficiency frontier *ABzDFG* are efficient and all interior portfolios are inefficient.

[5] A similar instance is the simultaneous purchase of a convertible bond with a short sale of the common stock. Other arbitrage situations would include the strategy of writing a put (or call) and simultaneously buying an equivalent call (put) or having a long and short position in nearly identical futures contracts traded on two different exchanges. All such positions presume a temporary disequilibrium in prices which, corrected through convergence, will bring profit to the arbitrager.

Figure 14.3
Investor's Efficient Frontier: All Risky Securities

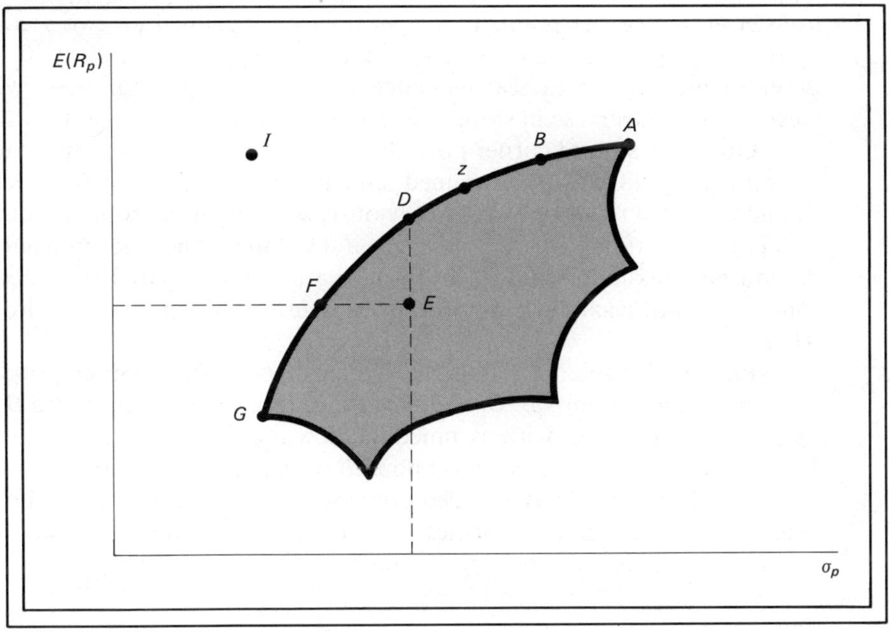

The number of feasible portfolios is nearly infinite and the identification of portfolios along the efficiency frontier is therefore a formidable conceptual and computational problem. In some cases graphic solution is possible; Chapter 15 will consider this possibility. More commonly, however, the identification of efficient portfolios requires solution of a mathematical programming problem on a high-speed computer. That procedure cannot be described here in detail but the general approach to the problem can be developed; it involves the concept of a corner portfolio.[6]

CORNER PORTFOLIOS

A number of portfolios on the efficiency frontier are *corner portfolios.* A corner portfolio is defined as one in which either (1) a new security is added to a previously efficient portfolio or (2) a security is dropped from a previously efficient portfolio. For example, assume that a population of 50 screened securities are analyzed to identify the set of efficient portfolios. The single security with the highest risk-return value, point *A* in Figure 14.3, provides a starting point. Next, expected returns, variances, and covariances are pairwise

[6] For a more detailed discussion of this computational process see William F. Sharpe, *Portfolio Theory and Capital Markets* (New York: McGraw-Hill, 1970).

compared for the point A security and each of the remaining 49 securities to identify the one to be added to the portfolio at the second corner point. The security to be added is the one that minimizes the slope of the efficiency frontier at that corner point. This is most easily explained for two securities by referring again to Figure 14.2 where increasing gain from diversification is represented by an increasing bulge in portfolio opportunities—with a corresponding decrease in slope at every risk-return frontier point.

Given the second corner portfolio, consisting of two securities, each of the remaining 48 will be examined similarly to determine if one security should be added to, or one of the previously selected ones dropped from, the next corner portfolio. In every case, when the slope of the efficient frontier is minimized, maximum gain from diversification is realized. This process is continued until each corner portfolio is identified along efficiency frontier $ABzDEFG$.

Part a of Table 14.3 illustrates three hypothetical corner portfolios corresponding to points B, D, and F in Figure 14.3. Corner portfolio B consists of three securities with assumed identification numbers 20, 13, and 47. The next corner portfolio occurs at point D where security number 9 is added. At F security number 20 is dropped from the set and the corner portfolio consists of three remaining securities—13, 47, and 9. Portfolio weights X_j of part a, Table 14.3, are arbitrary and illustrative.

Table 14.3
Corner and Noncorner Efficient Portfolios

a. Corner Portfolios (Security j)

Portfolio B		Portfolio D		Portfolio F	
j	X_j	j	X_j	j	X_j
20	.333	20	.167		
13	.334	13	.333	13	.100
47	.333	47	.333	47	.300
		9	.167	9	.600
	1.000		1.000		1.000

b. Noncorner Portfolio (z)
$(X_B = .50; X_D = .50)$

j	$X_B X_{B,j}$	$X_D X_{D,j}$	X_z
20	$(.50 \times .333)$	$+ (.50 \times .167) =$	.251
13	$(.50 \times .334)$	$+ (.50 \times .333) =$	.333
47	$(.50 \times .333)$	$+ (.50 \times .333) =$	.333
9	$(.50 \times .000)$	$+ (.50 \times .167) =$	.083
			1.000

Any two portfolios can be combined to form a third in the same manner that two individual securities can be combined to form a portfolio. If portfolios *B* and *D* are combined to form a new portfolio, *z*, expected return and risk will be measured in a similar manner to the two-security measures of Equations 14.9 and 14.10. Specifically, if X_B percentage of wealth is invested in portfolio *B* and X_D percentage is invested in portfolio *D*, expected return and standard deviation for portfolio *z* will be defined:

$$E(R_z) = X_B E(R_B) + X_D E(R_D), \qquad X_B + X_D = 1 \tag{14.12}$$

$$\sigma_z = \sqrt{X_B{}^2\sigma_B{}^2 + 2X_B X_D r_{BD}\sigma_B\sigma_D + X_D{}^2\sigma_D{}^2} \tag{14.13}$$

Every security held in either *B* or *D* will be held in combination *z* in proportions determined by the weighted average of percentages committed to each security in each of the adjacent portfolios. For security 20 of Table 14.3, for example, and with $X_B = X_D = .50$,

$$\begin{aligned} X_{z,20} &= X_B X_{B,20} + X_D X_{D,20} \\ &= (.50)(.333) + (.50)(.167) \\ &= .251 \end{aligned} \tag{14.14}$$

Part b of Table 14.3 illustrates Equation 14.14 for all four securities in combined portfolio z. The relationship examined there holds in general; weights for each security in any portfolio constructed from two other portfolios can be determined in this manner.

The efficient frontier of Figure 14.3 consists of expected return-risk loci for corner portfolios and other portfolios which are constructed from adjacent corner portfolios. The frontier is continuous since investors can allocate wealth among risk-return possibilities to achieve any desired point on the efficient curve.

The construction of the efficiency frontier has been outlined generally; specific application involves mathematical techniques beyond the level which is assumed here. At the same time, the analysis of corner portfolios does provide a preliminary identification of the input parameters which are required for portfolio construction. These are:

1. An estimate of the expected rate of return for each security for the investor's anticipated holding period.
2. An estimate of risk, measured by either the variance or the standard deviation of security rate of return.
3. An estimate of covariance among rates of return for all securities which are candidates for inclusion in the portfolio.

Expected return and risk are outputs of the security analysis process discussed in Chapters 5 through 9; the estimation of covariance is a problem which will be considered in the next chapter. With these inputs, and given access to computer facilities, efficient portfolios can be identified. Each investor, in turn, faces the problem of selecting one of the set of available efficient portfolios; this decision depends on individual attitudes toward the trade-off between risk and expected return.

Investor Preference and Portfolio Selection

Utility functions were considered in Chapter 4 from both a theoretical and a practical perspective. Expected utility, and not expected monetary value, was shown to be the correct object of choice. But the difficulty in measuring utility was also discussed and a pragmatic approach to decision making under risk was suggested. This chapter retains those views. At the same time, utility functions are a critical part of the portfolio selection process; for this reason it is important to consider the specific application of utility analysis to the efficient portfolio framework.

Chapter 4 discussed the utility of *wealth* but portfolio analysis depends upon *rate of return* utility. This is no problem, however, since there is a direct correspondence between rate of return and wealth. For a one-period rate of return R, current wealth W_0 is linked to period 1 wealth W_1:

$$W_1 = W_0(1 + R) = W_0 + RW_0 \qquad (14.15)$$

For a known and given W_0 utility can be expressed in terms of wealth W_1 or rate of return R; this is demonstrated in Figure 14.4 where the only change from one basis to another is a change in the scale of the horizontal axis. This chapter will therefore refer to rate of return utility.

The utility functions of Figure 14.4 imply positive but diminishing marginal utility; that is, they trace risk-return preference for *risk-averters* in terms discussed in Chapter 4 and illustrated in Figure 4.8(a). Positive marginal utility implies added satisfaction at higher rate of return levels; wealth, per se, is desirable. Diminishing marginal utility implies that added wealth provides added satisfaction at an increasingly smaller rate; risk, per se, is not desirable. Positive diminishing marginal utility results in the familiar concave downward function illustrated in Figure 14.4.[7]

INDIFFERENCE MAPS

Any cardinal utility value of the type portrayed in Figure 14.4 can be achieved at a number of different points in expected return-risk space. Point U in Figure 14.4, for example, might be realized with some low return–low risk

[7] Within a limited range of return levels, a concave downward utility curve can be approximated by a quadratic utility function having the form $U = a + bR - cR^2$, where U represents utility, R represents rate of return, and a, b, and c are positive constants. The values of the constant parameters (a, b, c), and the corresponding degree of concavity of the utility function, vary among investors depending on the extent of their absolute and relative risk aversion.

Figure 14.4
Hypothetical Utility Function (one-period return relative)

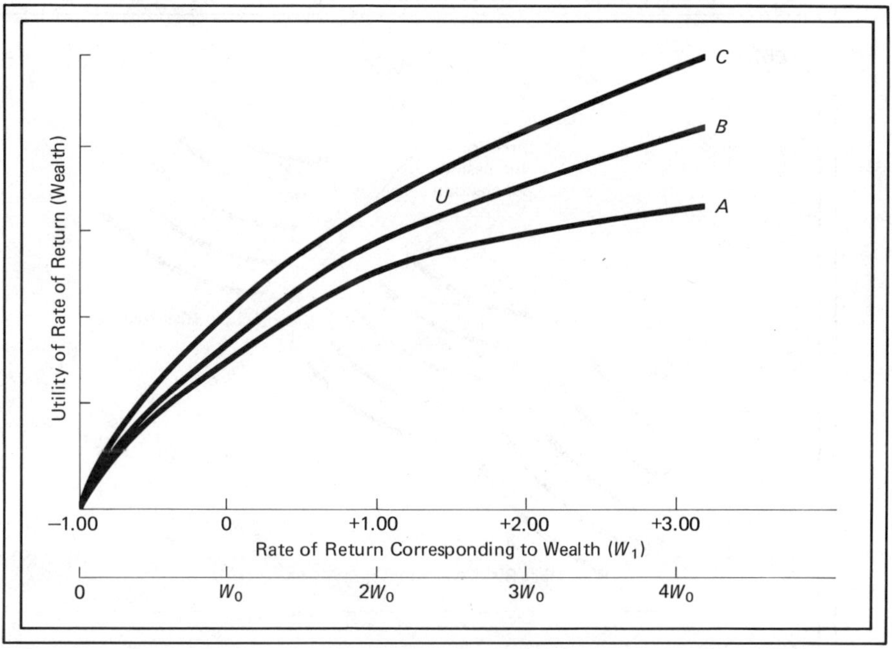

portfolio or it might result from some high return–high risk portfolio. While risk-return levels vary, the trade-off of one for the other would provide equal satisfaction for the investor with preferences represented by utility function *B* of Figure 14.4. This investor would be indifferent as to choice among different risk-return combinations which provide the same utility; the loci of these equivalent utility values is known as an *indifference curve.*

Figure 14.5 traces utility indifference curves for three hypothetical investors. Risk and return are both greater at point *Z* than they are at point *Y* but both points provide equal utility for the investor represented by the set of indifference curves labeled *B*. Thus utility is constant along the curve which passes through points *Y* and *Z*. In contrast, risk-return represented at point *X* is clearly preferred to either *Y* or *Z*; the indifference curve which includes *X*, accordingly, provides greater satisfaction than the curve containing *Y* and *Z*. The set or "family" of indifference curves—with each curve representing a different point on the utility function of Figure 14.4—is known as an *indifference map.* Utility increases from curve to curve in the direction indicated in Figure 14.5: upward and to the right.

Figure 14.5 portrays indifference maps for three different investors. Set *A* implies a large degree of risk aversion where safety of principal would be a primary investment objective; the utility function corresponding to

Figure 14.5
Indifference Maps for Three Investors with Varying Degrees of Risk Aversion

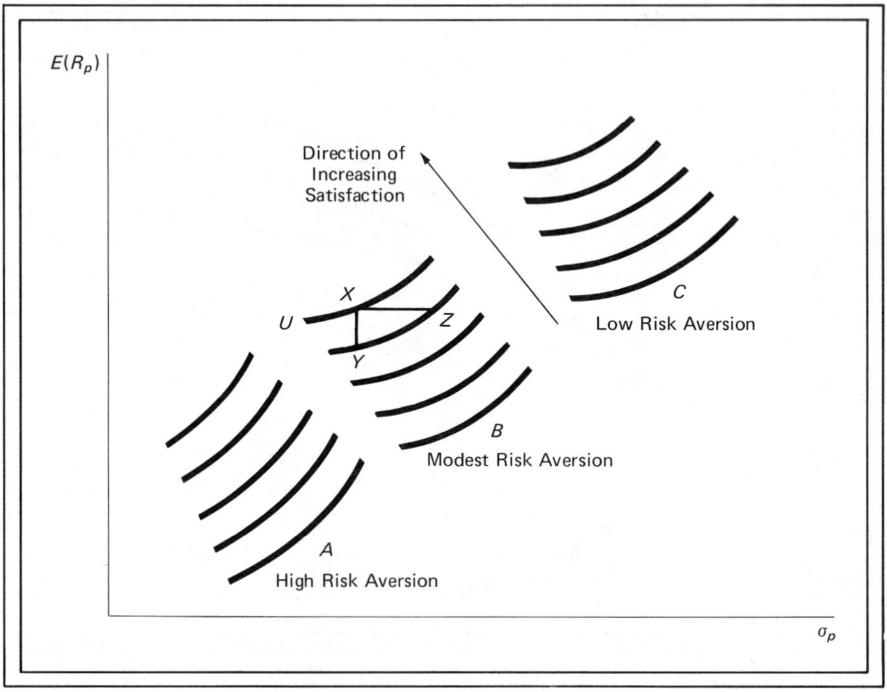

indifference map *A* would be very concave, as in utility function *A* of Figure 14.4. Indifference set *B* implies less dissatisfaction with loss relative to the satisfaction arising from gain. Set *C* implies an even greater willingness to accept risk in exchange for expected return; the utility function for *C*, although concave, would be closer to the straight line of risk neutrality than the utility function of either *A* or *B*.

PORTFOLIO SELECTION

The rational investor will attempt to maximize expected utility; this implies selection of the portfolio (or portfolios) which places that investor on the highest possible indifference curve on some relevant indifference map. This is illustrated in Figure 14.6; the highest attainable utility occurs at the point where indifference curve $I_3(U)$ is tangent to the efficient frontier. Utility is maximized by selecting portfolio *N*; it corresponds to the level designated by point *U* in utility function *B* of Figure 14.4. Indifference curves I_1 and I_2 represent greater utility but those levels cannot be achieved with the efficiency frontier portrayed in Figure 14.6.

Figure 14.6
Optimal Portfolio Selection: All Risky Securities

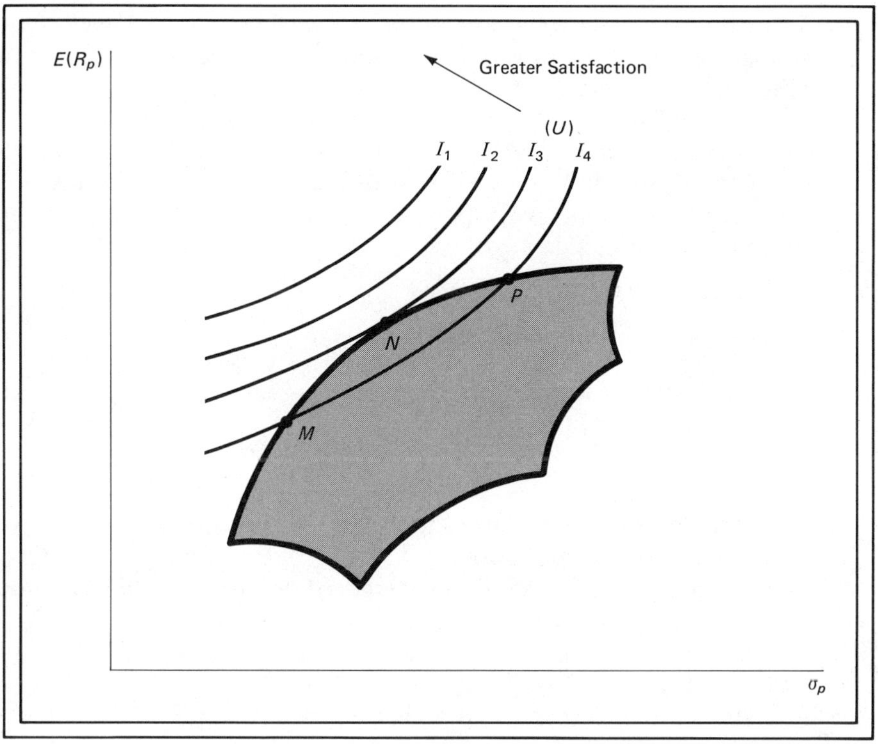

Suboptimal portfolios exist at efficient frontier points *M* and *P* and at inefficient interior points along or below indifference curve I_4. Portfolios *M* and *P* are inferior for the investor described by the indifference map of Figure 14.6; those portfolios would be optimal for other investors, however, with higher or lower risk aversion. Portfolios in the shaded interior region are not acceptable for any investor, whatever that investor's attitude toward risk, because expected utility could be increased by selecting one of the efficient portfolios. Risk aversion results in indifference curves which are concave upward; since the efficiency frontier is concave downward, the process described here insures a unique solution to the portfolio problem.

Lending and Borrowing Opportunity

The efficiency frontier described in the preceding sections of this chapter would be altered substantially if a risk-free security is included among available investment opportunities. While a risk-free security does not exist in the strict sense of the word, there are securities which promise return with relative certainty.[8] They are characterized by an absence of default risk and interest rate risk; full payment of principal (and interest) is assured without serious prospect of capital loss arising from changes in the level of interest rates. "Risk-free" securities of this type include cash, short-term treasury bills, and time deposits in banks or savings and loan associations; cash would be dominated by the other two positive return investments.

Lending is defined as the investment of some percentage of wealth in a risk-free security. If X_F of wealth is invested in a risk-free asset and X_M is invested in an efficient portfolio of risky assets, and if $X_F + X_M = 1$, return on combination C is defined:

$$R_C = X_F R_F + X_M R_M \qquad (14.16)$$

Expected return and standard deviation are:

$$E(R_C) = X_F R_F + X_M E(R_M) \qquad (14.17)$$

$$\sigma_C = \sqrt{{X_F}^2 {\sigma_F}^2 + 2 X_F X_M r_{FM} \sigma_F \sigma_M + {X_M}^2 {\sigma_M}^2}$$
$$= X_M \sigma_M \qquad (14.18)$$

Standard deviation σ_C collapses to $X_M \sigma_M$ because dispersion for a risk-free asset is zero by definition and ${\sigma_F}^2 = \sigma_F = 0$. Combination C is therefore linear in both expected return and standard deviation and portfolio opportunity C is measured along a straight line originating at R_F and tangent to the efficiency frontier at the risk-return locus for portfolio M. This is illusstrated in Figure 14.7.

In Figure 14.7 Q and M represent efficient portfolios of risky assets and S represents either a single security or an inefficient portfolio of securities. The risk-free rate of return is denoted by R_F. The combination of risky assets with a risk-free security provides alternative portfolios to those of the efficient frontier; $R_F Q$, $R_F S$, and $R_F LM$ are alternatives to investments in risky portfolios along BQM. The advantage enjoyed by the lending portfolio increases as the slope of the ray from R_F increases; in Figure 14.7 the slope is maximized at point M tangency with the efficiency frontier. The locus of expected return and risk points for lending portfolio C of Equations 14.17 and 14.18 is denoted by $R_F LM$. Points along $R_F LM$ are preferred to points along efficient frontier segment BQM; L is preferred to Q, for example, since it offers the same level of expected return at lesser risk. In this manner the efficient frontier is extended outward from $BQMA$ to $R_F LMA$.

Borrowing portfolios can be constructed in the same manner as lending portfolios. Assume that X_F percentage of total wealth is borrowed at a fixed

[8] Certainty is defined in the sense of a guaranteed nominal return and not in terms of real purchasing power. This is consistent with the general convention adopted here which focuses on monetary rate of return in lieu of real rate of return. Since relative returns are compared throughout the text, abstraction from price level change is defensible. In addition, risk arising from currency revaluation is ignored; "risk free" assumes certain payment in domestic currency.

Figure 14.7
Lending and Borrowing Opportunities

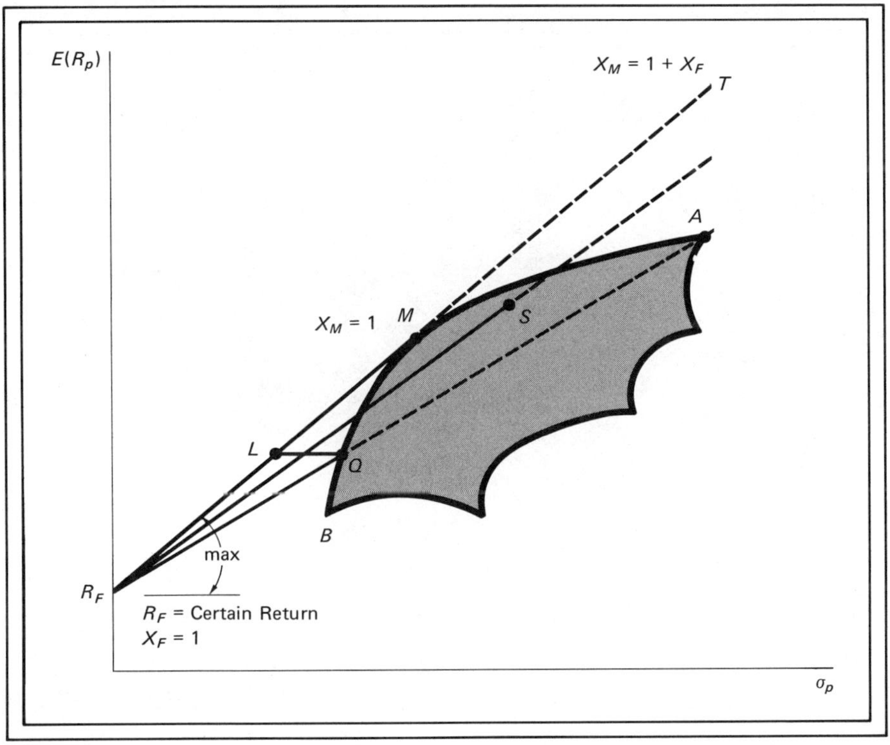

interest cost of R_F with proceeds invested in risky portfolio M; in this case the amount invested in risky assets exceeds the investor's total wealth. Expected return and risk would then be measured, as before,

$$E(R_C) = X_M E(R_M) - X_F R_F \tag{14.19}$$

$$\sigma_C = X_M \sigma_M \tag{14.20}$$

It is easily shown, proceeding as before, that borrowing portfolio C expected return-risk points fall along line segment MT of Figure 14.7. As before, portfolio opportunity MT dominates risky asset efficient frontier segment MA and the new efficiency frontier, assuming lending and borrowing opportunity at the same R_F value, becomes the straight line $R_F LMT$.

Figure 14.8 illustrates selection from among the set of efficient portfolios where lending and borrowing are possible at the same rate R_F. Lending opportunity allows the cautious investor to reach a higher indifference curve, at point L, for example, than would be possible if investment opportunity were limited to risky assets. In the same fashion borrowing is advantageous to an aggressive investor, increasing utility, for example, to the level at point

Figure 14.8
Portfolio Selection with Borrowing and Lending

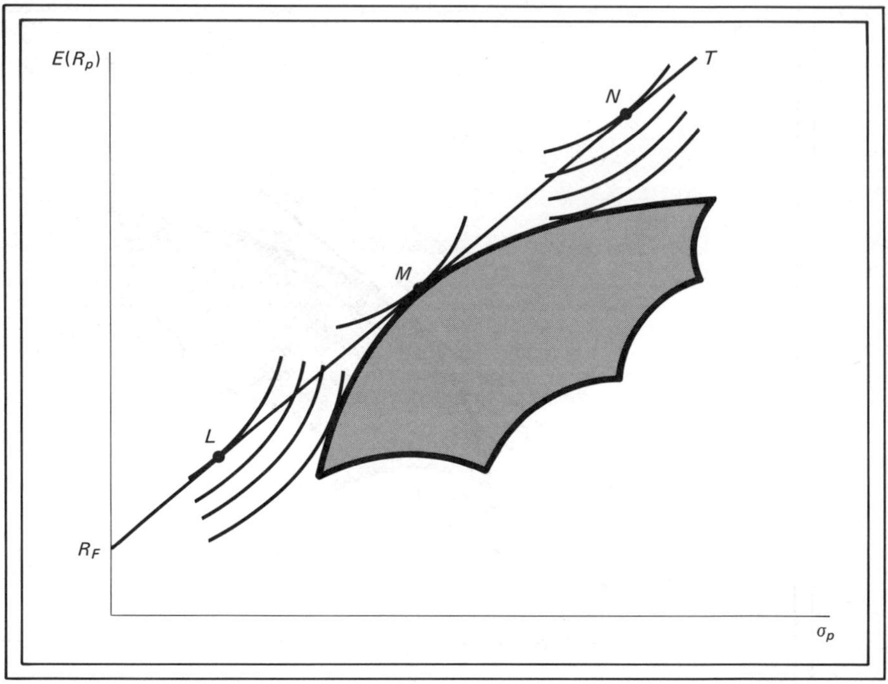

N. All investors, whatever their attitude toward risk, would want to hold optimal portfolio M;[9] this would be achieved by borrowing or lending.

With borrowing and lending opportunities available, the investor's portfolio decision process is greatly simplified because the optimal portfolio of risky securities can be determined independently of an investor's attitude toward risk.[10] The optimal combination can be determined graphically; given that solution an investor would then determine how much, if any, should be borrowed or loaned.

The assumption of a single borrowing-lending rate simplifies the analytical procedure discussed here. In reality, however, the borrowing rate

[9] Portfolio M may not be unique. It is possible that a number of portfolios exist which are perfectly positively correlated. In that event, the efficient set of risky securities will include a flat portion with the slope of $R_F LMNT$ in Figure 14.8. All portfolios in that flat section would be perfect substitutes for portfolio M.

[10] This important result was first identified by James Tobin, "Liquidity Preference as Behavior Towards Risk," *Review of Economic Studies*, February 1958, pp. 65–86. Since it separates selection of a risky portfolio from the investor's attitude toward risk, it is known as the *separation theorem.* Interestingly, Tobin's analysis was developed in support of Lord Keynes concept of a speculative demand for money. It chooses money as the risk-free security but, with the number of positive yield risk-free near-money assets which are available, money is an inferior choice for speculative balances.

Figure 14.9
Borrowing and Lending at Different Rates

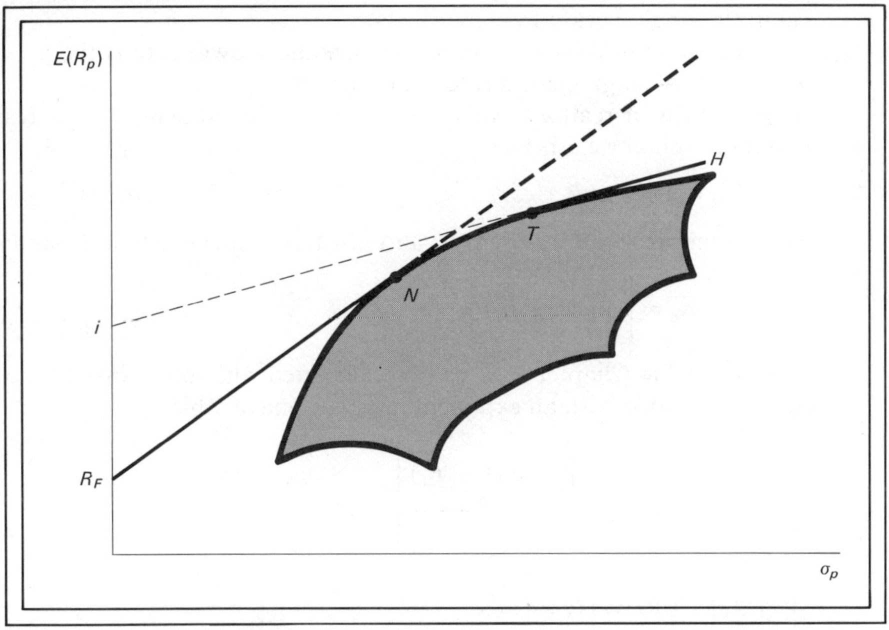

will be greater than the lending rate. This situation is portrayed in Figure 14.9 where the efficiency frontier is $R_F NTH$. Highly risk-averse investors will combine portfolio N and the risk-free security yielding R_F along line segment $R_F N$. Less risk-averse investors will then select one of the portfolios of risky securities in the curve segment NT. Beyond T increasing amounts of portfolio T will be purchased with money borrowed at interest rate i. Although different lending-borrowing rates tend to complicate the process, the basic impact on portfolio efficiency is unchanged.[11]

Long-Run Portfolio Growth

The portfolio measures discussed in this chapter are single-period values. The length of the period may vary—it may be a week, a month, a year, or some other calendar interval. But whatever the interval, portfolio analysis continues to be a one-period framework. For this reason wealth, invested

[11] Investors with strong credit ratings may find i to be only slightly greater than R_F. Those with poor credit may face a large differential between i and R_F with a relatively flat segment TH which provides little incentive for borrowing. Also, the relationship between i and R_F will vary for a single investor over time as conditions in the credit markets change. For a further discussion of these points, see K. L. Hastie, "The Determination of Optimal Investment Policy," *Management Science*, August 1967, pp. B757–B774.

to yield rate of return R, will grow during the period at growth rate R; stated differently, portfolio growth rate and realized rate of return are identical in the single-period framework.

In the multiple-period case the periodic growth rate is the geometric average $\bar{R}_g$ of single-period rates of return. $\bar{R}_g$ is the average internal rate of return which, if realized every period with reinvestment, would result in correct terminal wealth W_N:

$$W_N = W_0(1 + \bar{R}_g)^N \tag{14.21}$$

The geometric mean was defined and illustrated previously in Chapter 3:

$$1 + \bar{R}_g = \left[\prod_{t=1}^{N} (1 + \bar{R}_t)\right]^{1/N} \qquad [(3.7)]$$

As discussed in Chapter 3, $\bar{R}_g$ can be calculated with logarithms in the event that a calculator with an exponential key is unavailable:

$$\bar{R}_g = \text{antilog}\left[\frac{\sum_{t=1}^{N} \log(1 + \bar{R}_t)}{N}\right] - 1.0 \tag{14.22}$$

SECURITY GROWTH RATES

Under certain conditions the expected rate of growth in the value of an individual security can be estimated from the geometric mean of all possible one-period rates of return. The necessary conditions are:

1. Reinvestment of all interim proceeds (dividends and interest).
2. Maintenance of the original principal without increase or decrease.
3. Period-to-period stationarity and independence in the distribution of periodic rate of return.[12]

Under these circumstances the geometric mean can be calculated from Equation 14.22; this is illustrated in Table 14.4 for three securities, each of which has five equally likely one-period return relative outcomes. The arithmetic example of Table 14.4 is designed so that mean values for all three securities are the same (1.07); variances, on the other hand, differ from security to security. Importantly, an inverse relationship exists among geometric means and variances; as variance increases (.0000; .0146; .0234) the geometric mean decreases (1.070; 1.063; 1.059).

The example of Table 14.4 involves a limited number of return outcomes. In practice probability beliefs should be stated in greater detail but, as the number of outcomes increases, the process tends to become increasingly cumbersome. Fortunately, the geometric mean can be approximated on the basis of expected value and variance. Young and Trent tested the

[12] Since the return distribution is assumed to be stationary, each return outcome can be used as if it were an actual outcome over time. Over a prolonged time period each of the N outcomes would occur, on average, once every N periods.

Table 14.4
Security Growth Rates (return relatives)

		Security 1		Security 2		Security 3	
		Outcome	*Logarithm*	*Outcome*	*Logarithm*	*Outcome*	*Logarithm*
	1	1.07	.029384	1.00	.000000	1.12	.049218
	2	1.07	.029384	1.15	.060698	.80	−.096910
	3	1.07	.029384	.90	−.045757	1.17	.068186
	4	1.07	.029384	1.25	.096910	1.02	.008600
	5	1.07	.029384	1.05	.021189	1.24	.093422
Sum		5.35	.146920	5.35	.133040	5.35	.122516
Mean $[1 + E(R_j)]$		1.070		1.070		1.070	
Mean $[\log(1 + E(R_j))]$			.029384		.026608		.024503
Antilog$(1 + \bar{R}_g)$			1.070		1.063		1.059
$\text{var}(R_j)^a$		.0000		.0146		.0234	
$E(R_j) - \left[\frac{\text{var}(R_j)}{2(1 + E(R_j))}\right]$			1.070		1.063		1.059

[a] Calculation not shown; see Table 14.1 for methodology.

following equation, for security j,

$$\bar{R}_{gj} \approx E(R_j) - \left[\frac{\text{var}(R_j)}{2(1 + E(R_j))}\right] \tag{14.23}$$

and found it to be very accurate when applied to real data.[13] Equation 14.23 is illustrated in Table 14.4 and the values reported there are the same as Equation 14.22 values, to three decimal places.

PORTFOLIO GROWTH RATES

Portfolio growth rates can be approximated in the same manner; for portfolio geometric mean $\bar{R}_{gp}$,

$$\bar{R}_{gp} \approx E(R_p) - \left[\frac{\text{var}(R_p)}{2(1 + E(R_p))}\right] \tag{14.24}$$

The portfolio approximation of Equation (14.24) has been shown to be empirically more accurate than the security approximation of Equation 14.23; Young and Trent found that Equation 14.24 provided a reliable estimate for portfolios of NYSE firms with as few as four securities.[14]

[13] William E. Young and Robert H. Trent, "Geometric Mean Approximations of Individual Security and Portfolio Performance," *Journal of Financial and Quantitative Analysis* 4 (June 1969): 179–199.

[14] Ibid. For 392 four-stock portfolios, estimated annual growth rates averaged .998 percent of actual growth rates with a standard error of .009. Forty-nine 32-stock portfolios had growth-rate estimates averaging .999 percent of actual growth rates with a standard error of .003.

The portfolio growth rate depends upon *both* expected returns and variances of securities which are held in the portfolio; this is clear from the approximation of Equation 14.24. Since portfolio variance is highly dependent on covariances, long-run rate of growth can be increased by minimizing the average covariance, for given levels of expected return. In other words, expected return for every security in a portfolio may exceed expected return for every security in another with the growth rate of the second portfolio exceeding that of the first. Thc selection of securities with the highest expected returns does not insure the selection of a portfolio with the highest growth rate.

The point can be demonstrated by comparing growth rates for two portfolios consisting of equal dollar investment in three securities. Each security in the first portfolio offers a .50 probability of realizing either a 15 percent loss or a 50 percent gain. Returns for each of the three securities are perfectly correlated with each other and this is, in effect, an undiversified portfolio. Expected return and variance can be calculated for each security j and portfolio p:

$$E(R_j) = \frac{-.15 + .50}{2} = .1750, \text{ for } j = 1, 2, \text{ and } 3$$

$$E(R_p) = \frac{1}{3}(.175) + \frac{1}{3}(.175) + \frac{1}{3}(.175)$$

$$= .1750$$

$$\text{var}(R_j) = \frac{(-.15 - .175)^2 + (.50 - .175)^2}{2}$$

$$= .1056, \text{ for } j = 1, 2, \text{ and } 3$$

$$\text{var}(R_p) = \sum_i \sum_j X_i X_j r_{ij} \sigma_i \sigma_j,\ r_{ij} = +1, \text{ for all } i, j = 1, 2, 3$$

$$= \begin{bmatrix} \frac{1}{9}(.1056) & \frac{1}{9}(.1056) & \frac{1}{9}(.1056) \\ \frac{1}{9}(.1056) & \frac{1}{9}(.1056) & \frac{1}{9}(.1056) \\ \frac{1}{9}(.1056) & \frac{1}{9}(.1056) & \frac{1}{9}(.1056) \end{bmatrix}$$

$$= .1056$$

Security and portfolio growth rates can now be estimated from Equations 14.23 and 14.24; with perfect correlation they are equal and they approximate the geometric mean value of 12.9 percent:

$$\bar{R}_g = \sqrt{(.85)(1.50)} - 1 = .1292$$

$$\bar{R}_{gj} \approx \bar{R}_{gp} \approx .175 - \frac{.1056}{2(1.175)} = .1301$$

Each of the three securities in the second portfolio has a .50 probability of receiving either a 10 percent loss or a 40 percent gain. Returns for each security are independent of others in the portfolio; that is, the correlation coefficient r_{ij} is zero and the portfolio is diversified. Proceeding as before,

$$E(R_j) = \frac{-.10 + .40}{2} = .1500, \text{ for } j = 1, 2, \text{ and } 3$$

$$E(R_p) = \frac{1}{3}(.15) + \frac{1}{3}(.15) + \frac{1}{3}(.15)$$

$$= .1500$$

$$\text{var}(R_j) = \frac{(-.10 - .15)^2 + (.40 - .15)^2}{2}$$

$$= .0625, \text{ for } j = 1, 2, \text{ and } 3$$

$$\text{var}(R_p) = \sum_i \sum_j X_i X_j r_{ij} \sigma_i \sigma_j,\ r_{ij} = 0, \text{ for all } i, j = 1, 2, 3, i \neq j$$

$$= \begin{bmatrix} \frac{1}{9}(.0625) & \frac{1}{9}(.0000) & \frac{1}{9}(.0000) \\ \frac{1}{9}(.0000) & \frac{1}{9}(.0625) & \frac{1}{9}(.0000) \\ \frac{1}{9}(.0000) & \frac{1}{9}(.0000) & \frac{1}{9}(.0625) \end{bmatrix}$$

$$= .0208$$

Portfolio expected return and variance for this portfolio are both less than corresponding values for the first portfolio. Variance is less partly because security variance has decreased from .1056 to .0625 and partly because lack of correlation has resulted in zero covariances in off-diagonal elements. The net effect is a substantial decrease in portfolio variance and an increase in expected portfolio growth; security growth decreases slightly to 12.28 percent but portfolio growth increases to 14.10:

$$R_{gj} \approx .150 - \left[\frac{.0625}{2(1.15)}\right] = .1228$$

$$R_{gp} \approx .150 - \left[\frac{.0208}{2(1.15)}\right] = .1410$$

Expected return and variance for each security in the first portfolio exceeded expected return and variance for each security in the second portfolio but expected growth was greater for the second portfolio primarily because of the impact of zero covariances. Importantly, security and portfolio growth rates were less than the value of corresponding one-period rates of return; in the case of the second portfolio, for example, expected security and portfolio rates of return were 15 percent but estimated growth rates were, respectively, 12.28 and 14.10 percent. The relationship between expected rate of return and approximate rate of growth is implied by Equation 14.24: the two rates will be equal when there is no variance. Thus the difference between expected rate of return and portfolio rate of growth will *decrease*, other things equal, as:

1. Average correlation among security returns decreases, with average covariance and portfolio variance decreasing accordingly.
2. The number of securities in the portfolio increases.

As shown previously, portfolio variance becomes increasingly dependent upon covariances as the number of individual assets increases. As weights shift from security variances to covariances, portfolio variance decreases. In terms of the second portfolio described in the previous example, assume that equal dollar amounts can be invested in each of ten independent securities with the expected return (.150) and variance (.0625) assumed previously. This is similar to the ten-security case of Figure 14.1; portfolio variance would be .00625 and:

$$\bar{R}_{gp} \approx .150 - \left[\frac{.00625}{2.30}\right] = .1473$$

As the number of securities in the portfolio increases, the difference between expected rate of return and portfolio growth rate decreases. But the effect is not unlimited; at some point the impact of adding another security will become minimal. The remaining section of this chapter considers this problem.

Diversification and Unsystematic Risk

The risk associated with individual securities can be separated into two components: systematic risk and unsystematic risk.[15] Systematic risk depends upon factors which affect all securities; these include money and credit conditions, political events, and other forces which influence security returns generally. Unsystematic risk reflects factors which are unique to individual firms; these include changes in executive personnel, strikes, legal actions, and similar events. Systematic risk, because of its general nature, cannot be reduced through diversification. But average unsystematic risk can be decreased by combining securities in a portfolio. In other words, factors which are unique to individual securities tend to be offsetting in the aggregate.

[15] Systematic and unsystematic risk are important elements in the statement and development of portfolio theory. They will be considered more carefully in Chapter 15; they are introduced here to complete the description of the impact of diversification on portfolio risk.

A portfolio is a combination of individual securities. For this reason portfolio risk also consists of systematic and unsystematic components. Effective diversification reduces portfolio risk by decreasing average unsystematic variability; the systematic element is generally unresponsive to diversification. All risk is systematic for an efficient portfolio and a portfolio which is subject to unsystematic risk is inefficient. From an investor's viewpoint unsystematic risk is irrelevant for individual securities which are held as part of an efficient portfolio.

Evans and Archer studied the relationship between portfolio efficiency and the number of securities in the portfolio.[16] They found that average unsystematic risk can largely be eliminated, where securities are held in approximately equal proportion, in portfolios consisting of as few as eight to ten securities. They measured the mean semiannual standard deviation in rate of return for 60 randomly selected securities and then repeated the process for portfolios consisting of equal investment in 2 to 40 securities. In this manner systematic and unsystematic portfolio risk were observed empirically. For mean portfolio risk $\bar{\sigma}(R_p)$, mean security systematic risk $\bar{\sigma}(R_s)$, mean security unsystematic risk $\bar{\sigma}(R_u)$, and the number of securities in a portfolio (m), they tested the relationship:

$$\bar{\sigma}(R_p) = \bar{\sigma}(R_s) + \frac{\bar{\sigma}(R_u)}{m} \tag{14.25}$$

For the period tested, January, 1958, through June, 1967, mean security standard deviation was 20.54 percent; 11.91 percent was systematic and 8.63 percent was unsystematic. The portion of total variability (variance) which was caused by systematic factors was 33.6 percent.[17] Figure 14.10 traces Equation 14.25 for these values. As portfolio size increases unsystematic risk decreases rapidly and portfolio risk quickly converges to the systematic risk level. The values of Figure 14.10 are six-month values and they may be unrepresentative of current or future levels of risk. Nonetheless, the behavior pictured there provides strong support for the statement that efficiency can be realized with a very moderately sized portfolio.

Underdiversification occurs when a portfolio consists of too few securities to minimize unsystematic risk; there is general agreement that underdiversification is undesirable. But there is far less agreement on the related question of the possible effects of overdiversification. James Lorie has argued

[16] J. Evans and S. Archer, "Diversification and the Reduction of Dispersion: An Empirical Analysis," *Journal of Finance*, December 1968, pp. 761–767.

[17] For security variance $\sigma^2(R_j)$, the proportion is $[\sigma^2(R_s)]/[\sigma^2(R_j)] = [(11.91)^2]/[(20.54)^2] = .336$. Studies by Benjamin King, "Market and Industry Factors in Stock Price Behavior," *Journal of Business*, January 1966, pp. 139–190, and James Farrell, Jr., "Analyzing Covariation of Returns To Determine Homogeneous Stock Groupings," *Journal of Business*, April 1974, pp. 186–207, support the finding that in recent years about 30 to 34 percent of stock return variance is systematic. King further found that this level has declined historically from a high of 58 percent in the 1927–1935 period.

Figure 14.10
Portfolio Risk and the Extent of Portfolio Diversification

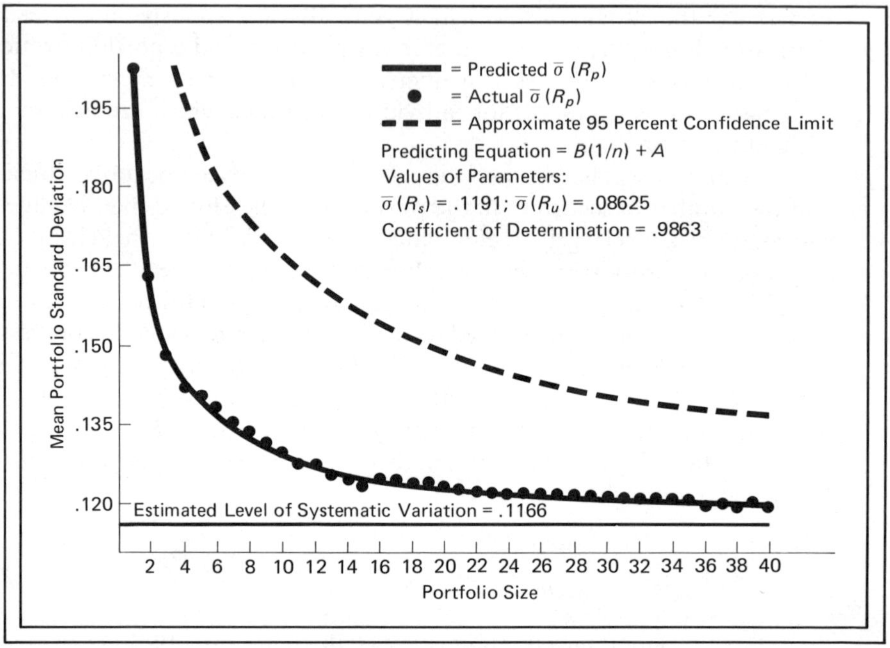

Source: J. Evans and S. Archer, "Diversification and the Reduction of Dispersion: An Empirical Analysis," *Journal of Finance*, December 1968, p. 765.

that small departures from perfect diversification—where all risk is systematic—can produce significant increases in portfolio variance.[18] Others would describe too large a portfolio as overdiversified. Beyond some portfolio size—say, 20—diminishing returns are realized from scale economies in transaction and information costs. Moreover, any advantage which is realized from identifying undervalued securities is lessened as the weight attaching to those securities decreases. In the final analysis the possibility of overdiversification is an empirical question which remains to be settled.

Investors' expectations are based upon analytical skills and perceptions of future events. Large numbers of investors share common, or homogeneous, expectations; this is evidenced by the popularity of mutual funds. Other investors form individual or heterogeneous expectations in the search for superior return on investment. In either case risk-adjusted rates of return are increased by the diversification effect which decreases unsystematic portfolio risk.

[18] James H. Lorie, "Diversification: Old and New," *The Journal of Portfolio Management*, Winter 1975, pp. 25–28.

Summary

This chapter introduced and analyzed principles of diversification. The relationship among rates of return, measured by the covariance, was shown to be the critical element in portfolio analysis. As portfolio size increases risk can be minimized by minimizing the average covariance. When risk is minimized for any given level of expected return, the portfolio in question is an efficient portfolio. Borrowing and lending opportunities increase portfolio efficiency. Long-run portfolio growth was described in terms of expected return and risk and the relationship between risk and portfolio size was then analyzed.

The next chapter considers the problem of applying the principles developed here; elements introduced in this chapter are examined in greater detail. This provides a basis for the discussion of portfolio revision and timing which is contained in Chapter 16.

Questions and Problems

1. The joint probability distribution of annual returns for Kellogg Corporation and Union Pacific in the years 1971–1975 were as follows:

Year	*Kellogg*	*Union Pacific*
1971	+.267	+.537
1972	+.148	+.131
1973	+.035	+.413
1974	+.023	−.227
1975	+.485	+.172

Calculate the average annual returns, standard deviations, and covariance of historical returns.

2. If the past five-year record is a fair estimate of next period's possible outcomes, calculate the return and risk to a portfolio consisting of equal dollar amounts of each stock in problem 1 above. What happens to these estimates if the returns in the next period are expected to be uncorrelated?
3. If the past five-year record in problem 1 is a fair estimate of long-run performance, what is the expected long-run growth rate of each security? Comment on the representativeness of the estimate.
4. You have identified two desirable portfolios and have labeled them A and B. Portfolio A appears too risky for your tastes and portfolio B, while safer, sacrifices too much in expected return. Having decided to divide your money equally between the portfolios, what portion of your wealth will be committed to each security?

Composition of Portfolio A		*Composition of Portfolio B*	
$X_{i,A}$	*Stock i*	$X_{j,B}$	*Stock j*
$\frac{1}{4}$	GM	$\frac{1}{5}$	GM
$\frac{1}{3}$	IBM	$\frac{1}{5}$	IBM
$\frac{1}{4}$	McDonalds	$\frac{1}{5}$	McDonalds
$\frac{1}{6}$	U.S. Steel	$\frac{1}{5}$	U.S. Steel
		$\frac{1}{5}$	Gulf Oil

5. Draw a representative efficient frontier of risky securities and an indifference curve in $E(R_P)$, σ_P space. Explain why the figures have the shape they do. Draw a lending line tangent to the efficient frontier; why is this line shaped as it is?
6. Identify what is meant by a security or portfolio's long-run rate of growth. How does this concept relate to $E(R_P)$, σ_P portfolio analysis? What assumptions are necessary to estimate growth rates from historical information?

Selected References

RATIONALE FOR DIVERSIFICATION

Brealey, Richard A., *An Introduction to Risk and Return from Common Stocks* (Cambridge, Mass.: M.I.T. Press, 1969).

Evans, John L., "An Examination of the Principle of Diversification," *Journal of Business Finance and Accounting*, Summer 1975, pp. 243–255.

Evans, J., and S. H. Archer, "Diversification and the Reduction of Dispersion: An Empirical Analysis," *Journal of Finance*, December 1968, pp. 761–767.

Lintner, John, "Security Prices, Risk, and Maximal Gains from Diversification," *Journal of Finance* 20, no. 4 (December 1965): 586–616.

Lorie, James H., "Diversification: Old and New," *The Journal of Portfolio Management*, Winter 1975, pp. 25–28.

Mao, James, "Essentials of Portfolio Diversification Strategy," *Journal of Finance* 25, no. 5 (December 1970): 1109–1124.

Renshaw, E. F., "Portfolio Balance Models in Perspective: Some Generalizations That Can Be Derived from the Two Asset Case," *Journal of Financial and Quantitative Analysis*, June 1967, pp. 138–139.

Samuelson, Paul, "General Proof that Diversification Pays," *Journal of Financial and Quantitative Analysis*, June 1967, pp. 107–22.

Shiskin, Julium, "Systematic Aspects of Stock Price Fluctuations," *Modern Developments in Investment Management*, ed. J. Lorie and K. Brealey (New York: Praeger, 1972).

PORTFOLIO CONSTRUCTION AND INVESTOR PREFERENCES

Black, Frank E., "Elements of Portfolio Construction," *Financial Analysts Journal* 25 (May–June 1969): 123–129.

Feldstein, M. S., "On the Measurement of Risk Aversion," *Southern Economic Journal*, July 1968, pp. 58–59.

Hamada, Robert S., "Investment Decision with a Mean-Variance Approach," *Quarterly Journal of Economics* 85 no. 4 (November 1971): 667–683.

Hastie, K. L., "The Determination of Optimal Investment Policy," *Management Science*, August 1967, pp. B757–774.

Markowitz, Harry, *Portfolio Selection: Efficient Diversification of Investments* (New York: Wiley 1959).

———, "Markowitz Revisited," *Financial Analysts Journal*, September–October 1976, pp. 47–62.

Pyle, David, and Stephen Turnvosky, "Safety First and Expected Utility Maximization in Mean-Standard Deviation Portfolio Analysis," *The Review of Economics and Statistics* 52, no. 1 (February 1970): 75–81.

Samuelson, Paul, "The Fundamental Approximation Theorem of Portfolio Analysis in Terms of Means, Variances, and Higher Moments," *Review of Economic Studies*, October 1970, pp. 537–542.

Sharpe, William F., *Portfolio Theory and Capital Markets* (New York: McGraw-Hill, 1970).

Tobin, James, "Liquidity Preference as Behavior Towards Risk," *Review of Economic Studies* 25 (February 1958): 65–86.

Upson, Roger, Paul Jessup, and Keishiro Matsumoto, "Portfolio Diversification Strategies," *Financial Analysts Journal*, May–June 1975, pp. 86–88.

Wallingford, B. A., "A Survey and Comparison of Portfolio Selection Models," *Journal of Financial and Quantitative Analysis*, June 1967, pp. 85–106.

Chapter 15
Portfolio Theory

The conceptual analysis of the preceding chapter did not consider the information and data costs required for a systematic approach to portfolio management. Ignoring these costs assumes that they are insignificant relative to the benefits provided in identifying properly diversified portfolios. In practice this is seldom the case. Security analysis requires estimation of security returns and their dispersion. Diversification requires more; additional estimates are required to specify the covariance expected between all pairs of security returns. For a screened population of m number of securities a total of

$$\frac{m(m-1)}{2}$$

estimates of covariances are needed. For a population of 50 securities, 1225 covariances are needed in addition to 50 estimates of expected return and 50 estimates of variance. When $m = 500$, 124,750 covariances are required. With over 1500 common stocks listed on the NYSE, an equivalent number on the AMEX, and even more over-the-counter, a reasonably representative screened population of common stocks alone results in an enormous data input problem.

The hazard of mechanistic generation of large numbers of covariances, based on historical observation, is obvious; quality of output depends critically on the accuracy of all inputs. Some method is needed to reduce security input requirements to a tractable number of forecastable estimates. A well-known method, the *single-index model*, is presented here in detail. The first section of the chapter identifies the general criteria and requirements of the single-index approach. Central to this approach is the division of security return into two *expected* components, one resulting from firm-related activity and the other from general economic conditions, together with one *unexpected* random element. Security risk is segmented into two parts: a systematic component and an unsystematic component. The latter, as will be shown, results from the random element of security return.

The single-index model is directly related to the concepts of security market efficiency and equilibrium. This body of knowledge is known as capital market theory and the second section outlines its application and importance in portfolio construction. The appendix to this chapter considers multi-index models and the potential impact of common industry and growth characteristics in estimating portfolio risk and return.

The Single-Index Model

Portfolio analysis with the complete set of inputs described in the preceding chapter is known as the *full covariance model;* this is the original portfolio model developed by Harry Markowitz in 1952.[1] A simplified model that greatly reduces both data and computations has since been developed by William Sharpe.[2] Sharpe's single-index model, also frequently referred to as the *market model*, is a simple linear expression identifying return on security j as the dependent variable R_{jt} and an index of return for a portfolio of securities as the independent variable R_{It}, in time period t. It is written as

$$R_{jt} = \alpha_j + \beta_j R_{It} + e_{jt} \tag{15.1}$$

The coefficients represented by the Greek symbols for alpha (α) and beta (β) are parameters which best identify the relationship in linear form. Their interpretation is specific and straightforward. Alpha is the intercept; it is the expected security return when the value of the index is zero. Beta is the slope which measures the average relationship between security and index return; it measures the average sensitivity of security return to index return. The product $\beta_j R_I$ is the portion of security return resulting from behavior

[1] Harry Markowitz, "Portfolio Selection," *The Journal of Finance* 11, no. 1 (March 1952): 77–91. Also see his *Portfolio Selection: Efficient Diversification of Investment* (New York: Wiley, 1959).

[2] William F. Sharpe, "A Simplified Model for Portfolio Analysis," *Management Science* 9 (January 1963): 277–293. Also see "Addendum," April 1963, p. 498.

of the index. In turn beta is the ratio of the security's covariance of return with the index and the variance of index return:

$$\beta_j = \frac{\text{cov}(R_j, R_I)}{\sigma_I^2} = \frac{r_{jI}\sigma_j\sigma_I}{\sigma_I^2} = \frac{r_{jI}\sigma_j}{\sigma_I} \tag{15.2}$$

If a security and the index had estimated standard deviations of return of .19 and .23 respectively, and if the correlation of their returns through time was +.60 then the security's beta would be estimated by Equation 15.2 as

$$\hat{\beta}_j = \frac{.60(.19)}{.23} = .50$$

The final term (e_{jt}) is the unexpected return resulting from influences not identified by the model. Frequently referred to as random or residual return, this third and unexpected component may take on any value, but over large numbers of observations it will average zero and it should demonstrate additional properties which will be discussed in subsequent paragraphs.

For a security having an alpha and beta estimated to be .02 and .50 respectively, in a period when the index is 12 percent the security's return would most likely be

$$R_{jt} = .02 + .50(.12) = .08$$

While 8 percent is the expected security return when the index is 12 percent, in any period actual return may differ from 8 percent. If the security's return were in fact 11 percent in period t, then by Equation 15.1

$$.11 = .02 + .50(.12) + e_{jt}$$
$$.11 = .08 + e_{jt}$$
$$.03 = e_{jt}$$

In other words, 3 percent of the stock's total return was unexpected. All elements of the single-index model are graphically illustrated in Figure 15.1. The model's features are highlighted in the next section and its application to portfolio construction is examined in greater detail.

DATA INPUT REDUCTION

The major benefit of the Sharpe index model is its reduction of the number of covariances through the assumption that the relationship among the returns to all pairs of securities occurs solely through their common association with an index. Thus the covariance of each security with the index, identified in Equation 15.2, suffices for portfolio construction, reducing the number of covariance computations to m.

The advantage of reducing covariance estimates exists with as few as four securities. When four securities are being considered the covariance

Figure 15.1
Components of the Single-Index Model

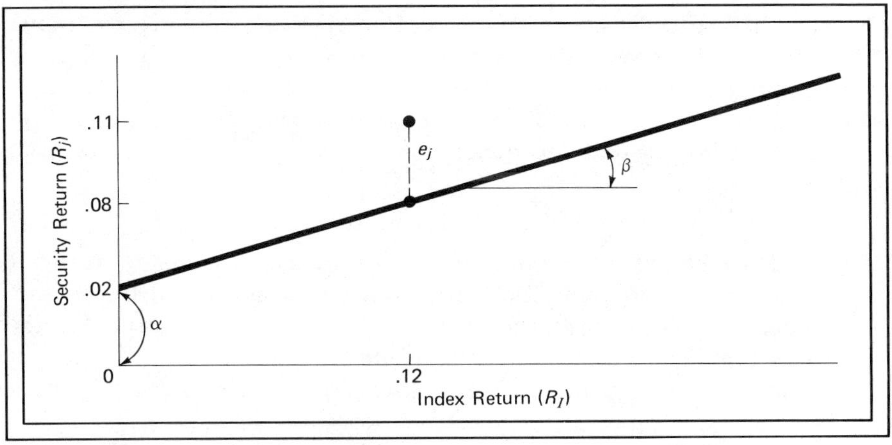

matrix for each method is

	Full Model				Single Model
Security	*1*	*2*	*3*	*4*	*Index*
1					cov(1, I)
2	cov(2, 1)				cov(2, I)
3	cov(3, 1)	cov(3, 2)			cov(3, I)
4	cov(4, 1)	cov(4, 2)	cov(4, 3)		cov(4, I)

The full covariance model required one-half of an $m \times (m - 1)$ matrix containing $1/2[4 \cdot 3] = 6$ necessary estimates of covariance. The single-index model requires only a $m \times 1$ matrix having $m = 4$ covariance estimates. For 50 securities only 50 covariances are required instead of the 1225 required for the full covariance model. When all necessary estimates are considered, including expected returns and variances, the two models compare as follows:

Estimates of	*Covariance*	*Return*	*Variance*	*Total*
Full model	$\frac{m(m-1)}{2}$	m	m	$\frac{m(m+3)}{2}$
Index model	m	$m + 1$	$m + 1$	$3m + 2$

Sharpe's single-index model results in costs as well as benefits. An appropriate measure of economic activity must be selected and its expected return and variance must be forecasted. Most commonly the index is specified as a measure of return to a broadly based sample of securities, that is, a market index. The index is more than an additional input; it is a "keystone" security in portfolio construction. Accurate estimation of index behavior thus becomes critical to successful portfolio building with the single-index method. Furthermore, the assumption that all relationships among securities' returns are captured by the association of each to a single index is imprecise. While the single-index approach provides a good approximation, the full covariance model will provide more accurate forecasts of portfolio risk providing that the quality of inputs into each model is the same.[3]

THE CHARACTERISTIC LINE

The straight line shown in Figure 15.1, which approximates the relationship between security and index returns, is commonly called the characteristic line. If the relationship between security and index return were exact, all observations of security return would plot on the characteristic line. All risk would be systematic, arising only from uncertainty as to the level of the index. For a perfectly diversified portfolio all risk is systematic, implying that residual return e_{jt} of Equation 15.1 would always be zero. Regressing a perfectly diversified portfolio's return on an index of market return would yield a perfect fit; this is signified by a coefficient of determination (the r^2 of regression analysis) of one.

Not all risk is systematic. Some risk, and for single securities most risk, is unsystematic. The characteristic line measures only the approximate relationship. Unsystematic risk is measured by the standard deviation or variance of the distribution of residual terms about the characteristic line. For the characteristic line to be properly fitted, the residuals must have the following properties:

1. $E(e_j) = 0$. This insures that the characteristic line is the best fit, for the sum of the squared deviations from the line will be a minimum.
2. $\text{cov}(e_j, R_I) = 0$. This states that unsystematic risk is invariant with respect to the level of index returns.
3. $\text{cov}(e_j, e_k) = 0$. This provides that the complete relationship between every pair of securities j and k is explained by their common relationship to the index.

Figure 15.2 illustrates the residual return behavior implicit in the relationship between security and index return. The total variability of security return can be expressed as

$$\sigma_j^2 = \beta_j^2 \sigma_I^2 + \sigma^2(e_j) \tag{15.3}$$

which corresponds to the identification of security risk in the previous chapter with two components: systematic risk and unsystematic risk. Systematic risk is the security beta squared times the variance of the market index. Unsystematic risk is the variance of deviations about the security's characteristic line.

[3] Single and full covariance models may be thought of as extreme points on a continuum. In between are procedures known as multi-index models. A multi-index model's virtue is increased accuracy and its vice is increased estimation and computational requirements. A discussion of multi-index models follows in the appendix to this chapter.

Figure 15.2
Unsystematic Risk and the Single-Index Model

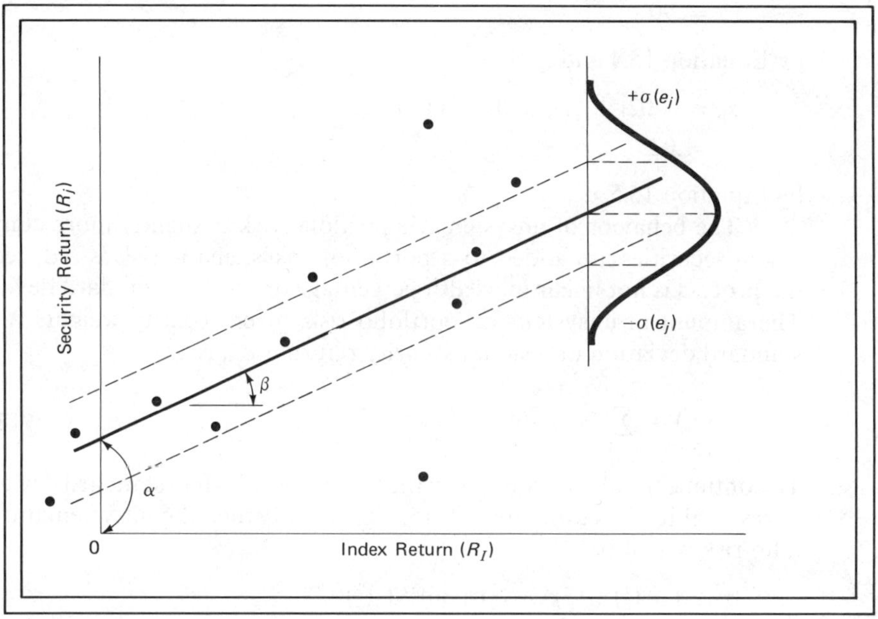

Because unsystematic risk is a very large component of total risk for individual securities, security alphas and betas have only limited use in predicting future security behavior. However, the stability gained through aggregation and averaging greatly enhances their value for describing the behavior of portfolios. Portfolio return R_p may also be defined with Equation 15.1 by substituting R_p for R_j. The relationship between security and portfolio characteristic lines can be summarized by the following:

1. The beta of a portfolio's characteristic line is a weighted average of the betas of component securities where weights are the percentage of wealth X_j allocated to the security:

$$\beta_p = \sum_{j=1}^{m} X_j\beta_j \quad \text{and} \quad \sum_{j=1}^{m} X_j = 1 \tag{15.4}$$

2. The alpha of a portfolio's characteristic line is similarly a weighted average of the component security alphas:

$$\alpha_p = \sum_{j=1}^{m} X_j\alpha_j \tag{15.5}$$

If a portfolio is to include three securities having individual alphas of .02, −.01, and .05 and individual betas of .50, 1.30, and .90, and if equal dollar amounts are placed in each security, the portfolio parameters would be

$$\beta_p = \tfrac{1}{3}(.50) + \tfrac{1}{3}(1.30) + \tfrac{1}{3}(.90)$$
$$= .90$$

by Equation 15.4 and

$$\alpha_p = \tfrac{1}{3}(.02) + \tfrac{1}{3}(-.01) + \tfrac{1}{3}(.05)$$
$$= .02$$

by Equation 15.5.

The behavior of unsystematic portfolio risk is slightly more complex. When securities are added to a portfolio, unsystematic risk is reduced but the process is not linear in wealth percentage or residual standard deviation. The amount of unsystematic portfolio risk, given security weights X_j and standard deviation of residual security return $\sigma(e_j)$, is

$$\sigma^2(e_p) = \sum_{j=1}^{m} X_j^2 \sigma^2(e_j) \tag{15.6}$$

To continue the above example, if the three securities had standard deviations of residual returns estimated at .15, .36, and .20, then the unsystematic portfolio risk would be

$$\sigma^2(e_p) = (\tfrac{1}{3})^2(.15)^2 + (\tfrac{1}{3})^2(.36)^2 + (\tfrac{1}{3})^2(.20)^2$$
$$= .021$$

by Equation 15.6 and

$$\sigma(e_p) = \sqrt{.021} = .146$$

The following paragraphs will summarize the interrelationships among total, systematic, and unsystematic portfolio risk.

PORTFOLIO VARIANCE

The major simplification of the single-index model is its reduction of the variance-covariance matrix to $2m + 1$ elements. Since by assumption each stock is related only to a market index, residual covariance for any two securities j and k is zero. Unsystematic risk may be estimated simply by subtracting the systematic element from total risk. Rearranging Equation 15.3,

$$\sigma^2(e_j) = \sigma_j^2 - \beta_j^2 \sigma_I^2 \tag{15.7}$$

Risk for any portfolio is given by

$$\sigma_p^2 = \sum_{j=1}^{m} X_j^2 \beta_j^2 \sigma_I^2 + \sum_{j=1}^{m} X_j^2 \sigma^2(e_j) \tag{15.8}$$

Equation 15.8 may be further simplified by substituting the calculation of portfolio beta from Equation 15.4, giving

$$\sigma_p^2 = \beta_p^2 \sigma_I^2 + \sum_{j=1}^{m} X_j^2 \sigma^2(e_j) \tag{15.8a}$$

The three equations above can be illustrated by continuing the example from the previous expressions. A security with a standard deviation equaling .19 was found by Equation 15.2 to have a beta of .5 with a market index having standard deviation of .23. With this information unsystematic security risk may be estimated by Equation 15.7 as

$$\sigma^2(e_j) = (.19)^2 - (.5)^2(.23)^2 = .0229$$

The square root of .0229 is 0.15, which was the standard deviation of unsystematic risk assumed for this security in the preceding illustration of Equation 15.6. In the example illustrating Equations 15.4 through 15.6 this security was combined with two riskier securities to give a portfolio beta of .90 and portfolio unsystematic risk (variance) of .021. Using these figures, the total risk of that portfolio may now be estimated with Equation 15.8a:

$$\sigma_p^2 = (.9)^2(.23)^2 + .021 = .064$$

or

$$\sigma_p = \sqrt{.064} = .253$$

Efficient portfolios have negligible unsystematic risk. Since $X_j < 1$, as the number of securities increases the sum of X_j^2 becomes very small. This is the way in which unsystematic risk vanishes. At the extreme unsystematic risk $[\sigma^2(e_p)]$ becomes zero,

$$\sigma^2(e_p) = \sum_{j=1}^{m} X_j^2 \sigma^2(e_j) \rightarrow 0 \text{ as } m \rightarrow \infty \qquad [(15.6a)]$$

leaving

$$\sigma_p^2 = \beta_p^2 \sigma_I^2 \quad \text{and} \quad \sigma_p = \beta_p \sigma_I \tag{15.9}$$

for efficient portfolios. Extremes are not usually relevant but this case is an exception. The previous chapter showed that portfolios of as few as $m = 10$ securities where $X_j = X_k = \cdots = 1/m$ eliminate most unsystematic risk. For any portfolio of m securities with equal allocation unsystematic risk reduces to[4]

$$\sigma^2(e_p) = \frac{1}{m}\,[\text{average } \sigma^2(e_j)] \qquad [(15.6b)]$$

[4] When $X_j = 1/m$,

$$\sum (X_j)^2(\sigma^2(e_j)) = \sum \left(\frac{1}{m}\right)^2 (\sigma^2(e_j)) = \left(\frac{1}{m}\right)^2 \sum \sigma^2(e_j) = \frac{1}{m}\left[\frac{\sum \sigma^2(e_j)}{m}\right]$$

In the preceding example illustrating Equation 15.6 equal allocation among three securities was assumed. The numeric solution was

$$\sigma^2(e_p) = (\tfrac{1}{3})^2(.15)^2 + (\tfrac{1}{3})^2(.36)^2 + (\tfrac{1}{3})^2(.20)^2 = .021$$

which may now be rearranged as

$$\sigma^2(e_p) = \frac{1}{3}\left[\frac{(.15)^2 + (.36)^2 + (.20)^2}{3}\right]$$

$$= \frac{1}{3}\,[\bar{\sigma}^2(e_j)] = \frac{1}{3}\,[.064] = .021$$

Rearranging in this manner shows that unsystematic portfolio risk is only one-third of the average unsystematic risk of its component securities. When $m = 10$, this expression is .10 [average $\bar{\sigma}^2(e_j)$] and portfolio unsystematic risk is only 10 percent of the average unsystematic risk of all securities. In portfolios where nearly all unsystematic risk is averaged away,

$$\sigma_p{}^2 \approx \beta_p{}^2\sigma_I{}^2 \tag{15.9a}$$

is a good approximation of portfolio risk. A portfolio with only three securities is obviously inefficient and its portfolio risk could not be approximated by Equation 15.9a. With total portfolio variance of .064 and unsystematic variance of .021, the portfolio contains 32.8 percent (.021/.064) more risk than necessary.

Estimates of unsystematic risk and total portfolio variability may be understated by the single-index model if securities in the portfolio are related beyond their common association with the market index. One condition of the single-index model is that $\text{cov}(e_j, e_k) = 0$ for all different securities. Stated simply, this assumption denies the existence of industry groupings or other elements of commonality among securities such as similar growth characteristics. Clearly this assumption is not correct but the seriousness of the inaccuracy is open to question. An investor can largely overlook the problem by avoiding a concentration of securities from the same industry in the portfolio. A more complete, but also more costly, procedure is to measure the impact of industry and other effects on portfolio risk directly. The importance of these factors as well as procedures for their measurement through use of multi-index models are discussed in the appendix to this chapter.

Capital Market Theory

Capital market theory is a statement about security pricing in a world where bright, well-informed, and risk-averse investors manage their wealth in a rational manner. It is an extension of the single-index model which substitutes the perspective of security markets as a whole for the view of a single investor. Since capital market theory is an abstraction, it relies on a number of simplifying assumptions. They include the following:

1. All investors share the same time frame and have common beliefs regarding the future.
2. All investors make their investment decisions solely on the basis of expected return and risk.
3. All investors may either borrow or lend at the same rate of interest, which is presumed to be risk-free.
4. All securities are properly priced; the markets are in equilibrium.

Furthermore, institutional realities such as transactions costs and taxes are ignored. Combined, these assumptions appear to portray an unreal world. No doubt they do. But, remarkably, studies have shown that security markets generally behave as if these assumptions are correct. Additionally, they allow development of a model, known as the capital asset pricing model, which provides a characterization of how security returns should behave when markets are in equilibrium.

THE CAPITAL ASSET PRICING MODEL

The capital asset pricing model is a representation of security pricing analogous to neoclassical models of production. The model assumes efficient markets where security values change in response to changing real economic conditions including the needs and preferences of investors. For any and all securities and portfolios, the capital asset pricing model states that the risk premium for any security j is related to the risk premium of the market M according to the relationship

$$E(R_j) - R_F = \beta_j^*[E(R_M) - R_F] \qquad (15.10)$$

Risk premium is the difference between the expected return on a risky security and the risk-free rate of interest (R_F). The constant of proportionality, β_j^*, may be interpreted as the true beta and the proper measure of risk for individual securities and portfolios under equilibrium market conditions.

The market portfolio M has a precise definition in the asset pricing model. Since all securities must be held and since markets are in equilibrium, the market portfolio contains all securities, each held in a proportion equaling the ratio of the security's market value to the total market value of all securities. Fortunately, security indexes which are less inclusive and which are weighted differently have proven to be suitable proxies in applications for valuation purposes, provided that they are selected carefully for the task at hand.[5] A broadly based security index I may therefore be used to represent the theoretical market portfolio M in actual applications of the asset pricing model.

[5] Frank K. Reilly, "Evidence Regarding a Segmented Stock Market," *Journal of Finance* 27 (June 1972): 607–626. A description of security indexes was provided in Chapter 3.

Figure 15.3
The Market Portfolio's Characteristic Line

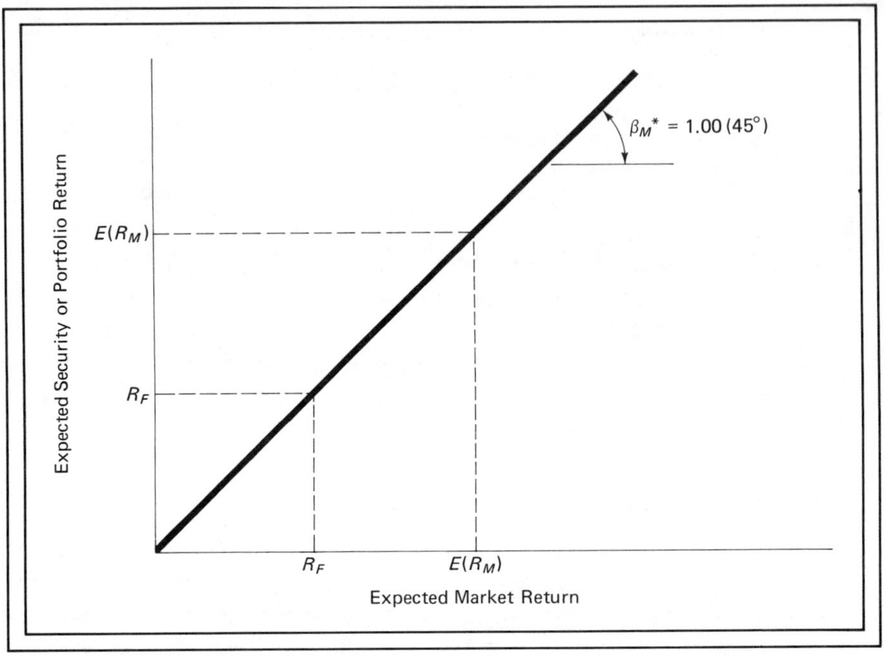

Applying the asset pricing model first requires identification of the market portfolio's characteristic line. Figure 15.3 supplies the appropriate illustration. With uniform scale on both axes, the market characteristic line is a straight line drawn 45° through the origin. Its slope, which equals the beta of the market portfolio, is one.[6] Since the market portfolio is all-inclusive, the average of all security betas equals one. Securities and portfolios with betas in excess of one are referred to as aggressive investments. They are more volatile, increasing or decreasing on average more than the market increases or decreases. Securities and portfolios having betas which are less than one are called defensive; they provide less movement than the market as a whole. Although betas for individual securities and small portfolios may be close to one, betas for very large portfolios of risky securities are commonly very close to one since they are good facsimiles of the market. The risk-free rate is identified on each axis in Figure 15.3. The market portfolio's characteristic line passes through the point of intersection of the lines drawn from and perpendicular to the risk-free points.

[6] This can be proven by recalling Equation 15.2 which defines $\beta_j = [\text{cov}(R_j, R_I)/\text{var}(R_I)]$. Using return to the market portfolio M as the proper index, the result becomes

$$\beta_M = \frac{\text{cov}(R_M, R_M)}{\sigma_M{}^2} = \frac{\sigma_M{}^2}{\sigma_M{}^2} = 1.00$$

Figure 15.4
Characteristic Lines of Hypothetical Securities

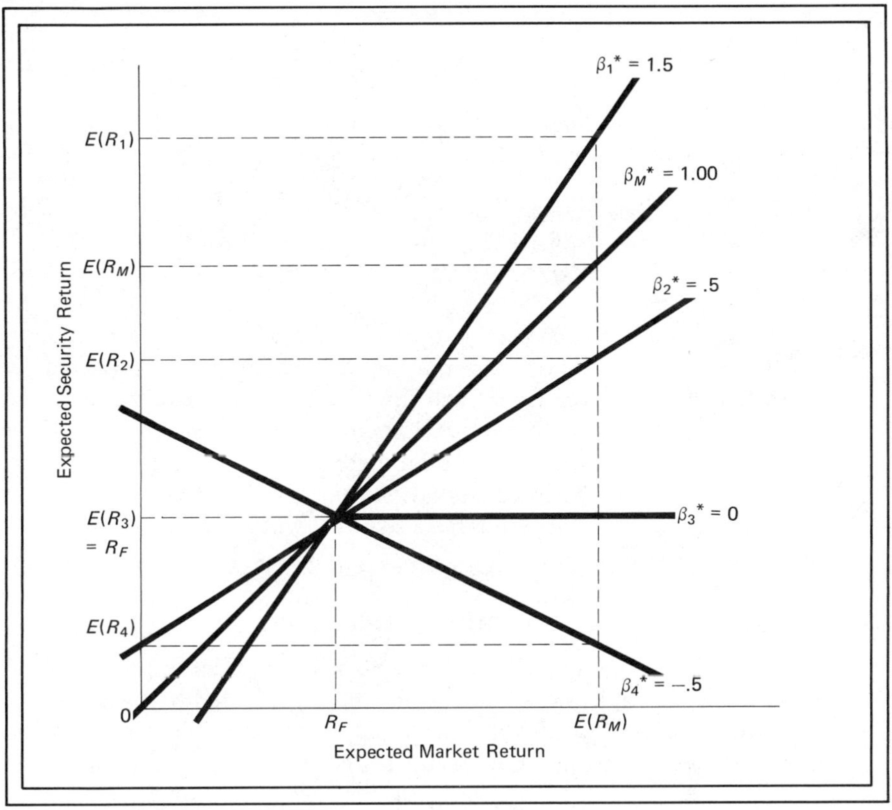

Assuming that equilibrium conditions prevail, every security's characteristic line will pass through two points:[7]

1. (E_j, E_M)
2. (R_F, R_F)

Figure 15.4 illustrates characteristic lines for four properly priced securities. One security is aggressive and three are defensive in differing degrees. Their expected return behavior over a period when market expectations are realized and alternatively when the market level remains unchanged is categorized in Table 15.1. The table highlights relationships requiring comment. First, it can be noted that any risky security having a beta of zero will have an expected return equaling the risk-free rate. Such a result is not a contradiction. A beta of zero implies that all risk is unsystematic and may be

[7] William F. Sharpe, *Portfolio Theory and Capital Markets* (New York: McGraw-Hill 1970), pp. 91–93.

Table 15.1
Relationship of Expected Security Return to Market Return

Market Outcomes	Security Expectations: Aggressive $\beta^* > 1.0$	Average $\beta^* = 1.0$	Defensive: $1.0 > \beta^* > 0$	$\beta^* = 0$	$\beta^* < 0$
$R_M = E(R_M)$	$E(R_j) > R_M$	$E(R_j) = R_M$	$R_F < E(R_j) < R_M$	$E(R_j) = R_F$	$E(R_j) < R_F$
$R_M = 0$	$E(R_j) < R_M$	$E(R_j) = 0$	$E(R_j) > 0$	$E(R_j) = R_F$	$E(R_j) > R_F$

eliminated by diversification. In the rare case of a negative beta security, one that moves contrary to the market, a normal level of expected return is less than the risk-free rate. Such low, conceivably negative, expected returns are justified owing to the fact that a negative beta security will do more to *reduce* total portfolio risk per dollar invested than will a risk-free security.[8] This result is evident by the observation that when the market does yield no (or negative) return a negative beta security will yield a positive return in excess of the risk-free rate.

IMPLICATIONS OF EQUILIBRIUM PRICING

The single-index model of Equation 15.1 has been used in the development of the theory of capital market equilibrium represented by the asset pricing model of Equation 15.10.[9] The relationship of the capital asset pricing model to the single-index model may be illustrated by rearranging Equation 15.10.

$$E(R_j) - R_F = \beta_j^*[E(R_M) - R_F]$$
$$E(R_j) = R_F + \beta_j^*E(R_M) - \beta_j^*R_F$$
$$E(R_j) = R_F - \beta_j^*R_F + \beta_j^*E(R_M)$$
$$E(R_j) = R_F(1 - \beta_j^*) + \beta_j^*E(R_M) \tag{15.10}$$

defining

$$\alpha^* = R_F(1 - \beta_j^*) \quad \text{and} \quad E(R_M) = E(R_I)$$
$$E(R_j) = \alpha_j^* + \beta_j^*E(R_I)$$

[8] All of these results follow directly from the equilibrium pricing conditions for all securities, which William Sharpe identifies as the Security Market Line. The Security Market Line is a linear relationship between securities returns and their covariances with the market's return. Ibid., pp. 86–91.

[9] Development of capital market theory is credited to William Sharpe, "Capital Asset Prices: A Theory of Market Equilibrium Under Conditions of Risk," *Journal of Finance* (1964): 425–442, and to John Lintner, "The Valuation of Risk Assets and the Selection of Risky Investments in Stock Portfolios and Capital Budgets," *Review of Economics and Statistics* (1965): 13–37. Refinement and clarification of the development has been provided by Eugene Fama, "Risk, Return, and Equilibrium: Some Clarifying Comments," *Journal of Finance*, March 1968, pp. 29–40.

whereas

$$R_{jt} = \alpha_j + \beta_j R_{It} + e_{jt} \qquad [(15.1)]$$

The two expressions are very similar but they are not identical: some subtle but important differences exist. The capital asset pricing model is more general since it is expressed only in terms of expected value; it does not presume a linear relationship over time between security and market returns as the single-index market model does. On the other hand, the market model may be a more valid expression of security return behavior when equilibrium market conditions are absent, since it portrays actual rather than normative market conditions. It is the task of security analysis to determine whether observed alpha and beta parameters for individual securities equal their true equilibrium counterparts, recognizing that divergence provides the opportunity for superior investment performance. Observed alphas and betas are commonly estimated through empirical application of the regression technique to Equation 15.1.

DIFFERENTIAL RETURN. Implications of the asset pricing model are most easily seen graphically in terms of excess returns. By subtracting the risk-free rate from all returns, the axes in Figure 15.4 are made to intersect at (R_F, R_F) instead of $(0, 0)$. In this manner the intercept of any security or portfolio characteristic line directly measures expected performance relative to the market. This technique was first developed by Michael Jensen who labeled the vertical intercept as *differential return.*[10] In market equilibrium, where all securities are properly priced, all differential returns are zero.[11] Undervalued securities will have positive differential returns and overvalued securities will have negative differential returns.

Consider three securities, *J*, *K*, and *L*, which are expected to yield 26, 10, and 9 percent, respectively, in the next year. Risk-free yield is 4 percent and the market in general is expected to provide a 12 percent return. Finally, the systematic risk of securities *J*, *K*, and *L* has been estimated by betas of 2.0, 1.0, and 0.5, respectively. With expected returns and betas, each characteristic line can be plotted as shown in Figure 15.5 by drawing a line with slope equaling beta through the point $[E(R_j) - R_F, E(R_m) - R_F]$. If all judgments are sound, securities *J* and *L* are bargains since they are undervalued in the current market. Security *K* is overpriced since its differential return is negative.

While the concept of differential return is valid for comparisons with the market, it is not accurate in making direct comparisons between two securities. One cannot say that because security *J*'s differential return of 6 percent exceeds security *L*'s differential return of 1 percent, security *J* represents the better buy. This is because security *J* has a larger beta signifying

[10] Michael Jensen, "Risk, the Pricing of Capital Assets, and the Evaluation of Investment Portfolios," *Journal of Business* 42, no. 2 (April 1969): 167–247.

[11] Figure 15.4 shows the equilibrium condition.

Figure 15.5
Characteristic Line and Differential Returns, Investor Estimates

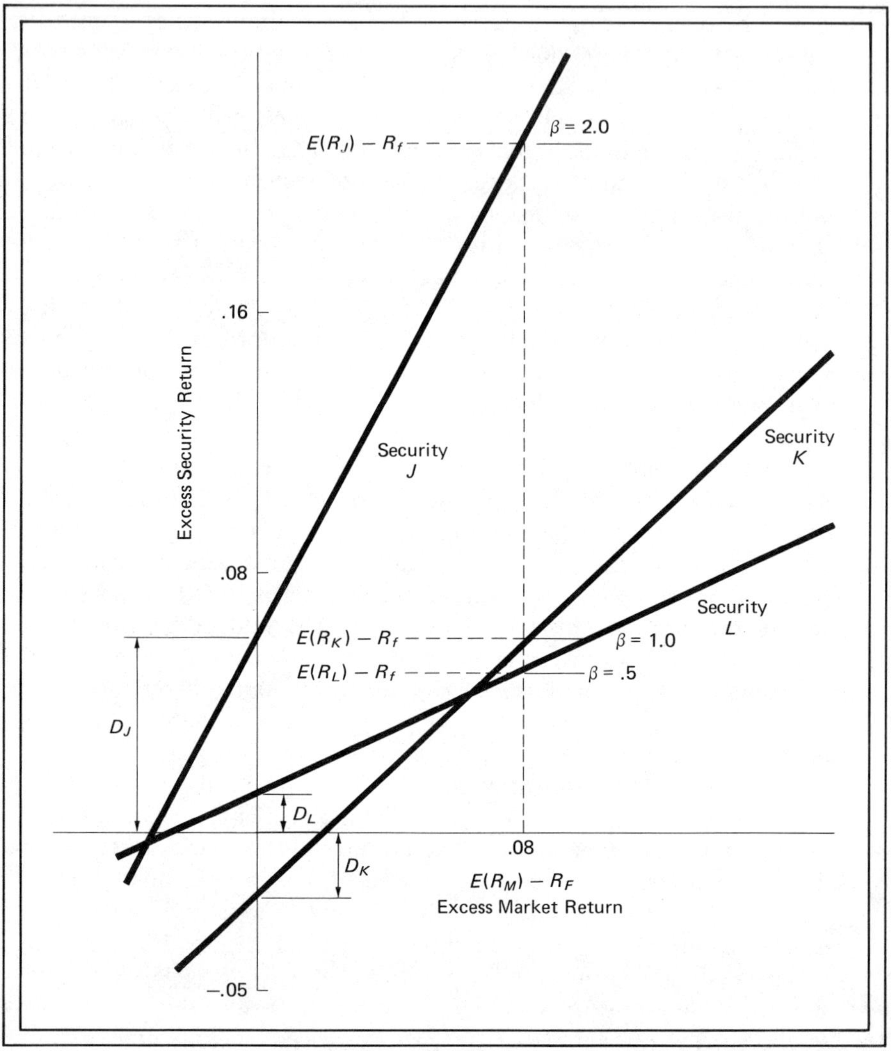

D_J, D_K, and D_L are differential returns to securities J, K, and L.

greater risk. Only in the case where one security has a larger differential return and the same or smaller beta is it necessarily superior.

SECURITY MARKET LINE. The capital asset pricing model identifies security return net of the risk-free rate as proportional to the expected net market return, where beta serves as the constant of proportionality. As a consequence of this relationship, all securities in equilibrium plot along a straight line called the security market line. Figure 15.6 illustrates a hypothetical security market line. It was plotted by drawing a line between the risk-free rate at beta of zero and the total market return at beta of one. The line is extended to negative values of beta to recognize that individual securities can (but, alas, seldom do) move on average contrary to other investments.

Further characteristics of the security market line can be shown by substituting the expression for beta (Equation 15.2) into the right-hand side of the capital asset pricing model (Equation 15.10):

$$E(R_j) = \frac{\text{cov}(j, M)}{\text{var}(M)}[E(R_M) - R_F] \tag{15.11}$$

Rearranging

$$E(R_j) = \frac{[E(R_M) - R_F]}{\text{var}(M)}[\text{cov}(j, M)] \tag{15.11a}$$

The first term of the second expression is a constant for all securities since it contains only market and risk-free information. This term is the slope of the security market line. The second term, security covariance with the market, is an alternative measure of security risk: it is simply the security beta with the constant [var(M)] removed. Either beta or covariance may be used as a measure or risk on the horizontal axis of Figure 15.6; beta is used here since its interpretation is more straightforward. Both represent the

Figure 15.6
The Security Market Line

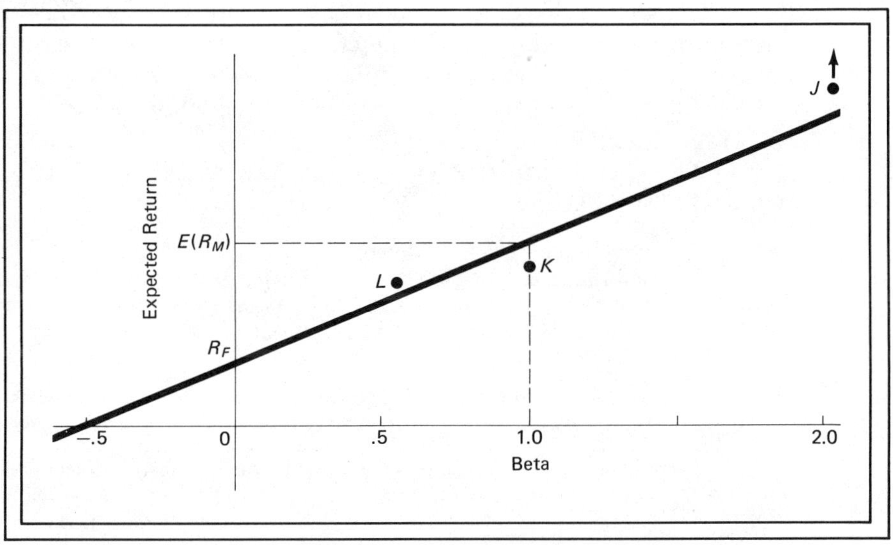

systematic and relevant risk to the pricing of all securities according to capital market theory.

Undervalued securities will plot above the security market line and overvalued securities will plot beneath it. The three securities whose differential returns were measured in the last section are also plotted on Figure 15.6. Since both procedures are similarly derived, the results should also be similar. This is confirmed by the graph's indication that securities *J* and *L* are undervalued and security *K* is overvalued.

BEHAVIOR OF ALPHA AND BETA

Extensive research has been conducted to increase understanding of the general properties and behavior of security and portfolio alphas and betas. Estimates of security betas derived from historical data are useful because factors affecting market, financial, and business risk are generally evolutionary in nature. Even so, individual security betas calculated from returns in a given period can explain only a third or so of the variation in betas observed during the next period. Historical betas are best calculated from the most recent six to seven years of return observations. Longer periods increase the likelihood that early observations are influenced by factors no longer representative of the firm's current operations and leverage. Shorter periods invite error resulting from placing excess weight on price observation not representative of normal performance. It appears that beta is not overly sensitive to the differencing interval over which it is calculated and it does not vary appreciably during bull and bear markets. Monthly, quarterly, or annual intervals all provide fairly reasonable estimates. Some researchers suggest that the interval between observations should be as short as possible, while others argue that because of possible short-run lead-lag relationships among returns of different securities the interval should be longer.[12] A policy of selecting an interval equal to or somewhat shorter than the future investment horizon selected is prudent in view of the current lack of consensus.

Other general properties of security beta may be summarized briefly by the following statements:

1. Almost without exception, common stock betas exceed zero. A study by Marshall Blume of all New York Stock Exchange common stocks over seven-year periods from 1926 to 1968 found less than one-fifth of 1 percent with negative betas.[13] Nearly all common stocks move with the market.

[12] Arguments for an "instantaneous" holding period have been presented by P. I. Cheng and M. K. Deets, "Systematic Risk and the Horizon Problem," *Journal of Financial and Quantitative Analysis* 8, no. 2 (March 1973): 299–307. The need for a longer interval has been made by R. M. Bear and A. K. Gehr, "Association of Returns to Alternative Investment Media: The Government Bond Common Stock Case," *Journal of Economics and Business* 28, no. 1 (Fall 1975): 68–74.

[13] Specifically, 7 of 4357 observations of security beta were negative. Marshall Blume, "On the Assessment of Risk," *Journal of Finance*, March 1971, pp. 1–10.

2. On the other side, rarely does a security beta exceed 2.50. If the market appreciates on average 11 percent per year, a stock having a beta of 2.5 would in normal times expect a corresponding return of 21.5 percent, assuming that the risk-free rate were 4 percent (by Equation 15.10). Firms can seldom obtain such superior performance for shareholders over sustained periods of time.
3. A slow but perceptible trend is evident in stock betas over time. Betas tend to converge toward the average value of 1.00. This is true for both defensive and aggressive securities and the tendency is greatest in the extremely low and high beta cases.[14]

Although individual stock betas are not constant or stationary over time, they behave as if they are for reasonably diversified portfolios. Again, in combination, estimation errors tend to be offsetting. This makes the error in estimating a portfolio beta much smaller than the errors of beta estimation for component securities. For portfolios containing 50 securities, estimation of future portfolio beta by extrapolating a historically derived beta may be as much as 96 percent accurate. With only a ten-stock portfolio, a naive predictive process can be expected to be 85 percent accurate.[15]

Historic measurement of a security or portfolio alpha is of very little value to the analyst in forming future return expectations. Previous positive or negative differential return is no indication that the investment in question is currently undervalued or overvalued. In recent times there has been evidence that high beta securities tend to have negative differential returns and low beta securities tend to have positive differential returns.[16] This condition can be characterized by an actual security market line with a less steep slope and greater intercept than would be expected according to the capital asset pricing model, a condition characterized in Figure 15.7.[17] Explanations for this observation involve the assumption of riskless borrowing and lending opportunities, problems in measuring market return, and differential tax policies on dividends and capital gains. Whatever the source, the implication is that on average defensive securities have performed relatively (but not absolutely) better, and aggressive securities worse, than would be expected according to the capital asset pricing model. The seriousness of this probable bias and its implications remains an active and unsettled issue in portfolio theory.

[14] Marshall Blume, "Betas and Their Regression Tendencies," *Journal of Finance*, June 1975, pp. 785–795. Also see Arthur E. Goodring and Terence P. O'Malley, "Market Phase and the Stationarity of Beta," *Journal of Financial and Quantitative Analysis*, December 1977, pp. 833–857.

[15] Blume, "On the Assessment of Risk," pp. 6–7.

[16] Merton H. Miller and Myron Scholes, "Rates of Return in Relation to Risk: A Reexamination of Some Recent Findings," in *Studies in the Theory of Capital Markets*, ed. Michael Jensen (New York: Praeger, 1972), pp. 47–78. A review of the testing of the asset pricing model is given by Franco Modigliani and Gerald Pogue, "An Introduction to Risk and Return (Part II)," *Financial Analysts Journal* 30, no. 3 (May–June 1974): 69–86.

[17] The actual intercept, R_Z in Figure 15.7, has been called the return to a "zero-beta risky portfolio" by Professors Black, Jensen, and Scholes who argue a two-factor model of the form $E(R_j) = E(R_Z) + [E(R_M) - E(R_Z)]\beta_j$ is superior in form to the capital asset pricing model. Fischer Black, Michael Jensen, and Myron Scholes, "The Capital Asset Pricing Model: Some Empirical Tests," in *Studies in the Theory of Capital Markets*, ed. Michael Jensen (New York: Praeger, 1972), pp. 79–121.

Figure 15.7
Theoretical and Observed Security Market Lines

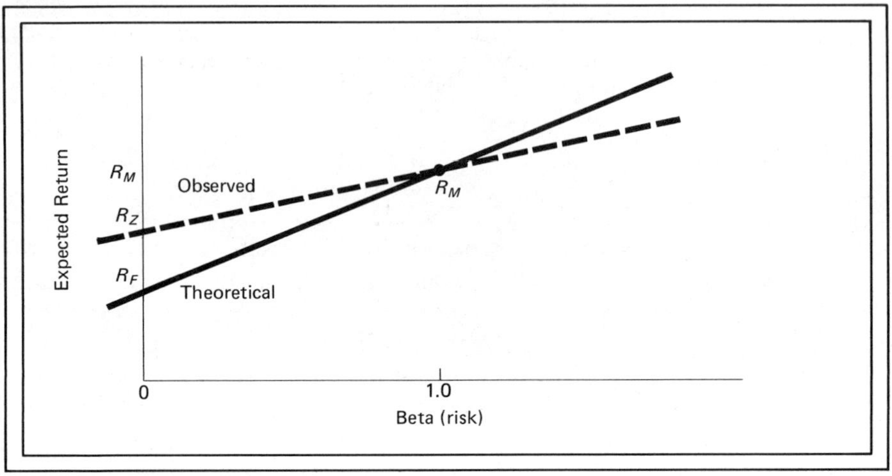

R_M is market index return, R_F is risk-free rate, and R_Z is zero beta portfolio return (see footnote 17).

Summary

This chapter has presented procedures for estimating efficient portfolios which simplify the exact methodologies discussed in the previous chapter. Based on the idea of a single-index model in which each security is related only to an index representative of all securities, the number of covariances necessary to identify portfolio risk is greatly reduced. However, this simplification is not costless; it comes at a potential loss of accuracy in estimating true portfolio risk. Studies have shown, however, that in practice the single-index model does as well as the full covariance model and may be superior when historical data are limited.[18]

The slope coefficient of the relationship between a security and an appropriate single index is the proper measure of security risk under the conditions of the single-index model. This coefficient is known as beta, and in combination with an estimate of return and variance provides identification of the efficient frontier either by graphic methods or alternatively by computer programming. A graphic procedure based on beta is illustrated in the following chapter along with methods of portfolio evaluation.

Multi-index models improve the accuracy of portfolio risk estimates where strong industry or growth relationships exist among securities in the

[18] George Frankfurter, Herbert R. Phillips, and John Seagle, "Performance of the Sharpe Portfolio Selection Model: A Comparison," *Journal of Financial and Quantitative Analysis* 11, no. 2 (June 1976): 204.

portfolio. Because multi-index models increase the complexity of portfolio construction, their value should be considered in light of their cost. The value of multi-index models is especially small when the analyst's confidence in estimates of future interrelationships is low. A discussion of multi-index models follows in the appendix to this chapter.

Appendix Multi-Index Models

The purpose of multi-index portfolio models is to describe more accurately actual relationships among securities returns than is possible using the single-index model. The perceived need for multi-index models results from the belief that a single-index model fails to capture all covariability among paired security returns. Should this be the case, portfolio risk is understated when covariability is positive or overstated when covariability is negative. In either case effective portfolio selection is not possible.

Consider two portfolios with equal expected return and equal portfolio risk when portfolio risk is measured by Equation 15.8. In one portfolio all conditions of the single-index model expressed by Equation 15.1 hold. The second portfolio, however, contains at least one pair of securities whose returns are related beyond their common association with the market.[19] This further association will make the second portfolio's actual risk something other than that predicted by a single index which assumes that additional relationships do not exist. Clearly one portfolio is preferred, but it cannot be identified by the single-index model. To deal with this shortcoming multi-index models may be employed. Conditioning security return on two or more indexes increases the likelihood that all intersecurity relations will be fully accounted for in the model.[20]

What indexes other than a general market index warrant possible consideration? A study by Benjamin King has shown that correlation of residual terms (e_j's) from a single-index model results from industry effects.[21] The principal findings of King were that the importance of a market factor has

[19] Precisely, the condition that $\text{cov}(e_j, e_k) = 0$ does not hold and residual returns are correlated over time. If the correlation is positive, risk will be increased. If the correlation is negative, risk will be reduced.

[20] A second effect is that the residual terms, the e_j's, will be smaller in absolute size on average since a multi-index model provides a better fit. In other words, more risk will appear to be systematic and less will appear to be unsystematic.

[21] Benjamin King, "Market and Industry Factors in Stock Price Behavior," *The Journal of Business* 39 (January 1966, Supplement): 139–190.

been declining secularly from an explanatory power of 58 percent during 1927–1935 to a low of 31 percent during 1952–1960, and that an industry factor has consistently explained an additional 10 percent of security return variance. By adding an index representing the firm's industry, some increased accuracy in estimating portfolio risk is possible. Bernell Stone developed a two-index model which incorporates both an equity market index and a bond market index, where the bond index adjusts for interest rate risk. Lloyd and Shick provided some empirical support for the Stone model but the relevance of this particular two-index model has not yet been fully demonstrated.[22]

In the same manner, James Farrell, Jr., demonstrated that indexes based on growth characteristics provide better risk estimates than those provided by the index model.[23] Farrell found that since 1960 a general market factor explains about 30 percent of security return variation and indexes based on a security's identification as a (1) growth, (2) stable, (3) cyclical, or (4) oil stock explained on average an additional 14 percent of return variation. Furthermore, Farrell determined that additional index categories contribute nothing: all pairwise covariation is accounted for by considering market, industry, and growth characteristics.

Both King's and Farrell's results highlight the unique characteristics of oil-related firms in periods prior to the emergence of world energy problems resulting from the OPEC (Organization of Petroleum Exporting Countries) cartel. In both studies the oil industry proved to be a unique group of securities, highly interdependent within itself and quite independent of all other categories. While this would be expected in the King study based on industry categories, oil's uniqueness is surprising in the Farrell study based on growth characteristics. Oils apparently do not associate with stable or cyclical firms as conventionally believed.

The format of a multi-index model is the same as that of a single-index model. In addition to a market index, assume that other relevant indexes have been identified. In all, the problem consists of m number of securities and n number of indexes. The return for each security may be expressed as

$$\begin{aligned} R_1 &= a_1 + \beta_{11}I_1 + \beta_{12}I_2 + \cdots + \beta_{1n}I_n + e_1 \\ &\vdots \\ R_j &= a_j + \beta_{j1}I_1 + \beta_{j2}I_2 + \cdots + \beta_{jn}I_n + e_j \\ &\vdots \\ R_m &= a_m + \beta_{m1}I_1 + \beta_{m2}I_2 + \cdots + \beta_{mn}I_n + e_m \end{aligned} \tag{15A.1}$$

[22] Bernell K. Stone, "Systematic Interest-Rate Risk in a Two-Index Model of Returns," *Journal of Financial and Quantitative Analysis*, (November 1974), pp. 709–721 and William P. Lloyd and Richard A Shick, "A Test of Stone's Two-Index Model of Returns," *Journal of Financial and Quantitative Analysis*, (September 1977), pp. 363–367. Additional support for Stone's argument of interest rate sensitivity is found in John D. Martin and Arthur J. Keown, "Interest Rate Sensitivity and Portfolio Risk," *Journal of Financial and Quantitative Analysis*, (June, 1977), pp. 181–189.

[23] James Farrell, Jr., "Analyzing Covariation of Returns To Determine Homogeneous Stock Groupings," *Journal of Business* 47 (April 1972): 186–207.

The conditions for the multi-index model to be properly specified are that the residual terms, the e_j's, have an expected value of zero and are uncorrelated with all other variables. It is the objective of multi-index models to achieve residual terms with these properties.

As before, a portfolio beta with respect to each specified index may be calculated by

$$\beta_{pK} = \sum_{j=1}^{m} X_j \beta_{jK} \tag{15A.2}$$

where here and in Equation 15A.3 below the subscripts K and L represent each index in the set of all n indexes. With all e_j terms in Equation 15.8a uncorrelated and with variances defied as $\sigma^2(e_j)$, portfolio risk will be measured as

$$\sigma_p{}^2 = \sum_{K=1}^{n} \sum_{L=1}^{n} \beta_{pK}\beta_{pL} \operatorname{cov}(K, L) + \sum_{j=1}^{m} X_j{}^2\sigma^2(e_j) \tag{15A.3}$$

The first right-hand term measures in substantial part the risk due to relationships among the indexes. As with individual securities, these require estimation of n variances and $(n^2 - n)/2$ covariances. If indexes could be assumed to be independent, residual covariances are zero and the expression for portfolio risk would collapse to $n + m$ terms, namely,

$$\sigma_p{}^2 = \sum_{K-1}^{n} \beta_{pK}{}^2\sigma_K{}^2 + \sum_{j=1}^{m} X_j{}^2\sigma^2(e_j) \tag{15A.4}$$

As before, for substantially diversified portfolios the second right-hand term can be expected to approach zero, with portfolio risk approaching its minimum—all systematic risk—where value is approximated by

$$\sigma_p{}^2 \approx \sum_{K=1}^{n} \beta_{pK}{}^2\sigma_K{}^2 \tag{15A.5}$$

But without some adjustment the assumption of index independence is unrealistic, which would destroy the relevance of Equation 15A.3 or 15A.4 for estimating portfolio risk.[24] Since one index represents overall market conditions and other indexes typically represent segments of the market, it must be presumed that they are related. It may be, however, that when other indexes are adjusted for general market conditions, they will be very nearly uncorrelated with each other. The indexes considered by both King and Farrell were predominantly uncorrelated or slightly negatively correlated with each other after removal of the market factor. This result assures that portfolio risk would not be underestimated by a procedure of removing the

[24] It would be necessary and proper to use Equation 15A.3 or substitute for equation 15A.5 the expression $\sigma_p{}^2 \approx \sum_{K=1}^{n} \sum_{L=1}^{n} \beta_{pK}{}^2\beta_{pL}{}^2 \operatorname{cov}(K, L)$ to determine portfolio risk in the case where interdependencies between indexes exist.

market index from all other indexes and then proceeding as if the indexes were uncorrelated.[25]

Using either Equation 15A.3 or deriving a specification for applying Equation 15A.4 involves estimation and computational requirements greater than those required for the single-index model. Individual circumstances and resources will dictate their potential use and value. The improvement which multi-index models offer remains a subject of debate.[26] But even if multi-index models are not computationally introduced into the analysis, it is important to recognize the influence which industry and growth factors have on diversification: concentration of security holdings in related industry and/or growth groupings should be avoided a priori.

Questions and Problems

1. Compare the number of inputs required to determine the efficient frontier when ten securities are being considered by the full covariance model (Markowitz) and the single-index model (Sharpe). Would raising the number of securities to 100 result in a tenfold increase in inputs to both models?
2. Identify accurately the differences between the security market line and the characteristic line.
3. A review of financial summaries identifies the return to General Motors common stock and to the NYSE composite index over recent years to be as follows:

Year	*GM*	*NYSE*
1970	+.223	−.018
1971	+.023	+.118
1972	+.056	+.136
1973	−.330	−.190
1974	−.294	−.317

[25] This procedure would be proper provided either industry or growth categories were considered alone but not both together. For example, even after removing the market some relationship would presumably exist between, say, an index of stable securities and an index of utilities. In the King and Farrell studies cited in footnotes 21 and 22, indexes were formed and adjusted for the market factor by the following procedure: (a) application of a single-index model, Equation 15.1, to the historical returns of all securities in the sample. Each residual is a market adjusted return for that particular security and period. (b) Residual returns, the e_j's, were then partitioned by cluster analysis into groups where each return was highly correlated with others in that group. (c) An index was formed for each group from the average residual return of all stocks in that group.

A more detailed discussion is provided by each author. For a more generalized analysis of the adjustment process see Sharpe, *Portfolio Theory and Capital Markets*, pp. 122–127, and pp. 294–302.

[26] Cohen and Pogue have argued that multi-index models are not superior to single-index models. K. Cohen and J. Pogue, "A Compound Evaluation of Alternative Portfolio Selection Models," *Journal of Business*, April 1967, pp. 166–193. On the other hand, Wallingford found that multi-index models do outperform single-index models, in at least some applications. R. Wallingford, "A Survey and Comparison of Portfolio Selection Models," *Journal of Financial and Quantitative Analysis*, June 1967, pp. 85–106. James Farrell, Jr., has argued convincingly that a four-index portfolio model provides superior performance to the single-index model with only a modest increase in required inputs and costs. James Farrell, Jr., "The Multi-Index Model and Practical Portfolio Analysis," Occasional Paper Number 4 (The Financial Analysts Research Foundation, 1976). Arguments questioning the practical significance of industry effects are found in John D. Martin and Robert C. Klemkosky, "The Effect of Homogeneous Stock Groupings on Portfolio Risk," *The Journal of Business*, July 1976, pp. 339–349.

a. Estimate graphically or calculate the regression equation representing the single-index model.
b. What are the values of GM's alpha and beta coefficients over this period?
c. What portion of GM's risk was systematic? Unsystematic?
d. GM's return in 1975 was .964 and the NYSE index yielded .324. Was this performance consistent with prior years?

4. Given your finding in part d of problem 3, it appears that individual security betas may be unstable from one period to the next. How then are they useful to portfolio construction?
5. Discuss how capital market theory relates to security analysis and portfolio construction.
6. Does it seem fair to state that good portfolio analysis is a substitute for security analysis?
7. The return for four securities may be expressed by a multi-index model such as

$$R_j = a_j + \beta_{j1}R_M + \beta_{j2}g^* + \beta_{j3}s^* + \beta_{j4}c^* + \beta_{j5}o^* + e_j$$

where g^*, s^*, c^*, and o^* are Farrell-type indexes representing growth, stable, cyclical, and oil companies, respectively. Each index has been constructed such that it bears no relationship to the market index R_M.

The model has provided the following beta and standard deviation estimates:

Stock Number		Index					
	R_M	g^*	s^*	c^*	o^*	$\sigma(e_j)$
$j = 1$	2.00	1.20	0	0	0	.14
2	.50	0	1.20	0	0	.10
3	1.10	0	0	1.00	0	.22
4	.80	0	0	0	1.00	.09
$\sigma(index)$ =	.08	.12	.04	.08	.06	

Which of the following portfolios will minimize risk?

	Percentage of Stocks			
Portfolio	X_1	X_2	X_3	X_4
1	.20	.20	.30	.30
2	.25	.25	.25	.25
3	.40	.40	.10	.10

Selected References

THE SINGLE-INDEX MODEL

Blume, Marshall E., "On the Assessment of Risk," *Journal of Finance* 26, no. 1 (March 1971): 1–10.

Frankfurter, George, "The Effect of 'Market Indexes' on the Ex-post Performance of the Sharpe Portfolio Selection Model," *Journal of Finance* 31 (June 1976): 949–955.

Frankfurter, George, Herbert Phillips, and John Seagle, "Performance of the Sharpe Portfolio Selection Model: A Comparison," *Journal of Financial and Quantitative Analysis* 11, no. 2 (June 1976): 195–204.

Jensen, Michael C., ed., *Studies in the Theory of Capital Markets* (New York: Praeger, 1972).

Martin, John D., and Robert C. Klemkosky, "Evidence of Heteroscedasticity in the Market Model," *Journal of Business*, January 1975, pp. 81–86.

Reilly, Frank K., "Evidence Regarding a Segmented Stock Market," *Journal of Finance* 27, no. 3 (June 1972): 607–625.

Robichek, Alexander A., and Richard A. Cohn, "The Economic Determinants of Systematic Risk," *Journal of Finance* 29, no. 2 (May 1974): 439–447.

Sharpe, W. F., "A Simplified Model for Portfolio Analysis," *Management Science* 9, no. 2 (January 1963): 277–293.

Smith, Keith, "Stock Price and Economic Indexes for Generating Efficient Portfolios," *Journal of Business* 42, no. 3 (July 1969): 326–336.

CAPITAL MARKET THEORY

Beaver, William, and James Manegold, "The Association Between Market-Determined and Accounting-Determined Measures of Systematic Risk: Some Further Evidence," *Journal of Financial and Quantitative Analysis*, June 1975, pp. 231–284.

Black, Fischer, "Capital Market Equilibrium with Restricted Borrowing," *Journal of Business* 45, no. 3 (July 1972): 444–454.

Blume, Marshall E., "Betas and Their Regression Tendencies," *Journal of Finance* 30, no. 3 (June 1975): 785–796.

Cheng, Pao, and M. King Deets, "Systematic Risk and the Horizon Problem," *Journal of Financial and Quantitative Analysis* 8, no. 2 (March 1973): 299–316.

Fabozzi, Frank J., and Jack C. Francis, "Stability Tests for Alphas and Betas Over Bull and Bear Market Conditions," *Journal of Finance*, September 1977, pp. 1093–1099.

Fama, Eugene F., "Risk, Return and Equilibrium: Some Clarifying Comments," *Journal of Finance* 23, no. 1 (March 1968): 29–40.

Gonedes, Nicholas, "A Note on Accounting-Based and Market-Based Estimates of Systematic Risk," *Journal of Financial and Quantitative Analysis* 10, no. 2 (June 1975): 355–366.

Jensen, Michael, "Risk, the Pricing of Capital Assets, and the Evaluation of Investment Portfolios," *Journal of Business* 42, no. 2 (April 1969): 167–247.

———, "Capital Markets: Theory and Evidence," *Bell Journal of Economics and Management Science*, Autumn 1972, pp. 357–398.

Levy, Robert A., "On the Short-Term Stationarity of Beta Coefficients," *Financial Analysts Journal*, November–December 1971, pp. 55–62.

Lintner, John, "The Valuation of Risk Assets and the Selection of Risky Investments in Stock Portfolios and Capital Budgets," *Review of Economics and Statistics* (1965): 13–37.

Rosenberg, Barr, and James Guy, "Prediction of Beta from Investment Fundamentals," Parts One and Two, *Financial Analysts Journal*, May–June 1976 and July–August 1976, pp. 60–71 and pp. 62–70.

Sharpe, William F., "Capital Asset Prices: A Theory of Market Equilibrium Under Conditions of Risk," *Journal of Finance* 29, no. 3 (September 1964): 425–442.

Thompson II, Donald J., "Sources of Systematic Risk in Common Stock," *The Journal of Business*, April 1976, pp. 173–188.

Welles, Chris, "The Beta Revolution: Learning to Live with Risk," *Institutional Investor*, September 1971, pp. 21–27ff.

MULTI-INDEX MODELS

Cohen, K., and J. Pogue, "An Empirical Evaluation of Alternative Portfolio Selection Models," *Journal of Business* 40, no. 2 (April 1967): 166–193.

Farrell, Jr., James L., "Analyzing Covariation of Returns to Determine Homogeneous Stock Groupings," *Journal of Business* 47, no. 2 (April 1974): 186–207.

——, "Homogeneous Stock Groupings," *Financial Analysts Journal*, May–June 1975, pp. 50–56.

King, Benjamin F., "Market and Industry Factors in Stock Price Behavior," *Journal of Business* 39, no. 1, part II (January 1966, Supplement): 139–190.

Wallingford, B. A., "A Survey and Comparison of Portfolio Selection Models," *Journal of Financial and Quantitative Analysis*, June 1967, pp. 85–106.

Chapter 16

Portfolio Construction and Evaluation

Chapters 14 and 15 reviewed some principles and introduced some models which can be applied in identifying efficient portfolios. This chapter begins with a step-by-step development of this process based upon graphic techniques which are useful in the absence of sophisticated computer software. In practice, of course, better resources would normally be available for investment analysts and managers. When portfolio construction has been illustrated, evaluation techniques will then be introduced and developed. A review of past performance provides the linkage between portfolio construction and the related tasks of portfolio maintenance and revision, which will be considered in the next chapter.

Building a Portfolio

With a well-defined set of risk and return projections, portfolio building consists of four basic and sequential procedures. The following paragraphs will discuss each of these in turn. Steps 1, 2, and 4 identify generally applicable procedures corresponding to the overall investment model that forms the basis of this text.[1] Step 3, which requires a specific portfolio-generating algorithm, is illustrated here by a simple model based on beta. This model provides reasonable approximations of the efficient set and it is appropriate when resources are limited.

STEP 1: CHOOSING A TIME HORIZON

Strictly speaking, portfolio models identify a single holding period during which there are no security transactions. Since portfolio management is an ongoing process, responsive to changes both environmentally and with respect to personal circumstances, this assumption only approximates reality. For this reason, many persons believe that time horizons should be limited to weekly or monthly intervals. If securities could be evaluated and exchanged costlessly, short time horizons would provide acceptable approximations of reality. However, accurate estimation of return incorporates transaction costs and trading lessens return to the extent of its real cost.

The choice of a time horizon for portfolio construction is theoretically arbitrary, provided only that all inputs can be estimated over the selected interval and the investor acts consistently by holding the portfolio unchanged during that interval. Practically speaking, the time horizon should not be longer than the period of time the investor is willing to hold the included securities. On the other hand, it should be sufficiently long so that transaction and analysis costs are small in comparison to expected return during the period. The minimum time horizon given information availability, costs of analysis, and the tax environment, is probably six months to a year and it may range up to two years. Under most conditions a one-year horizon is a suitable compromise, one which strains neither the credibility of economic forecasting nor the potential cost of analysis and revision.

STEP 2: PROVIDING CRITICAL INPUTS

The end product of meaningful security analysis is accurate estimation of the probability distribution of future security returns. Expected return and total variability about expected return are two critical statistical measures obtained from this process. Portfolio considerations require additional estimates of individual security performance with respect to specific assumptions pertaining to market and general economic conditions. This is necessary to formulate an estimate of the security's relationship with the market as measured by the security's covariance and beta coefficient.

[1] The model was first described in Chapter 1 and is portrayed graphically in Figure 1.1. In brief it shows security analysis and portfolio management as an integrated activity utilizing security analysis as the input and portfolio performance as the output; this is a circular process continuing through time as the portfolio is reevaluated and readjusted.

Identifying an appropriate market measure and accurately specifying the expected change and variability of estimate are critical for standard portfolio building procedures since they impact on the entire process, not just on individual securities. As with individual securities, historical behavior is likely to be a poor indication of future market outcomes. In addition to security and market estimates, two further inputs are required. One is estimation of the best borrowing and lending rates available; the other is identification of security groups with a greater common return behavior than is implied by their individual associations with the market.

STEP 3: A PORTFOLIO ESTIMATION MODEL

The following discussion is intended primarily to illustrate principles already presented; it is not intended as a generally suitable methodology in actual practice. The procedure is a partially naive portfolio-generating model, based on expected value and beta, which provides adequate first approximations of optimal security combinations when resources for investment analysis are limited. Specifically, the model is only appropriate when one or more of the following conditions hold:

1. The total population of securities under consideration is small (approximately twenty-five or less).
2. Software (portfolio computer programs) and hardware (computer facilities) are not available at a reasonable cost relative to the wealth available for investment.
3. Available wealth is small ($25,000 or less).
4. Investor confidence in one or more elements of the investment forecast is low.[2]

Pedagogically, the model illustrates basic concepts of portfolio construction.

To provide a portfolio model that is directly and easily solved for a small number of securities, several simplifying assumptions will be required. The model begins by specifying a variable, identified as λ (lambda), as a measure of the importance of return relative to risk.[3] Lambda is, in essence, a proxy for the investor's risk-return indifference map. Its range is

$$0 \leq \lambda \leq 1$$

When λ equals zero, the investor is indifferent toward risk, focusing only on maximizing expected return. When λ equals one, reducing risk to its minimum possible level is the basic objective. Values within the range represent less extreme feelings toward return relative to risk. For example, a λ of .5 indicates a position where equal percentage increases in risk and return are acceptable.

[2] It should be noted that under these conditions an investor might seriously consider one of the mutual funds described in Chapter 18 as an alternative to do-it-yourself investing. However, when an investor trusts his or her ability to identify undervalued securities, the techniques identified here provide the basis for potentially superior investment results.

[3] The procedure follows one originally suggested by William Sharpe, *Portfolio Theory and Capital Markets* (New York: McGraw-Hill, 1970), pp. 131–139.

Risk is assumed to be properly described by the portfolio beta. For fully diversified portfolios, as defined previously,

$$\sigma_p{}^2 = \beta_p{}^2\sigma_I{}^2 \quad \text{and} \quad \sigma_p = \beta_p\sigma_I \qquad [(15.9)]$$

where σ_I represents the standard deviation of the market expected return. Since σ_I is a constant for all securities and portfolios, portfolio risk for any efficient portfolio can be standardized by dividing Equation 15.9 by σ_I, giving

$$\beta_p = \frac{\sigma_p}{\sigma_I} \qquad (16.1)$$

Portfolio beta is thus a proper measure of portfolio risk when all risk is systematic. As stated before, most risk is systematic in portfolios of as few as eight to ten securities when wealth is equally divided among them. Strictly speaking, it is doubtful that portfolios with a limited number of securities will be totally efficient. However, this assumption is accurate enough to provide good approximations at low cost. By assuming that efficiency has been attained by selecting a minimum number of included securities and a maximum allocation of wealth to each, portfolio beta may be used as the measure of risk in the process of determining the efficient frontier.

Identification of the efficient frontier requires a two-stage process: (1) outline the efficient frontier for all risky securities, then (2) consider the impact of lending and borrowing. The first stage is the more tedious. It requires specifying the investment objective as

$$\max Z = (1 - \lambda)E_p - \lambda\beta_p \qquad (16.2)$$

Allowing λ to equal its extreme values shows the relation of this objective function to the investor's preferences, namely,

$$\max Z = E_p \quad \text{when} \quad \lambda = 0 \quad \text{(return maximizing)} \qquad (16.2a)$$

and

$$\max Z = -\beta_p \quad \text{when} \quad \lambda = 1 \quad \text{(risk minimizing)} \qquad (16.2b)$$

Equation 16.2a identifies the maximum return position while Equation 16.2b identifies the minimum risk position.

Figure 16.1(a) shows a typical efficient frontier of risky securities using β_p as the measure of risk. The relationship between the objective function Z and the efficient frontier of risky assets is shown by Figure 16.1(b) through 16.1(d) as λ varies over its 0 to 1 range. The relation between the objective function and all q individual securities under consideration can be seen by recalling the relationship between security and portfolio return and security and portfolio beta. Substituting,

$$\begin{aligned}\max Z = (1 - \lambda)&(X_1E_1 + X_2E_2 + \cdots + X_qE_q) \\ &- \lambda\,(X_1\beta_1 + X_2\beta_2 + \cdots + X_q\beta_q)\end{aligned} \qquad (16.2c)$$

Figure 16.1
E_p, β_p Efficient Frontier

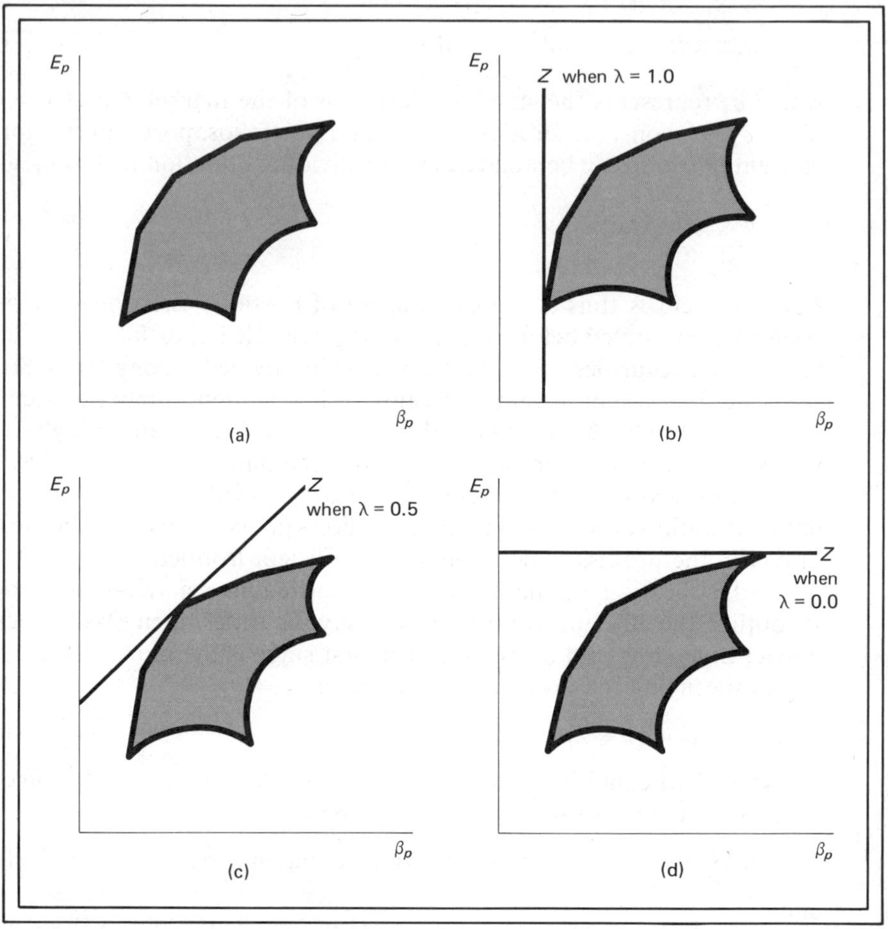

The objective function having been identified, portfolios are generated subject to both a minimum security and a maximum wealth allocation constraint. Since maximal diversification can generally be obtained when wealth is allocated to securities such that each receives a percentage of wealth no greater than $1/m$, where m is the minimum number of securities permitted in a portfolio, the constraint takes the form

$$X_j \leq \frac{1}{m} \tag{16.3}$$

where m is the minimum number of securities included in the portfolio.

To determine the securities included in the efficient set of portfolios,

Figure 16.2
*Figure of Merit, Five Securities**

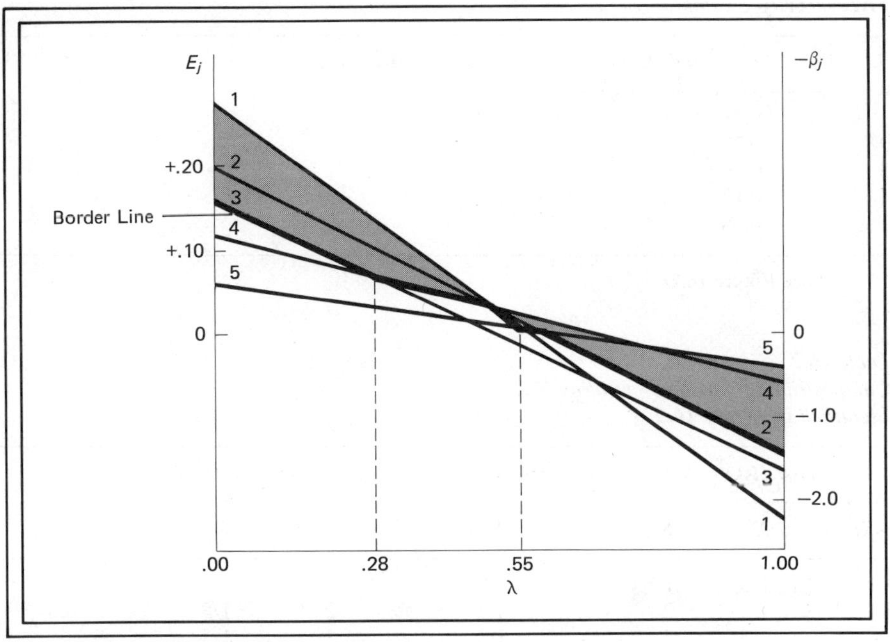

* Numbers correspond to securities identified in Table 16.2.

a "figure of merit" is calculated for each security.[4] The figure of merit is simply the investment objective of Equation 16.2 specified in terms of individual securities.

$$Z_j = (1 - \lambda)E_j - \lambda B_j \tag{16.4}$$

Computations for Equation 16.4 are straightforward since the expression is linear. Setting $\lambda = 0$ and $\lambda = 1$ provides two points which may be plotted on corresponding vertical axes representing E_j and $-\beta_j$. Connecting the two points for each and every security provides a complete graphic solution. This procedure is illustrated for five securities in Figure 16.2. The horizontal axis represents values of λ over its entire range. Necessary inputs are identified in Table 16.1.

Referring to Figure 16.2, the m securities (out of the set of $q = 5$ securities) with the largest Z_j values at each level of λ are included in the m-security portfolio. The mth line from the top over the range of λ is called the border line. The border line for portfolios having no less than $m = 3$ securities is the heavy line in Figure 16.2. All lines bordering and contained within

[4] The term "figure of merit" was introduced by William Sharpe, ibid., p. 135.

Table 16.1
Expected Return and Beta Estimates, Five-Security Example[a]

Security	*Expected Return* (E_j)	*Expected Beta* (β_j)
1	0.28	2.2
2	0.20	1.4
3	0.16	1.6
4	0.12	0.6
5	0.06	0.4

[a] See Figure 16.2.

Table 16.2
Composition of Corner Portfolios Identified in Figure 16.2

$\lambda = 0$ *(most risk)*		$\lambda = .28$ *(intermediate risk)*		$\lambda = .55$ *(least risk)*[a]	
Stock	X_j	*Stock*	X_j	*Stock*	X_j
1	1/3	1	1/3	5	1/3
2	1/3	2	1/3	2	1/3
3	1/3	4	1/3	4	1/3

[a] Over the range $.55 \le \lambda \le 1.0$ portfolio composition does not change; therefore the portfolio identified at $\lambda = .55$ provides the least possible risk given the inputs and constraint ($X_j \le 1/m$) of the problem.

the shaded area in Figure 16.2 identify the preferred three-security portfolios for varying levels of λ.

Whenever the border line bends owing to an intersection with a security line whose slope is less steep than itself, the intersection represents a corner portfolio where one security drops out *and* one security comes in. When the border line is intersected from above (moving left to right), no change in included securities takes place since the line intercepting the border line represents a security which is already in the portfolio. These intersections therefore are not corner portfolios. The activity at corner portfolios is constrained by the requirement that all efficient portfolios contain no more than $1/m$ of any one security. Since the portfolio identified at $\lambda = .00$ represents the greatest possible return, it too is a corner portfolio. The values of λ from Figure 16.2 corresponding to corner portfolios ($\lambda = .00$, .28, and .55) are identified graphically and are not part of any prior or subsequent calculations.

From Figure 16.2 the corner portfolios can be read off and identified as shown in Table 16.2. This table completely identifies the efficient frontier of risky securities since efficient portfolios between two adjacent corner portfolios are linear combinations of the two corner portfolios. Thus only the expected portfolio return and beta for each corner portfolio need be calculated. Calculating from data in Tables 16.1 and 16.2, the most risky portfolio has return and risk expectations of

$$E_p = \sum_{j=1}^{3} X_j E_j = \tfrac{1}{3}(.28) + \tfrac{1}{3}(.20) + \tfrac{1}{3}(.16) = .21$$

$$\beta_p = \sum_{j=1}^{3} X_j \beta_j = \tfrac{1}{3}(2.2) + \tfrac{1}{3}(1.4) + \tfrac{1}{3}(1.6) = 1.73$$

Corresponding calculations for the other corner portfolios permit identification of the efficient frontier of risky securities illustrated in Figure 16.3. The portfolio analysis is now almost complete. If a hypothetical investor with these expectations is able to borrow or lend without risk at a 6 percent rate, the optimal set of portfolios would be shown by line u in Figure 16.4(a). The corner portfolio at the point of tangency, u^*, is the optimal combination of risky securities under these assumptions.

The only remaining task is to select the most satisfying return and risk position on line u. Assuming this position is W^*, identified by a hypothetical indifference curve w in Figure 16.4(b), the expected return and risk is read

Figure 16.3
Efficient Frontier of Risky Securities

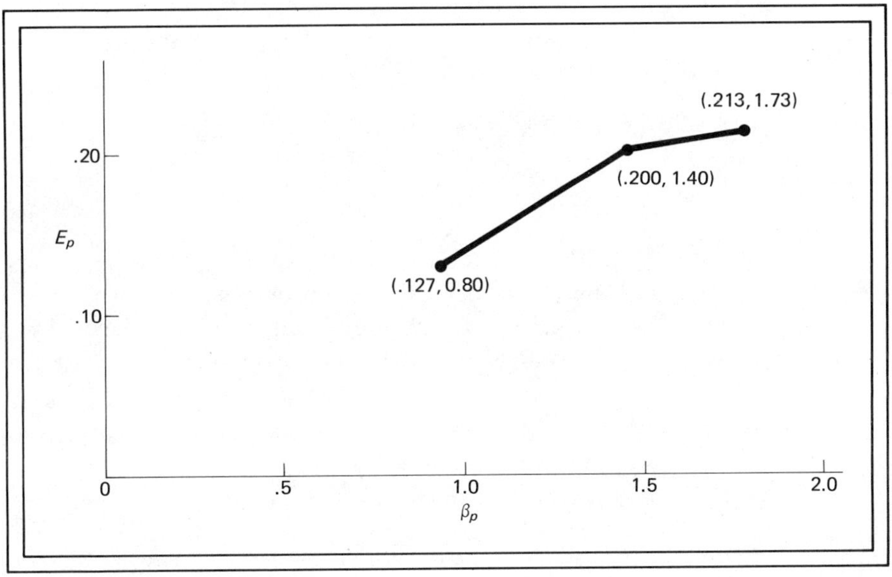

Figure 16.4
Efficient Frontier with Risk-Free Security

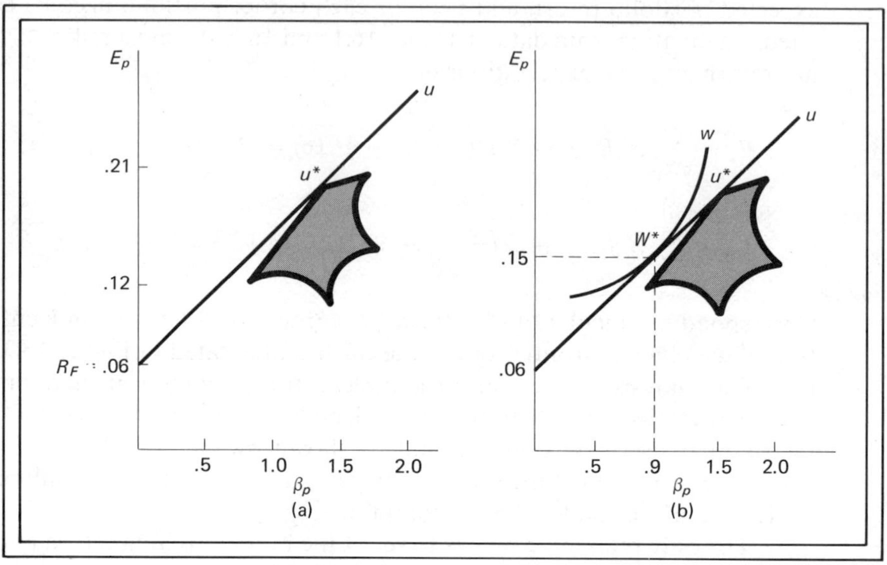

off the graph to be .15 and .90, respectively. The allocation of wealth necessary to obtain position W^* may be directly determined from

$$E_p = X_F R_F + (1 - X_F)E_{u^*}$$

since $X_F + X_{u^*} = 1$ and $X_{u^*} = 1 - X_F$

By substituting return expectations and solving for the portion of wealth allocated to the risk-free security,

$$.15 = X_F(.06) + (1 - X_F)(.20)$$
$$X_F = .36$$
$$X_{u^*} = 1 - .36 = .64$$

To obtain position W^*, 36 percent of wealth would be placed in a risk-free security and the remainder used to purchase risky portfolio u^*. The percentage of wealth going to each individual security is found by multiplying the percentage of wealth in u^* by the percentage of each stock in u^*:[5]

$.64(\frac{1}{3}) = .213$ percent	in stock 1
$.64(\frac{1}{3}) = .213$ percent	in stock 2
$.64(\frac{1}{3}) = .213$ percent	in stock 4

[5] A review of Chapter 14 is suggested if the reason for this procedure is not clear.

As required, the sum of the portions of wealth to each investment, including investment in the risk-free security, is unity, indicating that all wealth is invested.

The portfolio generating model described above greatly simplifies the task of portfolio construction. Its cost is the imprecision arising from the a priori presumption that all portfolios contain minimal levels of unsystematic risk. As indicated earlier, this presumption may be justified in practice only under highly constrained resource conditions.[6] It is very useful in demonstrating portfolio elements, however, since it operationalizes most aspects of mean-variance portfolio analysis in a straightforward manner. The next and final section considers several extensions of the procedure.

STEP 4: AN ONGOING PROCESS

Maintaining the attractiveness of a portfolio requires a strategy for portfolio maintenance and improvement. Procedures are required to monitor the performance of individual securities and to identify possible candidates for altering the composition of the portfolio. At this point, it is sufficient to point out that identification of a relevant security population and reapplication of the preceding three steps are basic to the maintenance procedure. Elements of portfolio maintenance and revision are discussed in the next chapter.

EXTENSIONS OF THE BETA MODEL

The portfolio selection model which was just described captures the essence of portfolio analysis in a manner permitting effective portfolio selection on a limited scale and in the absence of complex computational algorithms and computer hardware. This section concludes the illustration by considering two additional aspects of the procedure: (1) recognition of industry effects which, if ignored, may lead to suboptimal portfolio selection and (2) measurement of the extent of unsystematic risk remaining in selected portfolios.

INDUSTRY CONSTRAINTS. Industry effects may be controlled by constraining the maximum number of securities from the same broadly defined industry. The industry constraint is achieved by selecting the best securities in each industry classification where the number of securities exceeds the number allowed by the constraint. Selection within industry groupings precedes the

[6] There are other computational or graphic portfolio construction procedures that do not assume away unsystematic risk. Unfortunately those procedures are generally more complex and yet they retain one or more other limiting assumptions. See James C. T. Mao, "Essentials of Portfolio Diversification Strategy," *Journal of Finance* 25, no. 5 (December 1970): 1109–1131; Nancy I. Jacob, "A Limited-Diversification Portfolio Selection Model for the Small Investor," *Journal of Finance* 29, no. 4 (June 1974): 847–856; and Jack C. Francis, *Investments Analysis and Management* (New York: McGraw-Hill, 1976), app. A. "Markowitz Graphical Portfolio Analysis," pp. 420–438.

Figure 16.5
Identifying Best Oil Industry Securities

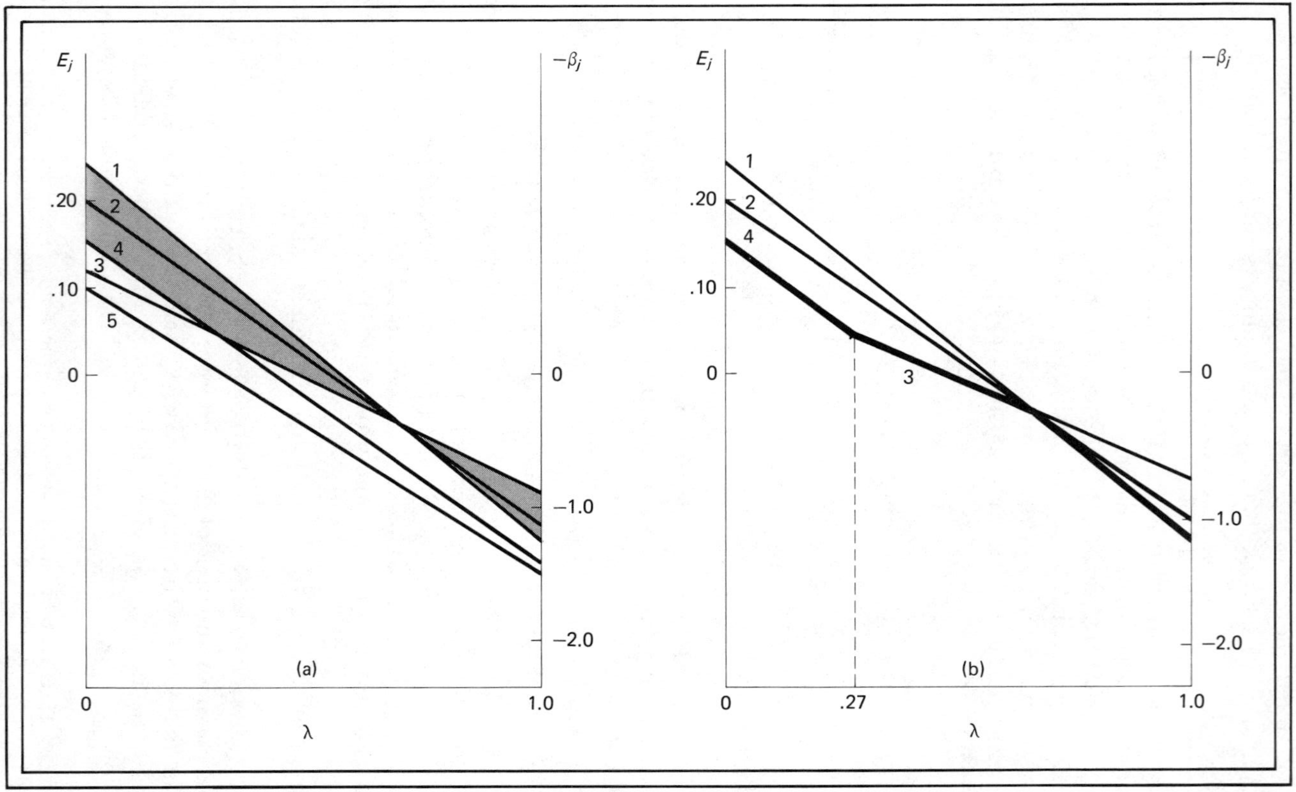

calculation of figures of merit for all securities. As an example, consider the possibility of constructing a portfolio where the minimum number of securities has been set at twelve with no more than three securities permitted from any one industry. The securities under review, however, include the following five firms from the oil industry:

1. Apache Corp.	$E(R) = .25,\ \beta = 1.10$
2. Ashland Oil	$E(R) = .20,\ \beta = 1.05$
3. Exxon	$E(R) = .12,\ \beta = .90$
4. Helmerich & Payne	$E(R) = .15,\ \beta = 1.30$
5. Natomas	$E(R) = .10,\ \beta = 1.40$

The figure of merit (Z_j) for each oil stock is drawn in Figure 16.5(a). As before, the third line from the top for all values of lambda (λ) is the border line. The three securities whose lines are on or above the border line (shaded area) are the three best stocks representing the industry. Security lines falling below the border line on Figure 16.5(b) have been deleted for clarity. By Figure 16.5(b) it is clear that Apache Corp. (1), Ashland Oil (2), and Helmerich & Payne (4) are the three best oil stocks for all values of lambda between 0 and .27. For values of lambda greater than .27, Exxon (3) replaces Helmerich & Payne.

A complete graphic solution would add all remaining securities to the surviving oil industry securities. If other industries exceeded their maximum, the process described by Figure 16.5 would be repeated until all industry constraints are satisfied and the results then merged on a single graph for a complete solution. The solution in this case would consist of selecting the twelve top security lines over the range of lambda from all candidates surviving the industry screening process.

TOTAL RISK. The expected value-beta estimating model presumes that all risk is systematic. This is a poor assumption when, as illustrated in an earlier example, there are only three securities in a corner portfolio. As the minimum security constraint is raised, systematic risk becomes a better estimate of total risk and the number of corner portfolios increases, giving the efficient surface a more curvilinear appearance (although it is still comprised of straight lines) than shown in Figure 16.3. With inputs of security return, beta, and variance, together with market return and variance, total portfolio risk, including unsystematic risk, can be measured for any corner portfolio.

Table 16.3 identifies an optimal corner portfolio which has resulted from an actual application of the beta model. The original total population consisted of twenty randomly selected stocks with a constraint that not fewer than six securities would be in the final set of portfolios. Portfolio risk, assuming that all risk is systematic, depends only on portfolio beta and market variability. For a portfolio of all stocks in Table 16.3 held in equal proportions, systematic risk, used as a proxy for total risk, suggests a standard deviation of 23 percent per year. Table 16.4 shows this calculation

Table 16.3
Securities in a Hypothetical Corner Portfolio (annual estimates)

Security	*Expected Return*	*Beta*	*Standard Deviation*
Am. Medical Int'l	.32	1.70	.50
Eastern Airlines	.30	1.40	.35
Apache Corp.	.25	1.10	.40
Continental Telephone	.22	.95	.24
Ashland Oil	.20	1.05	.28
Philadelphia Electric	.14	.70	.18
NYSE composite index	.12	1.00	.20

Table 16.4
Risk and Return of Sample Corner Portfolio

$$E_p = \sum_{j=1}^{6} X_j E_j = \tfrac{1}{6}(.32 + .30 + .25 + .22 + .20 + .14) = .238 \qquad \text{(Equation 14.2)}$$

$$\beta_p = \sum_{j=1}^{6} X_j \beta_j = \tfrac{1}{6}(1.70 + 1.40 + 1.10 + .95 + 1.05 + .70) = 1.150 \qquad \text{(Equation 15.4)}$$

$$\sigma_p = \beta_p \sigma_I = 1.150(.20) = .230 \qquad \text{(Equation 15.9)}$$

$$\sigma^2(e_j) = \sigma_j{}^2 - \beta_j{}^2 \sigma_I{}^2 \text{ for each stock in the portfolio} \qquad \text{(Equation 15.7)}$$

$$\sigma^2(e_1) = (.5)^2 - (1.70)^2(.20)^2 = .134 \text{ for stock 1}$$

$$(\sigma_p)^2 = \beta_p{}^2 \sigma_I{}^2 + \sum_{j=1}^{6} X_j{}^2 \sigma^2(e_j) \qquad \text{(Equation 15.8a)}$$

$$= (.23)^2 + (\tfrac{1}{6})^2 [.134 + .044 + .112 + .022 + .034 + .013]$$

$$= .053 + .010 = .063$$

$$\sigma_p = \sqrt{.063} = .251$$

$$\text{Percent unsystematic risk} = \frac{\sum X_j{}^2 \sigma^2(e_j)}{(\sigma_p)^2} = \frac{.010}{.063} = .153 \text{ or } 15.3 \text{ percent}$$

along with several other return and risk measures. Total risk of the portfolio, including the anticipated unsystematic component, is shown in Table 16.4 to slightly exceed 25 percent. By comparing the two variability estimates, the cost of the beta model's simplifying assumption and the specific constraint level is apparent. In this example the corner portfolio has slightly more than 15 percent greater variance than if all variability were systematic.

If the remaining 15 percent level of unsystematic risk is unacceptably high, the estimating procedure may be repeated with a constraint of more than six securities. It is conceivable that a lower constraint may be desired if fewer than six securities from the original population appear to be significantly undervalued. By accepting higher levels of unsystematic risk, larger excess returns would be captured if expectations are accurate.

Portfolio Evaluation

Portfolio evaluation requires measurement of return and risk after investment (ex post) in contrast to the task of forecasting return and risk before investment is made (ex ante). In discussing procedures of portfolio evaluation reference will be made to the optimal portfolio identified by the beta model in the previous section. Table 16.5 provides a summary of performance of each security in that portfolio and the NYSE composite index over the subsequent two-year period. The portfolio provided an average yearly return of .203 in contrast to an expected yearly return of .238. In an absolute sense, therefore, results were modestly disappointing. Overall, the portfolio provided a two-year return of 30.8 percent, in contrast to a market return of 17.5 percent. Judging simply by the market standard, the portfolio performed very well over the two-year period. But direct comparison of a portfolio's return with that of a market proxy, or for that matter any other portfolio, is insufficient because it ignores possible differences in risk. Portfolio performance should be evaluated by a joint criterion of return and risk as it is in the processes of security analysis and portfolio construction. Before considering measures inclusive of both return and risk, however, appropriate measures of risk for purposes of portfolio evaluation must first be identified.

Table 16.5
Observed Return Outcomes[a]

Security	*First Year Return*	*Second Year Return*	*Arithmetic Mean*	*Geometric Mean*	*Two-Year Return*
1. Am. Medical Int'l	−.404	1.704	.650	.270	.613
2. Apache Corp.	.055	.290	.172	.166	.360
3. Ashland Oil	−.189	.653	.232	.158	.341
4. Continental Telephone	−.157	.204	.024	.008	.016
5. Eastern Airlines	−.115	.478	.182	.143	.307
6. Philadelphia Electric	−.213	.546	.166	.103	.217
Portfolio	−.170	.577	.203	.144	.308
NYSE index (including dividends)	−.205	.478	.137	.084	.175
Risk-free return	.0600	.0600	.0600	.0600	.124

[a] Assumed from purchase of portfolio described in Tables 16.3 and 16.4.

This is a difficult task, for while it is easy to "see" return as time passes it is not as easy to "see" risk.

MEASURING RISK EX POST

The identification and meaning of risk after the fact (ex post) is not as easy or certain as the measurement of return. Actual return is the one and only point on a hypothetical distribution which is observable over any past period. The rest of the distribution is not observable, making measurement of risk exposure difficult. Three different procedures for measuring risk will be considered. First and most simply, ex ante portfolio risk estimators can serve as measures of actual risk exposure. This is an especially good assumption in the absence of any new knowledge that might influence the original return and risk estimates. This first estimating procedure (1) may be summarized as follows:

$$\sigma_p(1) = \sigma_p \quad \text{(ex ante)} \tag{16.5}$$

and

$$\beta_p(1) = \beta_p \quad \text{(ex ante)} \tag{16.5a}$$

Continuing the beta model portfolio example, the ex post risk proxy would be the original risk estimates determined in Table 16.4 from equations of the two previous chapters. Specifically, portfolio standard deviation and beta would be assumed to be:

$$\sigma_p(1) = .251 \quad \text{and} \quad \beta_p(1) = 1.150$$

As an alternative to these measurements, variability of return can be measured historically inclusive of the period which is being evaluated. Generally, variability should not be measured exclusively for the period under evaluation because that is too short a time for meaningful estimation. In some cases, however, it may be possible to divide the period into a sufficiently large number of subperiods and to derive risk measures from subperiod variability. For example, return over the two-year period described in Table 16.5 could be measured quarterly, monthly, or even weekly. But the relation between intraperiod variability and period risk exposure is not exact or obvious, and it may have little relation to the investor's perception of risk. This is especially true if the subperiod interval is very short in relation to the normal investment time horizon. A more satisfactory alternative would be to combine the period being evaluated with a sufficient number of equally long prior periods. For a total of T periods, a second measure of portfolio risk (2) would be calculated by:

$$\sigma_p^2(2) = 1/T \sum_{t=1}^{T} [R_{pt} - \bar{R}_p]^2 \tag{16.6}$$

The portfolio beta may be estimated from the series of T portfolio and market returns by using their observed variances and covariances. These values may be inserted into the formula for beta given in the previous chapter:

$$\beta_p(2) = \frac{\text{cov}(R_p, R_I)}{\sigma_I^{\,2}} \tag{16.7}$$

from Equation 15.2 *or* estimated directly by Equation 15.1.

To illustrate these calculations based on the beta model portfolio, one-year intervals will be assumed. From Table 16.5, portfolio returns for the two years were $-.170$ and $.577$. Assuming portfolio returns for the five preceding years of .237, .062, $-.087$, .364, and $-.195$, the average return over the extended seven-year period would be .113. From this historical record portfolio risk would be estimated from Equation 16.6 as

$$\sigma_p^{\,2}(2) = \frac{1}{7}\sum_{t=1}^{7} [R_{pt} - .113]^2 = .0730$$

$$\sigma_p(2) = \sqrt{.0730} = .270$$

The same procedure can be used to determine the variance of return for the NYSE index. Assuming that market variance was .048 (standard deviation of .220) and covariance of portfolio return was .053 (found by applying Equation 8A.16), portfolio beta can be calculated from Equation 16.7:

$$\beta_p(2) = \frac{.053}{.048} = 1.10$$

To the extent that expectations were originally based on historical relationships, risk measures $\sigma_p(1)$, $\beta_p(1)$ and $\sigma_p(2)$, $\beta_p(2)$ would very likely be similar because they are calculated over largely overlapping intervals. Only by chance could they be identical because $\sigma_p(2)$ and $\beta_p(2)$ include the period under evaluation which was unknown when $\sigma_p(1)$ and $\beta_p(1)$ were determined. Furthermore, $\sigma_p(1)$ and $\beta_p(1)$ should represent forecasts developed in consideration of future conditions, not simply as an extrapolation of historical behavior. The measures $\sigma_p(2)$ and $\beta_p(2)$ incorporate actual results, not expectations, and for this reason they may be considered the better measure of ex post risk despite the shortcomings already noted.

RISK BASED ON FORECASTING ERROR. A third form of risk measure directly considers the accuracy of investment forecasts of expected security return. Gerald Pogue has pointed out that identical portfolios held over the same time period could have different risks for different investors: high risk for those making inaccurate security forecasts and low risk for those forecasting accurately.[7] The measure of risk used to distinguish these variations in risk is

$$\sigma_p^{\,2}(3) = \sum_{j=1}^{m} X_j[R_j - E(R_j)]^2 \tag{16.8}$$

[7] Gerald A. Pogue, "An Intertemporal Model for Investment Management," *Journal of Bank Research* 1 (Spring 1970): 17–33.

which measures the dispersion of actual security returns from expected security returns, with each error weighed by the percentage of that security held in the portfolio. Again, given the expectations of the securities (j) in the beta portfolio (from Table 16.4) in comparison with the first year results (Table 16.5), forecasting error risk would be:

$$\sigma_p{}^2(3) = \sum_{j=1}^{6} X_j[R_{jt} - E(R_j)]^2 \qquad t = \text{year 1}$$

$$= \frac{1}{6}[1.1525] = .1921$$

$$\sigma_p(3) = \sqrt{.1921} = .438$$

In the second year, assuming that expectations remain unchanged, the standard deviation would be .622, higher than deviation for the first year. By this measure the second year risk was greater, although all error in the second year resulted from underestimation of return outcomes in contrast to the first year where all expected returns proved to be overly optimistic. Despite this limitation, $\sigma_p{}^2(3)$ provides some insight into the ability of security analysts to accurately forecast returns. Thus it may be concluded that $\sigma_p{}^2(3)$ is suitable as a measure of analysts' forecasting accuracy as distinguished from $\sigma_p{}^2(1)$ and $\sigma_p{}^2(2)$ which provide estimates of actual overall risk exposure.

REWARD TO VARIABILITY

In Chapter 14 an optimal portfolio of risky securities was identified from the set of portfolios on the investor's efficient frontier (recalling Figure 14.7). The basis of that identification was that a line drawn from the risk-free rate to the efficient frontier would just be tangent, and thus have the greatest slope, at that point. Investors could obtain any return and risk position along that line by combining ownership of the optimal portfolio with either borrowing or lending. The slope of the line measured the anticipated return for bearing risk to be received by the investor; notationally this slope was

$$\frac{E(R_p) - R_F}{\sigma_p} \tag{16.9}$$

which is at its highest value for all portfolios representing efficient combinations for the investor. The beta model portfolio has expected return of .238 and standard deviation of .251. If the risk-free return were .06, then the portfolio had an expected return to risk ratio of

$$\frac{.238 - .060}{.251} = .709$$

The numerator is the expected return in excess of the risk-free rate. The denominator is the risk incurred to obtain the excess return. The ratio .709

indicates that for each additional unit of risk borne, expected excess return increases by .709 units.[8] The concept is the same as the risk premium coefficient of variation described in Chapter 4 (Equation 4.10 and Figure 4.6), but it pertains here to portfolios rather than individual securities.

William Sharpe suggested a parallel measure for past portfolio performance known as the reward to vāriability ratio (R.V.).[9] Measuring historical performance over a period of years by the average annual return, $\bar{R}_p$, and the variability by the standard deviation about the historical average, σ_p, Sharpe's ratio is

$$\text{R.V.} = \frac{\bar{R}_p - R_F}{\sigma_p} \tag{16.10}$$

Using the reward to variability ratio, the performance of different portfolios can be ranked with the best having the highest ratio. An appropriate minimum standard is the reward to variability of the market portfolio as represented by a broadly based index. Successful security selection and portfolio construction should consistently result in higher reward to variability ratios for the portfolio than for the general market. The actual reward to variability ratio for the beta model portfolio and for the market, using $\sigma(2)$ risk measures of .270 and .220, respectively, were

$$\text{R.V. (portfolio)} = \frac{.203 - .060}{.270} = .530$$

and

$$\text{R.V. (market)} = \frac{.137 - .060}{.220} = .350$$

While the portfolio's return per unit of risk was lower than the .709 figure expected, it was superior to that achieved by the market in the same period. These results are illustrated in Figure 16.6. Historically, the return per unit of risk has been somewhat higher than the results of this example. Using a slightly different procedure, Soldofsky and Miller found that on average a 1.00 percent increase in standard deviation increased annual yield by 1.15

[8] If an investor were willing to accept a risk 20 percent greater than .251, return would increase by .20(.709)(.238 − .06) = .025 to a total expected return of .025 + .238 = .263. This position could be accomplished through borrowing money at 6 percent and using it to buy more of the portfolio promising 23.8 percent. Leverage provides the mechanism for increasing expected return to 26.3 percent. In this case money borrowed, as a percentage X of original capital, needs to be 14.2 percent and is found by:

$$\begin{aligned} .263 &= .238 + X(.238 - .060) \\ .263 - .238 &= X(.238 - .060) \\ .025 &= X(.178) \\ X &= .142 \end{aligned}$$

[9] William F. Sharpe, "Mutual Fund Performance," *Journal of Business* 39 (January 1966): 119–138.

Figure 16.6
Reward-to-Variability Lines

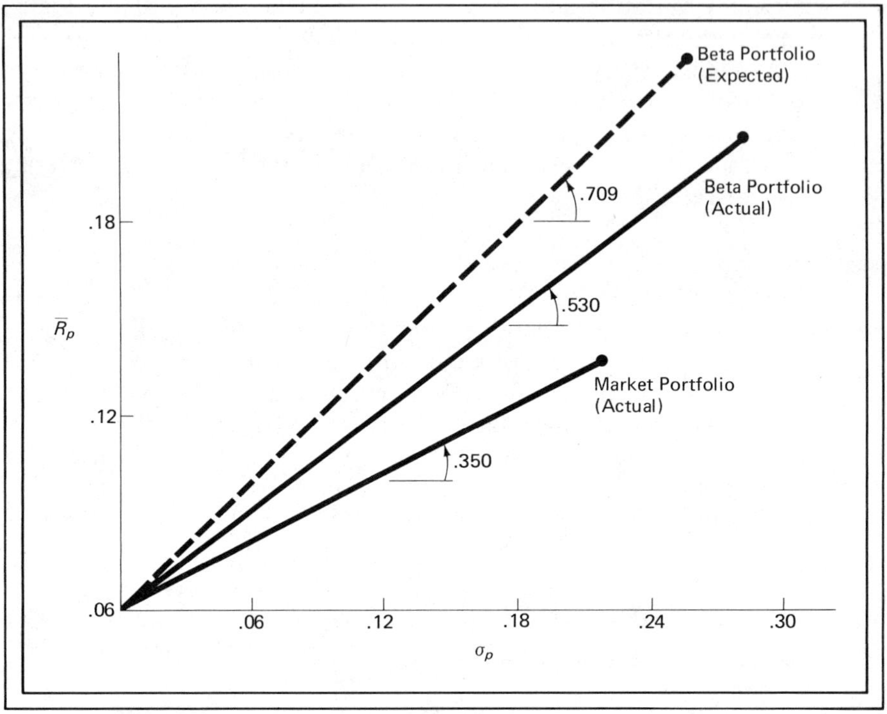

percent over the years 1950–1966 with a downward trend persisting throughout.[10] In an extension of this work Soldofsky and Jennings found that in the ten years ending in 1969 an average of .62 percent yield was gained for each 1.00 percent increase in standard deviation.[11] Relatively low returns for bearing risk have persisted through the mid-1970s.

A limitation of the reward to variability ratio is that it is a proper measure only when well-diversified portfolios are being considered. This is the case because total risk is used to appraise return. With efficient portfolios, all risk is systematic and differences in reward to variability ratios may be credited to the degree to which securities were initially under- or overvalued. For less than fully diversified portfolios, lower reward to variability ratios would occur even though undervalued securities were selected because risk is greater than necessary. Without further analysis it is difficult to say whether the beta model portfolio's performance resulted solely from security analysis

[10] Robert M. Soldofsky and Roger L. Miller, "Risk Premium Curves for Different Classes of Long Term Securities, 1950–1966," *Journal of Finance* 24 (June 1969): 429–445.

[11] Robert M. Soldofsky and Edward Jennings, "Risk Premium Curves: Empirical Evidence in Their Changing Position, 1950 to 1970," *Quarterly Review of Economics and Business* 13 (Spring 1973): 49–68.

or whether it was negatively influenced by inadequate diversification. Selecting $\sigma_p^2(2)$ and $\beta_p(2)$ risk estimates, the adequacy of portfolio diversification can be appraised ex post by Equation 15.6:

$$\sigma^2(e_p) = \sigma_p^{\ 2} - \beta_p^{\ 2}\sigma_m^{\ 2}$$
$$\sigma^2(e_p) = .073 - (1.10)^2(.048) = .0149$$

Solving for the percentage of risk which was unsystematic,

$$\frac{\sigma^2(e_p)}{\sigma_p^{\ 2}} = .204 \text{ or } 20.4 \text{ percent}$$

The portion of unsystematic risk was slightly higher than the expected level (from Table 16.4) of 15.3 percent but is low by the standards of an average portfolio containing only six securities.[12] These observations are important in considering potential revisions of the portfolio.

The reward to variability ratio may suffer from an additional limitation in practice. A study by Friend and Blume has found that a negative relationship exists between the reward to variability ratios of portfolios and the level of portfolio risk.[13] If the reward to variability ratio properly expresses return relative to risk, then the ratio should be independent of the level of risk in the portfolios being evaluated. Friend and Blume's finding of a negative relationship suggests that the ratio is in practice biased against high-risk portfolios. The seriousness of this bias as well as its causes and corrections have not yet been fully explored. But their findings do suggest caution until additional investigation substantiates or improves upon the reward to variability concept.

REWARD TO VOLATILITY AND DIFFERENTIAL RETURN

In consideration of single securities or less than fully diversified portfolios, two alternative and related measures are commonly used: the reward to volatility ratio and differential return. The reward to volatility ratio, developed by Jack Treynor,[14] is similar to the reward to variability ratio only with beta substituted for the standard deviation as the measure of risk. The reward to volatility ratio for security i is:

$$\text{R.B.} = \frac{\bar{R}_i - R_F}{\beta_i} \tag{16.11}$$

[12] From Figure 14.10, on average a six-stock portfolio appears to contain about 43 percent of unsystematic risk. This figure is obtained from the fact that an average six-stock portfolio has semiannual variance (read off the graph) of $(.14)^2$ whereas a completely diversified portfolio has variance of $(.117)^2$. Thus the variance relative of an average randomly selected portfolio is $(.14)^2/(.117)^2 = 1.43$, meaning that variance is 43 percent above the fully diversified minimum.

[13] Irwin Friend and Marshall Blume, "Measurement of Portfolio Performance Under Uncertainty," *American Economic Review* 60, no. 4 (September 1970): 561–576.

[14] Jack Treynor, "How To Rate Management of Investment Funds," *Harvard Business Review*, January–February 1965, pp. 63–75.

Higher reward to volatility ratios signify better security performance. The major advantage of the reward to volatility ratio over the reward to variability ratio is that it is a relevant measure of performance for all securities and portfolios, both inefficient and efficient.

Figure 16.7 graphically summarizes the reward to volatility ratios for each security in the beta model portfolio and the NYSE index. The reward to volatility ratio measures the slope of a line drawn from the risk-free rate through the security's location plotted in terms of its return and beta. Since the NYSE index represents the market and is therefore efficient, Figure 16.7 directly illustrates the superiority or inferiority of return performance realized by each individual security. The slope of a line drawn from the risk-free rate to each security's location on the graph identifies the reward to volatility ratio. The figure shows that of the six securities, five provided above average returns relative to their betas. Only one security provided a return below par, and it was this favorable ratio of winners to losers that enabled the beta model portfolio to outperform the market despite its retention of some unsystematic risk.

Differential return was mentioned briefly in the preceding chapter as a means of expressing the security valuation forecast in terms of its perceived current under- or overpricing by the market. The measure also may be used

Figure 16.7
Reward-to-Volatility Lines

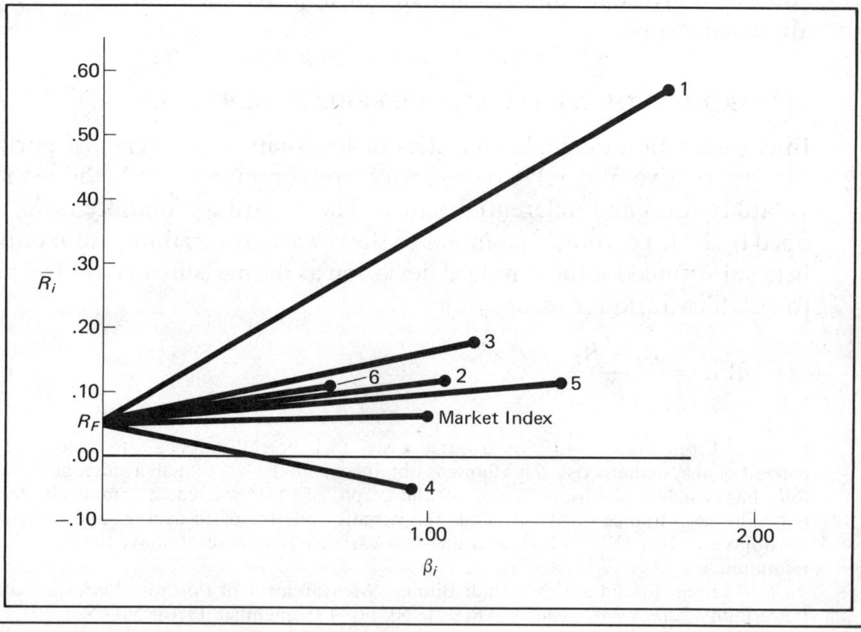

Numbers correspond to stocks in Table 16.5.

analogously to measure past performance. Recalling equilibrium conditions expressed by the capital asset pricing model for all securities:

$$E(R_i) - R_F = \beta_i[E(R_M) - R_F] \qquad [(15.10)]$$

If actual values from within the period being evaluated are substituted for expected values the expression becomes

$$\bar{R}_i - R_F = d_i + \beta_i(\bar{R}_M - R_F) \qquad (16.12)$$

The differential return, d_i, is the difference between the security's average return for bearing risk $(R_i - R_F)$ and the average return for bearing risk expected for a security having that level of systematic risk $\beta_i(\bar{R}_M - R_F)$. Since, in the absence of favorable new information, differential return of properly priced securities would be zero, positive differential returns indicate desirable results and negative differential returns reflect poor performance. Again referring to the beta model (Table 16.5), the best and worst performing securities had differential returns of

$$.650 - .060 = d_{\text{best}} + 1.70[.137 - .060]$$
$$d_{\text{best}} = .459 \quad \text{(Am. Medical Int'l)}$$

and

$$.024 - .060 = d_{\text{worst}} + .95[.137 - .060]$$
$$d_{\text{worst}} = -.109 \quad \text{(Continental Telephone)}$$

These differential returns are consistent with the findings of the reward to volatility analysis (see Figure 16.7). The worst security had a negative differential return indicating its performance was below the average of the market and therefore with hindsight it was a poor investment. However, this result by itself does not mean that the security should now be sold and replaced by another. That decision must be made as part of the portfolio revision process described in the next chapter.

Originally developed by Michael Jensen as a test of mutual fund performance, differential return bears a direct relationship to reward-to-volatility.[15] This is not surprising since both measures were developed from capital market theory and both use beta as the relevant measure of risk. Differential return has both limitations and advantages in comparison with other performance measures. Both result from the fact that, although it takes risk into account, differential return is an absolute (one-dimensional) measure. Because of this, differential returns may be directly compared to their expected level of zero but they cannot be compared to each other. The test for significance against a null hypothesis of zero is made by using the

[15] Michael C. Jensen, "Risk, the Pricing of Capital Assets, and the Evaluation of Investment Portfolios," *Journal of Business* 42 (April 1969): 167–247. Mutual fund performance is discussed in Chapter 18. The relationship between reward-to-volatility and differential return has been shown to be R.B. $= R_F + d_i/\beta_i$. Jack L. Treynor, "Discussion: The Performance of Mutual Funds in the Period 1945–1964," *Journal of Finance* 23 (May 1968): 418–419.

parameters of Equation 16.12 which are obtained by a regression based on intervals within the period under evaluation. This procedure is valid for either securities or portfolios. Alternatively, portfolio differential return may be tested cross-sectionally to determine if the securities selected for inclusion in the portfolio were on average significantly undervalued when purchased.

WEALTH MAXIMIZING

Portfolio theory and construction presume that investors seek to maximize their expected utility. An alternative presumption, originally suggested by Latane, is that investors attempt to maximize wealth; since there is a direct relationship between wealth accumulation and the rate of growth, maximizing wealth is equivalent to maximizing growth.[16] Unfortunately, difficulties in making the wealth maximization model operational and in forecasting the necessary security inputs sufficiently far into the future have so far limited the practical application of wealth maximizing models in ex ante portfolio selection.

The concept of wealth maximizing is, however, useful in evaluating the past performance of portfolios where a sufficient number of meaningful intervals are available to obtain valid growth rate measures. When an investor is comparing alternative portfolios, the one having the largest growth rate and hence greatest terminal wealth relative to initial investment would have been best. This generalization may be made because, coupled with borrowing or lending, the maximum growth portfolio would be the optimal risky portfolio for all investors regardless of their willingness to bear risk. Since for portfolio evaluation both beginning and current portfolio values are known along with the number of intervals (N), the rate of growth can be solved directly as the Nth root of the value relative minus one:

$$(1 + \bar{R}_g)^N = \frac{W_N}{W_0}$$

$$(1 + \bar{R}_g) = \left[\frac{W_N}{W_0}\right]^{1/N}$$

$$\bar{R}_g = \left[\frac{W_N}{W_0}\right]^{1/N} - 1$$

Annual growth rates for the beta model portfolio, summarized in Table 16.5, were calculated through application of the above equation. This solution presumes that no additions or withdrawals have taken place within the

[16] Henry A. Latané, "Criteria for Choice Among Risky Ventures," *Journal of Political Economy* 67, no 2 (April 1959): 144–155. Markowitz has argued that maximizing expected utility is consistent with maximizing expected growth as a general solution to the problem of investment for the long run. See Harry M. Markowitz, "Investment for the Long Run: New Evidence for an Old Rule," *Journal of Finance*, December 1976, pp. 1273–1286.

period being evaluated. The final section of this chapter will present a method of adjusting for variations in portfolio size over time.

THE CASH FLOW PROBLEM

All measures of actual portfolio performance discussed so far in this chapter presume no movement of cash in or out of the portfolio. When interim cash flows exist the investor can either (1) ignore changes in portfolio size or (2) weigh performance results by the relative amounts committed to the portfolio at different times.[17] The first procedure measures the growth of all funds kept in the portfolio over the entire period under consideration. In so doing, it provides an evaluation of security selection and portfolio diversification. But conventional procedures would no longer relate beginning with ending portfolio values because investment levels have been changed. The latter procedure maintains the association between beginning and ending wealth, thereby adding an evaluation of the timing decision to commit or withdraw funds to that of security selection per se.[18] The procedure assumes that any capital added or withdrawn earns a zero return for the time it is absent from the portfolio.

If cash movements are not considered an element of investment decision making, evaluation procedures would proceed as described earlier in this chapter. To consider cash flows, all individual return estimates are weighed by an amount equaling one plus (minus) funds added (withdrawn) as a percentage of the portfolio's value at the time the cash flow occurred. For example, suppose that an investor initially committed \$100,000 to the beta model portfolio and subsequently withdrew \$20,000 at the end of the first year. From Table 16.5, first year return is $-.170$ and second year return is $+.577$. Starting with \$100,000, the value of the portfolio at the end of the first year is

$$(1 - .170)(100{,}000) = 83{,}000$$

Withdrawing \$20,000 from this amount leaves \$63,000 which, at 57.7 percent the next year, would be worth a total of $(1.577)(\$63{,}000) = \$99{,}351$. By applying Equation 16.13, the annual growth of portfolio value is[19]

$$1 + \bar{R}_g = \left[\frac{97{,}351}{100{,}000}\right]^{1/2} = .997; \qquad \bar{R}_g = -.003$$

[17] It is assumed here that cash flows do not affect the composition of the portfolio in a way that significantly alters its risk. If a major change in composition has occurred, evaluation should begin from the point of change rather than attempt to encompass an earlier and different period.

[18] The dimension of timing is considered in the next chapter as part of the portfolio revision process.

[19] Alternatively, the growth rate could be determined through weighting the second year return as described earlier in the paragraph. The weight would be $[1 - (20{,}000/83{,}000)] = .759$, and the weighted second year return would be $(.759)(1.577) = 1.197$. The growth rate would be found by: $1 + \bar{R}_g = [(.830)(1.197)]^{1/2} = .997$; $\bar{R}_g = -.003$.

This is well below the .144 average rate of growth of the securities in the portfolio (from Table 16.5).

Cash additions would be evaluated in the same manner. If \$20,000 were added rather than withdrawn during the second year, then \$103,000 would have earned the .577 second year return resulting in an ending value of \$162,431. Overall growth would be

$$1 + \bar{R}_g = \left[\frac{162{,}431}{100{,}000}\right]^{1/2} = 1.274; \qquad \bar{R}_g = .274$$

Both rates are intuitively reasonable under their respective assumptions. If money is withdrawn prior to a winning year, poorer performance will result; alternatively, adding money will improve performance.

Summary

Selecting a time horizon, forming expectations in terms of probability beliefs, selecting a portfolio through modeling, and then monitoring, evaluating, and revising the portfolio through time comprise the major activities of investment management. This chapter has summarized the first three of these activities, drawing upon the principles developed in the two previous chapters. Portfolio construction was illustrated through introduction of a simplified beta model, and the results of this example were used illustratively throughout the rest of the chapter.

Portfolio evaluation provides information necessary for future estimates and revisions. The final part of the chapter considers the problems and procedures of portfolio evaluation. Once an adequate measure of risk exposure is identified, portfolio evaluation may proceed. Performance may be judged absolutely in relation to original expectations or relatively in relation to actual market conditions. The latter standard is more commonly used and may be measured by reward to variability ratios, reward to volatility ratios, or differential returns. The first measure is appropriate only for the investor's total portfolio, and most useful in this case only if the portfolio is efficient or very nearly so. Reward to volatility and differential return both measure performance of individual securities as well as portfolios.

An alternative evaluation criterion is that of maximizing portfolio growth. Since growth depends dually on period return and risk, growth maximizing is not the same as simply selecting the highest return investments. Growth maximizing is a long-run and multiperiod concept. In practice the single-period portfolio evaluation measures noted above are generally preferred because they are more easily interpreted and provide greater detail. In the next chapter portfolio revision procedures and the related topic of investment timing will be considered.

Questions and Problems

1. Review the steps outlined in the chapter for building a portfolio. In terms of emphasis, which areas are of greater concern to a professional security analyst as opposed to a financial advisor or consultant?
2. The illustrated graphic portfolio problem in the text identified a portfolio as the optimal combination of risky securities (Table 16.4). Under the assumption that next period's expectations will remain unchanged over succeeding periods, what is your estimate of the portfolio's long-run growth rate? What happens to your estimate if you believe the market portfolio's risk is $\sigma_M = .12$ instead of $\sigma_M = .20$ as given by Table 16.4?
3. A friend has requested that you suggest the best possible portfolios obtainable from a list of six favored securities. You first observe that the six securities represent substantially different lines of commerce, and then determine the following set of expectations:

	E_i	β_i	α_i
Stock 1	.09	.80	.15
2	.08	0	.20
3	.05	−.20	.35
4	.15	1.40	.30
5	.20	2.30	.35
6	.12	1.30	.20
Market	.12	1.00	.12

Using the decision rule that no more than one-third of your friend's money will be invested in any one stock, determine the efficient frontier. With a borrowing and lending rate of 8 percent, how do your results compare with putting everything in the safest portfolio? The riskiest portfolio? What should you advise?

4. What is an appropriate time frame in which to judge the success or failure of security selection and portfolio construction?
5. What are some of the problems encountered in evaluating portfolio performance?
6. Calculate the reward to variability ratios for the following portfolios:

	Portfolio B	*Portfolio S*	*Market Portfolio*	*Risk-free Return*
Average return	.10	.15	.12	.07
Beta	.40	1.10	1.00	0
Standard deviation	.18	.28	.22	0

What statements can you make about portfolios *B* and *S*? If the risk-free rate were .03, would these statements change? Is there any reasonable level of risk-free return that would have made these portfolios equally desirable? Does calculating their reward to volatility ratios provide any additional insights?

7. Rank the six stocks listed in Table 16.5 by their differential returns assuming a 6 percent risk-free rate and market return of 13.7 percent. Does this ranking necessarily show the relative desirability of each security? Why or why not? In this particular instance does the ranking in fact reflect desirability? (*Hint*: Compare to ranking based on reward to volatility.)

8. The six-stock beta model portfolio illustrated in the chapter had approximately 21 percent unsystematic risk. Referring back to the discussion in Chapter 14 (and especially Figure 14.10), how does this degree of unsystematic risk compare to what might reasonably be expected?
9. A portfolio successively earned 30 percent, −15 percent, and .10 percent over a three-year period. What was its annual rate of growth? Assuming that without disturbing portfolio composition an amount equaling 40 percent of the portfolio's value was withdrawn at the end of the first year, and a 20 percent addition was made at the end of the second year, what happened to the ending portfolio relative and implied rate of capital appreciation?

Selected References

PORTFOLIO BUILDING

Bear, Robert M., and Adam K. Gehr, "Association of Returns to Alternative Investment Media: The Government Bond-Common Stock Case," *Journal of Economics and Business* 28, no. 1 (Fall 1975): 68–74.

Beaver, W., P. Kettler, and Myron Scholes, "The Association Between Market Determined and Accounting Determined Risk Measures," *Accounting Review*, October 1970, pp. 654–682.

Blume, Marshall E., "Portfolio Theory: A Step Toward Its Practical Application," *Journal of Business*, April 1970, pp. 152–173.

Cheng, P. I., and M. K. Deets, "Systematic Risk and the Horizon Problem," *Journal of Financial and Quantitative Analysis* B, no. 2 (March 1973): 299–307.

Elton, Edwin J., Martin J. Gruber, and Manfred W. Padberg, "Simple Criteria for Optimal Portfolio Selection," *Journal of Finance*, December 1976, pp. 1341–1357.

Jacob, Nancy L., "A Limited Diversification Portfolio Selection Model for the Small Investor," *Journal of Finance* 29, no. 4 (June 1974): 847–856.

———, "The Measurement of Market Similarity for Securities Under Uncertainty," *Journal of Business* 43, no. 3 (July 1970): 328–353.

Mao, James C. T., "Essentials of Portfolio Diversification Strategy," *Journal of Finance* 25, no. 5 (December 1970): 1109–1131.

Officer, R. R., "The Variability of the Market Factor of the New York Stock Exchange," *Journal of Business*, July 1973, pp. 434–453.

Sharpe, William, *Portfolio Theory and Capital Markets* (New York: McGraw-Hill, 1970).

PORTFOLIO EVALUATION

Bierman, Jr., Harold, and Semour Smidt, "Application of the Capital Asset Pricing Model to Multi-period Investments," *Journal of Business Finance and Accounting* 2, no. 3 (Autumn 1975): 327–340.

Bower, Richard, and Donald Wippern, "Risk-Return Measurement in Portfolio Selection and Performance Appraisal Models: Progress Report," *Journal of Financial* and *Quantitative Analysis* 4, no. 4 (December 1969): 417–447.

Cranshaw, T. E., "The Evaluation of Investment Performance," *The Journal of Business*, October 1977, pp. 462–485.

Fleming, Robert M., "How Risky Is the Market?" *Journal of Business* 46, no. 3 (July 1973): 404–424.

Friend, Irwin, and Marshall Blume, "Measurement of Portfolio Performance Under Uncertainty," *American Economic Review* 60, no. 4 (September 1970): 561–576.

Jensen, Michael C., "Risk, the Pricing of Capital Assets, and the Evaluation of Investment Portfolios," *Journal of Business* 42, no. 2 (April 1969): 167–247.

Klemkosky, Robert C., "The Bias in Composite Performance Measures," *Journal of Financial and Quantitative Analysis* 8, no. 3 (June 1973): 505–514.

Latané, Henry A., "Criteria for Choice Among Risky Ventures," *Journal of Political Economy* 67, no. 2 (April 1959): 144–155.

Markowitz, Harry M., "Investment for the Long Run: New Evidence for an Old Rule," *Journal of Finance*, December 1976, pp. 1273–1286.

Matulich, Serge, "Portfolio Performance with Lending and Borrowing," *Journal of Business Finance and Accounting* 2, no. 3 (Autumn 1975): 341–348.

Pinches, George, and William Kinney, Jr., "The Measurement of the Volatility of Common Stock Prices," *Journal of Finance* 26 (March 1971): 119–125.

Pogue, Gerald A., "An Intertemporal Model for Investment Management," *Journal of Bank Research* 1 (Spring 1970): 17–33.

Samuelson, Paul, "The 'Fallacy' of Maximizing the Geometric Mean in Long Sequences of Investing or Gambling," *Proceedings of the National Academy of Science, U.S.A.*, October 1971, pp. 2493–2496.

Sharpe, William, "Mutual Fund Performance," *Journal of Business* 39 (January 1966): 119–138.

Soldofsky, Robert, and Edward Jennings, "Risk Premium Curves: Empirical Evidence in Their Changing Position, 1950–1970," *Quarterly Review of Economics and Business* 13 (Spring 1973): 49–68.

Soldofsky, Robert, and Roger Miller, "Risk Premium Curves for Different Classes of Long Term Securities, 1950–1966," *Journal of Finance* 24 (June 1969): 429–445.

Treynor, Jack, "Discussion: The Performance of Mutual Funds in the Period 1945–1964," *Journal of Finance* 23 (May 1968): 418–419.

——, "How To Note Management of Mutual Funds," *Harvard Business Review*, January–February 1965, pp. 63–75.

Chapter 17

Investment Maintenance and Revision

Investment management is a complex and ongoing professional occupation. Investment maintenance involves a constant monitoring of information that may affect security value. Revision involves making changes in the investment portfolio at appropriate times and in appropriate amounts. This chapter will discuss the rationale for portfolio revision and offer several procedures for measuring its potential effectiveness. As with all other aspects of investment activity, maintenance and revision raise many unsettled problems and challenges for the professional investor.

The chapter begins by exploring the basic motivation to rebalance and upgrade an existing portfolio. Revision must recognize the added expenses of tax and transaction costs which result from trading activity. A sequential approach to benefit-cost analysis is then presented as a useful way of determining the value of all potential changes which are under consideration. Timing of security transactions is another key dimension of investment maintenance and revision. The chapter concludes with a discussion of the difficulties presented by the timing question and an exploration of several possible solutions to the problem.

Portfolio Revision

A graphic model illustrating the need for portfolio revision is shown in Figure 17.1. The figure assumes that an investor had original return-risk expectations

Figure 17.1
The Portfolio Revision Problem

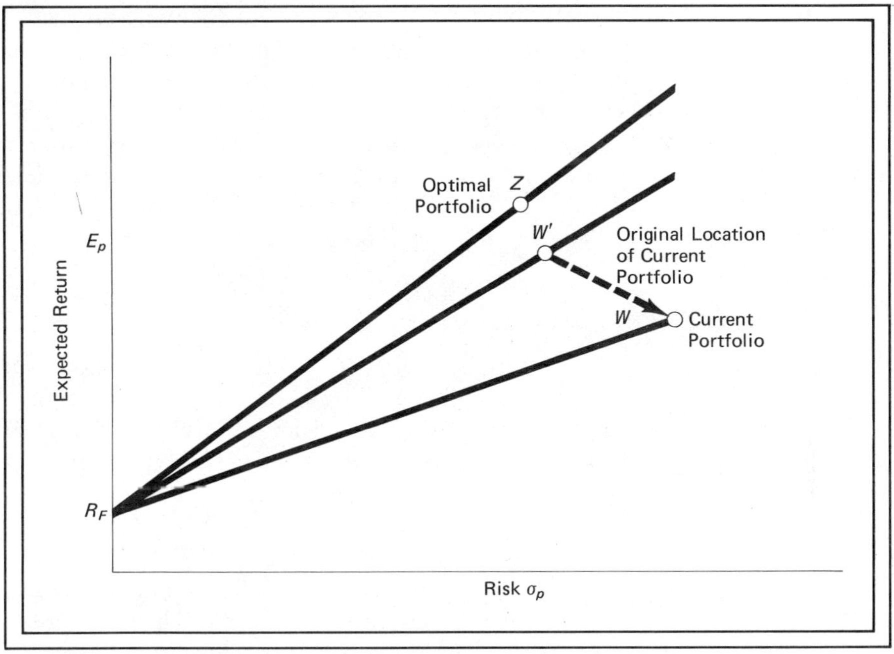

represented by point W'. Time has passed since portfolio W' was acquired and, based on current prices, the same portfolio now has expectations shown by W. The investor now envisions a different attainable portfolio with expectations of Z; future expectations for the portfolio which is currently held W are decidedly inferior to a new portfolio Z which the investor now perceives to be optimal.[1] Portfolio revision should employ methods for making a controlled transition from the current portfolio to the desired one. In keeping with the conventional treatment of security and portfolio analysis, portfolio revision will be viewed as a process of sequentially applying the single-period return and risk model over time. Although some authors argue that this procedure may lead to suboptimal results, others have demonstrated that one-period planning is consistent with long-run optimality.[2] The two

[1] Expectations may change because of changes in a firm's operations which have impact on its earnings, dividends, and total and/or systematic risk. Changed expectations could result from varying market conditions, interest rates, regulatory or tax conditions, or from other general factors. Changes might also result from the investor's altered needs and perceptions or simply from the fact that initially undervalued securities have become properly priced, thereby lowering their future potential.

[2] For the argument against one-period planning see Jan Mossin, "Optimal Multi-Period Portfolio Policies," *Journal of Business*, April 1969, pp. 215–229. The validity of single-period analysis has been shown by Eugene Fama, "Multiperiod Consumption-Investment Decisions," *American Economic Review*, March 1970, pp. 163–174.

basic motivations for portfolio revision are rebalancing and upgrading. Rebalancing is necessitated by cash flow needs arising from consumption and savings decisions and also by the desire to maintain adequate diversification in the face of changing relative market values. Upgrading seeks to improve the portfolio's future return prospects relative to risk. Both rebalancing and upgrading may occur at any time and should be considered at the completion of a normal forecasting period. In both cases the impact of taxes and transaction costs must be evaluated. This section considers each of these elements of investment management. The final question raised at the outset, investment timing, will be considered in the concluding section.

PORTFOLIO REBALANCING

The purpose of portfolio rebalancing is to maintain the original nature of the portfolio in the face of changing cash flows and market conditions. Presumably, rebalancing is not motivated by changes in expectations or new information which potentially affects investment performance. Instead, rebalancing is centered on liquidity needs and the strategy of maintaining the existing portfolio intact.

PERIODIC REBALANCING. The purpose of periodically rebalancing a portfolio is to restore portfolio composition as far as practicable. Through time, composition changes as relative market values change. The nature of this change is shown by the portfolio illustrated in Table 17.1. Data represent market values for five securities over the bull market year of 1975. Assuming that the five stocks were initially purchased in equal amounts, by the end of the year a far greater concentration of value is evident.[3]

The highest yielding security, Disney Productions, doubled its share within the portfolio while the poorest performer shrank in representation to about 11 percent. Over longer periods of time proportionality would likely become more divergent unless transactions occur to restore balance. In the absence of additional new capital, rebalancing requires selling of securities which have earned relatively higher returns in the past for additional purchases of securities which have had lower returns. *Fixed-target revision* strategy is the expression commonly given to this activity.

Fixed-target revision involves only securities which are already held in the portfolio. The objective is to restore original proportionality. If odd-lot holdings are avoided, rebalancing will produce a small cash residual which may be retained in a risk-free account for subsequent cash flow needs or investment decisions. Restoring the optimal portfolio illustrated in Table 17.1

[3] Actually, the majority of changes in stock values in this example occurred early in the year and shortly after the portfolio was created. Even though the time span was short, under these conditions the investor should have considered rebalancing earlier. An alternative strategy might employ writing a call or buying a put on the large gainers. Good investment management always requires flexibility and the ability to identify viable alternatives.

Table 17.1
Portfolio Composition After One Year[a]

	Initial		Year-end	
Stock	*Price*	*Percentage of Portfolio Value*	*Price*	*Percentage of Portfolio Value*
Disney Productions	22	.200	52	.330
DuPont	95	.200	132	.194
Int'l Paper	$36\frac{1}{2}$	.200	56	.214
Johnson & Johnson	83	.200	91	.153
Marine Midland	15	.200	$11\frac{3}{4}$	.109
		1.000		1.000

[a] Based on the 1975 experience. Year-end price includes dividends.

Table 17.2
Unsystematic and Systematic Risk

Stock	$\sigma^2(e)$	β
Disney Productions	.060	1.55
DuPont	.038	1.00
Int'l Paper	.048	1.15
Johnson & Johnson	.034	.90
Marine Midland	.031	.80

to approximately its original composition after one year would require selling some shares of Disney Productions and investing the proceeds in Johnson & Johnson and Marine Midland.

The benefits of fixed-target revision are threefold. First, unsystematic risk is usually reduced because unintended concentration is avoided. The first column of Table 17.2 contains estimates of unsystematic risk for each of the five securities listed in Table 17.1 based on historical data prior to 1975. Recalling the notion of unsystematic risk from Chapter 15, portfolio unsystematic risk would be found by applying

$$\sigma^2(e_p) = \sum_{j=1}^{m} X_j^{\,2}\sigma^2(e_j) \qquad [(15.6)]$$

In this case initial unsystematic risk was

$$\begin{aligned}\sigma^2(e_p) &= (\tfrac{1}{5})^2[.060 + .038 + .048 + .034 + .031] \\ &= .008\end{aligned}$$

But by the end of the year, using weights from Table 17.1, unsystematic risk has increased to

$$\sigma^2(e_p) = (.330)^2(.060) + (.194)^2(.038) + (.214)^2(.048) + (.153)^2(.034) + (.109)^2(.031)$$
$$= 0.11$$

Concentration has increased unsystematic risk.[4]

The second benefit of rebalancing is the restoration of the original level of systematic risk. Beta is a measure of systematic risk and portfolio beta is a weighted average of individual security betas. When proportional holdings change the portfolio beta will also change unless all securities have similar betas or their movements happen to be offsetting. From the betas in Table 17.2 and proportional holdings from Table 17.1, the original portfolio beta was (by Equation 15.4),

$$\beta_p = \tfrac{1}{5}[1.55 + 1.00 + 1.15 + .90 + .80]$$
$$= 1.08$$

In the absence of new information it may be assumed that end-of-year betas are unchanged from original estimates. At year-end portfolio beta was

$$\beta_p = .330(1.55) + .194(1.00) + .214(1.15) + .153(.90) + .109(.80)$$
$$= 1.18$$

Both systematic and unsystematic risk have increased over time. Although risk may either increase or decrease, increasing risk is typical under normally rising market conditions. In declining markets high beta securities should decline more than proportionally, producing a decline in portfolio systematic risk. But even in bear markets unsystematic risk would more likely increase. The larger the range of realized security yields within a portfolio, the larger should be the expected shift in portfolio risk.

The third potential benefit of portfolio rebalancing presumes convergence of security values to forecasted equilibrium levels. It is presumed that all securities held are thought initially to be undervalued. Some of these have appreciated more rapidly than others and, to the extent that this has occurred above levels warranted by risk differentials, the potential for future excess return is limited. By reallocating funds to securities where expected excess appreciation has not yet occurred, future portfolio performance may be enhanced. To test the return performance of a fixed target revision strategy, Latané and Young studied its effects relative to a buy and hold policy on port-

[4] An exception to this general result could occur where concentration exists in securities with unusually low levels of unsystematic risk. Assume that three stocks were $\sigma^2(e_1) = \sigma^2(e_2) = \sigma^2(e_3) = .100$ and proportional holdings change from $X_1 = X_2 = X_3$ to $X_1 = \frac{2}{3}$, $X_2 = X_3 = \frac{1}{6}$. By Equation 15.6 portfolio unsystematic risk rises from .033 to .050. But if instead $\sigma^2(e_1) = .05$ and $\sigma^2(e_2) = \sigma^2(e_3) = .20$, then the change of holdings would lower portfolio unsystematic risk from .050 to .033.

folios ranging in size from 4 to 32 securities.[5] Ignoring transaction costs, fixed-target revision was superior for nearly 75 percent of all portfolios constructed. Additionally, the superiority of fixed-target revision was related to the original procedure for security selection, working best when criteria were reward to volatility and expected return. Buying and holding the original portfolio provided good results when portfolios were comprised of randomly selected securities. Latané and Young further qualified their results by noting that the net superiority of fixed-target revision when transaction costs are considered is not clear: even maintaining the status quo is costly.

CASH FLOW NEEDS AND REINVESTMENT. Changes in the level of funds available for investment may occur periodically or unexpectedly. In either case money flows impact upon the nature and composition of the portfolio. If all investments were infinitely divisible, without cost or tax liability, additions or withdrawals could be spread across all individual securities in exact proportion to their value in the portfolio and portfolio composition would remain unchanged. In all but very large portfolios, or in the special case of a mutual fund, this policy is not practical owing to the high costs associated with a large number of small transactions. Other strategies are frequently necessary to accommodate interim cash flow needs effectively.

Substantial additions of capital should always be viewed as opportunities for upgrading the portfolio, which is the topic of the following section. For smaller savings and dividend flows, cash inflows may be accumulated in a liquid interest-bearing account until a position in risky securities becomes possible without incurring excessive transaction costs. As a general guideline, transaction costs in excess of 3 percent of investment value should be viewed as excessive. With respect to dividends, these arguments seem to imply that stock dividends paid in lieu of cash, as well as cash dividend reinvestment programs where firms retain dividends for additional purchases of company stock, would be beneficial.[6] However, although a potential transaction expense is avoided, these corporate programs eliminate the investor's choice of reinvestment and they generate odd-lot share holdings which may increase future selling costs. These drawbacks are less severe when additional funds are generally flowing into the portfolio and all security positions are viewed initially as long-term commitments.

When cash outflows are required partial liquidation becomes necessary. In this case it is desirable to maintain a high degree of diversification while also minimizing current tax liability. Unfortunately, these two objectives are usually in conflict. Diversification is impaired when undue concentration in one or more securities exists. Concentration occurs when one security has appreciated more rapidly in the past than others in the portfolio. But selling

[5] Henry A. Latané and William E. Young, "Test of Portfolio Building Rules," *Journal of Finance* 24, no. 4 (September 1969): 595–613.

[6] The nature and increasing popularity of corporate cash dividend reinvestment programs were noted in Chapter 6.

a portion of securities that have realized a large return produces the greatest possible capital gains tax liability. The opposite strategy, selling an unprofitable position, particularly if it is held less than one year, would have favorable tax consequences.[7] But securities that have appreciated less in value than the portfolio average will have shrunk proportionally over time, and their partial liquidation increases concentration of wealth in the remaining investments. The investor therefore faces a trade-off between increased unsystematic portfolio risk on one hand and a larger current tax liability on the other. Generally, when a portfolio is reasonably well-diversified at the outset a strategy having more favorable tax consequences will be optimal because small increases in unsystematic risk will have only a slight impact on total portfolio risk. When the portfolio is revised and upgraded, full diversification can be restored.

PORTFOLIO UPGRADING

Upgrading a portfolio involves the buying and selling of securities in response to the evaluation of new information. New information may impact on one security's prospects for future performance or it may lead to major changes in the size and composition of the entire portfolio. Important new information may be received at any time and data should be analyzed regularly in the process of systematic investment evaluation and revision.

Whatever the dimension of upgrading implied, the process of portfolio revision is illustrated in Figure 17.2. Over time, optimal portfolios will shift in return and risk space in accordance with changes in expectations about security returns, standard deviations, and covariances. Consider a portfolio which was purchased because it was perceived to be optimal where revised expectations now result in a new and different "optimal" portfolio, one which is superior in terms of risk-adjusted return. The currently owned portfolio, shown in Figure 17.2 as portfolio *W*, has shifted adversely from its original position because of changes in its composition and adjusted expectations. Any portfolio lying above a ray drawn from the current risk-free rate through *W*, including *X*, *Y*, and *Z*, would be an improvement. Portfolio *Z* is now the "optimal" portfolio as formerly described in Chapter 14 (see portfolio *M* on Figure 14.8).

From Figure 17.2, the problem of portfolio revision is clear. An investor who currently owns portfolio *W* would prefer to own portfolio *Z*. Unfortunately, however, taxes and transaction costs will be incurred in transforming *W* to *Z*. Accordingly, an analysis of the expected benefit of the transaction, in relation to its cost, is the central issue of portfolio revision. Intuitively, differences in composition between portfolios *W* and *Z* should seldom

[7] Capital losses realized within one year may be used in full to offset capital gains or ordinary income up to specified limits. Losses on positions held over one year receive only half value in offsetting income. For futures, the period is six months. The implications of tax treatment are reviewed in the next chapter.

Figure 17.2
Current, Interim, and Optimal Portfolios

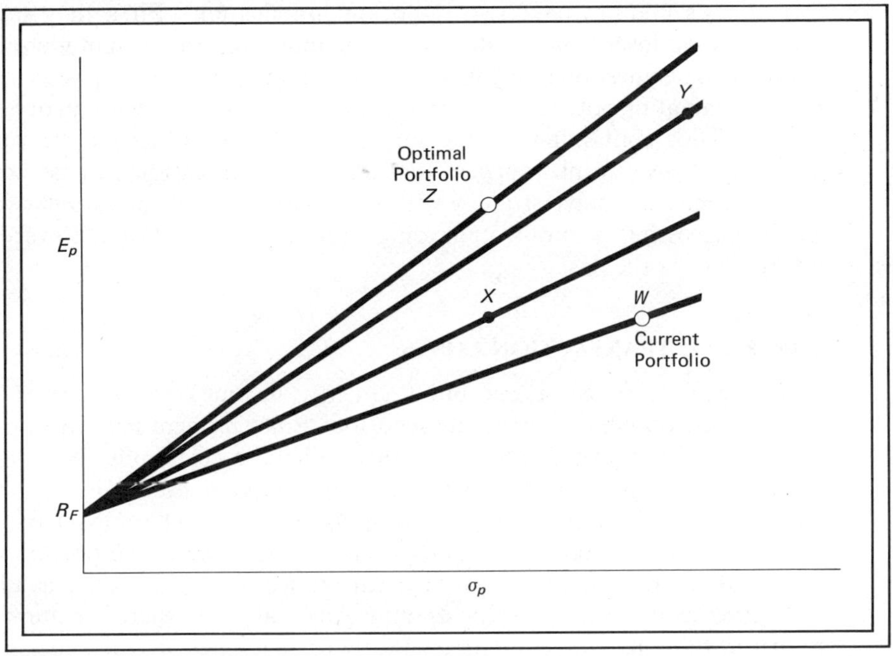

be extensive if initial expectations were reasonably accurate. Even if total costs exceed total benefits in moving to Z from W, a partial adjustment to some other portfolio (such as X or Y) may be justified. The potential benefits of revision, based solely upon observed portfolio performance, will be considered in the sections which follow; costs of revision will then be examined in detail and a benefit-cost sequential revision model will be introduced.

NAIVE REVISION. Robert Levy analyzed the upgrading of portfolios on the basis of "relative strength."[8] Levy tested the hypothesis that stocks which performed best in the recent past will continue to perform well in the future. Two hundred individual stocks were ranked by performance during the most recent six-month period and equal dollar amounts were assumed to be committed to the top securities. Portfolios ranging in size from 20 to 195 securities were then created every six months for a five-year period. After adjusting for transaction costs, only the 195-stock grouping outperformed the entire 200-stock population. The 195-security portfolio was the 200 portfolio less the five largest recent losers. Since at most 5 of 195 stocks changed every six

[8] Robert A. Levy, "The Principle of Portfolio Upgrading," *Industrial Management Review* 9, no. 2 (Fall 1967): 82–96.

months, transaction costs were low relative to smaller sized portfolios tested in the study.

Levy's findings have two important implications. First, they suggest that avoiding losers may in some cases be more important than identifying winners.[9] The question really is one of focus, and explicit emphasis on avoiding or eliminating potentially large negative yields would be a useful objective for portfolios containing a large number of securities. Second, and more generally, Levy's results suggest that simple extrapolation of past performance trends is a naive strategy with little if any positive investment value. To be successful, portfolio upgrading requires an orientation toward the future and not the past.

TAXES AND TRANSACTION COSTS

Brokerage fees, transfer taxes, and, frequently, income or capital gains taxes are the costs of selling and buying securities. Since prudent investment seeks maximum risk-adjusted *after-tax* return, all these costs must be fully accounted for in investment decision making. Individual federal tax liability and (negotiable) commissions vary among investors. The impact of taxes on revision may be considerable especially if the value of the portfolio has appreciated substantially. Current taxes reduce funds which are available for subsequent investment; postponing tax liabilities therefore improves return in the long run. Branch argues that the impact of year-end tax loss selling temporarily depresses prices of high risk securities which are already selling below recent price levels.[10] If this is true, it would represent another type of market centered special situation similar to those discussed in Chapter 10.

Portfolio rebalancing and upgrading most frequently involves the substitution of one risky security for another. To evaluate this "switching" operation requires complete specification of the new security's expected performance over a number of future periods. Using total percentage return over the extended horizon, to retain a single-period frame of reference, security switching is illustrated in Figure 17.3.[11] The figure assumes that a 100 percent gain has already been realized on a security which is currently held; the expected appreciation for that security is 27.6 percent over the next five

[9] This approach was also suggested by Charles Ellis, "The Loser's Game," *Financial Analysts Journal*, July–August 1975, pp. 19–26, and more recently in "Indexing Plus: By Avoiding Biggest Losers, You Can Easily Outperform the Stock Market," *The Wall Street Journal*, April 11, 1977, p. 24.

[10] Ben Branch, "A Tax Loss Trading Rule," *The Journal of Business*, April 1977, pp. 198–207.

[11] The discussion here appears to ignore possible differences in risk between the mutually exclusive securities. However, over an extended horizon of more than one period total return involves a compounded rate of periodic growth. Since growth is influenced by both period return and its variability, it is presumed that differences in risk are accounted for in extended-horizon expected returns.

Figure 17.3
Break-even Returns to Switching Securities: Text Example

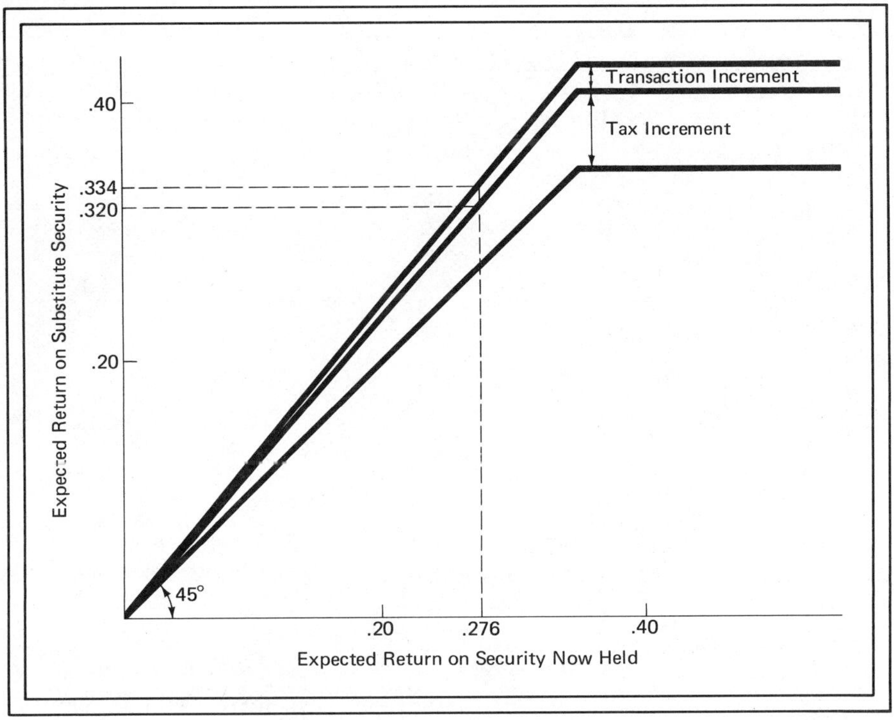

years,[12] the effective capital gains rate is 25 percent, and transaction expense is 1 percent.[13] The 45° line in Figure 17.3 recognizes that an investor would be indifferent between holding a security or trading it for another one of equal risk-adjusted expected return providing that switching is cost-free. The loss of reinvestment proceeds due to earlier payment of tax increases the slope of the break-even line and transaction costs increase it further. The five-year return of .276 is shown by the vertical broken line in the figure. Reading across from the horizontal broken line, a new security would have to yield 32 percent to provide the break-even return which just compensates for the current tax liability created by switching. Similarly, transaction costs raise the five-year break-even return to 33.4 percent. The methodology underlying the analysis of Figure 17.3 is developed in the following paragraphs.

[12] A 100 percent gain is not extreme. A security with an 11 percent rate of growth will double in value in seven years. If that rate of growth is sustained, the security would be worth eight times its original cost in 20 years.

[13] It is worth recalling that capital gains are taxed at one-half the investor's marginal ordinary income tax rate up to a maximum of 25 percent for capital gains not exceeding $50,000. Profits exceeding $50,000 may be taxed at rates up to 35 percent.

Table 17.3
Break-even Returns (assuming realized appreciation of 100 percent subject to a 25 percent tax rate)

Extended Horizon	*Extended Horizon*	
E[R(old)] (*1*)	*Tax Deferred*[a] (*2*)	*Tax Payable*[b] (*3*)
.04	.189	.046
.08	.234	.091
.12	.280	.137
.20	.371	.229
.30	.486	.343
.40	.600	.457
.60	.829	.686
.80	1.057	.914
1.00	1.286	1.143

[a] Calculated from

$$1 + E[R(\text{new})] = V\left[\frac{1 + E[R(\text{old})]}{1 + (V - 1)(1 - t_x)}\right]$$

where V = ratio of current to original value of stock now held and t_x = tax rate applicable on stock if it is sold.

[b] Calculated from Equation 17.1.

BREAK-EVEN RETURNS. Every individual case involves a different break-even analysis because the slopes of the lines in Figure 17.3 are unique to the circumstances involved. Required rates of return on prospective securities which make switching worthwhile under a limited but illustrative number of assumptions about expected return and time are given in Table 17.3. The values are only correct for a capital gains tax of 25 percent, zero transaction costs, and 100 percent capital appreciation in the security which is currently held. Column 2 of Table 17.3 assumes that no transactions take place at the end of the extended horizon; future tax liability is assumed to be indefinitely deferred. The general formula for calculating break-even returns under this assumption is also provided in the table. It should be noted that column 2 values are extremes because only in rare instances can taxes be put off indefinitely. When taxes are assumed to be due and payable at the end of the extended period, the differential return which is necessary to make switching attractive is smaller. End-of-period tax liability is the more likely case, and these values are given in column 3. To generalize the column 3 case, defining total return over the future horizon for current and prospective securities as $E[R(\text{old})]$ and $E[R(\text{new})]$, the ratio of current to original value of the stock now held as V, and the tax rate as t_x, switching becomes warranted when:

$$E[R(\text{new})] > E[R(\text{old})]\left[\frac{V}{V - t_x(V - 1)}\right] \tag{17.1}$$

For a security which has increased in price from \$7.50 to \$15.00 per share with dividends reinvested, $V = \$15.00/\$7.50$ or 2.00. With an expected aggregate return over an extended three-year period of 30 percent, and a 25 percent capital gains tax, switching would be profitable if the new opportunity earned a three-year rate of return in excess of 34.3 percent:

$$E[R(\text{new})] > .30\left[\frac{2.00}{2.00 - .25(2.0 - 1.0)}\right] = .343$$

This is the minimum return which is required if the investor plans to sell either security after three years. If the investor planned to hold the chosen security indefinitely, then by the column 1 formula provided in Table 17.3 the break-even rate on the new stock would be .486.[14] The higher rate reflects indefinite deferral of the tax liability on the security which is currently owned; if liquidation is intended, switching merely shifts the tax liability forward in time. A comparison of the two columns of Table 17.3 illustrates the critical role which assumptions about future actions have on current decisions.

Although it is not shown in the table, the break-even differential is directly related to realized appreciation (measured by V) because lesser tax liabilities on currently held investments make a greater portion of realized gains available for reinvestment. Additionally, it should be noted that when return has been negative switching may be advantageous even if the new security had a lower expected return. This would occur if the sale of a security resulted in a tax credit, freeing funds for reinvestment. Year-end tax switching is a well-publicized activity on Wall Street and the value of this strategy should be assessed by every investor. Additional tax considerations with respect to gains and losses are considered in the next chapter.

TRANSACTION COSTS. Transaction costs complicate the break-even formula; they also raise performance standards necessary to make switching attractive. With all transaction costs, brokerage fees, and transfer taxes expressed as a percentage of security value, a complete criterion for switching can be stated.[15] Defining f as the percentage transaction cost of buying or selling, the formula is:

$$E[R(\text{new})] > E[R(\text{old})] \times \left[\frac{V}{V(1-f)^2 - t_x(V-1)(1-f)} + \frac{f(2-f)}{(1-f)(1-t_x[f])}\right] \quad (17.2)$$

[14] By the formula in Table 17.3 the rate is:

$$1 + E[R(\text{new})] = 2\left[\frac{1.30}{1 + (1)(.75)}\right] = 2.60/1.75 = 1.486$$

After three years the securities are presumed to grow at equal rates.

[15] Charles C. Holt and John P. Shelton, "The Implications of the Capital Gains Tax for Investment Decision," *Journal of Finance*, December 1961, pp. 559–580.

Adding a total transaction cost of 2 percent to the example used to illustrate Equation 17.1 raises the minimum necessary extended horizon return to .399:

$$.30\left[\frac{2.0}{2.0(1-.02)^2-.25(2.0-1.0)(1-.02)}\right]+\left[\frac{.02(2-.02)}{(1-.02)(1-.20[.02])}\right]$$
$$=.30(1.194)+.041=.399$$

In other words, a new security must appreciate more than 39.9 percent, as opposed to the previous minimum return of 34.4 percent, to make switching attractive. Transaction costs have significantly increased performance demands upon the new security, even though they appear to be modest in size and they are amortized over a relatively long period of time.

Switching is a useful way of comparing new opportunities with current security positions and investors commonly tend to think in terms of paired relationships. Nevertheless, although it clearly shows the importance of cost considerations, the pairing process is not a desirable revision procedure. Just because stock ABC is not expected to earn enough to justify selling stock EFG does not necessarily mean that ABC should not be bought or that EFG should not be sold. Instead each decision must be evaluated on its own merit in terms of the effect on portfolio risk and return. The next section demonstrates a systematic procedure for portfolio revision which effectively implements the theory of portfolio building within the confines of varying cost considerations.

BENEFIT-COST REVISION STRATEGY

Previous chapters have been concerned with the identification of an optimal portfolio in terms of future return and risk. Given this efficient portfolio and a currently held portfolio which appears to be decidedly inefficient, the problem illustrated in Figure 17.2 is one of moving toward the desired position. But optimal portfolio *Z* was identified under the assumption that there are no cost differentials.[16] Given variations in tax and transaction costs when a portfolio is revised, the optimal revision would be some portfolio, such as *X* or *Y* (referring again to Figure 17.2), between *Z* and existing portfolio *W*.

Benefit-cost revision procedures are a sequential analysis of all changes necessary to progress from an existing portfolio to the new optimal one. The process occurs one step at a time where each decision involves only one security. With the opportunity to borrow or lend at known rates of interest, any desired level of risk can be achieved in the process of revising the existing

[16] More accurately, to ignore costs is to presume that they are zero, or at least the same, for all investments. The assumption is closest to reality when one is starting out with cash but even then the costs of buying stocks compared to those of buying bonds, risk-free claims, and other investments will be varied and they will have an impact on realized return.

portfolio. By limiting revision to the most advantageous changes, portfolios can be upgraded without excessive turnover. The value of an orderly and sequential revision strategy is the attainment of substantially higher expected return without excessive transaction costs. The application of benefit-cost procedures to every potential transaction is consistent with the methods most commonly taken in practice: investment managers tend to focus on individual transactions. In practice, however, insufficient consideration is sometimes given to systematic benefit-cost analysis.[17]

Revision benefit is measured as the dollar improvement in risk-equivalent expected portfolio return. Defining current portfolio dollar value V_p, unrevised return $E(R_p)$, and revised return $E(R_{pi})$, where $E(R_{pi})$ results from a change in the holdings of security i adjusted through borrowing and lending to the *same risk level*, the benefit of revising the security i position is represented by:

$$B[\Delta_i] = V_p[E(R_{pi}) - E(R_p)] \tag{17.3}$$

Similarly, the total cost of changing the position in security i involves transaction costs and, in the case of a sale, tax costs which were identified in the last section. Defining the market value of security i in the existing portfolio as M_i and with transaction costs defined again as a percentage, f, of market value, the cost of a purchase (+) can be expressed as:

$$C[\Delta_i^+] = M_i(f) \tag{17.4}$$

In the case of a sale (−), cost includes the tax liability. Defining the original gross cost of security i as M_{i0} and tax rate as t_x, total dollar cost of sales is:

$$C[\Delta_i^-] = [M_i(1 - f) - M_{i0}]t_x + M_i f \tag{17.5}$$

The first term within brackets is the percentage of market value lost to taxes and the second, as before, is the loss due to transaction expenses.

Having identified benefit and cost values for all securities which are candidates for potential sale or acquisition, the decision rule is:

$$\text{Max}\,\frac{B[\Delta_i]}{C[\Delta_i]} > 1.0 \tag{17.6}$$

where $B[\Delta_i]$ represents the dollar benefit of revising the position in security i and $C[\Delta_i]$ represents the cost of revision. If the maximum ratio of all possible changes is less than 1.00, no change should be made. If one or more ratios exceed 1.00, the individual change yielding the largest ratio should be made. Then, assuming that other ratios also exceed 1.00, the procedure is repeated where the new expected portfolio return, reflecting the preceding

[17] Critically, much of the problem stems from a lack of a common investment horizon for all securities. In practice some investments are undertaken for "long-term" potential while others are purchased for their "short-run" strength. Without a reasonable and common planning horizon, performance measurement and revision procedures are denied their full potential contribution to investment performance.

Table 17.4
Benefit-Cost Analysis

Stock	Change	Value Relative (V)	Transaction Expense (f)	\$ Cost (by Eq. 17.4 or 17.5)	\$ Benefit (by Eq. 17.3)	Ratio (by Eq. 17.6)
a	Sell	2.0	.02	2800[a]	2500[b]	.89
b	Buy	—	.02	300	900	3.00
c	Sell	.95	.03	89	1800	20.28

[a] For example, stock a which cost \$10,000 is now expected to be worth \$20,000 in a \$100,000 portfolio. By Equation 17.5, the cost of its sale with a 25 percent tax rate and 2 percent transaction cost would be [\$20,000(1 − .02) − \$10,000].25 + \$20,000(.02) = \$2800.

[b] Continuing the example, if the sale of stock a is expected to have a one-period effect of raising the risk-equivalent portfolio return from its current level of 9 percent to 11.5 percent, benefits would then be \$100,000[.115 − .09] = \$2500.

revision, is substituted for $E(R_p)$ in Equation 17.3. Portfolio values must be recalculated after each step in the revision process because every change in portfolio mix alters covariances and the desirability of additional revisions may be affected. This sequential procedure continues until no change yields a benefit-cost ratio in excess of 1.00. It is important to emphasize that revision involves both purchases and sales and both currently held and prospective securities. By this procedure the existing portfolio will converge on the optimal portfolio in the manner illustrated in Figure 17.2.

The basic mechanics of benefit-cost analysis can be illustrated through an example which is consistent with the portfolios shown in Figure 17.2. In that figure an investor who owns inefficient portfolio W would instead prefer efficient portfolio Z. In Table 17.4, portfolio Z is assumed to differ from W in that it contains one stock which is not in W and it omits two stocks which are in W. The potential costs and benefits of each change have been calculated by use of Equations 17.3–17.5. The resulting benefit-cost relationships are given in Table 17.4. The change with the largest benefit per unit of cost is the sale of stock c from portfolio W. The resulting portfolio is represented as portfolio X in Figure 17.2.

In examining the costs and benefits of selling stock *c*, three things should be noted:

1. The cost is very low. Selling expense is modest because the stock is currently held at a loss and the sale results in a tax credit that in this instance very nearly offsets transaction costs.[18]

[18] Stock c was assumed to cost \$10,000 originally; its sale involves the following expense: [9500(.97) − 10,000](.25) + 9500(.03) = −196.25 + 285.00 = 88.75. If the tax credit were much larger than 196.25, the "cost" of sale would be negative. This is both possible and consistent with the discussion in the chapter. But if the investor retained high expectations concerning the future potential of the stock, the beneficial effect of its sale would also be negative. In this very special case, if the loss of potential benefits exceeds the gain from sale, the stock should be retained. When the sale of a security implies both negative cost and positive benefit, the stock should be sold from the portfolio.

Figure 17.4
Risk Equivalent Return

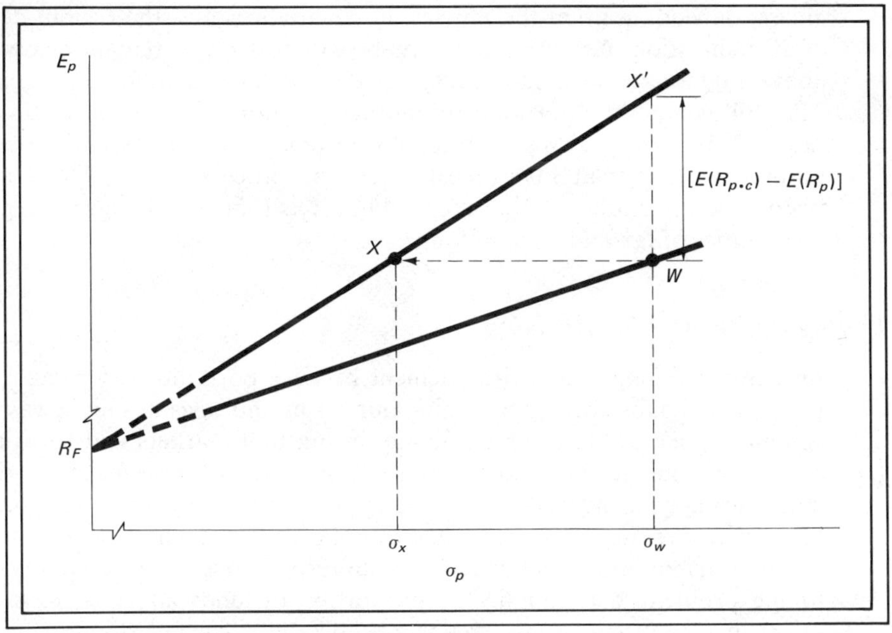

2. Benefits were based on the added return for a portfolio of *equal risk* to W. But the sale of stock c (with proceeds held as a risk-free investment) involves a reduction of actual risk. This is illustrated in Figure 17.4: improvement reflects the reduction of risk but benefit is measured in terms of risk-equivalent return. Risk-equivalent return is obtained by estimating the return and risk of portfolio X (portfolio W without stock c) and then levering X, borrowing along a line extrapolated from the risk-free rate through X. Borrowing, with proceeds invested in additional amounts of portfolio X, continues to point X' where the risk level is the same as the original portfolio W.[19] The difference between the return expected from levered portfolio X', labeled $E(R_{p.c})$ on Figure 17.4, and portfolio W, labeled $E(R_p)$, measures the benefit of selling stock c, according to the benefit expression given by Equation 17.3.
3. The single-period return and risk illustrated in Figures 17.2 and 17.4 is probably smaller than the extended horizon used to solve the benefit-cost equations. Specifically, return and risk corresponds to the single forecasting period defined in previous chapters. As suggested earlier in this chapter, adequate specification of benefits and costs for the purpose of revision may require projections beyond one period to an extended horizon.

Having selected the sale of stock c as the best change, the other two positions would then be reevaluated. Although their cost functions remain

[19] It is unlikely that an investor would actually lever portfolio X to X'; since the risk of portfolio W may no longer be relevant, there would be no reason for doing that. For purposes of measurement, however, the risk level of existing portfolio W serves as a point of reference. To measure benefit in one dimension based upon the change in expected return, the new portfolio X must first be adjusted to the same risk level as portfolio W.

unchanged, benefits will now be based on the relationship which each prospective change has to portfolio X. Benefits may increase or they may decrease, depending upon the impact on covariances and the overall degree of diversification. Assuming that new benefit-cost ratios remain below and above 1.00 for stocks a and b, respectively, the latter should be purchased. This will change the portfolio to another position—say, point Y—in Figure 17.2. If another reappraisal, based on portfolio Y, finds that stock a's ratio is still less than 1.00, then the revision process is complete. The investor's best portfolio would be Y, and not Z as Figure 17.2 suggested, given the realities of tax and transaction costs.

Timing and Portfolio Revision

Investment timing is a critical element because portfolio performance can be improved substantially by timing purchases and sales in such a way that common stock holdings predominate during bull markets and short-term debt (cash equivalents) or alternative debt-type or other securities predominate during bear markets. Profitable opportunities exist for bonds, futures, options, real estate, and other categories of investment where price behavior differs from common stock behavior with respect to level or variability. The timing problem, determining the proportion of funds allocated to investments in each category, is a "major mix" decision. The decision to vary this mix expands the investment problem from the level of individual security selection to the choice among different types of investment under differing economic conditions. The selection of attractive securities within each investment category is inadequate: in addition, an investor must concurrently analyze and select the best combination of investment categories to realize the highest possible risk-adjusted return.

For a total of m different investment categories, the market timing problem becomes one of varying the allocation of wealth among competing portfolios, each comprised of securities from different investment categories j. Notationally, with all wealth invested, the problem can be formulated as

$$1.0 = \sum_{j=1}^{m} X_j \tag{17.7}$$

where X_j is the percentage of wealth allocated to the best combination (portfolio) of securities in investment category j. This "major mix" concept was previously introduced in Chapter 14 for the two-category case of common stocks and a risk-free investment. However, in the one-period portfolio framework which was introduced there, timing was not a relevant consideration and the risk-free alternative was simply treated as another individual security. But in an ongoing situation, and with the explicit recognition of all investment alternatives, the major mix decision is an important intermediate step in the investment management process. Figure 17.5 illustrates the major mix problem during hypothetical bull and bear market

Figure 17.5
Optimal Portfolios in Bull and Bear Markets

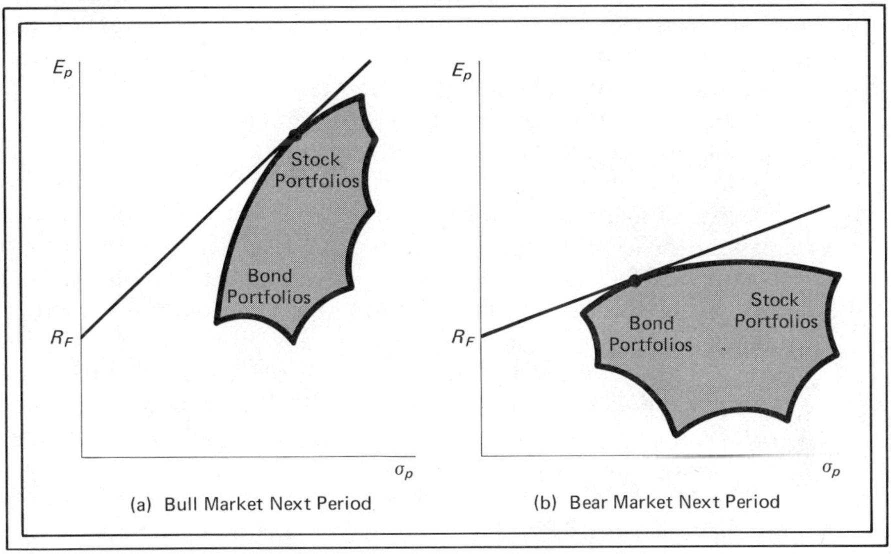

stages. In bullish markets, a 100 percent common stock position is probably optimal, as shown in part (a) of the figure. Under bearish conditions, on the other hand, a preferred portfolio would have larger proportions of debt and/or other types of securities. An accurate prediction of bull and bear market periods, if that were possible, would produce superior portfolio performance in terms of both greater return and lesser risk.

Given the reality of varying market conditions, investment timing can be approached either passively or actively. Three distinct approaches to timing are (1) ignoring the problem, (2) aggressive timing policies, and (3) defensive timing policies. The proper approach for any investment manager depends upon the confidence placed in market predictions and the manager's prevailing attitude toward risk. A high degree of confidence, based upon success in the past, may encourage an aggressive strategy in predicting major market cycles. Lesser confidence and/or a higher degree of risk aversion warrants some defensive strategy which is designed to minimize the effect of market cycles on portfolio value. Under some circumstances, including the acceptance of strong-form pricing efficiency, the investment manager may choose to ignore timing entirely while pursuing an investment policy which is independent of market conditions.

IGNORING THE PROBLEM

An investment manager who achieves superior portfolio performance through judgmental timing must be successful in predicting major changes in market prices. Common stocks have appreciated at an average rate of 7 to 10 percent per year; assuming that this average continues, 7 to 10 percent would be the expected range of performance under a naive buy and hold strategy. In markets where different types of securities are properly valued to reflect risk differentials at all times, attempts to react to market timing would only generate transaction costs which would lower performance below the level realized under a buy and hold strategy.

Ignoring the problem is not the same thing as the *buy and hold policy;* when timing is ignored, portfolio revision is accomplished without any consideration of significant market realignments. Buy and hold, in contrast, implies no revision at all; it assumes that financial markets are so completely price efficient that the cost associated with upgrading activities cannot be justified. In its extreme form, buy and hold reduces investment management to a one-time activity where any given portfolio is permitted to drift aimlessly with respect to return and risk characteristics. A modified buy and hold policy, where trading is permitted to maintain a constant level of risk, is a portfolio maintenance plan where restraint on trading may cause profitable opportunities to be overlooked.

The likelihood of profiting from a market timing strategy was explored by William Sharpe.[20] Sharpe observed that a perfect timing record in allocating funds among common stocks and short-term risk-free debt from 1946 to 1972 would have provided a 15.7 percent rate of capital growth compared with the 7.1 percent realized on common stocks during that period. The relationship between imperfect predictive accuracy and rate of return was then considered. A one-year predictive period was selected with the objective of classifying common stock performance in the coming year as "good" or "bad." Sharpe's findings are summarized in Figure 17.6, which relates the annual advantage of market timing with predictive accuracy. The sensitivity between yield and forecasting error is striking: correct identification of good and bad years must occur roughly three times out of four just to match the performance realized under a buy and hold strategy. Specifically, reading from the broken lines on Figure 17.6, a 1 percent excess annual return with equivalent risk required correct predictions 79 percent of the time. To achieve a long-run return which was 1 percent greater than the return under buy and hold required correct prediction of market direction 88 percent of the time. These demanding standards occurred because of transaction costs and the loss of capital appreciation when an unfavorable market prediction proved to be incorrect. However, Sharpe's methodology is inflexible in that a timing decision is required at a fixed time each year. A study by Russell Fuller suggests that the rewards and probabilities of successful timing improve by removing the holding period constraint. Fuller concludes that substantial benefits can result from timing and that the

[20] William F. Sharpe, "Likely Gains from Market Timing," *Financial Analysts Journal*, March–April 1975, pp. 60–69.

Figure 17.6
Annual Return Advantage from Market Timing

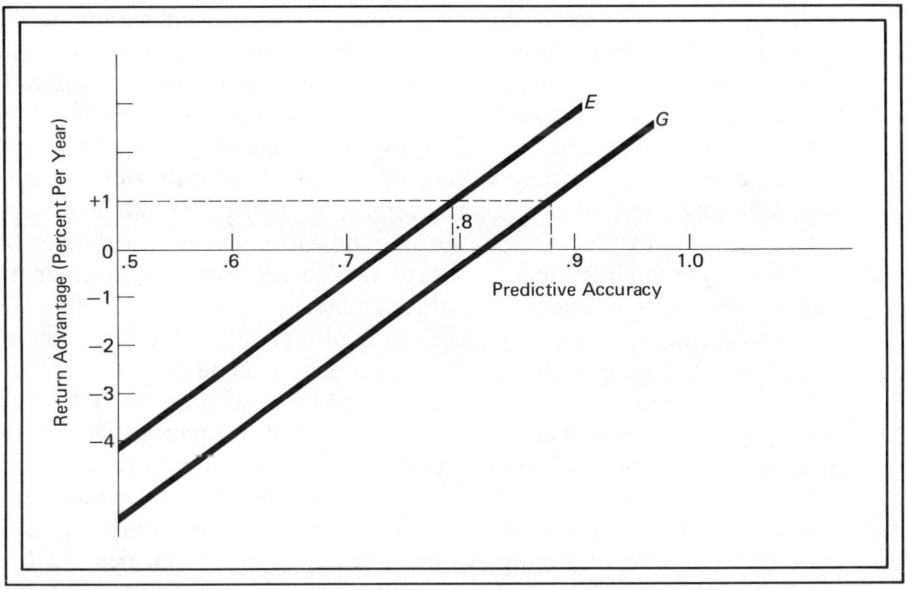

E is expected return, versus a mixture of stocks and cash equivalents with an equal standard deviation. *G* is geometric mean return, versus buying and holding stocks.

Source: W. F. Sharpe, "Likely Gains from Market Timing," *Financial Analysts Journal*, March–April 1975, p. 66.

timing of purchases is more critical than the timing of sales, especially when the investment horizon extends over many years.[21]

AGGRESSIVE TIMING POLICIES

Despite the discouraging implications of the Sharpe study, aggressive investors may benefit from decisions which are influenced by market timing considerations. For example, interim cash flows can be invested with recognition of timing factors; since transaction costs would be incurred in any event, the incremental cost of timing decisions would be reduced. Moreover, an investor may indeed be able to predict correctly major market variations with sufficient accuracy to justify timing strategies. Finally, although the Sharpe study required a prediction every year, investors may react to market cycles on a longer and more irregular basis.

[21] Russell J. Fuller, "Timing versus Selection: Which Holds the Key," *Journal of Portfolio Management*, Winter 1977, pp. 53–59.

MAJOR INDICATORS OF MARKET CYCLES. A tool which is frequently used to identify market peaks and troughs is the long-run moving average. This average is usually calculated from the preceding 180 to 200 daily values for some major index such as the Standard and Poor's "500" common stock index or the New York Stock Exchange index. The relevant index is interpreted by the ratio of current value to long-run moving average value. The key ratio of 1.00 indicates that the current level just equals the moving average. When the ratio rises above 1.00 from a lower position, it is interpreted as an indication of market strength; when the ratio moves in the opposite direction, falling below 1.00, a market decline is indicated. The moving average index has proven to be a helpful leading indicator of market behavior over the past 25 years. Unfortunately, its relevance with respect to future market behavior can be determined only after the fact.

Other aids of a basically technical nature are available for forecasting market trends. Some, including the length of skirt hemlines or astrological phases of the moon, can readily be dismissed by the serious analyst. Others, including the moving average described in the above paragraph and such indicators as the ratio of security price advances to security price declines, may provide helpful insights. Ultimately, the judgment of current and future market conditions rests with the analyst's perception of future events and their likelihood of becoming reality. Market timing strategies are a by-product of this fundamental forecasting activity.

DEFENSIVE TIMING POLICIES

In the absence of any strong belief concerning future market trends and cycles, an investment manager may attempt to minimize the impact of timing factors on long-run investment value. Any one of several plans which are designed to allocate funds systematically among major investment categories can be used. For example, portfolio revision may be combined with some strategy which allocates funds among common stocks and bonds according to a predetermined ratio or dollar value. Variable ratio, constant ratio, constant dollar, and dollar-cost averaging are alternative strategies which are available to an investor seeking relief from the timing problem. Dollar-cost averaging assumes that the investor has a fixed amount of savings available for investment each period; with fixed investment the number of shares purchased varies over the cycle. The other plans accommodate but do not require the investment of interim savings. Each plan is a mechanistic formula which is designed to reduce if not to eliminate the adverse consequences of cyclical price fluctuations. They are more effective under widely fluctuating and generally trendless conditions. Although they were popular when they were first publicized in the late 1930s, defensive plans have tended to lower return more proportionally than the lowering of risk in the generally rising markets of the 1950s and 1960s. Defensive plans have not worked well and for that reason they have not been popular recently.

Summary

Continuous investment management involves the evaluation of potential improvements in an existing portfolio. The need to revise portfolios occurs because investments and expectations both change over time. A portfolio which once appeared to be optimal may seem to be decidedly inferior at a later time. Unfortunately, however, portfolio improvement incurs certain costs as well as uncertain benefits. A systematic comparison of all costs relative to expected benefits provides a valid approach to portfolio revision.

The timing decision is but one dimension of the portfolio revision problem. The difficulty involved in solving the timing problem does not imply that forecasting is useless; instead, it suggests that investment decisions should be based upon expected trends in sales, earnings growth, and other conditions which are relevant to firm operations. The reallocation of savings among securities of the same general nature should be based upon expectations based upon fundamental characteristics. The reallocation of funds among different classes of investments, such as stocks versus bonds, is the essence of the timing problem. It requires considerable accuracy in forecasting interest rates, average price-earnings ratios, and other measures of relative performance to make this activity worthwhile.

Questions and Problems

1. Explain why there may be a difference between the optimal (efficient) portfolio as envisioned in Chapters 14 and 15 and the best portfolio for the investor based on procedures of portfolio revision.
2. What are the distinctions between rebalancing and upgrading investment portfolios?
3. Five years ago you purchased Howard Johnson's common stock at $8.00 per share. Its current price is now $12.50 and you expect a total return over the next two years of only 10 percent. Ramada Inn's stock, however, is expected to appreciate 25 percent over the same two-year period and possesses similar risk characteristics. Assuming a 25 percent capital gains tax, and the intention to hold either for two years, would switching be worthwhile? If a 2 percent transaction cost is considered would your answer change?
4. Can you think of any conditions whereby an investor would be better off selling one stock to buy another with a lower expected return?
5. Table 17.3 in the text illustrates break-even returns for switching in the case of 100 percent prior appreciation and a 25 percent tax rate. Assuming taxes are payable at the end of the forthcoming horizon, what happens to the level of additional return as (a) prior appreciation changes and (b) the tax rate changes?
6. Recalculate the values in Table 17.3 for expected return on the old security of 12 percent and 60 percent for the tax payable case with the added assumption of a 3 percent transaction cost. Comment on the impact of transaction costs in each case.
7. In Table 17.4 the example at the bottom (footnotes *a* and *b*) is based on the assumption that portfolio return rises to 11.5 percent. If the proceeds of selling stock a were invested risk free at 6 percent and this maintained the same level of risk as before, what does this imply about next period's expected return and risk for stock a?
8. What are the two basic ways investors have of earning above average returns? Discuss how these ways are related and how they may be implemented.
9. What are some weaknesses of formula plans as a defensive approach to timing and revision?

Selected References

PORTFOLIO REVISION

Chen, Andrew, Frank Jen, and Stanley Zionts, "The Optimal Portfolio Revision Policy," *Journal of Business* 44, no. 1 (January 1971): 51–61.

Fama, Eugene, "Multiperiod Consumption-Investment Decisions," *American Economic Review* 60, no. 1 (March 1970): 163–174.

Latané, Henry, Don Tuttle, and Charles Jones, *Security Analysis and Portfolio Management*, 2d ed. (New York: Ronald Press, 1975).

Schneller, Meir, "Mean-Variance Portfolio Composition When Investors' Revision Horizon is Very Long," *Journal of Finance* 30 (December 1975): 1293–1300.

Smith, Keith, "Alternative Procedures for Revising Investment Portfolios," *Journal of Financial and Quantitative Analysis* 3, no. 4 (December 1968): 371–404.

INVESTMENT TIMING AND PORTFOLIO REVISION

Branch, Ben, "The Predictive Power of Stock Market Indicators," *Journal of Financial and Quantitative Analysis*, June 1976, pp. 269–285.

Brown, Robert G., "Detection of Turning Points in a Time Series," *Decision Sciences* 2, no. 4 (October 1971): 383–404.

Christy, George A., "A Rationalization of the Stock-Bond Yield Spread," *Quarterly Review of Economics and Business* 7, no. 1 (Spring 1967): 63–70.

Cottle, C. C., and W. T. Whitman, *Investment Timing: The Formula Plan Approach* (New York: McGraw-Hill, 1953).

Dietz, Peter O., "Components of a Measurement Model: Rate of Return, Risk, and Timing," *Journal of Finance* 23, no. 2 (May 1968): 267–275.

Dince, Robert R., "Another View of Formula Planning," *Journal of Finance*, December 1964, pp. 678–688.

Haugen, Robert A., and A. James Heins, "Risk and the Rate of Return on Financial Assets: Some Old Wine in New Bottles," *Journal of Financial and Quantitative Analysis*, December 1975, pp. 775–784.

Latané, Henry, C. P. Jones, and R. D. Rieke, "Quarterly Earnings Reports and Subsequent Six-Month Holding Period Returns," *Journal of Business Research* 2 (April 1974): 119–132.

Niederhoffer, Victor, "The Analysis of World Events and Stock Prices," *Journal of Business* 44, no. 2 (April 1971): 193–219.

Okun, Arthur, "On the Appraisal of Cyclical Turning-Point Predictions," *Journal of Business* 33, no. 2 (April 1960): 101–120.

Sharpe, William F., "Bonds Versus Stocks: Some Lessons from Capital Market Theory," *Financial Analysts Journal*, November–December 1973, pp. 74–80.

———, "Likely Gains from Market Timing," *Financial Analysts Journal*, March–April 1975, pp. 60–69.

Wendt, Paul, "International Development and the Determination of Investment Policy," *Financial Analysts Journal*, January–February 1968, pp. 91+.

Chapter 18
Investment Management

The purpose of an investments course is to develop the techniques and abilities necessary for successful investment decision making. On a broader level, however, successful investment requires that all investment decisions carry out or at least be consistent with the investor's overall financial plan. Financial planning begins with a financial inventory of income earning ability, personal needs, and the willingness to bear risk. An honest estimate of current and future income streams and consumption patterns is a critical prerequisite to the planning process. Investment planning may then proceed sequentially through the following general activities:

1. Identifying current and future anticipated savings flows.
2. Allocating savings flows to competitive opportunities.
3. Managing the wealth accumulated through savings flows; preserving and redistributing capital as it appears to be necessary and prudent through time.

The focus of investment management is on the second and third activities where risk preferences in combination with identified investment opportunities structure investment choice and wealth allocation. In this final chapter three topics relating to the second and third activities listed above will be examined. The first is the systematic change in investor needs and preferences resulting from the process of aging. Following consideration of

Table 18.1
Life-Cycle Investment Priorities

Stage	Concern for: Liquidity	Income	Appreciation	Safety	Potential Tax Liability
Youth	High	Low	High	Low	Low
Middle age	Medium	Medium	Medium	Medium	Low
Retirement	Low	High	Low	High	Medium
Bequest	High	Low	Low	High	High

life-cycle investment patterns, the chapter will examine institutional investment services which provide an alternative to direct investment. Institutionally held portfolios represent a large portion of all savings. Professional management of other people's money is a major financial activity, with considerable resources within the financial community committed to security analysis activities. Finally, the tax environment and its implications for investment planning will be surveyed.

Life-Cycle Investment Priorities

Competitive investment opportunities differ in the characteristics of liquidity, income stream, appreciation, safety, and tax liability. Typically an investor's concern about each of these characteristics varies systematically over his or her lifetime. Long-run portfolio maintenance and revision discussed in the previous chapter will necessarily reflect adjustments resulting from changing priorities and needs of the investor, as well as adjustments for changing market conditions. The typical trend in emphasis of investment characteristics as one progresses from youth through middle age to retirement and beyond is suggested in Table 18.1. In the early career years preference is given to appreciation and liquidity. Middle age priorities are difficult to characterize because of differing financial needs and resources available at that time. As retirement approaches, greater concern is placed on income and safety of principal.

Portfolio characteristics of individual investors have been studied by Cohn. Lewellen, Lease, and Schlarbaum (hereafter (CLLS)).[1] A summary reflecting average individual portfolio holdings is provided in Table 18.2. Common stock is the largest component of the typical investor's assets,

[1] Richard A. Cohn, Wilber G. Lewellen, Ronald C. Lease, and Gary G. Schlarbaum, "Individual Investor Risk Aversion and Investment Portfolio Composition," *Journal of Finance* 30, no. 2 (May 1975): 605–620. Also Lewellen, Lease, and Schlarbaum, "The Individual Investor: Attributes and Attitudes," *Journal of Finance* 29, no. 2 (May 1974): 413–433.

Table 18.2
Individual Investor Portfolio Composition

Asset	*Percent Mean Portfolio Holdings*	*Percent Marketable Holdings*	*Percent with Zero Holdings*
Common stock	28.7	63.0	2
Preferred stock	1.4	3.1	69
Mutual fund shares	2.4	5.3	56
Government bonds	8.7	19.1	73
Corporate bonds	3.7	8.1	70
Stock options	.3	.7	87
Commodity futures	.3	.7	96
Savings accounts	6.3		16
Checking accounts	1.2		5
Home residence	11.7		18
Other real estate	15.8		51
Equity in own firm	13.5		79
Personal property	4.2		3
Other	1.8		84
Total	100.0	100.0[a]	

[a] Marketable holdings as percentage of total holdings 45.5 percent.

Source: Cohn, Lewellen, Lease, and Schlarbaum, "Individual Investor Risk Aversion and Investment Portfolio Composition," *Journal of Finance*, May 1975, p. 608.

followed by investment in real estate. All told, stocks and other marketable financial claims average nearly half of an investor's wealth. Nonmarket securities and property make up the rest. Because of the sampling techniques used in CLLS, the data in Table 18.2 are representative of the older and generally wealthier investor. In surveying these investors, CLLS learned that they generally adopted a fundamentalist long-run approach to investment decision making, used a market index as a benchmark to judge personal investment performance, and frequently supplemented direct security ownership with mutual fund shares and risk-free investments.

The concept of changing life-cycle priorities has several important implications for individual investors as well as the investment community as a whole. For individual investors, a major implication is the recognition that investment management is both a very personal and a constantly changing activity. Investment decision making, whether it is individual security selection or, alternatively, the choice among the professional investment services described in the next section, is best viewed as an adaptive and systematically changing process to implement a predetermined investment plan. Success, within the scope of such a plan, means achieving a return at least equal to and preferably in excess of the level achieved by the market after adjustment for risk differentials. On an aggregate level, it is worth noting that the average age of the population is shifting and will continue to shift upward in the foreseeable future as a result of demographic trends.

This phenomenon will probably alter the aggregate investment preferences of the financial community and cause a general realignment of investment values. A trend would be expected toward greater preference for large and stable dividends, tax-sheltered investments, and finally a reduced willingness to pay a premium for potential but uncertain growth.

Institutional Investment Services

Financial intermediaries offer a wide variety of institutional investment management services. These range from individual portfolio management offered by the trust departments of large commercial banks to group portfolio management provided by pension funds and insurance companies. The variety and popularity of institutional investment management does not necessarily mean, as some stock market officials have concluded, that individual investors are leaving the stock market. Instead it may suggest that many individuals have chosen professional management of their savings. At the end of 1975, institutions managed 40 percent of the value of all common stock in the United States while domestic investors held 54 percent and foreign investors held 6 percent.

INVESTMENT COMPANIES

The most direct and voluntary form of security investment substituting professional for individual choice is through purchase of investment company shares. The managers of investment companies use proceeds from the sale of fund shares to invest in other companies' securities in accordance with the stated policies and objectives of the investment company. Investment companies come in various types, sizes, and specializations, the majority of which will be discussed in the following paragraphs. All investment companies, numbering more than 1200 at the end of 1976, are subject to regulation by the Securities and Exchange Commission under the Investment Company Act of 1940 and the Investment Company Amendments Act of 1970. Persons advising others on securities transactions for compensation are also subject to regulation and registration under the Investment Advisors Act of 1940 and the aforementioned amendments act of 1970. These regulations, which cover the structure of fees, deceptive practices, financial reporting, and other areas, are designed to promote public confidence in the financial sector of the economy. The aggregate market value of assets controlled by investment companies exceeded $80 billion on June 30, 1976.

CLOSED-END INVESTMENT COMPANIES. A closed-end investment company issues shares in the same manner as a corporation. These shares are commonly equity but a closed-end fund may also issue bonds or other senior obligations. Investors purchase these shares as a new issue and they are subsequently traded as any other stock or bond. The market value of a fund's shares will fluctuate and at any time it may be above or below the net asset value of the investments held by the fund. When a closed fund's shares trade below net asset value it may reflect the market's belief that the securities held are worth less than the value claimed by the fund. A discount to asset value may also reflect a lack of liquidity for the fund's shares or simply pessimism by the market that the fund's investment portfolio taken as a whole is properly diversified and otherwise attractive. Regardless of the fund's share value, the capital available to the fund remains fixed unless a new public offering of additional stock is floated.

Closed-end funds have not grown in popularity as rapidly as other institutional investments. Over the past 30 years practically all of their growth has been through appreciation of portfolio values and not through new capital. As a result, their share of investment company assets shrank from 40 percent to a little more than 10 percent in recent years. As of June 30, 1976, the market value of their holdings was $9.3 billion. More aggressive management and more convenient and certain redemption procedures by open-end (mutual funds) companies are largely responsible for the decline in importance of closed-end funds.

A special category of closed-end funds is known as *dual funds.* Dual funds are of limited life, generally 15 years, and they offer the investor a choice of income shares or capital shares. Income shares comprise half the fund's capital and they receive all of the fund's dividend income. Income shareholders are guaranteed payments at minimum rate and should arrearages occur they are paid upon liquidation. Capital shareholders receive (only) the proceeds remaining at liquidation after income shareholders are satisfied, which would include any capital gains. There is a natural conflict of interest between capital and income shareholders which makes the management of dual funds a difficult task. As a result dual funds have not grown in popularity or number since their introduction in 1967.

OPEN-END INVESTMENT COMPANIES (MUTUAL FUNDS). Open-end investment companies, known as mutual funds, continuously stand ready to offer or redeem their own shares based on their current asset value. Net asset values are usually calculated twice a day, and redemption or sales value is based on the first calculation after the order is received. Ease of redemption is an attractive feature to investors, and it insures that management will remain sensitive to the needs and desires of its shareholders to insure a sufficient supply of investment capital. Most mutual funds (over 500) are "load funds" where the buyer pays a premium as high as 9 percent of asset value at the time of purchase as a sales charge. No-load funds sell shares directly to the public, thereby eliminating sales expenses. Since there appears to be no discernible difference in the performance of load versus no-load funds, a mutual fund buyer should probably search and select from the approximately 250 no-load funds currently available. The purchase of mutual funds through a broker or other advisor results in added transaction costs. Both load and no-load funds charge an annual fee based on the value of assets managed; these fees average three-tenths of 1 percent of net asset value.[2]

About 70 percent of all mutual funds offer investors an exclusive portfolio of common stocks. Many of these are extensively diversified while others concentrate on specific characteristics including growth, dividends, industry, country of origin, or countercyclical characteristics. Other funds "balance" their investments among bonds and stocks or they are restricted to bonds and preferred stock, tax-exempt securities, money market issues, or other specialties.[3] The market value of all mutual fund assets on June 30, 1976, was about $57 billion.

Mutual funds vary widely in size. While the majority of the more than five hundred funds in existence are valued at $10 million dollars or less, at least seven funds have assets in excess of $1 billion.[4] There appear to be some economies of scale in mutual fund operations. For every 1 percent increase in the size of assets, on average, expenses rise only seven-tenths of 1 percent. However, there is no evidence that large funds perform better or worse than smaller ones. In recent years the performance of mutual funds has not been outstanding. Many investors during the 1960s undoubtedly selected mutual funds on the assumption that professional management could achieve superior results. While professionally managed portfolios may do slightly better on a before-cost basis, costs have generally exceeded benefits. As a result mutual funds have an overall record to date which is slightly worse than that of the market as a whole.

Aside from management fees and loading costs, an important factor contributing to below average mutual fund performance has been high transaction costs resulting from aggressive trading practices. Historically mutual funds have had greater turnover than other institutional or individual investors, averaging 35 to 50 percent per year compared with 20 percent for other groups of investors. Aggressive capital gains oriented funds have had the highest turnover and in the early to mid 1970s they also realized the poorest return. Because of this, under generally bearish market conditions, net redemption of mutual fund shares has recently been greatest for aggressively

[2] Some mutual funds charge a redemption fee of up to 1 percent when sales are redeemed. Again, these costs should be considered by potential buyers.

[3] One special type is tax-free exchange funds. Tax-free exchange funds are formed by accepting securities from individual investors in exchange for shares in the fund. Under Section 351 of the Internal Revenue Code this one-time transaction permits an investor with sizable capital gains concentrated in a few securities to achieve broad diversification through the fund shares while postponing capital gains tax payment.

[4] The modest number of very large mutual funds and the large number of small ones means that mutual fund assets are highly concentrated. Thus the five largest funds (1 percent of total) hold 25 percent of assets and the top 25 funds hold 76 percent of all mutual fund assets. A detailed account of mutual funds and other institutional investors as of 1970 is found in the *Institutional Investor Study Report of the Securities and Exchange Commission* (92nd Congress, 1st Session), March 10, 1971.

managed stock funds.[5] In very recent periods the trading activity of mutual funds was less than in earlier years.

Mutual fund performance has been studied by William Sharpe, Michael Jensen, and others.[6] Additionally, the individual and collective performance of all mutual funds is monitored and reported by Wiesenberger Services. The Wiesenberger publication *Investment Companies*, available in larger libraries and by subscription (about $125 per year), provides a comprehensive survey, analysis, and explanation of all aspects of mutual fund operation. From these various studies and reports, mutual fund performance may be summarized by the following statements:

1. There are no persistently outstanding performers within the mutual fund industry. No management group exhibits a monopoly on superior research or inside information.
2. Mutual funds do an excellent job of attaining their stated risk objectives. Funds that emphasize safety of principal purchase only low-risk investments, and funds stating their intention to assume necessary risks for potential sizable capital gains invest in risky securities.
3. After all costs are considered, average mutual fund return—adjusted for risk—is slightly less than the yield that would be expected from broadly diversified and randomly selected portfolios held without revision.
4. On average mutual funds and other institutional investors held somewhat less risky portfolios than the market as a whole. Thus individual investors, as a group, must hold portfolios with higher than average risk.

Figure 18.1 illustrates the features outlined above. On balance they show that mutual funds have both good and bad features and their purchase should depend on the investor's particular needs and preferences. Investors who have the capability of selecting, on average, undervalued securities and who diversify adequately should have portfolios plotting above capital market line R_FM in Figure 18.1.

Almost all mutual funds are regulated investment companies for tax purposes where their income is passed directly to the shareholder without corporate tax. The tax exemption is based on the principle that shareholders should not gain or lose in tax liability by virtue of using an investment company rather than investing funds directly. Each year mutual funds send their stockholders a copy of the informational statement sent to the Internal Revenue Service. The statement shows the individual shareholder's portion of all capital gain and dividend distributions which, depending on the nature

[5] Redemptions of mutual fund shares have exceeded new sales since 1972 (1972–1976). In the first nine months of 1976, $2.67 billion equaling 104 percent of the $2.56 billion in net redemptions, came from mutual funds classified as having a growth orientation. Balanced, income, and bond funds had more sales than redemptions in the same period.

[6] William F. Sharpe, "Mutual Fund Performance," Part 2 *Journal of Business*, January 1966, pp. 119–138; Michael C. Jensen, "The Performance of Mutual Funds in the Period 1945–1964," *Journal of Finance*, May 1968, pp. 389–416; John C. Bogie, "Mutual Fund Performance Evaluation," *Financial Analysts Journal*, November–December 1970, pp. 25–33; Irwin Friend, Marshall Blume, and Jean Crockett, *Mutual Funds and Other Institutional Investors* (New York: McGraw-Hill, 1970); John C. McDonald, "Objectives and Performance of Mutual Funds, 1960–1969," *Journal of Financial and Quantitative Analysis*, June 1974, pp. 311–333.

Figure 18.1
Return and Risk Characteristics of Mutual Funds

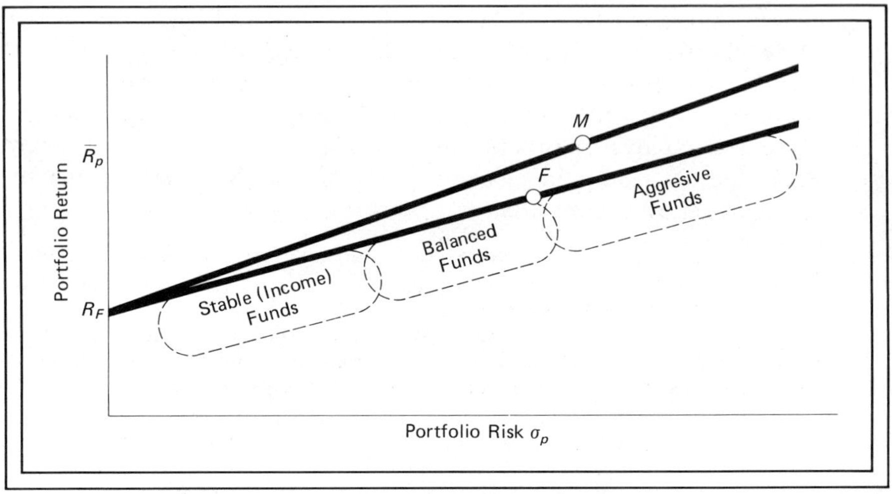

M is the market portfolio. *F* is the average mutual fund portfolio, and R_F is the risk-free return.

of the distribution, may or may not be taxable. A person investing in mutual funds does not need to do the record keeping necessary with direct ownership of securities. With mutual funds the investor pays taxes along the way rather than entirely at the time mutual fund shares are sold. An investor who purchased \$10,000 of a mutual fund and received \$18,000 in distributions over the years would pay tax on the distributions as they occur. Thus if the full value of the distributions were reinvested in shares and ultimately all shares were sold for \$30,000, tax would be owed at the capital gains rate on only \$2,000 dollars. The tax liability is calculated as follows:

Cost of fund shares	\$10,000
Distributions reinvested (tax paid when received)	18,000
Total cost of owned shares	\$28,000
Proceeds from sale	30,000
Taxable long-term gain	\$ 2,000

However, to the extent that mutual funds trade more frequently, tax liability of mutual fund shares occurs sooner. Earlier tax payment results in less capital available for reinvestment, resulting in a lower compounded rate of return. From a tax standpoint, therefore, mutual funds may work to the detriment of the investor.

Aside from the convenience of tax-record keeping, many mutual funds offer installment purchase plans and, in a few cases, installment redemption plans to facilitate retirement planning. Automatic reinvestment of dividend and capital gain proceeds is also common.

INDEX FUNDS. Index or "unit" funds are broadly diversified and essentially unmanaged portfolios designed to give investors a representative share of the market as a whole. Index funds duplicate in firm and market share the major stocks comprising the S&P 500 index. Thus if Xerox makes up 1 percent of the S&P 500 index by aggregate value, index funds would automatically invest 1 percent of capital in Xerox stock. The broad diversification of index funds virtually eliminates the chance of extraordinary gains or losses relative to the market. Investors remain fully exposed to market risk. Index funds by definition have a beta of 1.0, requiring investors with other risk preferences to either borrow or lend with risk-free securities as they desire. Turnover in index funds is much less than in other funds, reducing commission fees. Annual charges for management and expenses are only a small fraction of those charged by mutual funds.

The index fund concept was available only to wealthy investors until recently through a limited number of special bank trusts. Index funds for individual investors began late in 1976 with the introduction of the First Index Investment Trust. Because of the disappointing performance of mutual funds in the early 1970s, the index fund concept has initially been well received by investors. A growing number of pension fund administrators are relying on index funds for investing a portion of their assets. It is difficult to predict, however, if index funds with their guarantee of average return will remain popular with the investing public. Their rigid structure and indifference to timing have already been subjected to severe criticism.[7]

PENSION FUNDS

Employee pension funds have been the most rapidly growing and they are now one of the largest segments of institutionally managed portfolios. In dollar value nearly half of all pension funds are sponsored by various government agencies. Slightly more than half are private pension funds established by corporate employers. These funds promise future retirement payments to current employees and, where their rights have been "vested," to former employees. Private pension funds are either insured or uninsured. Uninsured pension funds, about two-thirds of the total, are usually managed by trust departments of large commercial banks. Some uninsured pension funds, called deposit administration plans, are managed by life insurance companies. Life insurance companies also manage all insured pension plans, guaranteeing payment of future annuity payments when due for these plans.

[7] Andrew B. Kim, "Is Indexing Really the Answer," *Journal of Portfolio Management*, Fall 1977, pp. 65–69. Also in the same issue see Edmond D. Villani, "The Theoretical Challenge to Index Funds," pp. 46–51, and Donald Shannon, Keith Johnson, and Gregory Neal, "How to Beat Those Index Funds," pp. 28–33.

PRIVATE PENSION PLANS. The attractiveness of a private pension fund depends on the company, the financial institution it selects to administer the plan (trustee), and the stipulations of the trust agreement outlining the rights and responsibilities of both parties. Generally the trustee is given wide discretion in the investment of funds provided by the company. The company, however, determines how the plan will be supported. Currently many companies carry unfunded pension fund liabilities, more than half of which are vested.[8] General Motors represents a case in point. In 1967 GM employed ten workers domestically for each GM pensioner. In 1977 the relationship of workers to pensioners was 4 to 1 and by 1995 is estimated to be 1 to 1.[9] At the end of 1976 GM reported $7.3 billion of unfunded actuarially computed prior service costs in a footnote in its 10-K report. This contingent liability nearly equaled the reported net pension fund reserves of $8.1 billion. At the same time GM reported record levels of net income and total assets as $2.9 and $24.4 billion, respectively. GM is not an exception; Fortune magazine reports that 10 of the top 100 companies in the Fortune 500 have unfunded vested liabilities equal to a third or more of their net worth.[10] Underfunding of pension obligations coupled with a general aging of the population may create serious problems in the future for some private as well as public pension plans. It will have an adverse impact on the future earnings growth of many firms as the percentage of income necessary to support pension obligations increases.

Owing to the geometric nature of compounding, small changes in the earnings of pension funds or changes in retirement age or other provisions cause large changes in probable funding requirements. A plan that appears to be fully funded or overfunded under one set of assumptions may be underfunded when key assumptions are changed. If actuarial assumptions are not realistic serious shortfalls may result.[11] Some firms commit themselves to fixed pension benefits while others agree only to certain standards of funding. In some cases firms commit themselves only in relation to their level of profits. Such plans, known as deferred profit-sharing plans, may replace or simply supplement regular pension benefits. Under a deferred profit-sharing plan the employer contributes a fixed percentage of profits or a fixed percent-

[8] Unfunded liabilities occur mainly from companies granting employees pension rights for service prior to the adoption or improvement of the pension plan. The basic guidelines for pension fund accounting are presented in Accounting Principles Board Opinion No. 8 "Accounting for the Cost of Pension Plans" (1966).

[9] *Business Week*, June 16, 1975, p. 80, and *Newsweek*, February 28, 1977, pp. 51–52.

[10] *Fortune*, November 1977, pp. 104–112+. A listing of the 10 firms is given on page 107.

[11] For example, to provide a new male employee aged 30 with a $1000 monthly pension at age 65 requires an annual contribution of $664 plus servicing costs providing contributions earn a simple 7 percent annual return. If only 5 percent is earned, contributions would need to be $1127 per year or 70 percent higher. If retirement age is lowered to 60 years, annual contributions would need to be raised by 69 percent. A decrease in employee turnover, especially among employees whose retirement rights are not yet vested, also increases employer pension liability. Recently won union rights regarding job security in many industries will probably decrease employee turnover in future years.

age of any profits over a specified level. Unfortunately the lack of detail provided by most firms about their pension costs and obligations prevents investors from accurately projecting the impact of the pension fund on future earnings and equity. Value Line provides estimates of unfunded pension liabilities for about half of the more than fifteen hundred firms which it surveys.

In 1974 Congress passed the Employee Retirement Income Security Act (ERISA). The major intent of ERISA was to improve employee vesting rights in private pension plans. Through creation of the Pension Benefit Guaranty Corporation, ERISA requires all employers to insure the solvency of each individual plan. In essence ERISA shifts the burden of pension risk from workers to company shareholders initially and then to shareholders of soundly financed programs through escalating premium assessments. Ultimately, by shifting private pensions to the public domain, ERISA places the final burden on taxpayers as guarantors of last resort, a policy with uncomfortable economic and political implications.[12] On matters of investment, an important provision of the act limits investment in the common stock of the employer, thereby reducing a potential pension fund abuse resulting from the firms' use of employees' money as a captive source of new capital.[13]

The effect of the new legislation on other aspects of pension fund investment practices is less clear. On one side, ERISA makes pension fund managers personally liable for losses resulting from imprudent investment judgments. Thus future investments may be more conservative with less emphasis on stocks and more emphasis on bonds. On the other side, ERISA's emphasis on prudent "experts" rather than on prudent "man" should permit recognition of the principles of diversification.[14] The recent interest by pension funds in index-fund investing results because indexing is a safe way of meeting the provisions of ERISA.

GOVERNMENT PENSION PLANS. Historically many government pension plans including Social Security have been poorly managed and funded. In large part this record is due to political pressures surrounding the operation of public plans. As a result of these pressures some funds are concentrated in obligations of the particular state or local municipality. A classic and continuing example is New York City and the pressures which its local civil employee pension funds face to purchase city bonds and notes which the general investing public rejects as too risky. However, not all state and local pension plans face unreasonable political pressure. Especially in recent years

[12] Jack L. Treynor, "The Principles of Corporate Pension Finance," *Journal of Finance*, May 1977, pp. 627–638.

[13] Such practices are still possible, however, providing that the plan is established through a special Employee Stock Ownership Trust. The practice may also occur in state and local pension funds not subject to ERISA legislation.

[14] Under former "prudent man" rules each security must be justified (only) in terms of its own characteristics. Robert C. Pozen, "The Prudent Man Rule and ERISA," *Financial Analysts Journal*, March–April 1977, pp. 30–35.

many public programs are increasing both stock purchases and their use of professional investment advisors. Similar to private plans, some public pension systems are transferring their investments to unit investment trusts (unmanaged index funds) organized by bank trust departments. Early in 1977, for example, three major New York City pension funds adopted indexing for a portion of their programs with funds to be managed by the Bankers Trust Company.

BANK TRUST SERVICES

Trust departments of major commercial banks administer the largest segment of institutionally managed funds in the United States. A trust account is a legal agreement by which wealth is administered on behalf of the owner (trustor) for the benefit of others (beneficiaries). Besides being established by individuals on behalf of other family members or through estate for designated heirs, trusts may be established for a variety of other purposes including pension funds, securing creditor accounts, and managing property in bankruptcy proceedings. Although any individual or corporation may be designated to manage funds placed in trust (act as trustee), most funds are placed in the stable and self-perpetuating care of bank trust departments or specialized trust companies.

Bank trust management is highly concentrated, with a small number of trust departments holding a majority of funds. Out of the approximately 4000 existing bank trust departments, the top 10 hold over a third of all assets. The largest 60 hold a combined two-thirds percentage.

Historically the majority of trust business centered around personal and estate trusts. These trusts are set up on an individual basis for accounts of sufficient size, generally taken to be $100,000 or more. For smaller trust accounts proceeds are commingled into a common trust fund. The common trust fund operates much as a mutual fund would, only in this case participation is limited to the bank's clients. Often a bank will establish more than one common fund to serve the differing needs and objectives of its trustors. Supervision of public and private pension fund assets has been a rapidly growing segment of bank trust department business. Today pension funds form the largest segment of business for most of the larger trust departments.

A bank's degree of control over investments placed in trust varies widely, depending on the nature of the trust account and the specific terms and conditions agreed to by the trustor. When banks have discretion over the investments in an account, they often limit equity participation to securities on an approved list. The list contains securities selected primarily for their defensive characteristics to minimize the chance of loss of principal. In recent years, however, a stronger performance orientation for certain accounts has been favored among many of the larger and more competitive trust departments. Although more aggressive investment practices may at times raise questions of preferential treatment among accounts as well as use of inside information,[15] the heightened competitive spirit in trust management, bringing as it has a greater emphasis on portfolio principles, should be viewed as a welcome trend.

OTHER INSTITUTIONAL INVESTORS

Other major categories of institutional investors include nonprofit organizations and insurance companies. Although these institutions provide benefits for individuals and society as a whole, their investment management activities are not directly on behalf of individual investors as is the case for investment companies, pension funds, and trusts. The portfolios of nonprofit organizations include those held by churches, hospitals, and museums, but the dominant categories are private foundations and university endowments. Foundations are established by gift, often a large single block of stock as was the case for the Ford Foundation, which is the nation's largest trust with assets over $3 billion. Provisions of the Tax Reform Act of 1969 require foundations to pay out all income and to diversify away any existing concentration in the stock of a single company to maintain a tax exempt status. University endowment funds are supported mainly by alumni contributions and they are used to support operating revenues, scholarships, and other university needs. In recent years many colleges have drawn upon both income and capital to support budget deficits. In both foundations and endowment funds there is a recent trend toward accepting greater investment risk in the hope of increasing return.

Insurance companies may generally be classified as life companies or property and casualty companies. Each may be either a mutual company owned by the policy holders or a profit-seeking company owned by stockholders. In either case the return earned on premium reserves is an important aspect of successful operation. Life companies are subject to more stringent state-imposed investment standards than are property and casualty companies. Life companies are limited in the amount of reserves that may be placed in equity and conventional mortgages. Quality standards for all investments are prevalent in the industry, and more reserves are required when they are invested in issues judged to be of lower quality according to standards of the National Association of Insurance Commissioners.

Despite these legal and quasi-legal restrictions which suggest a conservative portfolio policy, life companies commonly strive for an aggressive investment posture. This position is understandable given the competitive nature of the life insurance industry and the fact that liquidity needs are both minimal and highly predictable.

[15] Edward S. Herman and Carl F. Safanda, "Allocating Investment Information," *Financial Analysts Journal*, January–February 1973, pp. 23–28+. A classic illustration of potential problems involved is the Continental Illinois Bank and Trust Company's activity in the stock of Penn Central just prior to its filing for bankruptcy.

Table 18.3
Market Value of Stock Holdings of Institutional Investors and Others (billions of dollars–end of year)

	1970	1971	1972	1973	1974	1975
Private noninsured pension funds	67.1	88.7	115.2	90.5	63.3	88.6
Open-end investment companies	43.9	52.6	58.0	43.3	30.3	38.7
Other investment companies	6.2	6.9	7.4	6.6	4.7	6.0
Life insurance companies	15.4	20.6	26.8	25.9	21.9	28.3
Property-liability insurance companies[a]	13.2	16.6	21.8	19.7	12.8	14.3
Common trust funds	4.6	5.8	7.4	6.6	4.3	5.7
Personal trust funds	78.6	94.1	110.2	94.7	67.7	92.8
Mutual savings banks	2.8	3.5	4.5	4.2	3.7	4.4
State and local retirement funds	10.1	15.4	22.2	20.6	17.4	25.8
Foundations	22.0	25.0	28.5	24.5	18.4	22.7
Educational endowments	7.8	9.0	10.7	9.6	6.7	8.7
Subtotal	271.6	338.2	412.7	346.1	251.3	336.0
Less: Institutional holdings of investment company shares	4.9	5.8	6.5	6.3	5.8	7.8
Total institutional investors	266.8	332.4	406.2	339.8	245.4	328.2
Foreign investors[b]	28.7	32.9	41.3	37.0	28.2	48.2
Other domestic investors[c]	563.9	638.4	694.7	487.8	335.3	439.9
Total stock outstanding[d]	859.4	1003.7	1142.3	864.6	608.9	816.3

Source: Annual Report of the Securities and Exchange Commission, 1976.
[a] Excludes holdings of insurance company stock.
[b] Includes estimate of stock held as direct investment.
[c] Computed as residual. Includes both individuals and institutional groups not listed above.
[d] Includes both common and preferred stock. Excludes investment company shares but includes foreign issues outstanding in the United States.

SOME COMMENTS ON INSTITUTIONAL INVESTMENT MANAGEMENT

Over the past decade there have been numerous questions regarding the role and impact of institutional investors in our financial markets and social system as a whole. A special study commissioned by Congress and completed in 1970, the *Institutional Investor Study*, found little cause for concern.[16] The study concluded that institutional investors have in general had a favorable impact on the growth and development of the economy, and recent trends in their size and operation pose no serious threat to the public interest. Since the *Institutional Investor Study* the role of financial institutions on Wall Street has remained strong. Table 18.3 shows the market value of stock holdings for institutional investors and others since 1970. Pension funds and

[16] *Institutional Investor Study Report of the Securities and Exchange Commission*, March 10, 1971.

life insurance companies have been the large gainers. In total, proportional control of NYSE stocks by all institutions combined rose from 31.0 percent in 1970 to 40.2 percent in 1975. Traditionally, the NYSE membership has viewed institutional investors as an unwanted competitive threat. Pressures by Congress and the SEC in recent years have forced the exchange to grant institutions a larger direct role on Wall Street.[17]

The impact of institutional trading on stock prices has been the subject of careful studies by Alan Kraus and Hans Stoll and by Frank Reilly.[18] Because of the large size of institutional transactions and a possible tendency of institutional investors to think and act together, concern has been expressed that institutional trading unduly affects price behavior. However, Kraus and Stoll found little evidence to support concern in this area. While there is a tendency for similar institutions to follow a similar pattern of trading in some individual stocks, there is a more than compensatory tendency for different institutions to take offsetting positions. This was especially evident between the activities of mutual funds and bank trusts. For example, at a time when mutual funds collectively are net sellers of Xerox, bank managers are most likely net buyers. While offsetting transactions are not always present on individual transactions, large trading volumes and imbalances caused by institutional trading seldom have distinguishable influence on security pricing.

Kraus and Stoll's findings do not necessarily suggest that institutional trading cannot be troublesome in the future. Since many of the largest institutional investors hold sizable positions in the same stocks, their ability to liquidate securities on short notice without considerable price impact may be less than imagined.[19] Other critical questions arise from widespread institutional stock ownership. Top among these is the impact which institutions have on corporate management. Traditionally, institutional investors minimize involvement with corporate management, choosing instead to vote with management on all shareholder matters. Such a block of passive shareholders, however, may tend to make management less responsive to shareholders and society as a whole. Extending this argument, one may also question the impact of institutions on the distribution of wealth. While institutional investors contribute to aggregate economic growth over time through their favorable impact on savings flows, they may also contribute on balance to a less uniform distribution of wealth.

[17] Institutional membership, once denied by the NYSE, is now permitted provided that the institution does 80 percent or more of its trading with the general public. As a result of the Security Acts Amendments of 1975, passed by Congress, the SEC now has expanded power to decide what market activities may be anticompetitive.

[18] Alan Kraus and Hans R. Stoll, "Parallel Trading by Institutional Investors," *Journal of Financial and Quantitative Analysis* 7, no. 5 (December 1972): 2107–2138 and Frank K. Reilly, "Institutions on Trial: Not Guilty!" *Journal of Portfolio Management*, Winter 1977, pp. 5–10. See the discussion of institutional investors in Chapter 10 of this text.

[19] *Institutional Investor Study Report of the Securities and Exchange Commission*, Vol. 2 and Summary Vol., chap. IX.

Tax Aspects of Investment Management

Different investment strategies produce different tax consequences. Since the basic investment objective is to maximize risk-adjusted after-tax return, tax planning must be an integral feature of investment management. The general tax preference given capital gains relative to dividend and interest income has been referred to throughout the text. Chapter 17 provided procedures for calculating the tax consequences of portfolio revision decisions. This section will examine the tax code in more detail, considering the major tax implications relevant for retirement and estate planning as well as for ongoing investment management. This brief survey, however, is not intended to be comprehensive and, since tax codes change each year, investors should become fully aware of current tax laws as they apply to investment return and the investor's individual circumstances.

FEDERAL INCOME TAX

The federal tax system operates through application of a progressive rate of tax each year to all taxable income. To determine taxable income, the taxpayer first calculates adjusted gross income. Adjusted gross income includes almost all forms of income but it excludes two types of investment proceeds: (1) interest on state and municipal bonds, and (2) the first $100 of corporate dividends. Adjusted gross income also includes the net balance of profits and losses on sales of investments. Proper timing of purchases and sales resulting in capital gains and losses will be shown in the next paragraphs to be an important investment consideration. From adjusted gross income the taxpayer may subtract either a fixed standard deduction or the sum of a series of itemized deductions which are permitted by law. Subtracting these deductions gives a net income figure. Finally, subtracting a lump sum exemption from net income based on the number of dependents yields taxable income. A tax rate beginning at 14 percent on the first $500 of taxable income is then applied to determine tax liability. The tax rate rises on marginal taxable income up to a maximum rate of 50 percent on earned income and 70 percent on unearned income. For single taxpayers the maximum earned income rate applies to income over $38,000, and the maximum rate on other income applies to amounts over $100,000.

Tax planning aids the investor by increasing the percentage of money retained from successful investments and by reducing the loss of unsuccessful ones. Almost any bona fide investment qualifies for capital gain and loss consideration as long as it is not used in business or held for personal enjoyment. Tax savings are greatest for short-term losses (assets held less than one year) and long-term gain (assets held more than one year). Short-term losses may be used dollar for dollar to offset capital gains and, should they exceed gains, to offset up to $3000 of ordinary income. However, only half of all long-term losses may be used to offset capital gains or income. Any short- or long-term loss not used in the current year may be carried forward into subsequent tax years. Short-term gains not offset by losses are treated as income. Only one-half of all long-term gains are considered to be taxable income, and capital gain income is effectively taxed at half the investor's marginal tax rate. For gains up to $50,000 the maximum capital gains rate is 25 percent. Long-term gains above this amount are subject to tax at rates up to 35 percent. At the present time Congress and the president are considering the elimination of capital gains preference. The following paragraph presumes that current capital gains treatment will be retained. Wherever possible an investor should try to avoid long-term capital losses and short-term capital gains. When these are unavoidable, an attempt should be made to offset long-term losses with long-term gains and short-term losses against short-term gains so the full tax benefit of short-term losses will not be reduced. For example, consider the case of an investor who realized $10,000 of long-term gains (L.T.G.), $5000 of long-term losses (L.T.L.), $2000 of short-term gains (S.T.G.), and $5000 of short-term losses (S.T.L.) all in the same year. The taxable position would be:

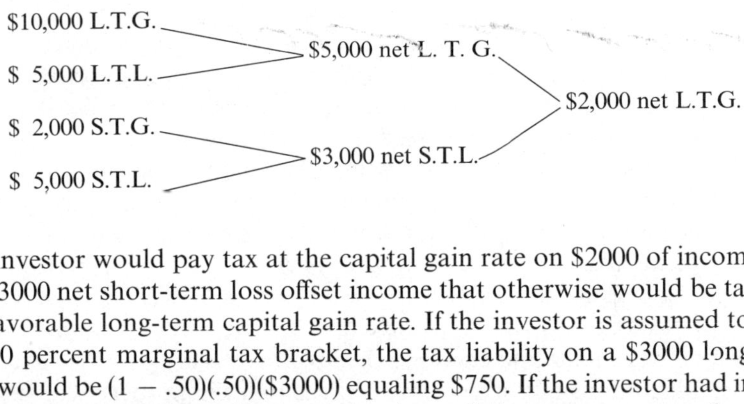

The investor would pay tax at the capital gain rate on $2000 of income. But the $3000 net short-term loss offset income that otherwise would be taxed at the favorable long-term capital gain rate. If the investor is assumed to be in the 50 percent marginal tax bracket, the tax liability on a $3000 long-term gain would be (1 – .50)(.50)($3000) equaling $750. If the investor had instead deferred at least $5000 of long-term gain until the next tax year, the $3000 net short-term loss would have been applied against ordinary income since the last $3000 of ordinary income is subject to a tax (1 – .50)($3000) equaling $1500. In other words, the example illustrates a tax liability which is $750 higher than it could have been. Other timing variations based on this example are possible, including postponing the short-term gain (with possible conversion to long-term status). But the point is clear: the way capital gains and losses are realized has significant impact on the overall after-tax return to investment.[20]

[20] For wealthy investors another consideration is the minimum tax provision which can reduce the value of long-term capital gains rate. One-half of long-term gains, along with other revenue categories such as accelerated depreciation, must be counted as a preference item. When preference items exceed the greater of one-half regular taxes owed or $10,000 the taxpayer is liable for the minimum tax figured at a 15 percent rate.

INCOME SHIFTING

Occasionally an investor can postpone receipt of income or transfer its possession to defer tax liability to a later time when it may be subject to a lower rate. An employee who is not covered by a corporate pension plan can set up an individual retirement account (IRA). Contributions of up to $1500 per year are permitted, and this limit will probably be raised by Congress in future years. Contributions are excluded from taxable income and their earnings will accumulate tax free. At retirement all proceeds will be taxed as ordinary income. However, income averaging may then be used to reduce overall tax liability. It is also possible to increase IRA contributions (currently by $250) for a taxpayer's spouse even if he or she is not employed.

For self-employed persons, including those engaged in part-time consulting, a Keogh retirement plan may be used. Keogh plans, created by the Self-Employed Individuals Tax Retirement Act of 1962 and subsequent amendments, currently permit up to $7500 per year in earned income to be shielded from tax. Furthermore, the taxpayer may retain considerable discretion over the investment decisions for assets invested in a Keogh or IRA plan. A potential drawback of the Keogh plan is that if the business employs others, they also must be covered after three years' service.

Other income-shifting strategies usually focus on deferred compensation or establishing special trusts. Persons receiving part of their compensation as a bonus may arrange with their employers to have it deferred until retirement when it will be taxed at a lower rate. To temporarily shift investment income to a beneficiary who presumably is in a lower tax bracket, a short-term trust agreement known as a Clifford Trust may be established. At the end of the trust period, which must be at least ten years, the income-producing assets revert back to the provider who then may be in a lower tax bracket because of retirement.[21]

A more permanent arrangement can be made by an irrevocable trust, but here all rights and claims to the investments are permanently transferred. An advantage of an irrevocable trust is that the property conveyed will not be taxed as part of an estate. Finally, charitable contributions can reduce income and estate taxes while in certain cases they can also continue to provide income. A charitable remainder trust or (if the charity has one) a pooled income fund can provide these advantages.

ESTATE AND INHERITANCE TAXES

A federal estate tax is imposed on the transfer of the net estate of every deceased person who was a U.S. citizen or resident. No investments are exempt from estate taxation; even state and municipal bonds are included in the

[21] Income paid from short-term trusts may subject the donor to gift taxes. However, there is a $3000 gift tax exclusion ($6000 for joint gifts) which would at least partially offset this tax liability.

tax base. For some individuals federal estate taxes are of little consequence because a credit of $47,000 permits the first $175,000 of net estate value to be exempt.[22] However, for the many individuals having a larger net estate at death, active estate planning can significantly affect the percentage of wealth transferred to heirs.

The federal estate tax liability is determined as follows. First, the gross estate value is calculated; this total includes all property interests of the deceased including trusts, life insurance, and real property owned within the United States including assets held in joint tenancy. Allowed deductions are then subtracted from gross estate value to yield net estate value. Deductions include all final expenses, including debts payable. For property passing to a surviving spouse, a marital deduction of the greater of $250,000 or 50 percent of the adjusted (after other deductions) estate value is permitted. A progressive estate tax ranging from 30 to 70 percent is next applied to the net estate value. The resulting gross estate tax is then reduced by credits for amounts paid in state inheritance taxes and gift taxes previously paid on property which is included in the gross estate.[23]

With one exception (Nevada) all states impose taxes on the transfer of property at death. Many states pattern their inheritance laws after the federal law but have both smaller exemptions and lower tax rates. Often the rate varies according to the closeness of the relationship between the deceased and the heir: property transferred to a distant relative or friend is taxed at a higher rate than that transferred to a brother or a daughter. Only property within the state's jurisdiction is subject to tax and many states exempt life insurance. Because the federal tax credit for state inheritance taxes usually equals the state tax owed, differences in state taxing policy make little difference to the total estate tax liability.

Because individual circumstances vary considerably, estate tax planning must be an individual matter requiring expert consultation and guidance. However, a few general observations on estate planning are worth noting:

1. Planning will be successful only with a carefully drawn and legally prepared will. Will making is not an appropriate do-it-yourself project.
2. Management of estate affairs—selection of the executor who carries out the terms of the will and the trustee who manages assets left on behalf of others—should be entrusted to an organization such as a bank or similar qualified financial institution. For reasons of ill health or the like, individuals named to these responsibilities may not function when they are needed as effectively as anticipated when the will was drawn.
3. Careful estate planning can minimize tax liabilities but it usually cannot

[22] The credit is somewhat lower in years immediately prior to 1981.

[23] Property transferred in contemplation of death is included in the estate. Any gift made within three years of death is considered to be so contemplated. Since the Tax Reform Act of 1976, gifts are taxed at the same rate as estates thus reducing a former tax advantage of transferring wealth by gift. However, the first $3000 ($6000 jointly with spouse) of a gift to any recipient is tax-free and there is no limit on the number of separate recipients. Also a gift tax marital deduction permits a total of $100,000 in tax-free gifts to a spouse, with only half of all excess subject to tax.

eliminate them entirely. Therefore the estate should have sufficient liquid assets to pay all taxes and expenses.

4. The form of ownership of real property can have a significant impact on tax and other estate costs. The best ownership form varies according to the circumstances.
5. Assigning life insurance policies to heirs removes them from the estate for tax purposes. In many cases, however, a gift tax liability will be incurred.
6. A variety of special trusts may be established which could reduce tax liability. These may be testamentary trusts established by the will to become effective at the legator's death, or inter vivos (living trusts) effective when made, that is, prior to the legator's death.
7. While minimizing the final tax burden is an important consideration, the primary concern should be achieving the desired distribution of the estate, not avoiding taxes.

Summary

Individual investment management is an ongoing and evolutionary process. The investor faces different needs at different stages of life. Youth, middle years, retirement, and estate planning identify four major life-cycle periods. Investment maintenance and revision include a gradual shifting of investments to meet changing priorities. Generally speaking, increasing age brings with it increasing emphasis on surety of principal and income and concern for the tax consequences of investment.

A large number of financial institutions provide investment consulting and management services. Some are direct and voluntary, as in the case of mutual funds and bank trust accounts. Other services including private or public pension fund programs provide the investor with little if any direct control over their operation. Typically only self-employed persons can determine the investment portfolio of funds allocated to retirement and many of these persons prefer to allocate that responsibility to professionally managed life insurance or bank trust accounts specifically created for this purpose. The investment practices of other institutions such as insurance companies, foundations, and educational endowment funds provide indirect benefits to individuals and society as a whole through lower costs and increased public services.

The performance of financial institutions has been mixed. Institutional management generally achieves desired levels of risk, diversifies adequately, and meets other investment objectives. But very few, if any, institutional investors persistently outperform the market as a whole. In part this is due to broad diversification: it is hard to outperform the market when one is "a piece of the rock."

Laws governing tax liability of investment income are complex and they are changing constantly. Careful planning can usually reduce tax liability, thereby increasing real return to investment. Timing of capital gains and losses, sheltering income in tax-deferred programs, and proper estate planning are three areas of major importance in tax planning.

Questions and Problems

1. How do investment objectives formulated in youth compare with those contemplated as retirement nears?
2. What are some important differences among closed-end investment companies, mutual funds, and index funds?
3. How would you summarize the historical performance of mutual funds? Does their record compare favorably with the results to be expected from a self-maintained investment management program?
4. Should public or privately sponsored retirement programs be thought of as substitutes for or complements to a self-sponsored savings and investment program?
5. Identify the principal uses of bank trust accounts. Why have bank trusts become the largest institutional holder of professionally managed assets?
6. A current revision of portfolio holdings suggests that switching is advisable which would result in a short-term loss of $10,000 and a long-term gain of $15,000. Assuming an investor in a 35 percent marginal tax bracket, what timing strategies might improve after tax return and how could they be implemented without significantly altering risk?
7. Because of other pressing commitments, a wealthy investor prefers to purchase mutual funds rather than manage a portfolio. The investor is in the 35 percent tax bracket and chooses four stocks on the basis of the following expectations:

Fund	*Income*	*Percent Expected Return*	*Percent Standard Deviation*	*Percent Load Charge*
A	Tax free	6	± 8	3
B	All interest & dividend	9	±12	6
C	50 percent interest, 50 percent capital gain	10	±16	0
D	All capital gain	12.5	±28	8

   Ignoring the income tax dividend exclusion, and possible small variation in annual fees, and assuming $100,000 is available to invest for 5 years, which fund should be purchased? (If necessary, use 5 percent as a risk-free rate.)
8. Provide a brief appraisal of the trend toward institutional ownership of stock in the United States.

Selected References

LIFE-CYCLE INVESTMENT PRIORITIES

Cohn, Richard A., Wilber G. Lewellen, Ronald C. Lease, and Gary G. Schlarbaum, "Individual Investor Risk Aversion and Investment Portfolio Composition," *Journal of Finance* 30, no. 2 (May 1975): 605–620.

Gooding, Arthur E., "Quantification of Investors' Perceptions of Common Stocks: Risk and Return Dimensions," *Journal of Finance* 30, no. 5 (December 1975): 1301–1316.

Lewellen, Wilber G., Ronald C. Lease, and Gary G. Schlarbaum, "The Individual Investor: Attributes and Attitudes," *Journal of Finance* 29, no. 2 (May 1974): 413–433.

Schoeplein, Robert N., "The Effects of Pension Plans on Other Retirement Saving," *Journal of Finance* 25, no. 3 (June 1970): 633–638.

INSTITUTIONAL INVESTMENT SERVICES

Boudreaux, Kenneth J., "Discounts and Premiums on Closed-End Mutual Funds: A Study in Valuation," *Journal of Finance*, May 1973, pp. 515–522.

Carlson, Robert S., "Aggregate Performance of Mutual Funds, 1948–1967," *Journal of Financial and Quantitative Analysis* 5, no. 1 (March 1970): 1–32.

Friend, Irwin, Marshall Blume, and Jean Crockett. *Mutual Funds and Other Institutional Investors* (New York: McGraw-Hill, 1970).

Good, Walter, Robert Ferguson, and Jack Treynor, "An Investor's Guide to the Index Fund Controversy," *Financial Analysts Journal*, November–December 1975, pp. 27–36.

Jensen, Michael C., "The Performance of Mutual Funds in the Period 1945–1964," *Journal of Finance* 23, no. 2 (May 1968): 389–416.

Kraus, Alan, and Hans R. Stoll, "Parallel Trading by Institutional Investors," *Journal of Financial and Quantitative Analysis* 7, no. 5 (December 1972): 2107–2138.

McDonald, John G., "Objectives and Performance of Mutual Funds, 1960–1969," *Journal of Financial and Quantitative Analysis* 9, no. 3 (June 1974): 311–333.

Murray, Roger F., "Indirect Investment in the Securities Market and the Individual Investor," *Journal of Contemporary Business*, Winter 1974, pp. 63–71.

Pozen, Robert C., "The Prudent Man Rule and ERISA," *Financial Analysts Journal*, March–April 1977, pp. 30–35.

Reilly, Frank K., "Institutions on Trial: Not Guilty," *The Journal of Portfolio Management* 3, no. 2 (Winter 1977): 5–10.

Roenfeldt, Rodney L., and Donald L. Tuttle, "An Examination of the Discounts and Premiums of Closed-End Investment Companies," *Journal of Business Research*, Fall 1973, pp. 129–140.

Institutional Investor Study Report of the Securities and Exchange Commission (92d Congress, 1st Session), March 10, 1971.

Securities and Exchange Commission, *Annual Report*, 1976.

Sharpe, William F., "Corporate Pension Fund Policy," *Journal of Financial Economics* 3, no. 3 (June 1976): 183–193.

Smith, Keith V., and John C. Schreiner, "Direct vs. Indirect Diversification," *Financial Analysts Journal*, September–October 1970, pp. 33–38.

Tepper, Irwin, "Risk vs. Return in Pension Fund Investment," *Harvard Business Review*, March–April 1977, pp. 100–107.

TAX ASPECTS OF INVESTMENT MANAGEMENT

Cornfeld, Dave L., et al., "Analyzing the 1976 Tax Reform Act (Part I)," *The Journal of Taxation*, December 1976, pp. 331–369.

Howe, Garry F., "Taxation of Trusts and Beneficiaries Changed by Provisions of Tax Reform Act of 1976," *Taxation for Accountants* 17, no. 6 (December 1976): 346–353.

Pedrick, Willard H., "Estate Planning and Future Shock," *Taxes* 55, no, 4 (April 1977): 226–238.

Rose, Michael D., and Joseph S. Platt, *A Federal Taxation Primer* (Indianapolis: Bobbs-Merrill, 1973).

Sacher, Charles P., "Tax Planning for the Moderately Wealthy Family in Light of the Tax Reform Act of 1976," *Taxation for Accountants* 18, no. 6 (June 1977): 334–343.

Willis, James R., "The '76 Act and the Individual Taxpayer," *The Tax Advisor*, March 1977, pp. 143–161.

Appendix

Compound Interest Relationships

Introduction

Rate of interest (or rate of return) is a periodic concept. It measures the return on investment relative to the amount invested during any period of time; that is, it is the ratio of interest received to funds invested. If \$100 invested in a savings account is credited with \$2 in interest at the end of a three-month period, the periodic (quarterly) rate of interest is 2 percent. For a rate of interest r,

$$
\begin{aligned}
r &= \frac{\text{interest}}{\text{investment}} \\
&= \frac{2.00}{100.00} \\
&= .02
\end{aligned}
\tag{A.1}
$$

Funds invested at the beginning of a period are often referred to, at that point in time, as *present value* (PV) of the investment. Total value of the investment at the end of the period, including interest earned, is similarly referred to as *future value* (FV). Present value and future value are linked by a *return relative* or *accumulation factor.* The accumulation factor consists of the sum of 1 plus the rate of interest. For present value PV, future value FV, and accumulation factor $1 + r$, for one time period,

$$FV = PV(1 + r) \tag{A.2}$$

In the example of the savings account,

$$\begin{aligned} FV &= 100.00(1.02) \\ &= 102.00 \end{aligned}$$

Return relative, the accumulation factor, is the ratio of future value to present value. Solving Equation A.2 for the accumulation factor,

$$1 + r = \frac{FV}{PV}$$

$$\begin{aligned} 1 + r &= \frac{102.00}{100.00} \\ &= 1.02 \end{aligned} \tag{A.3}$$

The value 1 in the accumulation factor represents the principal amount invested; that is, it is 100 percent of the sum which earns interest during the period. With r added, with interest added to principal, present value accumulates to future value at the end of the period.

Present value and future value can be defined for any number of periods desired. If, over a number of periods, interest accrues only on the original principal invested, interest earned is said to be *simple interest.* If the savings account of the example above earned simple interest, \$2.00 would be earned in each of the four quarters of the year and total interest for the year would be \$8.00. This is equivalent to an annual rate of interest of 8 percent, four times the quarterly rate. But interest can also accrue on interest earned during past periods; this case is said to be *compound interest.* If the savings account provided for compound interest, with quarterly compounding, the value of \$102.00 at the end of the first quarter would be invested for another quarter to yield \$104.04; \$104.04 would yield \$106.12 at the end of the third quarter; and \$106.12 would provide a future value of \$108.24 at the end of the year:

1. $100.00(1.02) = 102.00$
2. $102.00(1.02) = 104.04$
3. $104.04(1.02) = 106.12$
4. $106.12(1.02) = 108.24$

While this calculation is correct, it is unnecessarily cumbersome. It can be simplified by generalizing the accumulation factor to a multiperiod formulation. Future value of \$108.24 can be calculated:

$$\begin{aligned} FV &= 100.00(1.02)(1.02)(1.02)(1.02) \\ &= 100.00(1.02)^4 \\ &= 108.24 \end{aligned}$$

The multiperiod accumulation factor is the one-period factor raised to a power equal to the number of periods during which interest compounds:

$$\text{accumulation factor} = (1 + r)^n \tag{A.4}$$

In Equation A.4 r is the periodic rate of interest and n is the number of periods from the time of present value to the time of future value. Periods of accumulation are defined generally; they are not associated with any specific calendar period. In Equation A.4 n may represent a number of days, or months, or years, or any other desired time period. Equation A.5 provides a generalized definition of the relationship between present and future values:

$$FV = PV(1 + r)^n \tag{A.5}$$

Compound Interest Elements

Compound interest problems may involve a *single investment* or a *series of investments* during the time interval from present to future. The savings account example provides an illustration of a single investment; \$100.00 invested at present accrues to a value of \$108.24 four quarters later. A series of investments can be illustrated by assuming that \$100.00 is invested at the *beginning* of each quarter, for four quarters, at a rate of interest of 2 percent per period. At the end of the year future value would be \$420.40:

Quarter		
1	$100.00(1.02)^4 =$	108.24
2	$100.00(1.02)^3 =$	106.12
3	$100.00(1.02)^2 =$	104.04
4	$100.00(1.02)^1 =$	102.00
		420.40

When a series of payments is involved, it is called an *annuity*. If principal is invested at the *beginning* of each period, with future value defined at the *end* of the terminal period, it is said to be an *annuity due*; the example given above, with terminal value of \$420.40, is an example of an annuity due. If principal is invested at the *end* of each period, with future value again defined at the *end* of the terminal period, it is said to be an *ordinary annuity*. In the case of the four investments of \$100.00 per quarter, assume that each payment is deposited at the *end* of the quarter. The first payment would then accrue interest only for three periods, from the second through the fourth.

Figure A.1
Compound Interest Accumulation Factors

	Future Value (FV)	Present Value (PV)
Single Payment	$(1+r)^n$ **Table A.1**	$\dfrac{1}{(1+r)^n}$ or $(1+r)^{-n}$ **Table A.2**
Series of Fixed Payments	$(1+r)^0+(1+r)^1+\cdots+(1+r)^{n-2}+(1+r)^{n-1}$ or $\dfrac{(1+r)^n-1}{r}$ **Table A.3**	$(1+r)^{-1}+(1+r)^{-2}+\cdots+(1+r)^{n-1}+(1+r)^n$ or $\dfrac{1-(1+r)^{-n}}{r}$ **Table A.4**

Other returns would similarly be reduced and the last payment would earn no interest since accumulation factor $(1 + r)^0$ is equal to 1; in this case future value would be \$412.16:

Quarter 1	$100.00(1.02)^3 =$	106.12
2	$100.00(1.02)^2 =$	104.04
3	$100.00(1.02)^1 =$	102.00
4	$100.00(1.02)^0 =$	100.00
		412.16

Most investment problems involve ordinary annuities; the discussion which follows will generally focus on the ordinary annuity in lieu of the annuity due.

In addition to periodic rate of interest r and the number of periods n, compound interest problems may involve (1) future value *and/or* present value and (2) *either* a single payment or a series of fixed payments. This presents four different types of relationships with four different accumulation factors, as summarized in Figure A.1. The meaning of each accumulation factor in each of the four quadrants of that figure will be considered in turn.

FUTURE VALUE OF A SINGLE PAYMENT

The accumulation factor in this case has already been considered; it is the value $(1 + r)^n$ of Equation A.4. For given values of r and n, a numerical value exists for accumulation factor $(1 + r)^n$; given this value, the future value of a single payment is the product of the factor and present value. In the case of investment of \$100.00 for four quarters at an interest rate of 2 percent per quarter, compounded quarterly, the accumulation factor $(1.02)^4$ is equal to 1.0824. Each dollar invested accumulates to \$1.0824 at the end of the year; an investment of \$100.00 amounts to:

$$\begin{aligned} \text{FV} &= \text{PV}(1 + r)^n \\ &= 100.00(1.02)^4 \\ &= 100.00(1.0824) \\ &= 108.24 \end{aligned}$$

The factor $(1 + r)^n$ can easily be evaluated, for all permutations of r and n, if a calculator with an exponential key is available. It can also be evaluated by use of logarithm tables or by multiplying $(1 + r)$ by itself n times, but these operations are tedious and tables of values of $(1 + r)^n$ exist for easy reference. Table A.1 provides values for this accumulation factor for selected values of r and n; it is easily verified from that table that $(1.02)^4$ is equal to 1.0824.

PRESENT VALUE OF A SINGLE PAYMENT

Problems involving present value of a single payment are also easily solved. In this case the accumulation factor is $(1 + r)^{-n}$; solving Equation A.5 for present value:

$$\text{FV} = \text{PV}(1 + r)^n$$

$$\text{PV} = \frac{\text{FV}}{(1 + r)^n} = \text{FV}\left[\frac{1}{(1 + r)^n}\right] = \text{FV}(1 + r)^{-n} \tag{A.6}$$

Table A.2 provides values for the factor $(1 + r)^{-n}$ for selected values of r and n; when future value is multiplied by the relevant Table A.2 value, present value results. Reversing the savings account problem, what sum must be invested today at 2 percent per quarter, compounded quarterly, in order to have \$108.24 at the end of the year? The answer of course is \$100.00; from Table A.2, the accumulation factor is .9238:

$$\begin{aligned} \text{PV} &= \text{FV}(1 + r)^{-n} \\ &= 108.24(1.02)^{-4} \\ &= 108.24(.9238) \\ &= 100.00 \end{aligned}$$

Table A.2 values are reciprocals of Table A.1 values. That is,

$$(1 + r)^{-n} = \frac{1}{(1 + r)^n}$$

and, in the examples given, it is easily verified that:

$$.9238 = \frac{1}{1.0824}$$

FUTURE VALUE OF A SERIES OF PAYMENTS

Problems involving a series of payments appear to be more complex than those involving a single payment, but they are solved just as easily if payments are constant. In that event the constant can be factored and an accumulation factor can be defined. For a fixed payment each period of R dollars, and for an ordinary annuity,

$$\begin{aligned} \text{FV} &= R(1+r)^{n-1} + R(1+r)^{n-2} + \cdots + R(1+r)^1 + R(1+r)^0 \\ &= R[(1+r)^{n-1} + (1+r)^{n-2} + \cdots + (1+r)^1 + (1+r)^0] \\ &= R \sum_{t=0}^{n-1} (1+r)^t \end{aligned} \tag{A.7}$$

The summation term in brackets in Equation A.7 seems formidable but it is easily reduced, since it is a geometric progression, to:[1]

[1] A geometric progression is a sequence of numbers where each term after the first is found by multiplying by some constant. In this case the constant is the accumulation factor and succeeding terms beyond the first are calculated:

$$\begin{aligned} (1+r)^0 &= (1+r)^0 \\ (1+r)^0(1+r)^1 &= (1+r)^1 \\ (1+r)^1(1+r)^1 &= (1+r)^2 \\ (1+r)^2(1+r)^1 &= (1+r)^3 \end{aligned}$$

etc.

Geometric progressions have useful properties. For example, the sum $\sum$ of terms in a geometric progression can be solved by the formula:

$$\sum = \frac{f - ck}{1 - c}$$

where

f = the first term in the summation
c = the geometric constant
k = the last term in the summation

In this case, summing from period 0 through $n - 1$, and with geometric constant $(1 + r)$,

$$\begin{aligned} \sum &= \frac{(1+r)^0 - (1+r)(1+r)^{n-1}}{1-(1+r)} \\ &= \frac{1-(1+r)^n}{-r} \\ &= \frac{(1+r)^n - 1}{r} \end{aligned}$$

$$FV = R\left[\frac{(1+r)^n - 1}{r}\right] \tag{A.7a}$$

Given R, and values for the accumulation factor (in brackets) from Table A.3, problems involving future value of a series of fixed payments can be solved. Recalling the problem where \$100.00 was invested at the end of each of four quarters, with interest of 2 percent per quarter compounded quarterly, future value of \$412.16 is calculated more easily than before:[2]

$$\begin{aligned} FV &= 100.00\left[\frac{(1.02)^4 - 1}{.02}\right] \\ &= 100.00[4.1216] \\ &= 412.16 \end{aligned}$$

Table A.3 values can be calculated from Table A.1 values; from Equation A.7:

$$\begin{aligned} (1.02)^3 &= 1.0612 \\ (1.02)^2 &= 1.0404 \\ (1.02)^1 &= 1.0200 \\ (1.02)^0 &= 1.0000 \\ \sum &= 4.1216 \end{aligned}$$

While either table can be used to solve the problem, Table A.3 is the easier of the two and it is preferable when periodic payments are constant. But if payments are variable, Table A.1 must be used. For example, assume that payments of \$100.00, \$200.00, and \$400.00 are received at the end of each of the next three years; future value at the end of the third year is \$724.36 if funds are invested at 6 percent per year:

$$\begin{aligned} 100.00(1.06)^2 &= 100.00(1.1236) = 112.36 \\ 200.00(1.06)^1 &= 200.00(1.0600) = 212.00 \\ 400.00(1.06)^0 &= 400.00(1.0000) = 400.00 \\ & \qquad\qquad\qquad\qquad\quad 724.36 \end{aligned}$$

[2] This problem, and Table A.3, both involve an *ordinary annuity*. The accumulation factor for an *annuity due* can be calculated as follows:

$$\text{factor for annuity due} = (1 + r)\ \text{factor for ordinary annuity}$$

In the example given, to convert to an annuity due,

$$\begin{aligned} \text{factor} &= (1.02)(4.1216) \\ &= 4.2040 \end{aligned}$$

and

$$100.00[4.2040] = 420.40$$

as calculated previously.

PRESENT VALUE OF A SERIES OF PAYMENTS

The fourth accumulation factor is used to calculate the present value of a series of payments. For a fixed payment of R dollars per period,

$$\begin{aligned}\text{PV} &= \frac{R}{(1+r)} + \frac{R}{(1+r)^2} + \cdots + \frac{R}{(1+r)^{n-1}} + \frac{R}{(1+r)^n} \\ &= R[(1+r)^{-1} + (1+r)^{-2} + \cdots + (1+r)^{-(n-1)} + (1+r)^{-n}] \\ &= R\sum_{t=1}^{n}(1+r)^{-t} \\ &= R\left[\frac{1-(1+r)^{-n}}{r}\right] \qquad \text{(A.8)}\end{aligned}$$

Table A.4 provides present value factors for different values of r and n for the bracketed term. To illustrate its use, assume that $100.00 is received at the end of each of the next four periods; if the interest rate is 5 percent per period, present value is $354.60:

$$\begin{aligned}\text{PV} &= 100.00[3.5460] \\ &= 354.60\end{aligned}$$

Present value factors in Table A.4 can be derived from Table A.2 values; this is useful when payments are variable. The present value of $200.00 per period for the next two periods followed by $500.00 per period for the succeeding two periods, at 7 percent, is, from Table A.2:

$$\begin{aligned}200.00(1.07)^{-1} &= 200.00(.9346) = 186.92 \\ 200.00(1.07)^{-2} &= 200.00(.8734) = 174.68 \\ 500.00(1.07)^{-3} &= 500.00(.8163) = 408.15 \\ 500.00(1.07)^{-4} &= 500.00(.7629) = \underline{381.45} \\ & \qquad\qquad\qquad\qquad\quad 1151.20\end{aligned}$$

The same calculation can be performed with Table A.4 values:

Table A.4 PV, 4 years, at 7 percent	3.3872		
PV, years 1 and 2, at 7 percent	1.8080(200.00)	=	361.60
PV, years 3 and 4, at 7 percent	1.5792(500.00)	=	789.60
	Total		1151.20

PERIOD COMPOUNDING

Accumulation factors in Tables A.1 through A.4 are defined without respect to any particular calendar period. Variable n is general in that sense. But it is conventional to express periodic rates as annual rates for purposes of comparability; Equation A.9 relates period rates and annual rates:

$$(1 + r_a)^t = \left(1 + \frac{i}{c}\right)^{ct} \tag{A.9}$$

where

r_a = effective (compounded) annual rate of interest
i = nominal (simple) annual rate of interest
c = number of times per year interest is compounded
t = number of years in which interest is compounded

For example, $300.00 invested at 10 percent, compounded quarterly, will accumulate to $598.95 in seven years:

$$\text{FV} = 300.00\left(1 + \frac{.10}{4}\right)^{4 \times 7}$$

$$= 300.00(1.025)^{28}$$

$$= 300.00(1.9965)$$

$$= 598.95$$

The compound interest effect can be substantial. A nominal annual return of 12 percent increases significantly as the frequency of compounding increases:[3]

Annual	$(1.12)^1$	= 1.1200
Semiannual	$(1.06)^2$	= 1.1236
Quarterly	$(1.03)^4$	= 1.1255
Monthly	$(1.01)^{12}$	= 1.1268
Daily		1.1275
Continuously		1.1275

Moving from annual to monthly compounding increases rate of return by 68 basis points (.0068); for daily compounding the increase is three-fourths of one percent (.0075). Proper use of appendix tables requires careful identification of the calendar periods involved in a given situation.

[3] Data for daily compounding are not available in Table A.1. Continuous compounding is calculated by raising the irrational number e to the it power. That is, for $t = 1$,

$$e^{it} = e^{.12} = 1.1275$$

rounded to four decimal places.

Solving Compound Interest Problems

The discussion in the preceding section introduced four formulas (Equations A.5–A.8) employing the compound interest variables summarized below:

Compound Interest Variables

1. r, interest rate	Always involved
2. n, number of periods	Always involved
3. PV, present value	Two of three involved
4. FV, future value	Two of three involved
5. R, series of periodic payments	Two of three involved

Every compound interest problem involves four of those variables: r, n, and two from the set of PV, FV, and R. Of the four variables, values will be given for three, and the fourth, the unknown, can then be evaluated. Thus compound interest problems are easily solved. First, identify the three variables with given values as well as the fourth one, the unknown. Next, identify the proper formula (table) from the matrix of Figure A.2. The remaining step is arithmetic.

To illustrate the process, how long does it take to accumulate \$709.25 if \$500.00 is invested today at 6 percent compounded annually? This problem involves FV(709.25), PV(500.00), r(.06), and n(unknown). It is a single payment problem that can be solved from either of the upper quadrants of Figure A.2. Using Table A.1, the solution is six years:

$$\begin{aligned} \text{FV} &= \text{PV}(1 + r)^n \\ 709.25 &= 500.00(1.06)^n \\ 1.4185 &= (1.06)^n \\ n &= 6 \end{aligned}$$

Again, what is the periodic monthly payment which is required to amortize a \$20,000.00 home mortgage over eight years if the nominal interest rate is 12 percent? This problem involves present value and a series of payments; the relevant formula (table) is contained in the southeast quadrant. PV(20,000.00), r(.01), and n(96) are given; R is unknown:

$$20{,}000.00 = R\left[\frac{1 - (1.01)^{-96}}{.10}\right]$$

$$20{,}000.00 = R[61.5277]$$

$$R = \frac{20{,}000.00}{61.5277} = 325.06$$

With variables identified, and the correct formula located, problem solutions are easily calculated.

Figure A.2
Compound Interest Variables

	Future Value (FV)	Present Value (PV)
Single Payment	FV PV *r* *n* **Table A.1**	PV FV *r* *n* **Table A.2**
Series of Payments	FV *R* *r* *n* **Table A.3**	PV *R* *r* *n* **Table A.4**

Electronic Calculators

With the development of increasingly efficient and inexpensive electronic calculators, compound interest tables may soon be as obsolete as some now believe the slide rule to be. Nonetheless, the material provided in this appendix remains valuable for an understanding of relationships underlying computations. In addition, the methodology is still relevant: one of the more popular calculators currently available has basic finance routines which call for entry of three known variables, from left to right, from the set of n, r, R, PV, and FV; the problem is solved by depressing the fourth key, for the unknown value. The process is the one described in the last section, except for the substitution of the calculator routine for the compound interest table.[4]

Questions and Problems

1. An individual places $1000 in a bank time deposit, with interest credited at 6 percent compounded quarterly. What is the balance in the account after six and a half years?
2. A corporation is required to establish a sinking fund to retire a $10,000,000 bond issue ten years from now; what constant payment is required at the end of each year if sinking fund assets earn 8 percent per year compounded annually?
3. A corporate bond with a face value of $1000 is priced to yield 9 percent interest compounded semiannually. The coupon rate for the bond is also 9 percent, with semiannual payment; that is, the bondholder receives $45 interest every six months. At what price would the bond sell for today if it matures ten years from today, with the first interest payment due in six months?

[4] The calculator referred to is the Hewlett-Packard 80; more complicated problems are solved with somewhat more complicated routines than those described here.

4. Assume the same facts as in problem 3 above, except that the bond sells to yield 8 percent. What is the price under this assumption? What if the yield were 10 percent?
5. What is the yield on a mortgage which originated today in the amount of $10,000.00 if the monthly payment is $193.33 and it is due in five years?
6. Consider the present value factors in Tables A.2 and A.4 at 5 and 6 percent; describe the behavior of the values as r and n vary. What is the present value of $100 per year, at 5 percent, if that sum is received each year for the next ten years? Twenty years? One hundred years? Forever?
7. Internal Revenue regulations allow taxpayers to use a number of different methods of calculating depreciation, including the straight line (SL) and the sum-of-the-years digits (SYD) methods. Depreciation for an asset costing $21,000 which has no salvage value is given below; assumed useful life is six years.

Year	*SL*	*SYD*
1	$3500	$6000
2	3500	5000
3	3500	4000
4	3500	3000
5	3500	2000
6	3500	1000

If the taxpayer who owns this asset has the opportunity of investing money at 8 percent per year in any year, what is the advantage of selecting one method over another? Assume an effective tax rate of 40 percent.

Table A.1

Future Value of $1.00 for n Periods

n	r: 0.005	0.010	0.015	0.020	0.025	0.030	0.035
1	1.0050	1.0100	1.0150	1.0200	1.0250	1.0300	1.0350
2	1.0100	1.0201	1.0302	1.0404	1.0506	1.0609	1.0712
3	1.0151	1.0303	1.0457	1.0612	1.0769	1.0927	1.1087
4	1.0202	1.0406	1.0614	1.0824	1.1038	1.1255	1.1475
5	1.0253	1.0510	1.0773	1.1041	1.1314	1.1593	1.1877
6	1.0304	1.0615	1.0934	1.1262	1.1597	1.1941	1.2293
7	1.0355	1.0721	1.1098	1.1487	1.1887	1.2299	1.2723
8	1.0407	1.0829	1.1265	1.1717	1.2184	1.2668	1.3168
9	1.0459	1.0937	1.1434	1.1951	1.2489	1.3048	1.3629
10	1.0511	1.1046	1.1605	1.2190	1.2801	1.3439	1.4106
11	1.0564	1.1157	1.1779	1.2434	1.3121	1.3842	1.4600
12	1.0617	1.1268	1.1956	1.2682	1.3449	1.4258	1.5111
13	1.0670	1.1381	1.2136	1.2936	1.3785	1.4685	1.5640
14	1.0723	1.1495	1.2318	1.3195	1.4130	1.5126	1.6187
15	1.0777	1.1610	1.2502	1.3459	1.4483	1.5580	1.6753
16	1.0831	1.1726	1.2690	1.3728	1.4845	1.6047	1.7340
17	1.0885	1.1843	1.2880	1.4002	1.5216	1.6528	1.7947
18	1.0939	1.1961	1.3073	1.4282	1.5597	1.7024	1.8575
19	1.0994	1.2081	1.3270	1.4568	1.5987	1.7535	1.9225
20	1.1049	1.2202	1.3469	1.4859	1.6386	1.8061	1.9898
21	1.1104	1.2324	1.3671	1.5157	1.6796	1.8603	2.0594
22	1.1160	1.2447	1.3876	1.5460	1.7216	1.9161	2.1315
23	1.1216	1.2572	1.4084	1.5769	1.7646	1.9736	2.2061
24	1.1272	1.2697	1.4295	1.6084	1.8087	2.0328	2.2833
25	1.1328	1.2824	1.4509	1.6406	1.8539	2.0938	2.3632
26	1.1385	1.2953	1.4727	1.6734	1.9003	2.1566	2.4460
27	1.1442	1.3082	1.4948	1.7069	1.9478	2.2213	2.5316
28	1.1499	1.3213	1.5172	1.7410	1.9965	2.2879	2.6202
29	1.1556	1.3345	1.5400	1.7758	2.0464	2.3566	2.7119
30	1.1614	1.3478	1.5631	1.8114	2.0976	2.4273	2.8068
31	1.1672	1.3613	1.5865	1.8476	2.1500	2.5001	2.9050
32	1.1730	1.3749	1.6103	1.8845	2.2038	2.5751	3.0067
33	1.1789	1.3887	1.6345	1.9222	2.2589	2.6523	3.1119
34	1.1848	1.4026	1.6590	1.9607	2.3153	2.7319	3.2209
35	1.1907	1.4166	1.6839	1.9999	2.3732	2.8139	3.3336
36	1.1967	1.4308	1.7091	2.0399	2.4325	2.8983	3.4503
48	1.2705	1.6122	2.0435	2.5871	3.2715	4.1323	5.2136
60	1.3489	1.8167	2.4432	3.2810	4.3998	5.8916	7.8781
72	1.4320	2.0471	2.9212	4.1611	5.9172	8.4000	11.9043
84	1.5204	2.3067	3.4926	5.2773	7.9580	11.9764	17.9883
96	1.6141	2.5993	4.1758	6.6929	10.7026	17.0755	27.1815

Table A.1
(*continued*)

n	r = 0.040	0.045	0.050	0.055	0.060	0.065	0.070
1	1.0400	1.0450	1.0500	1.0550	1.0600	1.0650	1.0700
2	1.0816	1.0920	1.1025	1.1130	1.1236	1.1342	1.1449
3	1.1249	1.1412	1.1576	1.1742	1.1910	1.2079	1.2250
4	1.1699	1.1925	1.2155	1.2388	1.2625	1.2865	1.3108
5	1.2167	1.2462	1.2763	1.3070	1.3382	1.3701	1.4026
6	1.2653	1.3023	1.3401	1.3788	1.4185	1.4591	1.5007
7	1.3159	1.3609	1.4071	1.4547	1.5036	1.5540	1.6058
8	1.3686	1.4221	1.4775	1.5347	1.5938	1.6550	1.7182
9	1.4233	1.4861	1.5513	1.6191	1.6895	1.7626	1.8385
10	1.4802	1.5530	1.6289	1.7081	1.7908	1.8771	1.9672
11	1.5395	1.6229	1.7103	1.8021	1.8983	1.9992	2.1049
12	1.6010	1.6959	1.7959	1.9012	2.0122	2.1291	2.2522
13	1.6651	1.7722	1.8856	2.0058	2.1329	2.2675	2.4098
14	1.7317	1.8519	1.9799	2.1161	2.2609	2.4149	2.5785
15	1.8009	1.9353	2.0789	2.2325	2.3966	2.5718	2.7590
16	1.8730	2.0224	2.1829	2.3553	2.5404	2.7390	2.9522
17	1.9479	2.1134	2.2920	2.4848	2.6928	2.9170	3.1588
18	2.0258	2.2085	2.4066	2.6215	2.8543	3.1067	3.3799
19	2.1068	2.3079	2.5270	2.7656	3.0256	3.3086	3.6165
20	2.1911	2.4117	2.6533	2.9178	3.2071	3.5236	3.8697
21	2.2788	2.5202	2.7860	3.0782	3.3996	3.7527	4.1406
22	2.3699	2.6337	2.9253	3.2475	3.6035	3.9966	4.4304
23	2.4647	2.7522	3.0715	3.4262	3.8197	4.2564	4.7405
24	2.5633	2.8760	3.2251	3.6146	4.0489	4.5331	5.0724
25	2.6658	3.0054	3.3864	3.8134	4.2919	4.8277	5.4274
26	2.7725	3.1407	3.5557	4.0231	4.5494	5.1415	5.8074
27	2.8834	3.2820	3.7335	4.2444	4.8223	5.4757	6.2139
28	2.9987	3.4297	3.9201	4.4778	5.1117	5.8316	6.6488
29	3.1187	3.5840	4.1161	4.7241	5.4184	6.2107	7.114
30	3.2434	3.7453	4.3219	4.9840	5.7435	6.6144	7.6123
31	3.3731	3.9139	4.5380	5.2581	6.0881	7.0443	8.1451
32	3.5081	4.0900	4.7649	5.5473	6.4534	7.5022	8.7153
33	3.6484	4.2740	5.0032	5.8524	6.8406	7.9898	9.325
34	3.7943	4.4664	5.2533	6.1742	7.2510	8.5092	9.9781
35	3.9461	4.6673	5.5160	6.5138	7.6861	9.0623	10.6766
36	4.1039	4.8774	5.7918	6.8721	8.1473	9.6513	11.4239
48	6.5705	8.2715	10.4013	13.0653	16.3939	20.5485	25.7289
60	10.5196	14.0274	18.6792	24.8398	32.9877	43.7498	57.946
72	16.8423	23.7888	33.5451	47.2256	66.3777	93.1476	130.506
84	26.9650	40.3430	60.2422	89.7856	133.5650	198.3202	293.925
96	43.1718	68.4170	108.1864	170.7010	268.7590	422.2429	661.976

Table A.1

(continued)

n	r: 0.075	0.080	0.085	0.090	0.095	0.100	0.105
1	1.0750	1.0800	1.0850	1.0900	1.0950	1.1000	1.1050
2	1.1556	1.1664	1.1772	1.1881	1.1990	1.2100	1.2210
3	1.2423	1.2597	1.2773	1.2950	1.3129	1.3310	1.3492
4	1.3355	1.3605	1.3859	1.4116	1.4377	1.4641	1.4909
5	1.4356	1.4693	1.5037	1.5386	1.5742	1.6105	1.6474
6	1.5433	1.5869	1.6315	1.6771	1.7238	1.7716	1.8204
7	1.6590	1.7138	1.7701	1.8280	1.8876	1.9487	2.0116
8	1.7835	1.8509	1.9206	1.9926	2.0669	2.1436	2.2228
9	1.9172	1.9990	2.0839	2.1719	2.2632	2.3579	2.4562
10	2.0610	2.1589	2.2610	2.3674	2.4782	2.5937	2.7141
11	2.2156	2.3316	2.4532	2.5804	2.7137	2.8531	2.9991
12	2.3818	2.5182	2.6617	2.8127	2.9715	3.1384	3.3140
13	2.5604	2.7196	2.8879	3.0658	3.2537	3.4523	3.6619
14	2.7524	2.9372	3.1334	3.3417	3.5629	3.7975	4.0464
15	2.9589	3.1722	3.3997	3.6425	3.9013	4.1772	4.4713
16	3.1808	3.4259	3.6887	3.9703	4.2719	4.5950	4.9408
17	3.4194	3.7000	4.0023	4.3276	4.6778	5.0545	5.4596
18	3.6758	3.9960	4.3425	4.7171	5.1222	5.5599	6.0320
19	3.9515	4.3157	4.7116	5.1417	5.6088	6.1159	6.6663
20	4.2479	4.6610	5.1120	5.6044	6.1416	6.7275	7.3662
21	4.5664	5.0338	5.5466	6.1088	6.7251	7.4002	8.1397
22	4.9089	5.4365	6.0180	6.6586	7.3639	8.1403	8.9944
23	5.2771	5.8715	6.5296	7.2579	8.0635	8.9543	9.9388
24	5.6729	6.3412	7.0846	7.9111	8.8296	9.8497	10.9823
25	6.0983	6.8485	7.6868	8.6231	9.6684	10.8347	12.1355
26	6.5557	7.3964	8.3401	9.3992	10.5869	11.9182	13.4097
27	7.0474	7.9881	9.0490	10.2451	11.5926	13.1100	14.8177
28	7.5759	8.6271	9.8182	11.1671	12.6939	14.4210	16.3736
29	8.1441	9.3173	10.6528	12.1722	13.8998	15.8631	18.0928
30	8.7550	10.0627	11.5583	13.2677	15.2203	17.4494	19.9926
31	9.4116	10.8677	12.5407	14.4618	16.6662	19.1943	22.0918
32	10.1174	11.7371	13.6067	15.7633	18.2495	21.1138	24.4114
33	10.8763	12.6760	14.7632	17.1820	19.9832	23.2252	26.9746
34	11.6920	13.6901	16.0181	18.7284	21.8816	25.5477	29.8069
35	12.5689	14.7853	17.3796	20.4140	23.9604	28.1024	32.9367
36	13.5115	15.9682	18.8569	22.2512	26.2366	30.9127	36.3950
48	32.1815	40.2106	50.1912	62.5852	77.9611	97.0172	120.6117
60	76.6492	101.2571	133.5932	176.0313	231.6579	304.4816	399.7023
72	182.5616	254.9825	355.5831	495.1170	688.3615	955.5938	1324.5978
84	434.8215	642.0893	946.4507	1392.5982	2045.4365	2999.0628	4389.6648
96	1035.6489	1616.8902	2519.1549	3916.9119	6077.9265	9412.3437	1.455E+04

NOTE: NUMBERS GREATER THAN 9999.99 ARE EXPRESSED IN SCIENTIFIC NOTATION

Table A.1
(*continued*)

n	r = 0.110	0.115	0.120	0.130	0.140	0.150	0.160
1	1.1100	1.1150	1.1200	1.1300	1.1400	1.1500	1.1600
2	1.2321	1.2432	1.2544	1.2769	1.2996	1.3225	1.3456
3	1.3676	1.3862	1.4049	1.4429	1.4815	1.5209	1.5609
4	1.5181	1.5456	1.5735	1.6305	1.6890	1.7490	1.8106
5	1.6851	1.7234	1.7623	1.8424	1.9254	2.0114	2.1003
6	1.8704	1.9215	1.9738	2.0820	2.1950	2.3131	2.4364
7	2.0762	2.1425	2.2107	2.3526	2.5023	2.6600	2.8262
8	2.3045	2.3889	2.4760	2.6584	2.8526	3.0590	3.2784
9	2.5580	2.6636	2.7731	3.0040	3.2519	3.5179	3.8030
10	2.8394	2.9699	3.1058	3.3946	3.7072	4.0456	4.4114
11	3.1518	3.3115	3.4785	3.8359	4.2262	4.6524	5.1173
12	3.4985	3.6923	3.8960	4.3345	4.8179	5.3503	5.9360
13	3.8833	4.1169	4.3635	4.8980	5.4924	6.1528	6.8858
14	4.3104	4.5904	4.8871	5.5348	6.2613	7.0757	7.9875
15	4.7846	5.1183	5.4736	6.2543	7.1379	8.1371	9.2655
16	5.3109	5.7069	6.1304	7.0673	8.1372	9.3576	10.7480
17	5.8951	6.3632	6.8660	7.9861	9.2765	10.7613	12.4677
18	6.5436	7.0949	7.6900	9.0243	10.5752	12.3755	14.4625
19	7.2633	7.9108	8.6128	10.1974	12.0557	14.2318	16.7765
20	8.0623	8.8206	9.6463	11.5231	13.7435	16.3665	19.4608
21	8.9492	9.8350	10.8038	13.0211	15.6676	18.8215	22.5745
22	9.9336	10.9660	12.1003	14.7138	17.8610	21.6447	26.1864
23	11.0263	12.2271	13.5523	16.6266	20.3616	24.8915	30.3762
24	12.2392	13.6332	15.1786	18.7881	23.2122	28.6252	35.2364
25	13.5855	15.2010	17.0001	21.2305	26.4619	32.9190	40.8742
26	15.0799	16.9491	19.0401	23.9905	30.1666	37.8568	47.4141
27	16.7386	18.8982	21.3249	27.1093	34.3899	43.5353	55.0004
28	18.5799	21.0715	23.8839	30.6335	39.2045	50.0656	63.8004
29	20.6237	23.4948	26.7499	34.6158	44.6931	57.5755	74.0085
30	22.8923	26.1967	29.9599	39.1159	50.9502	66.2118	85.8499
31	25.4104	29.2093	33.5551	44.2010	58.0832	76.1435	99.5859
32	28.2056	32.5683	37.5817	49.9471	66.2148	87.5651	115.5196
33	31.3082	36.3137	42.0915	56.4402	75.4849	100.6998	134.0027
34	34.7521	40.4898	47.1425	63.7774	86.0528	115.8048	155.4432
35	38.5749	45.1461	52.7996	72.0685	98.1002	133.1755	180.3141
36	42.8181	50.3379	59.1356	81.4374	111.8342	153.1519	209.1643
48	149.7970	185.8633	230.3908	352.9923	538.8065	819.4007	1241.6051
60	524.0572	686.2653	897.5969	1530.0535	2595.9187	4383.9987	7370.2014
72	1833.3884	2533.9057	3497.0161	6632.0521	1.251E+04	2.346E+04	4.375E+04
84	6414.0186	9355.9709	1.362E+04	2.875E+04	6.026E+04	1.255E+05	2.597E+05
96	2.244E+04	3.455E+04	5.308E+04	1.246E+05	2.903E+05	6.714E+05	1.542E+06

NOTE: NUMBERS GREATER THAN 9999.99 ARE EXPRESSED IN SCIENTIFIC NOTATION

Table A.1
(continued)

n	r = 0.170	0.180	0.190	0.200	0.210	0.220	0.230
1	1.1700	1.1800	1.1900	1.2000	1.2100	1.2200	1.2300
2	1.3689	1.3924	1.4161	1.4400	1.4641	1.4884	1.5129
3	1.6016	1.6430	1.6852	1.7280	1.7716	1.8158	1.8609
4	1.8739	1.9388	2.0053	2.0736	2.1436	2.2153	2.2889
5	2.1924	2.2878	2.3864	2.4883	2.5937	2.7027	2.8153
6	2.5652	2.6996	2.8398	2.9860	3.1384	3.2973	3.4628
7	3.0012	3.1855	3.3793	3.5832	3.7975	4.0227	4.2593
8	3.5115	3.7589	4.0214	4.2998	4.5950	4.9077	5.2389
9	4.1084	4.4355	4.7854	5.1598	5.5599	5.9874	6.4439
10	4.8068	5.2338	5.6947	6.1917	6.7275	7.3046	7.9259
11	5.6240	6.1759	6.7767	7.4301	8.1403	8.9117	9.7489
12	6.5801	7.2876	8.0642	8.9161	9.8497	10.8722	11.9912
13	7.6987	8.5994	9.5964	10.6993	11.9182	13.2641	14.7491
14	9.0075	10.1472	11.4198	12.8392	14.4210	16.1822	18.1414
15	10.5387	11.9737	13.5895	15.4070	17.4494	19.7423	22.3140
16	12.3303	14.1290	16.1715	18.4884	21.1138	24.0856	27.4462
17	14.4265	16.6722	19.2441	22.1861	25.5477	29.3844	33.7588
18	16.8790	19.6733	22.9005	26.6233	30.9127	35.8490	41.5233
19	19.7484	23.2144	27.2516	31.9480	37.4043	43.7358	51.0737
20	23.1056	27.3930	32.4294	38.3376	45.2593	53.3576	62.8206
21	27.0336	32.3238	38.5910	46.0051	54.7637	65.0963	77.2694
22	31.6293	38.1421	45.9233	55.2061	66.2641	79.4175	95.0413
23	37.0062	45.0076	54.6487	66.2474	80.1795	96.8894	116.9008
24	43.2973	53.1090	65.0320	79.4968	97.0172	118.2050	143.7880
25	50.6578	62.6686	77.3881	95.3962	117.3909	144.2101	176.8593
26	59.2697	73.9490	92.0918	114.4755	142.0429	175.9364	217.5369
27	69.3455	87.2598	109.5893	137.3706	171.8719	214.6424	267.5704
28	81.1342	102.9666	130.4112	164.8447	207.9651	261.8637	329.1115
29	94.9271	121.5005	155.1893	197.8136	251.6377	319.4737	404.8072
30	111.0647	143.3706	184.6753	237.3763	304.4816	389.7579	497.9129
31	129.9456	169.1774	219.7636	284.8516	368.4228	475.5046	612.4328
32	152.0364	199.6293	261.5187	341.8219	445.7916	580.1156	753.2924
33	177.8826	235.5625	311.2073	410.1863	539.4078	707.7411	926.5496
34	208.1226	277.9638	370.3366	492.2235	652.6834	863.4441	1139.6560
35	243.5035	327.9973	440.7006	590.6682	789.7470	1053.4018	1401.7769
36	284.8991	387.0368	524.4337	708.8019	955.5938	1285.1502	1724.1856
48	1874.6550	2820.5665	4229.1603	6319.7487	9412.3437	1.397E+04	2.067E+04
60	1.234E+04	2.056E+04	3.410E+04	5.635E+04	9.271E+04	1.519E+05	2.479E+05
72	8.117E+04	1.498E+05	2.750E+05	5.024E+05	9.132E+05	1.652E+06	2.973E+06
84	5.341E+05	1.092E+06	2.218E+06	4.479E+06	8.994E+06	1.796E+07	3.565E+07
96	3.514E+06	7.956E+06	1.789E+07	3.994E+07	8.859E+07	1.952E+08	4.275E+08

NOTE: NUMBERS GREATER THAN 9999.99 ARE EXPRESSED IN SCIENTIFIC NOTATION

Table A.1
(*continued*)

n	r = 0.240	0.250	0.260	0.270	0.280	0.290	0.300
1	1.2400	1.2500	1.2600	1.2700	1.2800	1.2900	1.3000
2	1.5376	1.5625	1.5876	1.6129	1.6384	1.6641	1.6900
3	1.9066	1.9531	2.0004	2.0484	2.0972	2.1467	2.1970
4	2.3642	2.4414	2.5205	2.6014	2.6844	2.7692	2.8561
5	2.9316	3.0518	3.1758	3.3038	3.4360	3.5723	3.7129
6	3.6352	3.8147	4.0015	4.1959	4.3980	4.6083	4.8268
7	4.5077	4.7684	5.0419	5.3288	5.6295	5.9447	6.2749
8	5.5895	5.9605	6.3528	6.7675	7.2058	7.6686	8.1573
9	6.9310	7.4506	8.0045	8.5948	9.2234	9.8925	10.6045
10	8.5944	9.3132	10.0857	10.9153	11.8059	12.7614	13.7858
11	10.6571	11.6415	12.7080	13.8625	15.1116	16.4622	17.9216
12	13.2148	14.5519	16.0120	17.6053	19.3428	21.2362	23.2981
13	16.3863	18.1899	20.1752	22.3588	24.7588	27.3947	30.2875
14	20.3191	22.7374	25.4207	28.3957	31.6913	35.3391	39.3738
15	25.1956	28.4217	32.0301	36.0625	40.5648	45.5875	51.1859
16	31.2426	35.5271	40.3579	45.7994	51.9230	58.8079	66.5417
17	38.7408	44.4089	50.8510	58.1652	66.4614	75.8621	86.5042
18	48.0386	55.5112	64.0722	73.8698	85.0706	97.8622	112.4554
19	59.5679	69.3889	80.7310	93.8147	108.8904	126.2422	146.1920
20	73.8641	86.7362	101.7211	119.1446	139.3797	162.8524	190.0496
21	91.5915	108.4202	128.1685	151.3137	178.4060	210.0796	247.0645
22	113.5735	135.5253	161.4924	192.1683	228.3596	271.0027	321.1839
23	140.8312	169.4066	203.4804	244.0538	292.3003	349.5935	417.5391
24	174.6306	211.7582	256.3853	309.9483	374.1444	450.9756	542.8008
25	216.5420	264.6978	323.0454	393.6344	478.9049	581.7585	705.6410
26	268.5121	330.8722	407.0373	499.9157	612.9982	750.4685	917.3333
27	332.9550	413.5903	512.8670	634.8929	784.6377	968.1044	1192.5333
28	412.8642	516.9879	646.2124	806.3140	1004.3363	1248.8546	1550.2933
29	511.9516	646.2349	814.2276	1024.0187	1285.5504	1611.0225	2015.3813
30	634.8199	807.7936	1025.9267	1300.5038	1645.5046	2078.2190	2619.9956
31	787.1767	1009.7420	1292.6677	1651.6398	2106.2458	2680.9025	3405.9943
32	976.0991	1262.1774	1628.7613	2097.5826	2695.9947	3458.3642	4427.7926
33	1210.3629	1577.7218	2052.2392	2663.9299	3450.8732	4461.2898	5756.1304
34	1500.8500	1972.1523	2585.8215	3383.1910	4417.1177	5755.0639	7482.9696
35	1861.0540	2465.1903	3258.1350	4296.6525	5653.9106	7424.0324	9727.8604
36	2307.7070	3081.4879	4105.2501	5456.7487	7237.0056	9577.0018	1.265E+04
48	3.050E+04	4.484E+04	6.573E+04	9.607E+04	1.400E+05	2.034E+05	2.946E+05
60	4.030E+05	6.525E+05	1.053E+06	1.691E+06	2.708E+06	4.319E+06	6.864E+06
72	5.326E+06	9.496E+06	1.685E+07	2.978E+07	5.237E+07	9.172E+07	1.599E+08
84	7.038E+07	1.382E+08	2.699E+08	5.242E+08	1.013E+09	1.948E+09	3.726E+09
96	9.300E+08	2.011E+09	4.321E+09	9.229E+09	1.960E+10	4.136E+10	8.681E+10

NOTE: NUMBERS GREATER THAN 9999.99 ARE EXPRESSED IN SCIENTIFIC NOTATION

Table A.2

Future Value of $1.00 for n Periods

n	r = 0.005	0.010	0.015	0.020	0.025	0.030	0.035
1	0.9950	0.9901	0.9852	0.9804	0.9756	0.9709	0.9662
2	0.9901	0.9803	0.9707	0.9612	0.9518	0.9426	0.9335
3	0.9851	0.9706	0.9563	0.9423	0.9286	0.9151	0.9019
4	0.9802	0.9610	0.9422	0.9238	0.9060	0.8885	0.8714
5	0.9754	0.9515	0.9283	0.9057	0.8839	0.8626	0.8420
6	0.9705	0.9420	0.9145	0.8880	0.8623	0.8375	0.8135
7	0.9657	0.9327	0.9010	0.8706	0.8413	0.8131	0.7860
8	0.9609	0.9235	0.8877	0.8535	0.8207	0.7894	0.7594
9	0.9561	0.9143	0.8746	0.8368	0.8007	0.7664	0.7337
10	0.9513	0.9053	0.8617	0.8203	0.7812	0.7441	0.7089
11	0.9466	0.8963	0.8489	0.8043	0.7621	0.7224	0.6849
12	0.9419	0.8874	0.8364	0.7885	0.7436	0.7014	0.6618
13	0.9372	0.8787	0.8240	0.7730	0.7254	0.6810	0.6394
14	0.9326	0.8700	0.8118	0.7579	0.7077	0.6611	0.6178
15	0.9279	0.8613	0.7999	0.7430	0.6905	0.6419	0.5969
16	0.9233	0.8528	0.7880	0.7284	0.6736	0.6232	0.5767
17	0.9187	0.8444	0.7764	0.7142	0.6572	0.6050	0.5572
18	0.9141	0.8360	0.7649	0.7002	0.6412	0.5874	0.5384
19	0.9096	0.8277	0.7536	0.6864	0.6255	0.5703	0.5202
20	0.9051	0.8195	0.7425	0.6730	0.6103	0.5537	0.5026
21	0.9006	0.8114	0.7315	0.6598	0.5954	0.5375	0.4856
22	0.8961	0.8034	0.7207	0.6468	0.5809	0.5219	0.4692
23	0.8916	0.7954	0.7100	0.6342	0.5667	0.5067	0.4533
24	0.8872	0.7876	0.6995	0.6217	0.5529	0.4919	0.4380
25	0.8828	0.7798	0.6892	0.6095	0.5394	0.4776	0.4231
26	0.8784	0.7720	0.6790	0.5976	0.5262	0.4637	0.4088
27	0.8740	0.7644	0.6690	0.5859	0.5134	0.4502	0.3950
28	0.8697	0.7568	0.6591	0.5744	0.5009	0.4371	0.3817
29	0.8653	0.7493	0.6494	0.5631	0.4887	0.4243	0.3687
30	0.8610	0.7419	0.6398	0.5521	0.4767	0.4120	0.3563
31	0.8567	0.7346	0.6303	0.5412	0.4651	0.4000	0.3442
32	0.8525	0.7273	0.6210	0.5306	0.4538	0.3883	0.3326
33	0.8482	0.7201	0.6118	0.5202	0.4427	0.3770	0.3213
34	0.8440	0.7130	0.6028	0.5100	0.4319	0.3660	0.3105
35	0.8398	0.7059	0.5939	0.5000	0.4214	0.3554	0.3000
36	0.8356	0.6989	0.5851	0.4902	0.4111	0.3450	0.2898
48	0.7871	0.6203	0.4894	0.3865	0.3057	0.2420	0.1918
60	0.7414	0.5504	0.4093	0.3048	0.2273	0.1697	0.1269
72	0.6983	0.4885	0.3423	0.2403	0.1690	0.1190	0.0840
84	0.6577	0.4335	0.2863	0.1895	0.1257	0.0835	0.0556
96	0.6195	0.3847	0.2395	0.1494	0.0934	0.0586	0.0368

Table A.2
(continued)

n	r = 0.040	0.045	0.050	0.055	0.060	0.065	0.070
1	0.9615	0.9569	0.9524	0.9479	0.9434	0.9390	0.9346
2	0.9246	0.9157	0.9070	0.8985	0.8900	0.8817	0.8734
3	0.8890	0.8763	0.8638	0.8516	0.8396	0.8278	0.8163
4	0.8548	0.8386	0.8227	0.8072	0.7921	0.7773	0.7629
5	0.8219	0.8025	0.7835	0.7651	0.7473	0.7299	0.7130
6	0.7903	0.7679	0.7462	0.7252	0.7050	0.6853	0.6663
7	0.7599	0.7348	0.7107	0.6874	0.6651	0.6435	0.6227
8	0.7307	0.7032	0.6768	0.6516	0.6274	0.6042	0.5820
9	0.7026	0.6729	0.6446	0.6176	0.5919	0.5674	0.5439
10	0.6756	0.6439	0.6139	0.5854	0.5584	0.5327	0.5083
11	0.6496	0.6162	0.5847	0.5549	0.5268	0.5002	0.4751
12	0.6246	0.5897	0.5568	0.5260	0.4970	0.4697	0.4440
13	0.6006	0.5643	0.5303	0.4986	0.4688	0.4410	0.4150
14	0.5775	0.5400	0.5051	0.4726	0.4423	0.4141	0.3878
15	0.5553	0.5167	0.4810	0.4479	0.4173	0.3888	0.3624
16	0.5339	0.4945	0.4581	0.4246	0.3936	0.3651	0.3387
17	0.5134	0.4732	0.4363	0.4024	0.3714	0.3428	0.3166
18	0.4936	0.4528	0.4155	0.3815	0.3503	0.3219	0.2959
19	0.4746	0.4333	0.3957	0.3616	0.3305	0.3022	0.2765
20	0.4564	0.4146	0.3769	0.3427	0.3118	0.2838	0.2584
21	0.4388	0.3968	0.3589	0.3249	0.2942	0.2665	0.2415
22	0.4220	0.3797	0.3418	0.3079	0.2775	0.2502	0.2257
23	0.4057	0.3634	0.3256	0.2919	0.2618	0.2349	0.2109
24	0.3901	0.3477	0.3101	0.2767	0.2470	0.2206	0.1971
25	0.3751	0.3327	0.2953	0.2622	0.2330	0.2071	0.1842
26	0.3607	0.3184	0.2812	0.2486	0.2198	0.1945	0.1722
27	0.3468	0.3047	0.2678	0.2356	0.2074	0.1826	0.1609
28	0.3335	0.2916	0.2551	0.2233	0.1956	0.1715	0.1504
29	0.3207	0.2790	0.2429	0.2117	0.1846	0.1610	0.1406
30	0.3083	0.2670	0.2314	0.2006	0.1741	0.1512	0.1314
31	0.2965	0.2555	0.2204	0.1902	0.1643	0.1420	0.1228
32	0.2851	0.2445	0.2099	0.1803	0.1550	0.1333	0.1147
33	0.2741	0.2340	0.1999	0.1709	0.1462	0.1252	0.1072
34	0.2636	0.2239	0.1904	0.1620	0.1379	0.1175	0.1002
35	0.2534	0.2143	0.1813	0.1535	0.1301	0.1103	0.0937
36	0.2437	0.2050	0.1727	0.1455	0.1227	0.1036	0.0875
48	0.1522	0.1209	0.0961	0.0765	0.0610	0.0487	0.0389
60	0.0951	0.0713	0.0535	0.0403	0.0303	0.0229	0.0173
72	0.0594	0.0420	0.0298	0.0212	0.0151	0.0107	0.0077
84	0.0371	0.0248	0.0166	0.0111	0.0075	0.0050	0.0034
96	0.0232	0.0146	0.0092	0.0059	0.0037	0.0024	0.0015

Table A.2
(*continued*)

n	r = 0.075	0.080	0.085	0.090	0.095	0.100	0.105
1	0.9302	0.9259	0.9217	0.9174	0.9132	0.9091	0.9050
2	0.8653	0.8573	0.8495	0.8417	0.8340	0.8264	0.8190
3	0.8050	0.7938	0.7829	0.7722	0.7617	0.7513	0.7412
4	0.7488	0.7350	0.7216	0.7084	0.6956	0.6830	0.6707
5	0.6966	0.6806	0.6650	0.6499	0.6352	0.6209	0.6070
6	0.6480	0.6302	0.6129	0.5963	0.5801	0.5645	0.5493
7	0.6028	0.5835	0.5649	0.5470	0.5298	0.5132	0.4971
8	0.5607	0.5403	0.5207	0.5019	0.4838	0.4665	0.4499
9	0.5216	0.5002	0.4799	0.4604	0.4418	0.4241	0.4071
10	0.4852	0.4632	0.4423	0.4224	0.4035	0.3855	0.3684
11	0.4513	0.4289	0.4076	0.3875	0.3685	0.3505	0.3334
12	0.4199	0.3971	0.3757	0.3555	0.3365	0.3186	0.3018
13	0.3906	0.3677	0.3463	0.3262	0.3073	0.2897	0.2731
14	0.3633	0.3405	0.3191	0.2992	0.2807	0.2633	0.2471
15	0.3380	0.3152	0.2941	0.2745	0.2563	0.2394	0.2236
16	0.3144	0.2919	0.2711	0.2519	0.2341	0.2176	0.2024
17	0.2925	0.2703	0.2499	0.2311	0.2138	0.1978	0.1832
18	0.2720	0.2502	0.2303	0.2120	0.1952	0.1799	0.1658
19	0.2531	0.2317	0.2122	0.1945	0.1783	0.1635	0.1500
20	0.2354	0.2145	0.1956	0.1784	0.1628	0.1486	0.1358
21	0.2190	0.1987	0.1803	0.1637	0.1487	0.1351	0.1229
22	0.2037	0.1839	0.1662	0.1502	0.1358	0.1228	0.1112
23	0.1895	0.1703	0.1531	0.1378	0.1240	0.1117	0.1006
24	0.1763	0.1577	0.1412	0.1264	0.1133	0.1015	0.0911
25	0.1640	0.1460	0.1301	0.1160	0.1034	0.0923	0.0824
26	0.1525	0.1352	0.1199	0.1064	0.0945	0.0839	0.0746
27	0.1419	0.1252	0.1105	0.0976	0.0863	0.0763	0.0675
28	0.1320	0.1159	0.1019	0.0895	0.0788	0.0693	0.0611
29	0.1228	0.1073	0.0939	0.0822	0.0719	0.0630	0.0553
30	0.1142	0.0994	0.0865	0.0754	0.0657	0.0573	0.0500
31	0.1063	0.0920	0.0797	0.0691	0.0600	0.0521	0.0453
32	0.0988	0.0852	0.0735	0.0634	0.0548	0.0474	0.0410
33	0.0919	0.0789	0.0677	0.0582	0.0500	0.0431	0.0371
34	0.0855	0.0730	0.0624	0.0534	0.0457	0.0391	0.0335
35	0.0796	0.0676	0.0575	0.0490	0.0417	0.0356	0.0304
36	0.0740	0.0626	0.0530	0.0449	0.0381	0.0323	0.0275
48	0.0311	0.0249	0.0199	0.0160	0.0128	0.0103	0.0083
60	0.0130	0.0099	0.0075	0.0057	0.0043	0.0033	0.0025
72	0.0055	0.0039	0.0028	0.0020	0.0015	0.0010	7.549E-04
84	0.0023	0.0016	0.0011	7.181E-04	4.889E-04	3.334E-04	2.278E-04
96	9.656E-04	6.185E-04	3.970E-04	2.553E-04	1.645E-04	1.062E-04	6.874E-05

NOTE: NUMBERS LESS THAN 0.0010 ARE EXPRESSED IN SCIENTIFIC NOTATION

Table A.2
(continued)

n	r = 0.110	0.115	0.120	0.130	0.140	0.150	0.160
1	0.9009	0.8969	0.8929	0.8850	0.8772	0.8696	0.8621
2	0.8116	0.8044	0.7972	0.7831	0.7695	0.7561	0.7432
3	0.7312	0.7214	0.7118	0.6931	0.6750	0.6575	0.6407
4	0.6587	0.6470	0.6355	0.6133	0.5921	0.5718	0.5523
5	0.5935	0.5803	0.5674	0.5428	0.5194	0.4972	0.4761
6	0.5346	0.5204	0.5066	0.4803	0.4556	0.4323	0.4104
7	0.4817	0.4667	0.4523	0.4251	0.3996	0.3759	0.3538
8	0.4339	0.4186	0.4039	0.3762	0.3506	0.3269	0.3050
9	0.3909	0.3754	0.3606	0.3329	0.3075	0.2843	0.2630
10	0.3522	0.3367	0.3220	0.2946	0.2697	0.2472	0.2267
11	0.3173	0.3020	0.2875	0.2607	0.2366	0.2149	0.1954
12	0.2858	0.2708	0.2567	0.2307	0.2076	0.1869	0.1685
13	0.2575	0.2429	0.2292	0.2042	0.1821	0.1625	0.1452
14	0.2320	0.2178	0.2046	0.1807	0.1597	0.1413	0.1252
15	0.2090	0.1954	0.1827	0.1599	0.1401	0.1229	0.1079
16	0.1883	0.1752	0.1631	0.1415	0.1229	0.1069	0.0930
17	0.1696	0.1572	0.1456	0.1252	0.1078	0.0929	0.0802
18	0.1528	0.1409	0.1300	0.1108	0.0946	0.0808	0.0691
19	0.1377	0.1264	0.1161	0.0981	0.0829	0.0703	0.0596
20	0.1240	0.1134	0.1037	0.0868	0.0728	0.0611	0.0514
21	0.1117	0.1017	0.0926	0.0768	0.0638	0.0531	0.0443
22	0.1007	0.0912	0.0826	0.0680	0.0560	0.0462	0.0382
23	0.0907	0.0818	0.0738	0.0601	0.0491	0.0402	0.0329
24	0.0817	0.0734	0.0659	0.0532	0.0431	0.0349	0.0284
25	0.0736	0.0658	0.0588	0.0471	0.0378	0.0304	0.0245
26	0.0663	0.0590	0.0525	0.0417	0.0331	0.0264	0.0211
27	0.0597	0.0529	0.0469	0.0369	0.0291	0.0230	0.0182
28	0.0538	0.0475	0.0419	0.0326	0.0255	0.0200	0.0157
29	0.0485	0.0426	0.0374	0.0289	0.0224	0.0174	0.0135
30	0.0437	0.0382	0.0334	0.0256	0.0196	0.0151	0.0116
31	0.0394	0.0342	0.0298	0.0226	0.0172	0.0131	0.0100
32	0.0355	0.0307	0.0266	0.0200	0.0151	0.0114	0.0087
33	0.0319	0.0275	0.0238	0.0177	0.0132	0.0099	0.0075
34	0.0288	0.0247	0.0212	0.0157	0.0116	0.0086	0.0064
35	0.0259	0.0222	0.0189	0.0139	0.0102	0.0075	0.0055
36	0.0234	0.0199	0.0169	0.0123	0.0089	0.0065	0.0048
48	0.0067	0.0054	0.0043	0.0028	0.0019	0.0012	8.054E-04
60	0.0019	0.0015	0.0011	6.536E-04	3.852E-04	2.281E-04	1.357E-04
72	5.454E-04	3.946E-04	2.860E-04	1.508E-04	7.996E-05	4.263E-05	2.286E-05
84	1.559E-04	1.069E-04	7.340E-05	3.479E-05	1.660E-05	7.969E-06	3.851E-06
96	4.457E-05	2.895E-05	1.884E-05	8.025E-06	3.445E-06	1.489E-06	6.487E-07

NOTE: NUMBERS LESS THAN 0.0010 ARE EXPRESSED IN SCIENTIFIC NOTATION

Table A.2 (continued)

n	r = 0.170	0.180	0.190	0.200	0.210	0.220	0.230
1	0.8547	0.8475	0.8403	0.8333	0.8264	0.8197	0.8130
2	0.7305	0.7182	0.7062	0.6944	0.6830	0.6719	0.6610
3	0.6244	0.6086	0.5934	0.5787	0.5645	0.5507	0.5374
4	0.5337	0.5158	0.4987	0.4823	0.4665	0.4514	0.4369
5	0.4561	0.4371	0.4190	0.4019	0.3855	0.3700	0.3552
6	0.3898	0.3704	0.3521	0.3349	0.3186	0.3033	0.2888
7	0.3332	0.3139	0.2959	0.2791	0.2633	0.2486	0.2348
8	0.2848	0.2660	0.2487	0.2326	0.2176	0.2038	0.1909
9	0.2434	0.2255	0.2090	0.1938	0.1799	0.1670	0.1552
10	0.2080	0.1911	0.1756	0.1615	0.1486	0.1369	0.1262
11	0.1778	0.1619	0.1476	0.1346	0.1228	0.1122	0.1026
12	0.1520	0.1372	0.1240	0.1122	0.1015	0.0920	0.0834
13	0.1299	0.1163	0.1042	0.0935	0.0839	0.0754	0.0678
14	0.1110	0.0985	0.0876	0.0779	0.0693	0.0618	0.0551
15	0.0949	0.0835	0.0736	0.0649	0.0573	0.0507	0.0448
16	0.0811	0.0708	0.0618	0.0541	0.0474	0.0415	0.0364
17	0.0693	0.0600	0.0520	0.0451	0.0391	0.0340	0.0296
18	0.0592	0.0508	0.0437	0.0376	0.0323	0.0279	0.0241
19	0.0506	0.0431	0.0367	0.0313	0.0267	0.0229	0.0196
20	0.0433	0.0365	0.0308	0.0261	0.0221	0.0187	0.0159
21	0.0370	0.0309	0.0259	0.0217	0.0183	0.0154	0.0129
22	0.0316	0.0262	0.0218	0.0181	0.0151	0.0126	0.0105
23	0.0270	0.0222	0.0183	0.0151	0.0125	0.0103	0.0086
24	0.0231	0.0188	0.0154	0.0126	0.0103	0.0085	0.0070
25	0.0197	0.0160	0.0129	0.0105	0.0085	0.0069	0.0057
26	0.0169	0.0135	0.0109	0.0087	0.0070	0.0057	0.0046
27	0.0144	0.0115	0.0091	0.0073	0.0058	0.0047	0.0037
28	0.0123	0.0097	0.0077	0.0061	0.0048	0.0038	0.0030
29	0.0105	0.0082	0.0064	0.0051	0.0040	0.0031	0.0025
30	0.0090	0.0070	0.0054	0.0042	0.0033	0.0026	0.0020
31	0.0077	0.0059	0.0046	0.0035	0.0027	0.0021	0.0016
32	0.0066	0.0050	0.0038	0.0029	0.0022	0.0017	0.0013
33	0.0056	0.0042	0.0032	0.0024	0.0019	0.0014	0.0011
34	0.0048	0.0036	0.0027	0.0020	0.0015	0.0012	8.775E-04
35	0.0041	0.0030	0.0023	0.0017	0.0013	9.493E-04	7.134E-04
36	0.0035	0.0026	0.0019	0.0014	0.0010	7.781E-04	5.800E-04
48	5.334E-04	3.545E-04	2.365E-04	1.582E-04	1.062E-04	7.157E-05	4.837E-05
60	8.107E-05	4.865E-05	2.932E-05	1.775E-05	1.079E-05	6.583E-06	4.034E-06
72	1.232E-05	6.676E-06	3.636E-06	1.990E-06	1.095E-06	6.055E-07	3.364E-07
84	1.872E-06	9.160E-07	4.509E-07	2.232E-07	1.112E-07	5.569E-08	2.805E-08
96	2.845E-07	1.257E-07	5.591E-08	2.504E-08	1.129E-08	5.122E-09	2.339E-09

NOTE: NUMBERS LESS THAN 0.0010 ARE EXPRESSED IN SCIENTIFIC NOTATION

Table A.2
(continued)

n	r: 0.240	0.250	0.260	0.270	0.280	0.290	0.300
1	0.8065	0.8000	0.7937	0.7874	0.7813	0.7752	0.7692
2	0.6504	0.6400	0.6299	0.6200	0.6104	0.6009	0.5917
3	0.5245	0.5120	0.4999	0.4882	0.4768	0.4658	0.4552
4	0.4230	0.4096	0.3968	0.3844	0.3725	0.3611	0.3501
5	0.3411	0.3277	0.3149	0.3027	0.2910	0.2799	0.2693
6	0.2751	0.2621	0.2499	0.2383	0.2274	0.2170	0.2072
7	0.2218	0.2097	0.1983	0.1877	0.1776	0.1682	0.1594
8	0.1789	0.1678	0.1574	0.1478	0.1388	0.1304	0.1226
9	0.1443	0.1342	0.1249	0.1164	0.1084	0.1011	0.0943
10	0.1164	0.1074	0.0992	0.0916	0.0847	0.0784	0.0725
11	0.0938	0.0859	0.0787	0.0721	0.0662	0.0607	0.0558
12	0.0757	0.0687	0.0625	0.0568	0.0517	0.0471	0.0429
13	0.0610	0.0550	0.0496	0.0447	0.0404	0.0365	0.0330
14	0.0492	0.0440	0.0393	0.0352	0.0316	0.0283	0.0254
15	0.0397	0.0352	0.0312	0.0277	0.0247	0.0219	0.0195
16	0.0320	0.0281	0.0248	0.0218	0.0193	0.0170	0.0150
17	0.0258	0.0225	0.0197	0.0172	0.0150	0.0132	0.0116
18	0.0208	0.0180	0.0156	0.0135	0.0118	0.0102	0.0089
19	0.0168	0.0144	0.0124	0.0107	0.0092	0.0079	0.0068
20	0.0135	0.0115	0.0098	0.0084	0.0072	0.0061	0.0053
21	0.0109	0.0092	0.0078	0.0066	0.0056	0.0048	0.0040
22	0.0088	0.0074	0.0062	0.0052	0.0044	0.0037	0.0031
23	0.0071	0.0059	0.0049	0.0041	0.0034	0.0029	0.0024
24	0.0057	0.0047	0.0039	0.0032	0.0027	0.0022	0.0018
25	0.0046	0.0038	0.0031	0.0025	0.0021	0.0017	0.0014
26	0.0037	0.0030	0.0025	0.0020	0.0016	0.0013	0.0011
27	0.0030	0.0024	0.0019	0.0016	0.0013	0.0010	8.386E-04
28	0.0024	0.0019	0.0015	0.0012	9.957E-04	8.007E-04	6.450E-04
29	0.0020	0.0015	0.0012	9.765E-04	7.779E-04	6.207E-04	4.962E-04
30	0.0016	0.0012	9.747E-04	7.689E-04	6.077E-04	4.812E-04	3.817E-04
31	0.0013	9.904E-04	7.736E-04	6.055E-04	4.748E-04	3.730E-04	2.936E-04
32	0.0010	7.923E-04	6.140E-04	4.767E-04	3.709E-04	2.892E-04	2.258E-04
33	8.262E-04	6.338E-04	4.873E-04	3.754E-04	2.898E-04	2.242E-04	1.737E-04
34	6.663E-04	5.071E-04	3.867E-04	2.956E-04	2.264E-04	1.738E-04	1.336E-04
35	5.373E-04	4.056E-04	3.069E-04	2.327E-04	1.769E-04	1.347E-04	1.028E-04
36	4.333E-04	3.245E-04	2.436E-04	1.833E-04	1.382E-04	1.044E-04	7.908E-05
48	3.279E-05	2.230E-05	1.521E-05	1.041E-05	7.144E-06	4.917E-06	3.394E-06
60	2.481E-06	1.532E-06	9.501E-07	5.913E-07	3.693E-07	2.315E-07	1.457E-07
72	1.878E-07	1.053E-07	5.934E-08	3.358E-08	1.909E-08	1.090E-08	6.253E-09
84	1.421E-08	7.237E-09	3.706E-09	1.908E-09	9.871E-10	5.134E-10	2.684E-10
96	1.075E-09	4.973E-10	2.314E-10	1.084E-10	5.103E-11	2.418E-11	1.152E-11

NOTE: NUMBERS LESS THAN 0.0010 ARE EXPRESSED IN SCIENTIFIC NOTATION

Table A.3

Future Value of $1.00 per Period for n Periods

n	r: 0.005	0.010	0.015	0.020	0.025	0.030	0.035
1	1.0000	1.0000	1.0000	1.0000	1.0000	1.0000	1.0000
2	2.0050	2.0100	2.0150	2.0200	2.0250	2.0300	2.0350
3	3.0150	3.0301	3.0452	3.0604	3.0756	3.0909	3.1062
4	4.0301	4.0604	4.0909	4.1216	4.1525	4.1836	4.2149
5	5.0503	5.1010	5.1523	5.2040	5.2563	5.3091	5.3625
6	6.0755	6.1520	6.2296	6.3081	6.3877	6.4684	6.5502
7	7.1059	7.2135	7.3230	7.4343	7.5474	7.6625	7.7794
8	8.1414	8.2857	8.4328	8.5830	8.7361	8.8923	9.0517
9	9.1821	9.3685	9.5593	9.7546	9.9545	10.1591	10.3685
10	10.2280	10.4622	10.7027	10.9497	11.2034	11.4639	11.7314
11	11.2792	11.5668	11.8633	12.1687	12.4835	12.8078	13.1420
12	12.3356	12.6825	13.0412	13.4121	13.7956	14.1920	14.6020
13	13.3972	13.8093	14.2368	14.6803	15.1404	15.6178	16.1130
14	14.4642	14.9474	15.4504	15.9739	16.5190	17.0863	17.6770
15	15.5365	16.0969	16.6821	17.2934	17.9319	18.5989	19.2957
16	16.6142	17.2579	17.9324	18.6393	19.3802	20.1569	20.9710
17	17.6973	18.4304	19.2014	20.0121	20.8647	21.7616	22.7050
18	18.7858	19.6147	20.4894	21.4123	22.3863	23.4144	24.4997
19	19.8797	20.8109	21.7967	22.8406	23.9460	25.1169	26.3572
20	20.9791	22.0190	23.1237	24.2974	25.5447	26.8704	28.2797
21	22.0840	23.2392	24.4705	25.7833	27.1833	28.6765	30.2695
22	23.1944	24.4716	25.8376	27.2990	28.8629	30.5368	32.3289
23	24.3104	25.7163	27.2251	28.8450	30.5844	32.4529	34.4604
24	25.4320	26.9735	28.6335	30.4219	32.3490	34.4265	36.6665
25	26.5591	28.2432	30.0630	32.0303	34.1578	36.4593	38.9499
26	27.6919	29.5256	31.5140	33.6709	36.0117	38.5530	41.3131
27	28.8304	30.8209	32.9867	35.3443	37.9120	40.7096	43.7591
28	29.9745	32.1291	34.4815	37.0512	39.8598	42.9309	46.2906
29	31.1244	33.4504	35.9987	38.7922	41.8563	45.2189	48.9108
30	32.2800	34.7849	37.5387	40.5681	43.9027	47.5754	51.6227
31	33.4414	36.1327	39.1018	42.3794	46.0003	50.0027	54.4295
32	34.6086	37.4941	40.6883	44.2270	48.1503	52.5028	57.3345
33	35.7817	38.8690	42.2986	46.1116	50.3540	55.0778	60.3412
34	36.9606	40.2577	43.9331	48.0338	52.6129	57.7302	63.4532
35	38.1454	41.6603	45.5921	49.9945	54.9282	60.4621	66.6740
36	39.3361	43.0769	47.2760	51.9944	57.3014	63.2759	70.0076
48	54.0978	61.2226	69.5652	79.3535	90.8596	104.4084	120.3883
60	69.7700	81.6697	96.2147	114.0515	135.9916	163.0534	196.5169
72	86.4089	104.7099	128.0772	158.0570	196.6891	246.6672	311.5525
84	104.0739	130.6723	166.1726	213.8666	278.3206	365.8805	485.3791
96	122.8285	159.9273	211.7202	284.6467	388.1058	535.8502	748.0431

Table A.3
(*continued*)

	r						
n	0.040	0.045	0.050	0.055	0.060	0.065	0.070
1	1.0000	1.0000	1.0000	1.0000	1.0000	1.0000	1.0000
2	2.0400	2.0450	2.0500	2.0550	2.0600	2.0650	2.0700
3	3.1216	3.1370	3.1525	3.1680	3.1836	3.1992	3.2149
4	4.2465	4.2782	4.3101	4.3423	4.3746	4.4072	4.4399
5	5.4163	5.4707	5.5256	5.5811	5.6371	5.6936	5.7507
6	6.6330	6.7169	6.8019	6.8881	6.9753	7.0637	7.1533
7	7.8983	8.0192	8.1420	8.2669	8.3938	8.5229	8.6540
8	9.2142	9.3800	9.5491	9.7216	9.8975	10.0769	10.2598
9	10.5828	10.8021	11.0266	11.2563	11.4913	11.7319	11.9780
10	12.0061	12.2882	12.5779	12.8754	13.1808	13.4944	13.8164
11	13.4864	13.8412	14.2068	14.5835	14.9716	15.3716	15.7836
12	15.0258	15.4640	15.9171	16.3856	16.8699	17.3707	17.8885
13	16.6268	17.1599	17.7130	18.2868	18.8821	19.4998	20.1406
14	18.2919	18.9321	19.5986	20.2926	21.0151	21.7673	22.5505
15	20.0236	20.7841	21.5786	22.4087	23.2760	24.1822	25.1290
16	21.8245	22.7193	23.6575	24.6411	25.6725	26.7540	27.8881
17	23.6975	24.7417	25.8404	26.9964	28.2129	29.4930	30.8402
18	25.6454	26.8551	28.1324	29.4812	30.9057	32.4101	33.9990
19	27.6712	29.0636	30.5390	32.1027	33.7600	35.5167	37.3790
20	29.7781	31.3714	33.0660	34.8683	36.7856	38.8253	40.9955
21	31.9692	33.7831	35.7193	37.7861	39.9927	42.3490	44.8652
22	34.2480	36.3034	38.5052	40.8643	43.3923	46.1016	49.0057
23	36.6179	38.9370	41.4305	44.1118	46.9958	50.0982	53.4361
24	39.0826	41.6892	44.5020	47.5380	50.8156	54.3546	58.1767
25	41.6459	44.5652	47.7271	51.1526	54.8645	58.8877	63.2490
26	44.3117	47.5706	51.1135	54.9660	59.1564	63.7154	68.6765
27	47.0842	50.7113	54.6691	58.9891	63.7058	68.8569	74.4838
28	49.9676	53.9933	58.4026	63.2335	68.5281	74.3326	80.6977
29	52.9663	57.4230	62.3227	67.7114	73.6398	80.1642	87.3465
30	56.0849	61.0071	66.4388	72.4355	79.0582	86.3749	94.4608
31	59.3283	64.7524	70.7608	77.4194	84.8017	92.9892	102.0730
32	62.7015	68.6662	75.2988	82.6775	90.8898	100.0335	110.2182
33	66.2095	72.7562	80.0638	88.2248	97.3432	107.5357	118.9334
34	69.8579	77.0303	85.0670	94.0771	104.1838	115.5255	128.2588
35	73.6522	81.4966	90.3203	100.2514	111.4348	124.0347	138.2369
36	77.5983	86.1640	95.8363	106.7652	119.1209	133.0969	148.9135
48	139.2632	161.5879	188.0254	219.3684	256.5645	300.7469	353.2701
60	237.9907	289.4980	353.5837	433.4504	533.1282	657.6898	813.5204
72	396.0566	506.4182	650.9027	840.4647	1089.6286	1417.6557	1850.0922
84	649.1251	874.2893	1184.8448	1614.2833	2209.4167	3035.6961	4184.6506
96	1054.2960	1498.1551	2143.7282	3085.4732	4462.6505	6480.6599	9442.5233

Table A.3

(continued)

n	r = 0.075	0.080	0.085	0.090	0.095	0.100	0.105
1	1.0000	1.0000	1.0000	1.0000	1.0000	1.0000	1.0000
2	2.0750	2.0800	2.0850	2.0900	2.0950	2.1000	2.1050
3	3.2306	3.2464	3.2622	3.2781	3.2940	3.3100	3.3260
4	4.4729	4.5061	4.5395	4.5731	4.6070	4.6410	4.6753
5	5.8084	5.8666	5.9254	5.9847	6.0446	6.1051	6.1662
6	7.2440	7.3359	7.4290	7.5233	7.6189	7.7156	7.8136
7	8.7873	8.9228	9.0605	9.2004	9.3426	9.4872	9.6340
8	10.4464	10.6366	10.8306	11.0285	11.2302	11.4359	11.6456
9	12.2298	12.4876	12.7512	13.0210	13.2971	13.5795	13.8684
10	14.1471	14.4866	14.8351	15.1929	15.5603	15.9374	16.3246
11	16.2081	16.6455	17.0961	17.5603	18.0385	18.5312	19.0387
12	18.4237	18.9771	19.5492	20.1407	20.7522	21.3843	22.0377
13	20.8055	21.4953	22.2109	22.9534	23.7236	24.5227	25.3517
14	23.3659	24.2149	25.0989	26.0192	26.9774	27.9750	29.0136
15	26.1184	27.1521	28.2323	29.3609	30.5402	31.7725	33.0600
16	29.0772	30.3243	31.6320	33.0034	34.4416	35.9497	37.5313
17	32.2580	33.7502	35.3207	36.9737	38.7135	40.5447	42.4721
18	35.6774	37.4502	39.3230	41.3013	43.3913	45.5992	47.9317
19	39.3532	41.4463	43.6654	46.0185	48.5135	51.1591	53.9645
20	43.3047	45.7620	48.3770	51.1601	54.1222	57.2750	60.6308
21	47.5525	50.4229	53.4891	56.7645	60.2638	64.0025	67.9970
22	52.1190	55.4568	59.0356	62.8733	66.9889	71.4027	76.1367
23	57.0279	60.8933	65.0537	69.5319	74.3529	79.5430	85.1311
24	62.3050	66.7648	71.5832	76.7898	82.4164	88.4973	95.0699
25	67.9779	73.1059	78.6678	84.7009	91.2459	98.3471	106.0522
26	74.0762	79.9544	86.3546	93.3240	100.9143	109.1818	118.1877
27	80.6319	87.3508	94.6947	102.7231	111.5012	121.0999	131.5974
28	87.6793	95.3388	103.7437	112.9682	123.0938	134.2099	146.4151
29	95.2553	103.9659	113.5620	124.1354	135.7877	148.6309	162.7887
30	103.3994	113.2832	124.2147	136.3075	149.6875	164.4940	180.8815
31	112.1544	123.3459	135.7730	149.5752	164.9078	181.9434	200.8741
32	121.5659	134.2135	148.3137	164.0370	181.5741	201.1378	222.9658
33	131.6834	145.9506	161.9203	179.8003	199.8236	222.2515	247.3772
34	142.5596	158.6267	176.6836	196.9823	219.8068	245.4767	274.3518
35	154.2516	172.3168	192.7017	215.7108	241.6885	271.0244	304.1588
36	166.8205	187.1021	210.0813	236.1247	265.6489	299.1268	337.0955
48	415.7533	490.1322	578.7198	684.2804	810.1164	960.1723	1139.1588
60	1008.6565	1253.2133	1559.9198	1944.7921	2427.9781	3034.8164	3797.1651
72	2420.8213	3174.7814	4171.5662	5490.1891	7235.3844	9545.9382	1.261E+04
84	5784.2865	8013.6168	1.112E+04	1.546E+04	2.152E+04	2.998E+04	4.180E+04
96	1.380E+04	2.020E+04	2.963E+04	4.351E+04	6.397E+04	9.411E+04	1.385E+05

NOTE: NUMBERS GREATER THAN 9999.99 ARE EXPRESSED IN SCIENTIFIC NOTATION

Table A.3
(*continued*)

n	r 0.110	0.115	0.120	0.130	0.140	0.150	0.160
1	1.0000	1.0000	1.0000	1.0000	1.0000	1.0000	1.0000
2	2.1100	2.1150	2.1200	2.1300	2.1400	2.1500	2.1600
3	3.3421	3.3582	3.3744	3.4069	3.4396	3.4725	3.5056
4	4.7097	4.7444	4.7793	4.8498	4.9211	4.9934	5.0665
5	6.2278	6.2900	6.3528	6.4803	6.6101	6.7424	6.8771
6	7.9129	8.0134	8.1152	8.3227	8.5355	8.7537	8.9775
7	9.7833	9.9349	10.0890	10.4047	10.7305	11.0668	11.4139
8	11.8594	12.0774	12.2997	12.7573	13.2328	13.7268	14.2401
9	14.1640	14.4663	14.7757	15.4157	16.0853	16.7858	17.5185
10	16.7220	17.1300	17.5487	18.4197	19.3373	20.3037	21.3215
11	19.5614	20.0999	20.6546	21.8143	23.0445	24.3493	25.7329
12	22.7132	23.4114	24.1331	25.6502	27.2707	29.0017	30.8502
13	26.2116	27.1037	28.0291	29.9847	32.0887	34.3519	36.7862
14	30.0949	31.2207	32.3926	34.8827	37.5811	40.5047	43.6720
15	34.4054	35.8110	37.2797	40.4175	43.8424	47.5804	51.6595
16	39.1899	40.9293	42.7533	46.6717	50.9804	55.7175	60.9250
17	44.5008	46.6362	48.8837	53.7391	59.1176	65.0751	71.6730
18	50.3959	52.9993	55.7497	61.7251	68.3941	75.8364	84.1407
19	56.9395	60.0942	63.4397	70.7494	78.9692	88.2118	98.6032
20	64.2028	68.0051	72.0524	80.9468	91.0249	102.4436	115.3797
21	72.2651	76.8257	81.6987	92.4699	104.7684	118.8101	134.8405
22	81.2143	86.6606	92.5026	105.4910	120.4360	137.6316	157.4150
23	91.1479	97.6266	104.6029	120.2048	138.2970	159.2764	183.6014
24	102.1742	109.8536	118.1552	136.8315	158.6586	184.1678	213.9776
25	114.4133	123.4868	133.3339	155.6196	181.8708	212.7930	249.2140
26	127.9988	138.6878	150.3339	176.8501	208.3327	245.7120	290.0883
27	143.0786	155.6369	169.3740	200.8406	238.4993	283.5688	337.5024
28	159.8173	174.5351	190.6989	227.9499	272.8892	327.1041	392.5028
29	178.3972	195.6067	214.5828	258.5834	312.0937	377.1697	456.3032
30	199.0209	219.1014	241.3327	293.1992	356.7868	434.7451	530.3117
31	221.9132	245.2981	271.2926	332.3151	407.7370	500.9569	616.1616
32	247.3236	274.5074	304.8477	376.5161	465.8202	577.1005	715.7475
33	275.5292	307.0757	342.4294	426.4632	532.0350	664.6655	831.2671
34	306.8374	343.3895	384.5210	482.9034	607.5199	765.3654	965.2698
35	341.5896	383.8792	431.6635	546.6808	693.5727	881.1702	1120.7130
36	380.1644	429.0254	484.4631	618.7493	791.6729	1014.3457	1301.0270
48	1352.6996	1607.5069	1911.5898	2707.6334	3841.4753	5456.0047	7753.7818
60	4755.0658	5958.8287	7471.6411	1.176E+04	1.854E+04	2.922E+04	4.606E+04
72	1.666E+04	2.203E+04	2.913E+04	5.101E+04	8.933E+04	1.564E+05	2.734E+05
84	5.830E+04	8.135E+04	1.135E+05	2.211E+05	4.304E+05	8.366E+05	1.623E+06
96	2.040E+05	3.004E+05	4.423E+05	9.585E+05	2.074E+06	4.476E+06	9.635E+06

NOTE: NUMBERS GREATER THAN 9999.99 ARE EXPRESSED IN SCIENTIFIC NOTATION

Table A.3
(continued)

n	r = 0.170	0.180	0.190	0.200	0.210	0.220	0.230
1	1.0000	1.0000	1.0000	1.0000	1.0000	1.0000	1.0000
2	2.1700	2.1800	2.1900	2.2000	2.2100	2.2200	2.2300
3	3.5389	3.5724	3.6061	3.6400	3.6741	3.7084	3.7429
4	5.1405	5.2154	5.2913	5.3680	5.4457	5.5242	5.6038
5	7.0144	7.1542	7.2966	7.4416	7.5892	7.7396	7.8926
6	9.2068	9.4420	9.6830	9.9299	10.1830	10.4423	10.7079
7	11.7720	12.1415	12.5227	12.9159	13.3214	13.7396	14.1708
8	14.7733	15.3270	15.9020	16.4991	17.1189	17.7623	18.4300
9	18.2847	19.0859	19.9234	20.7989	21.7139	22.6700	23.6690
10	22.3931	23.5213	24.7089	25.9587	27.2738	28.6574	30.1128
11	27.1999	28.7551	30.4035	32.1504	34.0013	35.9620	38.0388
12	32.8239	34.9311	37.1802	39.5805	42.1416	44.8737	47.7877
13	39.4040	42.2187	45.2445	48.4966	51.9913	55.7459	59.7788
14	47.1027	50.8180	54.8409	59.1959	63.9095	69.0100	74.5280
15	56.1101	60.9653	66.2607	72.0351	78.3305	85.1922	92.6694
16	66.6488	72.9390	79.8502	87.4421	95.7799	104.9345	114.9834
17	78.9792	87.0680	96.0218	105.9306	116.8937	129.0201	142.4295
18	93.4056	103.7403	115.2659	128.1167	142.4413	158.4045	176.1883
19	110.2846	123.4135	138.1664	154.7400	173.3540	194.2535	217.7116
20	130.0329	146.6280	165.4180	186.6880	210.7584	237.9893	268.7853
21	153.1385	174.0210	197.8474	225.0256	256.0176	291.3469	331.6059
22	180.1721	206.3448	236.4385	271.0307	310.7813	356.4432	408.8753
23	211.8013	244.4868	282.3618	326.2369	377.0454	435.8607	503.9166
24	248.8076	289.4945	337.0105	392.4842	457.2249	532.7501	620.8174
25	292.1049	342.6035	402.0425	471.9811	554.2422	650.9551	764.6054
26	342.7627	405.2721	479.4306	567.3773	671.6330	795.1653	941.4647
27	402.0323	479.2211	571.5224	681.8528	813.6759	971.1016	1159.0016
28	471.3778	566.4809	681.1116	819.2233	985.5479	1185.7440	1426.5719
29	552.5121	669.4475	811.5228	984.0680	1193.5129	1447.6077	1755.6835
30	647.4391	790.9480	966.7122	1181.8816	1445.1507	1767.0813	2160.4907
31	758.5038	934.3186	1151.3875	1419.2579	1749.6323	2156.8392	2658.4036
32	888.4494	1103.4960	1371.1511	1704.1095	2118.0551	2632.3439	3270.8364
33	1040.4858	1303.1253	1632.6698	2045.9314	2563.8467	3212.4595	4024.1287
34	1218.3684	1538.6878	1943.8771	2456.1176	3103.2545	3920.2006	4950.6783
35	1426.4910	1816.6516	2314.2137	2948.3411	3755.9379	4783.6447	6090.3344
36	1669.9945	2144.6489	2754.9143	3539.0094	4545.6848	5837.0466	7492.1113
48	1.102E+04	1.566E+04	2.225E+04	3.159E+04	4.482E+04	6.351E+04	8.989E+04
60	7.256E+04	1.142E+05	1.795E+05	2.817E+05	4.415E+05	6.905E+05	1.078E+06
72	4.774E+05	8.322E+05	1.448E+06	2.512E+06	4.348E+06	7.507E+06	1.293E+07
84	3.142E+06	6.065E+06	1.167E+07	2.240E+07	4.283E+07	8.162E+07	1.550E+08
96	2.067E+07	4.420E+07	9.414E+07	1.997E+08	4.219E+08	8.874E+08	1.859E+09

NOTE: NUMBERS GREATER THAN 9999.99 ARE EXPRESSED IN SCIENTIFIC NOTATION

Table A.3
(*continued*)

n	r = 0.240	0.250	0.260	0.270	0.280	0.290	0.300
1	1.0000	1.0000	1.0000	1.0000	1.0000	1.0000	1.0000
2	2.2400	2.2500	2.2600	2.2700	2.2800	2.2900	2.3000
3	3.7776	3.8125	3.8476	3.8829	3.9184	3.9541	3.9900
4	5.6842	5.7656	5.8480	5.9313	6.0156	6.1008	6.1870
5	8.0484	8.2070	8.3684	8.5327	8.6999	8.8700	9.0431
6	10.9801	11.2588	11.5442	11.8366	12.1359	12.4423	12.7560
7	14.6153	15.0735	15.5458	16.0324	16.5339	17.0506	17.5828
8	19.1229	19.8419	20.5876	21.3612	22.1634	22.9953	23.8577
9	24.7125	25.8023	26.9404	28.1287	29.3692	30.6639	32.0150
10	31.6434	33.2529	34.9449	36.7235	38.5926	40.5564	42.6195
11	40.2379	42.5661	45.0306	47.6388	50.3985	53.3178	56.4053
12	50.8950	54.2077	57.7386	61.5013	65.5100	69.7800	74.3270
13	64.1097	68.7596	73.7506	79.1066	84.8529	91.0161	97.6250
14	80.4961	86.9495	93.9258	101.4654	109.6117	118.4108	127.9125
15	100.8151	109.6868	119.3465	129.8611	141.3029	153.7500	167.2863
16	126.0108	138.1085	151.3766	165.9236	181.8677	199.3374	218.4722
17	157.2534	173.6357	191.7345	211.7230	233.7907	258.1453	285.0139
18	195.9942	218.0446	242.5855	269.8882	300.2521	334.0074	371.5180
19	244.0328	273.5558	306.6577	343.7580	385.3227	431.8696	483.9734
20	303.6006	342.9447	387.3887	437.5726	494.2131	558.1118	630.1655
21	377.4648	429.6809	489.1098	556.7173	633.5927	720.9642	820.2151
22	469.0563	538.1011	617.2783	708.0309	811.9987	931.0438	1067.2796
23	582.6298	673.6264	778.7707	900.1993	1040.3583	1202.0465	1388.4635
24	723.4610	843.0329	982.2511	1144.2531	1332.6586	1551.6400	1806.0026
25	898.0916	1054.7912	1238.6363	1454.2014	1706.8031	2002.6156	2348.8033
26	1114.6336	1319.4890	1561.6818	1847.8358	2185.7079	2584.3741	3054.4443
27	1383.1457	1650.3612	1968.7191	2347.7515	2798.7061	3334.8426	3971.7776
28	1716.1007	2063.9515	2481.5860	2982.6443	3583.3438	4302.9470	5164.3109
29	2128.9643	2580.9394	3127.7984	3788.9583	4587.6801	5551.8016	6714.6042
30	2640.9164	3227.1743	3942.0260	4812.9771	5873.2306	7162.8241	8729.9855
31	3275.7363	4034.9678	4967.9527	6113.4809	7518.7351	9241.0431	1.135E+04
32	4062.9130	5044.7098	6260.6204	7765.1207	9624.9810	1.192E+04	1.476E+04
33	5039.0122	6306.8872	7889.3817	9862.7033	1.232E+04	1.538E+04	1.918E+04
34	6249.3751	7884.6091	9941.6210	1.253E+04	1.577E+04	1.984E+04	2.494E+04
35	7750.2251	9856.7613	1.253E+04	1.591E+04	2.019E+04	2.560E+04	3.242E+04
36	9611.2791	1.232E+04	1.579E+04	2.021E+04	2.584E+04	3.302E+04	4.215E+04
48	1.271E+05	1.794E+05	2.528E+05	3.558E+05	4.999E+05	7.013E+05	9.821E+05
60	1.679E+06	2.610E+06	4.048E+06	6.264E+06	9.670E+06	1.489E+07	2.288E+07
72	2.219E+07	3.798E+07	6.482E+07	1.103E+08	1.871E+08	3.163E+08	5.331E+08
84	2.932E+08	5.527E+08	1.038E+09	1.942E+09	3.618E+09	6.716E+09	1.242E+10
96	3.875E+09	8.043E+09	1.662E+10	3.418E+10	6.998E+10	1.426E+11	2.894E+11

NOTE: NUMBERS GREATER THAN 9999.99 ARE EXPRESSED IN SCIENTIFIC NOTATION

Table A.4

Present Value of $1.00 per Period for n Periods

n	r = 0.005	0.010	0.015	0.020	0.025	0.030	0.035
1	0.9950	0.9901	0.9852	0.9804	0.9756	0.9709	0.9662
2	1.9851	1.9704	1.9559	1.9416	1.9274	1.9135	1.8997
3	2.9702	2.9410	2.9122	2.8839	2.8560	2.8286	2.8016
4	3.9505	3.9020	3.8544	3.8077	3.7620	3.7171	3.6731
5	4.9259	4.8534	4.7826	4.7135	4.6458	4.5797	4.5151
6	5.8964	5.7955	5.6972	5.6014	5.5081	5.4172	5.3286
7	6.8621	6.7282	6.5982	6.4720	6.3494	6.2303	6.1145
8	7.8230	7.6517	7.4859	7.3255	7.1701	7.0197	6.8740
9	8.7791	8.5660	8.3605	8.1622	7.9709	7.7861	7.6077
10	9.7304	9.4713	9.2222	8.9826	8.7521	8.5302	8.3166
11	10.6770	10.3676	10.0711	9.7868	9.5142	9.2526	9.0016
12	11.6189	11.2551	10.9075	10.5753	10.2578	9.9540	9.6633
13	12.5562	12.1337	11.7315	11.3484	10.9832	10.6350	10.3027
14	13.4887	13.0037	12.5434	12.1062	11.6909	11.2961	10.9205
15	14.4166	13.8651	13.3432	12.8493	12.3814	11.9379	11.5174
16	15.3399	14.7179	14.1313	13.5777	13.0550	12.5611	12.0941
17	16.2586	15.5623	14.9076	14.2919	13.7122	13.1661	12.6513
18	17.1728	16.3983	15.6726	14.9920	14.3534	13.7535	13.1897
19	18.0824	17.2260	16.4262	15.6785	14.9789	14.3238	13.7098
20	18.9874	18.0456	17.1686	16.3514	15.5892	14.8775	14.2124
21	19.8880	18.8570	17.9001	17.0112	16.1845	15.4150	14.6980
22	20.7841	19.6604	18.6208	17.6580	16.7654	15.9369	15.1671
23	21.6757	20.4558	19.3309	18.2922	17.3321	16.4436	15.6204
24	22.5629	21.2434	20.0304	18.9139	17.8850	16.9355	16.0584
25	23.4456	22.0232	20.7196	19.5235	18.4244	17.4131	16.4815
26	24.3240	22.7952	21.3986	20.1210	18.9506	17.8768	16.8904
27	25.1980	23.5596	22.0676	20.7069	19.4640	18.3270	17.2854
28	26.0677	24.3164	22.7267	21.2813	19.9649	18.7641	17.6670
29	26.9330	25.0658	23.3761	21.8444	20.4535	19.1885	18.0358
30	27.7941	25.8077	24.0158	22.3965	20.9303	19.6004	18.3920
31	28.6508	26.5423	24.6461	22.9377	21.3954	20.0004	18.7363
32	29.5033	27.2696	25.2671	23.4683	21.8492	20.3888	19.0689
33	30.3515	27.9897	25.8790	23.9886	22.2919	20.7658	19.3902
34	31.1955	28.7027	26.4817	24.4986	22.7238	21.1318	19.7007
35	32.0354	29.4086	27.0756	24.9986	23.1452	21.4872	20.0007
36	32.8710	30.1075	27.6607	25.4888	23.5563	21.8323	20.2905
48	42.5803	37.9740	34.0426	30.6731	27.7732	25.2667	23.0912
60	51.7256	44.9550	39.3803	34.7609	30.9087	27.6756	24.9447
72	60.3395	51.1504	43.8447	37.9841	33.2401	29.3651	26.1713
84	68.4530	56.6485	47.5786	40.5255	34.9736	30.5501	26.9831
96	76.0952	61.5277	50.7017	42.5294	36.2626	31.3812	27.5203

Table A.4
(continued)

n	r = 0.040	0.045	0.050	0.055	0.060	0.065	0.070
1	0.9615	0.9569	0.9524	0.9479	0.9434	0.9390	0.9346
2	1.8861	1.8727	1.8594	1.8463	1.8334	1.8206	1.8080
3	2.7751	2.7490	2.7232	2.6979	2.6730	2.6485	2.6243
4	3.6299	3.5875	3.5460	3.5052	3.4651	3.4258	3.3872
5	4.4518	4.3900	4.3295	4.2703	4.2124	4.1557	4.1002
6	5.2421	5.1579	5.0757	4.9955	4.9173	4.8410	4.7665
7	6.0021	5.8927	5.7864	5.6830	5.5824	5.4845	5.3893
8	6.7327	6.5959	6.4632	6.3346	6.2098	6.0888	5.9713
9	7.4353	7.2688	7.1078	6.9522	6.8017	6.6561	6.5152
10	8.1109	7.9127	7.7217	7.5376	7.3601	7.1888	7.0236
11	8.7605	8.5289	8.3064	8.0925	7.8869	7.6890	7.4987
12	9.3851	9.1186	8.8633	8.6185	8.3838	8.1587	7.9427
13	9.9856	9.6829	9.3936	9.1171	8.8527	8.5997	8.3577
14	10.5631	10.2228	9.8986	9.5896	9.2950	9.0138	8.7455
15	11.1184	10.7395	10.3797	10.0376	9.7122	9.4027	9.1079
16	11.6523	11.2340	10.8378	10.4622	10.1059	9.7678	9.4466
17	12.1657	11.7072	11.2741	10.8646	10.4773	10.1106	9.7632
18	12.6593	12.1600	11.6896	11.2461	10.8276	10.4325	10.0591
19	13.1339	12.5933	12.0853	11.6077	11.1581	10.7347	10.3356
20	13.5903	13.0079	12.4622	11.9504	11.4699	11.0185	10.5940
21	14.0292	13.4047	12.8212	12.2752	11.7641	11.2850	10.8355
22	14.4511	13.7844	13.1630	12.5832	12.0416	11.5352	11.0612
23	14.8568	14.1478	13.4886	12.8750	12.3034	11.7701	11.2722
24	15.2470	14.4955	13.7986	13.1517	12.5504	11.9907	11.4693
25	15.6221	14.8282	14.0939	13.4139	12.7834	12.1979	11.6536
26	15.9828	15.1466	14.3752	13.6625	13.0032	12.3924	11.8258
27	16.3296	15.4513	14.6430	13.8981	13.2105	12.5750	11.9867
28	16.6631	15.7429	14.8981	14.1214	13.4062	12.7465	12.1371
29	16.9837	16.0219	15.1411	14.3331	13.5907	12.9075	12.2777
30	17.2920	16.2889	15.3725	14.5337	13.7648	13.0587	12.4090
31	17.5885	16.5444	15.5928	14.7239	13.9291	13.2006	12.5318
32	17.8736	16.7889	15.8027	14.9042	14.0840	13.3339	12.6466
33	18.1476	17.0229	16.0025	15.0751	14.2302	13.4591	12.7538
34	18.4112	17.2468	16.1929	15.2370	14.3681	13.5766	12.8540
35	18.6646	17.4610	16.3742	15.3906	14.4982	13.6870	12.9477
36	18.9083	17.6660	16.5469	15.5361	14.6210	13.7906	13.0352
48	21.1951	19.5356	18.0772	16.7902	15.6500	14.6359	13.7305
60	22.6235	20.6380	18.9293	17.4499	16.1614	15.0330	14.0392
72	23.5156	21.2881	19.4038	17.7968	16.4156	15.2195	14.1763
84	24.0729	21.6714	19.6680	17.9793	16.5419	15.3070	14.2371
96	24.4209	21.8974	19.8151	18.0753	16.6047	15.3482	14.2641

Table A.4
(*continued*)

n	r: 0.075	0.080	0.085	0.090	0.095	0.100	0.105
1	0.9302	0.9259	0.9217	0.9174	0.9132	0.9091	0.9050
2	1.7956	1.7833	1.7711	1.7591	1.7473	1.7355	1.7240
3	2.6005	2.5771	2.5540	2.5313	2.5089	2.4869	2.4651
4	3.3493	3.3121	3.2756	3.2397	3.2045	3.1699	3.1359
5	4.0459	3.9927	3.9406	3.8897	3.8397	3.7908	3.7429
6	4.6938	4.6229	4.5536	4.4859	4.4198	4.3553	4.2922
7	5.2966	5.2064	5.1185	5.0330	4.9496	4.8684	4.7893
8	5.8573	5.7466	5.6392	5.5348	5.4334	5.3349	5.2392
9	6.3789	6.2469	6.1191	5.9952	5.8753	5.7590	5.6463
10	6.8641	6.7101	6.5613	6.4177	6.2788	6.1446	6.0148
11	7.3154	7.1390	6.9690	6.8052	6.6473	6.4951	6.3482
12	7.7353	7.5361	7.3447	7.1607	6.9838	6.8137	6.6500
13	8.1258	7.9038	7.6910	7.4869	7.2912	7.1034	6.9230
14	8.4892	8.2442	8.0101	7.7862	7.5719	7.3667	7.1702
15	8.8271	8.5595	8.3042	8.0607	7.8282	7.6061	7.3938
16	9.1415	8.8514	8.5753	8.3126	8.0623	7.8237	7.5962
17	9.4340	9.1216	8.8252	8.5436	8.2760	8.0216	7.7794
18	9.7060	9.3719	9.0555	8.7556	8.4713	8.2014	7.9451
19	9.9591	9.6036	9.2677	8.9501	8.6496	8.3649	8.0952
20	10.1945	9.8181	9.4633	9.1285	8.8124	8.5136	8.2309
21	10.4135	10.0168	9.6436	9.2922	8.9611	8.6487	8.3538
22	10.6172	10.2007	9.8098	9.4424	9.0969	8.7715	8.4649
23	10.8067	10.3711	9.9629	9.5802	9.2209	8.8832	8.5656
24	10.9830	10.5288	10.1041	9.7066	9.3341	8.9847	8.6566
25	11.1469	10.6748	10.2342	9.8226	9.4376	9.0770	8.7390
26	11.2995	10.8100	10.3541	9.9290	9.5320	9.1609	8.8136
27	11.4414	10.9352	10.4646	10.0266	9.6183	9.2372	8.8811
28	11.5734	11.0511	10.5665	10.1161	9.6971	9.3066	8.9422
29	11.6962	11.1584	10.6603	10.1983	9.7690	9.3696	8.9974
30	11.8104	11.2578	10.7468	10.2737	9.8347	9.4269	9.0474
31	11.9166	11.3498	10.8266	10.3428	9.8947	9.4790	9.0927
32	12.0155	11.4350	10.9001	10.4062	9.9495	9.5264	9.1337
33	12.1074	11.5139	10.9678	10.4644	9.9996	9.5694	9.1707
34	12.1929	11.5869	11.0302	10.5178	10.0453	9.6086	9.2043
35	12.2725	11.6546	11.0878	10.5668	10.0870	9.6442	9.2347
36	12.3465	11.7172	11.1408	10.6118	10.1251	9.6765	9.2621
48	12.9190	12.1891	11.5303	10.9336	10.3913	9.8969	9.4448
60	13.1594	12.3766	11.6766	11.0480	10.4809	9.9672	9.5000
72	13.2603	12.4510	11.7316	11.0887	10.5110	9.9895	9.5166
84	13.3027	12.4805	11.7523	11.1031	10.5212	9.9967	9.5216
96	13.3205	12.4923	11.7600	11.1083	10.5246	9.9989	9.5232

Table A.4
(continued)

n	r: 0.110	0.115	0.120	0.130	0.140	0.150	0.160
1	0.9009	0.8969	0.8929	0.8850	0.8772	0.8696	0.8621
2	1.7125	1.7012	1.6901	1.6681	1.6467	1.6257	1.6052
3	2.4437	2.4226	2.4018	2.3612	2.3216	2.2832	2.2459
4	3.1024	3.0696	3.0373	2.9745	2.9137	2.8550	2.7982
5	3.6959	3.6499	3.6048	3.5172	3.4331	3.3522	3.2743
6	4.2305	4.1703	4.1114	3.9975	3.8887	3.7845	3.6847
7	4.7122	4.6370	4.5638	4.4226	4.2883	4.1604	4.0386
8	5.1461	5.0556	4.9676	4.7988	4.6389	4.4873	4.3436
9	5.5370	5.4311	5.3282	5.1317	4.9464	4.7716	4.6065
10	5.8892	5.7678	5.6502	5.4262	5.2161	5.0188	4.8332
11	6.2065	6.0697	5.9377	5.6869	5.4527	5.2337	5.0286
12	6.4924	6.3406	6.1944	5.9176	5.6603	5.4206	5.1971
13	6.7499	6.5835	6.4235	6.1218	5.8424	5.5831	5.3423
14	6.9819	6.8013	6.6282	6.3025	6.0021	5.7245	5.4675
15	7.1909	6.9967	6.8109	6.4624	6.1422	5.8474	5.5755
16	7.3792	7.1719	6.9740	6.6039	6.2651	5.9542	5.6685
17	7.5488	7.3291	7.1196	6.7291	6.3729	6.0472	5.7487
18	7.7016	7.4700	7.2497	6.8399	6.4674	6.1280	5.8178
19	7.8393	7.5964	7.3658	6.9380	6.5504	6.1982	5.8775
20	7.9633	7.7098	7.4694	7.0248	6.6231	6.2593	5.9288
21	8.0751	7.8115	7.5620	7.1016	6.6870	6.3125	5.9731
22	8.1757	7.9027	7.6446	7.1695	6.7429	6.3587	6.0113
23	8.2664	7.9845	7.7184	7.2297	6.7921	6.3988	6.0442
24	8.3481	8.0578	7.7843	7.2829	6.8351	6.4338	6.0726
25	8.4217	8.1236	7.8431	7.3300	6.8729	6.4641	6.0971
26	8.4881	8.1826	7.8957	7.3717	6.9061	6.4906	6.1182
27	8.5478	8.2355	7.9426	7.4086	6.9352	6.5135	6.1364
28	8.6016	8.2830	7.9844	7.4412	6.9607	6.5335	6.1520
29	8.6501	8.3255	8.0218	7.4701	6.9830	6.5509	6.1656
30	8.6938	8.3637	8.0552	7.4957	7.0027	6.5660	6.1772
31	8.7331	8.3980	8.0850	7.5183	7.0199	6.5791	6.1872
32	8.7686	8.4287	8.1116	7.5383	7.0350	6.5905	6.1959
33	8.8005	8.4562	8.1354	7.5560	7.0482	6.6005	6.2034
34	8.8293	8.4809	8.1566	7.5717	7.0599	6.6091	6.2098
35	8.8552	8.5030	8.1755	7.5856	7.0700	6.6166	6.2153
36	8.8786	8.5229	8.1924	7.5979	7.0790	6.6231	6.2201
48	9.0302	8.6489	8.2972	7.6705	7.1296	6.6585	6.2450
60	9.0736	8.6830	8.3240	7.6873	7.1401	6.6651	6.2492
72	9.0860	8.6922	8.3310	7.6911	7.1423	6.6664	6.2499
84	9.0895	8.6947	8.3327	7.6920	7.1427	6.6666	6.2500
96	9.0905	8.6954	8.3332	7.6922	7.1428	6.6667	6.2500

Table A.4
(continued)

n	r 0.170	0.180	0.190	0.200	0.210	0.220	0.230
1	0.8547	0.8475	0.8403	0.8333	0.8264	0.8197	0.8130
2	1.5852	1.5656	1.5465	1.5278	1.5095	1.4915	1.4740
3	2.2096	2.1743	2.1399	2.1065	2.0739	2.0422	2.0114
4	2.7432	2.6901	2.6386	2.5887	2.5404	2.4936	2.4483
5	3.1993	3.1272	3.0576	2.9906	2.9260	2.8636	2.8035
6	3.5892	3.4976	3.4098	3.3255	3.2446	3.1669	3.0923
7	3.9224	3.8115	3.7057	3.6046	3.5079	3.4155	3.3270
8	4.2072	4.0776	3.9544	3.8372	3.7256	3.6193	3.5179
9	4.4506	4.3030	4.1633	4.0310	3.9054	3.7863	3.6731
10	4.6586	4.4941	4.3389	4.1925	4.0541	3.9232	3.7993
11	4.8364	4.6560	4.4865	4.3271	4.1769	4.0354	3.9018
12	4.9884	4.7932	4.6105	4.4392	4.2784	4.1274	3.9852
13	5.1183	4.9095	4.7147	4.5327	4.3624	4.2028	4.0530
14	5.2293	5.0081	4.8023	4.6106	4.4317	4.2646	4.1082
15	5.3242	5.0916	4.8759	4.6755	4.4890	4.3152	4.1530
16	5.4053	5.1624	4.9377	4.7296	4.5364	4.3567	4.1894
17	5.4746	5.2223	4.9897	4.7746	4.5755	4.3908	4.2190
18	5.5339	5.2732	5.0333	4.8122	4.6079	4.4187	4.2431
19	5.5845	5.3162	5.0700	4.8435	4.6346	4.4415	4.2627
20	5.6278	5.3527	5.1009	4.8696	4.6567	4.4603	4.2786
21	5.6648	5.3837	5.1268	4.8913	4.6750	4.4756	4.2916
22	5.6964	5.4099	5.1486	4.9094	4.6900	4.4882	4.3021
23	5.7234	5.4321	5.1668	4.9245	4.7025	4.4985	4.3106
24	5.7465	5.4509	5.1822	4.9371	4.7128	4.5070	4.3176
25	5.7662	5.4669	5.1951	4.9476	4.7213	4.5139	4.3232
26	5.7831	5.4804	5.2060	4.9563	4.7284	4.5196	4.3278
27	5.7975	5.4919	5.2151	4.9636	4.7342	4.5243	4.3316
28	5.8099	5.5016	5.2228	4.9697	4.7390	4.5281	4.3346
29	5.8204	5.5098	5.2292	4.9747	4.7430	4.5312	4.3371
30	5.8294	5.5168	5.2347	4.9789	4.7463	4.5338	4.3391
31	5.8371	5.5227	5.2392	4.9824	4.7490	4.5359	4.3407
32	5.8437	5.5277	5.2430	4.9854	4.7512	4.5376	4.3421
33	5.8493	5.5320	5.2462	4.9878	4.7531	4.5390	4.3431
34	5.8541	5.5356	5.2489	4.9898	4.7546	4.5402	4.3440
35	5.8582	5.5386	5.2512	4.9915	4.7559	4.5411	4.3447
36	5.8617	5.5412	5.2531	4.9929	4.7569	4.5419	4.3453
48	5.8792	5.5536	5.2619	4.9992	4.7614	4.5451	4.3476
60	5.8819	5.5553	5.2630	4.9999	4.7619	4.5454	4.3478
72	5.8823	5.5555	5.2631	5.0000	4.7619	4.5455	4.3478
84	5.8823	5.5556	5.2632	5.0000	4.7619	4.5455	4.3478
96	5.8824	5.5556	5.2632	5.0000	4.7619	4.5455	4.3478

Table A.4
(continued)

n	r 0.240	0.250	0.260	0.270	0.280	0.290	0.300
1	0.8065	0.8000	0.7937	0.7874	0.7812	0.7752	0.7692
2	1.4568	1.4400	1.4235	1.4074	1.3916	1.3761	1.3609
3	1.9813	1.9520	1.9234	1.8956	1.8684	1.8420	1.8161
4	2.4043	2.3616	2.3202	2.2800	2.2410	2.2031	2.1662
5	2.7454	2.6893	2.6351	2.5827	2.5320	2.4830	2.4356
6	3.0205	2.9514	2.8850	2.8210	2.7594	2.7000	2.6427
7	3.2423	3.1611	3.0833	3.0087	2.9370	2.8682	2.8021
8	3.4212	3.3289	3.2407	3.1564	3.0758	2.9986	2.9247
9	3.5655	3.4631	3.3657	3.2728	3.1842	3.0997	3.0190
10	3.6819	3.5705	3.4648	3.3644	3.2689	3.1781	3.0915
11	3.7757	3.6564	3.5435	3.4365	3.3351	3.2388	3.1473
12	3.8514	3.7251	3.6059	3.4933	3.3868	3.2859	3.1903
13	3.9124	3.7801	3.6555	3.5381	3.4272	3.3224	3.2233
14	3.9616	3.8241	3.6949	3.5733	3.4587	3.3507	3.2487
15	4.0013	3.8593	3.7261	3.6010	3.4834	3.3726	3.2682
16	4.0333	3.8874	3.7509	3.6228	3.5026	3.3896	3.2832
17	4.0591	3.9099	3.7705	3.6400	3.5177	3.4028	3.2948
18	4.0799	3.9279	3.7861	3.6536	3.5294	3.4130	3.3037
19	4.0967	3.9424	3.7985	3.6642	3.5386	3.4210	3.3105
20	4.1103	3.9539	3.8083	3.6726	3.5458	3.4271	3.3158
21	4.1212	3.9631	3.8161	3.6792	3.5514	3.4319	3.3198
22	4.1300	3.9705	3.8223	3.6844	3.5558	3.4356	3.3230
23	4.1371	3.9764	3.8273	3.6885	3.5592	3.4384	3.3254
24	4.1428	3.9811	3.8312	3.6918	3.5619	3.4406	3.3272
25	4.1474	3.9849	3.8342	3.6943	3.5640	3.4423	3.3286
26	4.1511	3.9879	3.8367	3.6963	3.5656	3.4437	3.3297
27	4.1542	3.9903	3.8387	3.6979	3.5669	3.4447	3.3305
28	4.1566	3.9923	3.8402	3.6991	3.5679	3.4455	3.3312
29	4.1585	3.9938	3.8414	3.7001	3.5687	3.4461	3.3317
30	4.1601	3.9950	3.8424	3.7009	3.5693	3.4466	3.3321
31	4.1614	3.9960	3.8432	3.7015	3.5697	3.4470	3.3324
32	4.1624	3.9968	3.8438	3.7019	3.5701	3.4473	3.3326
33	4.1632	3.9975	3.8443	3.7023	3.5704	3.4475	3.3328
34	4.1639	3.9980	3.8447	3.7026	3.5706	3.4477	3.3329
35	4.1644	3.9984	3.8450	3.7028	3.5708	3.4478	3.3330
36	4.1649	3.9987	3.8452	3.7030	3.5709	3.4479	3.3331
48	4.1665	3.9999	3.8461	3.7037	3.5714	3.4483	3.3333
60	4.1667	4.0000	3.8462	3.7037	3.5714	3.4483	3.3333
72	4.1667	4.0000	3.8462	3.7037	3.5714	3.4483	3.3333
84	4.1667	4.0000	3.8462	3.7037	3.5714	3.4483	3.3333
96	4.1667	4.0000	3.8462	3.7037	3.5714	3.4483	3.3333

Table A.5

Common Logarithms

	1.00	1.10	1.20	1.30	1.40
0.00	0.000000	0.041393	0.079181	0.113943	0.146128
0.01	0.004321	0.045323	0.082785	0.117271	0.149219
0.02	0.008600	0.049218	0.086360	0.120574	0.152288
0.03	0.012837	0.053078	0.089905	0.123852	0.155336
0.04	0.017033	0.056905	0.093422	0.127105	0.158362
0.05	0.021189	0.060698	0.096910	0.130334	0.161368
0.06	0.025306	0.064458	0.100371	0.133539	0.164353
0.07	0.029384	0.068186	0.103804	0.136721	0.167317
0.08	0.033424	0.071882	0.107210	0.139879	0.170262
0.09	0.037426	0.075547	0.110590	0.143015	0.173186

	1.50	1.60	1.70	1.80	1.90
0.00	0.176091	0.204120	0.230449	0.255273	0.278754
0.01	0.178977	0.206826	0.232996	0.257679	0.281033
0.02	0.181844	0.209515	0.235528	0.260071	0.283301
0.03	0.184691	0.212188	0.238046	0.262451	0.285557
0.04	0.187521	0.214844	0.240549	0.264818	0.287802
0.05	0.190332	0.217484	0.243038	0.267172	0.290035
0.06	0.193125	0.220108	0.245513	0.269513	0.292256
0.07	0.195900	0.222716	0.247973	0.271842	0.294466
0.08	0.198657	0.225309	0.250420	0.274158	0.296665
0.09	0.201397	0.227887	0.252853	0.276462	0.298853

	2.00	2.10	2.20	2.30	2.40
0.00	0.301030	0.322219	0.342423	0.361728	0.380211
0.01	0.303196	0.324282	0.344392	0.363612	0.382017
0.02	0.305351	0.326336	0.346353	0.365488	0.383815
0.03	0.307496	0.328380	0.348305	0.367356	0.385606
0.04	0.309630	0.330414	0.350248	0.369216	0.387390
0.05	0.311754	0.332438	0.352183	0.371068	0.389166
0.06	0.313867	0.334454	0.354108	0.372912	0.390935
0.07	0.315970	0.336460	0.356026	0.374748	0.392697
0.08	0.318063	0.338456	0.357935	0.376577	0.394452
0.09	0.320146	0.340444	0.359835	0.378398	0.396199

	2.50	2.60	2.70	2.80	2.90
0.00	0.397940	0.414973	0.431364	0.447158	0.462398
0.01	0.399674	0.416641	0.432969	0.448706	0.463893
0.02	0.401401	0.418301	0.434569	0.450249	0.465383
0.03	0.403121	0.419956	0.436163	0.451786	0.466868
0.04	0.404834	0.421604	0.437751	0.453318	0.468347
0.05	0.406540	0.423246	0.439333	0.454845	0.469822
0.06	0.408240	0.424882	0.440909	0.456366	0.471292
0.07	0.409933	0.426511	0.442480	0.457882	0.472756
0.08	0.411620	0.428135	0.444045	0.459392	0.474216
0.09	0.413300	0.429752	0.445604	0.460898	0.475671

Table A.5
(continued)

	3.00	3.10	3.20	3.30	3.40
0.00	0.477121	0.491362	0.505150	0.518514	0.531479
0.01	0.478566	0.492760	0.506505	0.519828	0.532754
0.02	0.480007	0.494155	0.507856	0.521138	0.534026
0.03	0.481443	0.495544	0.509203	0.522444	0.535294
0.04	0.482874	0.496930	0.510545	0.523746	0.536558
0.05	0.484300	0.498311	0.511883	0.525045	0.537819
0.06	0.485721	0.499687	0.513218	0.526339	0.539076
0.07	0.487138	0.501059	0.514548	0.527630	0.540329
0.08	0.488551	0.502427	0.515874	0.528917	0.541579
0.09	0.489958	0.503791	0.517196	0.530200	0.542825

	3.50	3.60	3.70	3.80	3.90
0.00	0.544068	0.556303	0.568202	0.579784	0.591065
0.01	0.545307	0.557507	0.569374	0.580925	0.592177
0.02	0.546543	0.558709	0.570543	0.582063	0.593286
0.03	0.547775	0.559907	0.571709	0.583199	0.594393
0.04	0.549003	0.561101	0.572872	0.584331	0.595496
0.05	0.550228	0.562293	0.574031	0.585461	0.596597
0.06	0.551450	0.563481	0.575188	0.586587	0.597695
0.07	0.552668	0.564666	0.576341	0.587711	0.598791
0.08	0.553883	0.565848	0.577492	0.588832	0.599883
0.09	0.555094	0.567026	0.578639	0.589950	0.600973

	4.00	4.10	4.20	4.30	4.40
0.00	0.602060	0.612784	0.623249	0.633468	0.643453
0.01	0.603144	0.613842	0.624282	0.634477	0.644439
0.02	0.604226	0.614897	0.625312	0.635484	0.645422
0.03	0.605305	0.615950	0.626340	0.636488	0.646404
0.04	0.606381	0.617000	0.627366	0.637490	0.647383
0.05	0.607455	0.618048	0.628389	0.638489	0.648360
0.06	0.608526	0.619093	0.629410	0.639486	0.649335
0.07	0.609594	0.620136	0.630428	0.640481	0.650308
0.08	0.610660	0.621176	0.631444	0.641474	0.651278
0.09	0.611723	0.622214	0.632457	0.642465	0.652246

	4.50	4.60	4.70	4.80	4.90
0.00	0.653213	0.662758	0.672098	0.681241	0.690196
0.01	0.654177	0.663701	0.673021	0.682145	0.691081
0.02	0.655138	0.664642	0.673942	0.683047	0.691965
0.03	0.656098	0.665581	0.674861	0.683947	0.692847
0.04	0.657056	0.666518	0.675778	0.684845	0.693727
0.05	0.658011	0.667453	0.676694	0.685742	0.694605
0.06	0.658965	0.668386	0.677607	0.686636	0.695482
0.07	0.659916	0.669317	0.678518	0.687529	0.696356
0.08	0.660865	0.670246	0.679428	0.688420	0.697229
0.09	0.661813	0.671173	0.680336	0.689309	0.698101

Table A.5
(*continued*)

	5.00	5.10	5.20	5.30	5.40
0.00	0.698970	0.707570	0.716003	0.724276	0.732394
0.01	0.699838	0.708421	0.716838	0.725095	0.733197
0.02	0.700704	0.709270	0.717671	0.725912	0.733999
0.03	0.701568	0.710117	0.718502	0.726727	0.734800
0.04	0.702431	0.710963	0.719331	0.727541	0.735599
0.05	0.703291	0.711807	0.720159	0.728354	0.736397
0.06	0.704151	0.712650	0.720986	0.729165	0.737193
0.07	0.705008	0.713491	0.721811	0.729974	0.737987
0.08	0.705864	0.714330	0.722634	0.730782	0.738781
0.09	0.706718	0.715167	0.723456	0.731589	0.739572

	5.50	5.60	5.70	5.80	5.90
0.00	0.740363	0.748188	0.755875	0.763428	0.770852
0.01	0.741152	0.748963	0.756636	0.764176	0.771587
0.02	0.741939	0.749736	0.757396	0.764923	0.772322
0.03	0.742725	0.750508	0.758155	0.765669	0.773055
0.04	0.743510	0.751279	0.758912	0.766413	0.773786
0.05	0.744293	0.752048	0.759668	0.767156	0.774517
0.06	0.745075	0.752816	0.760422	0.767898	0.775246
0.07	0.745855	0.753583	0.761176	0.768638	0.775974
0.08	0.746634	0.754348	0.761928	0.769377	0.776701
0.09	0.747412	0.755112	0.762679	0.770115	0.777427

	6.00	6.10	6.20	6.30	6.40
0.00	0.778151	0.785330	0.792392	0.799341	0.806180
0.01	0.778874	0.786041	0.793092	0.800029	0.806858
0.02	0.779596	0.786751	0.793790	0.800717	0.807535
0.03	0.780317	0.787460	0.794488	0.801404	0.808211
0.04	0.781037	0.788168	0.795185	0.802089	0.808886
0.05	0.781755	0.788875	0.795880	0.802774	0.809560
0.06	0.782473	0.789581	0.796574	0.803457	0.810233
0.07	0.783189	0.790285	0.797268	0.804139	0.810904
0.08	0.783904	0.790988	0.797960	0.804821	0.811575
0.09	0.784617	0.791691	0.798651	0.805501	0.812245

	6.50	6.60	6.70	6.80	6.90
0.00	0.812913	0.819544	0.826075	0.832509	0.838849
0.01	0.813581	0.820201	0.826723	0.833147	0.839478
0.02	0.814248	0.820858	0.827369	0.833784	0.840106
0.03	0.814913	0.821514	0.828015	0.834421	0.840733
0.04	0.815578	0.822168	0.828660	0.835056	0.841359
0.05	0.816241	0.822822	0.829304	0.835691	0.841985
0.06	0.816904	0.823474	0.829947	0.836324	0.842609
0.07	0.817565	0.824126	0.830589	0.836957	0.843233
0.08	0.818226	0.824776	0.831230	0.837588	0.843855
0.09	0.818885	0.825426	0.831870	0.838219	0.844477

Table A.5
(*continued*)

	7.00	7.10	7.20	7.30	7.40
0.00	0.845098	0.851258	0.857332	0.863323	0.869232
0.01	0.845718	0.851870	0.857935	0.863917	0.869818
0.02	0.846337	0.852480	0.858537	0.864511	0.870404
0.03	0.846955	0.853090	0.859138	0.865104	0.870989
0.04	0.847573	0.853698	0.859739	0.865696	0.871573
0.05	0.848189	0.854306	0.860338	0.866287	0.872156
0.06	0.848805	0.854913	0.860937	0.866878	0.872739
0.07	0.849419	0.855519	0.861534	0.867467	0.873321
0.08	0.850033	0.856124	0.862131	0.868056	0.873902
0.09	0.850646	0.856729	0.862728	0.868644	0.874482

	7.50	7.60	7.70	7.80	7.90
0.00	0.875061	0.880814	0.886491	0.892095	0.897627
0.01	0.875640	0.881385	0.887054	0.892651	0.898176
0.02	0.876218	0.881955	0.887617	0.893207	0.898725
0.03	0.876795	0.882525	0.888179	0.893762	0.899273
0.04	0.877371	0.883093	0.888741	0.894316	0.899821
0.05	0.877947	0.883661	0.889302	0.894870	0.900367
0.06	0.878522	0.884229	0.889862	0.895423	0.900913
0.07	0.879096	0.884795	0.890421	0.895975	0.901458
0.08	0.879669	0.885361	0.890980	0.896526	0.902003
0.09	0.880242	0.885926	0.891537	0.897077	0.902547

	8.00	8.10	8.20	8.30	8.40
0.00	0.903090	0.908485	0.913814	0.919078	0.924279
0.01	0.903633	0.909021	0.914343	0.919601	0.924796
0.02	0.904174	0.909556	0.914872	0.920123	0.925312
0.03	0.904716	0.910091	0.915400	0.920645	0.925828
0.04	0.905256	0.910624	0.915927	0.921166	0.926342
0.05	0.905796	0.911158	0.916454	0.921686	0.926857
0.06	0.906335	0.911690	0.916980	0.922206	0.927370
0.07	0.906874	0.912222	0.917506	0.922725	0.927883
0.08	0.907411	0.912753	0.918030	0.923244	0.928396
0.09	0.907949	0.913284	0.918555	0.923762	0.928908

	8.50	8.60	8.70	8.80	8.90
0.00	0.929419	0.934498	0.939519	0.944483	0.949390
0.01	0.929930	0.935003	0.940018	0.944976	0.949878
0.02	0.930440	0.935507	0.940516	0.945469	0.950365
0.03	0.930949	0.936011	0.941014	0.945961	0.950851
0.04	0.931458	0.936514	0.941511	0.946452	0.951338
0.05	0.931966	0.937016	0.942008	0.946943	0.951823
0.06	0.932474	0.937518	0.942504	0.947434	0.952308
0.07	0.932981	0.938019	0.943000	0.947924	0.952792
0.08	0.933487	0.938520	0.943495	0.948413	0.953276
0.09	0.933993	0.939020	0.943989	0.948902	0.953760

Table A.5
(continued)

	9.00	9.10	9.20	9.30	9.40
0.00	0.954243	0.959041	0.963788	0.968483	0.973128
0.01	0.954725	0.959518	0.964260	0.968950	0.973590
0.02	0.955207	0.959995	0.964731	0.969416	0.974051
0.03	0.955688	0.960471	0.965202	0.969882	0.974512
0.04	0.956168	0.960946	0.965672	0.970347	0.974972
0.05	0.956649	0.961421	0.966142	0.970812	0.975432
0.06	0.957128	0.961895	0.966611	0.971276	0.975891
0.07	0.957607	0.962369	0.967080	0.971740	0.976350
0.08	0.958086	0.962843	0.967548	0.972203	0.976808
0.09	0.958564	0.963316	0.968016	0.972666	0.977266

	9.50	9.60	9.70	9.80	9.90
0.00	0.977724	0.982271	0.986772	0.991226	0.995635
0.01	0.978181	0.982723	0.987219	0.991669	0.996074
0.02	0.978637	0.983175	0.987666	0.992111	0.996512
0.03	0.979093	0.983626	0.988113	0.992554	0.996949
0.04	0.979548	0.984077	0.988559	0.992995	0.997386
0.05	0.980003	0.984527	0.989005	0.993436	0.997823
0.06	0.980458	0.984977	0.989450	0.993877	0.998259
0.07	0.980912	0.985426	0.989895	0.994317	0.998695
0.08	0.981366	0.985875	0.990339	0.994757	0.999131
0.09	0.981819	0.986324	0.990783	0.995196	0.999565

Index

81 82 9 8 7 6 5 4 3